PENGUIN BOOKS

INDIA'S STRUGGLE FOR INDEPENDENCE

Bipan Chandra was born in Kangra, Himachal Pradesh. He was educated at Forman Christian College, Lahore, and at Stanford University, California. He has been Professor of Modern History at Jawaharlal Nehru University (JNU) since 1971. Dr. Chandra is the author of several books on Indian nationalism.

Mridula Mukherjee was educated at Lady Shriram College, New Delhi, and at JNU. She teaches at the Centre for Historical Studies, JNU, where she is presently Associate Professor in Modern Indian History.

Aditya Mukherjee, who is married to Mridula Mukherjee, was educated at St. Stephen's College, New Delhi and at JNU. He teaches at the Centre for Historical Studies, JNU, where he is currently Associate Professor in Contemporary Indian History.

K.N. Panikkar was educated at Madras and Rajasthan Universities and is currently Professor of Modern Indian History at the Centre for Historical Studies, JNU, New Delhi.

Sucheta Mahajan was educated at Indraprastha College, New Delhi, and at JNU. She teaches history at Indraprastha College.

Bipan Chandra, Mridula Mukherjee, Aditya Mukherjee and Sucheta Mahajan are presently working on a multi-volume history of India's struggle for freedom.

INDIA'S STRUGGLE FOR INDEPENDENCE
1857-1947

BIPAN CHANDRA

MRIDULA MUKHERJEE ADITYA MUKHERJEE
K.N. PANIKKAR SUCHETA MAHAJAN

PENGUIN BOOKS

Penguin Books India (P) Ltd.,
B4/246 Safdarjung Enclave, New Delhi 110029 India
Penguin Books Ltd. Harmondsworth, Middlesex, England
Penguin Books USA Inc, 375 Hudson Street,
N.Y. New York 10014 USA.
Penguin Books Canada Ltd. 2801 John Street, Markham, Ontario,
Canada L3R 1B4
Penguin Books (N.Z.) Ltd. 182-190 Wairau Road, Auckland 10, New Zealand

First published by Viking 1988
Published in Penguin Books 1989
Reprinted 1989(twice), 1990(twice), 1991, 1992(twice), 1993
Copyright © Bipan Chandra, 1987, 1988, 1989

Some of the material in this book first appeared in *The Telegraph* , Calcutta.

Typeset in Times Roman by Macro Graphics, New Delhi.
Made and printed in India by Ananda Offset Private Ltd, Calcutta

To Romila Thapar and S. Gopal

Contents

Acknowledgements

This work is partly the result of an ongoing research project on the history of the Indian national movement conducted under the direction of Bipan Chandra and financed by the Indian Council of Social Science Research. A special feature of the project is that apart from utilizing traditional sources such as archives, private papers, institutional papers, and newspapers, it has attempted to use the experience and understanding of the grass-roots level participants in the national movement. We are extremely thankful to more than 1500 freedom fighters who gave freely of their time and extended us generous hospitality when we interviewed them. Along with Bipan Chandra, three of the contributors to the volume — Mridula Mukherjee, Aditya Mukherjee, and Sucheta Mahajan — are members of this project. We are grateful to K.N. Panikkar for contributing two chapters to the book.

We have benefitted immensely from our long-term interaction with S. Gopal and Romila Thapar. Many colleagues and students — V. Ramakrishna, D.N. Gupta, Prem Choudhry, Mohinder Singh, Sashi Joshi, Bhagwan Josh, Lajpat Jagga, A. Murali, K. Gopalan Kutty, C.S. Krishna, Gyan Kudaisya, Visalakshi Menon, A. Thomas, Vineeta Damodaran, Harjot Oberoi, Neerja Singh, C. Chandermohan — have enabled us to evolve our ideas and have also helped in several other ways.

Many friends — P.C. Joshi, B.D. Talib, Barun De, S. Bhattacharya, V.N. Datta, Ravinder Kumar, Hitesh Sanyal, Randhir Singh, Mohit Sen, Kewal Varma, Pramod Kumar — have deepened our knowledge of the subject through discussions and criticism.

We would like to thank the Directors and the staff of the National Archives and various state archives, the Nehru Memorial Museum and Library, the Jawaharlal Nehru University Library and other libraries in Delhi and other parts of the country for allowing us to use their facilities. We are, in particular, thankful to B.R. Nanda, V.C. Joshi, D.N. Panigrahi and Harideo Sharma of the Nehru Memorial Museum and Library for their assistance. As usual, Usha Chandra has contributed in multiple ways to the making of this volume.

We would also like to thank the publishers, and especially David Davidar and Sudha Sadhanand, for their interest and co-operation in seeing the book through its many stages. We also wish to thank J.S. Baweja who rendered invaluable assistance by cheerfully typing the manuscript under tremendous pressure.

A Note on Style

In order to ensure the continuity of the book's narrative the authors of the various chapters are mentioned here and nowhere else in the volume. The Introduction and Chapters 2, 3, 4, 5, 7, 8, 9, 11, 18, 19, 20, 23, 24, 25, 26, 30, 31, 32, 33, 34, 38 and 39 have been written by Bipan Chandra; Chapters 1 and 6, have been written by K.N. Panikkar; Chapters 10, 17 and 29 have been written by Aditya Mukherjee; Chapters 12, 13, 14, 15, 16, 21, 22, 27, 28 and 35 have been written by Mridula Mukherjee; and Chapters 36 and 37 have been written by Sucheta Mahajan.

A Note on Style

In order to ensure the continuity of the book's narrative, the authors of the various chapters are mentioned here and nowhere else in the volume. The Introduction and Chapters 2, 3, 4, 5, 7, 8, 9, 11, 16, 19, 20, 23, 24, 25, 26, 30, 31, 32, 33, 34, 38 and 39 have been written by Bipan Chandra. Chapters 1 and 6 have been written by K.N. Panikkar. Chapters 10, 17 and 29 have been written by Aditya Mukherjee. Chapters 12, 13, 14, 15, 16, 21, 22, 27, 28 and 35 have been written by Mridula Mukherjee, and Chapters 36 and 37 have been written by Sucheta Mahajan.

Introduction

The Indian national movement was undoubtedly one of the biggest mass movements modern society has ever seen. It was a movement which galvanized millions of people of all classes and ideologies into political action and brought to its knees a mighty colonial empire. Consequently, along with the British, French, Russian, Chinese, Cuban and Vietnamese revolutions, it is of great relevance to those wishing to alter the existing political and social structure.

Various aspects of the Indian national movement, especially Gandhian political strategy, are particularly relevant to these movements in societies that broadly function within the confines of the rule of law, and are characterized by a democratic and basically civil libertarian polity. But it is also relevant to other societies. We know for a fact that even Lech Walesa consciously tried to incorporate elements of Gandhian strategy in the Solidarity Movement in Poland.

The Indian national movement, in fact, provides the only actual historical example of a semi-democratic or democratic type of political structure being successfully replaced or transformed. It is the only movement where the broadly Gramscian theoretical perspective of a war of position was successfully practised; where state power was not siezed in a single historical moment of revolution, but through prolonged popular struggle on a moral, political and ideological level; where reserves of counter-hegemony were built up over the years through progressive stages; where the phases of struggle alternated with 'passive' phases.

The Indian national movement is also an example of how the constitutional space offered by the existing structure could be used without getting coopted by it. It did not completely reject this space, as such rejection in democratic societies entails heavy costs in terms of hegemonic influence and often leads to isolation — but entered it and used it effectively in combination with non-constitutional struggle to overthrow the existing structure.

The Indian national movement is perhaps one of the best examples of the creation of an extremely wide movement with a common aim in which diverse political and ideological currents could co-exist and work — and simultaneously continue to contend for overall ideological and political hegemony over it. While intense debate on all basic issues was allowed, the diversity and tension did not weaken the cohesion and striking power of the movement; on the contrary, this diversity and atmosphere of freedom and debate became a major source of its strength.

Today, over forty years after independence, we are still close enough to the freedom struggle to feel its warmth and yet far enough to be able to analyse it coolly, and with the advantage of hindsight. Analyse it we must, for our past, present and future are inextricably linked to it. Men and women in every age and society make their own history,but they do not make it in a historical vacuum, *de novo.* Their efforts, however innovative, at finding solutions to their problems in the present and charting out their future, are guided and circumscribed, moulded and conditioned, by their respective histories, their inherited economic, political and ideological structures. To make myself clearer, the path that India has followed since 1947 has deep roots in the struggle for independence. The political and ideological features, which have had a decisive impact on post-independence development, are largely a legacy of the freedom struggle. It is a legacy that belongs to all the Indian people, regardless of which party or group they belong to now, for the 'party' which led this struggle from 1885 to 1947 was not then a party but a movement — all political trends from the Right to the Left were incorporated in it.

*

What are the outstanding features of the freedom struggle? A major aspect is the values and modern ideals on which the movement itself was based and the broad socio-economic- and political vision of its leadership (this vision was that of a democratic, civil libertarian and secular India, based on a self-reliant, egalitarian social order and an independent foreign policy).

The movement popularized democratic ideas and institutions in India.

The nationalists fought for the introduction of a representative government on the basis of popular elections and demanded that elections be based on adult franchise. The Indian National Congress was organized on a democratic basis and in the form of a parliament. It not only permitted but encouraged free expression of opinion within the party and the movement; some of the most important decisions in its history were taken after heated debates and on the basis of open voting.

From the beginning, the nationalists fought against attacks by the State on the freedoms of the Press, expression and association, and made the struggle for these freedoms an integral part of the national movement. During their brief spell in power, from 1937-39, the Congress ministries greatly extended the scope of civil liberties. The defence of civil liberties was not narrowly conceived in terms of one political group, but was extended to include the defence of other groups whose views were politically and ideologically different. The Moderates defended Tilak, the Extremist, and non-violent Congressmen passionately defended revolutionary terrorists and communists alike during their trials. In 1928, the Public Safety Bill and Trade Disputes' Bill were opposed not only by Motilal Nehru but also by conservatives like Madan Mohan Malaviya and M.R. Jayakar. It was this strong civil libertarian and democratic tradition of the national movement which was reflected in the Constitution of independent India.

The freedom struggle was also a struggle for economic development. In time an economic ideology developed which was to dominate the views of independent India. The national movement accepted, with near unanimity, the need to develop India on the basis of industrialization which in turn was to be independent of foreign capital and was to rely on the indigenous capital goods sector. A crucial role was assigned to the public sector and, in the 1930s, there was a commitment to economic planning.

From the initial stages, the movement adopted a pro-poor orientation which was strengthened with the advent of Gandhi and the rise of the leftists who struggled to make the movement adopt a socialist outlook. The movement also increasingly moved towards a programme of radical agrarian reform. However, socialism did not, at any stage, become the official goal of the Indian National Congress though there was a great deal of debate around it within the national movement and the Indian National Congress during the 1930s and 1940s. For various reasons, despite the existence of a powerful leftist trend within the nationalist mainstream, the dominant vision within the Congress did not transcend the parameters of a capitalist conception of society.

The national movement was, from its early days, fully committed to secularism. Its leadership fought hard to inculcate secular values among the people and opposed the growth of communalism. And, despite the partition of India and the accompanying communal holocaust. it did succeed in enshrining secularism in the Constitution of free India.

It was never inward looking. Since the days of Raja Rammohan Roy, Indian leaders had developed a broad international outlook. Over the years, they evolved a policy of opposition to imperialism on a world-wide scale and solidarity with anti-colonial movements in other parts of the world. They established the principle that Indians should hate British imperialism but not the British people. Consequently, they were supported by a large number of English men, women and political groups. They maintained close links with the progressive, anti-colonial and anti-capitalist forces of the world. A non-racist, anti-imperialist outlook, which continues to characterize Indian foreign policy, was thus part of the legacy of the anti-imperialist struggle.

*

This volume has been written within a broad frame work that the authors, their colleagues and students have evolved and are in the process of evolving through on-going research on and study of the Indian national movement. We have in the preparation of this volume extensively used existing published and unpublished monographs, archival material, private papers, and newspapers. Our understanding also owes a great deal to our recorded interviews with over 1,500 men and women who participated in the movement from 1918 onwards. However, references to these sources have, for the ease of the reader and due to constraints of space, been kept to the minimum and, in fact, have been confined mostly to citations of quoted statements and to works readily available in a good library.

For the same reason, though the Indian national movement has so far been viewed from a wide variety of historiographic perspectives ranging from the hard-core imperialist to the Marxist, and though various stereotypes and shibboleths about it exist, we have generally avoided entering into a debate with those whose positions and analyses differ from our own — except occasionally, as in the case of Chapter 4, on the origin of the Indian National Congress, which counters the hoary perennial theory of the Congress being founded as a safety valve. In all fairness to the reader, we have only briefly delineated the basic contours of major historiographical trends, indicated our differences with them, and outlined the alternative framework within which this volume has been written.

*

We differ widely from the imperialist approach which first emerged in the official pronouncements of the Viceroys, Lords Dufferin, Curzon and Minto, and the Secretary of State, George Hamilton. It was first cogently put forward by V. Chirol, the Rowlatt (Sedition) Committee Report, Verney Lovett, and the Montagu-Chelmsford Report. It was theorized, for the first time, by Bruce T. McCully, an American scholar, in 1940. Its liberal version was adopted by Reginald Coupland and, after 1947, by Percival Spear, while its conservative version was refurbished and developed at length by Anil Seal and J.A. Gallagher and their students and followers after 1968. Since the liberal version is no longer fashionable in academic circles, we will ignore it here due to shortage of space.

The conservative colonial administrators and the imperialist school of historians, popularly known as the Cambridge School, deny the existence of colonialism as an economic, political, social and cultural structure in India. Colonialism is seen by them primarily as foreign rule. They either do not see or vehemently deny that the economic, social, cultural and political development of India required the overthrow of colonialism. Thus, their analysis of the national movement is based on the denial of the basic contradiction between the interests of the Indian people and of British colonialism and causative role this contradiction played in the rise of the national movement. Consequently, they implicitly or explicitly deny that the Indian national movement represented the Indian side of this contradiction or that it was anti-imperialist, that is, it opposed British imperialism in India. They see the Indian struggle against imperialism as a mock battle ('mimic warfare'), 'a Dassehra duel between two hollow statues, locked in motiveless and simulated combat.'[1] The denial of the central contradiction vitiates the entire approach of these scholars though their meticulous research does help others to use it within a different framework.

The imperialist writers deny that India was in the process of becoming a nation and believe that what is called India in fact consisted of religions, castes, communities and interests. Thus, the grouping of Indian politics around the concept of an Indian nation or an Indian people or social classes is not recognised by them. There were instead, they said, pre-existing Hindu-Muslim, Brahmin, Non-Brahmin, Aryan, Bhadralok (cultured people) and other similar identities. They say that these prescriptive groups based on caste and religion are the real basis of political organization and, as such, caste and religion-based politics are primary and nationalism a mere cover. As Seal puts it: 'What from a distance appear as their political strivings were often, on close examination, their efforts to conserve or improve the position of their own prescriptive groups.'[2] (This also makes Indian nationalism, says Seal, different from the nationalism of China, Japan, the Muslim countries and Africa).[3]

If the Indian national movement did not express the interests of the Indian people vis-a-vis imperialism, then whose interests did it represent? Once again the main lines of the answer and argument were worked out by late 19th century and early 20th century officials and imperialist spokesmen. The national movement, assert the writers of the imperialist school, was not a people's movement but a product of the needs and interests of the elite groups who used it to serve either their own narrow interests or the interests of their prescriptive groups. Thus, the elite groups, and their needs and interests, provide the origin as well as the driving force of the idea, ideology and movement of nationalism. These groups were sometimes formed around religious or caste identities and sometimes through political connections built around patronage. But, in each case, these groups had a narrow, selfish interest in opposing British rule or each other. Nationalism, then, is seen primarily as a mere ideology which these elite groups used to legitimize their narrow ambitions and to mobilize public support. The national movement was merely an instrument used by the elite groups to mobilize the masses and to satisfy their own interests.

Gallagher, Seal and their students have added to this viewpoint. While Dufferin, Curzon, Chirol, Lovett, McCully, and B.B. Misra talked of the frustrated educated middle classes using nationalism to fight the 'benevolent Raj', Seal develops a parallel view, as found in Chirol and the Rowlatt Committee Report, that the national movement represented the struggle of one Indian elite group against another for British favours. As he puts it: 'It is misleading to view these native mobilizations as directed chiefly against foreign overlordship. Much attention has been paid to the apparent conflicts between imperialism and nationalism; it would be at least equally profitable to study their real partnership'.[4] The main British contribution to the rise and growth of the national movement, then, was that British rule sharpened mutual jealousies and struggles among Indians and created new fields and institutions for their mutual rivalry.

Seal, Gallagher and their students also extended the basis on which the elite groups were formed. They followed and added to the viewpoint of the British historian Lewis Namier and contended that these groups were formed on the basis of patron-client relationships. They theorize that, as the British extended administrative, economic and political power to the localities and provinces, local potentates started organizing politics by acquiring clients and patrons whose interests they served, and who in turn served their interests. Indian politics began to be formed through the links of this patron-client chain. Gradually, bigger leaders emerged who undertook to act as brokers to link together the politics of the local potentates, and eventually, because British rule encompassed the whole of India, all-India brokers emerged. To operate successfully, these all-India brokers needed province level brokers at the lower levels, and needed to involve clients in the national movement. The second level leaders are also described as sub-contractors. Seal says the chief political brokers were Gandhi, Nehru, and Patel. And according to these historians, the people themselves, those whose fortunes were affected by all this power brokering, came in only in 1918. After that, we are told, their existential grievances such as war, inflation, disease, drought or depression — which had nothing to do with colonialism — were cleverly used to bamboozle them into participating in this factional struggle of the potentates.

Thus, this school of historians treats the Indian national movement as a cloak for the struggle for power between various sections of the Indian elite, and between them and the foreign elite, thus effectively denying its existence and legitimacy as a movement of the Indian people for the overthrow of imperialism and for the establishment of an independent nation state. Categories of nation, class, mobilization, ideology, etc., which are generally used by historians to analyze national movements and revolutionary processes in Europe, Asia and Africa are usually missing from their treatment of the Indian national movement. This view not only denies the existence of colonial exploitation and

underdevelopment, and the central contradiction, but also any idealism
on the part of those who sacrificed their lives for the anti-imperialist
cause. As S. Gopal has put it: 'Namier was accused of taking the mind
out of politics; this School has gone further and taken not only the
mind but decency, character, integrity and selfless commitment out of
the Indian national movement.'[5] Moreover, it denies any intelligent or
active role to the mass of workers, peasants, lower middle class and
women in the anti-imperialist struggle. They are treated as a child-
people or dumb creatures who had no perception of their needs and interests. One wonders why the colonial rulers did not succeed in mobilizing
them behind their own politics!

*

A few historians have of late initiated a new trend, described by its proponents as subaltern, which dismisses all previous historical writing,
including that based on a Marxist perspective, as elite historiography,
and claims to replace this old, 'blinkered' historiography with what it
claims is a new people's or subaltern approach.

For them, the basic contradiction in Indian society in the colonial
epoch was between the elite, both Indian and foreign, on the one hand,
and the subaltern groups, on the other, and not between colonialism and
the Indian people. They believe that the Indian people were never united
in a common anti-imperialist struggle, that there was no such entity as
the Indian national movement. Instead, they assert that there were two
distinct movements or streams, the real anti-imperialist stream of the
subalterns and the bogus national movement of the elite. The elite
stream, led by the 'official' leadership of the Indian National Congress,
was little more than a cloak for the struggle for power among the elite.
The subaltern school's characterization of the national movement bears a
disturbing resemblance to the imperialist and neo-imperialist characterization of the national movement, the only difference being that, while
neo-imperialist historiography does not split the movement but charac-
terizes the entire national movement in this fashion, 'subaltern'
historiography first divides the movement into two and then accepts the
neo-imperialist characterization for the 'elite' stream. This approach is
also characterized by a generally ahistorical glorification of all forms of
popular militancy and consciousness and an equally ahistorical contempt
for all forms of initiative and activity by the intelligentsia, organized

party leaderships and other 'elites'. Consequently, it too denies the legitimacy of the actual, historical anti-colonial struggle that the Indian people waged. The new school, which promised to write a history based on the people's own consciousness, is yet to tap new sources that may be more reflective of popular perceptions; its 'new' writing continues to be based on the same old 'elite' sources.

*

The other major approach is nationalist historiography. In the colonial period, this school was represented by political activists such as Lajpat Rai, A.C. Mazumdar, R.G. Pradhan, Pattabhi Sitaramayya, Surendranath Banerjea, C.F. Andrews, and Girija Mukerji. More recently, B.R. Nanda, Bisheshwar Prasad and Amles Tripathi have made distinguished contributions within the framework of this approach. The nationalist historians, especially the more recent ones, show an awareness of the exploitative character of colonialism, but on the whole they feel that the national movement was the result of the spread and realization of the idea or spirit of nationalism or liberty. They also take full cognizance of the process of India becoming a nation, and see the national movement as a movement of the people.

Their major weakness, however, is that they tend to ignore or, at least, underplay the inner contradictions of Indian society both in terms of class and caste. They tend to ignore the fact that while the national movement represented the interests of the people or nation as a whole (that is, of all classes vis-a-vis colonialism) it only did so from a particular class perspective, and that, consequently, there was a constant struggle between different social, ideological perspectives for hegemony over the movement. They also usually take up the position adopted by the right wing of the national movement and equate it with the movement as a whole. Their treatment of the strategic and ideological dimensions of the movement is also inadequate.

*

The Marxist school emerged on the scene later. Its foundations, so far as the study of the national movement is concerned, were laid by R. Palme Dutt and A.R. Desai; but several others have developed it over the years. Unlike the imperialist school, the Marxist historians clearly see the primary contradiction, as well as the process of the nation-in-the-making, and unlike the nationalists, they also take full note of the inner contradictions of Indian society.

However, many of them — and Palme Dutt in particular — are not able to fully integrate their treatment of the primary anti-imperialist contradiction and the secondary inner contradictions, and tend to counterpose the anti-imperialist struggle to the class or social struggle. They also tend to see the movement as a structured bourgeois movement, if not the bourgeoisie's movement, and miss its open-ended and all-class character. They see the bourgeoisie as playing the dominant role in the movement — they tend to equate or conflate the national leadership with the bourgeoisie or capitalist class. They also interpret the class character of the movement in terms of its forms of struggle (i.e., in its non-violent character) and in the fact that it made strategic retreats and compromises. A few take an even narrower view. They suggest that access to financial resources determined the ability to influence the course and direction of nationalist politics. Many of the Marxist writers also do not do an actual detailed historical investigation of the strategy, programme, ideology, extent and forms of mass mobilization, and strategic and tactical manoeuvres of the national movement.

*

Our own approach, while remaining, we believe, within the broad Marxist tradition, tries to locate the issues — of the nature of the contradictions in colonial India; the relationship between the primary and the secondary contradictions; the class character of the movement; the relationship between the bourgeoisie and other social classes and the Indian National Congress and its leadership, i.e., the relationship between class and party; the relationship between forms of struggle (including non-violence) and class character, ideology, strategy and mass character of the movement and so on — in a framework which differs in many respects from the existing approaches, including the classical Marxist approach of Palme Dutt and A.R. Desai. The broad contours of that framework are outlined below.

*

In our view, India's freedom struggle was basically the result of a fundamental contradiction between the interests of the Indian people and that of British colonialism. From the beginning itself, India's national leaders grasped this contradiction. They were able to see that India was regressing economically and undergoing a process of underdevelopment. In time they were able to evolve a scientific analysis of colonialism. In fact, they were the first in the 19th century to develop an economic critique of colonialism and lay bare its complex structure. They were also able to see the distinction between colonial policy and the imperatives of the colonial structure. Taking the social experience of the Indian people as colonized subjects and recognizing the common interests of the Indian people vis-a-vis colonialism, the national leaders gradually evolved a clear-cut anti-colonial ideology on which they based the national movement. This anti-colonial ideology and critique of colonialism were disseminated during the mass phase of the movement.

The national movement also played a pivotal role in the historical process through which the Indian people got formed into a nation or a people. National leaders from Dadabhai Naoroji, Surendranath Banerjea and Tilak to Gandhiji and Nehru accepted that India was not yet a fully structured nation but a nation-in-the-making and that one of the major objectives and functions of the movement was to promote the growing unity of the Indian people through a common struggle against colonialism. In other words, the national movement was seen both as a product of the process of the nation-in-the-making and as an active agent of the process. This process of the nation-in-the-making was never *counterposed* to the diverse regional, linguistic and ethnic identities in India. On the contrary, the emergence of a national identity and the flowering of other narrower identities were seen as processes deriving strength from each other.

The pre-nationalist resistance to colonial rule failed to understand the twin phenomena of colonialism and the nation-in-the-making. In fact, these phenomena were not visible, or available to be grasped, on the surface. They had to be grasped through hard analysis. This analysis and political consciousness based on it were then taken to the people by intellectuals who played a significant role in arousing the inherent, instinctive, nascent, anti-colonial consciousness of the masses.

*

As explained in Chapter 38, the Indian national movement had a certain specific, though untheorized, strategy of struggle within which its various phases and forms of struggle were integrated, especially after 1918. This strategy was formed by the waging of hegemonic struggle for the minds and hearts of the Indian people. The purpose was to destroy the two basic constituents of colonial hegemony* or the belief system through which the British secured the acquiescence of the Indian people in their rule: that British rule was benevolent or for the good of the Indians and that it was invincible or incapable of being overthrown. Replying to the latter aspect, Jawaharlal Nehru wrote in *The Discovery of India*: 'The essence of his (Gandhiji's) teaching was fearlessness . . . not merely bodily courage but the absence of fear from the mind . . . But the dominant impulse in India under British rule was that of fear, pervasive, oppressing, strangling fear; fear of the army, the police, the widespread secret service; fear of the official class; fear of laws meant to suppress and of prison; fear of the landlord's agents; fear of the money-lender; fear of unemployment and starvation, which were always on the threshold. It was against this all-pervading fear that Gandhiji's quiet and determined voice was raised: Be not afraid.'6

*

And how was nationalist hegemony to be evolved? In the case of a popular anti-imperialist movement, we believe, the leadership, acting within a particular ideological framework, exercises hegemony by taking up the anti-colonial interests of the entire colonized people and by

---

*Relying basically on Gramsci, we have used the concept of hegemony in an amended form since exercise of hegemony in a colonial society both by the colonial rulers and the opposing anti-imperialist forces occurs in a context different from an independent capitalist society. The concept of hegemony, as used by us, means exercise of leadership as opposed to pure domination. More specifically, it relates to the capacity of, as also the strategy through which, the rulers or dominant classes or leadership of popular movements organize consent among the ruled or the followers and exercise moral and ideological leadership over them. According to Gramsci, in the case of class hegemony, the hegemonic class is able to make compromises with a number of allied classes by taking up their causes and interests and thus emerges as the representative of the current interests of the entire society. It unifies these allies under its own leadership through 'a web of institutions, social relations and ideas.' The Gramscian concept of hegemony is of course opposed to an economistic notion of movements and ideologies which concentrate primarily on immediate class interests in politics and ideology and tend to make a direct correlation between the two and sometimes even to derive the latter from the former.

unifying them by adjusting the class interests of the different classes, strata and groups constituting the colonized people. The struggle for ideological hegemony within a national movement pertains to changing the relative balance of advantages flowing from such adjustment and not to the question of adjustment itself. In the colonial situation the anti-imperialist struggle was primary and the social — class and caste — struggles were secondary, and, therefore, struggles within Indian society were to be initiated and then compromised rather than carried to an extreme, with all mutually hostile classes and castes making concessions.

Further, the nationalist strategy alternated between phases of massive mass struggle which broke existing laws and phases of intense political-agitational work within the legal framework. The strategy accepted that mass movements by their very nature had ups and downs, troughs and peaks, for it was not possible for the vast mass of people to engage continuously in a long-drawn-out extra legal struggle that involved considerable sacrifice. This strategy also assumed freedom struggle advancing through stages, though the country was not to advance to freedom till the threshold of the last stage was crossed.

Constructive work — organized around the promotion of *khadi*, national education, Hindi-Muslim unity, the boycott of foreign cloth and liquor, the social upliftment of the Harijans (low caste 'untouchables') and tribal people and the struggle against untouchability — formed an important part of nationalist strategy especially during its constitutional phases. This strategy also involved participation in the colonial constitutional structure without falling prey to it or without getting co-opted by it.

And what was the role of non-violence? It was not, we believe, a mere dogma of Gandhiji nor was it dictated by the interests of the propertied classes. It was an essential part of a movement whose strategy involved the waging of a hegemonic struggle based on a mass movement which mobilized the people to the widest possible extent.

The nationalist strategy of a war of position, of hegemonic struggle, was also linked to the semi-hegemonic or legal authoritarian character of the colonial state which functioned through the rule of law, a rule-bound bureaucracy and a relatively independent judiciary while simultaneously enacting and enforcing extremely repressive laws and which extended a certain amount of civil liberties in normal times and curtailed them in periods of mass struggle. It also constantly offered constitutional and economic concessions though it always retained the basics of state power in its own hands.

Seen from this point of view, the peaceful and negotiated nature of the transfer of power in 1947 was no accident, nor was it the result of a compromise by a tired leadership, but was the result of the character and strategy of the Indian national movement, the culmination of a war of position where the British recognized that the Indian people were no longer willing to be ruled by them and the Indian part of the colonial apparatus could no longer be trusted to enforce a rule which the people did not want. The British recognized that they had lost the battle of hegemony or war of position and decided to retreat rather than make a futile attempt to rule such a vast country by threat of a sword that was already breaking in their hands.

Seen in this strategic perspective, the various negotiations and agreements between the rulers and the nationalist leadership, the retreat of the movement in 1922 and 1934, the compromise involved in the Gandhi-Irwin Pact and the working of constitutional reforms after 1922 and in 1937 also have to be evaluated differently from that done by writers such as R. Palme Dutt. This we have done in the chapters dealing with these issues.

*

The Indian national movement was a popular, multi-class movement. It was not a movement led or controlled by the bourgeoisie, nor did the bourgeoisie exercise exclusive influence over it. Moreover, its multi-class, popular, and open-ended character meant that it was open to the alternative hegemony of socialist ideas.

The national movement did, in fact, undergo constant ideological transformation. In the late 1920s and 1930s, Jawaharlal Nehru, Subhas Bose, the Communists, the Congress Socialists, and other Left-minded socialist groups and individuals made an intense effort to give the movement and the National Congress a socialistic direction. One aspect of this was the effort to organize the peasants in *kisan sabhas*, the workers in trade unions and the youth in youth leagues and student unions. The other was the effort to give the entire national movement a socialist ideological orientation, to make it adopt a socialist vision of free India. This effort did achieve a certain success and socialist ideas spread widely and rapidly. Almost all young intellectuals of the 1930s and

1940s belonged to some shade of pink or red. *Kisan sabhas* and trade unions also tended to shift to the Left. Also important in this respect was the constant development of Gandhiji's ideas in a radical direction. But, when freedom came, the Left had not yet succeeded, for various reasons, in establishing the hegemony of socialist ideas over the national movement and the dominant vision within the movement remained that of bourgeois development. Thus, we suggest, the basic weakness of the movement was located in its ideological structure.

*

The Indian National Congress, being a movement and not just a party, included within its fold, individuals and groups which subscribed to widely divergent political and ideological perspectives. Communists, Socialists and Royists worked within the Congress as did constitution-alists like Satyamurthy and K.M. Munshi. At the same time, the national movement showed a remarkable capacity to remain united despite diversity. A lesson was learnt from the disastrous split of 1907 and the Moderates and Extremists, constitutionalists and non-constitutionalists and leftists and rightists did not split the Indian National Congress thereafter, even in the gravest crises.

There were, of course, many other streams flowing into the swelling river of India's freedom struggle. The Indian National Congress was the mainstream but not the only stream. We have discussed many of these streams in this volume: the pre-Congress peasant and tribal movements, the Revolutionary Terrorists, the Ghadar and Home Rule Movements, the Akali and Temple Reform movements of the 1920s, the struggle in the legislatures and in the Press, the peasant and working class struggles, the rise of the Left inside and outside the Congress, the state people's movements, the politics of the capitalist class, the Indian National Army, the RIN Revolt, etc. We have, as a matter of fact, devoted nearly half of this volume to political movements which formally happened outside the Congress. But we do not treat these 'non-Congress' movements as 'parallel' streams, as some have maintained. Though they were outside the Congress, most of them were not really separate from it. They cannot be artificially counterposed to the movement led by the Congress, which, with all its positive and negative features, was the actual anti-imperialist movement of the Indian people incorporating their historical energies and genius, as is the case with any genuine mass movement.

In fact, nearly all these movements established a complex relationship with the Congress mainstream and at no stage became alternatives to the Congress. They all became an integral part of the Indian national movement. The only ones which may be said to have formed part of an alternative stream of politics were the communal and casteist movements which were not nationalist or anti-imperialist but in fact betrayed loyalist pro-colonial tendencies.

*

In time, the Indian National Movement developed into one of the greatest mass movements in world history. It derived its entire strength, especially after 1918, from the militancy and self-sacrificing spirit of the masses. *Satyagraha* as a form of struggle was based on the active participation of the people and on the sympathy and support of the non-participating millions. Several *Satyagraha* campaigns — apart from innumerable mass agitational campaigns — were waged between 1919 and 1942. Millions of men and women were mobilized in myriad ways; they sustained the movement by their grit and determination. Starting out as a movement of the nationalist intelligentsia, the national movement succeeded in mobilizing the youth, women, the urban petty bourgeoisie, the urban and rural poor, urban and rural artisans, peasants, workers, merchants, capitalists, and a large number of small landlords.

The movement in its various forms and phases took modern politics to the people. It did not, in the main, appeal to their pre-modern consciousness based on religion, caste and locality or loyalty to the traditional rulers or chieftains. It did not mobilize people ideologically around religion, caste or region. It fought for no benefits on that basis. People did not join it as Brahmins, or Patidars, or Marathas, or Harijans. It made no appeal to religious or caste identities, though in some cases caste structure was used in villages to enforce discipline in a movement whose motivation and demands had nothing to do with caste.

Even while relying on the popular consciousness, experience, perception of oppression, and the needed remedies, on notions of good rule or utopia the movement did not merely reflect the existing consciousness but also made every effort to radically transform it in the course of the struggle. Consequently it created space for as well as got integrated with other modern, liberationist movements — movements of women, youth, peasants, workers, Harijans and other lower castes. For example, the social and religious reform movements which developed during the 19th century as part of the defence against colonialization of Indian culture merged with the national movement. Most of them became a part of the broad spectrum of the national movement in the 20th century. But, in the end, the national movement had to surrender in part before communalism. We have tried to examine, at some length, the rise and growth of communalism and the reasons for the partial failure of the national movement to counter its challenge. The national movement also failed to undertake a cultural revolution despite some advances in the social position of women and lower castes. Moreover, it was unable to take the 'cultural defence' of the late 19th century's social and religious reforms back to the rationalist critical phase of the early 19th century. It also could not fully integrate the cultural struggle with the political struggle despite Gandhiji's efforts in that direction.

The national movement was based on an immense faith in the capacity of the Indian people to make sacrifices. At the same time, it recognized the limits on this capacity and did not make demands based on unrealistic and romantic notions. After all, while a cadre-based movement can base itself on exceptional individuals capable of making uncommon sacrifices, a mass movement, even while having exceptional individuals as leaders, has to rely on the masses with all their normal strengths and weaknesses. It is these common people who had to perform uncommon tasks. 'The nation has got energy of which you have no conception but I have,' Gandhiji told K.F. Nariman in 1934. At the same time, he said, a leadership should not 'put an undue strain on the energy.'[7]

As a mass movement, the Indian national movement was able to tap the diverse energies, talents and capacities of a large variety of people. It had a place for all — old and young, rich and poor, women and men, the intellectuals and the masses. People participated in it in varied ways: from jail-going *Satyagraha* and picketing to participation in public meetings and demonstrations, from going on *hartals* and strikes to cheering the *jathas* of Congress volunteers from the sidelines, from voting for nationalist candidates in municipal, district, provincial and central elections to participating in constructive programmes, from becoming 4-*anna* (25 *paise*) members of the Congress to wearing *khadi* and a Gandhi cap, from contributing funds to the Congress to feeding and giving shelter to Congress agitators, from distributing and reading the *Young India* and the *Harijan* or the illegal *Patrikas* (bulletins) to staging and attending nationalist dramas and poetry festivals, and from writing and reading nationalist novels, poems and stories to walking and singing in the *prabhat pheries* (parties making rounds of a town or part of it).

The movement and the process of mass mobilization were also an expression of the immense creativity of the Indian people. They were able to give a full play to their innovativeness and initiative.

The movement did not lack exceptional individuals, both among leaders and followers. It produced thousands of martyrs. But as heroic were those who worked for years, day after day, in an unexciting, humdrum fashion, forsaking their homes and careers, and losing their lands and very livelihood — whose families were often short of daily bread and whose children went without adequate education or health care.

1 The First Major Challenge: The Revolt of 1857

It was the morning of 11 May 1857. The city of Delhi had not yet woken up when a band of *sepoys* from Meerut, who had defied and killed the European officers the previous day, crossed the Jamuna, set the toll house on fire and marched to the Red Fort. They entered the Red Fort through the Raj Ghat gate, followed by an excited crowd, to appeal to Bahadur Shah II, the Moghul Emperor — a pensioner of the British East India Company, who possesed nothing but the name of the mighty *Mughals* — to become their leader, thus, give legitimacy to their cause. Bahadur Shah vacillated as he was neither sure of the intentions of the sepoys nor of his own ability to play an effective role. He was however persuaded, if not coerced, to give in and was proclaimed the *Shahenshah-e-Hindustan*. The sepoys, then, set out to capture and control the imperial city of Delhi. Simon Fraser, the Political Agent, and several other Englishmen were killed; the public offices were either occupied or destroyed. The Revolt of 1857, an unsuccessful but heroic effort to eliminate foreign rule, had begun. The capture of Delhi and the proclamation of Bahadur Shah as the Emperor of Hindustan gave a positive political meaning to the Revolt and provided a rallying point for the rebels by recalling the past glory of the imperial city.

The Revolt at Meerut and the capture of Delhi was the precursor to a widespread mutiny by the sepoys and rebellion almost all over North India, as well as Central and Western India. South India remained quiet and Punjab and Bengal were only marginally affected. Almost half the Company's sepoy strength of 2,32,224 opted out of their loyalty to their regimental colours and overcame the ideology of the army, meticulously constructed over a period of time through training and discipline.

*

Even before the Meerut incident, there were rumblings of resentment in various cantonments. The 19th Native Infantry at Berhampur, which refused to use the newly introduced Enfield rifle, was disbanded in March 1857. A young sepoy of the 34th Native Infantry, Mangal Pande, went a step further and fired at the Sergeant Major of his regiment. He was overpowered and executed and his regiment, too, was disbanded. The 7th Oudh Regiment which defied its officers met with a similar fate.

Within a month of the capture of Delhi, the Revolt spread to different parts of the country: Kanpur, Lucknow, Benares, Allahabad, Bareilly, Jagdishpur and Jhansi. The rebel activity was marked by intense anti-British feelings, and the administration was invariably toppled. In the absence of any leaders from their own ranks, the insurgents turned to the traditional leaders of Indian society — the territorial aristocrats and feudal chiefs who had suffered at the hands of the British.

At Kanpur, the natural choice was Nana Saheb, the adopted son of the last Peshwa, Baji Rao II. He had refused the family title and, banished from Poona, was living near Kanpur. Begum Hazrat Mahal took over the reigns at Lucknow, where popular sympathy was overwhelmingly in favour of the deposed Nawab. Her son, Birjis Qadir, was proclaimed the Nawab and a regular administration was organized with important offices shared equally by Muslims and Hindus.

At Barielly, Khan Bahadur, a descendant of the former ruler of Rohilkhand, was placed in command. Living on a pension granted by the British, he was not too enthusiastic about this and had in fact, warned the Commissioner of the impending mutiny. Yet, once the Revolt broke out, he assumed the administration, organized an army of 40,000 soldiers and offered stiff resistance to the British.

*

In Bihar, the Revolt was led by Kunwar Singh, the *zamindar* of Jagdishpur, a 70-year-old man on the brink of bankruptcy. He nursed a grudge against the British. He had been deprived of his estates by them and his repeated appeals to be entrusted with their management again fell on deaf ears. Even though he had not planned an uprising, he unhesitatingly joined the sepoys when they reached Arrah from Dinapore.

The most outstanding leader of the Revolt was Rani Lakshmibhai, who assumed the leadership of the sepoys at Jhansi. Lord Dalhousie, the Governor-General, had refused to allow her adopted son to succeed to the throne after her husband died and had annexed the state by the application of the Doctrine of Lapse. The Rani had tried everything to reverse the decision. She even offered to keep Jhansi 'safe' for the British if they would grant her wishes. When it was clear nothing was working she joined the sepoys and, in time, became one of the most formidable enemies the British had to contend with.

The Revolt was not confined to these major centres. It had embraced almost every cantonment in the Bengal and a few in Bombay. Only the Madras army remained totally loyal. Why did the sepoys revolt? It was considered prestigious to be in the service of the Company; it provided economic stability. Why, then, did the sepoys choose to forego these advantages for the sake of an uncertain future? A proclamation issued at Delhi indicates the immediate cause: 'It is well known that in these days all the English have entertained these evil designs — first, to destroy the religion of the whole Hindustani Army, and then to make the people by compulsion Christians. Therefore, we, solely on account of our religion, have combined with the people, and have not spared alive one infidel, and have re-established the Delhi dynasty on these terms.'[1]

It is certainly true that the conditions of service in the Company's army and cantonments increasingly came into conflict with the religious beliefs and prejudices of the sepoys, who were predominantly drawn from the upper caste Hindus of the North Western Provinces and Oudh. Initially, the administration sought to accommodate the sepoys' demands: facilities were provided to them to live according to the dictates of their caste and religion. But, with the extension of the Army's operation not only to various parts of India, but also to countries outside, it was not possible to do so any more. Moreover, caste distinctions and segregation within a regiment were not conducive to the cohesiveness of a fighting unit. To begin with, the administration thought of an easy way out: discourage the recruitment of Brahmins; this apparently did not succeed and, by the middle of the nineteenth century, the upper castes predominated in the Bengal Army, for instance.

The unhappiness of the sepoys first surfaced in 1824 when the 47th Regiment at Barrackpur was ordered to go to Burma. To the religious Hindu, crossing the sea meant loss of caste. The sepoys, therefore, refused to comply. The regiment was disbanded and those who led the opposition were hanged. The religious sensibilities of the sepoys who participated in the Afghan War were more seriously affected. During the arduous and disastrous campaigns, the fleeing sepoys were forced to eat and drink whatever came their way. When they returned to India, those at home correctly sensed that they could not have observed caste stipulations and, therefore, were hesitant to welcome them back into the *biradiri*(caste fraternity). Sitaram who had gone to Afghanistan found himself an outcaste not only in his village, but even in his own barracks. The prestige of being in the pay of the Company was not enough to hold his position in society; religion and caste proved to be more powerful.[2]

*

The rumours about the Government's secret designs to promote conversions to Christianity further exasperated the sepoys. The official-missionary nexus gave credence to the rumour. In some cantonments, missionaries were permitted to preach openly and their diatribe against other religions angered the sepoys. The reports about the mixing of bone dust in *atta* and the introduction of the Enfield rifle enhanced the sepoys' growing disaffection with the Government. The cartridges of the new rifle had to be bitten off before loading and the grease was reportedly made of beef and pig fat. The army administration did nothing to allay these fears, and the sepoys felt their religion was in real danger.

The sepoys' discontent was not limited to religion alone. They were equally unhappy with their emoluments. A sepoy in the infantry got seven rupees a month. A *sawar* in the cavalry was paid Rs. 27, out of which he had to pay for his own uniform, food and the upkeep of his mount, and he was ultimately left with only a rupee or two. What was more galling was the sense of deprivation compared to his British counterparts. He was made to feel a subordinate at every step and was discriminated against racially and in matters of promotion and privileges. 'Though he might give the signs of a military genius of Hyder,' wrote T.R. Holmes, 'he knew that he could never attain the pay of an English subaltern and that the rank to which he might attain, after 30 years of faithful service, would not protect him from the insolent dictation of an ensign fresh from England.'[3]

The discontent of the sepoys was not limited to matters military, they reflected the general disenchantment with and opposition to British rule. The sepoy, in fact, was a 'peasant in uniform,' whose consciousness was not divorced from that of the rural population. A military officer had warned Dalhousie about the possible consequences of his policies: 'Your army is derived from the peasantry of the country who have rights and if those rights are infringed upon, you will no longer have to depend on the fidelity of the army . . . *If you infringe the institutions of the people of India, that army will sympathise with them; for they are* part of the population, and in every infringement you may make upon the rights of the individuals, you infringe upon the rights of men who are either themselves in the army or upon their sons, their fathers or their relations.'[4]

*

Almost every agricultural family in Oudh had a representative in the army; there were 75,000 men from Oudh. Whatever happened there was of immediate concern to the sepoy. The new land revenue system introduced after the annexation and the confiscation of lands attached to charitable institutions affected his well-being. That accounted for the 14,000 petitions received from the sepoys about the hardships of the revenue system. A proclamation issued by the Delhi rebels clearly reflected the sepoy's awareness of the misery brought about by British rule. The mutiny in itself, therefore, was a revolt against the British and, thus, a political act. What imparted this character to the mutiny was the sepoy's identity of interests with the general population.

The Revolt of the sepoys was accompanied by a rebellion of the civil population, particularly in the North Western Provinces and Oudh, the two areas from which the sepoys of the Bengal army were recruited. Except in Muzzafarnagar and Saharanpur, civil rebellion followed the Revolt of the sepoys. The action of the sepoys released the rural population from fear of the state and the control exercised by the administration. Their accumulated grievances found immediate expression and they rose *en masse* to give vent to their opposition to British rule. Government buildings were destroyed, the "treasury was plundered, the magazine was sacked, barracks and court houses were burnt and prison gates were flung open." The civil rebellion had a broad social base, embracing all sections of society — the territorial magnates, peasants, artisans, religious mendicants and priests, civil servants, shopkeepers and boatmen. The Revolt of the sepoys, thus, resulted in a popular uprising.

*

The reason for this mass upsurge has to be sought in the nature of British rule which adversely affected the interests of almost all sections of society. Under the burden of excessive taxes the peasantry became progressively indebted and impoverished. The only interest of the Company was the realization of maximum revenue with minimum effort. Consequently, settlements were hurriedly undertaken, often without any regard for the resources of the land. For instance, in the district of Bareilly in 1812, the settlement was completed in the record time of ten months with a dramatic increase of Rs. 14,73,188 over the earlier settlement. Delighted by this increase, the Government congratulated the officers for their 'zeal, ability and indefatigable labour.' It did not occur to the authorities that such a sharp and sudden increase would have disastrous consequences on the cultivators. Naturally, the revenue could not be collected without coercion and torture: in Rohilkhand there were as many as 2,37,388 coercive collections during 1848-56. Whatever the conditions, the Government was keen on collecting revenue. Even in very adverse circumstances, remissions were rarely granted. A collector who repeatedly reported his inability to realize revenue from an estate, as only grass was grown there, was told that grass was a very good produce and it should be sold for collecting revenue![5]

The traditional landed aristocracy suffered no less. In Oudh, which was a storm centre of the Revolt, the *taluqdars* lost all their power and privileges. About 21,000 *taluqdars* whose estates were confiscated suddenly found themselves without a source of income, 'unable to work, ashamed to beg, condemned to penury.' These dispossessed *taluqdars* smarting under the humiliation heaped on them, seized the opportunity presented by the Sepoy Revolt to oppose the British and regain what they had lost.

*

British rule also meant misery to the artisans and handicraftsmen. The annexation of Indian states by the Company cut off their major source of patronage. Added to this, British policy discouraged Indian handicrafts and promoted British goods. The highly skilled Indian craftsmen were deprived of their source of income and were forced to look for alternate sources of employment that hardly existed, as the destruction of Indian handicrafts was not accompanied by the development of modern industries.

The reforming zeal of British officials under the influence of utilitarianism had aroused considerable suspicion, resentment, and opposition. The orthodox Hindus and Muslims feared that through social legislation the British were trying to destroy their religion and culture. Moreover, they believed that legislation was undertaken to aid the missionaries in their quest for evangelization. The orthodox and the religious, therefore, arrayed against the British. Several proclamations of the rebels expressed this cultural concern in no uncertain terms.

The coalition of the Revolt of the sepoys and that of the civil population made the 1857 movement an unprecedented popular upsurge. Was it an organized and methodically planned Revolt or a spontaneous insurrection? In the absence of any reliable account left behind by the rebels it is difficult to be certain. The attitude and activities of the leaders hardly suggest any planning or conspiracy on their part and if at all it existed it was at an embryonic stage.

When the sepoys arrived from Meerut, Bahadur Shah seems to have been taken by surprise and promptly conveyed the news to the Lt. Governor at Agra. So did Rani Lakshmibhai of Jhansi who took quite some time before openly joining the rebels. Whether Nana Saheb and Maulvi Ahmad Shah of Faizabad had established links with various cantonments and were instrumental in instigating Revolt is yet to be proved beyond doubt. Similarly, the message conveyed by the circulation of *chappatis* and lotus flowers is also uncertain. The only positive factor is that within a month of the Meerut incident the Revolt became quite widespread.

*

Even if there was no planning and organization before the revolt, it was important that it was done, once it started. Immediately after the capture of Delhi a letter was addressed to the rulers of all the neighbouring states and of Rajasthan soliciting their support and inviting them to participate. In Delhi, a court of administrators was established which was responsible for all matters of state. The court consisted of ten members, six from the army and four from the civilian departments. All decisions were taken by a majority vote. The court conducted the affairs of the state in the name of the Emperor. 'The Government at Delhi,' wrote a British official, 'seems to have been a sort of constitutional Milocracy. The king was king and honoured as such, like a constitutional monarch; but instead of a Parliament, he had a council of soldiers, in whom power rested, and of whom he was no degree a military commander.'[6] In other centres, also, attempts were made to bring about an organization.

Bahadur Shah was recognized as the Emperor by all rebel leaders. Coins were struck and orders were issued in his name. At Bareilly, Khan Bahadur Khan conducted the administration in the name of the Mughal Emperor. It is also significant that the first impulse of the rebels was always to proceed to Delhi whether they were at Meerut, Kanpur or Jhansi. The need to create an organization and a political institution to preserve the gains was certainly felt. But in the face of the British counter-offensive, there was no chance to build on these early nebulous ideas.

For more than a year, the rebels carried on their struggle against heavy odds. They had no source of arms and ammunition; what they had captured from the British arsenals could not carry them far. They were often forced to fight with swords and pikes against an enemy supplied with the most modern weapons. They had no quick system of communication at their command and, hence, no coordination was possible. Consequently, they were unaware of the strength and weaknesses of their compatriots and as a result could not come to each other's rescue in times of distress. Every one was left to play a lonely hand.

*

Although the rebels received the sympathy of the people, the country as a whole was not behind them. The merchants, intelligentsia and Indian rulers not only kept aloof, but actively supported the British. Meetings were organized in Calcutta and Bombay by them to pray for the success of the British. Despite the Doctrine of Lapse, the Indian rulers who expected their future to be safer with the British liberally provided them with men and materials. Indeed, the sepoys might have made a better fight of it if they had received their support.

Almost half the Indian soldiers not only did not Revolt but fought against their own countrymen. The recapture of Delhi was effected by five columns consisting of 1700 British troops and 3200 Indians. The blowing up of Kashmere Gate was conducted by six British officers and

NCOs and twenty-four Indians, of whom ten were Punjabis and fourteen were from Agra and Oudh.

Apart from some honourable exceptions like the Rani of Jhansi, Kunwar Singh and Maulvi Ahmadullah, the rebels were poorly served by their leaders. Most of them failed to realize the significance of the Revolt and simply did not do enough. Bahadur Shah and Zeenat Mahal had no faith in the sepoys and negotiated with the British to secure their safety. Most of the *taluqdars* tried only to protect their own interests. Some of them, like Man Singh, changed sides several times depending on which side had the upper hand.

Apart from a commonly shared hatred for alien rule, the rebels had no political perspective or a definite vision of the future. They were all prisoners of their own past, fighting primarily to regain their lost privileges. Unsurprisingly, they proved incapable of ushering in a new political order. John Lawrence rightly remarked that 'had a single leader of ability arisen among them (the rebels) we must have been lost beyond redemption.'

That was not to be, yet the rebels showed exemplary courage, dedication and commitment. Thousands of men courted death, fighting for a cause they held dear. Their heroism alone, however, could not stem the onslaught of a much superior British army. The first to fall was Delhi on 20 September 1857 after a prolonged battle. Bahadur Shah, who took refuge in Humayun's tomb, was captured, tried and deported to Burma. With that the back of the Revolt was broken, since Delhi was the only possible rallying point. The British military then dealt with the rebels in one centre after another. The Rani of Jhansi died fighting on 17 June 1858. General Hugh Rose, who defeated her, paid high tribute to his enemy when he said that 'here lay the woman who was the only man among the rebels.' Nana Saheb refused to give in and finally escaped to Nepal in the beginning of 1859, hoping to renew the struggle. Kunwar Singh, despite his old age, was too quick for the British troops and constantly kept them guessing till his death on 9 May 1858. Tantia Tope, who successfully carried on guerrilla warfare against the British until April 1859, was betrayed by a *zamindar*, captured and put to death by the British.

Thus, came to an end the most formidable challenge the British empire had to face in India. It is a matter of speculation as to what the course of history would have been had the rebels succeeded. Whether they would have 'put the clock back' and resurrected and reinforced a feudal order need not detain us here; although that was not necessarily the only option. Despite the sepoys' limitations and weaknesses, their effort to emancipate the country from foreign rule was a patriotic act and a progressive step. If the importance of a historical event is not limited to its immediate achievements, the Revolt of 1857 was not a pure historical tragedy. Even in failure it served a grand purpose: a source of inspiration for the national liberation movement which later achieved what the Revolt could not.

2 Civil Rebellions and Tribal Uprisings

The Revolt of 1857 was the most dramatic instance of traditional India's struggle against foreign rule. But it was no sudden occurrence. It was the culmination of a century long tradition of fierce popular resistance to British domination.

The establishment of British power in India was a prolonged process of piecemeal conquest and consolidation and the colonialization of the economy and society. This process produced discontent, resentment and resistance at every stage.

This popular resistance took three broad forms: civil rebellions, tribal uprisings and peasant movements. We will discuss the first two in this chapter.

*

The series of civil rebellions, which run like a thread through the first 100 years of British rule, were often led by deposed *rajas* and *nawabs* or their descendants, uprooted and impoverished *zamindars*, *landlords* and *poligars* (landed military magnates in South India), and ex-retainers and officials of the conquered Indian states. The backbone of the rebellions, their mass base and striking power came from the rack-rented peasants, ruined artisans and demobilized soldiers.

These sudden, localized revolts often took place because of local grievances although for short periods they acquired a broad sweep, involving armed bands of a few hundreds to several thousands.

The major cause of all these civil rebellions taken as a whole was the rapid changes the British introduced in the economy, administration and land revenue system. These changes led to the disruption of the agrarian society, causing prolonged and widespread suffering among its constit-uents. Above all, the colonial policy of intensifying demands for land revenue and extracting as large an amount as possible produced a verit-able upheaval in Indian villages. In Bengal, for example, in less than thirty years land revenue collection was raised to nearly double the amount collected under the *Mughals*. The pattern was repeated in other parts of the country as British rule spread. And aggravating the unhap-piness of the farmers was the fact that not even a part of the enhanced revenue was spent on the development of agriculture or the welfare of the cultivator.

Thousands of *zamindars* and *poligars* lost control over their land and its revenues either due to the extinction of their rights by the colonial state or by the forced sale of their rights over land because of their ina-bility to meet the exorbitant land revenue demanded. The proud *zamindars* and *poligars* resented this loss even more when they were displaced by rank outsiders — government officials and the new men of money — merchants and moneylenders. Thus they, as also the old chiefs, who had lost their principalities, had personal scores to settle with the new rulers.

Peasants and artisans, as we have seen earlier, had their own reasons to rise up in arms and side with the traditional elite. Increasing demands for land revenue were forcing large numbers of peasants into growing indebtedness or into selling their lands. The new landlords, bereft of any traditional paternalism towards their tenants, pushed up rents to rui-nous heights and evicted them in the case of non-payment. The economic decline of the peasantry was reflected in twelve major and numerous minor famines from 1770 to 1857.

The new courts and legal system gave a further fillip to the dispos-sessors of land and encouraged the rich to oppress the poor. Flogging, torture and jailing of the cultivators for arrears of rent or land revenue or interest on debt were quite common. The ordinary people were also hard hit by the prevalence of corruption at the lower levels of the police, judiciary and general administration. The petty officials enriched themselves freely at the cost of the poor. The police looted, oppressed and tortured the common people at will. William Edwards, a British official, wrote in 1859 that the police were 'a scourge to the people' and that 'their oppression and exactions form one of the chief grounds of dissatisfaction with our government.'

The ruin of Indian handicraft industries, as a result of the imposition of free trade in India and levy of discriminatory tariffs against Indian goods in Britain, pauperized millions of artisans. The misery of the artisans was further compounded by the disappearance of their traditional patrons and buyers, the princes, chieftains, and *zamindars*.

The scholarly and priestly classes were also active in inciting hatred and rebellion against foreign rule. The traditional rulers and ruling elite had financially supported scholars, religious preachers, priests, *pandits* and *maulvis* and men of arts and literature. With the coming of the British and the ruin of the traditional landed and bureaucratic elite, this patronage came to an end, and all those who had depended on it were impoverished.

Another major cause of the rebellions was the very foreign character of British rule. Like any other people, the Indian people too felt humiliated at being under a foreigner's heel. This feeling of hurt pride inspired efforts to expel the foreigner from their lands.

The civil rebellions began as British rule was established in Bengal and Bihar, and they occurred in area after area as it was incorporated into colonial rule. There was hardly a year without armed opposition or a decade without a major armed rebellion in one part of the country or the other. From 1763 to 1856, there were more than forty major rebellions apart from hundreds of minor ones.

Displaced peasants and demobilized soldiers of Bengal led by religious monks and dispossessed *zamindars* were the first to rise up in the Sanyasi rebellion, made famous by Bankim Chandra Chatterjee in his novel *Anand Math*, that lasted from 1763 to 1800. It was followed by the Chuar uprising which covered five districts of Bengal and Bihar from 1766 to 1772 and then, again, from 1795 to 1816. Other major rebellions in Eastern India were those of Rangpur and Dinajpur, 1783; Bishnupur and Birbhum, 1799; Orissa *zamindars*, 1804-17; and Sambalpur, 1827-40.

In South India, the Raja of Vizianagram revolted in 1794, the *poligars* of Tamil Nadu during the 1790's, of Malabar and coastal Andhra during the first decade of the 19th century, of Parlekamedi during 1813-14. Dewan Velu Thampi of Travancore organized a heroic revolt in 1805. The Mysore peasants too revolted in 1830-31. There were major uprisings in Vizagapatam from 1830-34, Ganjam in 1835 and Kurnool in 1846-47.

In Western India, the chiefs of Saurashtra rebelled repeatedly from 1816 to 1832. The Kolis of Gujarat did the same during 1824-28, 1839 and 1849. Maharashtra was in a perpetual state of revolt after the final defeat of the Peshwa. Prominent were the Bhil uprisings, 1818-31; the Kittur uprising, led by Chinnava, 1824; the Satara uprising, 1841; and the revolt of the Gadkaris, 1844.

Northern India was no less turbulent. The present states of Western U.P. and Haryana rose up in arms in 1824. Other major rebellions were those of Bilaspur, 1805; the *taluqdars* of Aligarh, 1814-17; the Bundelas of Jabalpur, 1842; and Khandesh, 1852. The second Punjab War in 1848-49 was also in the nature of a popular revolt by the people and the army.

These almost continuous rebellions were massive in their totality, but were wholly local in their spread and isolated from each other. They were the result of local causes and grievances, and were also localized in their effects. They often bore the same character not because they represented national or common efforts but because they represented common conditions though separated in time and space.

Socially, economically and politically, the semi-feudal leaders of these rebellions were backward looking and traditional in outlook. They still lived in the old world, blissfully unaware and oblivious of the modern world which had knocked down the defences of their society. Their resistance represented no societal alternative. It was centuries-old in form and ideological and cultural content. Its basic objective was to restore earlier forms of rule and social relations. Such backward looking and scattered, sporadic and disunited uprisings were incapable of fending off or overthrowing foreign rule. The British succeeded in pacifying the rebel areas one by one. They also gave concessions to the less fiery rebel chiefs and *zamindars* in the form of reinstatement, the restoration of their estates and reduction in revenue assessments so long as they agreed to live peacefully under alien authority. The more recalcitrant ones were physically wiped out. Velu Thampi was, for example, publicly hanged even after he was dead.

The suppression of the civil rebellions was a major reason why the Revolt of 1857 did not spread to South India and most of Eastern and Western India. The historical significance of these civil uprisings lies in that they established strong and valuable local traditions of resistance to British rule. The Indian people were to draw inspiration from these traditions in the later nationalist struggle for freedom.

*

The tribal people, spread over a large part of India, organized hundreds of militant outbreaks and insurrections during the 19th century. These uprisings were marked by immense courage and sacrifice on their part and brutal suppression and veritable butchery on the part of the rulers. The tribals had cause to be upset for a variety of reasons. The colonial administration ended their relative isolation and brought them fully within the ambit of colonialism. It recognized the tribal chiefs as *zamindars* and introduced a new system of land revenue and taxation of tribal products. It encouraged the influx of Christian missionaries into the tribal areas. Above all, it introduced a large number of moneylenders, traders and revenue farmers as middlemen among the tribals. These middlemen were the chief instruments for bringing the tribal people within the vortex of the colonial economy and exploitation. The middlemen were outsiders who increasingly took possession of tribal lands and ensnared the tribals in a web of debt. In time, the tribal people increasingly lost their lands and were reduced to the position of agricultural labourers, share-croppers and rack-rented tenants on the land they had earlier brought under cultivation and held on a communal basis.

Colonialism also transformed their relationship with the forest. They had depended on the forest for food, fuel and cattle-feed. They practised shifting cultivation (*jhum, podu,* etc.), taking recourse to fresh forest lands when their existing lands showed signs of exhaustion. The colonial government changed all this. It usurped the forest lands and placed restrictions on access to forest products, forest lands and village common lands. It refused to let cultivation shift to new areas.

Oppression and extortion by policemen and other petty officials further aggravated distress among the tribals. The revenue farmers and government agents also intensified and expanded the system of *begar* —making the tribals perform unpaid labour.

All this differed in intensity from region to region, but the complete disruption of the old agrarian order of the tribal communities provided the common factor for all the tribal uprisings. These uprisings were broad-based, involving thousands of tribals, often the entire population of a region.

The colonial intrusion and the triumvirate of trader, moneylender and revenue farmer in sum disrupted the tribal identity to a lesser or greater degree. In fact, ethnic ties were a basic feature of the tribal rebellions. The rebels saw themselves not as a discreet class but as having a tribal identity. At this level the solidarity shown was of a very high order. Fellow tribals were never attacked unless they had collaborated with the enemy.

At the same time, not all outsiders were attacked as enemies. Often there was no violence against the non-tribal poor, who worked in tribal villages in supportive economic roles, or who had social relations with the tribals, such as *telis, gwalas, lohars*, carpenters, potters, weavers, washermen, barbers, drummers, and bonded labourers and domestic servants of the outsiders. They were not only spared, but were seen as allies. In many cases, the rural poor formed a part of the rebellious tribal bands.

The rebellions normally began at the point where the tribals felt so oppressed that they felt they had no alternative but to fight. This often took the form of spontaneous attacks on outsiders, looting their property and expelling them from their villages. This led to clashes with the colonial authorities. When this happened, the tribals began to move towards armed resistance and elementary organization.

Often, religious and charismatic leaders — messiahs — emerged at this stage and promised divine intervention and an end to their suffering at the hands of the outsiders, and asked their fellow tribals to rise and rebel against foreign authority. Most of these leaders claimed to derive their authority from God. They also often claimed that they possessed magical powers, for example, the power to make the enemies' bullets ineffective. Filled with hope and confidence, the tribal masses tended to follow these leaders to the very end.

The warfare between the tribal rebels and the British armed forces was totally unequal. On one side were drilled regiments armed with the latest weapons and on the other were men and women fighting in roving bands armed with primitive weapons such as stones, axes, spears and bows and arrows, believing in the magical powers of their commanders. The tribals died in lakhs in this unequal warfare.

*

Among the numerous tribal revolts, the Santhal *hool* or uprising was the most massive. The Santhals, who live in the area between Bhagalpur and Rajmahal, known as Daman-i-koh, rose in revolt; made a determined attempt to expel the outsiders — the *dikus* — and proclaimed the complete 'annihilation' of the alien regime. The social conditions which drove them to insurrection were described by a contemporary in the *Calcutta Review* as follows:'*Zamindars*, the police, the revenue and court alas have exercised a combined system of extortions, oppressive exactions, forcible dispossession of property, abuse and personal violence and a variety of petty tyrannies upon the timid and yielding Santhals. Usurious interest on loans of money ranging from 50 to 500 per cent; false measures at the *haut* and the market; wilful and uncharitable trespass by the rich by means of their untethered cattle, *tattoos*, ponies and even elephants, on the growing crops of the poorer race; and such like illegalities have been prevalent.'[1]

The Santhals considered the *dikus* and government servants morally corrupt being given to beggary, stealing, lying and drunkenness.

By 1854, the tribal heads, the *majhis* and *parganites*, had begun to meet and discuss the possibility of revolting. Stray cases of the robbing of *zamindars* and moneylenders began to occur. The tribal leaders called an assembly of nearly 6000 Santhals, representing 400 villages, at Bhaganidihi on 30 June 1855. It was decided to raise the banner of revolt, get rid of the outsiders and their colonial masters once and for all, and usher in *Satyug*, 'The Reign of Truth,' and 'True Justice.'

The Santhals believed that their actions had the blessings of God. Sido and Kanhu, the principal rebel leaders, claimed that Thakur (God) had communicated with them and told them to take up arms and fight for independence. Sido told the authorities in a proclamation: 'The Thacoor has ordered me saying that the country is not *Sahibs* . . . The Thacoor himself will fight. Therefore, you *Sahibs* and Soldiers (will) fight the Thacoor himself.'[2]

The leaders mobilized the Santhal men and women by organizing huge processions through the villages accompanied by drummers and other musicians. The leaders rode at the head on horses and elephants and in *palkis*. Soon nearly 60,000 Santhals had been mobilized. Forming bands of 1,500 to 2,000, but rallying in many thousands at the call of drums on particular occasions, they attacked the *mahajans* and *zamindars* and their houses, police stations, railway construction sites, the *dak* (post) carriers — in fact all the symbols of *diku* exploitation and colonial power.

The Santhal insurrection was helped by a large number of non-tribal and poor *dikus*. *Gwalas* (milkmen) and others helped the rebels with provisions and services; *lohars* (blacksmiths) accompanied the rebel bands, keeping their weapons in good shape.

Once the Government realized the scale of the rebellion, it organized a major military campaign against the rebels. It mobilized tens of regiments under the command of a major-general, declared Martial Law in the affected areas and offered rewards of upto Rs. 10,000 for the capture of various leaders.

The rebellion was crushed ruthlessly. More than 15,000 Santhals were killed while tens of villages were destroyed. Sido was betrayed and captured and killed in August 1855 while Kanhu was arrested by accident at the tail-end of the rebellion in February 1866. And 'the Rajmahal Hills were drenched with the blood of the fighting Santhal peasantry.' One typical instance of the heroism of Santhal rebels has been narrated by L.S.S. O'Malley: 'They showed the most reckless courage, never knowing when they were beaten and refusing to surrender. On one occasion, forty-five Santhals took refuge in a mud hut which they held against the Sepoys. Volley after volley was fired into it . . . Each time the Santhals replied with a discharge of arrows. At last, when their fire ceased, the Sepoys entered the hut and found only one old man was left alive. A Sepoy called on him to surrender, whereupon the old man rushed upon him and cut him down with his battle axe.'[3]

*

I shall describe briefly three other major tribal rebellions. The *Kols* of Chhotanagpur rebelled from 1820 to 1837. Thousands of them were massacred before British authority could be re-imposed. The hill tribesmen of Rampa in coastal Andhra revolted in March 1879 against the depredations of the government-supported *mansabdar* and the new restrictive forest regulations. The authorities had to mobilize regiments of infantry, a squadron of cavalry and two companies of sappers and miners before the rebels, numbering several thousands, could be defeated by the end of 1880.

The rebellion (*ulgulan*) of the Munda tribesmen, led by Birsa Munda, occurred during 1899-1900. For over thirty years the Munda *sardars* had been struggling against the destruction of their system of common land holdings by the intrusion of *jagirdars*, *thikadars* (revenue farmers) and merchant moneylenders.

Birsa, born in a poor share-cropper household in 1874, had a vision of God in 1895. He declared himself to be a divine messenger, possessing miraculous healing powers. Thousands gathered around him seeing in him a Messiah with a new religious message. Under the influence of the *sardars*, the religious movement soon acquired an agrarian and political content. Birsa began to move from village to village, organizing rallies and mobilizing his followers on religious and political grounds. On Christmas Eve, 1899, Birsa proclaimed a rebellion to establish Munda rule in the land and encouraged 'the killing of *thikadars* and *jagirdars* and Rajas and *Hakims* (rulers) and Christians.' *Satyug* would be established in place of the present-day *Kalyug*. He declared that 'there was going to be a fight with the *dikus*, the ground would be as red as the red flag with their blood.'[4] The non-tribal poor were not to be attacked.

To bring about liberation, Birsa gathered a force of 6,000 Mundas armed with swords, spears, battle-axes, and bows and arrows. He was, however, captured in the beginning of February 1900 and he died in jail in June. The rebellion had failed. But Birsa entered the realms of legend.

3 Peasant Movements and Uprisings After 1857

It is worth taking a look at the effects of colonial exploitation of the Indian peasants. Colonial economic policies, the new land revenue system, the colonial administrative and judicial systems, and the ruin of handicrafts leading to the over-crowding of land, transformed the agrarian structure and impoverished the peasantry. In the vast *zamindari* areas, the peasants were left to the tender mercies of the *zamindars* who rack-rented them and compelled them to pay illegal dues and perform *begar*. In *Ryotwari* areas, the Government itself levied heavy land revenue. This forced the peasants to borrow money from the moneylenders. Gradually, over large areas, the actual cultivators were reduced to the status of tenants-at-will, share-croppers and landless labourers, while their lands, crops and cattle passed into the hands of landlords, trader-moneylenders and rich peasants.

When the peasants could take it no longer, they resisted against the oppression and exploitation; and, they found whether their target was the indigenous exploiter or the colonial administration, that their real enemy, after the barriers were down, was the colonial state.

One form of elemental protest, especially when individuals and small groups found that collective action was not possible though their social condition was becoming intolerable, was to take to crime. Many dispossessed peasants took to robbery, dacoity and what has been called social banditry, preferring these to starvation and social degradation.

*

The most militant and widespread of the peasant movements was the

Indigo Revolt of 1859-60. The indigo planters, nearly all Europeans, compelled the tenants to grow indigo which they processed in factories set up in rural (*mofussil*) areas. From the beginning, indigo was grown under an extremely oppressive system which involved great loss to the cultivators. The planters forced the peasants to take a meager amount as advance and enter into fraudulent contracts. The price paid for the indigo plants was far below the market price. The comment of the Lieutenant Governor of Bengal, J.B. Grant, was that 'the root of the whole question is the struggle to make the *raiyats* grow indigo plant, without paying them the price of it.'[1] The peasant was forced to grow indigo on the best land he had whether or not he wanted to devote his land and labour to more paying crops like rice. At the time of delivery, he was cheated even of the due low price. He also had to pay regular bribes to the planter's officials. He was forced to accept an advance. Often he was not in a position to repay it, but even if he could he was not allowed to do so. The advance was used by the planters to compel him to go on cultivating indigo.

Since the enforcement of forced and fraudulent contracts through the courts was a difficult and prolonged process, the planters resorted to a reign of terror to coerce the peasants. Kidnapping, illegal confinement in factory godowns, flogging, attacks on women and children, carrying off cattle, looting, burning and demolition of houses and destruction of crops and fruit trees were some of the methods used by the planters. They hired or maintained bands of *lathiyals* (armed retainers) for the purpose.

In practice, the planters were also above the law. With a few exceptions, the magistrates, mostly European, favoured the planters with whom they dined and hunted regularly. Those few who tried to be fair were soon transferred. Twenty-nine planters and a solitary Indian *zamindar* were appointed as Honorary Magistrates in 1857, which gave birth to the popular saying '*je rakhak se bhakak*' (Our protector is also our devourer).

The discontent of indigo growers in Bengal boiled over in the autumn of 1859 when their case seemed to get Government support. Misreading an official letter and exceeding his authority, Hem Chandra Kar, Deputy Magistrate of Kalaroa, published on 17 August a proclamation to policemen that 'in cases of disputes relating to Indigo *Ryots*, they (*ryots*) shall retain possession of their own lands, and shall sow on them what crops they please, and the Police will be careful that no

Indigo Planter nor anyone else be able to interface in the matter.'2

The news of Kar's proclamation spread all over Bengal, and peasants felt that the time for overthrowing the hated system had come. Initially, the peasants made an attempt to get redressal through peaceful means. They sent numerous petitions to the authorities and organized peaceful demonstrations. Their anger exploded in September 1859 when they asserted their right not to grow indigo under duress and resisted the physical pressure of the planters and their *lathiyals* backed by the police and the courts.

The beginning was made by the *ryots* of Govindpur village in Naida district when, under the leadership of Digambar Biswas and Bishnu Biswas, ex-employees of a planter, they gave up indigo cultivation. And when, on 13 September, the planter sent a band of 100 *lathiyals* to attack their village, they organized a counter force armed with lathis and spears and fought back.

The peasant disturbances and indigo strikes spread rapidly to other areas. The peasants refused to take advances and enter into contracts, pledged not to sow indigo, and defended themselves from the planters' attacks with whatever weapons came to hand — spears, slings, lathis, bows and arrows, bricks, bhel-fruit, and earthen-pots (thrown by women).

The indigo strikes and disturbances flared up again in the spring of 1860 and encompassed all the indigo districts of Bengal. Factory after factory was attacked by hundreds of peasants and village after village bravely defended itself. In many cases, the efforts of the police to intervene and arrest peasant leaders were met with an attack on policemen and police posts.

The planters then attacked with another weapon, their *zamindari* powers. They threatened the rebellious *ryots* with eviction or enhancement of rent. The *ryots* replied by going on a rent strike. They refused to pay the enhanced rents; and they physically resisted attempts to evict them. They also gradually learnt to use the legal machinery to enforce their rights. They joined together and raised funds to fight court cases filed against them, and they initiated legal action on their own against the planters. They also used the weapon of social boycott to force a planter's servants to leave him.

Ultimately, the planters could not withstand the united resistance of the *ryots*, and they gradually began to close their factories. The cultivation of indigo was virtually wiped out from the districts of Bengal by the end of 1860.

A major reason for the success of the Indigo Revolt was the tremendous initiative, cooperation, organization and discipline of the *ryots*. Another was the complete unity among Hindu and Muslim peasants. Leadership for the movement was provided by the more well-off *ryots* and in some cases by petty *zamindars*, moneylenders and ex-employees of the planters.

A significant feature of the Indigo Revolt was the role of the intelligentsia of Bengal which organized a powerful campaign in support of the rebellious peasantry. It carried on newspaper campaigns, organized mass meetings, prepared memoranda on peasants' grievances and supported them in their legal battles. Outstanding in this respect was the role of Harish Chandra Mukherji, editor of the *Hindoo Patriot*. He published regular reports from his correspondents in the rural areas on planters' oppression, officials' partisanship and peasant resistance. He himself wrote with passion, anger and deep knowledge of the problem which he raised to a high political plane. Revealing an insight into the historical and political significance of the Indigo Revolt, he wrote in May 1860: 'Bengal might well be proud of its peasantry . . . Wanting power, wealth, political knowledge and even leadership, the peasantry of Bengal have brought about a revolution inferior in magnitude and importance to none that has happened in the social history of any other country . . . With the Government against them, the law against them, the tribunals against them, the Press against them, they have achieved a success of which the benefits will reach all orders and the most distant generations of our countrymen.'[3]

Din Bandhu Mitra's play, *Neel Darpan*, was to gain great fame for vividly portraying the oppression by the planters.

The intelligentsia's role in the Indigo Revolt was to have an abiding impact on the emerging nationalist intellectuals. In their very political childhood they had given support to a popular peasant movement against the foreign planters. This was to establish a tradition with long term implications for the national movement.

Missionaries were another group which extended active support to the indigo *ryots* in their struggle.

The Government's response to the Revolt was rather restrained and not as harsh as in the case of civil rebellions and tribal uprisings. It had just undergone the harrowing experience of the Santhal uprising and the Revolt of 1857. It was also able to see, in time, the changed temper of the peasantry and was influenced by the support extended to the Revolt by the intelligentsia and the missionaries. It appointed a commission to inquire into the problem of indigo cultivation. Evidence brought before the Indigo Commission and its final report exposed the coercion and corruption underlying the entire system of indigo cultivation. The result was the mitigation of the worst abuses of the system. The Government issued a notification in November 1860 that *ryots* could not be compelled to sow indigo and that it would ensure that all disputes were settled by legal means. But the planters were already closing down the factories — they felt that they could not make their enterprises pay without the use of force and fraud.

*

Large parts of East Bengal were engulfed by agrarian unrest during the 1870s and early 1880s. The unrest was caused by the efforts of the *zamindars* to enhance rent beyond legal limits and to prevent the tenants from acquiring occupancy rights under Act X of 1859. This they tried to achieve through illegal coercive methods such as forced eviction and seizure of crops and cattle as well as by dragging the tenants into costly litigation in the courts.

The peasants were no longer in a mood to tolerate such oppression. In May 1873, an agrarian league or combination was formed in Yusufshahi Parganah in Pabna district to resist the demands of the *zamindars*. The league organized mass meetings of peasants. Large crowds of peasants would gather and march through villages frightening the *zamindars* and appealing to other peasants to join them. The league organized a rent-strike — the *ryots* were to refuse to pay the enhanced rents — and challenged the *zamindars* in the courts. Funds were raised from the *ryots* to meet the costs. The struggle gradually spread throughout Pabna and then to the other districts of East Bengal. Everywhere agrarian leagues were organized, rents were withheld and *zamindars* fought in the courts. The main form of struggle was that of legal resistance. There was very little violence — it only occurred when the *zamindars* tried to compel the *ryots* to submit to their terms by force. There were only a few cases of looting of the houses of the *zamindars*. A few attacks on police stations took place and the peasants also resisted attempts to execute court decrees. But such cases were rather rare. Hardly any *zamindar* or *zamindar's* agent was killed or seriously injured. In the course of the movement, the *ryots* developed a strong awareness of the law and their legal rights and the ability to combine and form associations for peaceful agitation.

Though peasant discontent smouldered till 1885, many of the disputes were settled partially under official pressure and persuasion and partially out of the *zamindar's* fear that the united peasantry would drag them into prolonged and costly litigation. Many peasants were able to acquire occupancy rights and resist enhanced rents.

The Government rose to the defence of the *zamindars* wherever violence took place. Peasants were then arrested on a large scale. But it assumed a position of neutrality as far as legal battles or peaceful agitations were concerned. The Government also promised to undertake legislation to protect the tenants from the worst aspects of *zamindari* oppression, a promise it fulfilled however imperfectly in 1885 when the Bengal Tenancy Act was passed.

What persuaded the *zamindars* and the colonial regime to reconcile themselves to the movement was the fact that its aims were limited to the redressal of the immediate grievances of the peasants and the enforcement of the existing legal rights and norms. It was not aimed at the *zamindari* system. It also did not have at any stage an anti-colonial political edge. The agrarian leagues kept within the bounds of law, used the legal machinery to fight the *zamindars*, and raised no anti-British demands. The leaders often argued that they were against *zamindars* and not the British. In fact, the leaders raised the slogan that the peasants want 'to be the *ryots* of Her Majesty the Queen and of Her only.' For this reason, official action was based on the enforcement of the Indian Penal Code and it did not take the form of armed repression as in the case of the Santhal and Munda uprisings.

Once again the Bengal peasants showed complete Hindu-Muslim solidarity, even though the majority of the *ryots* were Muslim and the majority of *zamindars* Hindu. There was also no effort to create peasant solidarity on the grounds of religion or caste.

In this case, too, a number of young Indian intellectuals supported the peasants' cause. These included Bankim Chandra Chatterjea and R.C. Dutt. Later, in the early 1880s, during the discussion of the Bengal Tenancy Bill, the Indian Association, led by Surendranath Banerjea, Anand Mohan Bose and Dwarkanath Ganguli, campaigned for the rights of tenants, helped form *ryot'* unions, and organized huge meetings of upto 20,000 peasants in the districts in support of the Rent Bill.

The Indian Association and many of the nationalist newspapers went further than the Bill. They asked for permanent fixation of the tenant's rent. They warned that since the Bill would confer occupancy rights even on non-cultivators, it would lead to the growth of middlemen — the *jotedars* — who would be as oppressive as the *zamindars* so far as the actual cultivators were concerned. They, therefore, demanded that the right of occupancy should go with actual cultivation of the soil, that is, in most cases to the under-*ryots* and the tenants-at-will.

*

A major agrarian outbreak occurred in the Poona and Ahmednagar districts of Maharashtra in 1875. Here, as part of the Ryotwari system, land revenue was settled directly with the peasant who was also recognized as the owner of his land. Like the peasants in other Ryotwari areas, the Deccan peasant also found it difficult to pay land revenue without getting into the clutches of the moneylender and increasingly losing his land. This led to growing tension between the peasants and the moneylenders most of whom were outsiders — Marwaris or Gujaratis.

Three other developments occurred at this time. During the early 1860s, the American Civil War had led to a rise in cotton exports which had pushed up prices. The end of the Civil War in 1864 brought about an acute depression in cotton exports and a crash in prices. The ground slipped from under the peasants' feet. Simultaneously, in 1867, the Government raised land revenue by nearly 50 per cent. The situation was worsened by a succession of bad harvests.

To pay the land revenue under these conditions, the peasant had to go to the moneylender who took the opportunity to further tighten his grip on the peasant and his land. The peasant began to turn against the perceived cause of his misery, the moneylender. Only a spark was needed to kindle the fire.

A spontaneous protest movement began in December 1874 in Kardah village in Sirur *taluq*. When the peasants of the village failed to convince the local moneylender, Kalooram, that he should not act on a court decree and pull down a peasant's house, they organised a complete social boycott of the 'outsider' moneylenders to compel them to accept their demands in a peaceful manner. They refused to buy from their shops. No peasant would cultivate their fields. The *bullotedars*

(village servants) — barbers, washermen, carpenters, ironsmiths, shoe-
makers and others would not serve them. No domestic servant would
work in their houses and when the socially isolated moneylenders
decided to run away to the *taluq* headquarters, nobody would agree to
drive their carts. The peasants also imposed social sanctions against
those peasants and *bullotedars* who would not join the boycott of moneylenders. This social boycott spread rapidly to the villages of Poona,
Ahmednagar, Sholapur and Satara districts.

The social boycott was soon transformed into agrarian riots when it
did not prove very effective. On 12 May, peasants gathered in Supa, in
Bhimthari *taluq*, on the bazar day and began a systematic attack on the
moneylenders' houses and shops. They seized and publicly burnt debt
bonds and deeds — signed under pressure, in ignorance, or through
fraud — decrees, and other documents dealing with their debts. Within
days the disturbances spread to other villages of the Poona and
Ahmednagar districts.

There was very little violence in this settling of accounts. Once the
moneylenders' instruments of oppression — debt bonds — were surrendered, no need for further violence was felt. In most places, the
'riots' were demonstrations of popular feeling and of the peasants
newly acquired unity and strength. Though moneylenders' houses and
shops were looted and burnt in Supa, this did not occur in other places.

The Government acted with speed and soon succeeded in repressing
the movement. The active phase of the movement lasted about three
weeks, though stray incidents occurred for another month or two. As in
the case of the Pabna Revolt, the Deccan disturbances had very limited
objectives. There was once again an absence of anti-colonial consciousness. It was, therefore, possible for the colonial regime to extend them a
certain protection against the moneylenders through the Deccan
Agriculturists' Relief Act of 1879.

Once again, the modern nationalist intelligentsia of Maharashtra supported the peasants' cause. Already, in 1873-74, the Poona Sarvajanik
Sabha, led by Justice Ranade, had organized a successful campaign
among the peasants, as well as at Poona and Bombay, against the land
revenue settlement of 1867. Under its impact, a large number of peasants had refused to pay the enhanced revenue. This agitation had
generated a mentality of resistance among the peasants which contributed to the rise of peasant protest in 1875. The Sabha as well as many

of the nationalist newspapers also supported the D.A.R. Bill.

*

Peasant resistance also developed in other parts of the country. Mappila outbreaks were endemic in Malabar. Vasudev Balwant Phadke, an educated clerk, raised a Ramosi peasant force of about 50 in Maharashtra during 1879, and organized social banditry on a significant scale. The Kuka Revolt in Punjab was led by Baba Ram Singh and had elements of a messianic movement. It was crushed when 49 of the rebels were blown up by a cannon in 1872. High land revenue assessment led to a series of peasant riots in the plains of Assam during 1893-94. Scores were killed in brutal firings and bayonet charges.

*

There was a certain shift in the nature of peasant movements after 1857. Princes, chiefs and landlords having been crushed or co-opted, peasants emerged as the main force in agararian movements. They now fought directly for their own demands, centered almost wholly on economic issues, and against their immediate enemies, foreign planters and indigenous *zamindars* and moneylenders. Their struggles were directed towards specific and limited objectives and redressal of particular grievances. They did not make colonialism their target. Nor was their objective the ending of the system of their subordination and exploitation. They did not aim at 'turning the world upside down.'

The territorial reach of these movements was also limited. They were confined to particular localities with no mutual communication or linkages. They also lacked continuity of struggle or long-term organization. Once the specific objectives of a movement were achieved, its organization, as also peasant solidarity built around it, dissolved and disappeared. Thus, the Indigo strike, the Pabna agrarian leagues and the social-boycott movement of the Deccan *ryots* left behind no successors. Consequently, at no stage did these movements threaten British supremacy or even undermine it.

Peasant protest after 1857 often represented an instinctive and spontaneous response of the peasantry to its social condition. It was the result of excessive and unbearable oppression, undue and unusual deprivation and exploitation, and a threat to the peasant's existing, established position. The peasant often rebelled only when he felt that it was not possible to carry on in the existing manner.

He was also moved by strong notions of legitimacy, of what was justifiable and what was not. That is why he did not fight for land ownership or against landlordism but against eviction and undue enhancement of rent. He did not object to paying interest on the sums he had borrowed; he hit back against fraud and chicanery by the moneylender and when the latter went against tradition in depriving him of his land. He did not deny the state's right to collect a tax on land but objected when the level of taxation overstepped all traditional bounds. He did not object to the foreign planter becoming his *zamindar* but resisted the planter when he took away his freedom to decide what crops to grow and refused to pay him a proper price for his crop.

The peasant also developed a strong awareness of his legal rights and asserted them in and outside the courts. And if an effort was made to deprive him of his legal rights by extra-legal means or by manipulation of the law and law courts, he countered with extra-legal means of his own. Quite often, he believed that the legally-constituted authority approved his actions or at least supported his claims and cause. In all the three movements discussed here, he acted in the name of this authority, the *sarkar*.

In these movements, the Indian peasants showed great courage and a spirit of sacrifice, remarkable organizational abilities, and a solidarity that cut across religious and caste lines. They were also able to wring considerable concessions from the colonial state. The latter, too, not being directly challenged, was willing to compromise and mitigate the harshness of the agrarian system though within the broad limits of the colonial economic and political structure. In this respect, the colonial regime's treatment of the post-1857 peasant rebels was qualitatively different from its treatment of the participants in the civil rebellions, the Revolt of 1857 and the tribal uprisings which directly challenged colonial political power.

A major weakness of the 19th century peasant movements was the lack of an adequate understanding of colonialism — of colonial economic structure and the colonial state — and of the social framework of the movements themselves. Nor did the 19th century peasants possess a new ideology and a new social, economic and political programme based on an analysis of the newly constituted colonial society. Their struggles, however militant, occurred within the framework of the old societal order. They lacked a positive conception of an alternative society — a conception which would unite the people in a common struggle on a wide regional and all-India plane and help develop long-term political movements. An all-India leadership capable of evolving a strategy of struggle that would unify and mobilize peasants and other sections of society for nation-wide political activity could be formed only on the basis of such a new conception, such a fresh vision of society. In the absence of such a new ideology, programme, leadership and strategy of struggle, it was not too difficult for the colonial state, on the one hand, to reach a conciliation and calm down the rebellious peasants by the grant of some concessions and, on the other hand, to suppress them with the full use of its force. This weakness was, of course, not a blemish on the character of the peasantry which was perhaps incapable of grasping on its own the new and complex phenomenon of colonialism. That needed the efforts of a modern intelligentsia which was itself just coming into existence.

Most of these weaknesses were overcome in the 20th century when peasant discontent was merged with the general anti-imperialist discontent, and their political activity became a part of the wider anti-imperialist movement. And, of course, the peasants' participation in the larger national movement not only strengthened the fight against the foreigner, it also, simultaneously, enabled them to organize powerful struggles around their class demands and to create modern peasant organizations.

4 Foundation of the Congress: The Myth

Indian National Congress was founded in December 1885 by seventy-two political workers. It was the first organized expression of Indian nationalism on an all-India scale. A.O. Hume, a retired English ICS officer, played an important role in its formation. But why was it founded by these seventy-two men and why at that time?

A powerful and long-lasting myth, the myth of 'the safety valve,' has arisen around this question. Generations of students and political activists have been fed on this myth. But despite widespread popular belief, this myth has little basis in historical fact.

The myth is that the Indian National Congress was started by A.O. Hume and others under the official direction, guidance and advice of no less a person than Lord Dufferin, the Viceroy, to provide a safe, mild, peaceful, and constitutional outlet or *safety valve* for the rising discontent among the masses, which was inevitably leading towards a popular and violent revolution. Consequently, the revolutionary potential was nipped in the bud. The core of the myth, that a violent revolution was on the cards at the time and was avoided only by the foundation of the Congress, is accepted by most writers; the liberals welcome it, the radicals use it to prove that the Congress has always been compromising if not loyalist vis-a-vis imperialism, the extreme right use it to show that the Congress has been anti-national from the beginning. All of them agree that the manner of its birth affected the basic character and future work of the Congress in a crucial manner.

In his *Young India* published in 1916, the Extremist leader Lala Lajpat Rai used the safety-valve theory to attack the Moderates in the Congress. Having discussed the theory at length and suggested that the

Congress 'was a product of Lord Dufferin's brain,' he argued that 'the Congress was started more with the object of saving the British Empire from danger than with that of winning political liberty for India. The interests of the British Empire were primary and those of India only secondary.' And he added: 'No one can say that the Congress has not been true to that ideal.' His conclusion was: 'So this is the genesis of the Congress, and this is sufficient to condemn it in the eyes of the advanced Nationalists.'[1]

More than a quarter century later, R. Palme Dutt's authoritative work *India Today* made the myth of the safety-valve a staple of left-wing opinion. Emphasizing the myth, Dutt wrote that the Congress was brought into existence through direct Governmental initiative and guidance and through 'a plan secretly pre-arranged with the Viceroy' so that it (the Government) could use it 'as an intended weapon for safeguarding British rule against the rising forces of popular unrest and anti-British feeling.' It was 'an attempt to defeat, or rather forestall, an impending revolution.' The Congress did, of course, in time become a nationalist body; 'the national character began to overshadow the loyalist character.' It also became the vehicle of mass movements. But the 'original sin' of the manner of its birth left a permanent mark on its politics. Its 'two-fold character' as an institution which was created by the Government and yet became the organizer of the anti-imperialist movement 'ran right through its history.' It both fought and collaborated with imperialism. It led the mass movements and when the masses moved towards the revolutionary path, it betrayed the movement to imperialism. The Congress, thus, had two strands: 'On the one hand, the strand of cooperation with imperialism against the "menace" of the mass movement; on the other hand, the strand of leadership of the masses in the national struggle.' This duality of the Congress leadership from Gokhale to Gandhi, said Dutt, in fact reflected the two-fold and vacillating character of the Indian bourgeoisie itself; 'at once in conflict with the British bourgeoisie and desiring to lead the Indian people, yet feeling that "too rapid" advance may end in destroying its privileges along with those of the imperialists.' The Congress had, thus, become an organ of opposition to real revolution, that is, a violent revolution. But this role did not date from Gandhiji; 'this principle was implanted in it by imperialism at the outset as its intended official role.' The culmination of this dual role was its 'final capitulation with the Mountbatten Settlement.'[2]

Earlier, in 1939, M.S. Golwalkar, the RSS chief, had also found the safety-valve theory handy in attacking the Congress for its secularism and, therefore, anti-nationalism. In his pamphlet *We* Golwalkar complained that Hindu national consciousness had been destroyed by those claiming to be 'nationalists' who had pushed the 'notions of democracy' and the perverse notion that 'our old invaders and foes,' the Muslims, had something in common with Hindus. Consequently, 'we have allowed our foes to be our friends and with our hands are undermining true nationality.' In fact, the fight in India was not between Indians and the British only. It was 'a triangular fight.' Hindus were at war with Muslims on the one hand and with the British on the other. What had led Hindus to enter the path of 'denationalization,' said Golwalkar, were the aims and policy laid down by Hume, Cotton, and Wedderburn in 1885; 'the Congress they founded as a "safety valve" to "seething nationalism," as a toy which would lull the awakening giant into slumber, an instrument to destroy National consciousness, has been, as far as they are concerned, a success.'[3]

The liberal C.F. Andrews and Girija Mukerji fully accepted the safety-valve theory in their work, *The Rise and Growth of the Congress in India* published in 1938. They were happy with it because it had helped avoid 'useless bloodshed.' Before as well as after 1947, tens of scholars and hundreds of popular writers have repeated some version of these points of view.

*

Historical proof of the safety-valve theory was provided by the seven volumes of secret reports which Hume claimed to have read at Simla in the summer of 1878 and which convinced him of the existence of 'seething discontent' and a vast conspiracy among the lower classes to violently overthrow British rule.

Before we unravel the mystery of the seven volumes, let us briefly trace the history of its rise and growth. It was first mentioned in William Wedderburn's biography of A.O. Hume published in 1913. Wedderburn (ICS) found an undated memorandum in Hume's papers which dealt with the foundation of the Congress. He quoted at length from this document.[4] To keep the mystery alive so that the reader may go along with the writer step by step towards its solution, I will withhold an account of Wedderburn's writing, initially giving only those paragraphs which were quoted by the subsequent writers. According to Lajpat Rai, despite the fact that Hume was 'a lover of liberty and wanted political liberty for India under the aegis of the British crown,' he was above all 'an English patriot.' Once he saw that British rule was threatened with 'an impending calamity,' he decided to create a safety valve for the discontent.

As decisive proof of this Lajpat Rai provided a long quotation from Hume's memorandum that Wedderburn had mentioned along with his own comments in his book.[5] Since this passage is quoted or cited by all subsequent authors, it is necessary to reproduce it here at length.

' "I was shown," wrote Hume, "several large volumes containing a vast number of entries; English abstracts or translations — longer or shorter — of vernacular reports or communications of one kind or another, all arranged according to districts (not identical with ours) . . . The number of these entries was enormous; there were said, at the time, to be communications from over 30,000 different reporters." He (Hume) mentions that he had the volumes in his possession only for a week . . . Many of the entries reported conversations between men of the lowest classes, "all going to show that these poor men were pervaded with a sense of the hopelessness of the existing state of affairs; that they were convinced that they would starve and die, and that they wanted to do *something,* and stand by each other, and *that something meant violence* . . . a certain small number of the educated classes, at the time desperately, perhaps unreasonably, bitter against the Government, would join the movement, assume here and there the lead, give the outbreak cohesion, and direct it as a national revolt." '

Very soon, the seven volumes, whose character, origin, etc., were left undefined in Lajpat Rai's quotation, started undergoing a metamorphosis. In 1933, in Gurmukh Nihal Singh's hands, they became 'government reports.'[6] Andrews and Mukerji transformed them into 'several volumes of secret reports from the CID' which came into Hume's possession 'in his official capacity.'[7] The classical and most influential statement came from R. Palme Dutt. After quoting the passage quoted by Lajpat Rai from Wedderburn, Dutt wrote: 'Hume in his official capacity had received possession of the voluminous secret police reports.'[8] Numerous other historians of the national movement, including recent ones such as R.C. Majumdar and Tara Chand, were to accept this product of the creative imagination of these writers as historical fact.

So deeply rooted had become the belief in Hume's volumes as official documents that in the 1950s a large number of historians and would-be historians, including the present writer, devoted a great deal of time and energy searching for them in the National Archives. And when their search proved futile, they consoled themselves with the thought that the British had destroyed them before their departure in 1947. Yet only if the historians had applied a minimum of their historiographic sense to the question and looked at the professed evidence a bit more carefully, they would not have been taken for a ride. Three levels of historical evidence and logic were available to them even before the private papers of Ripon and Dufferin became available.

The first level pertains to the system under which the Government of India functioned in the 1870s. In 1878, Hume was Secretary to the Department of Revenue, Agriculture and Commerce. How could the Secretary of these departments get access to Home Department files or CID reports? Also he was then in Simla while Home Department files were kept in Delhi; they were not sent to Simla. And from where would 30,000 reporters come? The intelligence department could not have employed more than a few hundred persons at the time! And, as Lajpat Rai noted, if Congress was founded out of the fear of an outbreak, why did Hume and British officialdom wait for seven long years?

If these volumes were not government documents, what were they? The clue was there in Wedderburn's book and it was easily available if a writer would go to the book itself and not rely on extracts from it reproduced by previous authors as nearly all the later writers seem to have done. This brings us to the second level of historical evidence already available in Wedderburn.

The passages quoted by Lajpat Rai, R. Palme Dutt and others are on pages 80-81 of Wedderburn's book. Two pages earlier, pages 78-80, and one page later, 82-83, Wedderburn *tells the reader what these volumes were and who provided them* to Hume. The heading of the section where the quoted passages occur is 'Indian religious leaders.' In the very beginning of the section, Wedderburn writes that a warning of the threatened danger came to Hume 'from a very special source, that is, from the leaders among those devoted, in all parts of India, to a religious life.' Hume referred in his memorandum to "the legions of secret quasi-religious orders, with literally their millions of members, which form so important a factor in the Indian problem." These religious sects and orders were headed by *Gurus,* "men of the highest quality who . . . have purged themselves from earthly desires, and fixed their desires on the highest good." And "these religious leaders, through their *Chelas* or disciples, are fully informed of all that goes on under the surface, and their influence is great in forming public opinion." It was with these *Gurus,* writes Wedderburn, 'that Mr. Hume came in touch, towards the end of Lord Lytton's Viceroyalty.' These *Gurus* approached Hume because Hume was a keen student of Eastern religions, but also because they "feared that the ominous 'unrest' throughout the country . . . would lead to terrible outbreak" and it was only men like Hume who had access to the Government who could help 'avert a catastrophe.' "This," wrote Hume, "is how the case was put to me." With this background the passages on pages 80-81 become clearer.

In other words, the evidence of the seven volumes was shown to Hume by the *Gurus* who had been sent reports by thousands of *Chelas.* But why should Hume believe that these reports 'must necessarily be true?' Because *Chelas* were persons of a special breed who did not belong to any particular sect or religion or rather belonged to all religions. Moreover they were 'bound by vows and conditions, over and above those of ordinary initiates of low grade.' They were 'all initiates in some of the many branches of the secret knowledge' and were 'all bound by vows, they *cannot* practically break, to some farther advanced seeker than themselves.' The leaders were of '*no* sect and *no* religion, but of *all* sects and *all* religions.' But why did hardly anyone in India know of the existence of these myriads of *Gurus* and *Chelas*? Because, explained Hume, absolute secrecy was an essential feature in their lives. They had communicated with Hume only because they were anxious to avert calamity.

And, finally, we come to the third level of historiography, the level of profound belief and absolute fantasy. The full character of the *Gurus* and *Chelas* was still not revealed by Wedderburn, for he was sheltering the reputation of his old friend, as friendly biographers usually do. The impression given by him was that these *Gurus* and *Chelas* were ordinary mortal men. This was, however, not the case. Reconstructing the facts on the basis of some books on Theosophy and Madame Blavatsky and the private papers of the Viceroys Ripon and Dufferin, we discover that these *Gurus* were persons who, because of their practice of 'peculiar Eastern religious thought,' were supposed to possess supernatural, occult powers; they could communicate and direct from thousands of miles, enter any place, go anywhere, sit anywhere unseen, and direct men's thoughts and opinions without their being aware of it.

*

In 1881, Hume came under the spell of Madame Blavatsky who claimed to be in touch with these *Gurus* who were described by her as *mahatmas*. These *mahatmas* lived as part of a secret brotherhood in Tibet, but they could contact or 'correspond' with persons anywhere in the world because of their occult powers. Blavatsky enabled Hume to get in touch with one of these *mahatmas* named 'Koot Hoomi Lal Singh.' It is this invisible brotherhood that gathered secret information on Indian affairs through their *Chelas*. In a book published in 1880, A.P. Sinnet, editor of the *Pioneer* and another follower of Blavatsky, had quoted a letter from Koot Hoomi that these *mahatmas* had used their power in 1857 to control the Indian masses and saved the British empire and that they would do the same in future.

Hume believed all this. He was keen to acquire these occult powers by which the *Chelas* could know all about the present and the future. He started a 'correspondence' with the *mahatmas* in Tibet. By 1883 Hume had quarrelled with Blavatsky, but his faith in the *Gurus* or *mahatmas* continued unabated. He also began to use his connection with the *mahatmas* to promote political objectives dear to his heart — attempting to reform Indian administration and make it more responsive to Indian opinion.

In December 1883, he wrote to Ripon: 'I am associated with men, who though never seen by the masses . . . are yet reverenced by them as Gods, . . . and who feel every pulse of public feeling.' He claimed a superior knowledge 'of the native mind' because 'a body of men, mostly of Asiatic origin . . . who possess facilities which no other man or body of men living do, for gauging the feelings of the natives . . . have seen fit . . . to give me their confidence to a certain limited extent.' In January 1884, he informed Ripon that even earlier, in 1848, he had been in contact with the brotherhood or association of his mystical advisers and that it was their intervention which had defeated the revolutions of 1848 in Europe and the 'mutiny' of 1857. From distant Tibet they were now acting through him and others like him to help Ripon introduce reforms and avoid 'the possibility of such a cataclysm recurring.' This association of *mahatmas* was also helping him, he told

Ripon, to persuade the Queen to give a second term as Viceroy to Ripon and to 'tranquilize the native press.'[9]

Hume tried to play a similar role with Dufferin, but more hesitatingly, not sharing with him the information that his advisers were astral, occult figures, so that even many historians have assumed that these advisers were his fellow Congress leaders! Only once did he lift the veil before Dufferin when the latter during 1887 angrily pressed him to reveal the source through which he claimed to have gained access to the Viceroy's secret letter to the Secretary of State. Pressed to the wall, Hume told him copies of the letter had been obtained by his friends through occult methods or 'through the medium of supernatural photography.' And when Dufferin showed him the original letter, proving that the copy was false, Hume had no answer.[10]

Once earlier, too, Hume had indirectly tried to tell Duferrin that his advisers were not ordinary political leaders but 'advanced initiates' and *mahatmas*; but he had done so in a guarded fashion. In a letter to Dufferin in November 1886, he said that he had been trying to persuade those who had shown him the volumes in Simla to also show them to Dufferin so that the Viceroy could get their veracity checked by his own sources. But, 'at present they say that this is impossible.' Nor would they agree to communicate with the Viceroy directly. '*Most* of them, I believe, *could* not. You have not done, and would not do, what is required to enable them to communicate with you directly after their fashion.' But there was hope. 'My own special friend' who spent more than a month with Hume in Simla (in 1878), and who was often in India might agree to see the Viceroy. Hume suggested: 'if ever a native gentleman comes to the Private Secretary and says that Mr. Hume said the Viceroy would like to see him, see him at once. You will not talk to him ten minutes without finding out that he is no ordinary man. You may never get the chance — goodness knows — they move in a mysterious way their wonders to perform.'[11]

But Hume was worried that he could offer no visible or direct proof of his knowledge or connections. He told the Viceroy that he was 'getting gradually very angry and disgusted' because he was not able to get 'this vouching for directly.' None of the 'advanced initiates' under whose 'advice and guidance' he was working would 'publicly stand by me,' so that most Europeans in India 'look upon me either as a lunatic or a liar.' And hence, he informed the Viceroy, while he had decided to continue the political work, he had decided to 'drop all references to my friends'[12] Thus, it turns out that the seven volumes which Hume saw were prepared by *mahatmas* and *Gurus*, and his friends and advisers were these occult figures and not Congressmen!

*

Further proof offered for the safety-valve theory was based on W.C. Bonnerjee's statement in 1898 in *Indian Politics* that the Congress, 'as it was originally started and as it has since been carried on, is in reality the work of the Marquis of Dufferin and Ava.' He stated that Hume had, in 1884, thought of bringing together leading political Indians once a year "to discuss social matters" and did not "desire that politics should form part of their discussion." But Dufferin asked Hume to do the opposite and start a body to discuss politics so that the Government could keep itself informed of Indian opinion. Such a body could also perform 'the functions which Her Majesty's Opposition did in England.'[13]

Clearly, either W.C. Bonnerjee's memory was failing or he was trying to protect the National Congress from the wrath of the late 19th century imperialist reaction, for contemporary evidence clearly indicated the opposite. All the discussions Hume had with Indian leaders regarding the holding of an annual conference referred to a political gathering. Almost the entire work of earlier associations like the Bombay Presidency Association, Poona Sarvajanik Sabha, Madras Mahajan Sabha and Indian Association was political. Since his retirement from the Indian Civil Service in 1882, Hume had been publicly urging Indians to take to politics. He had also been asking his Indian friends not to get divided on social questions.

When, in January 1885, his friend B.M. Malabari wrote some editorials in the *Indian Spectator* urging educated Indians to inaugurate a movement for social reform, Hume wrote a letter to the *Indian Spectator* criticizing Malabari's proposals, warning against the dangerous potential of such a move, and arguing that political reforms should take precedence over social reform.[14] Dufferin, on his part, in his St. Andrews' Day dinner speech in 1888, publicly criticized the Congress for pursuing politics to serve narrow interests rather than take to social reform which would benefit millions.[15] Earlier he had expressed the same sentiment in a private letter to the Secretary of State.

A perusal of Dufferin's private papers, thrown open to scholars in the late 1950s, should have put an end to the myth of Dufferin s sponsorship of or support to the Congress. It was only after Hume had sent him a copy of the letter to the *Indian Spectator* with a covering note deprecating Malabari's views on social reform that Dufferin *expressed agreement with Hume* and asked him to meet him. Definite confirmation of the fact that Hume never proposed a social gathering but rather a political one comes in Dufferin's letter to Lord Reay, Governor of Bombay, after his first meeting with Hume in May 1885: "At his last interview he told me that he and his friends were going to assemble a political convention of delegates, as far as I understood, on the lines adopted by O'Connell previous to Catholic emancipation."[16]

Neither Dufferin and his fellow-liberal Governors of Bombay and Madras nor his conservative officials like Alfred and J.B. Lyall, D.M. Wallace, A. Colvin and S.C. Bayley were sympathetic to the Congress. It was not only in 1888 that Dufferin attacked the Congress in a vicious manner by writing that he would consider 'in what way the happy despatch may be best applied to the Congress,' for 'we cannot allow the Congress to continue to exist.'[17] In May 1885 itself, he had written to Reay asking him to be careful about Hume's Congress, telling him that it would be unwise to identify with either the reformers or the reactionaries.[18] Reay in turn, in a letter in June 1885, referred with apprehension to the new political activists as 'the National Party of India' and warned against Indian delegates, like Irish delegates, making their appearance on the British political scene. Earlier, in May, Reay had cautioned Dufferin that Hume was 'the head-centre of an organization . . . (which) has for its object to bring native opinion into a focus.'[19]

In fact, from the end of May 1885, Dufferin had grown cool to Hume and began to keep him at an arm's length. From 1886 onwards he also began to attack the 'Bengali *Baboos* and Mahratta Brahmins' for being 'inspired by questionable motives' and for wanting to start Irish-type revolutionary agitations in India.[20] And, during May-June 1886, he was describing Hume as 'cleverish, a little cracked, excessively vain, and absolutely indifferent to truth,' his main fault being that he was 'one of the chief stimulants of the Indian Home Rule movement.'[21]

To conclude, it is high time that the safety-valve theory of the genesis of the Congress was confined to the care of the *mahatmas* from whom perhaps it originated!

5 Foundation of
The Indian National Congress:The Reality

In the last chapter we began the story of the foundation of the Indian National Congress. We could not, however, make much headway because the cobwebs had to be cleared, the myth of the safety-valve had to be laid to rest, the mystery of the 'missing volumes' had to be solved, and Hume's *mahatmas* had to be sent back to their resting place in Tibet. In this chapter we resume the more serious part of the story of the emergence of the Indian National Congress as the apex nationalist organization that was to guide the destiny of the Indian national movement till the attainment of independence.

The foundation of the Indian National Congress in 1885 was not a sudden event, or a historical accident. It was the culmination of a process of political awakening that had its beginnings in the 1860s and 1870s and took a major leap forward in the late 1870s and early 1880s. The year 1885 marked a turning point in this process, for that was the year the political Indians, the modern intellectuals interested in politics, who no longer saw themselves as spokesmen of narrow group interests, but as representatives of national interest vis-a-vis foreign rule, as a 'national party,' saw their efforts bear fruit. The all-India nationalist body that they brought into being was to be the platform, the organizer, the headquarters, the symbol of the new national spirit and politics.

British officialdom, too, was not slow in reading the new messages that were being conveyed through the nationalist political activity leading to the founding of the Congress, and watched them with suspicion, and a sense of foreboding. As this political activity gathered force, the prospect of disloyalty, sedition and Irish-type agitations began to haunt the Government.

The official suspicion was not merely the over-anxious response of an administration that had not yet recovered from the mutiny complex, but was, in fact, well-founded. On the surface, the nationalist Indian demands of those years — no reduction of import duties on textile imports, no expansion in Afghanistan or Burma, the right to bear arms, freedom of the Press, reduction of military expenditure, higher expenditure on famine relief, Indianization of the civil services, the right of Indians to join the semi-military volunteer corps, the right of Indian judges to try Europeans in criminal cases, the appeal to British voters to vote for a party which would listen to Indians — look rather mild, especially when considered separately. But these were demands which a colonial regime could not easily concede, for that would undermine its hegemony over the colonial people. It is true that any criticism or demand no matter how innocuous its appearance but which cannot be accommodated by a system is in the long-run subversive of the system.

The new political thrust in the years between 1875 and 1885 was the creation of the younger, more radical nationalist intellectuals most of whom entered politics during this period. They established new associations, having found that the older associations were too narrowly conceived in terms of their programmes and political activity as well as social bases. For example, the British Indian Association of Bengal had increasingly identified itself with the interests of the *zamindars* and, thus, gradually lost its anti-British edge. The Bombay Association and Madras Native Association had become reactionary and moribund. And so the younger nationalists of Bengal, led by Surendranath Banerjea and Anand Mohan Bose, founded the Indian Association in 1876. Younger men of Madras — M. Viraraghavachariar, G. Subramaniya Iyer, P. Ananda Charlu and others — formed the Madras Mahajan Sabha in 1884. In Bombay, the more militant intellectuals like K. T. Telang and Pherozeshah Mehta broke away from older leaders like Dadabhai Framji and Dinshaw Petit on political grounds and formed the Bombay Presidency Association in 1885. Among the older associations only the Poona Sarvajanik Sabha carried on as before. But, then, it was already in the hands of nationalist intellectuals.

A sign of new political life in the country was the coming into existence during these years of nearly all the major nationalist newspapers which were to dominate the Indian scene till 1918 — The *Hindu, Tribune, Bengalee, Mahratta* and *Kesari*. The one exception was the *Amrita Bazar Patrika* which was already edited by new and younger men. It became an English language newspaper only in 1878.

By 1885, the formation of an all-India political organization had become an objective necessity, and the necessity was being recognized by nationalists all over the country. Many recent scholars have furnished detailed information on the many moves that were made in that direction from 1877. These moves acquired a greater sense of urgency especially from 1883 and there was intense political activity. The *Indian Mirror* of Calcutta was carrying on a continuous campaign on the question. The Indian Association had already in December 1883 organized an All-India National Conference and given a call for another one in December 1885. (Surendranath Banerjea, who was involved in the All-India National Conference, could not for that reason attend the founding session of the National Congress in 1885).

Meanwhile, the Indians had gained experience, as well as confidence, from the large number of agitations they had organized in the preceding ten years. Since 1875, there had been a continuous campaign around cotton import duties which Indians wanted to stay in the interests of the Indian textile industry. A massive campaign had been organized during 1877-88 around the demand for the Indianization of Government services. The Indians had opposed the Afghan adventure of Lord Lytton and then compelled the British Government to contribute towards the cost of the Second Afghan War. The Indian Press had waged a major campaign against the efforts of the Government to control it through the Vernacular Press Act. The Indians had also opposed the effort to disarm them through the Arms Act. In 1881-82 they had organized a protest against the Plantation Labour and the Inland Emigration Act which condemned plantation labourers to serfdom. A major agitation was organized during 1883 in favour of the Ilbert Bill which would enable Indian magistrates to try Europeans. This Bill was successfully thwarted by the Europeans. The Indians had been quick to draw the political lesson. Their efforts had failed because they had not been coordinated on an all-India basis. On the other hand, the Europeans had acted in a concerted manner. Again in July 1883 a massive all-India effort was made to raise a National Fund which would be used to promote political agitation in India as well as England. In 1885, Indians fought for the right to join the volunteer corps restricted to Europeans, and then organized an appeal to British voters to vote for those candidates who were friendly towards India. Several Indians were sent to Britain to put the Indian case before British voters through public speeches, and other means.

*

It, thus, becomes clear that the foundation of the Congress was the natural culmination of the political work of the previous years. By 1885, a stage had been reached in the political development of India when certain basic tasks or objectives had to be laid down and struggled for. Moreover, these objectives were correlated and could only be fulfilled by the coming together of political workers in a single organization formed on an all-India basis. The men who met in Bombay on 28 December 1885 were inspired by these objectives and hoped to initiate the process of achieving them. The success or failure and the future character of the Congress would be determined not by who founded it but by the extent to which these objectives were achieved in the initial years.

*

India had just entered the process of becoming a nation or a people. The first major objective of the founders of the Indian national movement was to promote this process, to weld Indians into a nation, to create an Indian people. It was common for colonial administrators and ideologues to assert that Indians could not be united or freed because they were not a nation or a people but a geographical expression, a mere congeries of hundreds of diverse races and creeds. The Indians did not deny this but asserted that they were now becoming a nation. India was as Tilak, Surendranath Banerjea and many others were fond of saying — a nation-in-the-making. The Congress leaders recognized that objective historical forces were bringing the Indian people together. But they also realized that the people had to become subjectively aware of the objective process and that for this it was necessary to promote the feeling of national unity and nationalism among them.

Above all, India being a nation-in-the-making, its nationhood could not be taken for granted. It had to be constantly developed and consolidated. The promotion of national unity was a major objective of the Congress and later its major achievement. For example, P. Ananda Charlu in his presidential address to the Congress in 1891 described it 'as a mighty nationalizer,' and said that this was its most 'glorious' role.[1] Among the three basic aims and objectives of the Congress laid down by its first President, W.C. Bonnerji, was that of 'the fuller development and consolidation of those sentiments of national unity.'[2] The Russian traveller, I.P. Minayeff, wrote in his diary that, when travelling with Bonnerji, he asked, 'what practical results did the Congress leaders expect from the Congress,' Bonnerji replied: 'Growth of national feeling and unity of Indians.'[3] Similarly, commenting on the first Congress session, the *Indu Prakash* of Bombay wrote: 'It marks the beginning of a new life . . . it will greatly help in creating a national feeling and binding together distant people by common sympathies, and common ends.'[4]

The making of India into a nation was to be a prolonged historical process. Moreover, the Congress leaders realized that the diversity of India was such that special efforts unknown to other parts of the world would have to be made and national unity carefully nurtured. In an effort to reach all regions, it was decided to rotate the Congress session among different parts of the country. The President was to belong to a region other than where the Congress session was being held.

To reach out to the followers of all religions and to remove the fears of the minorities, a rule was made at the 1888 session that no resolution was to be passed to which an overwhelming majority of Hindu or Muslim delegates objected.[5] In 1889, a minority clause was adopted in the resolution demanding reform of legislative councils. According to the clause, wherever Parsis, Christians, Muslims or Hindus were a minority their number elected to the Councils would not be less than their proportion in the population.[6] The reason given by the mover of the resolution was that India was not yet a homogenous country and political methods here had, therefore, to differ from those in Europe.

The early national leaders were also determined to build a secular nation, the Congress itself being intensely secular.

*

The second major objective of the early Congress was to create a common political platform or programme around which political workers in different parts of the country could gather and conduct their political activities, educating and mobilizing people on an all-India basis. This was to be accomplished by taking up those grievances and fighting for those rights which Indians had in common in relation to the rulers.

For the same reason the Congress was not to take up questions of social reform. At its second session, the President of the Congress,

Dadabhai Naoroji, laid down this rule and said that 'A National Congress must confine itself to questions in which the entire nation has a direct participation.' Congress was, therefore, not the right place to discuss social reforms. 'We are met together,' he said, 'as a political body to represent to our rulers our political aspirations.'[7]

*

Modern politics — the politics of popular participation, agitation, mobilisation — was new to India. The notion that politics was not the preserve of the few but the domain of everyone was not yet familiar to the people. No modern political movement was possible till people realized this. And, then, on the basis of this realization, an informed and determined political opinion had to be created. The arousal, training, organization and consolidation of public opinion was seen as a major task by the Congress leaders. All initial activity of the early nationalists was geared towards this end.

The first step was seen to be the politicization and unification of the opinion of the educated, and then of other sections. The primary objective was to go beyond the redressal of immediate grievances and organize *sustained* political activity along the lines of the Anti-Corn Law League (formed in Britain by Cobden and Bright in 1838 to secure reform of Corn Laws). The leaders as well as the people also had to gain confidence in their own capacity to organize political opposition to the most powerful state of the day.

All this was no easy task. A prolonged period of politicization would be needed. Many later writers and critics have concentrated on the methods of political struggle of the early nationalist leaders, on their petitions, prayers and memorials. It is, of course, true that they did not organize mass movements and mass struggles. But the critics have missed out the most important part of their activity — that all of it led to politics, to the politicization of the people. Justice Ranade, who was known as a political sage, had, in his usual perceptive manner, seen this as early as 1891. When the young and impatient twenty-six-year-old Gokhale expressed disappointment when the Government sent a two-line reply to a carefully and laboriously prepared memorial by the Poona Sarvajanik Sabha, Ranade reassured him: 'You don't realize our place in the history of our country. These memorials are nominally addressed to Government, in reality they are addressed to the people, so that they may learn how to think in these matters. This work must be done for many years, without expecting any other result, because politics of this kind is altogether new in this land.'[8]

*

As part of the basic objective of giving birth to a national movement, it was necessary to create a common all-India national-political leadership, that is, to construct what Antonio Gramsci, the famous Italian Marxist, calls the headquarters of a movement. Nations and people become capable of meaningful and effective political action only when they are organized. They become a people or 'historical subjects' only when they are organized as such. The first step in a national movement is taken when the 'carriers' of national feeling or national identity begin to organize the people. But to be able to do so successfully, these 'carriers' or leaders must themselves be unified; they must share a collective identification, that is, they must come to know each other and share and evolve a common outlook, perspective, sense of purpose, as also common feelings. According to the circular which, in March 1885, informed political workers of the coming Congress session, the Congress was intended 'to enable all the most earnest labourers in the cause of national progress to become personally known to each other.'[9] W.C. Bonnerji, as the first Congress President, reiterated that one of the Congress objectives was the 'eradication, by direct friendly personal intercourse, of all possible race, creed, or provincial prejudices amongst all lovers of our country,' and 'the promotion of personal intimacy and friendship amongst all the more earnest workers in our country's cause in (all) parts of the Empire.'[10]

In other words, the founders of the Congress understood that the first requirement of a national movement was a national leadership. The social-ideological complexion that this leadership would acquire was a question that was different from the main objective of the creation of a national movement. This complexion would depend on a host of factors: the role of different social classes, ideological influences, outcomes of ideological struggles, and so on.

*

The early nationalist leaders saw the internalization and indigenization of political democracy as one of their main objectives. They based their politics on the doctrine of the sovereignty of the people, or, as Dadabhai Naoroji put it, on 'the new lesson that Kings are made for the people, not peoples for their Kings.'

From the beginning, the Congress was organized in the form of a Parliament. In fact, the word Congress was borrowed from North American history to connote an assembly of the people. The proceedings of the Congress sessions were conducted democratically, issues being decided through debate and discussion and occasionally through voting. It was, in fact, the Congress, and not the bureaucratic and authoritarian colonial state, as some writers wrongly argue, which indigenized, popularized and rooted parliamentary democracy in India.

Similarly, the early national leaders made maintenance of civil liberties and their extension an integral part of the national movement. They fought against every infringement of the freedom of the Press and speech and opposed every attempt to curtail them. They struggled for separation of the judicial and executive powers and fought against racial discrimination.

*

It was necessary to evolve an understanding of colonialism and then a nationalist ideology based on this understanding. In this respect, the early nationalist leaders were simultaneously learners and teachers. No ready-made anti-colonial understanding or ideology was available to them in the 1870s and 1880s. They had to develop their own anti-colonial ideology on the basis of a concrete study of the reality and of their own practice.

There could have been no national struggle without an ideological struggle clarifying the concept of *we* as a nation against colonialism as an enemy. They had to find answers to many questions. For example, is Britain ruling India for India's benefit? Are the interests of the rulers and the ruled in harmony, or does a basic contradiction exist between the two? Is the contradiction of the Indian people with British bureaucrats in India, or with the British Government, or with the system of colonialism as such? Are the Indian people capable of fighting the mighty British empire? And how is the fight to be waged?

In finding answers to these and other questions many mistakes were made. For example, the early nationalists failed to understand, at least till the beginning of the 20th century, the character of the colonial state. But, then, some mistakes are an inevitable part of any serious effort to grapple with reality. In a way, despite mistakes and setbacks, it was perhaps no misfortune that no ready-made, cut and dried, symmetrical formulae were available to them. Such formulae are often lifeless and, therefore, poor guides to action.

True, the early national leaders did not organize mass movements against the British. But they did carry out an ideological struggle against them. It should not be forgotten that nationalist or anti-imperialist struggle is a struggle *about* colonialism before it becomes a struggle against colonialism. And the founding fathers of the Congress carried out this 'struggle about colonialism' in a brilliant fashion.

*

From the beginning, the Congress was conceived not as a party but as a movement. Except for agreement on the very broad objectives discussed earlier, it did not require any particular political or ideological commitment from its activists. It also did not try to limit its following to any social class or group. As a movement, it incorporated different political trends, ideologies and social classes and groups so long as the commitment to democratic and secular nationalism was there. From the outset, the Congress included in the ranks of its leadership persons with diverse political thinking, widely disparate levels of political militancy and varying economic approaches.

To sum up: The basic objectives of the early nationalist leaders were to lay the foundations of a secular and democratic national movement, to politicize and politically educate the people, to form the headquarters of the movement, that is, to form an all-India leadership group, and to develop and propagate an anti-colonial nationalist ideology.

History will judge the extent of the success or failure of the early national movement not by an abstract, ahistorical standard but by the extent to which it was able to attain the basic objectives it had laid down for itself. By this standard, its achievements were quite substantial and that is why it grew from humble beginnings in the 1880s into the most spectacular of popular mass movements in the 20th century. Historians are not likely to disagree with the assessment of its work in the early phase by two of its major leaders. Referring to the preparatory nature of the Congress work from 1885 to 1905, Dadabhai Naoroji wrote to D.E. Wacha in January 1905: 'The very discontent and impatience it (the Congress) has evoked against itself as slow and non-progressive among the rising generation are among its best results or fruit. It is its own evolution and progress . . . (the task is) to evolve the required revolution — whether it would be peaceful or violent. The character of the revolution will depend upon the wisdom or unwisdom of the British Government and action of the British people.'[11]

And this is how G.K. Gokhale evaluated this period in 1907: 'Let us not forget that we are at a stage of the country's progress when our achievements are bound to be small, and our disappointments frequent and trying. That is the place which it has pleased Providence to assign to us in this struggle, and our responsibility is ended when we have done the work which belongs to that place. It will, no doubt, be given to our countrymen of future generations to serve India by their successes; we, of the present generation, must be content to serve her mainly by our failures. For, hard though it be, out of those failures the strength will come which in the end will accomplish great tasks.'[12]

*

As for the question of the role of A.O. Hume, if the founders of the Congress were such capable and patriotic men of high character, why did they need Hume to act as the chief organizer of the Congress? It is undoubtedly true that Hume impressed — and quite rightly — all his liberal and democratic contemporaries, including Lajpat Rai, as a man of high ideals with whom it was no dishonour to cooperate. But the real answer lies in the conditions of the time. Considering the size of the Indian subcontinent, there were very few political persons in the early 1880s and the tradition of open opposition to the rulers was not yet firmly entrenched.

Courageous and committed persons like Dadabhai Naoroji, Justice Ranade, Pherozeshah Mehta, G. Subramaniya Iyer and Surendranath Banerjea (one year later) cooperated with Hume because they did not want to arouse official hostility at such an early stage of their work. They assumed that the rulers would be less suspicious and less likely to attack a potentially subversive organization if its chief organizer was a retired British civil servant. Gokhale, with his characteristic modesty and political wisdom, stated this explicitly in 1913: 'No Indian could have started the Indian National Congress . . . if an Indian had . . . come forward to start such a movement embracing all India, the officials in India would not have allowed the movement to come into existence. If the founder of the Congress had not been a great Englishman and a distinguished ex-official, such was the distrust of political agitation in those days that the authorities would have at once found some way or the other to suppress the movement.'13

In other words, if Hume and other English liberals hoped to use the Congress as a safety-valve, the Congress leaders hoped to use Hume as a lightning conductor. And as later developments show, it was the Congress leaders whose hopes were fulfilled.

6 Socio-Religious Reforms and the National Awakening

'I regret to say,' wrote Raja Rammohan Roy in 1828, 'that the present system of religion adhered to by the Hindus is not well calculated to promote their political interest. The distinctions of castes introducing innumerable divisions and sub-divisions among them has entirely deprived them of patriotic feeling, and the multitude of religious rites and ceremonies and the laws of purification have totally disqualified them from undertaking any difficult enterprise. It is, I think, necessary that some change should take place in their religion atleast for the sake of their political advantage and social comfort.'[1] Written at a time when Indians had just begun to experience the intellectual and cultural turmoil that characterized social life in nineteenth century India this represented the immediate Indian response. The British conquest and the consequent dissemination of colonial culture and ideology had led to an inevitable introspection about the strengths and weaknesses of indigenous culture and institutions. The response, indeed, was varied but the need to reform social and religious life was a commonly shared conviction. The social base of this quest which has generally, but not altogether appropriately been called the renaissance, was the newly emerging middle class and the traditional as well as western educated intellectuals. The socio-cultural regeneration in nineteenth century India was occasioned by the colonial presence, but not created by it.

The spirit of reform embraced almost the whole of India beginning with the efforts of Raja Rammohan Roy in Bengal leading to the formation of the Brahmo Samaj in 1828. Apart from the Brahmo Samaj, which had branches in several parts of the country, the Paramahansa Mandali and the Prarthana Samaj in Maharashtra and the Arya Samaj in Punjab and North India were some of the prominent movements among the Hindus. There were several other regional and caste movements like the Kayasth Sabha in Uttar Pradesh and the Sarin Sabha in Punjab. The backward castes also started the work of reformation with the Satya Sodhak Samaj in Maharashtra and the Sri Narayana Dharma Paripalana Sabha in Kerala. The Ahmadiya and Aligarh movements, the Singh Sabha and the Rehnumai Mazdeyasan Sabha represented the spirit of reform among the Muslims, the Sikhs and the Parsees respectively. Despite being regional in scope and content and confined to a particular religion, their general perspectives were remarkably similar; they were regional and religious manifestations of a common consciousness.

Although religious reformation was a major concern of these movements, none of them were exclusively religious in character. Strongly humanist in inspiration, the idea of otherworldliness and salvation were not a part of their agenda; instead their attention was focused on worldly existence. Raja Rammohan Roy was prepared to concede the possible existence of the otherworld mainly due to its utilitarian value. Akshay Kumar Dutt and Ishwarchandra Vidyasagar were agnostics who refused to be drawn into any discussion on supernatural questions. Asked about the existence of God, Vidyasagar quipped that he had no time to think about God, since there was much to be done on earth. Bankimchandra Chatterjee and Vivekananda emphasized the secular use of religion and used spirituality to take cognizance of the material conditions of human existence.

Given the inter-connection between religious beliefs and social practices, religious reformation was a necessary pre-requisite for social reform. 'The Hindu meets his religion at every turn. In eating, in drinking, moving, sitting, standing, he is to adhere to sacred rules, to depart from which is sin and impiety.'[2] Similarly, the social life of the Muslims was strongly influenced by religious tenets. Religion was the dominant ideology of the times and it was not possible to undertake any social action without coming to grips with it.

*

Indian society in the nineteenth century was caught in a vicious web created by religious superstitions and social obscurantism. Hinduism, as

Max Weber observed, had 'become a compound of magic, animism and superstition' and abominable rites like animal sacrifice and physical torture had replaced the worship of God. The priests exercised an overwhelming and, indeed, unhealthy influence on the minds of the people. Idolatry and polytheism helped to reinforce their position. As suggested by Raja Rammohan Roy, their monopoly of scriptural knowledge and of ritual interpretation imparted a deceptive character to all religious systems. The faithful lived in submission, not only to God, the powerful and unseen, but even to the whims, fancies and wishes of the priests. There was nothing that religious ideology could not persuade people to do — women even went to the extent of offering themselves to priests to satisfy their carnal pleasures.

Social conditions were equally depressing. The most distressing was the position of women. The birth of a girl was unwelcome, her marriage a burden and her widowhood inauspicious. Attempts to kill girl infants at birth were not unusual. Those who escaped this initial brutality were subjected to the violence of marriage at a tender age. Often the marriage was a device to escape social ignomiy and, hence, marital life did not turn out to be a pleasant experience. An eighty-year-old Brahman in Bengal had as many as two hundred wives, the youngest being just eight years old. Several women hardly had a married life worth the name, since their husbands participated in nuptial ceremonies for a consideration and rarely set eyes on their wives after that. Yet when their husbands died they were expected to commit Sati which Rammohan described as 'murder according to every *shastra.*'[3] If they succeeded in overcoming this social coercion, they were condemned, as widows, to life-long misery, neglect and humiliation.

Another debilitating factor was caste. It sought to maintain a system of segregation, hierarchically ordained on the basis of ritual status. The rules and regulations of caste hampered social mobility, fostered social divisions and sapped individual initiative. Above all was the humiliation of untouchability which militated against human dignity.

There were innumerable other practices marked by constraint, credulity, status, authority, bigotry and blind fatalism. Rejecting them as features of a decadent society, the reform movements sought to create a social climate for modernization. In doing so, they referred to a golden past when no such malaise existed. The nineteenth century situation was the result of an accretionary process; a distortion of a once ideal past. The reformers' vision of the future, however, was not based on this idealization. It was only an aid and an instrument — since practices based on faith cannot be challenged without bringing faith itself into question. Hence, Raja Rammohan Roy, demonstrated that *sati* had no religious sanction, Vidyasagar did not 'take up his pen in defence of widow marriage' without being convinced about scriptural support and Dayanand based his anti-castesim on Vedic authority.

This, however, did not mean a subjection of the present to the past nor a blind resurrection of tradition. 'The dead and the buried,' maintained Mahadev Govind Ranade, the doyen of reformers in Maharashtra, 'are dead, buried, and burnt once for all and the dead past cannot, therefore, be revived except by a reformation of the old materials into new organized forms.'[4] Neither a revival of the past nor a total break with tradition was contemplated.

*

Two important intellectual criteria which informed the reform movements were rationalism and religious universalism. Social relevance was judged by a rationalist critique. It is difficult to match the uncompromising rationalism of the early Raja Rammohan Roy or Akshay Kumar Dutt. Rejecting supernatural explanations, Raja Rammohan Roy affirmed the principle of casuality linking the whole phenomenal universe. To him demonstrability was the sole criterion of truth. In proclaiming that 'rationalism is our only preceptor,' Akshay Kumar went a step further. All natural and social phenomena, he held, could be analyzed and understood by purely mechanical processes. This perspective not only enabled them to adopt a rational approach to tradition but also to evaluate the contemporary socio-religious practices from the standpoint of social utility and to replace faith with rationality. In the Brahmo Samaj, it led to the repudiation of the infallibility of the Vedas, and in the Aligarh movement, to the reconciliation of the teachings of Islam with the needs of the modern age. Holding that religious tenets were not immutable, Syed Ahmed Khan emphasized the role of religion in the progress of society: if religion did not keep pace with and meet the demands of the time it would get get fossilized as in the case of Islam in India.

The perspectives on reform were not always influenced by religious considerations. A rational and secular outlook was very much evident in posing an alternative to prevalent social practices. In advocating widow marriage and opposing polygamy and child marriage, Akshay Kumar was not concerned about religious sanction or whether they existed in the past. His arguments were mainly based on their effects on society. Instead of depending on the scriptures, he cited medical opinion against child marriage. He held very advanced ideas about marriage and family: courtship before marriage, partnership and equality as the basis of married life and divorce by both law and custom. In Maharashtra, as compared to other regions, there was less dependence on religion as an aid to social reform. To Gopal Hari Deshmukh, popularly known as Lokahitavadi, whether social reforms had the sanction of religion was immaterial. If religion did not sanction these, he advocated that religion itself should be changed as it was made by man and what was laid down in the scriptures need not necessarily be of contemporary relevance.

Although the ambit of reforms were particularistic, their religious perspective was universalistic. Raja Rammohan Roy considered different religions as national embodiments of universal theism. The Brahmo Samaj was initially conceived by him as a universalist church. He was a defender of the basic and universal principles of all religions — the monotheism of the Vedas and the unitarianism of Christianity — and at the same time attacked polytheism of Hinduism and the trinitarianism of Christianity. Syed Ahmed Khan echoed the same idea: all prophets had the same *din* (faith) and every country and nation had different prophets. This perspective found clearer articulation in Keshub Chandra Sen's ideas. He said 'our position is not that truths are to be found in all religions, but all established religions of the world are true.' He also gave expression to the social implications of this universalist perspective: 'Whoever worships the True God daily must learn to recognize all his fellow countrymen as brethren. Caste would vanish in such a state of society. If I believe that my God is one, and that he has created us all, I must at the same time instinctively, and with all the warmth of natural feelings, look upon all around me — whether Parsees, Hindus, Mohammadans or Europeans — as my brethren.'[5]

The universalist perspective was not a purely philosophic concern; it strongly influenced the political and social outlook of the time. till religious particularism gained ground in the second half of the nineteenth century. For instance, Raja Rammohan Roy considered Muslim lawyers to be more honest than their Hindu counterparts and Vidyasagar did not discriminate against Muslims in his humanitarian activities. Even to Bankim, who is credited with a Hindu outlook, *dharma* rather than religious belonging was the criterion for determining superiority. Yet, 'Muslim yoke' and 'Muslim tyranny' were epithets often used to describe the pre-colonial rule. This, however, was not a religious but a political attitude, influenced by the arbitrary character of pre-colonial political institutions. The emphasis was not on the word 'Muslim' but on the word 'tyranny.' This is amply clear from Syed Ahmed Khan's description of the pre-colonial system: 'The rule of the former emperors and *rajas* was neither in accordance with the Hindu nor the Mohammadan religion. It was based upon nothing but tyranny and oppression; the law of might was that of right; the voice of the people was not listened to.'[6] The yardstick obviously was not religious identity, but liberal and democratic principles. This, however, does not imply that religious identity did not influence the social outlook of the people; in fact, it did very strongly. The reformers' emphasis on universalism was an attempt to contend with it. However, faced with the challenge of colonial culture and ideology, universalism, instead of providing the basis for the development of a secular ethos, retreated into religious particularism.

*

The nineteenth century witnessed a cultural-ideological struggle against the backward elements of traditional culture, on the one hand, and the fast hegemonizing colonial culture and ideology on the other. The initial reforming efforts represented the former. In the religious sphere they sought to remove idolatry, polytheism and priestly monopoly of religious knowledge and to simplify religious rituals. They were important not for purely religious reasons but equally for their social implications. They contributed to the liberation of the individual from conformity born out of fear and from uncritical submission to the exploitation of the priests. The dissemination of religious knowledge through translation of religious texts into vernacular languages and the right granted to the laity to interpret scriptures represented an important initial breach in the stranglehold of misinterpreted religious dogmas. The simplification of rituals made worship a more intensely personal experience without the mediation of intermediaries. The individual was, thus, encouraged to exercise his freedom.

The socially debilitating influence of the caste system which perpetuated social distinctions was universally recognized as an area which called for urgent reform. It was morally and ethically abhorrent; more importantly, it militated against patriotic feelings and negated the growth of democratic ideas. Raja Rammohan Roy initiated, in ideas but not in practice, the opposition which became loud and clear as the century progressed. Ranade, Dayanand and Vivekananda denounced the existing system of caste in no uncertain terms. While the reform movements generally stood for its abolition, Dayanand gave a utopian explanation for *chaturvarna* (four-fold *varna* division of Hindu society) and sought to maintain it on the basis of virtue. 'He deserves to be a Brahman who has acquired the best knowledge and character, and an ignorant person is fit to be classed as a *shudra*,' he argued.[7] Understandably the most virulent opposition to caste came from lower caste movements. Jyotiba Phule and Narayana Guru were two unrelenting critics of the caste system and its consequences. A conversation between Gandhiji and Narayana Guru is significant. Gandhiji, in an obvious reference to *Chaturvarna* and the inherent differences in quality between man and man, observed that all leaves of the same tree are not identical in shape and texture. To this Narayana Guru pointed out that the difference is only superficial, but not in essence: the juice of all leaves of a particular tree would be the same in content.[8] It was he who gave the call — 'one religion, one caste and one God for mankind' which one of his disciples, Sahadaran Ayyapan, changed into 'no religion, no caste and no God for mankind.'

The campaign for the improvement of the condition and status of women was not a purely humanitarian measure either. No reform could be really effective without changes in the domestic conditions, the social space in which the initial socialization of the individual took place. A crucial role in this process was played by women. Therefore, there could be no reformed men and reformed homes without reformed women. Viewed from the standpoint of women, it was, indeed, a limited perspective. Nevertheless, it was realized that no country could ever make 'significant progress in civilization whose females were sunk in ignorance.'

If the reform movements had totally rejected tradition, Indian society would have easily undergone a process of westernization. But the reformers were aiming at modernization rather than westernization. A blind initiation of western cultural norms was never an integral part of reform.

To initiate and undertake these reforms which today appear to be modest, weak and limited was not an easy proposition. It brought about unprecedented mental agony and untold domestic and social tension. Breaking the bonds of tradition created emotional and sentimental crises for men and women caught between two worlds. The first widow marriage in Bengal attracted thousands of curious spectators. To the first such couple in Maharashtra the police had to give lathis to protect themselves! Rukmabhai, who refused to accept her uneducated and unaccomplished husband, virtually unleashed a storm. Faced with the prospect of marrying a young girl much against his conviction, Ranade spent several sleepless nights. So did Lokahitavadi, Telang and a host of others who were torn between traditional sentiments and modern commitments. Several however succumbed to the former, but it was out of this struggle that the new men and the new society evolved in India.

*

Faced with the challenge of the intrusion of colonial culture and ideology, an attempt to reinvigorate traditional institutions and to realize the potential of traditional culture developed during the nineteenth century. The initial expression of the struggle against colonial domination manifested itself in the realm of culture as a result of the fact that the principles on which the colonial state functioned were not more retrogressive than those of the pre-colonial state. All intrusions into the cultural realm were more intensely felt. Therefore, a defence of indigenous culture developed almost simultaneously with the colonial conquest.

This concern embraced the entire cultural existence, the way of life and all signifying practices like language, religion, art and philosophy. Two features characterized this concern; the creation of an alternate cultural-ideological system and the regeneration of traditional institutions. The cultivation of vernacular languages, the creation of an alternate system of education, the efforts to regenerate Indian art and literature, the emphasis on Indian dress and food, the defence of religion and the attempts to revitalize the Indian system of medicine, the attempt to probe the potentialities of pre-colonial technology and to reconstruct traditional knowledge were some of the expressions of this concern. The early inklings of this can be discerned in Raja Rammohan Roy's debates with the Christian missionaries, in the formation and activities of Tattvabodhini Sabha, in the memorial on education signed by 70,000 inhabitants of Madras and in the general resentment against the Lex Loci Act.[9] (the Act proposed in 1845 and passed in 1850 provided the right to inherit ancestral property to Hindu converts to Christianity). A more definite articulation, however, was in the ideas and activities of later movements generally characterized as conservative and revivalist. Strongly native in tendency, they were clearly influenced by the need to defend indigenous culture against colonial cultural hegemony. In this specific historical sense, they were not necessarily retrogressive, for underlying these efforts was the concern with the revival of the cultural personality, distorted, if not destroyed, by colonial domination. More so because it formed an integral element in the formation of national consciousness. Some of these tendencies however, were not able to transcend the limits of historical necessity and led to a sectarian and obscurantist outlook. This was possibly a consequence of the lack of integration between the cultural and political struggles, resulting in cultural backwardness, despite political advance.

The cultural-ideological struggle, represented by the socio-religious movements, was an integral part of the evolving national consciousness. This was so because it was instrumental in bringing about the initial intellectual and cultural break which made a new vision of the future possible. Second, it was a part of the resistance against colonial cultural and ideological hegemony. Out of this dual struggle evolved the modern cultural situation: new men, new homes and a new society.

7 An Economic Critique of Colonialism

Of all the national movements in colonial countries, the Indian national movement was the most deeply and firmly rooted in an understanding of the nature and character of colonial economic domination and exploitation. Its early leaders, known as Moderates, were the first in the 19th century to develop an economic critique of colonialism. This critique was, also, perhaps their most important contribution to the development of the national movement in India — and the themes built around it were later popularized on a massive scale and formed the very pith and marrow of the nationalist agitation through popular lectures, pamphlets, newspapers, dramas, songs, and *prabhat pheries*.

Indian intellectuals of the first half of the 19th century had adopted a positive attitude towards British rule in the hope that Britain, the most advanced nation of the time, would help modernize India. In the economic realm, Britain, the emerging industrial giant of the world, was expected to develop India's productive forces through the introduction of modern science and technology and capitalist economic organization. It is not that the early Indian nationalists were unaware of the many political, psychological and economic disabilities of foreign domination, but they still supported colonial rule as they expected it to rebuild India as a spit image of the Western metropolis.

The process of disillusionment set in gradually after 1860 as the reality of social development in India failed to conform to their hopes. They began to notice that while progress in new directions was slow and halting, overall the country was regressing and underdeveloping. Gradually, their image of British rule began to take on darker hues; and they began to probe deeper into the reality of British rule and its impact on India.

Three names stand out among the large number of Indians who initiated and carried out the economic analysis of British rule during the years 1870-1905. The tallest of the three was Dadabhai Naoroji, known in the pre-Gandhian era as the Grand Old Man of India. Born in 1825, he became a successful businessman but devoted his entire life and wealth to the creation of a national movement in India. His near contemporary, Justice Mahadev Govind Ranade, taught an entire generation of Indians the value of modern industrial development. Romesh Chandra Dutt, a retired ICS officer, published *The Economic History of India* at the beginning of the 20th century in which he examined in minute detail the entire economic record of colonial rule since 1757.

These three leaders along with G.V. Joshi, G. Subramaniya Iyer, G.K. Gokhale, Prithwis Chandra Ray and hundreds of other political workers and journalists analysed every aspect of the economy and subjected the entire range of economic issues and colonial economic policies to minute scrutiny. They raised basic questions regarding the nature and purpose of British rule. Eventually, they were able to trace the process of the colonialization of the Indian economy and conclude that colonialism was the main obstacle to India's economic development.

They clearly understood the fact that the essence of British imperialism lay in the subordination of the Indian economy to the British economy. They delineated the colonial structure in all its three aspects of domination through trade, industry and finance. They were able to see that colonialism no longer functioned through the crude tools of plunder and tribute and mercantilism but operated through the more disguised and complex mechanism of free trade and foreign capital investment. The essence of 19th century colonialism, they said, lay in the transformation of India into a supplier of food stuffs and raw materials to the metropolis, a market for the metropolitan manufactures, and a field for the investment of British capital.

The early Indian national leaders were simultaneously learners and teachers. They organized powerful intellectual agitations against nearly all the important official economic policies. They used these agitations to both understand and to explain to others the basis of these policies in the colonial structure. They advocated the severance of India's economic subservience to Britain in every sphere of life and agitated for an alternative path of development which would lead to an independent economy. An important feature of this agitation was the use of bold, hard-hitting and colourful language.

*

The nationalist economic agitation started with the assertion that Indians were poor and were growing poorer every day. Dadabhai Naoroji made poverty his special subject and spent his entire life awakening the Indian and British public to the 'continuous impoverishment and exhaustion of the country' and 'the wretched, heart-rending, blood-boiling condition of India.' Day after day he declaimed from public platforms and in the Press that the Indian 'is starving, he is dying off at the slightest touch, living on insufficient food.'[1]

The early nationalists did not see this all-encompassing poverty as inherent and unavoidable, a visitation from God or nature. It was seen as man-made and, therefore, capable of being explained and removed. As R.C. Dutt put it: 'If India is poor today, it is through the operation of economic causes.'[2] In the course of their search for the causes of India's poverty, the nationalists underlined factors and forces which had been brought into play by the colonial rulers and the colonial structure.

The problem of poverty was, moreover, seen as the problem of increasing the 'productive capacity and energy' of the people, in other words as the problem of national development. This approach made poverty a broad national issue and helped to unite, instead of divide, different regions and sections of Indian society.

Economic development was seen above all as the rapid development of modern industry. The early nationalists accepted with remarkable unanimity that the complete economic transformation of the country on the basis of modern technology and capitalist enterprise was the primary goal of all their economic policies. Industrialism, it was further believed, represented, to quote G.V. Joshi, 'a superior type and a higher stage of civilization;'[3] or, in the words of Ranade, factories could 'far more effectively than Schools and Colleges give a new birth to the activities of the Nation.'[4] Modern industry was also seen as a major force which could help unite the diverse peoples of India into a single national entity having common interests. Surendranath Banerjea's newspaper the *Bengalee* made the point on 18 January 1902: 'The agitation for political rights may bind the various nationalities of India together for a time. The community of interests may cease when these rights are achieved. But the commercial union of the various Indian nationalities, once established, will never cease to exist. Commercial and industrial activity is, therefore, a bond of very strong union and is, therefore, a mighty factor in the formation of a great Indian nation.'

Consequently, because of their whole-hearted devotion to the cause of industrialization, the early nationalists looked upon all other issues such as foreign trade, railways, tariffs, currency and exchange, finance, and labour legislation in relation to this paramount aspect.

*

At the same time, nearly all the early nationalists were clear on one question: However great the need of India for industrialization, it had to be based on Indian capital and not foreign capital.[5] Ever since the 1840s, British economists, statesmen and officials had seen the investment of foreign capital, along with law and order, as the major instrument for the development of India. John Stuart Mill and Alfred Marshall had put forward this view in their economic treatises. In 1899, Lord Curzon, the Viceroy, said that foreign capital was 'a *sine qua non* to the national advancement' of India.[6]

The early nationalists disagreed vehemently with this view. They saw foreign capital as an unmitigated evil which did not develop a country but exploited and impoverished it. Or, as Dadabhai Naoroji popularly put it, foreign capital represented the 'despoilation' and 'exploitation' of Indian resources.[7] Similarly, the editor of the *Hindustan Review and Kayastha Samachar* described the use of foreign capital as 'a system of international depradation.'[8]

They further argued that instead of encouraging and augmenting Indian capital, foreign capital replaced and suppressed it, led to the drain of capital from India and further strengthened the British hold over the Indian economy. To try to develop a country through foreign capital, they said, was to barter the entire future for the petty gains of today. Bipin Chandra Pal summed up the nationalist point of view in 1901 as follows: 'The introduction of foreign, and mostly British, capital for working out the natural resources of the country, instead of being a help, is, in fact, the greatest of hindrances to all real improvements in the economic condition of the people. It is as much a political, as it is an economic danger. And the future of New India absolutely depends upon an early and radical remedy of this two-edged evil.'[9]

In essence, the early nationalists asserted that genuine economic development was possible only if Indian capital itself initiated and developed the process of industrialization. Foreign capital would neither undertake nor could it fulfill this task.

According to the early nationalists, the political consequences of foreign capital investment were no less harmful, for the penetration of a country by foreign capital inevitably led to its political subjugation. Foreign capital investment created vested interests which demanded security for investors and, therefore, perpetuated foreign rule. 'Where foreign capital has been sunk in a country,' wrote the *Hindu* in its issue dated 23 September 1889, 'the administration of that country becomes at once the concern of the bondholders.' It added: '(if) the influence of foreign capitalists in the land is allowed to increase, then adieu to all chances of success of the Indian National Congress whose voice will be drowned in the tremendous uproar of "the empire in danger" that will surely be raised by the foreign capitalists.'

*

A major problem the early nationalists highlighted was that of the progressive decline and ruin of India's traditional handicrafts. Nor was this industrial prostration accidental, they said. It was the result of the deliberate policy of stamping out Indian industries in the interests of British manufactures.

The British administrators, on the other hand, pointed with pride to the rapid growth of India's foreign trade and the rapid construction of railways as instruments of India's development as well as proof of its growing prosperity. However, the nationalists said that because of their negative impact on indigenous industries, foreign trade and railways represented not economic development but colonialization and underdevelopment of the economy. What mattered in the case of foreign trade, they maintained, was not its volume but its pattern or the nature of goods internationally exchanged and their impact on national industry and agriculture. And this pattern had undergone drastic changes during the 19th century, the bias being overwhelmingly towards the export of raw materials and the import of manufactured goods.

Similarly, the early nationalists pointed out that the railways had not been coordinated with India's industrial needs. They had, therefore, ushered in a commercial and not an industrial revolution which enabled imported foreign goods to undersell domestic industrial products. Moreover, they said that the benefits of railway construction in terms of encouragement to the steel and machine industry and to capital investment — what today we would call backward and forward linkages — had been reaped by Britain and not India. In fact, remarked G.V. Joshi, expenditure on railways should be seen as Indian subsidy to British industries.[10] Or, as Tilak put it, it was like 'decorating another's wife.'[11]

According to the early nationalists, a major obstacle to rapid industrial development was the policy of free trade which was, on the one hand, ruining India's handicraft industries and, on the other, forcing the infant and underdeveloped modern industries into a premature and unequal and, hence, unfair and disastrous competition with the highly organized and developed industries of the West. The tariff policy of the Government convinced the nationalists that British economic policies in India were basically guided by the interests of the British capitalist class.

The early nationalists strongly criticized the colonial pattern of finance. Taxes were so raised, they averred, as to overburden the poor while letting the rich, especially the foreign capitalists and bureaucrats, go scot-free. To vitiate this, they demanded the reduction of land revenue and abolition of the salt tax and supported the imposition of income tax and import duties on products which the rich and the middle classes consumed.

On the expenditure side, they pointed out that the emphasis was on serving Britain's imperial needs while the developmental and welfare departments were starved. In particular, they condemned the high expenditure on the army which was used by the British to conquer and maintain imperialist control over large parts of Asia and Africa.

*

The focal point of the nationalist critique of colonialism was the drain theory.[12] The nationalist leaders pointed out that a large part of India's capital and wealth was being transferred or 'drained' to Britain in the form of salaries and pensions of British civil and military officials working in India, interest on loans taken by the Indian Government, profits of British capitalists in India, and the Home Charges or expenses of the Indian Government in Britain.

This drain took the form of an excess of exports over imports for which India got no economic or material return. According to the nationalist calculations, this drain amounted to one-half of government revenues, more than the entire land revenue collection, and over one-third of India's total savings. (In today's terms this would amount to eight per cent of India's national income).

The acknowledged high-priest of the drain theory was Dadabhai Naoroji. It was in May 1867 that Dadabhai Naoroji put forward the idea that Britain was draining and 'bleeding' India. From then on for nearly half a century he launched a raging campaign against the drain, hammering at the theme through every possible form of public communication.

The drain, he declared, was the basic cause of India's poverty and the fundamental evil of British rule in India. Thus, he argued in 1880: 'It is not the pitiless operations of economic laws, but it is the thoughtless and pitiless action of the British policy; it is the pitiless eating of India's substance in India, and the further pitiless drain to England; in short, it is the pitiless *perversion* of economic laws by the sad bleeding to which India is subjected, that is destroying India.'[13]

Other nationalist leaders, journalists and propagandists followed in the foot-steps of Dadabhai Naoroji. R.C. Dutt, for example, made the drain the major theme of his *Economic History of India*. He protested that 'taxation raised by a king, says the Indian poet, is like the moisture sucked up by the sun, to be returned to the earth as fertilizing rain; but the moisture raised from the Indian soil now descends as fertilizing rain largely on other lands, not on India ... So great an Economic Drain out of the resources of a land would impoverish the most prosperous countries on earth; it has reduced India to a land of famines more frequent, more widespread, and more fatal, than any known before in the history of India, or of the world.'[14]

The drain theory incorporated all the threads of the nationalist critique of colonialism, for the drain denuded India of the productive capital its agriculture and industries so desperately needed. Indeed, the drain theory was the high water-mark of the nationalist leaders' comprehensive, inter-related and integrated economic analysis of the colonial situation. Through the drain theory, the exploitative character of British rule could be made visible. By attacking the drain, the nationalists were able to call into question, in an uncompromising manner, the economic essence of imperialism.

Moreover, the drain theory possessed the great political merit of being easily grasped by a nation of peasants. Money being transferred from one country to another was the most easily understood of the theories of economic exploitation, for the peasant daily underwent this experience vis-a-vis the state, landlords, moneylenders, lawyers and priests. No other idea could arouse people more than the thought that they were being taxed so that others in far off lands might live in comfort.

'No drain' was the type of slogan that all successful movements need — it did not have to be proved by sophisticated and complex arguments. It had a sort of immanent quality about it; it was practically self-evident. Nor could the foreign rulers do anything to appease the people on this question. Modern colonialism was inseparable from the drain. The contradiction between the Indian people and British imperialism was seen by people to be insoluble except by the overthrow of British rule. It was, therefore, inevitable that the drain theory became the main staple of nationalist political agitation during the Gandhian era.

*

This agitation on economic issues contributed to the undermining of the ideological hegemony of the alien rulers over Indian minds, that is, of the foundations of colonial rule in the minds of the people. Any regime is politically secure only so long as the people have a basic faith in its moral purpose, in its benevolent character — that is, they believe that the rulers are basically motivated by the desire to work for their welfare. It is this belief which leads them to support the regime or to at least acquiesce in its continuation. It provides legitimacy to a regime — in this belief lie its moral foundations.

The secret of British power in India lay not only in physical force but also in moral force, that is, in the belief sedulously inculcated by the rulers for over a century that the British were the *Mai-Baap* of the common people of India — the first lesson in primary school language textbooks was most often on 'the benefits of British rule.' The nationalist economic agitation gradually undermined these moral foundations. It corroded popular confidence in the benevolent character of British rule — in its good results as well as its good intentions.

The economic development of India was offered as the chief justification for British rule by the imperialist rulers and spokesmen. The

Indian nationalists controverted it forcefully and asserted that India was economically backward precisely because the British were ruling it in the interests of British trade, industry and capital, and that poverty and backwardness were the inevitable consequences of colonial rule. Tilak's newspaper, the *Kesari*, for example, wrote on 28 January 1896: 'Surely India is treated as a vast pasture for the Europeans to feed upon.' And P. Ananda Charlu, an ex-President of the Congress, said in the Legislative Council: 'While India is safe-guarded against foreign inroads by the strong arm of the British power, she is defenceless in matters where the English and Indian interests clash and where (as a Tamil saying puts it) the very fence begins to feed on the crop.'[15]

The young intellectual from Bihar, Sachidanand Sinha, summed up the Indian critique in a pithy manner in *Indian People* on 27 February 1903: 'Their work of administration in Lord Curzon's testimony is only the handmaid to the task of exploitation. Trade cannot thrive without efficient administration, while the latter is not worth attending to in the absence of profits of the former. So always with the assent and often to the dictates of the Chamber of Commerce, the Government of India is carried on, and this is the "White Man's Burden."

It was above all Dadabhai Naoroji who in his almost daily articles and speeches hammered home this point. 'The face of beneficence,' he said, was a mask behind which the exploitation of the country was carried on by the British though 'unaccompanied with any open compulsion or violence to person or property which the world can see and be horrified with.' And, again: 'Under the present evil and unrighteous administration of Indian expenditure, the romance is the beneficence of the British Rule, the reality is the "bleeding" of the British Rule.'[16] Regarding the British claim of having provided security of life and property, Dadabhai wrote: 'The romance is that there is security of life and property in India; the reality is that there is no such thing. There is security of life and property in one sense or way, i.e., the people are secure from any violence from each other or from Native despots . . . But from England's own grasp there is no security of property at all, and, as a consequence, no security for life . . . What is secure, and well secure, is that England is perfectly safe and secure . . . to carry away from India, and to eat up in India, her property at the present rate of 30,000,000 or 40,00,000 £ a year . . . To millions in India life is simply "half-feeding," or starvation, or famine and disease.'[17]

With regard to the benefits of law and order, Dadabhai said: 'There is an Indian saying: "Pray strike on the back, but don't strike on the belly." Under the "native despot the people keep and enjoy what they produce, though at times they suffer some violence on the back. Under the British Indian despot the man is at peace, there is no violence; his substance is drained away, unseen, peaceably and subtly — he starves in peace, and peaceably perishes in peace, with law and order!"[18]

*

The corrosion of faith in British rule inevitably spread to the political field. In the course of their economic agitation, the nationalist leaders linked nearly every important economic question with the politically subordinated status of the country. Step by step, issue by issue, they began to draw the conclusion that since the British Indian administration was 'only the handmaid to the task of exploitation,' pro-Indian and developmental policies would be followed only by a regime in which Indians had control over political power.

The result was that even though most of the early nationalist leaders were moderate in politics and political methods, and many of them still professed loyalty to British rule, they cut at the political roots of the empire and sowed in the land the seeds of disaffection and disloyalty and even sedition. This was one of the major reasons why the period 1875 to 1905 became a period of intellectual unrest and of spreading national consciousness — the seed-time of the modern Indian national movement.

While until the end of the 19th century, Indian nationalists confined their political demands to a share in political power and control over the purse, by 1905 most of the prominent nationalists were putting forward the demand for some form of self-government. Here again, Dadabhai Naoroji was the most advanced. Speaking on the drain at the International Socialist Congress in 1904, he put forward the demand for 'self-government' and treatment of India 'like other British Colonies.'[19] A year later, in 1905, in a message to the Benares session of the Indian National Congress, Dadabhai categorically asserted: 'Self-government is the only remedy for India's woes and wrongs.'[20] And, then, as the President of the 1906 session of the Congress at Calcutta, he laid down the goal of the national movement as "self-government or *Swaraj*," like that of the United Kingdom or the Colonies.'[21]

While minds were being prepared and the goal formed, the mass struggle for the political emancipation of the country was still in the womb of time. But the early nationalists were laying strong and enduring foundations for the national movement to grow upon. They sowed the seeds of nationalism well and deep. They did not base their nationalism primarily on appeals to abstract or shallow sentiments or on obscurantist appeals to the past. They rooted their nationalism in a brilliant scientific analysis of the complex economic mechanism of modern colonialism and of the chief contradiction between the interests of the Indian people and British rule.

The nationalists of the 20th century were to rely heavily on the main themes of their economic critique of colonialism. These themes were then to reverberate in Indian cities, towns and villages, carried there by the youthful agitators of the Gandhian era. Based on this firm foundation, the later nationalists went on to stage powerful mass agitations and mass movements. At the same time, because of this firm foundation, they would not, unlike in China, Egypt and many other colonial and semi-colonial countries, waver in their anti-imperialism.

8 The Fight to Secure Press Freedom

Almost from the beginning of the 19th century, politically conscious Indians had been attracted to modern civil rights, especially the freedom of the Press. As early as 1824, Raja Rammohan Roy had protested against a regulation restricting the freedom of the Press. In a memorandum to the Supreme Court, he had said that every good ruler 'will be anxious to afford every individual the readiest means of bringing to his notice whatever may require his interference. To secure this important object, the unrestricted liberty of publication is the only effectual means that can be employed.'[1]

In the period from 1870 to 1918, the national movement had not yet resorted to mass agitation through thousands of small and large *maidan* meetings, nor did political work consist of the active mobilization of people in mass struggles. The main political task still was that of politicization, political propaganda and education and formation and propagation of nationalist ideology. The Press was the chief instrument for carrying out this task, that is, for arousing, training, mobilizing and consolidating nationalist public opinion.

Even the work of the National Congress was accomplished during these years largely through the Press. The Congress had no organization of its own for carrying on political work. Its resolutions and proceedings had to be propagated through newspapers. Interestingly, nearly one-third of the founding fathers of the Congress in 1885 were journalists.

Powerful newspapers emerged during these years under distinguished and fearless journalists. These were the *Hindu* and *Swadesamitran* under the editorship of G. Subramaniya Iyer, *Kesari* and *Mahratta* under B.G. Tilak, *Bengalee* under Surendranath Banerjea, *Amrita Bazar Patrika* under Sisir Kumar Ghosh and Motilal Ghosh, *Sudharak* under G.K. Gokhale, *Indian Mirror* under N.N. Sen, *Voice of India* under Dadabhai Naoroji, *Hindustani* and *Advocate* under G.P. Varma and *Tribune* and *Akhbar-i-Am* in Punjab, *Indu Prakash, Dnyan Prakash, Kal* and *Gujarati* in Bombay, and *Som Prakash, Banganivasi* and *Sadharani* in Bengal. In fact, there hardly existed a major political leader in India who did not possess a newspaper or was not writing for one in some capacity or the other.

The influence of the Press extended far beyond its literate subscribers. Nor was it confined to cities and large towns. A newspaper would reach remote villages and would then be read by a reader to tens of others. Gradually library movements sprung up all over the country. A local 'library' would be organized around a single newspaper. A table, a bench or two or a *charpoy* would constitute the capital equipment. Every piece of news or editorial comment would be read or heard and thoroughly discussed. The newspaper not only became the political educator; reading or discussing it became a form of political participation.

Newspapers were not in those days business enterprises, nor were the editors and journalists professionals. Newspapers were published as a national or public service. They were often financed as objects of philanthropy. To be a journalist was often to be a political worker and an agitator at considerable self-sacrifice. It was, of course, not very expensive to start a newspaper, though the editor had usually to live at a semi-starvation level or earn his livelihood through a supplementary source. The *Amrita Bazar Patrika* was started in 1868 with printing equipment purchased for Rs. 32. Similarly, Surendranath Banerjea purchased the goodwill of the *Bengalee* in 1879 for Rs. 10 and the press for another Rs. 1600.

Nearly all the major political controversies of the day were conducted through the Press. It also played the institutional role of opposition to the Government. Almost every act and every policy of the Government was subjected to sharp criticism, in many cases with great care and vast learning backing it up. 'Oppose, oppose, oppose' was the motto of the Indian Press. Regarding the role of the nationalist Press, Lord Dufferin, the Viceroy, wrote as early as March 1886: 'Day after day, hundreds of sharp-witted *babus* pour forth their indignation against their English oppressors in very pungent and effective diatribe.' And again in May:

'In this way there can be no doubt there is generated in the minds of those who read these papers . . . a sincere conviction that we are all of us the enemies of mankind in general and of India in particular.'[2]

To arouse political consciousness, to inculcate nationalism, to expose colonial rule, to 'preach disloyalty' was no easy task, for there had existed since 1870 Section 124A of the Indian Penal Code according to which 'whoever attempts to excite feelings of disaffection to the Government established by law in British India' was to be punished with transportation for life or for any term or with imprisonment upto three years. This clause was, moreover, later supplemented with even more strident measures.

Indian journalists adopted several clever strategems and evolved a distinctive style of writing to remain outside the reach of the law. Since Section 124A excluded writings of persons whose loyalty to the Government was undoubted, they invariably prefaced their vitriolic writing with effusive sentiments of loyalty to the Government and the Queen. Another strategem was to publish anti-imperialist extracts from London-based socialist and Irish newspapers or letters from radical British citizens knowing that the Indian Government could not discriminate against Indians by taking action against them without touching the offending Britishers. Sometimes the extract from the British newspaper would be taken without quotation marks and acknowledgment of the source, thus teasing the British-Indian bureaucracy into contemplating or taking action which would have to be given up once the real source of the comment became known. For example, a sympathetic treatment of the Russian terrorist activities against Tsarism would be published in such a way that the reader would immediately draw a parallel between the Indian Government and the Revolutionary Terrorists of Bengal and Maharashtra. The officials would later discover that it was an extract from the *Times*, London, or some such other British newspaper.

Often the radical expose would take the form of advice and warning to the Government as if from a well-wisher, as if the writer's main purpose was to save the authorities from their own follies! B.G. Tilak and Motilal Ghosh were experts at this form of writing. Some of the more daring writers took recourse to irony, sarcasm, banter, mock-seriousness and burlesque.

In all cases, nationalist journalists, especially of Indian language newspapers, had a difficult task to perform, for they had to combine simplicity with subtlety — simplicity was needed to educate a semi-literate public, subtlety to convey the true meaning without falling foul of the law. They performed the task brilliantly, often creatively developing the languages in which they were writing, including, surprisingly enough, the English language.

The national movement from the beginning zealously defended the freedom of the Press whenever the Government attacked it or tried to curtail it. In fact, the struggle for the freedom of the Press became an integral part of the struggle for freedom.

*

Indian newspapers began to find their feet in the 1870s. They became highly critical of Lord Lytton's administration, especially regarding its inhuman approach towards the victims of the famine of 1876-77. As a result the government decided to make a sudden strike at the Indian language newspapers, since they reached beyond the middle class readership. The Vernacular Press Act of 1878, directed only against Indian language newspapers, was conceived in great secrecy and passed at a single sitting of the Imperial Legislative Council. The Act provided for the confiscation of the printing press, paper and other materials of a newspaper if the Government believed that it was publishing seditious materials and had flouted an official warning.

Indian nationalist opinion firmly opposed the Act. The first great demonstration on an issue of public importance was organized in Calcutta on this question when a large meeting was held in the Town Hall. Various public bodies and the Press also campaigned against the Act. Consequently, it was repealed in 1881 by Lord Ripon.

The manner in which the Indian newspapers cleverly fought such measures was brought out by a very amusing and dramatic incident. The Act was in particular aimed at the *Amrita Bazar Patrika* which came out at the time in both Bengali and English. The objective was to take summary action against it. But when the officials woke up the morning after the Act was passed, they discovered to their dismay that the *Patrika* had foxed them; overnight, the editors had converted it into an English newspaper!

*

Another remarkable journalistic coup occurred in 1905. Delivering the

Convocation Address at Calcutta University, Lord Curzon, the Viceroy, said that 'the highest ideal of truth is to a large extent a Western conception. Undoubtedly, truth took a high place in the moral codes of the West before it had been similarly honoured in the East.'[3] The insinuation was that the British had taught this high conception of truth to Indians.

Next day, the *Amrita Bazar Patrika* came out with this speech on the front page along with a box reproducing an extract from Curzon's book the *Problems of the East* in which he had taken credit for lying while on a visit to Korea. He had written that he had told the President of the Korean Foreign Office that he was forty when he was actually thirty-three because he had been told that in the East respect went with age. He had ascribed his youthful appearance to the salubrious climate of Korea! Curzon had also recorded his reply to the President's question whether he was a near relation of Queen Victoria as follows: ' "No," I replied, "I am not." But observing the look of disgust that passed over his countenance, I was fain to add, "I am, however, as yet an unmarried man," with which unscrupulous suggestion I completely regained the old gentleman's favour.'[4]

The whole of Bengal had a hearty laugh at the discomfiture of the strait-laced Viceroy, who had not hesitated to insult an entire people and who was fond of delivering homilies to Indians. The *Weekly Times* of London also enjoyed the episode. Lord Curzon's 'admiration for truth,' it wrote, 'was perhaps acquired later on in life, under his wife's management. It is pre-eminently a Yankee quality.' (Curzon's wife was an American heiress).

*

Surendranath Banerjea, one of the founding fathers of the Indian national movement, was the first Indian to go to jail in performance of his duty as a journalist. A dispute concerning a family idol, a *saligram*, had come up before Justice Norris of the Calcutta High Court. To decide the age of the idol, Norris ordered it to be brought to the Court and pronounced that it could not be a hundred years old. This action deeply hurt the sentiments of the Bengali Hindus. Banerjea wrote an angry editorial in the *Bengalee* of 2 April 1883. Comparing Norris with the notorious Jeffreys and Seroggs (British judges in the 17th century, notorious for infamous conduct as judges), he said that Norris had done enough 'to show how unworthy he is of his high office.' Banerjea suggested that 'some public steps should be taken to put a quietus to the wild eccentricities of this young and raw Dispenser of Justice.'

Immediately, the High Court hauled him up for contempt of court before a bench of five judges, four of them Europeans. With the Indian judge, Romesh Chandra Mitra, dissenting, the bench convicted and sentenced him to two months imprisonment. Popular reaction was immediate and angry. There was a spontaneous *hartal* in the Indian part of Calcutta. Students demonstrated outside the court smashing windows and pelting the police with stones. One of the rowdy young men was Asutosh Mukherjea who later gained fame as a distinguished Vice-Chancellor of Calcutta University. Demonstrations were held all over Calcutta and in many other towns of Bengal as also in Lahore, Amritsar, Agra, Fyzabad, Poona and other cities. Calcutta witnessed for the first time several largely attended open-air meetings.

*

But the man who is most frequently associated with the struggle for the freedom of the Press during the nationalist movement is Bal Gangadhar Tilak, the outstanding leader of militant nationalism. Born in 1856, Tilak devoted his entire life to the service of his country.

In 1881, along with G.G. Agarkar, he founded the newspapers *Kesari* (in Marathi) and *Mahratta* (in English). In 1888, he took over the two papers and used their columns to spread discontent against British rule and to preach national resistance to it. Tilak was a fiery and courageous journalist whose style was simple and direct and yet highly readable.

In 1893, he started the practice of using the traditional religious Ganapati festival to propagate nationalist ideas through patriotic songs and speeches. In 1896, he started the Shivaji festival to stimulate nationalism among young Maharashtrians. In the same year, he organized an all-Maharashtra campaign for the boycott of foreign cloth in protest against the imposition of the excise duty on cotton. He was, perhaps, the first among the national leaders to grasp the important role that the lower middle classes, peasants, artisans and workers could play in the national movement and, therefore, he saw the necessity of bringing them into the Congress fold. Criticizing the Congress for ignoring the peasant, he wrote in the *Kesari* in early 1897: 'The country's emancipation can only be achieved by removing the clouds of lethargy and indifference which have been hanging over the peasant, who is the soul of India. We must remove these clouds, and for that we must completely identify ourselves with the peasant — we must feel that he is ours and we are his.' Only when this is done would 'the Government realize that to despise the Congress is to despise the Indian Nation. Then only will the efforts of the Congress leaders be crowned with success.'5

In pursuance of this objective, he initiated a no-tax campaign in Maharashtra during 1896-97 with the help of the young workers of the Poona Sarvajanik Sabha. Referring to the official famine-code, whose copies he got printed in Marathi and distributed by the thousand, he asked the famine-stricken peasants of Maharashtra to withhold payment of land revenue if their crops had failed.

In 1897, plague broke out in Poona and the Government had to undertake severe measures of segregation and house-searches. Unlike many other leaders, Tilak stayed in Poona, supported the Government and organized his own measures against the plague. But he also criticized the harsh and heartless manner in which the officials dealt with the plague-stricken people. Popular resentment against the official plague measures resulted in the assassination of Rand, the Chairman of the Plague Committee in Poona, and Lt. Ayerst by the Chapekar brothers on 27 June 1898.

The anti-plague measures weren't the only practices that made the people irate. Since 1894, anger had been rising against the Government because of its tariff, currency and famine policy. A militant trend was rapidly growing among the nationalists and there were hostile comments in the Press. The Government was determined to check this trend and teach a lesson to the Press. Tilak was by now well-known in Maharashtra, both as a militant nationalist and as a hostile and effective journalist. The Government was looking for an opportunity to make an example of him. The Rand murder gave them the opportunity. The British-owned Press and the bureaucracy were quick to portray the Rand murder as a conspiracy by the Poona Brahmins led by Tilak.

The Government investigated the possibility of directly involving Tilak in Rand's assassination. But no proof could be found. Moreover, Tilak had condemned the assassination describing it as the horrible work of a fanatic, though he would not stop criticizing the Government, asserting that it was a basic function of the Press to bring to light the unjust state of affairs and to teach people how to defend their rights.

And so, the Government decided to arrest him under Section 124A of the Indian Penal Code on the charge of sedition, that is, spreading disaffection and hatred against the Government.

Tilak was arrested on 27 July 1897 and tried before Justice Strachey and a jury of six Europeans and three Indians. The charge was based on the publication in the *Kesari* of 15 June of a poem titled 'Shivaji's Utterances' read out by a young man at the Shivaji Festival and on a speech Tilak had delivered at the Festival in defence of Shivaji's killing of Afzal Khan.

In 'Shivaji's Utterances,' the poet had shown Shivaji awakening in the present and telling his countrymen: 'Alas! Alas! I now see with my own eyes the ruin of my country . . . Foreigners are dragging out Lakshmi violently by the hand (*kar* in Marathi which also means taxes) and by persecution . . . The wicked Akabaya (misfortune personified) stalks with famine through the whole country . . . How have all these kings (leaders) become quite effeminate like helpless figures on the chess-board?'

Tilak's defence of Shivaji's killing of Afzal Khan was portrayed by the prosecution as an incitement to kill British officials. The overall accusation was that Tilak propagated the views,in his newspaper, that the British had no right to stay in India and any and all means could be used to get rid of them.

Looking back, it is clear that the accusation was not wrong. But the days when, under Gandhiji's guidance, freedom fighters would refuse to defend themselves and openly proclaim their sedition were still far off. The politics of sacrifice and open defiance of authority were still at an early stage. It was still necessary to claim that anti-colonial activities were being conducted within the limits of the law. And so Tilak denied the official charges and declared that he had no intention of preaching disaffection against alien rule. Within this 'old' style of facing the rulers, Tilak set a high example of boldness and sacrifice. He was aware that he was initiating a new kind of politics which must gain the confidence and faith of the people by the example of a new type of leader, while carefully avoiding premature radicalism which would invite repression by the Government and lead to the cowing down of the people and, consequently, the isolation of the leaders from the people.

Pressure was brought upon Tilak by some friends to withdraw his remarks and apologise. Tilak's reply was: 'My position (as a leader) amongst the people entirely depends upon my character . . . Their

(Government's) object is to humiliate the Poona leaders, and I think in me they will not find a "kutcha"(weak) reed . . . Then you must remember beyond a certain stage we are all servants of the people. You will be betraying and disappointing them if you show a lamentable want of courage at a critical time.'[6]

Judge Strachey's partisan summing up to the jury was to gain notoriety in legal circles, for he defined disaffection as 'simply the absence of affection' which amounted to the presence of hatred, enmity, disloyalty and every other form of ill-will towards the Government! The jury gave a 6 to 3 verdict holding Tilak guilty, the three dissenters being its Indian members. The Judge passed a barbarous sentence of rigorous imprisonment for eighteen months, and this when Tilak was a member of the Bombay Legislative Council! Simultaneously several other editors of Bombay Presidency were tried and given similar harsh sentences.

Tilak's imprisonment led to widespread protests all over the country. Nationalist newspapers and political associations, including those run by Tilak's critics like the Moderates, organized a country-wide movement against this attack on civil liberties and the freedom of the Press. Many newspapers came out with black borders on the front page. Many published special supplements hailing Tilak as a martyr in the battle for the freedom of the Press. Addressing Indian residents in London, Dadabhai Naoroji accused the Government of initiating Russian (Tsarist) methods of administration and said that gagging the Press was simply suicidal.[7]

Overnight Tilak became a popular all-India leader and the title of Lokamanya (respected and honoured by the people) was given to him. He became a hero, a living symbol of the new spirit of self-sacrifice, — a new leader who preached with his deeds. When at the Indian National Congress session at Amraoti in December 1897, Surendranath Banerjea made a touching reference to Tilak and said that 'a whole nation is in tears,' the entire audience stood up and enthusiastically cheered.[8]

In 1898, the Government amended Section 124A and added a new Section 153A to the penal code, making it a criminal offence for anyone to attempt 'to bring into contempt' the Government of India or to create hatred among different classes, that is vis-a-vis Englishmen in India. This once again led to nation-wide protest.

The Swadeshi and Boycott Movement, which we shall look at in more detail later on in Chapter 10, led to a new wave of repression in the country. The people once again felt angry and frustrated. This frustration led the youth of Bengal to take to the path of individual terrorism. Several cases of bomb attacks on officials occurred in the beginning of 1908. The Government felt unnerved. Once again newspapers became a major target. Fresh laws for controlling the Press were enacted, prosecutions against a large number of newspapers and their editors were launched and the Press was almost completely suppressed. In this atmosphere, it was inevitable that the Government's attention would turn towards Lokamanya Tilak, the mainstay of the Boycott movement and militant politics outside Bengal.

Tilak wrote a series of articles on the arrival of the 'Bomb' on the Indian scene. He condemned the use of violence and individual killings — he described Nihilism as 'this poisonous tree' — but, simultaneously, he held the Government responsible for suppressing criticism and dissent and the urge of the people for greater freedom. In such an atmosphere, he said 'violence, however deplorable, became inevitable.' As he wrote in one of his articles: 'When the official class begins to overawe the people without any reason and when an endeavour is made to produce despondency among the people by unduly frightening them, then the sound of the bomb is spontaneously produced to impart to the authorities the true knowledge that the people have reached a higher stage than the vapid one in which they pay implicit regard to such an illiberal policy of repression.'9

Once again, on 24 June 1908, Tilak was arrested and tried on the charge of sedition for having published these articles. Once again Tilak pleaded not guilty and behaved with exemplary courage. A few days before his arrest, a friendly police officer warned him of the coming event and asked Tilak to take precautionary steps. Tilak laughed and said: 'The Government has converted the entire nation into a prison and we are all prisoners. Going to prison only means that from a big cell one is confined to a smaller one.'10 In the court, Tilak posed the basic question: 'Tilak or no Tilak is not the question. The question is, do you really intend as guardians of the liberty of the Press to allow as much liberty here in India as is enjoyed by the people of England?'11

Once again the Jury returned a verdict of guilty with only the two Indian members opposing the verdict. Tilak's reply was: 'There are higher powers that rule the destiny of men and nations; and it may be the will of Providence that the cause which I represent may prosper more by my sufferings than by my remaining free.' Justice Davar awarded him the sentence of six years' transportation and after some time the Lokamanya was sent to a prison in Mandalay in Burma.

The public reaction was massive. Newspapers proclaimed that they would defend the freedom of the Press by following Tilak's example. All markets in Bombay city were closed on 22 July, the day his conviction was announced, and remained closed for a week. The workers of all the textile mills and railway workshops went on strike for six days. Efforts to force them to go back to work led to a battle between them and the police. The army was called out and at the end of the battle sixteen workers lay dead in the streets with nearly fifty others seriously injured. Lenin hailed this as the entrance of the Indian working class on the political stage.[12]

Echoes of Tilak's trial were to be heard in another not-so-distant court when Gandhiji, his political successor, was tried in 1922 for the same offence of sedition under the same Section 124A for his articles in *Young India*. When the Judge told him that his offence was similar to Tilak's and that he was giving him the same sentence of six years' imprisonment, Gandhiji replied: 'Since you have done me the honour of recalling the trial of the late Lokamanya Bal Gangadhar Tilak, I just want to say that I consider it to be the proudest privilege and honour to be associated with his name.'[13]

The only difference between the two trials was that Gandhiji had pleaded guilty to the charges. This was also a measure of the distance the national movement had travelled since 1908. Tilak's contribution to this change in politics and journalism had been momentous.

9 Propaganda in the Legislatures

Legislative Councils in India had no real official power till 1920. Yet, work done in them by the nationalists helped the growth of the national movement.

*

The Indian Councils Act of 1861 enlarged the Governor-General's Executive Council for the purpose of making laws. The Governor-General could now add from six to twelve members to the Executive Council. At least half of these nominees had to be non-officials, Indian or British. This council came to be known as the Imperial Legislative Council. It possessed no powers at all. It could not discuss the budget or a financial measure or any other important bill without the previous approval of the Government. It could not discuss the actions of the administration. It could not, therefore, be seen as some kind of parliament, even of the most elementary kind. As if to underline this fact, the Council met, on an average, for only twenty-five days in a year till 1892.

The Government of India remained, as before 1858, an alien despot. Nor was this accidental. While moving the Indian Councils Bill of 1861, the Secretary of State for India, Charles Wood, said: 'All experience teaches us that where a dominant race rules another, the mildest form of government is despotism.' A year later he wrote to Elgin, the Viceroy, that 'the only government suitable for such a state of things as exists in India is a despotism controlled from home.'[1] This 'despotism controlled from home' was to remain the fundamental feature of the

Government of India till 15 August 1947.

What was the role of Indian members in this Legislative Council? The Government had decided to add them in order to represent Indian views, for many British officials and statesmen had come to believe that one reason for the Revolt of 1857 was that Indian views were not known to the rulers. But, in practice, the Council did not serve even this purpose. Indian members were few in number — in thirty years, from 1862 to 1892, only forty-five Indians were nominated to it. Moreover, the Government invariably chose rulers of princely states or their employees, big *zamindars*, big merchants or retired high government officials as Indian members. Only a handful of political figures and independent intellectuals such as Syed Ahmed Khan (1878-82), Kristodas Pal (1883), V.N. Mandlik (1884-87), K.L. Nulkar (1890-91) and Rash Behari Ghosh (1892) were nominated. The overwhelming majority of Indian nominees did not represent the Indian people or emerging nationalist opinion. It was, therefore, not surprising that they completely toed the official line. There is the interesting story of Raja Dig Vijay Singh of Balarampur — nominated twice to the Council — who did not know a word of English. When asked by a relative how he voted one way or the other, he replied that he kept looking at the Viceroy and when the Viceroy raised his hand he did so too and when he lowered it he did the same!

The voting record of Indian nominees on the Council was poor. When the Vernacular Press Bill came up before the Council, only one Indian member, Maharaja Jotendra Mohan Tagore, the leader of the *zamindari*-dominated British Indian Association was present. He voted for it. In 1885, the two spokesmen of the *zamindars* in the Council helped emasculate the pro-tenant character of the Bengal Tenancy Bill at a time when nationalist leaders like Surendranath Banerjea were agitating to make it more pro-tenant. In 1882, Jotendra Mohan Tagore and Durga Charan Laha, the representative of Calcutta's big merchants, opposed the reduction of the salt tax and recommended the reduction of the licence tax on merchants and professionals instead.[2] The nationalists were demanding the opposite. In 1888, Peary Mohan Mukherjea and Dinshaw Petit, representatives of the big *zamindars* and big merchants respectively, supported the enhancement of the salt tax along with the non-official British members representing British business in India.[3]

By this time nationalists were quite active in opposing the salt tax and reacted strongly to this support. In the newspapers and from the

Congress platform they described Mukherjea and Petit as 'gilded shams" and 'magnificent non-entities.' They cited their voting behaviour as proof of the nationalist contention that the existing Legislative Councils were unrepresentative of Indian opinion. Madan Mohan Malaviya said at the National Congress session of 1890: 'We would much rather that there were no non-official members at all on the Councils than that there should be members who are not in the least in touch with the people and who . . . betray a cruel want of sympathy with them.' Describing Mukherjea and Petit as 'these big honourable gentlemen, enjoying private incomes and drawing huge salaries,' he asked rhetorically: 'Do you think, gentlemen, such members would be appointed to the Council if the people were allowed any voice in their selection?' The audience shouted 'No, no, never.'[4]

However, despite the early nationalists believing that India should eventually become self-governing, they moved very cautiously in putting forward political demands regarding the structure of the state, for they were afraid of the Government declaring their activities seditious and disloyal and suppressing them. Till 1892, their demand was limited to the expansion and reform of the Legislative Councils. They demanded wider participation in them by a larger number of elected Indian members as also wider powers for the Councils and an increase in the powers of the members to 'discuss and deal with' the budget and to question and criticize the day-to-day administration.

*

The nationalist agitation forced the Government to make some changes in legislative functioning by the Indian Councils Act of 1892. The number of additional members of the Imperial and Provincial Legislative Councils was increased from the previous six to ten to ten to sixteen. A few of these members could be elected indirectly through municipal committees, district boards, etc., but the official majority remained. The members were given the right to discuss the annual budget but they could neither vote on it nor move a motion to amend it. They could also ask questions but were not allowed to put supplementary questions or to discuss the answers. The 'reformed' Imperial Legislative Council met, during its tenure till 1909, on an average for only thirteen days in a year, and the number of unofficial Indian members present was only five out of twenty-four!

The nationalists were totally dissatisfied with the Act of 1892. They saw in it a mockery of their demands. The Councils were still impotent; despotism still ruled. They now demanded a majority for non-official elected members with the right to vote on the budget and, thus, to control the public purse. They raised the slogan 'no taxation without representation.' Gradually, they raised their demands. Many leaders — for example, Dadabhai Naoroji in 1904, G.K. Gokhale in 1905 and Lokamanya Tilak in 1906 began to put forward the demand for self-government on the model of the self-governing colonies of Canada and Australia.

*

Lord Dufferin, who had prepared the outline of the Act of 1892, and other British statesmen and administrators had seen in the Legislative Councils a device to incorporate the more vocal Indian political leaders into the colonial political structure where they could, in a manner of speaking, let off their political steam. They knew that the members of the Councils enjoyed no real powers; they could only make wordy speeches and indulge in empty rhetorics, and the bureaucracy could afford to pay no attention to them.

But the British policy makers had reckoned without the political capacities of the Indian leaders who soon transformed the powerless and impotent councils, designed as mere machines for the endorsement of government policies and measures and as toys to appease the emerging political leadership, into forums for ventilating popular grievances, mercilessly exposing the defects and shortcomings of the bureaucratic administration, criticizing and opposing almost every government policy and proposal, and raising basic economic issues, especially relating to public finance. They submitted the acts and policies of the Government to a ruthless examination regarding both their intention and their method and consequence. Far from being absorbed by the Councils, the nationalist members used them to enhance their own political stature in the country and to build a national movement. The safety valve was transformed into a major channel for nationalist propaganda. By sheer courage, debating skill, fearless criticism, deep knowledge and careful marshalling of data they kept up a constant campaign against the Government in the Councils undermining its political and moral influence and generating a powerful anti-imperialist sentiment.

Their speeches began to be reported at length in the newspapers and widespread public interest developed in the legislative proceedings.

The new Councils attracted some of the most prominent nationalist leaders. Surendranath Banerjea, Kalicharan Banerjee, Ananda Mohan Bose, Lal Mohan Ghosh, W.C. Bonnerji and Rash Behari Ghosh from Bengal, P. Ananda Charlu, C. Sankaran Nair and Vijayaraghavachariar from Madras, Madan Mohan Malaviya, Ayodhyanath and Bishambhar Nath from U.P., B.G. Tilak, Pherozeshah Mehta, R.M. Sayani, Chimanlal Setalvad, N.G. Chandravarkar and G.K. Gokhale from Bombay, and G.M. Chitnavis from Central Provinces were some of the Congressmen who served as members of the Provincial or Central Legislative Councils from 1893 to 1909.

The two men who were most responsible for putting the Councils to good use and introducing a new spirit in them were Pherozeshah Mehta and Gopal Krishna Gokhale. Both men were political Moderates. Both became famous for being fearlessly independent and the *bete noir* of British officialdom in India.

*

Born in 1845 in Bombay, Pherozeshah Mehta came under Dadabhai Naoroji's influence while studying law in London during the 1860s. He was one of the founders of the Bombay Presidency Association as also the Indian National Congress. From about the middle of the 1890s till his death in 1915 he was a dominant figure in the Indian National Congress and was often accused of exercising autocratic authority over it. He was a powerful debater and his speeches were marked by boldness, lucidity, incisiveness, a ready wit and quick repartee, and a certain literary quality.

Mehta's first major intervention in the Imperial Legislative Council came in January 1895 on a Bill for the amendment of the Police Act of 1861 which enhanced the power of the local authorities to quarter a punitive police force in an area and to recover its cost from selected sections of the inhabitants of the area. Mehta pointed out that the measure was an attempt to convict and punish individuals without a judicial trial under the garb of preserving law and order. He argued: 'I cannot conceive of legislation more empirical, more retrograde, more open to abuse, or more demoralizing. It is impossible not to see that it is a piece of that empirical legislation so dear to the heart of executive officers, which will not and cannot recognize the scientific fact that the punishment and suppression of crime without injuring or oppressing innocence must be controlled by judicial procedure.' Casting doubts on the capacity and impartiality of the executive officers entrusted with the task of enforcing the Act, Mehta said: 'It would be idle to believe that they can be free from the biases, prejudices, and defects of their class and position.'[5] Nobody would today consider this language and these remarks very strong or censorious. But they were like a bomb thrown into the ranks of a civil service which considered itself above such criticism. How dare a mere 'native' lay his sacrilegious hands on its fair name and reputation and that too in the portals of the Legislative Council? James Westland, the Finance Member, rose in the house and protested against 'the new spirit' which Mehta 'had introduced into the Council.' He had moreover uttered 'calumnies' against and 'arraigned as a class as biased, prejudiced, utterly incapable of doing the commonest justice . . . a most distinguished service,' which had 'contributed to the framing and consolidation of the Empire.' His remarks had gravely detracted 'from the reputation which this Council has justly acquired for the dignity, the calmness and the consideration which characterize its deliberations.'[6] In other words, Mehta was accused of changing the role and character of the colonial legislatures.

The Indian reaction was the very opposite. Pherozeshah Mehta won the instant approval of political Indians, even of his political opponents like Tilak, who readily accepted Westland's description that 'a new spirit' had entered the legislatures. People were accustomed to such criticism coming from the platform or the Press but that the 'dignified' Council halls could reverberate with such sharp and fearless criticism was a novel experience. The *Tribune* of Lahore commented: 'The voice that has been so long shut out from the Council Chamber — the voice of the people has been admitted through the open door of election . . . Mr. Mehta speaks as the representative of the people . . . Sir James Westland's protest is the outcry of the bureaucrat rapped over the knuckles in his own stronghold.'[7]

The bureaucracy was to smart under the whiplash of Mehta's rapier-like wit almost every time he spoke in the Council. We may give a few more examples of the forensic skill with which he regaled the Indians and helped destroy the moral influence and prestige of the British Indian Government and its holier-than-thou bureaucracy. The educated

Indians and higher education were major bugbears of the imperialist administrators then as they are of the imperialist schools of historians today. Looking for ways and means of cutting down higher education because it was producing 'discontented and seditious *babus*,' the Government hit upon the expedient of counterposing to expenditure on primary education of the masses that on the college education of the elites.

Pointing to the real motives behind this move to check the spread of higher education, Mehta remarked: 'It is very well to talk of "raising the subject to the pedestal of the ruler" but when the subject begins to press close at your heels, human nature is after all weak, and the personal experience is so intensely disagreeable that the temptation to kick back is almost irresistible.' And so, most of the bureaucrats looked upon 'every Indian college (as) a nursery for hatching broods of vipers; the less, therefore, the better.'[8]

In another speech, commenting on the official desire to transfer public funds from higher to primary education, he said he was reminded of 'the amiable and well-meaning father of a somewhat numerous family, addicted unfortunately to slipping off a little too often of an evening to the house over the way, who, when the mother appealed to him to do something for the education of the grown-up boys, begged of her with tears in his eyes to consider if her request was not unreasonable, when there was not even enough food and clothes for the younger children. The poor woman could not gainsay the fact, with the hungry eyes staring before her; but she could not help bitterly reflecting that the children could have food and clothes, and education to boot, if the kindly father could be induced to be good enough to spend a little less on drink and cards. Similarly, gentlemen, when we are reminded of the crying wants of the poor masses for sanitation and pure water and medical relief and primary education, might we not respectfully venture to submit that there would be funds, and to spare, for all these things, and higher education too, if the enormous and growing resources of the country were not ruthlessly squandered on a variety of whims and luxuries, on costly residences and sumptuous furniture, on summer trips to the hills, on little holiday excursions to the frontiers, but above and beyond all, on the lavish and insatiable humours of an irresponsible military policy, enforced by the very men whose view and opinions of its necessity cannot but accommodate themselves to their own interests and ambitions.'[9]

The officials were fond of blaming the Indian peasant's poverty and indebtedness on his propensity to spend recklessly on marriages and festivals. In 1901, a Bill was brought in the Bombay Legislative Council to take away the peasant's right of ownership of land to prevent him from bartering it away because of his thriftlessness. Denying this charge and opposing the bill, Mehta defended the right of the peasant to have some joy, colour, and moments of brightness in his life. In the case of an average Indian peasant, he said, 'a few new earthenware, a few wild flowers, the village tom-tom, a stomach-full meal, bad areca-nut and betel-leaves and a few stalks of cheap tobacco, and in some cases a few cheap tawdry trinkets, exhaust the joys of a festive occasion in the life of a household which has known only an unbroken period of unshrinking labour from morn to sunset.'[10] And when the Government insisted on using its official majority to push through the Bill, Mehta along with Gokhale, G.K. Parekh, Balachandra Krishna and D.A. Khare took the unprecedented step of organizing the first walk-out in India's legislative history. Once again officialdom was furious with Mehta. The *Times of India*, then British-owned, even suggested that these members should be made to resign their seats!

Criticizing the Government's excise policy for encouraging drinking in the name of curbing it, he remarked in 1898 that the excise department 'seems to follow the example of the preacher who said that though he was bound to teach good principles, he was by no means bound to practice them.'[11]

Pherozeshah Mehta retired from the Imperial Legislative Council in 1901 due to bad health. He got elected in his place thirty-five-year-old Gokhale, who had already made his mark as the Secretary of the Poona Sarvajanik Sabha and the editor of the *Sudharak*. In 1897, as a witness in London before the Royal Commission on Expenditure in India, Gokhale had outshone veterans like Surendranath Banerjea, D.E. Wacha, G. Subramaniya Iyer and Dadabhai Naoroji. Gokhale was to prove a more than worthy successor to Mehta.

*

Gopal Krishna Gokhale was an outstanding intellectual who had been carefully trained in Indian economics by Justice Ranade and G.V. Joshi. He was no orator. He did not use strong and forceful language as Tilak, Dadabhai Naoroji and R.C. Dutt did. Nor did he take recourse, as

Mehta did, to humour, irony and sarcasm. As a speaker he was gentle, reasonable, courteous, non-flamboyant and lucid. He relied primarily upon detailed knowledge and the careful, cool and logical marshalling and analysis of data. Consequently, while his speeches did not entertain or hurt, they gradually took hold of the listener's or reader's attention by their sheer intellectual power.

Gokhale was to gain great fame for his budget speeches which used to be reported extensively by the newspapers and whose readers would wait eagerly for their morning copy. He was to transform the Legislative Council into an open university for imparting political education to the people.

His very first budget speech on 26 March 1902 established him as the greatest parliamentarian that India has produced. The Finance Member, Edward Law, had just presented a budget with a seven-crore-rupees surplus for which he had received with great pride the congratulations of the house. At this point Gokhale rose to speak. He could not, he said, 'conscientiously join in the congratulations' because of the huge surplus. On the contrary, the surplus budget 'illustrated the utter absence of a due correspondence between the condition of the country and the condition of the finances of the country.' In fact, this surplus coming in times of serious depression and suffering, constituted 'a wrong to the community.' The keynote of his speech was the poverty of the people. He examined the problem in all its aspects and came to the conclusion that the material condition of the mass of the people was 'steadily deteriorating' and that the phenomenon was 'the saddest in the whole range of the economic history of the world.' He then set out to analyze the budget in detail. He showed how land revenue and the salt tax had been going up even in times of drought and famine. He asked for the reduction of these two taxes and for raising the minimum level of income liable to income tax to Rs. 1,000 so that the lower middle classes would not be harassed. He condemned the large expenditure on the army and territorial expansion beyond Indian frontiers and demanded greater expenditure on education and industry instead. The management of Indian finances, he said, revealed that Indian interests were invariably subordinated to foreign interests. He linked the poor state of Indian finances and the poverty of the people with the colonial status of the Indian economy and polity. And he did all this by citing at length from the Government's own blue books.[12]

Gokhale's first budget speech had 'an electrifying effect' upon the people. As his biographer, B.R. Nanda, has put it: 'Like Byron, he could have said that he woke up one fine morning and found himself famous.'[13] He won instant praise even from his severest critics and was applauded by the entire nationalist Press. It was felt that he had raised Indian pride many notches higher. The *Amrita Bazar Patrika*, which had missed no opportunity in the past to berate and belittle him, gave unstinted expression to this pride: 'We had ever entertained the ambition of seeing some Indian member openly and fearlessly criticizing the Financial Statement of the Government. But this ambition was never satisfied. When members had ability, they had not the requisite courage. When they had the requisite courage, they had not the ability . . . For the first time in the annals of British rule in India, a native of India has not only succeeded in exposing the fallacies which underlie these Government statements, but has ventured to do it in an uncompromising manner.'[14] All this well-deserved acclaim did not go to Gokhale's head. He remained unassuming and modest as before. To G.V. Joshi (leading economist and one of his *gurus*), he wrote: 'Of course it is your speech more than mine and I almost feel I am practicing a fraud on the public in that I let all the credit for it come to me.'[15]

In the next ten years, Gokhale was to bring this 'mixture of courage, tenacity and ability' to bear upon every annual budget and all legislation, highlighting in the process the misery and poverty of the peasant, the drain of wealth from India, the Government neglect of industrial development, the taxation of the poor, the lack of welfare measures such as primary education and health and medical facilities, the official efforts to suppress the freedom of the Press and other civil liberties, the enslavement of Indian labourers in British colonies, the moral dwarfing of Indians, the underdevelopment of the Indian economy and the complete neglect and subordination of Indian interests by the rulers.

Officials from the Viceroy downwards squirmed with impotent fury under his sharp and incisive indictments of their policies. In 1904, Edward Law, the Finance Member, cried out in exasperation: 'When he takes his seat at this Council table he unconsciously perhaps adopts the role and demeanour of the habitual mourner, and his sad wails and lamentations at the delinquencies of Government are as piteous as long practice and training can make them.'[16] Such was the fear Gokhale's budget speeches aroused among officials that in 1910, Lord Minto, the Viceroy, asked the Secretary of State to appoint R.W. Carlyle as Revenue Member because he had come to know privately of 'an

intended attack in which Gokhale is interested on the whole of our revenue system and it is important that we should be well prepared to meet
it.'[17]

Gokhale was to be repaid in plenty by the love and recognition of his
own people. Proud of his legislative achievements, they were to confer
on him the title of 'the leader of the opposition.' Gandhiji was to
declare him his political *guru*. And Tilak, his lifelong political opponent, said at his funeral: 'This diamond of India, this jewel of
Maharashtra, this prince of workers, is taking eternal rest on the funeral
ground. Look at him and try to emulate him.'[18]

10 *The Swadeshi Movement — 1903-1908*

With the start of the Swadeshi movement at the turn of the century , the Indian national movement took a major leap forward. Women, students and a large section of the urban and rural population of Bengal and other parts of India became actively involved in politics for the first time. The next half a decade saw the emergence of almost all the major political trends of the Indian national movement. From conservative moderation to political extremism, from terrorism to incipient social-ism, from petitioning and public speeches to passive resistance and boycott, all had their origins in the movement. The richness of the movement was not confined to politics alone. The period saw a break-through in Indian art, literature, music, science and industry. Indian society, as a whole, was experimenting and the creativity of the people expanded in every direction.

*

The Swadeshi movement had its genesis in the anti-partition movement which was started to oppose the British decision to partition Bengal. There was no questioning the fact that Bengal with a population of 78 million (about a quarter of the population of British India) had indeed become administratively unwieldy. Equally there was no escaping the fact that the real motive for partitioning Bengal was political. Indian nationalism was gaining in strength and partition expected to weaken what was perceived as the nerve centre of Indian nationalism at that time. The attempt, in the words of Lord Curzon, the Viceroy, (1899-1905) was to 'dethrone Calcutta' from its position as the 'centre from which the Congress Party is manipulated throughout Bengal, and indeed, the whole of India . . . The centre of successful intrigue,' and 'divide the Bengali speaking population.'[1] Risley, the Home Secretary to Government of India, was more blunt. He said on 6 December, 1904: 'Bengal united, is power. Bengal divided, will pull several different ways. That is what the Congress leaders feel: their apprehensions are perfectly correct and they form one of the great merits of the scheme . . in this scheme . . . one of our main objects is to split up and thereby weaken a solid body of opponents to our rule.'[2]

Curzon reacted sharply to the almost instant furore that was raised in Bengal over the partition proposals and wrote to the Secretary of State. 'If we are weak enough to yield to their clamour now, we shall not be able to dismember or reduce Bengal again: and you will be cementing and solidifying a force already formidable, and certain to be a source of increasing trouble in the future.'[3] The partition of the state intended to curb Bengali influence by not only placing Bengalis under two administrations but by reducing them to a minority in Bengal itself as in the new proposal Bengal proper was to have seventeen million Bengali and thirty-seven million Oriya and Hindi speaking people! Also, the partition was meant to foster another kind of division — this time on the basis of religion. The policy of propping up Muslim communalists as a counter to the Congress and the national movement, which was getting increasingly crystallized in the last quarter of the 19th century, was to be implemented once again. Curzon's speech at Dacca, betrayed his attempt to 'woo the Muslims' to support partition. With partition, he argued , Dacca could become the capital of the new Muslim majority province (with eighteen million Muslims and twelve million Hindus) 'which would invest the Mohammedans in Eastern Bengal with a unity which they have not enjoyed since the days of the old Mussulman Viceroys and Kings.'[4] The Muslims would thus get a 'better deal' and the eastern districts would be freed of the 'pernicious influence of Calcutta.'

And even Lord Minto, Curzon's successor, who was critical of the way in which partition was imposed disregarding public opinion, saw that it was good political strategy; Minto argued that 'from a political point of view alone, putting aside the administrative difficulties of the old province, I believe partition to have been very necessary . . .'5

The Indian nationalists clearly saw the design behind the partition and condemned it unanimously. The anti-partition and Swadeshi movement had begun.

*

In December 1903, the partition proposals became publicly known. An immediate and spontaneous protest followed. The strength of this protest can be gauged from the fact that in the first two months following the announcement 500 protest meetings were held in East Bengal alone, especially in Dacca, Mymensingh and Chittagong. Nearly fifty thousand copies of pamphlets giving a detailed critique of the partition proposals were distributed all over Bengal. Surendranath Bannerjee, Krishna Kumar Mitra, Prithwishchandra Ray and other leaders launched a powerful press campaign against the partition proposals through journals and newspapers like the *Bengalee*, *Hitabadi* and *Sanjibani*. Vast protest meetings were held in the town hall of Calcutta in March 1904 and January 1905, and numerous petitions (sixty-nine memoranda from the Dacca division alone), some of them signed by as many as 70,000 people — a very large number keeping in view the level of politicization in those days — were sent to the Government of India and the Secretary of State. Even, the big *zamindars* who had hitherto, been loyal to the Raj joined forces with the Congress leaders who were mostly intellectuals and political workers drawn from journalism, law and other liberal professions.

This was the phase, 1903 to mid-1905, when moderate techniques of petitions, memoranda, speeches, public meetings and press campaigns held full sway. The objective was to turn to public opinion in India and England against the partition proposals by preparing a foolproof case against them. The hope was that this would yield sufficient pressure to prevent this injustice from occurring.

*

The Government of India, however, remained unmoved. Despite the widespread protest voiced against the partition proposals, the decision to partition Bengal was announced on 19 July 1905. It was obvious to the nationalists that their moderate methods were not working and that a different kind of strategy was needed. Within days of the government announcement numerous spontaneous protest meetings were held in mofussil towns such as Dinajpur, Pabna, Faridpur, Tangail, Jessore, Dacca, Birbhum, and Barisal. It was in these meetings that the pledge to boycott foreign goods was first taken. In Calcutta, students organized a number of meeting against partition and for Swadeshi.

The formal proclamation of the Swadeshi movement was, made on the 7 August 1905, in a meeting held at the Calcutta town hall. The movement, hitherto, sporadic and spontaneous, now had a focus and a leadership that was coming together. At the 7 August meeting, the famous Boycott Resolution was passed. Even Moderate leaders like Surendranath Bannerjea toured the country urging the boycott of Manchester cloth and Liverpool salt. On September 1, the Government announced that partition was to be effected on 16 October 1905. The following weeks saw protest meetings being held almost everyday all over Bengal; some of these meetings, like the one in Barisal, drew crowds of ten to twelve thousand. That the message of boycott went home is evident from the fact that the value of British cloth sold in some of the mofussil districts fell by five to fifteen times between September 1904 and September 1905.

The day partition took effect — 16 October 1905 — was declared a day of mourning throughout Bengal. People fasted and no fires were lit at the cooking hearth. In Calcutta a *hartal* was declared. People took out processions and band after band walked barefoot, bathed in the Ganges in the morning and then paraded the streets singing *Bande Mataram* which, almost spontaneously, became the theme song of the movement. People tied *rakhis* on each other's hands as a symbol of the unity of the two halves of Bengal. Later in the day Anandamohan Bose and Surendranath Bannerjea addressed two huge mass meetings which drew crowds of 50,000 to 75,000 people. These were, perhaps, the largest mass meetings ever to be held under the nationalist banner this far. Within a few hours of the meetings, a sum of Rs. 50,000 was raised for the movement.

It was apparent that the character of the movement in terms of both its goals and social base had begun to expand rapidly. As Abdul Rasul, President of the Barisal Conference, April 1906, put it: 'What we could not have accomplished in 50 or 100 years, the great disaster, the partition of Bengal, has done for us in six months. Its fruits have been the great national movement known as the Swadeshi movement.'6

The message of Swadeshi and the boycott of foreign goods soon spread to the rest of the country: Lokamanya Tilak took the movement to different parts of India, especially Poona and Bombay; Ajit Singh and Lala Lajpat Rai spread the Swadeshi message in Punjab and other parts of northern India; Syed Haidar Raza led the movement in Delhi; Rawalpindi, Kangra, Jammu, Multan and Hardwar witnessed active participation in the Swadeshi movement; Chidambaram Pillai took the movement to the Madras presidency, which was also galvanized by Bipin Chandra Pal's extensive lecture tour.

The Indian National Congress took up the Swadeshi call and the Banaras Session, 1905, presided over by G.K. Gokhale, supported the Swadeshi and boycott movement for Bengal. The militant nationalists led by Tilak, Bipin Chandra Pal, Lajpat Rai and Aurobindo Ghosh were, however, in favour of extending the movement to the rest of India and carrying it beyond the programme of just Swadeshi and boycott to a full fledged political mass struggle. The aim was now Swaraj and the abrogation of partition had become the 'pettiest and narrowest of all political objects.'[7] The Moderates, by and large, were not as yet willing to go that far. In 1906, however, the Indian National Congress at its Calcutta Session, presided over by Dadabhai Naoroji, took a major step forward. Naoroji in his presidential address declared that the goal of the Indian National Congress was 'self-government or Swaraj like that of the United Kingdom or the Colonies.'[8] The differences between the Moderates and the Extremists, especially regarding the pace of the movement and the techniques of struggle to be adopted, came to a head in the 1907 Surat session of the Congress where the party split with serious consequences for the Swadeshi movement.

*

In Bengal, however, after 1905, the Extremists acquired a dominant influence over the Swadeshi movement. Several new forms of mobilization and techniques of struggle now began to emerge at the popular level. The trend of 'mendicancy,' petitioning and memorials was on the retreat. The militant nationalists put forward several fresh ideas at the theoretical, propagandistic and programmatic plane. Political independence was to be achieved by converting the movement into a mass movement through the extension of boycott into a full-scale movement of non-cooperation and passive resistance. The technique of 'extended boycott' was to include, apart from boycott of foreign goods, boycott of government schools and colleges, courts, titles and government services and even the organization of strikes. The aim was to 'make the administration under present conditions impossible by an organized refusal to do anything which shall help either the British Commerce in the exploitation of the country or British officialdom in the administration of it.'[9] While some, with remarkable foresight, saw the tremendous potential of large scale peaceful resistance — ' . . . if . . . the *Chowkidar*, the constable, the deputy and the munsif and the clerk, not to speak of the sepoy all resign their respective functions, *feringhee* rule in the country may come to an end in a moment. No powder and shot will be needed, no sepoys will have to be trained . . .'[10] Others like Aurobindo Ghosh (with his growing links with revolutionary terrorists) kept open the option of violent resistance if British repression was stepped up.

Among the several forms of struggle thrown up by the movement, it was the boycott of foreign goods which met with the greatest visible success at the practical and popular level. Boycott and public burning of foreign cloth, picketing of shops selling foreign goods, all became common in remote corners of Bengal as well as in many important towns and cities throughout the country. Women refused to wear foreign bangles and use foreign utensils, washermen refused to wash foreign clothes and even priests declined offerings which contained foreign sugar.

The movement also innovated with considerable success different forms of mass mobilization. Public meetings and processions emerged as major methods of mass mobilization and simultaneously as forms of popular expression. Numerous meetings and processions, organized at the district, *taluqa* and village levels, in cities and towns, both testified to the depth of Swadeshi sentiment and acted as vehicles for its further spread. These forms were to retain their pre-eminence in later phases of the national movement.

Corps of volunteers (or *samitis* as they were called) were another major form of mass mobilization widely used by the Swadeshi movement. The Swadesh Bandhab Samiti set up by Ashwini Kumar Dutt, a school teacher, in Barisal was the most well-known volunteer organization of them all. Through the activities of this Samiti, whose 159 branches reached out to the remotest corners of the district, Dutt was able to generate an unparalleled mass following among the predominantly Muslim peasantry of the region. The *samitis* took the Swadeshi message to the villages through magic lantern lectures and swadeshi songs, gave physical and moral training to their members, did social work during famines and epidemics, organized schools, training in swadeshi craft and arbitration courts. By August 1906 the Barisal Samiti reportedly settled 523 disputes through eighty-nine arbitration committees. Though the *samitis* struck their deepest roots in Barisal, they had expanded to other parts of Bengal as well. British officialdom was genuinely alarmed by their activities, their growing popularity with the rural masses.

The Swadeshi period also saw the creative use of traditional popular festivals and *melas* as a means of reaching out to the masses. The Ganapati and Shivaji festivals, popularized by Tilak, became a medium for Swadeshi propaganda not only in Western India but also in Bengal. Traditional folk theatre forms such as *jatras* were extensively used in disseminating the Swadeshi message in an intelligible form to vast sections of the people, many of whom were being introduced to modern political ideas for the first time.

Another important aspect of the Swadeshi movement was the great emphasis given to self-reliance or 'Atmasakti' as a necessary part of the struggle against the Government. Self-reliance in various fields meant the re-asserting of national dignity, honour and confidence. Further, self-help and constructive work at the village level was envisaged as a means of bringing about the social and economic regeneration of the villages and of reaching the rural masses. In actual terms this meant social reform and campaigns against evils such as caste oppression, early marriage, the dowry system, consumption of alcohol, etc. One of the major planks of the programme of self-reliance was Swadeshi or national education. Taking a cue from Tagore's Shantiniketan, the Bengal National College was founded, with Aurobindo as the principal. Scores of national schools sprang up all over the country within a short period. In August 1906, the National Council of Education was established. The Council, consisting of virtually all the distinguished persons of the country at the time, defined its objectives in this way . . . 'to organize a system of Education Literary, Scientific and Technical — on National lines and under National control'[11] from the primary to the university level. The chief medium of instruction was to be the vernacular to enable the widest possible reach. For technical education, the Bengal Technical Institute was set up and funds were raised to send students to Japan for advanced learning.

Self-reliance also meant an effort to set up Swadeshi or indigenous enterprises. The period saw a mushrooming of Swadeshi textile mills, soap and match factories, tanneries, banks, insurance companies, shops, etc. While many of these enterprises, whose promoters were more endowed with patriotic zeal than with business acumen were unable to survive for long, some others such as Acharya P.C.Ray's Bengal Chemicals Factory, became successful and famous.

It was, perhaps, in the cultural sphere that the impact of the Swadeshi movement was most marked. The songs composed at that time by Rabindranath Tagore, Rajani Kanta Sen, Dwijendralal Ray, Mukunda Das, Syed Abu Mohammed, and others later became the moving spirit for nationalists of all hues, 'terrorists, Gandhian or Communists' and are still popular. Rabindranath's '*Amar Sonar Bangla*,' written at that time, was to later inspire the liberation stuggle of Bangladesh and was adopted as the national anthem of the country in 1971. The Swadeshi influence could be seen in Bengali folk music popular among Hindu and Muslim villagers (Palligeet and Jari Gan) and it evoked collections of Indian fairy tales such as, *Thakurmar Jhuli* (Grandmother's tales) written by Dakshinaranjan Mitra Majumdar which delights Bengali children to this day. In art, this was the period when Abanindranath Tagore broke the domination of Victorian naturalism over Indian art and sought inspiration from the rich indigenous traditions of Mughal, Rajput and Ajanta paintings. Nandalal Bose, who left a major imprint on Indian art, was the first recipient of a scholarship offered by the Indian Society of Oriental Art founded in 1907. In science, Jagdish Chandra Bose, Pradullachandra Roy, and others pioneered original research that was praised the world over.

*

In sum, the Swadeshi movement with its multi-faceted programme and activity was able to draw for the first time large sections of society into active participation in modern nationalist politics and still larger sections into the ambit of modern political ideas.

The social base of the national movement was now extended to include a certain *zamindari* section, the lower middle class in the cities and small towns and school and college students on a massive scale. Women came out of their homes for the first time and joined processions and picketing. This period saw, again for the first time, an attempt being made to give a political direction to the economic grievances of the working class. Efforts were made by Swadeshi leaders, some of whom were influenced by international socialist currents such as those in Germany and Russia, to organize strikes in foreign managed concerns such as the Eastern Indian Railway and Clive Jute Mills, etc.

While it is argued that the movement was unable to make much headway in mobilizing the peasantry especially its lower rungs, except in certain areas, such as the district of Barisal, there can be no gainsaying the fact that even if the movement was able to mobilize the peasantry only in a limited area that alone would count for a lot. This is so because the peasant participation in the Swadeshi movement marked the very beginnings of modern mass politics in India. After all, even in the later, post-Swadeshi movements, intense political mobilization and activity among the peasantry largely remained concentrated in specific pockets. Also, while it is true that during the Swadeshi phase the peasantry was not organized around peasant demands, and that the peasants in most parts did not actively join in certain forms of struggle such as, boycott or passive resistance, large sections of the peasants, through meetings, *jatras*, constructive work, and so on were exposed for the first time to modern nationalist ideas and politics.

The main drawback of the Swadeshi movement was that it was not able to garner the support of the mass of Muslims and especially of the Muslim peasantry. The British policy of consciously attempting to use communalism to turn the Muslims against the Swadeshi movement was to a large extent responsible for this. The government was helped in its designs by the peculiar situation obtaining in large parts of Bengal where Hindus and Muslims were divided along class lines with the former being the landlords and the latter constituting the peasantry . This was the period when the All India Muslim League was set up with the active guidance and support of the government. More specifially, in Bengal, people like Nawab Salimullah of Dacca were propped up as centres of opposition to the Swadeshi movement. *Mullahs* and *maulvis* were pressed into service and, unsurprisingly, at the height of the Swadeshi movement communal riots broke out in Bengal.

Given this background, some of the forms of mobilization adopted by the Swadeshi movement had certain unintended negative consequences. The use of traditional popular customs, festivals and institutions for mobilizing the masses — a technique used widely in most parts of the world to generate mass movements, especially in the initial stages — was misinterpreted and distorted by communalists backed by the state. The communal forces saw narrow religious identities in the traditional forms utilized by the Swadeshi movement whereas in fact these forms generally reflected common popular cultural traditions which had evolved as a synthesis of different religious practices prevalent among the people.

*

By mid-1908, the open movement with its popular mass character had all but spent itself. This was due to several reasons. First, the government, seeing the revolutionary potential of the movement, came down with a heavy hand. Repression took the form of controls and bans on public meetings, processions and the press. Student participants were expelled from government schools and colleges, debarred from government service, fined and at times beaten up by the police. The case of the 1906 Barisal Conference, where the police forcibly dispersed the conference and brutally beat up a large number of the participants, is a telling example of the government's attitude and policy.

Second, the internal squabbles, and especially, the split, in 1907,in the Congress, the apex all-India organisation, weakened the movement. Also, though the Swadeshi movement had spread outside Bengal, the rest of the country was not as yet fully prepared to adopt the new style and stage of politics. Both these factors strengthened the hands of the government. Between 1907 and 1908, nine major leaders in Bengal including Ashwini Kumar Dutt and Krishna Kumar Mitra were deported, Tilak was given a sentence of six years imprisonment, Ajit Singh and Lajpat Rai of Punjab were deported and Chidambaram Pillai and Harisarvottam Rao from Madras and Andhra were arrested. Bipin Chandra Pal and Aurobindo Ghosh retired from active politics, a decision not unconnected with the repressive measures of the government. Almost with one stroke the entire movement was rendered leaderless.

Third, the Swadeshi movement lacked an effective organization and party structure. The movement had thrown up programmatically almost the entie gamut of Gandhian techniques such as passive resistance, non-violent non-cooperation, the call to fill the British jails, social reform, constructive work, etc. It was, however, unable to give these techniques a centralized, disciplined focus, carry the bulk of political India, and convert these techniques into actual, practical political practice, as

Gandhiji was able to do later.

Lastly, the movement declined partially because of the very logic of mass movements itself — they cannot be sustained endlessly at the same pitch of militancy and self-sacrifice, especially when faced with severe repression, but need to pause, to consolidate its forces for yet another struggle.

However, the decline of the open movement by mid-1908 engendered yet another trend in the Swadeshi phase i.e., the rise of revolutionary terrorism. The youth of the country, who had been part of the mass movement, now found themselves unable to disappear tamely into the background once the movement itself grew moribund and Government repression was stepped up. Frustrated some among them opted for 'individual heroism' as distinct from the earlier attempts at mass action.

*

With the subsiding of the mass movement, one era in the Indian freedom struggle was over. It would be wrong, however, to see the Swadeshi movement as a failure. The movement made a major contribution in taking the idea of nationalism, in a truely creative fashion, to many sections of people, hitherto untouched by it. By doing so, it further eroded the hegemony of colonial ideas and institutions. Swadeshi influence in the realm of culture and ideas was crucial in this regard and has remained unparalleld in Indian history, except, perhaps, for the cultural upsurge of the 1930s, this time under the influence of the Left.

Further, the movement evolved several new methods and techniques of mass mobilization and mass action though it was not able to put them all into practice successfully. Just as the Moderate's achievement in the realm of developing an economic critique of colonialism is not minimized by the fact that they could not themselves carry this critique to large masses of people, similarly the achievement of the Extremists and the Swadeshi movement in evolving new methods of mass mobilization and action is not diminished by the fact that they could not themselves fully utilize these methods. The legacy they bequeathed was one on which the later national movement was to draw heavily.

The Swadeshi movement was only the first round in the national popular struggle against colonialism. It was to borrow the imagery used by Antonio Gramsci an important 'battle' in the long drawn out and complex 'war of position' for Indian independence.

11 The Split in the Congress and the Rise of Revolutionary Terrorism

The Indian National Congress split in December 1907. Almost at the same time revolutionary terrorism made its appearance in Bengal. The two events were not unconnected.

*

By 1907, the Moderate nationalists had exhausted their historical role. Their achievements, as we have seen in the previous chapter, were immense, considering the low level of political consciousness and the immense difficulties they had to face when they began.

Their failures too were numerous. They lacked faith in the common people, did no work among them and consequently failed to acquire any roots among them. Even their propaganda did not reach them. Nor did they organize any all-India campaigns and when, during 1905-07, such an all-India campaign did come up in the form of the Swadeshi and Boycott Movement, they were not its leaders (though the Bengal Moderates did play an active role in their own province). Their politics were based on the belief that they would be able to persuade the rulers to introduce economic and political reforms but their practical achievements in this respect were meagre. Instead of respecting them for their moderation, the British treated them with contempt, sneered at their politics, and met popular agitations with repression.

Their basic failure, however, was that of not keeping pace with events. They could not see that their own achievements had made their politics obsolete. They failed to meet the demands of the new stage of the national movement. Visible proof of this was their failure to attract the younger generation.

*

The British had been suspicious of the National Congress from its inception. But they had not been overtly hostile, in the first few years of its existence because they believed its activities would remain academic and confined to a handful of intellectuals. However, as soon as it became apparent that the Congress would not remain so narrowly confined, and that it was becoming a focus of Indian nationalism, the officials turned openly critical of the Congress, the nationalist leaders and the Press.

They now began to brand the nationalists as 'disloyal babus,' 'seditious Brahmins,' and 'violent villains.' The Congress was described as 'a factory of sedition' and Congressmen as 'disappointed candidates for office and discontented lawyers who represent no one but themselves.' In 1888, Dufferin, the Viceroy, attacked the National Congress in a public speech and ridiculed it as representing only the elite — 'a microscopic minority.'[1] George Hamilton, Secretary of State for India, accused the Congress leaders of possessing 'seditious and double sided character.'[2]

This hostility did not abate when the Moderates, who then controlled the Congress, began to distance themselves from the rising militant nationalist tendencies of certain sections of the Congress which became apparent when the government unleashed a repressive policy against the Indian Press in 1897. Instead the British appeared even more eager to attack and finish the Congress. Why was this so? First, because however moderate and loyal in their political perception the Moderates were, they were still nationalists and propagators of anti-colonialist politics and ideas. As Curzon, the Viceroy, put it in 1905: 'Gokhale either does not see where he is going, or if he does see it, then he is dishonest in his pretensions. You cannot awaken and appeal to the spirit of nationality in India and at the same time, profess loyal acceptance of British rule.'[3] Or, as George Hamilton, the Secretary of State, had complained to Dadabhai Naoroji in 1900: 'You announce yourself as a sincere supporter of British rule; you vehemently denounce the conditions and consequences which are inseparable from the maintenance of that rule.'[4]

Second, the British policy-makers felt that the Moderate-led

Congress could be easily finished because it was weak and without a popular base. Curzon, in particular, supported by George Hamilton, pursued this policy. He declared in 1900: 'The Congress is tottering to its fall, and one of my greatest ambitions while in India is to assist it to a peaceful demise.'[5] In 1903, he wrote to the Madras Governor: 'My policy, ever since I came to India, has been to reduce the Congress to impotence.'[6] In 1904, he had insulted the Congress by refusing to meet its delegation headed by its President.

This policy was changed once the powerful Swadeshi and Boycott Movement began and the militant nationalist trend became strong. An alternative policy of weakening the national movement was now to be followed. Instead of sneering at the Moderates, the policy was to be that of 'rallying' them as John Morley, the new Secretary of State for India, put it in 1907. The new policy, known as the policy of the carrot and the stick, was to be a three pronged one. It may be described as a policy of repression-conciliation-suppression. The Extremists, as we shall refer to the militant nationalists from now on, were to be repressed, though mildly in the first stage, the purpose being to frighten the Moderates. The Moderates were then to be placated through some concessions and promises and hints were to be given that further concessions would be forthcoming if they disassociated themselves from the Extremists. The entire objective of the new policy was to isolate the Extremists. Once the Moderates fell into the trap, the Extremists could be suppressed through the use of the full might of the state. The Moderates, in turn, could then be ignored. Unfortunately, for the national movement, neither the Moderates nor the Extremists were able to understand the official strategy and consequently suffered a number of reverses.

*

The Government of India, headed by Lord Minto as Viceroy and John Morley as the Secretary of State, offered a bait of fresh reforms in the Legislative Councils and in the beginning of 1906 began discussing them with the Moderate leadership of the Congress. The Moderates agreed to cooperate with the Government and discuss the reforms even while a vigorous popular movement, which the Govenment was trying to suppress, was going on in the country. The result was a total split in the nationalist ranks.

Before we take up this split at some length, it is of some interest to note that the British were to follow this tactic of dividing the Moderates from the militants in later years also — for example in 1924, vis-a-vis *Swarajists*, in 1936, vis-a-vis Nehru and the leftists, and so on. The difference was that in the later years the national leadership had learnt a lesson from the events of 1907-1909, and refused to rise to the bait, remaining united despite deep differences.

*

There was a great deal of public debate and disagreement among Moderates and Extremists in the years 1905-1907, even when they were working together against the partitioning of Bengal. The Extremists wanted to extend the Swadeshi and the Boycott Movement from Bengal to the rest of the country. They also wanted to gradually extend the boycott from foreign goods to every form of association or cooperation with the colonial Government. The Moderates wanted to confine the boycott part of the movement to Bengal and were totally opposed to its extension to the Government.

Matters nearly came to a head at the Calcutta Congress in 1906 over the question of its Presidentship. A split was avoided by choosing Dadabhai Naoroji, who was respected by all the nationalists as a great patriot. Four compromise resolutions on the Swadeshi, Boycott, National Education, and Self-Government demands were passed. Throughout 1907 the two sides fought over differing interpretations of the four resolutions. By the end of 1907, they were looking upon each other as the main political enemy. The Extremists were convinced that the battle for freedom had begun as the people had been roused. They felt it was time for the big push and in their view the Moderates were a big drag on the movement. Most of them, led by Aurobindo Ghose, felt that the time had come to part company with the Moderates, push them out of the leadership of the Congress, and split the organization if the Moderates could not be deposed.

Most of the Moderates, led by Pherozeshah Mehta, were no less determined on a split. To remain with the Extremists was, they felt, to enter dangerous waters. They were afraid that the Congress organization, built carefully over the last twenty years, would be shattered. The Government was bound to suppress any large-scale anti-imperialist movement; why invite premature repression? As Gokhale put it in

1907, 'You (the Extremists) do not realize the enormous reserve of power behind the Government. If the Congress were to do anything such as you suggest, the Government would have no difficulty in throttling it in five minutes.'[7] Minto and Morley were holding up hopes of brighter prospects . Many Moderates thought that their dream of Indians sharing political and administrative power was going to come true. Any hasty action by the Congress under Extremist pressure could annoy the Liberals in power in Britain. Why not get rid of the Extremists while there was still time?

As H.A. Wadya, representing Pherozeshah Mehta's thinking, wrote in an article in which, after referring to the Extremists as 'the worst enemies of our cause,' said: 'The union of these men with the Congress is the union of a diseased limb to a healthy body, and the only remedy is surgical severance, if the Congress is to be saved from death by blood poisoning.'[8]

Both sides had it wrong — from the nationalist point of view as well as their own factional point of view. The Moderates did not see that the colonial state was negotiating with them not because of their inherent political strength but because of the fear of the Extremists. The Extremists did not see that the Moderates were their natural outer defence line (in terms of civil liberties and so on) and that they did not possess the required strength to face the colonial state's juggernaut. Neither saw that in a vast country like India ruled by a powerful imperialist nation only a broad-based united movement had any chance of success. It wasn't as though the whole leadership was blind to the danger. The main public leaders of the two wings, Tilak (of the Extremists) and Gokhale (of the Moderates) were mature politicians who had a clear grasp of the dangers of disunity in the nationalist ranks. Tilak did not want the united national front to break. He saw clearly that a powerful movement could not be built up at that stage nor political demands successfully pressed on the rulers without the unity of different political trends. His tactics were to organize massive support for his political line and, thus, force a favourable compromise on the Moderates. But having roused his followers in Maharashtra and pushed on by the more extreme elements of Bengal, Tilak found that he could not afford to dismount from the tiger he found himself riding. When it came to the crunch, he had to go with the more extreme leaders like Aurobindo Ghose.

Gokhale, too, saw the dangers of a split in the nationalist ranks and tried to avoid it. Already, in October 1907, he had written to a friend: 'If a split does come it means a disaster, for the Bureaucracy will then put down both sections without much difficulty.'9 But he did not have the personality to stand upto a wilful autocrat like Pherozeshah Mehta. He, too, kunckled under pressure of his own extremists.

The Congress session was held on 26 December, 1907 at Surat, on the banks of the river Tapti. The Extremists were excited by the rumours that the Moderates wanted to scuttle the four Calcutta resolutions. The Moderates were deeply hurt by the ridicule and venom poured on them in mass meetings held at Surat on the previous three days. The delegates, thus, met in an atmosphere surcharged with excitement and anger.

The Extremists wanted a guarantee that the four resolutions would be passed. To force the Moderates to do so they decided to object to the duly elected President for the year, Rash Behari Ghose. Both sides came to the session prepared for a confrontation. In no time, the 1600 delegates were shouting, coming to blows and hurling chairs at each other. In the meantime, some unknown person hurled a shoe at the dais which hit Pherozeshah Mehta and Surendranath Banerjea. The police came and cleared the hall. The Congress session was over. The only victorious party was the rulers. Minto immediately wrote to Morley that the 'Congress collapse' at Surat was 'a great triumph for us.'10

Tilak had seen the coming danger and made last minute efforts to avoid it. But he was helpless before his followers. Lajpat Rai, a participant in the events from the Extremist side, wrote later: 'Instead of leading his party, he (Tilak) allowed himself to be led by some of its wild spirits. Twice on my request, at Surat, he agreed to waive his opposition to the election of Dr. Rash Behari Ghose and leave the matter of the four Calcutta resolutions to the Subjects Committee, but the moment I left him he found himself helpless before the volume of opinion that surrounded him.'11

The suddenness of the Surat fiasco took Tilak by surprise. He had not bargained for it because, as Aurobindo Ghose wrote later, Tilak viewed the split as a 'catastrophe.' He valued the Congress 'as a great national fact and for its unrealized possibilities.'12 He now tried to undo the damage. He sent a virtual letter of regret to his opponents, accepted Rash Behari Ghose as the President of the Congress and offered his cooperation in working for Congress unity. But Pherozeshah Mehta and his colleagues would not relent. They thought they were on a sure wicket. The Government immediately launched a massive attack on the Extremists. Extremist newspapers were suppressed. Tilak, their main leader, was sent to Mandalay jail for six years. Aurobindo Ghose, their ideologue, was involved in a revolutionary conspiracy case and immediately after being judged innocent gave up politics and escaped to Pondicherry to take up religion. B.C. Pal temporarily retired from politics and Lajpat Rai, who had been a helpless onlooker at Surat, left for Britain in 1908 to come back in 1909 and then to go off to the United States for an extended stay. The Extremists were not able to organize an effective alternative party or to sustain the movement. The Government had won, at least for the moment.

The Moderates were indulging their own foolish beliefs. They gave up all the radical measures adopted at the Benares and Calcutta sessions of the Congress, spurned all overtures for unity from the Extremists and excluded them from the party. They thought they were going to rebuild, to quote Pherozeshah Mehta, a 'resuscitated, renovated, reincarnated Congress.' But the spirit had gone out of the Congress and all efforts to restore it failed. They had lost the respect and support of the political Indians, especially the youth, and were reduced to a small coterie. Most of the Moderate leaders withdrew into their shells; only Gokhale plodded on, with the aid of a small band of co-workers from the Servants of India Society. And the vast majority of politically conscious Indians extended their support, however passive, to Lokamanya Tilak and the militant nationalists.

After 1908 the national movement as a whole declined. In 1909, Aurobindo Ghose noted the change: 'When I went to jail the whole country was alive with the cry of Bande Matram, alive with the hope of a nation, the hope of millions of men who had newly risen out of degradation. When I came out of jail I listened for that cry, but there was instead a silence. A hush had fallen on the country.'[13] But while the upsurge was gone, the aroused nationalist sentiments did not disappear. The people waited for the next phase. In 1914, Tilak was released and he picked up the threads of the movement.

*

The Moderates and the country as a whole were disappointed by the 'constitutional' reforms of 1909. The Indian Councils Act of 1909 increased the number of elected members in the Imperial Legislative

Council and the provincial legislative councils. Most of the elected members were still elected indirectly. An Indian was to be appointed a member of the Governor-General's Executive Council. Of the sixty-eight members of the Imperial Legislative Council, thrity-six were officials and five were nominated non-officials. Out of twenty-seven elected members, six were elected by big landlords and two by British capitalists. The Act permitted members to introduce resolutions; it also increased their power to ask questions. Voting on separate budget items was allowed. But the reformed councils still enjoyed no real power and remained mere advisory bodies. They also did not introduce an element of democracy or self-government. The undemocratic, foreign and exploitative character of British rule remained unchanged.

Morley openly declared in Parliament: 'If it could be said that this chapter of reforms led directly or neccessarily up to the establishment of a Parliamentary system in India, I, for one, would have nothing at all to do with it.'[14]

The real purpose of the Morley-Minto Reforms was to divide the nationalist ranks and to check the growing unity among Indians by encouraging the growth of Muslim communalism. To achieve the latter objective, the Reforms introduced the system of separate electorates under which Muslims could only vote for Muslim candidates in constituencies specially reserved for them. This was done to encourage the notion that the political, economic and cultural interests of Hindus and Muslims were separate and not common. The institution of separate electorates was one of the poisonous trees which was to yield a bitter harvest in later years.

*

The end of 1907 brought another political trend to the fore. The impatient young men of Bengal took to the path of individual heroism and revolutionary terrorism (a term we use without any pejorative meaning and for want of a different term). This was primarily because they could find no other way of expressing their patriotism. It is necessary at this point to reiterate the fact that, while the youth of Bengal might have been incensed at the official arrogance and repression and the 'mendicancy' of the Congress Moderates, they were also led to 'the politics of the bomb' by the Extremists' failure to give a positive lead to the people. The Extremists had made a sharp and on the whole correct and effective critique of the Moderates. They had rightly emphasized the role of the masses and the need to go beyond propaganda and agitation. They had advocated persistent opposition to the Government and put forward a militant programme of passive resistance and boycott of foreign cloth, foreigners' courts, education, and so on. They had demanded self-sacrifice from the youth. They had talked and written about direct action.

But they had failed to find forms through which all these ideas could find practical expression. They could neither create a viable organization to lead the movement nor could they really define the movement in a way that differed from that of the Moderates. They were more militant, their critique of British rule was couched in stronger language, they were willing to make greater sacrifices and undergo greater suffering, but they did not know how to go beyond more vigorous agitation. They were not able to put before people new forms of political struggle or mass movements. Consequently, they too had come to a political dead end by the end of 1907. Perhaps that is one reason why they expended so much of their energy in criticizing the Moderates and capturing the Congress. Unsurprisingly, the Extremists' waffling failed to impress the youth who decided to take recourse to physical force. The *Yugantar*, a newspaper echoing this feeling of disaffection, wrote in April 1906, after the police assault on the peaceful Barisal Conference: 'The thirty crores of people inhabiting India must raise their sixty crores of hands to stop this curse of oppression. Force must be stopped by force.'[15]

But the question was what form would this movement based on force take. Organizing a popular mass uprising would necessarily be an uphill and prolonged task. Many thought of trying to subvert the loyalty of the army, but they knew it would not be easy. However, these two objectives were kept as long-term goals and, for the present, revolutionary youth decided to copy the methods of the Irish nationalists and Russian nihilists and populists. That is to say, they decided to organize the assassination of unpopular British officials. Such assassinations would strike terror into the hearts of the rulers, arouse the patriotic instincts of the people, inspire them and remove the fear of authority from their minds. Each assassination, and if the assassins were caught, the consequent trial of the revolutionaries involved, would act as 'propaganda by deed.' All that this form of struggle needed was numbers of young people ready to sacrifice their lives. Inevitably, it appealed to the idealism of the youth; it aroused their latent sense of heroism. A steadily increasing number of young men turned to this form of political struggle.

Here again the Extremist leadership let the young people down. While it praised their sense of self-sacrifice and courage, it failed to provide a positive outlet for their revolutionary energies and to educate them on the political difference between a revolution based on the activity of the masses and a revolutionary feeling based on individual action, however heroic. It also failed to oppose the notion that to be a revolutionary meant to be a believer in violent action. In fact, Aurobindo Ghose encouraged this notion. Perhaps the actions of the Extremist leadership were constrained by the feeling that it was not proper to politically criticize the heroic youth who were being condemned and hunted by the authorities. But this failure to politically and ideologically oppose the young revolutionaries proved a grievous error, for it enabled the individualistic and terrorist conception of revolution to take root in Bengal.

In 1904, V.D. Savarkar organized *Abhinav Bharat* as a secret society of revolutionaries. After 1905 several newspapers openly (and a few leaders secretly) began to advocate revolutionary terrorism. In 1907, an unsuccessful attempt was made on the life of the Lieutenant-Governor of Bengal. In April 1908, Prafulla Chaki and Khudiram Bose threw a bomb at a carriage which they believed was occupied by Kingsford, the unpopular judge at Muzzafarpur. Unfortunately, they killed two English ladies instead. Prafulla Chaki shot himself dead while Khudiram Bose was tried and hanged. Thousands wept at his death and he and Chaki entered the ranks of popular nationalist heroes about whom folk songs were composed and sung all over the country.

The era of revolutionary terrorism had begun. Very soon secret societies of revolutionaries came up all over the country, the most famous and long lasting being *Anushilan Samity* and *Jugantar*. Their activities took two forms — the assassination of oppressive officials and informers and traitors from their own ranks and dacoities to raise funds for purchase of arms, etc. The latter came to be popularly known as Swadeshi dacoities! Two of the most spectacular revolutionary terrorist actions of the period were the unsuccessful attempt under the leadership of Rash Behari Bose and Sachin Sanyal to kill the Viceroy, Lord Hardinge who was wounded by the bomb thrown at him while he was riding an elephant in a state procession — and the assassination of

Curzon-Wylie in London by Madan Lal Dhingra. In all 186 revolutionaries were killed or convicted between the years 1908-1918. The revolutionary terrorists also established centres abroad. The more famous of them were Shyamji Krishnavarma, V.D. Savarkar and Har Dayal in London and Madame Cama and Ajit Singh in Europe.

Revolutionary terrorism gradually petered out. Lacking a mass base, despite remarkable heroism, the individual revolutionaries, organized in small secret groups, could not withstand suppression by the still strong colonial state. But despite their small numbers and eventual failure, they made a valuable contribution to the growth of nationalism in India. As a historian has put it, 'they gave us back the pride of our manhood.'[16]

12 World War I and Indian Nationalism: The Ghadar

The outbreak of the First World War in 1914 gave a new lease of life to the nationalist movement which had been dormant since the heady days of the Swadeshi movement. Britain's difficulty was India's 'opportunity.' This opportunity was seized, in different ways and with varying success, by the *Ghadar* revolutionaries based in North America and by Lokamanya Tilak, Annie Besant and their Home Rule Leagues in India. The Ghadarites attempted a violent overthrow of British rule, while the Home Rule Leaguers launched a nation-wide agitation for securing Home Rule or *Swaraj*.

*

The West Coast of North America had, since 1904, become home to a steadily increasing number of Punjabi immigrants. Many of these were land-hungry peasants from the crowded areas of Punjab, especially the Jullundur and Hoshiarpur districts, in search of some means of survival. Some of them came straight from their villages in Punjab while others had emigrated earlier to seek employment in various places in the Far East, in the Malay States, and in Fiji. Many among them were ex-soldiers whose service in the British Indian Army had taken them to distant lands and made them aware of the opportunities to be had there. Pushed out from their homes by economic hardship and lured by the prospect of building a new and prosperous life for themselves and their kin, they pawned their belongings, mortgaged or sold their land, and set out for the promised lands.

The welcome that awaited the travel-weary immigrants in Canada and the USA was, however, not what they had expected. Many were refused entry, especially those who came straight from their villages and did not know Western ways and manners; those who were allowed to stay not only had to face racial contempt but also the brunt of the hostility of the White labour force and unions who resented the competition they offered. Agitations against the entry of the Indians were launched by native American labourers and these were supported by politicians looking for the popular vote.

Meanwhile, the Secretary of State for India had his own reasons for urging restrictions on immigration. For one, he believed that the terms of close familiarity of Indians with Whites which would inevitably take place in America was not good for British prestige; it was by prestige alone that India was held and not by force. Further, he was worried that the immigrants would get contaminated by socialist ideas, and that the racial discrimination to which they were bound to be subjected would become the source of nationalist agitation in India.[1] The combined pressure resulted in an effective restriction on Indian immigration into Canada in 1908. Tarak Nath Das, an Indian student, and one of the first leaders of the Indian community in North America to start a paper (called *Free Hindustan*) realized that while the British government was keen on Indians going to Fiji to work as labourers for British planters, it did not want them to go to North America where they might be infected by ideas of liberty.

*

The discriminatory policies of the host countries soon resulted in a flurry of political activity among Indian nationalists. As early as 1907, Ramnath Puri, a political exile on the West Coast, issued a *Circular-e-Azadi* (Circular of Liberty) in which he also pledged support to the Swadeshi movement; Tarak Nath Das in Vancouver started the *Free Hindustan* and adopted a very militant nationalist tone; G.D. Kumar set up a *Swadesh Sevak* Home in Vancouver on the lines of the *India House* in London and also began to bring out a Gurmukhi paper called *Swadesh Sevak* which advocated social reform and also asked Indian troops to rise in revolt against the British. In 1910, Tarak Nath Das and G.D. Kumar, by now forced out of Vancouver, set up the United India House in Seattle in the US, where every Saturday they lectured to a group of twenty-five Indian labourers. Close links also developed between the United India House group, consisting mainly of radical nationalist students, and the Khalsa Diwan Society, and in 1913 they decided to send a deputation to meet the Colonial Secretary in London and the Viceroy and other officials in India. The Colonial Secretary in London could not find the time to see them even though they waited for a whole month, but in India they succeeded in meeting the Viceroy and the Lieutenant Governor of the Punjab. But, more important, their visit became the occasion for a series of public meetings in Lahore, Ludhiana, Ambala, Ferozepore, Jullundur, Amritsar, Lyallpur, Gujranwala, Sialkot and Simla and they received enthusiastic support from the press and the general public.[2]

The result of this sustained agitation, both in Canada and the United States, was the creation of a nationalist consciousness and feeling of solidarity among immigrant Indians. Their inability to get the Government of India or the British Government to intercede on their behalf regarding immigration restrictions and other disabilities, such as those imposed by the Alien Land law which practically prohibited Indians from owning land in the US, led to an impatience and a mood of discontent which blossomed into a revolutionary movement.

*

The first fillip to the revolutionary movement was provided by the visit to Vancouver, in early 1913, of Bhagwan Singh, a Sikh priest who had worked in Hong Kong and the Malay States. He openly preached the gospel of violent overthrow of British rule and urged the people to adopt *Bande Mataram* as a revolutionary salute. Bhagwan Singh was externed from Canada after a stay of three months.

The centre of revolutionary activity soon shifted to the US, which provided a relatively free political atmosphere. The crucial role was now played by Lala Har Dayal, a political exile from India. Har Dayal arrived in California in April 1911, taught briefly at Stanford University, and soon immersed himself in political activity. During the summer of 1912, he concentrated mainly on delivering lectures on the anarchist and syndicalist movements to various American groups of intellectuals, radicals and workers, and did not show much interest in the problems that were agitating the immigrant Indian community. But the bomb attack on Lord Hardinge, the Viceroy of India, in Delhi on 23 December, 1912, excited his imagination and roused the dormant Indian revolutionary in him. His faith in the possibility of a revolutionary overthrow of the British regime in India was renewed, and he issued a *Yugantar Circular* praising the attack on the Viceroy.

Meanwhile, the Indians on the West Coast of the US had been in search of a leader and had even thought of inviting Ajit Singh, who had become famous in the agitation in Punjab in 1907. But Har Dayal was already there and, after December 1912, showed himself willing to play an active political role. Soon the Hindi Association was set up in Portland in May 1913.

At the very first meeting of the Association, held in the house of Kanshi Ram, and attended among others by Bhai Parmanand, Sohan Singh Bhakna, and Harnam Singh 'Tundilat,' Har Dayal set forth his plan of action: 'Do not fight the Americans, but use the freedom that is available in the US to fight the British; you will never be treated as equals by the Americans until you are free in your own land; the root cause of Indian poverty and degradation is British rule and it must be overthrown, not by petitions but by armed revolt; carry this message to the masses and to the soldiers in the Indian Army; go to India in large numbers and enlist their support.' Har Dayal's ideas found immediate acceptance. A Working Committee was set up and the decision was taken to start a weekly paper, *The Ghadar*, for free circulation, and to set up a headquarters called *Yugantar Ashram* in San Francisco. A series of meetings held in different towns and centres and finally a representatives' meeting in Astoria confirmed and approved the decisions of the first meeting at Portland. The *Ghadar* movement had begun.

*

The *Ghadar* militants immediately began an extensive propaganda campaign; they toured extensively, visiting mills and farms where most of the Punjabi immigrant labour worked. The *Yugantar Ashram* became the home and headquarters and refuge of these political workers.

On 1 November 1913, the first issue of *Ghadar*, in Urdu, was published and on 9 December, the Gurmukhi edition.The name of the paper left no doubts as to its aim. *Ghadar* meant Revolt. And if any doubts remained, they were to be dispelled by the caption on the masthead: *Angrezi Raj ka Dushman* or 'An Enemy of British Rule.' On the front page of each issue was a feature titled *Angrezi Raj Ka Kacha Chittha* or 'An Expose of British Rule.' This *Chittha* consisted of fourteen points enumerating the harmful effects of British rule, including the drain of wealth, the low per capita income of Indians, the high land tax, the contrast between the low expenditure on health and the high expenditure on the military, the destruction of Indian arts and industries, the recurrence of famines and plague that killed millions of Indians, the use of Indian tax payers' money for wars in Afghanistan, Burma, Egypt, Persia and China, the British policy of promoting discord in the Indian States to extend their own influence, the discriminatory lenient treatment given to Englishmen who were guilty of killing Indians or dishonouring Indian women, tl e policy of helping Christian missionaries with money raised from Hindus and Muslims, the effort to foment discord between Hindus and Muslims: in sum, the entire critique of British rule that had been formulated by the Indian national movement was summarized and presented every week to *Ghadar* readers. The last two points of the *Chittha* suggested the solution: (1) The Indian population numbers seven crores in the Indian States and 24 crores in British India, while there are only 79,614 officers and soldiers and 38,948 volunteers who are Englishmen. (2) Fifty-six years have lapsed since the Revolt of 1857; now there is urgent need for a second one.[3]

Besides the powerful simplicity of the *Chittha*, the message was also conveyed by serializing Savarkar's *The Indian War of Independence — 1857. The Ghadar* also contained references to the contributions of Lokamanya Tilak, Sri Aurobindo, V.D. Savarkar, Madame Cama, Shyamji Krishna Varma, Ajit Singh and Sufi Amba Prasad, as well as highlights of the daring deeds of the *Anushilan Samiti*, the *Yugantar* group and the Russian secret societies.[4]

But, perhaps, the most powerful impact was made by the poems that appeared in *The Ghadar*, soon collected and published as *Ghadar di Goonj* and distributed free of cost. These poems were marked as much by their secular tone as by their revolutionary zeal, as the following extract demonstrates:[5]

> Hindus, Sikhs, Pathans and Muslims,
> Pay attention ye all people in the army.
> Our country has been plundered by the British,
> We have to wage a war against them.
> We do not need *pandits* and *quazis*,
> We do not want to get our ship sunk.
> The time of worship is over now,
> It is time to take up the sword.

The Ghadar was circulated widely among Indians in North America, and within a few months it had reached groups settled in the Philippines, Hong Kong, China, the Malay States, Singapore, Trinidad, the Honduras, and of course, India. It evoked an unprecedented response, becoming the subject of lively discussion and debate. The poems it carried were recited at gatherings of Punjabi immigrants, and were soon popular everywhere.

Unsurprisingly, *The Ghadar*, succeeded, in a very brief time, in changing the self-image of the Punjabi immigrant from that of a loyal soldier of the British Raj to that of a rebel whose only aim was to destroy the British hold on his motherland. *The Ghadar* consciously made the Punjabi aware of his loyalist past, made him feel ashamed of it, and challenged him to atone for it in the name of his earlier tradition of resistance to oppression:[6]

> Why do you disgrace the name of Singhs?
> How come! you have forgotten the majesty of 'Lions'
> Had the like of Dip Singh been alive today
> How could the Singhs have been taunted?
> People say that the Singhs are no good
> Why did you turn the tides during the Delhi mutiny?
> Cry aloud, 'Let us kill the Whites'
> Why do you sit quiet, shamelessly
> Let the earth give way so we may drown
> To what good were these thirty crores born.

The message went home, and ardent young militants began thirsting for 'action.' Har Dayal himself was surprised by the intensity of the response. He had, on occasion, spoken in terms of 'ten years' or 'some years' when asked how long it would take to organize the revolution in India. But those who read the heady exhortations of *The Ghadar* were too impatient, and ten years seemed a long time.

*

Finally, in 1914, three events influenced the course of the *Ghadar* movement: the arrest and escape of Har Dayal, the *Komagata Maru* incident, and the outbreak of the First World War.

Har Dayal was arrested on 25 March 1914 on the stated ground of his anarchist activities though everybody suspected that the British government had much to do with it. Released on bail, he used the opportunity to slip out of the country.With that, his active association with the *Ghadar* movement came to an abrupt end.

Meanwhile, in March 1914, the ship, *Komagatu Maru* had begun its fateful voyage to Canada. Canada had for some years imposed very strict restrictions on Indian immigration by means of a law that forbade entry to all, except those who made a continuous journey from India. This measure had proved effective because there were no shipping lines that offered such a route. But in November 1913, the Canadian Supreme Court allowed entry to thrity-five Indians who had not made a continuous journey. Encouraged by this judgement, Gurdit Singh, an Indian contractor living in Singapore, decided to charter a ship and carry to Vancouver, Indians who were living in various places in East and South-East Asia. Carrying a total of 376 Indian passengers, the ship began its journey to Vancouver. *Ghadar* activists visited the ship at Yokohama in Japan, gave lectures and distributed literature. The press in Punjab warned of serious consequences if the Indians were not allowed entry into Canada. The press in Canada took a different view and some newspapers in Vancouver alerted the people to the 'Mounting Oriental Invasion.' The Government of Canada had, meanwhile, plugged the legal loopholes that had resulted in the November Supreme Court judgement. The battle lines were clearly drawn.

When the ship arrived in Vancouver, it was not allowed into the port and was cordoned off by the police. To fight for the rights of the passengers, a 'Shore Committee' was set up under the leadership of Husain Rahim, Sohan Lal Pathak and Balwant Singh, funds were raised, and protest meetings organized. Rebellion against the British in India was threatened. In the United States, under the leadership of Bhagwan Singh, Barkatullah, Ram Chandra and Sohan Singh Bhakna, a powerful campaign was organized and the people were advised to prepare for rebellion.

Soon the *Komagata Maru* was forced out of Canadian waters. Before it reached Yokohama, World War I broke out, and the British Government passed orders that no passenger be allowed to disembark anywhere on the way — not even at the places from where they had joined the ship — but only at Calcutta. At every port that the ship touched, it triggered off a wave of resentment and anger among the Indian community and became the occasion for anti-British mobilization. On landing at Budge Budge near Calcutta, the harassed and irate passengers, provoked by the hostile attitude of the authorities, resisted the police and this led to a clash in which eighteen passengers were killed, and 202 arrested. A few of them succeeded in escaping.

The third and most important development that made the *Ghadar* revolution imminent was the outbreak of the World War I. After all, this was the opportunity they had been told to seize. True, they were not really prepared, but should they now let it just pass by? A special meeting of the leading activists of the *Ghadar* movement decided that the opportunity must be seized, that it was better to die than to do nothing at all, and that their major weakness, the lack of arms, could be overcome by going to India and winning over the Indian soldiers to their cause. The *Ailan-e-Jung* or Proclamation of War of the *Ghadar* Party was issued and circulated widely. Mohammed Barkatullah, Ram Chandra and Bhagwan Singh organized and addressed a series of public meetings to exhort Indians to go back to India and organize an armed revolt. Prominent leaders were sent to persuade Indians living in Japan, the Philippines, China, Hong Kong, The Malay States, Singapore and Burma to return home and join the rebels. The more impatient among the *Ghadar* activists, such as Kartar Singh Sarabha, later hanged by the British in a conspiracy case, and Raghubar Dayal Gupta, immediately left for India.

*

The Government of India, fully informed of the *Ghadar* plans, which were, in any case, hardly a secret, armed itself with the Ingress into India Ordinance and waited for the returning emigrants. On arrival, the emigrants were scrutinized, the 'safe' ones allowed to proceed home, the more 'dangerous' ones arrested and the less 'dangerous' ones ordered not to leave their home villages. Of course, some of 'the dangerous' ones escaped detection and went to Punjab to foment rebellion. Of an estimated 8000 emigrants who returned to India, 5000 were allowed to proceed unhindered. Precautionary measures were taken for roughly 1500 men. Upto February 1915, 189 had been interned and 704 restricted to their villages. Many who came via colombo and South India succeeded in reaching Punjab without being found out.

But Punjab in 1914 was very different from what the Ghadarites had been led to expect — they found the Punjabis were in no mood to join the romantic adventure of the *Ghadar*. The militants from abroad tried their best, they toured the villages, addressed gatherings at melas and festivals, all to no avail. The Chief Khalsa Diwan, proclaiming its loyalty to the sovereign, declared them to be 'fallen' Sikhs and criminals, and helped the Government to track them down.[7]

Frustrated and disillusioned with the attitude of the civilian population, the Ghadarites turned their attention to the army and made a number of naive attempts in November 1914 to get the army units to mutiny. But the lack of an organized leadership and central command frustrated all the *Ghadar's* efforts.

Frantically, the *Ghadar* made an attempt to find a leader; Bengali revolutionaries were contacted and through the efforts of Sachindranath Sanyal and Vishnu Ganesh Pingley, Rash Behari Bose, the Bengali revolutionary who had become famous by his daring attack on Hardinge, the Viceroy, finally arrived in Punjab in mid-January 1915 to assume leadership of the revolt.

Bose established a semblance of an organization and sent out men to contact army units in different centres, (from Bannu in the North West Frontier to Faizabad and Lucknow in the U.P.) and report back by 11 February 1915. The emissaries returned with optimistic reports, and the date for the mutiny was set first for 21 and then for 19 February. But the Criminal Investigation Department (CID) had succeeded in penetrating the organization, from the very highest level down, and the Government succeeded in taking effective pre-emptive measures. Most of the leaders were arrested, though Bose escaped. For all practical purposes, the *Ghadar* movement was crushed. But the Government did not stop there. In what was perhaps the most repressive action experienced by the national movement this far, Conspiracy trials were held in Punjab and Mandalay, forty-five revolutionaries were sentenced to death and over 200 to long terms of imprisonment. An entire generation of the nationalist leadership of Punjab was, thus, politically beheaded.

Some Indian revolutionaries who were operating from Berlin, and who had links with the *Ghadar* leader Ram Chandra in America, continued, with German help, to make attempts to organize a mutiny among Indian troops stationed abroad. Raja Mahendra Pratap and Barkatullah tried to enlist the help of the Amir of Afghanistan and even, hopefully, set up a Provisional Government in Kabul, but these and other attempts failed to record any significant success. It appeared that violent opposition to British rule was fated to fail.

*

Should we, therefore, conclude that the Ghadarites fought in vain? Or that, because they could not drive out the British, their movement was a failure? Both these conclusions are not necessarily correct because the success or failure of a political movement is not always to be measured in terms of its achievement of stated objectives. By that measure, all the major national struggles whether of 1920-22, 1930-34, or 1942 would have to be classified as failures, since none of them culminated in Indian independence. But if success and failure are to be measured in terms of the deepening of nationalist consciousness, the evolution and testing of new strategies and methods of struggle, the creation of traditions of resistance, of secularism, of democracy, and of egalitarianism, then, the Ghadarites certainly contributed their share to the struggle for India's freedom.

Ironic though it may seem, it was in the realm of ideology that *Ghadar* success was the greatest. Through the earlier papers, but most of all through *The Ghadar* itself, the entire nationalist critique of colonialism, which was the most solid and abiding contribution of the moderate nationalists, was carried, in a powerful and simple form, to the mass of Indian immigrants, many of whom were poor workers and agricultural labourers. This huge propaganda effort motivated and educated an entire generation. Though a majority of the leaders of the *Ghadar* movement, and most of the participants, were drawn from among the Sikhs, the ideology that was created and spread through *The Ghadar* and *Ghadar Ki Goonj* and other publications was strongly secular in tone. Concern with religion was seen as petty and narrow-minded, and unworthy of revolutionaries. That this was not mere brave talk is seen by the ease with which leaders belonging to different religions and regions were accepted by the movement. Lala Har Dayal was a Hindu, and so were Ram Chandra and many others, Barkatullah was a Muslim and Rash Behari Bose a Hindu and a Bengali! But perhaps much more important, the Ghadarites consciously set out to create a secular consciousness among the Punjabis. A good example of this is the way in which the term *Turka Shahi* (Turkish rule), which in Punjabi was a synonym for oppression and high-handed behaviour, was sought to be reinterpreted; and the Punjabis were urged to look upon the 'Turks' (read Muslims) as their brothers who fought hard for the country's freedom. Further, the nationalist salute *Bande Mataram* (and not any Sikh religious greeting such as *Sat Sri Akal*) was urged upon and adopted as the rallying cry of the *Ghadar* movement. The *Ghadar*ites sought to give a new meaning to religion as well. They urged that religion lay not in observing the outward forms such as those signified by long hair and *Kirpan* (sword), but in remaining true to the model of good behaviour that was enjoined by all religious teachings.[8]

The ambiguities that remained in the *Ghadar* ideological discourse, such as those evidenced by Har Dayal's advocacy of Khilafat as a religious cause of the Muslims, or when the British policy of not allowing Sikhs to carry arms was criticized, etc., were a product of the transitional stage in the evolution of a secular nationalist ideology that was spanned by the *Ghadar* movement and its leaders. Also, the defence of religious interests has to be seen as part of the whole aspect of cultural defence against colonialism, and not necessarily as an aspect of communalism or communal ideology and consciousness.

Nor did the Ghadarites betray any narrow regional loyalties. Lokamanya Tilak, Aurobindo Ghose, Khudi Ram Bose, Kanhia lal Dutt, Savarkar were all the heroes of the *Ghadars*. Rash Behari Bose was importuned and accepted as the leader of the abortive *Ghadar* revolt in 1915. Far from dwelling on the greatness of the Sikhs or the Punjabis, the *Ghadars* constantly criticized the loyalist role played by the Punjabis during 1857. Similarly, the large Sikh presence in the British Indian Army was not hailed as proof of the so-called 'martial' traditions of the Sikhs, as became common later, but was seen as a matter of shame and Sikh soldiers were asked to revolt against the British. The self-image of the Punjabi, and especially of the Punjabi Sikh, that was created by the *Ghadar* movement was that of an Indian who had betrayed his motherland in 1857 by siding with the foreigner and who had, therefore, to make amends to *Bharat Mata*, by fighting for her honour. In the words of Sohan Singh Bhakna, who later became a major peasant and Communist leader: 'We were not Sikhs or Punjabis. Our religion was patriotism.'[9]

Another marked feature of *Ghadar* ideology was its democratic and egalitarian content. It was clearly stated by the Ghadarites that their objective was the establishment of an independent republic of India. Also, deeply influenced as he was by anarchist and syndicalist movements, and even by socialist ideas, Har Dayal imparted to the movement an egalitarian ideology. Perhaps this facilitated the transformation of many Ghadarites into peasant leaders and Communists in the '20s and '30s.

Har Dayal's other major contribution was the creation of a truly internationalist outlook among the *Ghadar* revolutionaries. His lectures and articles were full of references to Irish, Mexican, and Russian revolutionaries. For example, he referred to Mexican revolutionaries as 'Mexican Ghadarites.'[10] *Ghadar* militants were thus distinguished by their secular, egalitarian, democratic and non-chauvinistic internationalist outlook.

This does not, however, mean that the *Ghadar* movement did not suffer from any weaknesses. The major weakness of the *Ghadar* leaders was that they completely under-estimated the extent and amount of preparation at every level — organizational, ideological, strategic, tactical, financial — that was necessary before an attempt at an armed revolt could be organized. Taken by surprise by the outbreak of the war and roused to a fever-pitch by the Komagata Maru episode, they sounded the bugles of war without examining the state of their army. They forgot that to mobilize a few thousand discontented immigrant Indians, who were already in a highly charged emotional state because of the racial discrimination they suffered at the hands of white foreigners, was very different from the stupendous task of mobilizing and motivating lakhs of peasants and soldiers in India. They underestimated the strength of the British in India, both their armed and organizational might as well as the ideological foundations of their rule, and led themselves to imagine that all that the masses of India lacked was a call to revolt, which, once given, would strike a fatal blow to the tottering structure of British rule.

The *Ghadar* movement also failed to generate an effective and sustained leadership that was capable of integrating the various aspects of the movement. Har Dayal himself was temperamentally totally unsuited to the role of an organizer; he was a propagandist, an inspirer, an ideologue. Even his ideas did not form a structured whole but remained a shifting amalgam of various theories that attracted him from time to time. Further, his departure from the U.S. at a critical stage left his compatriots floundering.[11]

Another major weakness of the movement was its almost nonexistent organizational structure; the *Ghadar* movement was sustained more by the enthusiasm of the militants than by their effective organization.

These weaknesses of understanding, of leadership, of organization, all resulted in what one can only call a tremendous waste of valuable human resources. If we recall that forty Ghadarites were sentenced to be hanged and over 200 given long terms of imprisonment, we can well realize that the particular romantic adventure of 1914-15 resulted in the beheading of an entire generation of secular nationalist leadership, who could perhaps have, if they had remained politically effective, given an entirely different political complexion to Punjab in the following years. They would certainly have, given their strong secular moorings, acted as a bulwark against the growth of communal tendencies that were to raise their heads in later years. That this is not just wild speculation is seen from the fact that, in the late '20s, and ,'30s, the few surviving Ghadarites helped lay the foundations of a secular national and peasant movement in Punjab.

13 The Home Rule Movement and Its Fallout

The romantic adventure of the *Ghadar* revolutionaries was the dramatic response of Indians living abroad to the First World War. We now turn to the less charged, but more effective, Indian response — the Home Rule League movement, led by Lokamanya Tilak and Annie Besant.

*

On 16 June 1914, Bal Gangadhar Tilak was released after serving a prison sentence of six years, most of which he had spent in Mandalay in Burma. He returned to a India very different to the one he had been banished from. Aurobindo Ghose, the firebrand of the Swadeshi days, had taken *sanyas* in Pondicherry, and Lala Lajpat Rai was away in the United States of America. The Indian National Congress had yet to recover from the combined effects of the split at Surat in 1907, the heavy government repression of the activists of the Swadeshi movement, and the disillusionment of the Moderates with the constitutional reforms of 1909.

Tilak initially concentrated all his attention on seeking readmission, for himself and other Extremists, into the Indian National Congress. He was obviously convinced that the sanction of this body, that had come to symbolize the Indian national movement, was a necessary pre-condition for the success of any political action. To conciliate the Moderates and convince them of his *bona fides*, as well as to stave off any possible government repression, he publicly declared: 'I may state once for all that we are trying in India, as the Irish Home-rulers have been doing in Ireland, for a reform of the system of administration and not for the overthrow of Government; and I have no hesitation in saying that the acts of violence which have been committed in the different parts of India are not only repugnant to me, but have, in my opinion, only unfortunately retarded to a great extent, the pace of our political progress.'[1] He further assured the Government of his loyalty to the Crown and urged all Indians to assist the British Government in its hour of crisis.

Many of the Moderate leaders of the Congress were also unhappy with the choice they had made in 1907 at Surat, and also with the fact that the Congress had lapsed into almost total inactivity. They were, therefore, quite sympathetic to Tilak's overtures. Further, they were under considerable pressure from Mrs. Annie Besant, who had just joined the Indian National Congress and was keen to arouse nationalist political activity, to admit the Extremists.

Annie Besant, already sixty-six in 1914, had begun her political career in England as a proponent of Free Thought, Radicalism, Fabianism and Theosophy, and had come to India in 1893 to work for the Theosophical Society. Since 1907, she had been spreading the message of Theosophy from her headquarters in Adyar, a suburb of Madras, and had gained a large number of followers among the educated members of many communities that had experienced no cultural revival of their own. In 1914, she decided to enlarge the sphere of her activities to include the building of a movement for Home Rule on the lines of the Irish Home Rule League. For this, she realized it was necessary both to get the sanction of the Congress, as well as the active cooperation of the Extremists. She devoted her energies, therefore, to persuading the Moderate leaders to open the doors of the Congress to Tilak and his fellow-Extremists.

But the annual Congress session in December 1914 was to prove a disappointment — Pherozeshah Mehta and his Bombay Moderate group succeeded, by winning over Gokhale and the Bengal Moderates, in keeping out the Extremists. Tilak and Besant thereupon decided to revive political activity on their own, while maintaining their pressure on the Congress to re-admit the Extremist group.

*

In early 1915, Annie Besant launched a campaign through her two papers, *New India* and *Commonweal*, and organized public meetings and conferences to demand that India be granted self-government on the lines of the White colonies after the War. From April 1915, her tone became more peremptory and her stance more aggressive.

Meanwhile, Lokamanya began his political activities, but, not yet having gained admittance into the Congress, was careful that he did not in any way alarm the Moderates or appear to be by-passing the Congress. This is clear from the fact that at the meeting of his followers convened at Poona in May 1915, it was decided that their initial phase of action would be to set up an agency 'to enlighten the villagers regarding the objects and work of the Congress.'[2] The local associations that were set up in many Maharashtra towns in August and September of that year also concentrated more on emphasizing the need for unity in the Congress than on the stepping up of political activity. While sometimes resorting to threats to pressurize the more conservative among the Moderates, Tilak still hoped to persuade the majority to accept him because of his reasonableness and caution.

His efforts and those of Annie Besant were soon to meet with success, and at the annual session of the Congress in December 1915 it was decided that the Extremists be allowed to rejoin the Congress. The opposition from the Bombay group had been greatly weakened by the death of Pherozeshah Mehta. But Annie Besant did not succeed in getting the Congress and the Muslim League to support her decision to set up Home Rule Leagues. She did manage, however, to persuade the Congress to commit itself to a programme of educative propaganda and to a revival of the local level Congress committees. Knowing that the Congress, as constituted at the time, was unlikely to implement this, she had inserted a condition by which, if the Congress did not start this activity by September 1916, she would be free to set up her own League.

Tilak, not bound by any such commitment, and having gained the right of readmission, now took the lead and set up the Home Rule League at the Bombay Provincial Conference held at Belgaum in April 1916. Annie Besant's impatient followers, unhappy with her decision to wait till September, secured her permission to start Home Rule groups. Jamnadas Dwarkadas, Shankerlal Banker and Indulal Yagnik set up a Bombay paper *Young India* and launched an All India Propaganda Fund to publish pamphlets in regional languages and in English. In September 1916, as there were no signs of any Congress activity, Annie Besant announced the formation of her Home Rule League, with George Arundale, her Theosophical follower, as the Organizing Secretary. The two Leagues avoided any friction by demarcating their area of activity: Tilak's League was to work in Maharashtra, (excluding Bombay city), Karnataka the Central Provinces and Berar, and Annie Besant's

League was given charge of the rest of India. The reason the two Leagues did not merge was because, in Annie Besant's words, 'some of his followers disliked me and some of mine disliked him. We, however, had no quarrel with each other.'[3]

Tilak promoted the Home Rule campaign with a tour of Maharashtra and through his lectures clarified and popularized the demand for Home Rule. 'India was like a son who had grown up and attained majority. It was right now that the trustee or the father should give him what was his due. The people of India must get this effected. They have a right to do so.'[4] He also linked up the question of *swaraj* with the demand for the formation of linguistic states and education in the vernacular. 'Form one separate state each for Marathi, Telugu and Kanarese provinces . . . The principle that education should be given through the vernaculars is self-evident and clear. Do the English educate their people through the French language? Do Germans do it through English or the Turks through French?' At the Bombay Provincial Conference in 1915, he told V.B. Alur who got up to support his condolence resolution on Gokhale's death: 'Speak in Kannada to establish the right of Kannada language.'[5] It is clear that the Lokamanya had no trace of regional or linguistic Marathi chauvinism.

His stand on the question of non-Brahmin representation and on the issue of untouchability demonstrated that he was no casteist either. When the non-Brahmins in Maharashtra sent a separate memorandum to the Government dissociating themselves from the demands of the advanced classes, Tilak urged those who opposed this to be patient: 'If we can prove to the non-Brahmins, by example, that we are wholly on their side in their demands from the Government, I am sure that in times to come their agitation, now based on social inequality, will merge into our struggle.'[6] To the non-Brahmins, he explained that the real difference was not between Brahmin and non-Brahmin, but between the educated and the non-educated. Brahmins were ahead of others in jobs because they were more educated, and the Government, in spite of its sympathy for non-Brahmins and hostility towards Brahmins, was forced to look to the needs of the administration and give jobs to Brahmins. At a conference for the removal of untouchability, Tilak declared: 'If a God were to tolerate untouchability, I would not recognize him as God at all.'[7]

Nor can we discern in his speeches of this period any trace of religious appeal; the demand for Home Rule was made on a wholly secular basis. The British were aliens not because they belonged to another religion but because they did not act in the Indian interest. 'He who does what is beneficial to the people of this country, be he a Muhammedan or an Englishman, is not alien. 'Alienness' has to do with interests. Alienness is certainly not concerned with white or black skin . . . or religion.'[8]

Tilak's League furthered its propaganda efforts by publishing six Marathi and two English pamphlets, of which 47,000 copies were sold. Pamphlets were brought out in Gujarati and Kannada as well. The League was organized into six branches, one each in Central Maharashtra, Bombay city, Karnataka, and Central Provinces, and two in Berar.

As soon as the movement for Home Rule began to gather steam, the Government hit back, and it chose a particularly auspicious day for the blow. The 23rd of July, 1916, was Tilak's sixtieth birthday, and, according to custom, it was the occasion for a big celebration. A purse of Rs. one lakh was presented to him. The same day the Government offered him their own present: a notice asking him to show cause why he should not be bound over for good behaviour for a period of one year and demanding securities of Rs. 60,000. For Tilak, this was the best gift he could have wanted for his birthday. 'The Lord is with us,' he said, 'Home Rule will now spread like wildfire.'[9] Repression was sure to fan the fire of revolt.

Tilak was defended by a team of lawyers led by Mohammed Ali Jinnah. He lost the case in the Magistrate's Court but was exonerated by the High Court in November. The victory was hailed all over the country. Gandhiji's *Young India* summed up the popular feeling: 'Thus, a great victory has been won for the cause of Home Rule which has, thus, been freed from the chains that were sought to be put upon it.'[10] Tilak immediately pushed home the advantage by proclaiming in his public speeches that Home Rule now had the sanction of the Government and he and his colleagues intensified their propaganda campaign for Home Rule. By April 1917 Tilak had enlisted 14,000 members.

*

Meanwhile, Annie Besant had gone ahead with the formal founding of her League in September 1916. The organization of her League was much looser than that of Tilak's, and three members could form a branch while in the case of Tilak's League each of the six branches had a clearly defined area and activities. Two hundred branches of Besant's League were established, some consisting of a town and others of groups of villages. And though a formal Executive Council of seven members was elected for three years by thirty-four 'founding branches,' most of the work was carried on by Annie Besant and her lieutenants — Arundale, C.P. Ramaswamy Aiyar, and B.P. Wadia — from her headquarters at Adyar. Nor was there any organized method for passing on instructions — these were conveyed through individual members and through Arundale's column on Home Rule in '*New India*'. The membership of Annie Besant's League increased at a rate slower than that of Tilak's. By March 1917, her League had 7,000 members. Besides her existing Theosophical followers, many others including Jawaharlal Nehru in Allahabad and B. Chakravarti and J. Banerjee in Calcutta joined the Home Rule League. However, the strength of the League could not be judged from the number of branches because, while many were extremely active, others remained adjuncts of the Theosophical societies. In Madras city, for example, though the number of branches was very large, many were inactive, while the branch in Bombay city, the four branches in the U.P. towns, and many village branches in Gujarat were very active.

The main thrust of the activity was directed towards building up an agitation around the demand for Home Rule. This was to be achieved by promoting political education and discussion. Arundale, through *New India*, advised members to promote political discussions, establish libraries containing material on national politics, organize classes for students on politics, print and circulate pamphlets, collect funds, organize social work, take part in local government activities, arrange political meetings and lectures, present arguments to friends in favour of Home Rule and urge them to join the movement. At least some of these activities were carried on by many of the branches, and especially the task of promotion of political discussion and debate.

Some idea of the immensity of the propaganda effort that was launched can be gauged from the fact that by the time Annie Besant's League was formally founded in September 1916, the Propaganda Fund started earlier in the year had already sold 300,000 copies of twenty-six English pamphlets which focused mainly on the system of government existing in India and the arguments for self-government. After the founding of the League, these pamphlets were published again and, in addition, new ones in Indian languages were brought out. Most branches were also very active in holding public meetings and lectures. Further, they would always respond when a nation-wide call was given for protest on any specific issue. For example, when Annie Besant was externed from the Central Provinces and Berar in November 1916, most of the branches, at Arundale's instance, held meetings and sent resolutions of protest to the Viceroy and the Secretary of State. Tilak's externment from Punjab and Delhi in February 1917 elicited a similar response.

Many Moderate Congressmen, who were dissatisfied with the inactivity into which the Congress had lapsed, joined the Home Rule agitation. Members of Gokhale's Servants of India Society, though not permitted to become members of the League, were encouraged to add their weight to the demand for Home Rule by undertaking lecture tours and publishing pamphlets. Many other Moderate nationalists joined the Home Rule Leaguers in U.P. in touring the surrounding towns and villages in preparation for the Lucknow session of the Congress in December 1916. Their meetings were usually organized in the local Bar libraries, and attended by students, professionals, businessmen and, if it was a market day, by agriculturists. Speaking in Hindi, they contrasted India's current poverty with her glorious past, and also explained the main features of European independence movements. The participation of Moderates was hardly surprising, since the Home Rule Leagues were after all only implementing the programme of political propaganda and education that they had been advocating for so long.

*

The Lucknow session of the Congress in December 1916 presented the Home Rule Leaguers with the long-awaited opportunity of demonstrating their strength. Tilak's Home Rule League established a tradition that was to become an essential part of later Congress annual sessions — a special train, known variously as the 'Congress Special' and the 'Home Rule Special,' was organized to carry delegates from Western India to Lucknow. Arundale asked every member of the League to get himself elected as a delegate to the Lucknow session — the idea being quite simply to flood the Congress with Home Rule Leaguers.

Tilak and his men were welcomed back into the Congress by the Moderate president, Ambika Charan Mazumdar: 'After nearly 10 years of painful separation and wanderings through the wilderness of misunderstandings and the mazes of unpleasant controversies . . . both the wings of the Indian Nationalist party have come to realize the fact that united they stand, but divided they fall, and brothers have at last met brothers . . .'[11]

The Lucknow Congress was significant also for the famous Congress League Pact, popularly know as the Lucknow Pact. Both Tilak and Annie Besant had played a leading role in bringing about this agreement between the Congress and the League, much against the wishes of many important leaders, including Madan Mohan Malaviya. Answering the criticism that the Pact had acceded too much to the Muslim League, Lokamanya Tilak said: 'It has been said, gentlemen, by some that we Hindus have yielded too much to our Mohammedan brethren. I am sure I represent the sense of the Hindu community all over India when I say that we could not have yielded too much. I would not care if the rights of self-government are granted to the Mohammedan community only. I would not care if they are granted to the Rajputs. I would not care if they are granted to the lower and the lowest classes of the Hindu population provided the British Government consider them more fit than the educated classes of India for exercising those rights. I would not care if those rights are granted to any section of the Indian community . . . When we have to fight against a third party — it is a very important thing that we stand on this platform united, united in race, united in religion, united as regards all different shades of political creed.'[12]

Faced with such a stand by one who was considered the most orthodox of Hindus and the greatest scholar of the ancient religious texts, the opposition stood little chance of success, and faded away. And though the acceptance of the principle of separate electorates for Muslims was certainly a most controversial decision, it cannot be denied that the Pact was motivated by a sincere desire to allay minority fears about majority domination.

The Lucknow Congress also demanded a further dose of constitutional reforms as a step towards self-government. Though this did not go as far as the Home Rule Leaguers wished, they accepted it in the interest of Congress unity. Another very significant proposal made by Tilak — that the Congress should appoint a small and cohesive Working Committee that would carry on the day to day affairs of the Congress and be responsible for implementing the resolutions passed at the annual sessions, a proposal by which he hoped to transform the Congress from a deliberative body into one capable of leading a sustained movement — was unfortunately quashed by Moderate opposition. Four years later, in 1920, when Mahatma Gandhi prepared a reformed constitution for the Congress, this was one of the major changes considered necessary if the

Congress was to lead a sustained movement.

After the end of the Congress session, a joint meeting of the two Home Rule Leagues was held in the same *pandal*, and was attended by over 1,000 delegates. The Congress League Pact was hailed and the gathering was addressed by both Annie Besant and Tilak. On their return journeys, both the leaders made triumphant tours through various parts of North, Central and Eastern India.

The increasing popularity of the Home Rule movement soon attracted the Government's wrath. The Government of Madras was the most harsh and first came out with an order banning students from attending political meetings. This order was universally condemned and Tilak commented : 'The Government is fully aware that the wave of patriotism strikes the students most, and if at all a nation is to prosper, it is through an energetic new generation.'13

*

The turning point in the movement came with the decision of the Government of Madras in June 1917 to place Mrs. Besant and her associates, B.P. Wadia and George Arundale, under arrest. Their internment became the occasion for nation-wide protest. In a dramatic gesture, Sir S. Subramania Aiyar renounced his knighthood. Those who had stayed away, including many Moderate leaders like Madan Mohan Malaviya, Surendranath Banerjea and M.A. Jinnah now enlisted as members of the Home Rule Leagues to record their solidarity with the internees and their condemnation of the Government's action. At a meeting of the AICC on 28 July, 1917, Tilak advocated the use of the weapon of passive resistance or civil disobedience if the Government refused to release the internees. The proposal for adopting passive resistance was sent for comment to all the Provincial Congress Committees, and while Berar and Madras were willing to adopt it immediately, most of the others were in favour of waiting for more time before taking a decision. At Gandhiji's instance, Shankerlal Banker and Jamnadas Dwarkadas collected signatures of one thousand men willing to defy the internment orders and march to Besant's place of detention. They also began to collect signatures of a million peasants and workers on a petition for Home Rule. They made regular visits to Gujarat towns and villages and helped found branches of the League. In short, repression only served to harden the attitude of the agitators and strengthen their resolve to resist the government. Montagu, writing in his Diary, commented: '. . . . Shiva . . . cut his wife into fifty-two pieces only to discover that he had fifty-two wives. This is really what happens to the Government of India when it interns Mrs. Besant.'[14]

The Government in Britain decided to effect a change in policy and adopt a conciliatory posture. The new Secretary of State, Montagu, made a historic declaration in the House of Commons, on 20 August, 1917 in which he stated: 'The policy of His Majesty's Government . . . is that of the increasing association of Indians in every branch of the administration, and the gradual development of self-governing institutions, with a view to the progressive realization of responsible government in India as an integral part of the British Empire.'[15] This statement was in marked contrast to that of Lord Morley who, while introducing the Constitutional Reforms in 1909, had stated categorically that these reforms were in no way intended to lead to self-government. The importance of Montagu's Declaration was that after this the demand for Home Rule or self-government could no longer be treated as seditious.

This did not, however, mean that the British government was about to grant self-government. The accompanying clause in the statement which clarified that the nature and the timing of the advance towards responsible government would be decided by the Government alone gave it enough leeway to prevent any real transfer of power to Indian hands for a long enough time.

In keeping with the conciliatory stance of the Montagu Declaration, Annie Besant was released in September 1917. Annie Besant was at the height of her popularity and, at Tilak's suggestion, was elected President at the annual session of the Congress in December 1917.

*

During 1918, however, various factors combined to diffuse the energies that had concentrated in the agitation for Home Rule. The movement, instead of going forward after its great advance in 1917, gradually dissolved. For one, the Moderates who had joined the movement after Besant's arrest were pacified by the promise of reforms and by Besant's release. They were also put off by the talk of civil disobedience and did not attend the Congress from September 1918 onwards. The publication of the scheme of Government reforms in July 1918 further divided the nationalist ranks. Some wanted to accept it outright and others to reject it outright, while many felt that, though inadequate, they should be given a trial. Annie Besant herself indulged in a lot of vacillation on this question as well as on the question of passive resistance. At times she would disavow passive resistance, and at other times, under pressure from her younger followers, would advocate it. Similarly, she initially, along with Tilak, considered the reforms unworthy of Britain to offer and India to accept, but later argued in favour of acceptance. Tilak was more consistent in his approach, but given Besant's vacillations, and the change in the Moderate stance, there was little that he could do to sustain the movement on his own. Also, towards the end of the year, he decided to go to England to pursue the libel case that he had filed against Valentine Chirol, the author of *Indian Unrest*, and was away for many critical months. With Annie Besant unable to give a firm lead, and Tilak away in England, the movement was left leaderless.

The tremendous achievement of the Home Rule movement and its legacy was that it created a generation of ardent nationalists who formed the backbone of the national movement in the coming years when, under the leadership of the Mahatma, it entered its truly mass phase. The Home Rule Leagues also created organizational links between town and country which were to prove invaluable in later years. And further, by popularizing the idea of Home Rule or self-government, and making it a commonplace thing, it generated a widespread pro-nationalist atmosphere in the country.

By the end of the First World War, in 1918, the new generation of nationalists aroused to political awareness and impatient with the pace of change, were looking for a means of expressing themselves through effective political action. The leaders of the Home Rule League, who themselves were responsible for bringing them to this point, were unable to show the way forward. The stage was thus set for the entry of Mohandas Karamchand Gandhi, a man who had already made a name for himself with his leadership of the struggle of Indians in South Africa and by leading the struggles of Indian peasants and workers in Champaran, Ahmedabad and Kheda. And in March 1919, when he gave a call for a *Satyagraha* to protest against the obnoxious 'Rowlatt' Act, he was the rallying point for almost all those who had been awakened to politics by the Home Rule Movement.

14 Gandhiji's Early Career and Activism

When Mohandas Karamchand Gandhi called for a nation-wide *Satyagraha* against the Rowlatt Act in March 1919, his first attempt at leading an all-India struggle, he was already in his fiftieth year. To understand the man who was about to take over the reins of the Indian national movement and guide its destinies through its most climactic years, it is necessary to begin his story at least twenty-five years earlier, in 1893, when as a twenty-four old barrister, he began the struggle of Indians against racial discrimination in South Africa.

*

The young barrister who landed at Durban in 1893 on a one-year contract to sort out the legal problems of Dada Abdullah, a Gujarati merchant, was to all appearances an ordinary young man trying to make a living. But he was the first Indian barrister, the first highly-educated Indian, to have come to South Africa.

Indian immigration to South Africa had begun in 1890 when the White settlers recruited indentured Indian labour, mainly from South India, to work on the sugar plantations. In their wake had come Indian merchants, mostly Meman Muslims. Ex-indentured labourers, who had settled down in South Africa after the expiry of their contract, and their children, many born in South Africa itself, constituted the third group of Indians that was in South Africa prior to Gandhiji's arrival. None of these groups of Indians had much access to education and certainly very little education in English; even the wealthy merchants often knew only a smattering of English necessary to carry on their trade. The racial discrimination to which they were subjected, as part of their daily existence, they had come to accept as a way of life, and even if they resented it, they had little idea about how to challenge it.

But young Mohandas Gandhi was not used to swallowing racial insults in order to carry on with the business of making a living. He was the son of a *Dewan* (Minister) of an Indian state whose family, though in straitened economic circumstances, was widely respected in his native Kathiawad. Further, he had spent three years in London studying for the Bar. Neither in India nor in England had he ever come in contact with the overt racism that confronted him within days of his arrival in South Africa.

His journey from Durban to Pretoria, which he undertook within a week of his arrival on the continent, consisted of a series of racial humiliations. Apart from the famous incident in which he was bundled out of a first-class compartment by a White man and left to spend the night shivering in the waiting room, he was made to travel in the driver's box in a coach for which he had bought a first-class ticket; when he ignored the coach leader's order to vacate even that seat and sit on the foot-board, he was soundly thrashed. On reaching Johannesburg, he found that all the hotels became full up the moment he asked for a room to stay the night. Having succeeded in securing a first-class train ticket from Johannesburg to Pretoria (after quoting extensively from railway regulations), he was almost pushed out again from his railway compartment and was only saved this humiliation by the intervention of a European passenger.[1]

On his arrival in Pretoria, where he was to work on the civil suit that had brought him to South Africa, he immediately convened a meeting of the Indians there. He offered to teach English to anybody who wanted to learn and suggested that they organize themselves and protest against oppression. He voiced his protest through the press as well. In an indignant letter to the *Natal Advertiser*, he asked: 'Is this Christian-like, is this fair play, is this justice, is this civilization? I pause for a reply.'[2] Even though he had no plans of staying on in South Africa at that stage, he tried his best to arouse the Indians in Pretoria to a sense of their own dignity as human beings and persuade them to resist all types of racial disabilities.

Having settled the law suit for which he had come, Gandhiji prepared to leave for India. But on the eve of his departure from Durban, he raised the issue of the bill to disenfranchise Indians which was in the process of being passed by the Natal legislature. The Indians in South Africa begged Gandhiji to stay on for a month and organize their protest as they could not do so on their own, not knowing even enough English to draft petitions, and so on. Gandhiji agreed to stay on for a month and stayed for twenty years. He was then only twenty-five; when he left, he was forty-five.

Gandhiji's experience in South Africa was unique in one respect. By virtue of being a British-educated barrister, he demanded many things as a matter of right, such as first-class train tickets and rooms in hotels, which other Indians before him had never probably even had the courage to ask for. Perhaps, they believed that they were discriminated against because they were not 'civilized,' that is, 'westernized.' Gandhiji's experience, the first of a westernized Indian in South Africa, demonstrated clearly, to him and to them, that the real cause lay elsewhere, in the assumption of racial superiority by the White rulers.

His uniqueness in being the only western-educated Indian also simultaneously placed on his shoulders the responsibility of leading the struggle of the Indians against increasing racial discrimination. Wealthy Indian merchants, senior to the twenty-five-year-old barrister in experience and age, appointed him as their leader because he was the only one who could speak to the rulers in their own language, the only one who understood the intricacies of their laws and their system of government, the only one who could draft their petitions, create their organizations, and represent them before their rulers.

*

The story of Gandhiji in South Africa is a long one and we present it here in its briefest outline only to highlight the wide experience that Gandhiji had undergone before he came back to India.

Gandhiji's political activities from 1894 to 1906 may be classified as the 'Moderate' phase of the struggle of the South African Indians. During this phase, he concentrated on petitioning and sending memorials to the South African legislatures, the Colonial Secretary in London and the British Parliament. He believed that if all the facts of the case were presented to the Imperial Government, the British sense of justice and fair play would be aroused and the Imperial Government would intervene on behalf of Indians who were, after all, British subjects. His attempt was to unite the different sections of Indians, and to give their demands wide publicity. This he tried to do through the setting up of the Natal Indian Congress and by starting a paper called *Indian Opinion*. Gandhiji's abilities as an organizer, as a fund-raiser, as a journalist and as a propagandist, all came to the fore during this period. But, by 1906, Gandhiji, having fully tried the 'Moderate' methods of struggle, was becoming convinced that these would not lead anywhere.

The second phase of the struggle in South Africa, which began in 1906, was characterized by the use of the method of passive resistance or civil disobedience, which Gandhiji named *Satyagraha*. It was first used when the Government enacted legislation making it compulsory for Indians to take out certificates of registration which held their finger prints. It was essential to carry these on person at all times. At a huge public meeting held on 11 September, 1906, in the Empire Theatre in Johannesburg, Indians resolved that they would refuse to submit to this law and would face the consequences. The Government remained adamant, and so did the Indians. Gandhiji formed the Passive Resistance Association to conduct the campaign. The last date for registration being over, the government started proceedings against Gandhiji and twenty-six others. The passive resisters pleaded guilty, were ordered to leave the country and, on refusing to do so, were sent to jail. Others followed, and their numbers swelled to 155. The fear of jail had disappeared, and it was popularly called King Edward's Hotel.

General Smuts called Gandhiji for talks, and promised to withdraw the legislation if Indians voluntarily agreed to register themselves. Gandhiji accepted and was the first to register. But Smuts had played a trick; he ordered that the voluntary registrations be ratified under the law. The Indians under the leadership of Gandhiji retaliated by publicly burning their registration certificates.

Meanwhile, the Government brought in new legislation, this time to restrict Indian immigration. The campaign widened to oppose this. In August 1908, a number of prominent Indians from Natal crossed the frontier into Transvaal to defy the new immigration laws and were arrested. Other Indians from Transvaal opposed the laws by hawking without a licence; traders who had licences refused to produce them. All of them were jailed. Gandhiji himself landed in jail in October 1908 and, along with the other Indians, was sentenced to a prison term involving hard physical labour and miserable conditions. But imprisonment failed to crush the spirit of the resisters, and the Government resorted to deportation to India, especially of the poorer Indians.

Merchants were pressurized by threats to their economic interests.

At this stage, the movement reached an impasse. The more committed *Satyagrahis* continued to go in and out of jail, but the majority were showing signs of fatigue. The struggle was obviously going to be a protracted one, and the Government was in no mood to relent. Gandhiji's visit to London in 1909 to meet the authorities there yielded little result. The funds for supporting the families of the *Satyagrahis* and for running *Indian Opinion* were fast running out. Gandhiji's own legal practice had virtually ceased since 1906, the year he had started devoting all his attention to the struggle. At this point, Gandhiji set up Tolstoy Farm, made possible through the generosity of his German architect friend, Kallenbach, to house the families of the *Satyagrahis* and give them a way to sustain themselves. Tolstoy Farm was the precursor of the later Gandhian ashrams that were to play so important a role in the Indian national movement. Funds also came from India — Sir Ratan Tata sent Rs. 25,000 and the Congress and the Muslim League, as well as the Nizam of Hyderabad, made their contributions.

In 1911, to coincide with the coronation of King George V, an agreement was reached between the Government and the Indians which, however, lasted only till the end of 1912. Meanwhile, Gokhale paid a visit to South Africa, was treated as a guest of the Government and was made a promise that all discriminatory laws against Indians would be removed. The promise was never kept, and *Satyagraha* was resumed in 1913.

This time the movement was widened further to include resistance to the poll tax of three pounds that was imposed on all ex-indentured Indians. The inclusion of the demand for the abolition of this tax, a particularly heavy charge on poor labourers whose wages hardly averaged ten shillings a month, immediately drew the indentured and ex-indentured labourers into the struggle, and *Satyagraha* could now take on a truly mass character. Further fuel was added to the already raging fire by a judgement of the Supreme Court which invalidated all marriages not conducted according to Christian rites and registered by the Registrar of Marriages. By implication, Hindu, Muslim and Parsi marriages were illegal and the children born through these marriages illegitimate. The Indians treated this judgement as an insult to the honour of their women and many women were drawn into the movement because of this indignity.

Gandhiji decided that the time had now come for the final struggle into which all the resisters resources should be channelled. The campaign was launched by the illegal crossing of the border by a group of sixteen *Satyagrahis*, including Kasturba, Gandhiji's wife, who marched from Phoenix Settlement in Natal to Transvaal, and were immediately arrested. A group of eleven women then marched from Tolstoy Farm in Transvaal and crossed the border into Natal without a permit, and reached New Castle, a mining town. Here, they talked to the Indian mine workers, mostly Tamils, and before being arrested persuaded them to go on strike.

Gandhiji reached New Castle and took charge of the agitation. The employers retaliated by cutting off water and electricity to the workers' quarters, thus forcing them to leave their homes. Gandhiji decided to march this army of over two thousand men, women and children over the border and thus see them lodged in Transvaal jails. During the course of the march, Gandhiji was arrested twice, released, arrested a third time and sent to jail. The morale of the workers, however, was very high and they continued the march till they were put into trains and sent back to Natal, where they were prosecuted and sent to jail. The treatment that was meted out to these brave men and women in jail included starvation and whipping, and being forced to work in the mines by mounted military police. Gandhiji himself was made to dig stones and sweep the compound. He was kept in a dark cell, and taken to court handcuffed and manacled.

The Governments' action inflamed the entire Indian community; workers on the plantations and the mines went on a lightning strike. Gokhale toured the whole of India to arouse Indian public opinion and even the Viceroy, Lord Hardinge, condemned the repression as 'one that would not be tolerated by any country that calls itself civilized'[3] and called for a impartial enquiry into the charges of atrocities. The use of brutal force on unarmed and peaceful men and women aroused widespread indignation and condemnation.

Eventually, through a series of negotiations involving Gandhiji, the Viceroy, Lord Hardinge, C.F. Andrews and General Smuts, an agreement was reached by which the Government of South Africa conceded the major Indian demands relating to the poll tax, the registration certificates and marriages solemnized according to Indian rites, and promised to treat the question of Indian immigration in a sympathetic manner.

*

Non-violent civil disobedience had succeeded in forcing the opponent to the negotiating table and conceding the substance of the demands put forward by the movement. The blueprint for the 'Gandhian' method of struggle had been evolved and Gandhiji started back for his native land. The South African 'experiment' was now to be tried on a much wider scale on the Indian sub-continent.

In other respects, too, the South African experiment prepared Gandhiji for leadership of the Indian national struggle. He had had the invaluable experience of leading poor Indian labourers, of seeing their capacity for sacrifice and for bearing hardship, their morale in the face of repression. South Africa built up his faith in the capacity of the Indian masses to participate in and sacrifice for a cause that moved them.

Gandhiji also had had the opportunity of leading Indians belonging to different religions: Hindus, Muslims, Christians and Parsis were all united under his leadership in South Africa. They also came from different regions, being mainly Gujaratis and Tamils. They belonged to different social classes; rich merchants combined with poor indentured labourers. Women came along with the men.

Another aspect of the South African experience also stood Gandhiji in good stead. He learnt, the hardest way, that leadership involves facing the ire not only of the enemy but also of one's followers. There were two occasions on which Gandhiji was faced with a serious threat to his life. Once, when a white mob chased him down a street in Durban in 1896 and surrounded the house where he was staying, asking for his blood; he had to be whisked out in disguise. The second, when an Indian, a Pathan, who was angry with him because of an agreement he had reached with the Government assaulted him on the street. Gandhiji learnt that leaders often have to take hard decisions that are unpopular with enthusiastic followers.

South Africa, then, provided Gandhiji with an opportunity for evolving his own style of politics and leadership, for trying out new techniques of struggle, on a limited scale, untrammelled by the opposition of contending political currents. In South Africa, he had already taken the movement from its 'Moderate' phase into its 'Gandhian' phase. He already knew the strengths and the weaknesses of the Gandhian method and he was convinced that it was the best method around. It now remained for him to introduce it into India.

*

Gandhiji returned to India, in January 1915, and was warmly welcomed. His work in South Africa was well-known, not only to educated Indians, but, as he discovered on his visit to the Kumbh Mela at Hardwar, even to the masses who flocked to him for his 'darshan.' Gokhale had already hailed him as being 'without doubt made of the stuff of which heroes and martyrs are made.' The veteran Indian leader noticed in Gandhiji an even more important quality: 'He has in him the marvellous spiritual power to turn ordinary men around him into heroes and martyrs.'[4]

On Gokhale's advice, and in keeping with his own style of never intervening in a situation without first studying it with great care, Gandhiji decided that for the first year he would not take a public stand on any political issue. He spent the year travelling around the country, seeing things for himself, and in organizing his ashram in Ahmedabad where he, and his devoted band of followers who had come with him from South Africa, would lead a community life. The next year as well, he continued to maintain his distance from political affairs, including the Home Rule Movement that was gathering momentum at this time. His own political understanding did not coincide with any of the political currents that were active in India then. His faith in 'Moderate' methods was long eroded, nor did he agree with the Home Rulers that the best time to agitate for Home Rule was when the British were in difficulty because of the First World War.

Further, he was deeply convinced that none of these methods of political struggle were really viable; the only answer lay in *Satyagraha*. His reasons for not joining the existing political organizations are best explained in his own words: 'At my time of life and with views firmly formed on several matters, I could only join an organization to affect its policy and not be affected by it. This does not mean that I would not now have an open mind to receive new light. I simply wish to emphasize the fact that the new light will have to be specially dazzling in order to entrance me.'[5] In other words, he could only join an organization or a movement that adopted non-violent *Satyagraha* as its method of struggle.

That did not, however, mean that Gandhiji was going to remain politically idle. During the course of 1917 and early 1918, he was involved in three significant struggles — in Champaran in Bihar, in Ahmedabad and in Kheda in Gujarat. The common feature of these struggles was that they related to specific local issues and that they were fought for the economic demands of the masses. Two of these struggles, Champaran and Kheda, involved the peasants and the one in Ahmedabad involved industrial workers.

*

The story of Champaran begins in the early nineteenth century when European planters had involved the cultivators in agreements that forced them to cultivate indigo on 3/20th of their holdings (known as the *tinkathia* system). Towards the end of the nineteenth century, German synthetic dyes forced indigo out of the market and the European planters of Champaran, keen to release the cultivators from the obligation of cultivating indigo, tried to turn their necessity to their advantage by securing enhancements in rent and other illegal dues as a price for the release. Resistance had surfaced in 1908 as well, but the exactions of the planters continued till Raj Kumar Shukla, a local man, decided to follow Gandhiji all over the country to persuade him to come to Champaran to investigate the problem. Raj Kumar Shukla's decision to get Gandhiji to Champaran is indicative of the image he had acquired as one who fought for the rights of the exploited and the poor.

Gandhiji, on reaching Champaran, was ordered by the Commissioner to immediately leave the district. But to the surprise of all concerned, Gandhiji refused and preferred to take the punishment for his defiance of the law. This was unusual, for even Tilak and Annie Besant, when externed from a particular province, obeyed the orders even though they organized public protests against them. To offer passive resistance or civil disobedience to an unjust order was indeed novel. The Government of India, not willing to make an issue of it and not yet used to treating Gandhiji as a rebel, ordered the local Government to retreat and allow Gandhiji to proceed with his enquiry.

A victorious Gandhiji embarked on his investigation of the peasants' grievances. Here, too, his method was striking. He and his colleagues, who now included Brij Kishore, Rajendra Prasad and other members of the Bihar intelligentsia, Mahadev Desai and Narhari Parikh, two young men from Gujarat who had thrown in their lot with Gandhiji, and J.B.Kripalani, toured the villages and from dawn to dusk recorded the statements of peasants, interrogating them to make sure that they were giving correct information.

Meanwhile, the Government appointed a Commission of Inquiry to go into the whole issue, and nominated Gandhiji as one of its members. Armed with evidence collected from 8,000 peasants, he had little difficulty in convincing the Commission that the *tinkathia* system needed to be abolished and that the peasants should be compensated for the illegal enhancement of their dues. As a compromise with the planters, he agreed that they refund only twenty-five per cent of the money they had taken illegally from the peasants. Answering critics who asked why he did not ask for a full refund, Gandhiji explained that even this refund had done enough damage to the planters' prestige and position. As was often the case, Gandhiji's assessment was correct and, within a decade, the planters left the district altogether.

*

Gandhiji then turned his attention to the workers of Ahmedabad. A dispute was brewing between them and the mill owners over the question of a 'plague bonus' the employers wanted to withdraw once the epidemic had passed but the workers insisted it stay, since the enhancement hardly compensated for the rise in the cost of living during the War. The British Collector, who feared a showdown, asked Gandhiji to bring pressure on the mill owners and work out a compromise. Ambalal Sarabhai, one of the leading mill owners of the town, was a friend of Gandhiji, and had just saved the Sabarmati Ashram from extinction by a generous donation. Gandhiji persuaded the mill owners and the workers to agree to arbitration by a tribunal, but the mill owners, taking advantage of a stray strike, withdrew from the agreement. They offered a twenty per cent bonus and threatened to dismiss those who did not accept it.

The breach of agreement was treated by Gandhiji as a very serious affair, and he advised the workers to go on strike. He further suggested, on the basis of a thorough study of the production costs and profits of the industry as well as the cost of living, that they would be justified in demanding a thirty-five per cent increase in wages.

The strike began and Gandhiji addressed the workers every day on the banks of the Sabarmati River. He brought out a daily news bulletin, and insisted that no violence be used against employers or blacklegs. Ambalal Sarabhai's sister, Anasuya Behn, was one of the main lieutenants of Gandhiji in this struggle in which her brother, and Gandhiji's friend, was one of the main adversaries.

After some days, the workers began to exhibit signs of weariness. The attendance at the daily meetings began to decline and the attitude towards blacklegs began to harden. In this situation, Gandhiji decided to go on a fast to rally the workers and strengthen their resolve to continue. Also, he had promised that if the strike led to starvation he would be the first to starve, and the fast was a fulfilment of that promise. The fast, however, also had the effect of putting pressure on the mill owners and they agreed to submit the whole issue to a tribunal. The strike was withdrawn and the tribunal later awarded the thirty-five percent increase the workers had demanded.

*

The dispute in Ahmedabad had not yet ended when Gandhiji learnt that the peasants of Kheda district were in extreme distress due to a failure of crops, and that their appeals for the remission of land revenue were being ignored by the Government. Enquiries by members of the Servants of India Society, Vithalbhai Patel and Gandhiji confirmed the validity of the peasants' case. This was that as the crops were less than one-fourth of the normal yield, they were entitled under the revenue code to a total remission of the land revenue.

The *Gujarat Sabha*, of which Gandhiji was the President, played a leading role in the agitation. Appeals and petitions having failed, Gandhiji advised the withholding of revenue, and asked the peasants to 'fight unto death against such a spirit of vindictiveness and tyranny,'[6] and show that 'it is impossible to govern men without their consent.'[7] Vallabhbhai Patel, a young lawyer and a native of Kheda district, and other young men, including Indulal Yagnik, joined Gandhiji in touring the villages and urging the peasants to stand firm in the face of increasing government repression which included the seizing of cattle and household goods and the attachment of standing crops. The cultivators were asked to take a solemn pledge that they would not pay; those who could afford to pay were to take a vow that they would not pay in the interests of the poorer ryots who would otherwise panic and sell off their belongings or incur debts in order to pay the revenue. However, if the Government agreed to suspend collection of land revenue, the ones who could afford to do so could pay the whole amount .

The peasants of Kheda, already hard pressed because of plague, high prices and drought, were beginning to show signs of weakness when

Gandhiji came to know that the Government had issued secret instructions directing that revenue should be recovered only from those peasants who could pay. A public declaration of this decision would have meant a blow to government prestige, since this was exactly what Gandhiji had been demanding. In these circumstances, the movement was withdrawn. Gandhiji later recalled that by this time 'the people were exhausted' and he was actually 'casting about for some graceful way of terminating the struggle. . . '8

Champaran, Ahmedabad and Kheda served as demonstrations of Gandhiji's style and method of politics to the country at large. They also helped him find his feet among the people of India and study their problems at close quarters. He came to possess, as a result of these struggles, a surer understanding of the strengths and weaknesses of the masses, as well as of the viability of his own political style. He also earned the respect and commitment of many political workers, especially the younger ones, who were impressed by his identification with the problems of ordinary Indians, and his willingness to take up their cause.

*

It was this reservoir of goodwill, and of experience, that encouraged Gandhiji, in February 1919, to call for a nation-wide protest against the unpopular legislation that the British were threatening to introduce. Two bills, popularly known as the Rowlatt Bills after the man who chaired the Committee that suggested their introduction, aimed at severely curtailing the civil liberties of Indians in the name of curbing terrorist violence, were introduced in the Legislative Council. One of them was actually pushed through in indecent haste in the face of opposition from all the elected Indian members. This act of the Government was treated by the whole of political India as a grievous insult, especially as it came at the end of the War when substantial constitutional concessions were expected.

Constitutional protest having failed, Gandhiji stepped in and suggested that a *Satyagraha* be launched. A *Satyagraha Sabha* was formed, and the younger members of the Home Rule Leagues who were more than keen to express their disenchantment with the Government flocked to join it. The old lists of the addresses of Home Rule Leagues and their members were taken out, contacts established and propaganda begun.

The form of protest finally decided upon was the observance of a nation-wide *hartal* (strike) accompanied by fasting and prayer. In addition, it was decided that civil disobedience would be offered against specific laws.

The sixth of April was fixed as the date on which the *Satyagraha* would be launched. The movement that emerged was very different from the one that had been anticipated or planned. Delhi observed the *hartal* on 30 March because of some confusion about dates, and there was considerable violence in the streets. This seemed to set the pattern in most other areas that responded to the call; protest was generally accompanied by violence and disorder. Punjab, which was suffering from the after-effects of severe war-time repression, forcible recruitment, and the ravages of disease, reacted particularly strongly and both in Amritsar and Lahore the situation became very dangerous for the Government. Gandhiji tried to go to Punjab to help quieten the people, but the Government deported him to Bombay. He found that Bombay and even his native Gujarat, including Ahmedabad, were up in flames and he decided to stay and try and pacify the people.

Events in Punjab were moving in a particularly tragic direction. In Amritsar, the arrest of two local leaders on 10 April led to an attack on the town hall and the post office; telegraph wires were cut and Europeans including women were attacked. The army was called in and the city handed over to General Dyer, who issued an order prohibiting public meetings and assemblies. On 13 April, *Baisakhi* day, a large crowd of people, many of whom were visitors from neighbouring villages who had come to the town to attend the *Baisakhi* celebrations, collected in the Jallianwala Bagh to attend a public meeting. General Dyer, incensed that his orders were disobeyed, ordered his troops to fire upon the unarmed crowd. The shooting continued for ten minutes. General Dyer had not thought it necessary to issue any warning to the people nor was he deterred by the fact that the ground was totally hemmed in from all sides by high walls which left little chance for escape. The Government estimate was 379 dead, other estimates were considerably higher.

The brutality at Jallianwala Bagh stunned the entire nation. The response would come, not immediately, but a little later. For the moment, repression was intensified, Punjab placed under martial law and the people of Amritsar forced into indignities such as crawling on their bellies before Europeans. Gandhiji, overwhelmed by the total atmosphere of violence, withdrew the movement on 18 April.

That did not mean, however, that Gandhiji had lost faith either in his non-violent *Satyagraha* or in the capacity of the Indian people to adopt it as a method of struggle. A year later, he launched another nation-wide struggle, on a scale bigger than that of the Rowlatt *Satyagraha*. The wrong inflicted on Punjab was one of the major reasons for launching it.

The Mahatma's 'Indian Experiment' had begun.

15 The Non-Cooperation Movement — 1920-22

The last year of the second decade of the twentieth century found India highly discontented. With much cause. The Rowlatt Act, the Jallianwala Bagh massacre and martial law in Punjab had belied all the generous war-time promises of the British. The Montagu-Chelmsford Reforms, announced towards the end of 1919, with their ill-considered scheme of dyarchy satisfied few. The Indian Muslims were incensed when they discovered that their loyalty had been purchased during the War by assurances of generous treatment of Turkey after the War — a promise British statesman had no intention of fulfilling. The Muslims regarded the Caliph of Turkey as their spiritual head and were naturally upset when they found that he would retain no control over the holy places it was his duty as Caliph to protect. Even those who were willing to treat the happenings at Jallianwala Bagh and other places in Punjab as aberrations, that would soon be 'corrected', were disillusioned when they discovered that the Hunter Committee appointed by the Government to enquire into the Punjab disturbances was an eye wash and that the House of Lords had voted in favour of General Dyer's action, and that the British public had demonstrated its support by helping the Morning Post collect 30,000 pounds for General Dyer.

By the end of the first quarter of 1920, all the excuses in favour of the British Government were fast running out. The Khilafat leaders were told quite clearly that they should not expect anything more and the Treaty of Sevres signed with Turkey in May 1920 made it amply clear that the dismemberment of the Turkish Empire was complete. Gandhiji, who had been in close touch with the Khilafat leaders for quite some time, and was a special invitee to the Khilafat Conference in November 1919, had all along been very sympathetic to their cause, especially because he felt the British had committed a breach of faith by making promises that they had no intention of keeping. In February 1920, he suggested to the Khilafat Committee that it adopt a programme of non-violent non-cooperation to protest the Governments behaviour. On 9 June 1920, the Khilafat Committee at Allahabad unanimously accepted the suggestion of non-cooperation and asked Gandhiji to lead the movement.

Meanwhile, the Congress was becoming sceptical of any possibility of political advance through constitutional means. It was disgusted with the Hunter Committee Report especially since it was appraised of brutalities in Punjab by its own enquiry committee. In the circumstances, it agreed to consider non-cooperation. The AICC met in May 1920 and decided to convene a special session in September to enable the Congress to decide on its course of action.

It was apparent they had to work out something soon for it was clear that the people were chafing for action. Large numbers of them, who had been awakened to political consciousness by the incessant propaganda efforts that the nationalist leadership had been making for the previous four decades or more, were thoroughly outraged by what they perceived as insults by the British government. To swallow these insults appeared dishonourable and cowardly. Also many sections of Indian society suffered considerable economic distress. In the towns, the workers and artisans, the lower middle class and the middle class had been hit by high prices, and shortage of food and essential commodities. The rural poor and peasants were in addition victims of widespread drought and epidemics.

*

The movement was launched formally on 1 August, 1920, after the expiry of the notice that Gandhiji had given to the Viceroy in his letter of 22 June, in which he had asserted the right recognized 'from time immemorial of the subject to refuse to assist a ruler who misrules.'[1] Lokamanya Tilak passed away in the early hours of 1 August, and the day of mourning and of launching of the movement merged as people all over the country observed *hartal* and took out processions. Many kept a fast and offered prayers.

The Congress met in September at Calcutta and accepted non-co oper-ation as its own. The main opposition, led by C.R. Das, was to the boycott of legislative councils, elections to which were to be held very soon. But even those who disagreed with the idea of boycott accepted the Congress discipline and withdrew from the elections. The voters, too, largely stayed away.

By December, when the Congress met for its annual session at Nagpur, the opposition had melted away; the elections were over and, therefore, the boycott of councils was a non-issue, and it was C.R. Das who moved the main resolution on non-cooperation. The programme of non-cooperation included within its ambit the surrender of titles and hon-ours, boycott of government affiliated schools and colleges, law courts, foreign cloth, and could be extended to include resignation from govern-ment service and mass civil disobedience including the non-payment of taxes. National schools and colleges were to be set up, panchayats were to be established for settling disputes, hand-spinning and weaving was to be encouraged and people were asked to maintain Hindu-Muslim unity, give up untouchability and observe strict non-violence. Gandhiji prom-ised that if the programme was fully implemented, *Swaraj* would be ushered in within the year. The Nagpur session, thus, committed the Congress to a programme of extra-constitutional mass action. Many groups of revolutionary terrorists, especially in Bengal, also pledged support to the movement.

To enable the Congress to fulfill its new commitment, significant changes were introduced in its creed as well as in its organizational struc-ture. The goal of the Congress was changed from the attainment of self-Government by constitutional and legal means to the attainment of *Swaraj* by peaceful and legitimate means. The new constitution of the Congress, the handiwork of Gandhiji, introduced other important changes.

The Congress was now to have a Working Committee of fifteen members to look after its day-to-day affairs. This proposal, when first made by Tilak in 1916, had been shot down by the Moderate opposition. Gandhiji, too, knew that the Congress could not guide a sustained move-ment unless it had a compact body that worked round the year. Provincial Congress Committees were now to be organized on a linguis-tic basis, so that they could keep in touch with the people by using the local language. The Congress organization was to reach down to the village and the *mohalla* level by the formation of village and mohalla or ward committees. The membership fee was reduced to four annas per year to enable the poor to become members. Mass involvement would also enable the Congress to have a regular source of income. In other ways, too, the organizational structure was both streamlined and democratized. The Congress was to use Hindi as far as possible.

*

The adoption of the Non-Cooperation Movement (initiated earlier by the Khilafat Conference) by the Congress gave it a new energy and, from January 1921, it began to register considerable success all over the country. Gandhiji, along with the Ali brothers (who were the foremost Khilafat leaders), undertook a nation-wide tour during which he addressed hundreds of meetings and met a large number of political workers. In the first month itself, thousands of students (90000 according to one estimate) left schools and colleges and joined more than 800 national schools and colleges that had sprung up all over the country. The educational boycott was particularly successful in Bengal, where the students in Calcutta triggered off a province-wide strike to force the managements of their institutions to disaffiliate themselves from the Government. C.R.Das played a major role in promoting the movement and Subhas Bose became the principal of the National College in Calcutta. The Swadeshi spirit was revived with new vigour, this time as part of a nation-wide struggle. Punjab, too, responded to the educational boycott and was second only to Bengal, Lala Lajpat Rai playing a leading part here despite his initial reservations about this item of the programme. Other areas that were active were Bombay, U.P., Bihar, Orissa and Assam. Madras remained lukewarm.

The boycott of law courts by lawyers was not as successful as the educational boycott, but it was very dramatic and spectacular. Many leading lawyers of the country, like C.R. Das, Motilal Nehru, M.R.Jayakar, Saifuddin Kitchlew, Vallabhbhai Patel, C. Rajagopalachari, T.Prakasam and Asaf Ali gave up lucrative practices, and their sacrifice became a source of inspiration for many. In numbers again Bengal led, followed by Andhra Pradesh, U.P., Karnataka and Punjab.

But, perhaps, the most successful item of the programme was the boycott of foreign cloth. Volunteers would go from house to house collecting clothes made of foreign cloth, and the entire community would collect to light a bonfire of the goods. Prabhudas Gandhi, who accompanied Mahatma Gandhi on his nation-wide tour in the first part of 1921, recalls how at small way-side stations where their train would stop for a few minutes, Gandhiji would persuade the crowd, assembled to greet him, to at least discard their head dress on the spot. Immediately, a pile of caps, *dupattas*, and turbans would form and as the train moved out they would see the flames leaping upwards.[2] Picketing of shops selling foreign cloth was also a major form of the boycott. The value of imports of foreign cloth fell from Rs. 102 crore in 1920-21 to Rs. 57 crore in 1921-22. Another feature of the movement which acquired great popularity in many parts of the country, even though it was not part of the original plan, was the picketing of toddy shops. Government revenues showed considerable decline on this count and the government was forced to actually carry on propaganda to bring home to the people the healthy effects of a good drink.

The Government of Bihar and Orissa even compiled and circulated a list of all the great men in history (which included Moses, Alexander, Julius Caeser, Napoleon, Shakespeare, Gladstone, Tennyson and Bismarck) who enjoyed their liquor.

The AICC, at its session at Vijayawada in March 1921, directed that for the next three months Congressmen should concentrate on collection of funds, enrolment of members and distribution of *charkhas*. As a result, a vigorous membership drive was launched and though the target of one crore members was not achieved, Congress membership reached a figure roughly of 50 lakhs. The Tilak Swaraj Fund was oversubscribed, exceeding the target of rupees one crore. Charkhas were popularized on a wide scale and khadi became the uniform of the national movement. There was a complaint at a students meeting Gandhiji addressed in Madurai that khadi was too costly. Gandhiji retorted that the answer lay in wearing less clothes and, from that day, discarded his *dhoti* and *kurta* in favour of a *langot*.[3] For the rest of his life, he remained a 'half-naked fakir.'

In July 1921, a new challenge was thrown to the Government. Mohammed Ali, at the All India Khilafat Conference held at Karachi on 8 July, declared that it was 'religiously unlawful for the Muslims to continue in the British Army' and asked that this be conveyed to every Muslim in the Army.[4] As a result, Mohammed Ali, along with other leaders, was immediately arrested. In protest, the speech was repeated at innumerable meetings all over the country. On 4 October, forty-seven leading Congressmen, including Gandhiji, issued a manifesto repeating whatever Mohammed Ali had said and added that every civilian and member of the armed forces should sever connections with the repressive Government. The next day, the Congress Working Committee passed a similar resolution, and on 16 October, Congress committees all over the country held meetings at which the same resolution was adopted. The Government was forced to ignore the whole incident, and accept the blow to its prestige.

The next dramatic event was the visit of the Prince of Wales which began on 17 November, 1921. The day the Prince landed in Bombay was observed as a day of hartal all over the country. In Bombay, Gandhiji himself addressed a mammoth meeting in the compound of the Elphinstone Mill owned by the nationalist Umar Shobhani, and lighted a huge bonfire of foreign cloth. Unfortunately, however, clashes occurred between those who had gone to attend the welcome function and the crowd returning from Gandhiji's meeting. Riots followed , in which Parsis, Christians, Anglo-Indians became special targets of attack as identifiable loyalists. There was police firing, and the three-day turmoil resulted in fifty-nine dead. Peace returned only after Gandhiji had been on fast for three days. The whole sequence of events left Gandhiji profoundly disturbed and worried about the likelihood of recurrence of violence once mass civil disobedience was sanctioned.

The Prince of Wales was greeted with empty streets and downed shutters wherever he went. Emboldened by their successful defiance of the Government, non-cooperators became more and more aggressive. The Congress Volunteer Corps emerged as a powerful parallel police, and the sight of its members marching in formation and dressed in uniform was hardly one that warmed the Government's heart. The Congress had already granted permission to the PCCs to sanction mass civil disobedience wherever they thought the people were ready and in some areas, such as Midnapur district in Bengal, which had started a movement against Union Board Taxes[5],and Chirala-Pirala and Pedanandipadu taluqa in Guntur district of Andhra, no-tax movements were already in the offing.[6]

The Non-Cooperation Movement had other indirect effects as well. In the Avadh area of U.P., where kisan sabhas and a kisan movement had been gathering strength since 1918, Non-cooperation propaganda, carried on among others by Jawaharlal Nehru, helped to fan the already existing ferment, and soon it became difficult to distinguish between a Non-cooperation meeting and a kisan meeting.[7]In Malabar in Kerala, Non-cooperation and Khilafat propaganda helped to rouse the Muslim tenants against their landlords, but the movement here, unfortunately, at times took on a communal colour.[8]

In Assam, labourers on tea plantations went on strike. When the fleeing workers were fired upon, there were strikes on the steamer service, and on the Assam-Bengal Railway as well. J.M. Sengupta, the Bengali nationalist leader, played a leading role in these developments. In Midnapur, a cultivators' strike against a White zamindari company was led by a Calcutta medical student. Defiance of forest laws became popular in Andhra. Peasants and tribals in some of the Rajasthan states began movements for securing better conditions of life. In Punjab, the Akali movement for wresting control of the gurdwaras from the corrupt mahants (priests) was a part of the general movement of Non-cooperation, and the Akalis observed strict non-violence in the face of tremendous repression. [9]. The examples could be multiplied, but the point is that the spirit of unrest and defiance of authority engendered by the Non-Cooperation movement contributed to the rise of many local movements in different parts of the country, movements which did not often adhere strictly either to the programme of the Non-Cooperation Movement or even to the policy of non-violence.

*

In this situation, it was hardly surprising that the Government came to the conclusion that its earlier policy had not met with success and that the time to strike had arrived. In September 1920, at the beginning of the movement, the Government had thought it best to leave it alone as repression would only make martyrs of the nationalists and fan the spirit of revolt. In May 1921, it had tried, through the Gandhi-Reading talks, to persuade Gandhiji to ask the Ali brothers to withdraw from their speeches those passages that contained suggestions of violence; this was an attempt to drive a wedge between the Khilafat leaders and Gandhiji, but it failed. By December, the Government felt that things were really going too far and announced a change of policy by declaring the Volunteers Corps illegal and arresting all those who claimed to be its members.

C.R. Das was among the first to be arrested, followed by his wife Basantidebi, whose arrest so incensed the youth of Bengal that thousands came forward to court arrest. In the next two months, over 30,000 people were arrested from all over the country, and soon only Gandhiji out of the top leadership remained out of jail. In mid-December, there was an abortive attempt at negotiations, initiated by Malaviya, but the conditions offered were such that it meant sacrificing the Khilafat leaders, a course that Gandhiji would not accept. In any case, the Home Government had already decided against a settlement and ordered the Viceroy, Lord Reading, to withdraw from the negotiations. Repression continued, public meetings and assemblies were banned, newspapers gagged, and midnight raids on Congress and Khilafat offices became common.

Gandhiji had been under considerable pressure from the Congress rank and file as well as the leadership to start the phase of mass civil disobedience. The Ahmedabad session of the Congress in December 1921 had appointed him the sole authority on the issue. The Government showed no signs of relenting and had ignored both the appeal of the All-Parties Conference held in mid-January 1922 as well as Gandhiji's letter to the Viceroy announcing that, unless the Government lifted the ban on civil liberties and released political prisoners, he would be forced to go ahead with mass civil disobedience. The Viceroy was unmoved and, left with no choice, Gandhiji announced that mass civil disobedience would begin in Bardoli taluqa of Surat district, and that all other parts of the country should cooperate by maintaining total discipline and quiet so that the entire attention of the movement could be concentrated on Bardoli. But Bardoli was destined to wait for another six years before it could launch a no-tax movement. Its fate was decided by the action of members of a Congress and Khilafat procession in Chauri Chaura in Gorakhpur district of U.P. on 5 February 1922. Irritated by the behaviour of some policemen, a section of the crowd attacked them. The police opened fire. At this, the entire procession attacked the police and when the latter hid inside the police station, set fire to the building. Policemen who tried to escape were hacked to pieces and thrown into the fire. In all twenty-two policemen were done to death. On hearing of the incident, Gandhiji decided to withdraw the movement. He also persuaded the Congress Working Committee to ratify his decision and thus, on 12 February 1922, the Non-Cooperation Movement came to an end.

*

Gandhijis decision to withdraw the movement in response to the violence at Chauri Chaura raised a controversy whose heat can still be felt in staid academic seminars and sober volumes of history. Motilal Nehru, C.R. Das, Jawaharlal Nehru, Subhas Bose, and many others have recorded their utter bewilderment on hearing the news. They could not understand why the whole country had to pay the price for the crazy behaviour of some people in a remote village. Many in the country thought that the Mahatma had failed miserably as a leader and that his days of glory were over.

Many later commentators, following the tradition established by R. Palme Dutt in *India Today* [10], have continued to condemn the decision taken by Gandhiji, and seen in it proof of the Mahatma's concern for the propertied classes of Indian society. Their argument is that Gandhiji did not withdraw the movement simply because of his belief in the necessity of non-violence. He withdrew it because the action at Chauri Chaura was a symbol and an indication of the growing militancy of the Indian masses, of their growing radicalization, of their willingness to launch an attack on the status quo of property relations. Frightened by this radical possibility and by the prospect of the movement going out of his hands and into the hands of radical forces, and in order to protect the interests of landlords and capitalists who would inevitably be at the receiving end of this violence, Gandhiji cried halt to the movement. They have found supportive proof in the resolution of the Congress Working Committee of 12 February 1922 popularly known as the Bardoli resolution which, while announcing the withdrawal, asked the peasants to pay taxes and tenants to pay rents. This, they say, was the real though hidden motive behind the historic decision of February 1922.

It seems, however, that Gandhiji's critics have been less than fair to him. First, the argument that violence in a remote village could not be a sufficient cause for the decision is in itself a weak one. Gandhiji had repeatedly warned that he did not even want any non-violent movement in any other part of the country while he was conducting mass civil disobedience in Bardoli, and in fact had asked the Andhra PCC to withdraw the permission that it had granted to some of the District Congress Committees to start civil disobedience. One obvious reason for this was that, in such a situation of mass ferment and activity, the movement might easily take a violent turn, either due to its own volatile nature or because of provocation by the authorities concerned (as had actually happened in Bombay in November 1921 and later in Chauri Chaura); also if violence occurred anywhere it could easily be made the excuse by the Government to launch a massive attack on the movement as a whole. The Government could always cite the actual violence in one part as proof of the likelihood of violence in another part of the country, and thus justify its repression. This would upset the whole strategy of non-violent civil disobedience which was based on the principle that the forces of repression would always stand exposed since they would be using armed force against peaceful civil resisters. It was, therefore, not enough to assert that there was no connection between Chauri Chaura and Bardoli.

It is entirely possible that in Gandhiji's assessment the chances of his being allowed to conduct a mass civil disobedience campaign in Bardoli had receded further after Chauri Chaura. The Government would have had excuse to remove him and other activists from the scene and use force to cow down the people. Mass civil disobedience would be defeated even before it was given a fair trial. By taking the onus of withdrawal on himself and on the Working Committee, Gandhiji was protecting the movement from likely repression, and the people from demoralization. True, the withdrawal itself led to considerable demoralization, especially of the active political workers, but it is likely that the repression and crushing of the movement (as happened in 1932) would have led to even greater demoralization. Perhaps, in the long run, it was better to have felt that, if only Gandhiji had not withdrawn the movement, it would have surged forward, than to see it crushed and come to the conclusion that it was not possible for a mass movement to succeed in the face of government repression. It is necessary to remember that, after all, the Non-Cooperation Movement was the first attempt at an all-India mass struggle against the British, and a serious reverse at this elementary stage could have led to a prolonged period of demoralization and passivity.

The other argument that the real motive for withdrawal was the fear of the growth of radical forces and that Chauri Chaura was proof of the emergence of precisely such a radical sentiment is on even thinner ground. The crowd at Chauri Chaura had not demonstrated any intention of attacking landlords or overturning the structure of property relations, they were merely angered by the overbearing behaviour of policemen and vented their wrath by attacking them. Peasant unrest in most of Avadh and Malabar had died out long before this time, and the Eka movement that was on in some of the rural areas of Avadh showed no signs of wanting to abolish the *zamindari* system; it only wanted zamindars to stop 'illegal' cesses and arbitrary rent enhancements. In fact, one of the items of the oath that was taken by peasants who joined the Eka movement was that they would 'pay rent regularly at Kharif and Rabi.'[11] The no-tax movement in Guntur was very much within the framework of the Non-Cooperation Movement; it was directed against the government and remained totally peaceful. Moreover, it was already on the decline before February 1922.[12] It is difficult to discern where the threat from radical tendencies is actually located.

That the Bardoli resolution which announced the withdrawal also contained clauses which asked peasants to pay up taxes and tenants to pay up rents, and assured zamindars that the Congress had no intention of depriving them of their rights, is also no proof of hidden motives. The Congress had at no stage during the movement sanctioned non-payment of rent or questioned the rights of zamindars; the resolution was merely a reiteration of its position on this issue. Non-payment of taxes was obviously to cease if the movement as a whole was being withdrawn.

There are also some indications that Gandhiji's decision may have been prompted by the fact that in many parts of the country, by the second half of 1921, the movement had shown clear signs of being on the ebb. Students had started drifting back to schools and colleges, lawyers and litigants to law courts, the commercial classes showed signs of weariness and worry at the accumulating stocks of foreign cloth, attendance at meetings and rallies had dwindled, both in the urban and rural areas. This does not mean that in some pockets, like Bardoli in Gujarat or Guntur in Andhra, where intensive political work had been done, the masses were not ready to carry on the struggle. But the mass enthusiasm that was evident all over the country in the first part of 1921 had, perhaps, receded. The cadre and the active political workers were willing to carry on the fight, but a mass movement of such a nature required the active participation of the masses, and not only of the highly motivated among them. However, at the present stage of research, it is not possible to argue this position with great force; we only wish to urge the possibility that this too was among the factors that led to the decision to withdraw.

Gandhiji's critics often fail to recognize that mass movements have an inherent tendency to ebb after reaching a certain height, that the capacity of the masses to withstand repression, endure suffering and make sacrifice is not unlimited, that a time comes when breathing space is required to consolidate, recuperate, and gather strength for the next round of struggle, and that, therefore, withdrawal or a shift to a phase of non-confrontation is an inherent part of a strategy of political action that is based on the masses. Withdrawal is not tantamount to betrayal; it is an inevitable part of the strategy itself.

Of course, whether or not the withdrawal was made at the correct time can always be a matter open to debate. But perhaps Gandhiji had enough reasons to believe that the moment he chose was the right one. The movement had already gone on for over a year, the government was in no mood for negotiations, and Chauri Chaura presented an opportunity to retreat with honour, before the internal weaknesses of the movement became apparent enough to force a surrender or make the retreat look like a rout.

*

Gandhiji had promised Swaraj within a year if his programme was adopted. But the year was long over, the movement was withdrawn, and there was no sign of Swaraj or even of any tangible concessions. Had it all been in vain? Was the movement a failure?

One could hardly answer in the affirmative. The Non-Cooperation Movement had in fact succeeded on many counts. It certainly demonstrated that it commanded the support and sympathy of vast sections of the Indian people. After Non-cooperation, the charge of representing a 'microscopic minority,' made by the Viceroy, Dufferin, in 1888,[13] could never again be hurled at the Indian National Congress. Its reach among many sections of Indian peasants, workers, artisans, shopkeepers, traders, professionals, white-collar employees, had been demonstrated. The spatial spread of the movement was also nation-wide. Some areas were more active than others, but there were few that showed no signs of activity at all.

The capacity of the 'poor dumb millions' of India to take part in modern nationalist politics was also demonstrated. By their courage, sacrifice, and fortitude in the face of adversity and repression, they dispelled the notion that the desire for national freedom was the preserve of the educated and the rich and showed that it was an elemental urge common to all members of a subject nation. They may not as yet have fully comprehended all its implications, understood all the arguments put forth in its favour or observed all the discipline that the movement demanded for its successful conduct. This was, after all, for many of them, their first contact with the modern world of nationalist politics and the modern ideology of nationalism. This was the first time that nationalists from the towns, students from schools and colleges or even the educated and politically aware in the villages had made a serious attempt to bring the ideology and the movement into their midst. Its success was bound to be limited, the weaknesses many. There were vast sections of the masses that even then remained outside the ambit of the new awakening. But this was only the beginning and more serious and consistent efforts were yet in the offing. But the change was striking.

The tremendous participation of Muslims in the movement, and the maintenance of communal unity, despite the Malabar developments, was in itself no mean achievement. There is hardly any doubt that it was Muslim participation that gave the movement its truly mass character in many areas; at some places two-thirds of those arrested were Muslims. And it was, indeed, unfortunate that this most positive feature of the movement was not to be repeated in later years once communalism began to take its toll. The fraternization that was witnessed between Hindus and Muslims, with Gandhiji and other Congress leaders speaking from mosques, Gandhiji being allowed to address meetings of Muslim women in which he was the only male who was not blind-folded, all these began to look like romantic dreams in later years.

*

The retreat that was ordered on 12 February, 1922 was only a temporary one. The battle was over, but the war would continue. To the challenge thrown by Montagu and Birkenhead that 'India would not challenge with success the most determined people in the world, who would once again answer the challenge with all the vigour and determination at its command,'[14] Gandhiji, in an article written in Young India on 23 February 1922 *after* the withdrawal of the movement, replied: 'It is high time that the British people were made to realize that the fight that was commenced in 1920 is a fight to the finish, whether it lasts one month or one year or many months or many years and whether the representatives of Britain re-enact all the indescribable orgies of the Mutiny days with redoubled force or whether they do not.'[15]

16 *Peasant Movements and Nationalism in the 1920s*

Peasant discontent against established authority was a familiar feature of the nineteenth century. But in the twentieth century, the movements that emerged out of this discontent were marked by a new feature: they were deeply influenced by and in their turn had a marked impact on the ongoing struggle for national freedom. To illustrate the complex nature of this relationship, we will recount the story of three important peasant struggles that emerged in the second and third decade of the country: The *kisan sabha* and Eka movements in Avadh in U.P., the Mappila rebellion in Malabar and the Bardoli *Satyagraha* in Gujarat.

*

Following the annexation of Avadh in 1856, the second half of the nineteenth century had seen the strengthening of the hold of the *taluqdars* or big landlords over the agrarian society of the province. This had led to a situation in which exorbitant rents, illegal levies, renewal fees or *nazrana*, and arbitrary ejectments or *bedakhli* had made life miserable for the majority of the cultivators. The high price of food and other necessities that accompanied and followed World War I made the oppression all the more difficult to bear, and the tenants of Avadh were ripe for a message of resistance.

It was the more active members of the Home Rule League in U.P. who initiated the process of the organization of the peasants of the province on modern lines into *kisan sabhas*. The U.P. *Kisan Sabha* was set up in February 1918 through the efforts of Gauri Shankar Misra and Indra Narain Dwivedi, and with the support of Madan Mohan Malaviya. The U.P. *Kisan Sabha* demonstrated considerable activity, and by June 1919 had established at least 450 branches in 173 tehsils of the province. A consequence of this activity was that a large number of *kisan* delegates from U.P. attended the Delhi and Amritsar sessions of the Indian National Congress in December 1918 and 1919.

Towards the end of 1919, the first signs of grass-roots peasant activity were evident in the reports of a *nai-dhobi* band (a form of social boycott) on an estate in Pratapgarh district. By the summer of 1920, in the villages of *taluqdari* Avadh, *kisan* meetings called by village panchayats became frequent. The names of Jhinguri Singh and Durgapal Singh were associated with this development. But soon another leader, who became famous by the name of Baba Ramchandra, emerged as the rallying point.

Baba Ramachandra, a Brahmin from Maharashtra, was a wanderer who had left home at the age of thirteen, done a stint as an indentured labourer in Fiji and finally turned up in Fyzabad in U.P. in 1909. Till 1920, he had wandered around as a *sadhu*, carrying a copy of Tulsidas' *Ramayan* on his back, from which he would often recite verses to rural audiences. In the middle of 1920, however, he emerged as a leader of the peasants of Avadh, and soon demonstrated considerable leadership and organizational capacities.

In June 1920, Baba Ramachandra led a few hundred tenants from the Jaunpur and Pratapgarh districts to Allahabad. There he met Gauri Shankar Misra and Jawaharlal Nehru and asked them to visit the villages to see for themselves the living conditions of the tenants. The result was that, between June and August, Jawaharlal Nehru made several visits to the rural areas and developed close contacts with the *Kisan Sabha* movement.

*

Meanwhile, the kisans found sympathy in Mehta, the Deputy Commissioner of Pratapgarh, who promised to investigate complaints forwarded to him. The *Kisan Sabha* at village Roor in Pratapgarh district became the centre of activity and about one lakh tenants were reported to have registered their complaints with this Sabha on the payment of one anna each. Gauri Shankar Misra was also very active in Pratapgarh during this period, and was in the process of working out an agreement with Mehta over some of the crucial tenant complaints such as *bedakhli* and *nazrana*.

But, in August 1920, Mehta went on leave and the *taluqdars* used the opportunity to strike at the growing *kisan* movement. They succeeded in getting Ramachandra and thirty-two kisans arrested on a trumped-up charge of theft on 28 August 1920. Incensed at this, 4,000 to 5,000 kisans collected at Pratapgarh to see their leaders in jail and were dispersed after a great deal of persuasion.

Ten days later, a rumour that Gandhiji was coming to secure the release of Baba Ramachandra brought ten to twenty thousand kisans to Pratapgarh, and this time they returned to their homes only after Baba Ramachandra gave them *darshan* from atop a tree in a sugar-cane field. By now, their numbers had swelled to sixty thousand. Mehta was called back from leave to deal with the situation and he quickly withdrew the case of theft and attempted to bring pressure on the landlords to change their ways. This easy victory, however, gave a new confidence to the movement and it burgeoned forth.

Meanwhile, the Congress at Calcutta had chosen the path of non-cooperation and many nationalists of U.P. had committed themselves to the new political path. But there were others, including Madan Mohan Malaviya, who preferred to stick to constitutional agitation. These differences were reflected in the U.P. *Kisan Sabha* as well, and soon the Non-cooperators set up an alternative Oudh *Kisan Sabha* at Pratapgarh on 17 October 1920. This new body succeeded in integrating under its banner all the grassroots *kisan sabhas* that had emerged in the districts of Avadh in the past few months; through the efforts of Misra, Jawaharlal Nehru, Mata Badal Pande, Baba Ram Chandra, Deo Narayan Pande and Kedar Nath, the new organization brought under its wing, by the end of October, over 330 *kisan sabhas*. The Oudh *Kisan Sabha* asked the kisans to refuse to till *bedakhli* land, not to offer *hari* and *begar* (forms of unpaid labour), to boycott those who did not accept these conditions and to solve their disputes through panchayats. The first big show of strength of the Sabha was the rally held at Ayodhya, near Fyzabad town, on 20 and 21 December which was attended by roughly 100,000 peasants. At this rally, Baba Ram Chandra turned up bound in ropes to symbolize the oppression of the kisans. A marked feature of the *kisan sabha* movement was that kisans belonging to the high as well as the low castes were to be found in its ranks.

In January 1921, however, the nature of the peasant activity underwent a marked change. The centres of activity were primarily the districts of Rae Bareli, Fyzabad and, to a lesser extent, Sultanpur. The pattern of activity was the looting of bazaars, houses, granaries, and clashes with the police. A series of incidents, small and big, but similar in character, occurred. Some, such as the ones at Munshiganj and Karhaiya Bazaar in Rae Bareli, were sparked off by the arrests or rumours of arrest of leaders. The lead was often taken not by recognized *Kisan Sabha* activists, but by local figures — *sadhus*, holy men, and disinherited ex-proprietors.

The Government, however, had little difficulty in suppressing these outbreaks of violence. Crowds were fired upon and dispersed, leaders and activists arrested, cases launched and, except for a couple of incidents in February and March, the movement was over by the end of January itself. In March, the Seditious Meetings Act was brought in to cover the affected districts and all political activity came to a standstill. Nationalists continued to defend the cases of the tenants in the courts, but could do little else. The Government, meanwhile, pushed through the Oudh Rent (Amendment) Act, and though it brought little relief to the tenants, it helped to rouse hopes and in its own way assisted in the decline of the movement.

*

Towards the end of the year, peasant discontent surfaced again in Avadh, but this time the centres were the districts of Hardoi, Bahraich, and Sitapur in the northern part of the province. The initial thrust here was provided by Congress and Khilafat leaders and the movement grew under the name of the Ekta or unity movement. The main grievances here related to the extraction of a rent that was generally fifty per cent higher than the recorded rent, the oppression of *thekedars* to whom the work of rent-collection was farmed out and the practice of share-rents.

The Eka meetings were marked by a religious ritual in which a hole that represented the river Ganges was dug in the ground and filled with water, a priest was brought in to preside and the assembled peasants vowed that they would pay only the recorded rent but pay it on time, would not leave when ejected, would refuse to do forced labour, would give no help to criminals and abide by the panchayat decisions.

The Eka movement, however, soon developed its own grass-roots leadership in the form of Madari Pasi and other low-caste leaders who were not particularly inclined to accept the discipline of non-violence that the Congress and Khilafat leaders urged. As a result, the movement's contacts with the nationalists diminished and it went its own way. However, unlike the earlier *Kisan Sabha* movement that was based almost solely on tenants, the Eka movement included in its ranks many small *zamindars* who found themselves disenchanted with the Government because of its heavy land revenue demand. By March 1922, however, severe repression on the part of the authorities succeeded in bringing the Eka movement to its end.[1]

*

In August 1921, peasant discontent erupted in the Malabar district of Kerala. Here Mappila (Muslim) tenants rebelled. Their grievances related to lack of any security of tenure, renewal fees, high rents, and other oppressive landlord exactions. In the nineteenth century as well, there had been cases of Mappila resistance to landlord oppression but what erupted in 1921 was on a different scale together.

The impetus for resistance had first come from the Malabar District Congress Conference held at Manjeri in April 1920. This conference supported the tenants' cause and demanded legislation to regulate land-lord-tenant relations. The change was significant because earlier the landlords had successfully prevented the Congress from committing itself to the tenants' cause. The Manjeri conference was followed by the formation of a tenants' association at Kozhikode, and soon tenants' associations were set up in other parts of the district.

Simultaneously, the Khilafat movement was also extending its sweep. In fact, there was hardly any way one could distinguish between Khilafat and tenants' meetings, the leaders and the audience were the same, and the two movements were inextricably merged into one. The social base of the movement was primarily among the Mappila tenants, and Hindus were quite conspicuous by their absence, though the movement could count on a number of Hindu leaders.

Disturbed by the growing popularity of the Khilafat-cum-tenant agitation, which had received considerable impetus from the visits of Gandhiji, Shaukat Ali, and Maulana Azad, the Government issued prohibitory notices on all Khilafat meetings on 5 February 1921. On 18 February, all the prominent Khilafat and Congress leaders, Yakub Hasan, U. Gopala Menon, P. Moideen Koya and K. Madhavan Nair, were arrested. This resulted in the leadership passing into the hands of the local Mappila leaders.

Angered by repression and encouraged by rumours that the British, weakened as a result of the World War, were no longer in a position to take strong military action, the Mappilas began to exhibit increasing signs of turbulence and defiance of authority. But the final break came only when the District Magistrate of Eranad *taluq*, E.F. Thomas, on 20 August 1921, accompanied by a contingent of police and troops, raided the mosque at Tirurangadi to arrest Ali Musaliar, a Khilafat leader and a highly respected priest. They found only three fairly insignificant Khilafat volunteers and arrested them. However the news that spread was that the famous Mambrath mosque, of which Ali Musaliar was the priest, had been raided and destroyed by the British army. Soon Mappilas from Kottakkal, Tanur and Parappanagadi converged at Tirurangadi and their leaders met the British officers to secure the release of the arrested volunteers. The people were quiet and peaceful, but the police opened fire on the unarmed crowd and many were killed. A clash ensued, and Government offices were destroyed, records burnt and the treasury looted. The rebellion soon spread into the Eranad, Walluvanad and Ponnani *taluqs*, all Mappila strongholds.

In the first stage of the rebellion, the targets of attack were the unpopular *jenmies* (landlords), mostly Hindu, the symbols of Government authority such as *kutcheris* (courts), police stations, treasuries and offices, and British planters. Lenient landlords and poor Hindus were rarely touched. Rebels would travel many miles through territory populated by Hindus and attack only the landlords and burn their records. Some of the rebel leaders, like Kunhammed Haji, took special care to see that Hindus were not molested or looted and even punished those among the rebels who attacked the Hindus. Kunhammed Haji also did not discriminate in favour of Muslims : he ordered the execution and punishment of a number of pro-government Mappilas as well.

But once the British declared martial law and repression began in earnest, the character of the rebellion underwent a definite change. Many Hindus were either pressurized into helping the authorities or voluntarily gave assistance and this helped to strengthen the already existing anti-Hindu sentiment among the poor illiterate Mappilas who in any case were motivated by a strong religious ideology. Forced conversions, attacks on and murders of Hindus increased as the sense of desperation mounted. What had been largely an anti-government and anti-landlord affair acquired strong communal overtones.

The Mappilas' recourse to violence had in any case driven a wedge between them and the Non-Cooperation Movement which was based on the principle of non-violence. The communalization of the rebellion completed the isolation of the Mappilas. British repression did the rest and by December 1921 all resistance had come to a stop. The toll was heavy indeed : 2,337 Mappilas had lost their lives. Unofficial estimates placed the number at above 10,000. 45,404 rebels were captured or had surrendered. But the toll was in fact even heavier, though in a very different way. From then onwards, the militant Mappilas were so completely crushed and demoralized that till independence their participation in any form of politics was almost nil. They neither joined the national movement nor the peasant movement that was to grow in Kerala in later years under the Left leadership.[2]

*

The peasant movements in U.P. and Malabar were thus closely linked with the politics at the national level. In U.P., the impetus had come from the Home Rule Leagues and, later, from the Non-Cooperation and Khilafat movement. In Avadh, in the early months of 1921 when peasant activity was at its peak, it was difficult to distinguish between a Non-cooperation meeting and a peasant rally. A similar situation arose in Malabar, where Khilafat and tenants' meetings merged into one. But in both places, the recourse to violence by the peasants created a distance between them and the national movement and led to appeals by the nationalist leaders to the peasants that they should not indulge in violence. Often, the national leaders, especially Gandhiji, also asked the peasants to desist from taking extreme action like stopping the payment of rent to landlords.

This divergence between the actions and perceptions of peasants and local leaders and the understanding of the national leaders has often been interpreted as a sign of the fear of the middle class or bourgeois leadership that the movement would go out of its own 'safe' hands into that of supposedly more radical and militant leaders of the people. The call for restraint, both in the demands as well as in the methods used, is seen as proof of concern for the landlords and propertied classes of Indian society. It is possible, however, that the advice of the national leadership was prompted by the desire to protect the peasants from the consequences of violent revolt, consequences which did not remain hidden for long as both in U.P. and Malabar the Government launched heavy repression in order to crush the movements. Their advice that peasants should not push things too far with the landlords by refusing to pay rent could also stem from other considerations. The peasants themselves were not demanding abolition of rent or landlordism, they only wanted an end to ejectments, illegal levies, and exorbitant rents — demands which the national leadership supported. The recourse to extreme measures like refusal to pay rent was likely to push even the small landlords further into the lap of the government and destroy any chances of their maintaining a neutrality towards the on-going conflict between the government and the national movement.

*

The no-tax movement that was launched in Bardoli *taluq* of Surat district in Gujarat in 1928 was also in many ways a child of the Non-cooperation days. [3]Bardoli *taluq* had been selected in 1922 as the place from where Gandhiji would launch the civil disobedience campaign, but events in Chauri Chaura had changed all that and the campaign never took off. However, a marked change had taken place in the area because of the various preparations for the civil disobedience movement and the end result was that Bardoli had undergone a process of intense politicization and awareness of the political scene. The local leaders such as the brothers Kalyanji and Kunverji Mehta, and Dayalji Desai, had worked hard to spread the message of the Non-Cooperation Movement. These leaders, who had been working in the district as social reformers and political activists for at least a decade prior to Non-cooperation, had set up many national schools, persuaded students to leave government schools, carried out the boycott of foreign cloth and liquor, and had captured the Surat municipality.

After the withdrawal of the Non-Cooperation Movement, the Bardoli Congressmen had settled down to intense constructive work. Stung by Gandhiji's rebuke in 1922 that they had done nothing for the upliftment of the low-caste untouchable and tribal inhabitants [4] — who were known by the name of *Kaliparaj* (dark people) to distinguish them from the high caste or *Ujaliparaj* (fair people) and who formed sixty per cent of the population of the *taluq* — these men, who belonged to high castes, started work among the *Kaliparaj* through a network of six ashrams that were spread out over the *taluq*. These ashrams, many of which survive to this day as living institutions working for the education of the tribals, did much to lift the *taluq* out of the demoralization that had followed the withdrawal of 1922. Kunverji Mehta and Keshavji Ganeshji learnt the tribal dialect, and developed a '*Kaliparaj* literature' with the assistance of the educated members of the *Kaliparaj* community, which contained poems and prose that aroused the *Kaliparaj* against the *Hali* system under which they laboured as hereditary labourers for upper-caste landowners, and exhorted them to abjure intoxicating drinks and high marriage expenses which led to financial ruin. *Bhajan mandalis* consisting of *Kaliparaj* and *Ujaliparaj* members were used to spread the message. Night schools were started to educate the Kaliparaj and in 1927 a school for the education of *Kaliparaj* children was set up in Bardoli town. Ashram workers had to often face the hostility of upper-caste landowners who feared that all this would 'spoil' their labour. Annual *Kaliparaj* conferences were held in 1922 and, in 1927, Gandhiji, who presided over the annual conference, initiated an enquiry into the conditions of the *Kaliparaj*, who he also now renamed as *Raniparaj* or the inhabitants of the forest in preference to the derogatory term *Kaliparaj* or dark people. Many leading figures of Gujarat including Narhari Parikh and Jugatram Dave conducted the inquiry which turned into a severe indictment of the *Hali* system, exploitation by money lenders and sexual exploitation of women by upper-castes. As a result of this, the Congress had built up a considerable base among the *Kaliparaj*, and could count on their support in the future.

Simultaneously, of course, the Ashram workers had continued to work among the landowning peasants as well and had to an extent regained their influence among them. Therefore, when in January 1926 it became known that Jayakar, the officer charged with the duty of reassessment of the land revenue demand of the *taluq*, had recommended a thirty percent increase over the existing assessment, the Congress leaders were quick to protest against the increase and set up the Bardoli Inquiry Committee to go into the issue. Its report, published in July 1926, came to the conclusion that the increase was unjustified. This was followed by a campaign in the press, the lead being taken by *Young India* and *Navjivan* edited by Gandhiji. The constitutionalist leaders of the area, including the members of the Legislative Council, also took up the issue. In July 1927, the Government reduced the enhancement to 21.97 per cent.

But the concessions were too meagre and came too late to satisfy anybody. The constitutionalist leaders now began to advise the peasants to resist by paying only the current amount and withholding the enhanced amount. The 'Ashram' group, on the other hand, argued that the entire amount must be withheld if it was to have any effect on the government. However, at this stage, the peasants seemed more inclined to heed the advice of the moderate leaders.

Gradually, however, as the limitations of the constitutionalist leadership became more apparent, and their unwillingness to lead even a movement based on the refusal of the enhanced amount was clear, the peasants began to move towards the 'Ashram' group of Congress leaders. The latter, on their part, had in the meanwhile contacted Vallabhbhai Patel and were persuading him to take on the leadership of the movement. A meeting of representatives of sixty villages at Bamni in Kadod division formally invited Vallabhbhai to lead the campaign. The local leaders also met Gandhiji and after having assured him that the peasants were fully aware of the implications of such a campaign, secured his approval.

Patel reached Bardoli on 4 February and immediately had a series of meetings with the representatives of the peasants and the constitutionalist leaders. At one such meeting, the moderate leaders frankly told the audience that their methods had failed and they should now try Vallabhbhai's methods. Vallabhbhai explained to the peasants the consequences of their proposed plan of action and advised them to give the matter a week's thought. He then returned to Ahmedabad and wrote a letter to the Governor of Bombay explaining the miscalculations in the settlement report and requesting him to appoint an independent enquiry; else, he wrote, he would have to advise the peasants to refuse to pay the land revenue and suffer the consequences.

On 12 February, Patel returned to Bardoli and explained the situation, including the Government's curt reply, to the peasants' representatives. Following this, a meeting of the occupants of Bardoli *taluq* passed a resolution advising all occupants of land to refuse payment of the revised assessment until the Government appointed an independent tribunal or accepted the current amount as full payment. Peasants were asked to take oaths in the name of *Prabhu* (the Hindu name for god) and *Khuda* (the Muslim name for god) that they would not pay the land revenue. The resolution was followed by the recitation of sacred texts from the *Gita* and the *Koran* and songs from Kabir, who symbolized Hindu-Muslim unity. The *Satyagraha* had begun.

Vallabhbhai Patel was ideally suited for leading the campaign. A veteran of the Kheda *Satyagraha*, the Nagpur Flag *Satyagraha*, and the

Borsad Punitive Tax *Satyagraha*, he had emerged as a leader of Gujarat who was second only to Gandhiji. His capacities as an organizer, speaker, indefatigable campaigner, inspirer of ordinary men and women were already known, but it was the women of Bardoli who gave him the title of *Sardar*. The residents of Bardoli to this day recall the stirring effect of the Sardar's speeches which he delivered in an idiom and style that was close to the peasant's heart.

The Sardar divided the *taluq* into thirteen workers' camps or *Chhavanis* each under the charge of an experienced leader. One hundred political workers drawn from all over the province, assisted by 1,500 volunteers, many of whom were students, formed the army of the movement. A publications bureau that brought out the daily *Bardoli Satyagraha Patrika* was set up. This Patrika contained reports about the movement, speeches of the leaders, pictures of the *jabti* or confiscation proceedings and other news. An army of volunteers distributed this to the farthest corners of the *taluq*. The movement also had its own intelligence wing, whose job was to find out who the indecisive peasants were. The members of the intelligence wing would shadow them night and day to see that they did not pay their dues, secure information about Government moves, especially of the likelihood of *jabti* (confiscation) and then warn the villagers to lock up their houses or flee to neighbouring Baroda.

The main mobilization was done through extensive propaganda via meetings, speeches, pamphlets, and door to door persuasion. Special emphasis was placed on the mobilization of women and many women activists like Mithuben Petit, a Parsi lady from Bombay, Bhaktiba, the wife of Darbar Gopaldas, Maniben Patel, the Sardar's daughter, Shardaben Shah and Sharda Mehta were recruited for the purpose. As a result, women often outnumbered men at the meetings and stood firm in their resolve not to submit to Government threats. Students were another special target and they were asked to persuade their families to remain firm.

Those who showed signs of weakness were brought into line by means of social pressure and threats of social boycott. Caste and village panchayats were used effectively for this purpose and those who opposed the movement had to face the prospect of being refused essential services from sweepers, barbers, washermen, agricultural labourers, and of being socially boycotted by their kinsmen and neighbours. These threats were usually sufficient to prevent any weakening. Government officials faced the worst of this form of pressure. They were refused supplies, services, transport and found it almost impossible to carry out their official duties. The work that the Congress leaders had done among the *Kaliparaj* people also paid dividends during this movement and the government was totally unsuccessful in its attempts to use them against the upper caste peasants.

Sardar Patel and his colleagues also made constant efforts to see that they carried the constitutionalist and moderate leadership, as well as public opinion, with them on all important issues. The result of this was that very soon the Government found even its supporters and sympathizers, as well as impartial men, deserting its side. Many members of the Bombay Legislative Council like K.M. Munshi and Lalji Naranji, the representative of the Indian Merchants Chamber, who were not hot-headed extremists resigned their seats. By July 1928, the Viceroy, Lord Irwin, himself began to doubt the correctness of the Bombay Government's stand and put pressure on Governor Wilson to find a way out. Uncomfortable questions had started appearing in the British Parliament as well.

Public opinion in the country was getting more and more restive and anti-Government. Peasants in many parts of Bombay Presidency were threatening to agitate for revision of the revenue assessments in their areas. Workers in Bombay textile mills were on strike and there was a threat that Patel and the Bombay Communists would combine in bringing about a railway strike that would make movement of troops and supplies to Bardoli impossible. The Bombay Youth League and other organizations had mobilized the people of Bombay for huge public meetings and demonstrations. Punjab was offering to send *jathas* on foot to Bardoli. Gandhiji had shifted to Bardoli on 2 August , 1928, in order to take over the reins of the movement if Patel was arrested. All told, a retreat, if it could be covered up by a face saving device, seemed the best way out for the Government.

The face-saving device was provided by the Legislative Council members from Surat who wrote a letter to the Governor assuring him that his pre-condition for an enquiry would be satisfied. The letter contained no reference to what the pre-condition was (though everyone knew that it was full payment of the enhanced rent) because an understanding had already been reached that the full enhanced rent would not be paid. Nobody took the Governor seriously when he declared that he had secured an 'unconditional surrender.'[5] It was the Bardoli peasants who had won.

The enquiry, conducted by a judicial officer, Broomfield, and a revenue officer, Maxwell, came to the conclusion that the increase had been unjustified, and reduced the enhancement to 6.03 per cent. *The New Statesman* of London summed up the whole affair on 5 May 1929 : 'The report of the Committee constitutes the worst rebuff which any local government in India has received for many years and may have far-reaching results ... It would be difficult to find an incident quite comparable with this in the long and controversial annals of Indian Land Revenue.'6

The relationship of Bardoli and other peasant struggles with the struggle for freedom can best be described in Gandhiji's pithy words: 'Whatever the Bardoli struggle may be, it clearly is not a struggle for the direct attainment of *swaraj*. That every such awakening, every such effort as that of Bardoli will bring *swaraj* nearer and may bring it nearer even than any direct effort is undoubtedly true.'7

17 The Indian Working Class and the National Movement

The modern worker makes his appearance in India in the second half of the 19th century with the slow beginnings of modern industry and the growth of utilities like the railways and the post and the telegraph network. The process of the disparate groups of workers in various parts of country emerging as an organized, self-conscious, all India class is inextricably linked with the growth of the Indian national movement and the process of the Indian 'nation-in-the-making' because the notion of the Indian working class could not exist before the notion of the Indian 'people' had begun to take root.

*

Before the Indian nationalist intelligentsia began to associate itself with working class agitations towards the end of the 19th century, there were several agitations, including strikes by workers in the textile mills of Bombay, Calcutta, Ahmedabad, Surat, Madras, Coimbatore, Wardha, and so on, in the railways and in the plantations. However, they were mostly sporadic, spontaneous and unorganized revolts based on immediate economic grievances, and had hardly any wider political implications.

There were also some early attempts at organized effort to improve the condition of the workers. These efforts were made as early as the 1870s by philanthropists. In 1878, Sorabjee Shapoorji Bengalee tried unsuccessfully to introduce a Bill in the Bombay Legislative Council to limit the working hours for labour. In Bengal, Sasipada Banerjee, a

Brahmo Social reformer, set up a Workingmen's Club in 1870 and brought out a monthly journal called *Bharat Sramjeebi* (Indian Labour), with the primary idea of educating the workers. In Bombay, Narayan Meghajee Lokhanday brought out an Anglo-Marathi weekly called *Dina-Bandhu* (Friend of the Poor) in 1880, and started the Bombay Mill and Millhands' Association in 1890. Lokhanday held meetings of workers and in one instance sent a memorial signed by 5,500 mill workers, to the Bombay Factory Commission, putting forward some minimum workers' demands. All these efforts were admittedly of a philanthropic nature and did not represent the beginnings of an organized working class movement. Moreover, these philanthropists did not belong to the mainstream of the contemporary national movement.

The mainstream nationalist movement in fact was as yet, by and large, indifferent to the question of labour. The early nationalists in the beginning paid relatively little attention to the question of workers despite the truly wretched conditions under which they existed at that time. Also, they had a strikingly, though perhaps understandably, differential attitude towards the workers employed in European enterprises and those employed in Indian enterprises.

One major reason for the relatively lukewarm attitude of the early nationalists towards the question of workers was that, at this time, when the anti-imperialist movement was in its very infancy, the nationalists did not wish to, in any way, weaken the common struggle against British rule — the primary task to be achieved in a colonial situation — by creating any divisions within the ranks of the Indian people. Dadabhai Naoroji, in the very second session of the Indian national Congress (1886), made it clear that the Congress 'must confine itself to questions in which the entire nation has a direct participation, and it must leave the adjustment of social reforms and other class questions to class Congresses.'[1] Later, with the national movement gaining in strength, and the emergence within the nationalist ranks of ideological trends with less inhibitions towards labour and increasingly with an actively pro-labour orientation, efforts were made to organize labour and secure for it a better bargaining position vis-a-vis the more powerful classes in the common anti-imperialist front. While still endeavouring to maintain an anti-imperialist united front, unity was no longer sought at the unilateral cost of the worker and the oppressed but was to be secured through sacrifices or concessions from all classes including the powerful propertied classes.

At this stage, however, the nationalists were unwilling to take up the question of labour versus the indigenous employer. Most of the nationalist newspapers, in fact, denied the need for any government legislation to regulate working conditions and actively opposed the Factories Acts of 1881 and 1891. Similarly, strikes in Indian textiles mills were generally not supported. Apart from the desire not to create any divisions in the fledgling anti-imperialist movement, there were other reasons for the nationalist stance. The nationalists correctly saw the government initiative on labour legislation as dictated by British manufacturing interests which, when faced with growing Indian competition and a shrinking market in India, lobbied for factory legislation in India which would, for example, by reducing the working hours for labour, reduce the competitive edge enjoyed by Indian industry. Further, the early nationalists saw rapid industrialisation as the panacea for the problems of Indian poverty and degradation and were unwilling to countenance any measure which would impede this process. Labour legislation which would adversely affect the infant industry in India, they said, was like killing the goose that laid the golden egg. But there was also the nationalist newspaper, *Mahratta*, then under the influence of the radical thinker, G.S. Agarkar, which even at this stage supported the workers' cause and asked the millowners to make concessions to them. This trend was, however, still a very minor one.

The scenario completely altered when the question was of Indian labour employed in British-owned enterprises. Here the nationalists had no hesitation in giving full support to the workers. This was partially because the employer and the employed, in the words of P. Ananda Charlu, the Congress president in 1891, were not 'part and parcel of the same nation.'2

The Indian National Congress and the nationalist newspapers began a campaign against the manner in which the tea plantation workers in Assam were reduced to virtual slavery, with European planters being given powers, through legislation to arrest, punish and prevent the running away of labour. An appeal was made to national honour and dignity to protest against this unbridled exploitation by foreign capitalists aided by the colonial state.

It was not fortuitous, then, that perhaps the first organized strike by any section of the working class should occur in a British-owned and managed railway. This was the signallers' strike in May 1899 in the Great Indian Peninsular (GIP) Railway and the demands related to wages, hours of work and other conditions of service. Almost all nationalist newspapers came out fully in support of the strike, with Tilak's newspapers *Mahratta* and *Kesari* campaigning for it for months. Public meetings and fund collections in aid of the strikers were organized in Bombay and Bengal by prominent nationalists like Pherozeshah Mehta, D.E. Wacha and Surendranath Tagore. The fact that the exploiter in these cases was foreign was enough to make agitation against it a national issue and an integral part of the national movement.

At the turn of the century, with the growth of the working class, there emerged a new tendency among the nationalist intelligentsia. B.C.Pal and G.Subramania Iyer, for example, began to talk of the need for legislation to protect the workers, the weaker section, against the powerful capitalists. In 1903, G. Subramaniya Iyer urged that workers should combine and organize themselves into unions to fight for their rights and the public must give every help to the workers in achieving this task.[3]

*

The Swadeshi upsurge of 1903-8 was a distinct landmark in the history of the labour movement. An official survey pinpointed the rise of the 'professional agitator' and the 'power of organization' of labour into industrial strikes as the two distinct features of this period.[4] The number of strikes rose sharply and many Swadeshi leaders enthusiastically threw themselves into the tasks of organizing stable trade unions, strikes, legal aid, and fund collection drives. Public meetings in support of striking workers were addressed by national leaders like B.C. Pal, C.R. Das and Liaqat Hussain. Four prominent names among the Swadeshi leaders who dedicated themselves to labour struggles were Aswinicoomar Bannerji, Prabhat Kumar Roy Chowdhuri, Premtosh Bose and Apurba Kumar Ghose. They were active in a large number of strikes but their greatest success, both in setting up workers' organizations and in terms of popular support, was among workers in the Government Press, Railways and the jute industry — significantly all areas in which either foreign capital or the colonial state held sway.

Frequent processions in support of the strikers were taken out in the streets of Calcutta. People fed the processionists on the way. Large numbers including women and even police constables made contributions of money, rice, potatoes, and green vegetables. The first tentative attempts to form all-India unions were also made at this time, but these were unsuccessful. The differential attitude towards workers employed in European enterprises and those in Indian ones, however, persisted throughout this period.

Perhaps the most important feature of the labour movement during the Swadeshi days was the shift from agitations and struggles on purely economic questions to the involvement of the worker with the wider political issues of the day. The labour movement had graduated from relatively unorganized and spontaneous strikes on economic issues to organized strikes on economic issues with the support of the nationalists and then on to working class involvement in wider political movements.

The national upsurge on 16 October 1905, the day the partition of Bengal came into effect, included a spurt of working class strikes and *hartals* in Bengal. Workers in several jute mills and jute press factories, railway coolies and carters, all struck work. Workers numbering 12,000 in the Burn Company shipyard in Howrah struck work on being refused leave to attend the Federation Hall meeting called by the Calcutta Swadeshi leaders. Workers also went on strike when the management objected to their singing 'Bande Mataram' or tying *rakhis* on each others' wrists as a symbol of unity.

In Tuticorin, in Tamil Nadu, Subramaniya Siva campaigned for a strike in February-March 1908 in a foreign-owned cotton mill saying that strikes for higher wages would lead to the demise of foreign mills. When Siva and the famous Swadeshi leader Chidambaram Pillai were arrested, there were widespread strikes and riots in Tuticorin and Tirunelveli.

In Rawalpindi, in Punjab, the arsenal and railway engineering workers went on strike as part of the 1907 upsurge in the Punjab which had led to the deportation of Lajpat Rai and Ajit Singh. Perhaps the biggest political demonstration by the working class in this period occurred during Tilak's trial and subsequent conviction as has already been discussed earlier.

The Swadeshi period was also to see the faint beginnings of a socialist tinge among some of the radical nationalist leaders who were exposed to the contemporary Marxist and social democratic forces in Europe. The example of the working class movement in Russia as a mechanism of effective political protest began to be urged for emulation in India.

With the decline in the nationalist mass upsurge after 1908, the labour movement also suffered an eclipse. It was only with the coming of the next nationalist upsurge in the immediate post World-War I years that the working class movement was to regain its elan, though now on a qualitatively higher plane.

*

Beginning with the Home Rule Leagues in 1915 and continuing through the Rowlatt *Satyagraha* in 1919, the national movement once again reached a crescendo in the Non-Cooperation and Khilafat Movement in 1920-22. It was in this context that there occurred a resurgence of working class activity in the years from 1919 to 1922. The working class now created its own national-level organization to defend its class rights. It was in this period that the working class also got involved in the mainstream of nationalist politics to a significant extent.

The most important development was the formation of the All India Trade Union Congress (AITUC) in 1920. Lokmanya Tilak, who had developed a close association with Bombay workers, was one of the moving spirits in the formation of the AITUC, which had Lala Lajpat Rai, the famous Extremist leader from Punjab, as its first president and Dewan Chaman Lal, who was to become a major name in the Indian labour movement, as its general secretary. In his presidential address to the first AITUC, Lala Lajpat Rai emphasized that, '. . . Indian labour should lose no time to organize itself on a national scale . . . the greatest need in this country is to organize, agitate, and educate. We must organize our workers, make them class conscious ...' While aware that 'for some time to come' the workers will need all the help and guidance and cooperation they can get from such among the intellectuals as are prepared to espouse their cause, he maintained that 'eventually labour shall find its leaders from among its own ranks.'[5]

The manifesto issued to the workers by the AITUC urged them not only to organize themselves but also to intervene in nationalist politics: 'Workers of India! .... Your nation's leaders ask for *Swaraj*, you must not let them leave you out of the reckoning. Political freedom to you is of no worth without economic freedom. You cannot therefore afford to neglect the movement for national freedom. You are part and parcel of that movement. You will neglect it only at the peril of your liberty."[6]

Lajpat Rai was among the first in India to link capitalism with imperialism and emphasize the crucial role of the working class in fighting this combination. He said on 7 November, 1920 : 'India . . . has . . . been bled white by the forces of organized capital and is today lying prostrate at its feet. Militarism and Imperialism are the twin-children of capitalism; they are one in three and three in one. Their shadow, their fruit and their bark all are poisonous. It is only lately that an antidote has been discovered and that antidote is organized labour.'[7]

Reflecting the emerging change in nationalist attitudes towards labour employed in Indian enterprise, Lajpat Rai said. 'We are often told that in order successfully to compete with Manchester and Japan, capital in India should be allowed a high rate of profit and cheap labour is a necessity for that purpose . . . We are not prepared to admit the validity of this plea . . . An appeal to patriotism must affect the rich and the poor alike, in fact, the rich more than the poor . . . Surely . . . the way to develop Indian industries . . . is to be . . . (not) at the expense of labour alone . . . The Indian capitalist must meet labour half way and must come to an understanding with it on the basis of sharing the profits in a reasonable and just proportion . . . If, however, Indian capital wants to ignore the needs of labour and can think only of its huge profits, it should expect no response from labour and no sympathy from the general public.'[8]

Similarly at the second session of the AITUC, Dewan Chaman Lal while moving a resolution in favour of *Swaraj* pointed out that it was to be a *Swaraj*, not for the capitalists but for the workers.

Apart from Lajpat Rai, several of the leading nationalists of the time became closely associated with the AITUC. C.R. Das presided over its third and fourth sessions, and among the other prominent names were those of C.F. Andrews, J.M. Sengupta, Subhas Bose, Jawaharlal Nehru, and Satyamurti. The Indian National Congress at its Gaya session in 1922 welcomed the formation of the AITUC and formed a committee consisting of prominent Congressmen to assist its work.

C.R. Das, in his presidential address to the Gaya Congress, said that the Congress must 'take labour and the peasantry in hand . . . and organize them both from the point of view of their own special interests and also from the point of view of the higher ideal which demands satisfaction of their special interests and the devotion of such interests to the cause of *Swaraj*.' If this was not done, he warned, organization of workers and peasants would come up 'dissociated from the cause of *Swaraj*' and pursuing 'class struggles and the war of special interest.'9

The working class responded to the changed political atmosphere in a magnificent manner. In 1920, there were 125 unions with a total membership of 250,000, and a large proportion of these had been formed during 1919-20. The workers' participation in the major national political events was also very significant. In April 1919, following the repression in Punjab and Gandhiji's arrest, the working class in Ahmedabad and other parts of Gujarat resorted to strikes, agitations and demonstrations. In Ahmedabad, Government buildings were set on fire, trains derailed, and telegraph wires snapped. Suppression led to at least twenty-eight people being killed and 123 wounded. Waves of working class protest rocked Bombay and Calcutta.

Railway workers' agitations for economic demands and against racial discrimination also coincided with the general anti-colonial mass struggle. Between 1919 and 1921, on several occasions, railway workers struck in support of the Rowlatt agitation and the non-cooperation and Khilafat Movement. The call for an all-India general strike given by the North-Western Railway workers in April 1919 got an enthusiastic response in the northern region. Lajpat Jagga has shown that for railwaymen in large parts of the country Gandhiji came to symbolize resistance to colonial rule and exploitation, just as the Indian Railways symbolized the British Empire, 'the political and commercial will of the Raj.'10

In November 1921, at the time of the visit of the Prince of Wales, the workers responded to the Congress call of a boycott by a country-wide general strike. In Bombay, the textile factories were closed and about 1,40,000 workers were on the streets participating in the rioting and attacks on Europeans and Parsis who had gone to welcome the Prince of Wales. The spirit and the urges that moved the workers in these eventful years, the relationship seen between the nationalist upsurge and the workers' own aspirations, is best expressed in the words of Arjun Atmaram Alwe, an illiterate worker in a Bombay textile mill, who was later to become a major figure in the working class movement : 'While our struggle . . . was going on in this manner, the drum of political agitation was being beaten in the country. The Congress started a great agitation demanding rights for India to conduct her own administration. At that time we workers understood the meaning of this demand for *Swaraj* to be only this; that our indebtedness would disappear, the oppression of the moneylender would stop, our wages would increase, and the oppression of the owner on the worker, the kicks and blows with which they belabour us, would stop by legislation, and that as a result of it, the persecution of us workers would come to an end. These and other thoughts came into the minds of us workers, and a good many workers from among us, and I myself, enlisted ourselves as volunteers in the Non-Cooperation Movement.'[11]

Any discussion of these years would remain incomplete without mentioning the founding in 1918 by Gandhiji of the Ahmedabad Textile Labour Association (TLA) which, with 14,000 workers, on its rolls, was perhaps the largest single trade union of the time. Too often and too casually has Gandhiji's experiment based on the principle of trusteeship (the capitalist being the trustee of the workers' interest) and arbitration been dismissed as class collaborationist and against the interests of the workers. Apart from the fact that the TLA secured one of the highest hikes in wages (27 1/2 per cent) during a dispute in 1918, Gandhiji's conception of trusteeship also had a radical potential which is usually missed. As Acharya J.B. Kripalani, one of Gandhiji's staunchest followers, explained: 'The Trustee by the very term used means that he is not the owner. The owner is one whose interest he is called upon to protect,' i.e., the worker. Gandhiji himself told the textile workers of Ahmedabad 'that they were the real masters of the mills' and if the trustee, the millowner, did not act in the interest of the real owners, then the workers should offer *Satyagraha* to assert their rights.'[12] Gandhiji's philosophy for labour, with its emphasis on arbitration and trusteeship, also reflected the needs of the anti-imperialist movement which could ill-afford an all-out class war between the constituent classes of the emerging nation.

After 1922, there was again a lull in the working class movement, and a reversion to purely economic struggles, that is, to corporatism. The next wave of working class activity came towards the end of the 1920s, this time spurred by the emergence of a powerful and clearly defined Left Bloc in the national movement.

*

It was in the second half of the 1920s that a consolidation of various Left ideological trends occurred and began to have a significant impact on the national movement. Various Communist groups in different parts of India had by early 1927 organized themselves into the Workers' and Peasants' Parties (WPP), under the leadership of people like S.A. Dange, Muzaffar Ahmed, P.C. Joshi and Sohan Singh Josh. The WPPs, functioning as a left-wing within the Congress, rapidly gained in strength within the Congress organization at the provincial and the all-India levels.

Also, by working within a broad Left front under the WPPs, Communist influence in the trade union movement, marginal till early 1927, had become very strong indeed, by the end of 1928. In Bombay, following the historic six-month-long general strike by the textile workers (April-September 1928), the Communist-led Girni Kamgar Union (GKU) acquired a pre-eminent position. Its membership rose from 324 to 54,000 by the end of 1928. Communist influence also spread to workers in the railways, jute mills, municipalities, paper mills, etc., in Bengal and Bombay and in the Burma Oil Company in Madras. In the AITUC too, by the time of the 1928 Jharia session, the broad Left including the Communists had acquired a dominating position. This resulted in the corporatist trend led by people like N.M. Joshi splitting away from the AITUC at the subsequent session presided over by Jawaharlal Nehru. By the end of 1928, the government was anxiously reporting that 'there was hardly a single public utility service or industry which had not been affected in whole or in part, by the wave of communism which swept the country.'13

The workers under Communist and radical nationalist influence participated in a large number of strikes and demonstrations all over the country between 1927 and 1929. The AITUC in November 1927 took a decision to boycott the Simon Commission and many workers participated in the massive Simon boycott demonstrations. There were also numerous workers' meetings organized on May Day, Lenin Day, the anniversary of the Russian Revolution, and so on.

The government, nervous at the growing militancy and political involvement of the working class, and especially at the coming together of the nationalist and the Left trends, launched a two-pronged attack on the labour movement. On the one hand, it enacted repressive laws like the Public Safety Act and Trade Disputes Acts and arrested in one swoop virtually the entire radical leadership of the labour movement and launched the famous Meerut Conspiracy Case against them. On the other hand, it attempted, not without some success, to wean away through concessions (for example the appointment of the Royal Commission on Labour in 1929) a substantial section of the labour movement and commit it to the constitutionalist and corporatist mould.

The labour movement suffered a major setback partially due to this Government offensive and partially due to a shift in stance of the Communist-led wing of the movement. We shall look at this aspect in more detail later on; suffice it to say that from about the end of 1928, the Communists reversed their policy of aligning themselves with and working within the mainstream of the national movement. This led to the isolation of the Communists from the national movement and greatly reduced their hold over even the working class. The membership of the GKU fell from 54,000 in December 1928 to about 800 by the end of 1929. Similarly, the Communists got isolated within the AITUC and were thrown out in the split of 1931.

A CPI document of 1930 clearly brings out the impact of this dissociation from the Civil Disobedience Movement on the workers of Bombay: ' . . . we actually withdrew from the struggle (civil disobedience) and left the field entirely to the Congress. We limited our role to that of a small group. The result was . . . that in the minds of workers there grew an opinion that we are doing nothing and that the Congress is the only organization which is carrying on the fight against imperialism and therefore the workers began to follow the lead of the Congress.'[14]

Nevertheless, workers participated in the civil disobedience movement all over the country. The textiles workers of Sholapur, dock labourers of Karachi, transport and mill workers of Calcutta, and the mill workers of Madras heroically clashed with the government during the movement. In Sholapur, between the 7th and the 16th of May, the textile workers went on a rampage after the police fired to stop an anti-British procession. Government offices, law courts, police stations and railway stations were attacked and rebels virtually took over the city administration for some days. The national flag was hoisted over the town. The government had to declare martial law to crush the insurgents. Several workers were hanged or sentenced to long-terms of imprisonment.

In Bombay, where the Congress slogan during civil disobedience was that the 'workers and peasants are the hands and the feet of the Congress,'[15] about 20,000 workers mostly from the GIP Railway struck work on 4 February 1930. The day Gandhiji breached the salt law, 6 April, a novel form of *Satyagraha* was launched by the workers of GIP Railwaymen's Union. Batches of workers went to the suburban stations of North Bombay and prostrated themselves on the tracks with red flags posted in front of them. The police had to open fire to clear the tracks. On 6 July, Gandhi Day was declared by the Congress Working Committee to protest against large scale arrests, and about 50,000 people took part in the *hartal* that day with workers from forty-nine factories downing their tools.

*

There was a dip in the working class movement between 1931 and 1936. Neither did the workers take an active part in the Civil Disobedience Movement of 1932-34. The next wave of working class activity came with provincial autonomy and the formation of popular ministries during 1937-1939.

The Communists had, in the meantime, abandoned their suicidal sectarian policies and since 1934 re-entered the mainstream of nationalist politics. They also rejoined the AITUC in 1935. Left influence in nationalist politics and the trade union movement once again began to grow rapidly. The Communists, the Congress Socialists and the Left nationalists led by Jawaharlal Nehru and Subhas Bose now formed a powerful Left consolidation within the Congress and other mass organizations.

When the campaign for the 1937 elections began, the AITUC, barring a few centres, gave its support to the Congress candidates. The Congress election manifesto declared that the Congress would take steps for the settlement of labour disputes and take effective measures for securing the rights to form unions and go on strike. During the tenure of the Congress Provincial Governments the trade union movement showed a phenomenal rise. Between 1937 and 1939 the number of trade unions increased from 271 to 562 and the total membership of these unions increased from 261,047 to 399,159. The number of strikes also increased considerably.

One of the principal factors which gave a fillip to the trade union movement in this period was the increased civil liberties under the Congress Governments and the pro-labour attitude of many of the Congress ministries. It is significant that a peculiar feature of the strikes in this period was that a majority of them ended successfully, with full or partial victory for the workers.[16]

World War II began on 3 September 1939 and the working class of Bombay was amongst the first in the world to hold an anti-war strike on 2 October, 1939. About 90,000 workers participated in the strike. There were several strikes on economic issues all over the country despite the severe repression let loose by a government keen to prevent any disruption of the war effort.

However, with the Nazi attack on the Soviet Union in 1941, the Communists argued that the character of the War had changed from an imperialist war to a people's war. It was now the duty of the working class to support the Allied powers to defeat fascism which threatened the socialist fatherland. Because of this shift in policy, the Communist party dissociated itself from the Quit India movement launched by Gandhiji in August 1942. They also successfully followed a policy of industrial peace with employers so that production and war-effort would not be hampered.

The Quit India movement, however, did not leave the working class untouched, despite the Communist indifference or opposition to it. Immediately after the arrest of Gandhiji and other leaders on 9 August 1942, following the Quit India Resolution, there were strikes and *hartals* all over the country, lasting for about a week, by workers in Delhi, Lucknow, Kanpur, Bombay, Nagpur, Ahmedabad, Jamshedpur, Madras, Indore and Bangalore. The Tata Steel Plant was closed for thirteen days with the strikers' slogan being that they would not resume work till a national government was formed. In Ahmedabad, the textile strike lasted for about three-and-a-half months with the millowners in their national-ist euphoria actually cooperating! The participation of workers was, however, low in pockets of Communist influence though in many areas the Communist rank and file, actively joined the call of Quit India despite the party line.

*

There was a tremendous resurgence in working class activity between 1945-47. The workers in large numbers participated in the post-war political upsurge. They were part of the numerous meetings and demon-strations organized in towns and cities (especially in Calcutta) on the issue of the INA trials. Towards the end of 1945, the Bombay and Calcutta dock workers refused to load ships going to Indonesia with supplies for troops meant to suppress the national liberation struggles of South-East Asia.

Perhaps the most spectacular action by the workers in this period was the strike and *hartal* by the Bombay workers in solidarity with the mutiny of the naval ratings in 1946. On 22 February, two to three hundred thousand workers downed their tools, responding to a call given by the Communist Party and supported by the Socialists. Peaceful meetings and demonstrations developed into violent clashes as the police intervened. Barricades were set up on the streets which were the scene of pitched battles with the police and the army. Two army battalions were needed to restore order in the city; nearly 250 agitators laid down their lives.

The last years of colonial rule also saw a remarkably sharp increase in strikes on economic issues all over the country — the all India strike of the Post and Telegraph Department employees being the most well known among them. The pent-up economic grievances during the War, coupled with the problems due to post-war demobilization and the continuation of high prices, scarcity of food and other essentials, and a drop in real wages, all combined to drive the working class to the limits of its tolerance.

Also, the mood in anticipation of freedom was pregnant with expectation. Independence was seen by all sections of the Indian people as signalling an end to their miseries. The workers were no exception. They too were now struggling for what they hoped freedom would bring them as a matter of right.

18 The Struggles for Gurdwara Reform and Temple Entry

The rising tide of nationalism and democracy inevitably began to overflow from the political to the religious and social fields affecting the downtrodden castes and classes. And many nationalists began to apply the newly discovered technique of non-violent *Satyagraha* and mobilization of public opinion to issues which affected the internal structure of Indian society. Quite often this struggle to reform Indian social and religious institutions and practices led the reformers to clash with the colonial authorities. Thus, the struggle to reform Indian society tended to merge with the anti-imperialist struggle. This was in part the result of the fact that as the national movement advanced, the social base of colonialism was narrowed and the colonial authorities began to seek the support of the socially, culturally and economically reactionary sections of Indian society. This aspect of the national movement is well illustrated by the Akāli Movement in Punjab and the Temple Entry Movement in Kerala.

*

The Akali Movement developed on a purely religious issue but ended up as a powerful episode of India's freedom struggle. From 1920 to 1925 more than 30,000 men and women underwent imprisonment, nearly 400 died and over 2,000 were wounded.

The movement arose with the objective of freeing the Gurdwaras (Sikh temples) from the control of ignorant and corrupt *mahants* (priests). The Gurdwaras had been heavily endowed with revenue-free land and money by Maharaja Ranjit Singh, Sikh chieftains and other devout Sikhs during the 18th and 19th centuries. These shrines came to be managed during the 18th century by Udasi Sikh *mahants* who escaped the wrath of Mughal authorities because they did not wear their hair long . (Many ignorant people therefore believe that these *mahants* were Hindus. This is, of course, not true at all). In time corruption spread among these *mahants* and they began to treat the offerings and other income of the Gurdwaras as their personal income. Many of them began to live a life of luxury and dissipation. Apart from the *mahants*, after the British annexation of Punjab in 1849, some control over the Gurdwaras was exercised by Government-nominated managers and custodians, who often collaborated with *mahants*.

The Government gave full support to the *mahants*. It used them and the managers to preach loyalism to the Sikhs and to keep them away from the rising nationalist movement. The Sikh reformers and nationalists, on the other hand, wanted a thorough reformation of the Gurdwaras by taking them out of the control of the *mahants* and agents of the colonial regime. The nationalists were especially horrified by two incidents — when the priests of the Golden Temple at Amritsar issued a *Hukamnama* (directive from the Gurus or the holy seats of the Sikh authority) against the Ghadarites, declaring them renegades, and then honoured General Dyer, the butcher of Jallianwala massacre, with a *saropa* (robe of honour) and declared him to be a Sikh.

A Popular agitation for the reform of Gurdwaras developed rapidly during 1920 when the reformers organized groups of volunteers known as *jathas* to compel the *mahants* and the Government-appointed managers to hand over control of the Gurdwaras to the local devotees. The reformers won easy victories in the beginning with tens of Gurdwaras being liberated in the course of the year. Symbolic of this early success was the case of the Golden Temple and the Akal Takht. The reformers demanded that 'this foremost seat of Sikh faith should be placed in the hands of a representative body of the Sikhs,' and organized a series of public meetings in support of their demand. The Government did not want to antagonize the reformers at this stage and decided to stem the rising tide of discontent on such an emotional religious issue by appeasing the popular sentiment. It, therefore, permitted the Government-appointed manager to resign and, thus, let the control of the Temple pass effectively into the reformers' hands.

To control and manage the Golden Temple, the Akal Takht and other

Gurdwaras, a representative assembly of nearly 10,000 reformers met in November 1920 and elected a committee of 175 to be known as the Shiromani Gurdwara Prabhandak Committee (SGPC). At the same time, the need was felt for a central body which would organize the struggle on a more systematic basis. The Shiromani Akali Dal was established in December for this purpose. It was to be the chief organizer of the Akali *jathas* whose backbone was provided by Jat peasantry while their leadership was in the hands of the nationalist intellectuals. Under the influence of the contemporary Non-Cooperation Movement — and many of the leaders were common to both the movements — the Akali Dal and the SGPC accepted complete non-violence as their creed.

*

The Akali movement faced its first baptism by blood at Nankana, the birth place of Guru Nanak, in February 1921. The *mahant* of the Gurdwara there, Narain Das, was not willing to peacefully surrender his control to the Akalis. He gathered a force of nearly 500 mercenaries and armed them with guns, swords, lathis and other lethal weapons to meet the challenge of the peaceful Akali volunteers. On 20 February, an Akali *Jatha* entered the Gurdwara to pray. Immediately, the *mahant's* men opened fire on them and attacked them with other weapons. Nearly 100 Akalis were killed and a large number wounded. This enraged the Akali leadership and a large number of *jathas* under Kartar Singh Jhabbar's command marched into the Gurdwara and took complete control despite dire warnings by the Deputy Commissioner. The *mahant* had already been arrested. The Government policy was still of vacillation. On the one hand, it did not want to earn the ire of the Sikhs, and, on the other, it did not want to lose control over the Gurdwaras.

The Nankana tragedy was a landmark in the Akali struggle. As Kartar Singh Jhabbar, the liberator of the Nankana Gurdwara, put it, 'the happening had awakened the Sikhs from their slumber and the march towards *Swaraj* had been quickened.' The tragedy aroused the conscience of the entire country. Mahatma Gandhi, Maulana Shaukat Ali, Lala Lajpat Rai and other national leaders visited Nankana to show their solidarity.

The Government now changed its policy. Seeing the emerging integration of the Akali movement with the national movement, it decided to follow a two-pronged policy. To win over or neutralize the Moderates and those concerned purely with religious reforms, it promised and started working for legislation which would satisfy them. It decided to suppress the extremist or the anti-imperialist section of the Akalis in the name of maintaining law and order.

The Akalis, too, changed their policy. Heartened by the support of nationalist forces in the country, they extended the scope of their movement to completely root out Government interference in their religious places. They began to see their movement as an integral part of the national struggle. Consequently, within the SGPC, too, the non-cooperator nationalist section took control. In May 1921, the SGPC passed a resolution in favour of non-cooperation, for the boycott of foreign goods and liquor, and for the substitution of *panchayats* for the British courts of law. The Akali leaders, arrested for the breaking of law, also refused to defend themselves, denying the jurisdiction of foreign-imposed courts.

A major victory was won by the Akalis in the 'Keys Affair' in October 1921. The Government made an effort to keep possession of the keys of the *Toshakhana* of the Golden Temple. The Akalis immediately reacted, and organized massive protest meetings; tens of Akali *jathas* reached Amritsar immediately. The SGPC advised Sikhs to join the *hartal* on the day of the arrival of the Prince of Wales in India. The Government retaliated by arresting the prominent, militant nationalist leaders of the SGPC like Baba Kharak Singh and Master Tara Singh. But, instead of dying down, the movement began to spread to the remotest rural areas and the army. The Non-Cooperation Movement was at its height in the rest of the country. The Government once again decided not to confront Sikhs on a religious issue. It released all those arrested in the 'Keys Affair' and surrendered the keys of the *Toshakhana* to Baba Kharak Singh, head of the SGPC. Mahatma Gandhi immediately sent a telegram to the Baba: 'First battle for India's freedom won. Congratulations.'[1]

*

The culmination of the movement to liberate the Gurdwaras came with the heroic non-violent struggle around Guru-Ka-Bagh Gurdwara which shook the whole of India. Smarting under its defeat in the 'keys affair,' the Punjab bureaucracy was looking for an opportunity to teach the

Akalis a lesson and to recover its lost prestige. It was further emboldened by the fact that the Non-Cooperation Movement had been withdrawn in February 1922. It began to look for a pretext.

The pretext was provided by events at a little known village, Ghokewala, about 20 kilometers from Amritsar. The *mahant* of the Gurdwara Guru-Ka-Bagh had handed over the Gurdwara to the SGPC in August 1921, but claimed personal possession of the attached land. When the Akalis cut a dry *kikkar* tree on the land for use in the community kitchen, he complained to the police 'of the theft of his property from his land.' The officials seized this opportunity to provoke the Akalis. On 9 August 1922, five Akalis were arrested and put on trial. The Akali Dal reacted immediately to the new challenge. Akali *jathas* began to arrive and cut trees from the disputed land. The Government started arresting all of them on charges of theft and rioting. By 28 August more than 4,000 Akalis had been arrested.

The authorities once again changed their tactics. Instead of arresting the Akali volunteers they began to beat them mercilessly with lathis. But the Akalis stood their ground and would not yield till felled to the ground with broken bones and lacerated bodies. C.F. Andrews described the official action as 'inhuman, brutal, foul, cowardly and incredible to an Englishman and a moral defeat of England.'[2] The entire country was outraged. National leaders and journalists converged on Guru-Ka-Bagh. Massive protest meetings were organized all over Punjab. A massive Akali gathering at Amritsar on 10 September was attended by Swami Shraddhanand, Hakim Ajmal Khan and others. The Congress Working Committee appointed a committee to investigate the conduct of the police.

Once again the Government had to climb down. As a face-saving device, it persuaded a retired Government servant to lease the disputed land from the *mahant* and then allow the Akalis to cut the trees. It also released all the arrested Akali volunteers.

With the Gurdwaras under the control of the SGPC, the militant Akalis looked for some other opportunity of confronting the Government since they felt that the larger Gurdwara — the country — was not yet liberated. In September 1923, the SGPC took up the cause of the Maharaja of Nabha who had been forced by the Government to abdicate. This led to the famous *morcha* at Jaito in Nabha. But the Akalis could not achieve much success on the issue since it neither involved religion nor was there much support in the rest of the country.

In the meanwhile, the Government had succeeded in winning over the moderate Akalis with the promise of legislation which was passed in July 1925 and which handed over control over all the Punjab Gurdwaras to an elected body of Sikhs which also came to be called the SGPC.

Apart from its own achievement, the Akali movement made a massive contribution to the political development of Punjab. It awakened the Punjab peasantry. As Mohinder Singh, the historian of the Akali movement, has pointed out: 'It was only during the Akali movement that the pro-British feudal leadership of the Sikhs was replaced by educated middle-class nationalists and the rural and urban classes united on a common platform during the two-pronged Akali struggle.' This movement was also a model of a movement on a religious issue which was utterly non-communal. To further quote Mohinder Singh: 'It was this idea of liberation of the country from a foreign Government that united all sections of the Sikh community and brought the Hindus, the Muslims and the Sikhs of the province into the fold of the Akali movement.'[3] The Akali movement also awakened the people of the princely states of Punjab to political consciousness and political activity. There were also certain weaknesses with long-term consequences. The movement encouraged a certain religiosity which would be later utilized by communalism.

The Akali movement soon divided into three streams because it represented three distinct political streams, which had no reason to remain united as a distinct Akali party once Gurdwara reform had taken place. One of the movement's streams consisted of moderate, pro-Government men who were pulled into the movement because of its religious appeal and popular pressure. These men went back to loyalist politics and became a part of the Unionist Party. Another stream consisted of nationalist persons who joined the mainstream nationalist movement, becoming a part of the Gandhian or leftist Kirti-Kisan and Communist wings. The third stream, which kept the title of Akali, although it was not the sole heir of the Akali movement, used to the full the prestige of the movement among the rural masses, and became the political organ of Sikh communalism, mixing religion and politics and inculcating the ideology of political separation from Hindus and Muslims. In pre-1947 politics the Akali Dal constantly vacillated between nationalist and loyalist politics.

*

Till 1917, the **National Congress** had refused to take up social reform issues lest the growing political unity of the Indian people got disrupted. It reversed this position in 1917 when it passed a resolution urging upon the people 'the necessity, justice and righteousness of removing all disabilities imposed by custom upon the depressed classes.' At this stage, Lokamanya Tilak also denounced untouchability and asked for its removal. But they did not take any concrete steps in the direction. Among the national leaders, it was Gandhi who gave top priority to the removal of untouchability and declared that this was no less important than the political struggle for freedom.

In 1923, the Congress decided to take active steps towards the eradication of untouchability. The basic strategy it adopted was to educate and mobilize opinion among caste Hindus on the question. The nationalist challenge in this respect came to be symbolized by two famous struggles in Kerala.

The problem was particularly acute in Kerala where the depressed classes or *avarnas* (those without caste, later known as Harijans) were subjected to degrading and de-humanising social disabilities. For example, they suffered not only from untouchability but also *theendal* or distance pollution—the *Ezhavas* and *Pulayas* could not approach the higher castes nearer than 16 feet and 72 feet respectively. Struggle against these disabilities was being waged since the end of 19th century by several reformers and intellectuals such as Sri Narayana Guru, N. Kumaran Asan and T.K. Madhavan.

Immediately after the Kakinada session, the Kerala Provincial Congress Committee (KPCC) took up the eradication of untouchability as an urgent issue. While carrying on a massive propaganda campaign against untouchability and for the educational and social upliftment of the Harijans, it was decided to launch an immediate movement to open Hindu temples and all public roads to the *avarnas* or Harijans. This,it was felt, would give a decisive blow to the notion of untouchabili*y since it was basically religious in character and the *avarnas'* exclusion from the temples was symbolic of their degradation and oppression.

A beginning was made in Vaikom, a village in Travancore. There was a major temple there whose four walls were surrounded by temple roads which could not be used by *avarnas* like *Ezhavas* and *Pulayas*. The KPCC decided to use the recently acquired weapon of *Satyagraha* to fight untouchability and to make a beginning at Vaikom by defying the unapproachability rule by leading a procession of *savarnas* (caste

Hindus) and *avarnas* on the temple roads on 30 March 1924.

The news of the *Satyagraha* aroused immediate enthusiasm among political and social workers and led to an intense campaign to arouse the conscience of *savarnas* and mobilize their active support. Many *savarna* organizations such as the Nair Service Society, Nair *Samajam* and Kerala Hindu Sabha supported the *Satyagraha*. Yogakshema Sabha, the leading organization of the Namboodiris (highest Brahmins by caste), passed a resolution favouring the opening of temples to *avarnas*. The temple authorities and the Travancore Government put up barricades on the roads leading to the temple and the District Magistrate served prohibitory orders on the leaders of the *Satyagraha*. On 30th March, the Satyagrahis, led by K.P. Kesava Menon, marched from the *Satyagraha* camp towards the temple. They, as well as the succeeding batches of Satyagrahis, consisting of both *savarnas* and *avarnas*, were arrested and sentenced to imprisonment.

The Vaikom *Satyagraha* created enthusiasm all over the country and volunteers began to arrive from different parts of India. An Akali *jatha* arrived from Punjab. E.V. Ramaswami Naicker (popularly known as Periyar later) led a *jatha* from Madurai and underwent imprisonment. On the other hand, the orthodox and reactionary section of caste Hindus met at Vaikom and decided to boycott all pro-*Satyagraha* Congressmen and not to employ them as teachers or lawyers or to vote for them.

On the death of the Maharaja in August 1924, the Maharani, as Regent, released all the Satyagrahis. As a positive response to this gesture, it was decided to organize a *jatha* (a group of volunteers) of caste Hindus to present a memorial to the Maharani asking for the opening of the temple roads to all. Batches of caste Hindus from all over Kerala converged on Vaikom. On 31 October, a *jatha* of nearly one hundred caste Hindus started their march on foot to Trivandrum. It was given warm receptions at nearly 200 villages and towns on the way. By the time it reached Trivandrum, it consisted of over 1,000 persons. The Maharani, however, refused to accept their demand and the *Satyagraha* was continued.

In early March 1925, Gandhi began his tour of Kerala and met the Maharani and other officials. A compromise was arrived at. The roads around the temple were opened to *avarnas* but those in the *Sankethan* of the temple remained closed to them. In his Kerala tour, Gandhi did not visit a single temple because *avarnas* were kept out of them.

The struggle against untouchability and for the social and economic uplift of the depressed classes continued all over India after 1924 as a part of the Gandhian constructive programme. Once again the struggle was most intense in Kerala.

Prodded by K. Kelappan, the KPCC took up the question of temple entry in 1931 during the period when the Civil Disobedience Movement was suspended. A vast campaign of public meetings was organized throughout Malabar. The KPCC decided to make a beginning by organizing a temple entry *Satyagraha* at Guruvayur on 1st November 1931.

A *jatha* of sixteen volunteers, led by the poet Subramanian Tirumambu, who became famous as the 'Singing Sword of Kerala,' began a march from Cannanore in the north to Guruvayur on 21 October. The volunteers ranged from the lowliest of Harijans to the highest caste Namboodiris. The march stirred the entire country and aroused anit-caste sentiments. 1 November was enthusiastically observed as All-Kerala Temple Entry Day with a programme of prayers, processions, meetings, receptions and fund collections. It was also observed in cities like Madras, Bombay, Calcutta, Delhi and Colombo (Sri Lanka). The popular response was tremendous. Many all-India leaders visited Malabar. Money and volunteers poured in from everywhere. The youth were specially attracted and were in the forefront of the struggle. The anti-untouchability movement gained great popularity. Many religious devotees transferred the offerings they would have made to the temple to the *Satyagraha* camp, feeling that the camp was even more sacred than the temple.

The temple authorities also made arrangements. They put up barbed wire all around the temple and organized gangs of watchmen to keep the Satyagrahis out and to threaten them with beating.

On 1 November, sixteen white *khadi*-clad volunteers marched to the eastern gate of the temple where their way was barred by a posse of policemen headed by the Superintendent of Police. Very soon, the temple servants and local reactionaries began to use physical force against the peaceful and non-violent Satyagrahis while the police stood by. For example, P. Krishna Pillai and A.K. Gopalan, who were to emerge later as major leaders of the Communist movement in Kerala, were mercilessly beaten. The *Satyagraha* continued even after the Civil Disobedience Movement was resumed in January 1932 and all Congress

Committees were declared unlawful and most of the Congressmen leading the *Satyagraha* were imprisoned.

The *Satyagraha* entered a new phase on 21 September 1932 when K. Kelappan went on a fast unto death before the temple until it was opened to the depressed classes. The entire country was again stirred to its depths. Once again meetings and processions engulfed Kerala and many other parts of the country. Caste Hindus from Kerala as well as rest of India made appeals to the Zamorin of Calicut, custodian of the temple, to throw open the temples to all Hindus; but without any success.

Gandhiji made repeated appeals to Kelappan to break his fast, at least temporarily, with an assurance that he would himself, if necessary, undertake the task of getting the temple opened. Finally, Kelappan broke his fast on October 2, 1932. The *Satyagraha* was also suspended. But the temple entry campaign was carried on ever more vigorously.

A *jatha* led by A.K. Gopalan toured whole of Kerala on foot, carrying on propaganda and addressing massive meetings everywhere. Before it was disbanded the *jatha* had covered nearly 1,000 miles and addressed over 500 meetings.

Even though the Guruvayur temple was not opened immediately, the *Satyagraha* was a great success in broader terms. As A.K. Gopalan has recorded in his autobiography, 'although the Guruvayur temple was still closed to Harijans, I saw that the movement had created an impetus for social change throughout the country. It led to a transformation everywhere.'4

The popular campaign against untouchability and for temple entry continued in the succeeding years. In November 1936, the Maharaja of Travancore issued a proclamation throwing open all Government- controlled temples to all Hindus irrespective of caste. Madras followed suit in 1938 when its Ministry was headed by C.Rajagopalachari. Other provinces under Congress rule also took similar steps.

The temple entry campaign used all the techniques developed by the Indian people in the course of the nationalist struggle. Its organizers succeeded in building the broadest possible unity, imparting mass education, and mobilizing the people on a very wide scale on the question of untouchability. Of course, the problem of caste inequality, oppression and degradation was very deep-seated and complex, and temple entry alone could not solve it. But *Satyagrahas* like those of Vaikom and Guruvayur and the movements around them did make a massive contribution in this respect. As E.M.S. Namboodiripad was to write years later: 'Guruvayur Temple *Satyagraha* was an event that thrilled thousands of young men like me and gave inspiration to a vast majority of the people to fight for their legitimate rights with self-respect . . . It was the very same youth who gave this bold lead, who subsequently became founder-leaders of the worker-peasant organizations that were free from the malice of religious or communal considerations.'[5]

The main weakness of the temple entry movement and the Gandhian or nationalist approach in fighting caste oppression was that even while arousing the people against untouchability they lacked a strategy for ending the caste system itself. The strength of the national movement in this respect was to find expression in the Constitution of independent India which abolished caste inequality, outlawed untouchability and guaranteed social equality to all citizens irrespective of their caste. Its weakness has found expression in the growth of casteism and the continuous existence in practice of oppression and discrimination against the lower castes in post-1947 India.

19 The Years of Stagnation — Swarajists, No-changers and Gandhiji

The withdrawal of the Non-Cooperation Movement in February 1922 was followed by the arrest of Gandhiji in March and his conviction and imprisonment for six years for the crime of spreading disaffection against the Government. The result was the spread of disintegration, disorganization and demoralization in the nationalist ranks. There arose the danger of the movement lapsing into passivity. Many began to question the wisdom of the total Gandhian strategy. Others started looking for ways out of the impasse.

A new line of political activity, which would keep up the spirit of resistance to colonial rule, was now advocated by C.R. Das and Motilal Nehru. They suggested that the nationalists should end the boycott of the legislative councils, enter them, expose them as 'sham parliaments' and as 'a mask which the bureaucracy has put on,' and obstruct 'every work of the council.' This, they argued, would not be giving up non-cooperation but continuing it in a more effective form by extending it to the councils themselves. It would be opening a new front in the battle.

C.R. Das as the President of the Congress and Motilal as its Secretary put forward this programme of 'either mending or ending' the councils at the Gaya session of the Congress in December 1922. Another section of the Congress, headed by Vallabhbhai Patel, Rajendra Prasad and C. Rajagopalachari, opposed the new proposal which was consequently defeated by 1748 to 890 votes. Das and Motilal resigned from their respective offices in the Congress and on 1 January 1923 announced the formation of the Congress-Khilafat *Swaraj* Party better known later as the *Swaraj* Party. Das was the President and Motilal one of the Secretaries of the new party. The adherents of the council-entry programme came to be popularly known as 'pro-changers' and those still advocating boycott of the councils as 'no-changers.'

The *Swaraj* Party accepted the Congress programme in its entirety except in one respect — it would take part in elections due later in the year. It declared that it would present the national demand for self-government in the councils and in case of its rejection its elected members would adopt 'a policy of uniform, continuous and consistent obstruction within the councils, with a view to make the Government through the councils impossible.'[1] The councils would, thus, be wrecked from within by creating deadlocks on every measure that came before them.

Both Das (born in 1870) and Motilal (born in 1861) were highly successful lawyers who had once been Moderates but had accepted the politics of boycott and non-cooperation in 1920. They had given up their legal practice, joined the movement as wholetime workers and donated to the nation their magnificent houses in Calcutta and Allahabad respectively. They were great admirers of Gandhiji but were also his political equals. Both were brilliant and effective parliamentarians. One deeply religious and the other a virtual agnostic, both were secular to the core. Different in many ways, they complemented each other and formed a legendary political combination. Das was imaginative and emotional and a great orator with the capacity to influence and conciliate friends and foes. Motilal was firm, coolly analytical, and a great organizer and disciplinarian. They had such absolute trust and confidence in each other that each could use the other's name for any statement without prior consultation.

The no-changers, whose effective head was Gandhiji even though he was in jail, argued for the continuation of the full programme of boycott and non-cooperation, effective working of the constructive programme and quiet preparations for the resumption of the suspended civil disobedience.

*

The pro-changers and the no-changers were soon engaged in a fierce controversy. There was, of course, a lot of common ground between the two. Both agreed that civil disobedience was not possible immediately and that no mass movement could be carried on indefinitely or for a prolonged period. Hence, breathing time was needed and a temporary retreat from the active phase of the movement was on the agenda. Both also accepted that there was need to rest and to reinvigorate the anti-imperialist forces, overcome demoralization, intensify politicization, widen political participation and mobilization, strengthen organization, and keep up the recruitment, training and morale of the cadre. In fact, the national movement was facing the basic problem that any mass movement has to face: how were they to carry on political work in the movements' non-active phases?

It was in the answer to this last question that the two sides differed. The *Swarajists* said that work in the councils was necessary to fill in the temporary political void. This would keep up the morale of the politicized Indians, fill the empty newspaper spaces, and enthuse the people. Electioneering and speeches in the councils would provide fresh avenues for political agitation and propaganda.

Even without Congressmen, said the *Swarajists*, the councils would continue to function and, perhaps, a large number of people would participate in voting. This would lead to the weakening of the hold of the Congress. Morever, non-Congressmen would capture positions of vantage and use them to weaken the Congress. Why should such 'vantage points in a revolutionary fight be left in the hands of the enemy?' By joining the councils and obstructing their work, Congressmen would prevent undesirable elements from doing mischief or the Government from getting some form of legitimacy for their laws.

In other words, the *Swarajists* claimed that they would transform the legislatures into arenas of political struggle and that their intention was not to use them, as the Liberals desired, as organs for the gradual transformation of the colonial state, but to use them as the ground on which the struggle for the overthrow of the colonial state was to be carried out.

The no-changers opposed council-entry mainly on the ground that parliamentary work would lead to the neglect of constructive and other work among the masses, the loss of revolutionary zeal and political corruption. The legislators who would go into the councils with the aim of wrecking them would gradually give up the politics of obstruction, get sucked into the imperial constitutional framework, and start cooperating with the Government on petty reforms and piecemeal legislation. Constructive work among the masses, on the other hand, would prepare them for the next round of civil disobedience.

As the pro-changer no-changer clash developed, the atmosphere of dismay in nationalist ranks began to thicken, and they began to be haunted by the fear of the repetition of the disastrous split of 1907. Pressure began to develop on the leaders to put a check on their public bickerings.

Both groups of leaders began to pull back from the brink and move towards mutual accommodation. This trend was helped by several factors. First, the need for unity was felt very strongly by all the Congressmen. Secondly, not only the no-changers but also the *Swarajists* realized that however useful parliamentary work might be, the real sanctions which would compel the Government to accept national demands would be forged only by a mass movement outside the legislatures — and this would need unity. Lastly, both groups of leaders fully accepted the essentiality of Gandhiji's leadership.

Consequently, in a special session of the Congress held at Delhi in September 1923, the Congress suspended all propaganda against council-entry and permitted Congressmen to stand as candidates and exercise their franchise in forthcoming elections.

*

Gandhiji was released from jail on 5 February 1924 on health grounds. He was completely opposed to council-entry as also to the obstruction of work in the councils which he believed was inconsistent with non-violent non-cooperation. Once again a split in the Congress loomed on the horizon. The Government very much hoped for and banked on such a split. When releasing the Mahatma, the Bombay Government had suggested that he 'would denounce the *Swarajists* for their defection from the pure principle of non-cooperation, and thus considerably reduce in legislatures their power for harm.'[2] Similarly, Reading, the Viceroy, told the Secretary of State for India, on 6 June 1924: 'The probability of a split between *Swarajists* and Gandhiji is increasing . . . Moonje, (The *Swarijist* leader from the Central Provinces) adds that the *Swarajists* are now driven to concentrating all their energy on breaking Gandhiji's hold on the Congress.'[3]

But Gandhiji did not oblige. Step by step, he moved towards an accommodation with the *Swarajists*. In fact, his approach towards the *Swarajists* at this stage brings out some of the basic features of his political style, especially when dealing with co-workers with whom he differed, and is, therefore, worth discussing, however briefly.

Gandhiji's starting point was the fact that even when opposing the *Swarajist* leaders he had full trust in their bonafides. He described them as 'the most valued and respected leaders' and as persons who 'have made great sacrifices in the cause of the country and who yield to no one in their love of freedom of the motherland.'[4] Moreover, he and Das and Motilal Nehru throughout maintained warm personal relations based on mutual respect and regard. Immediately after his release, Gandhiji refused to publicly comment on council-entry till he had discussions with the *Swarajist* leaders. Even after meeting them, while he continued to believe in the futility and even harmful character of the *Swarajists* programme, he remained convinced that public opposition to the 'settled fact' of council-entry would be counterproductive.

The courageous and uncompromising manner in which the *Swarajists* had functioned in the councils convinced Gandhiji that, however politically wrong, they were certainly not becoming a limb of imperial administration. To the contrary, he noted, 'they have shown determination, grit, discipline and cohesion and have not feared to carry their policy to the point of defiance. Once assume the desirability of entering Councils and it must be admitted that they have introduced a new spirit into the Indian Legislatures.'[5]

Gandhiji was also pained by the bickerings in the worst of taste among the proponents of the two schools. As he wrote in April 1924: 'Even the "changers" and the "no-changers" have flung mud against one another. Each has claimed the monopoly of truth and, with an ignorant certainty of conviction, sworn at the other for his helpless stupidity.'[6] He was very keen to end such mud-slinging.

In any case, felt Gandhiji, council entry had already occurred and now to withdraw would be 'disastrous' and would be 'misunderstood' by the Government and the people 'as a rout and weakness.'[7] This would further embolden the Government in its autocratic behaviour and repressive policy and add to the state of political depression among the people.

The last straw came when the Government launched a full attack on civil liberties and the *Swarajists* in Bengal in the name of fighting terrorism. It promulgated an ordinance on 25 October 1924 under which it conducted raids on Congress offices and house searches and arrested a large number of revolutionary terrorists and *Swarajists* and other Congressmen including Subhas Chandra Bose and two *Swarajists* members of the Bengal legislature, Anil Baran Roy and S.C. Mitra.

Perceiving a direct threat to the national movement, Gandhiji's first reaction was anger. He wrote in *Young India* on 31 October: 'The Rowlatt Act is dead but the spirit that prompted it is like an evergreen. So long as the interest of Englishmen is antagonistic to that of Indians, so long must there be anarchic crime or the dread of it and an edition of the Rowlatt Act in answer.'[8]

As an answer to the Government's offensive against the *Swarajists*, he decided to show his solidarity with the *Swarajists* by 'surrendering' before them. As he wrote in *Young India*: 'I would have been false to the country if I had not stood by the *Swaraj* Party in the hour of its need . . . I must stand by it even though I do not believe in the efficacy of Council-entry or even some of the methods of conducting Council-Warfare.'[9] And again: 'Though an uncompromising No-changer, I must not only tolerate their attitude and work with them, but I must even strengthen them wherever I can.'[10]

On 6 November 1924, Gandhiji brought the strife between the *Swarajists* and no-changers to an end, by signing a joint statement with Das and Motilal that the *Swarajists* Party would carry on work in the legislatures on behalf of the Congress and as an integral part of the Congress. This decision was endorsed in December at the Belgaum session of the Congress over which Gandhiji presided. He also gave the *Swarajists* a majority of seats on his Working Committee.

*

Elections to the legislative councils were held in November 1923. The *Swarajist* manifesto, released on 14 October, took up a strong anti-imperialist position: 'The guiding motive of the British in governing India is to secure the selfish interests of their own country and the so-called reforms are a mere blind to further the said interests under the pretence of granting responsible government to India, the real object being to continue the exploitation of the unlimited resources of the country by keeping Indians permanently in a subservient position to Britain.'[11] It promised that the *Swarajists* would wreck the sham reforms from within the councils.

Even though the *Swarajists* got only a few weeks to prepare for the elections and the franchise was extremely narrow — only about 6.2 million or less than three per cent had the right to vote — they managed to do quite well. They won forty-two out of 101 elected seats in the Central Legislative Assembly; they got a clear majority in the

Central Provinces ; they were the largest party in Bengal; and they fared quite well in Bombay and U.P., though not in Madras and 'Punjab because of strong casteist and communal currents.

In the Central Legislative Assembly, the *Swarajists* succeeded in building a common political front with the Independents led by M.A. Jinnah, the Liberals, and individuals such as Madan Mohan Malaviya. They built similar coalitions in most of the provinces. And they set out to inflict defeat after defeat on the Government.

The legislatures, reformed in 1919, had a 'semblance' of power without any real authority. Though they had a majority of elected members, the executive at the centre or in the provinces was outside their control, being responsible only to the British Government at home. Moreover, the Viceroy or the Governor could certify any legislation, including a budgetary grant, if it was rejected in the legislature. The *Swarajists* forced the Government to certify legislation repeatedly at the centre as well as in many of the provinces, thus exposing the true character of the reformed councils. In March 1925, they succeeded in electing Vithalbhai Patel, a leading *Swarajist*, as the President of the Central Legislative Assembly.

Though intervening on every issue and often outvoting the Government, the *Swarajists* took up at the centre three major sets of problems on which they delivered powerful speeches which were fully reported in the Press and followed avidly every morning by the readers. One was the problem of constitutional advance leading to self-Government; second of civil liberties, release of political prisoners, and repeal of repressive laws; and third of the development of indigenous industries.

In the very first session, Motilal Nehru put forward the national demand for the framing of a new constitution, which would transfer real power to India. This demand was passed by 64 votes to 48. It was reiterated and passed in September 1925 by 72 votes to 45. The Government had also to face humiliation when its demands for budgetary grants under different heads were repeatedly voted out. On one such occasion, Vithalbhai Patel told the Government: 'We want you to carry on the administration of this country by veto and by certification. We want you to treat the Government of India Act as a scrap of paper which I am sure it has proved to be.'12

Similarly, the Government was defeated several times on the question of the repeal of repressive laws and regulations and release of political prisoners. Replying to the official criticism of the revolutionary terrorists, C.S. Ranga Iyer said that the Government officials were themselves 'criminals of the worst sort, assassins of the deepest dye, men who are murdering the liberties of a liberty-loving race.'[13] Lala Lajpat Rai said: 'Revolutions and revolutionary movements are only natural . . . there can be no progress in the world without revolutions and revolutionary movements.'[14] C.R. Das was no less critical of the Government's repressive policy. He told the Bengal Provincial Conference: 'Repression is a process in the consolidation of arbitrary power — and I condemn the violence of the Government for repression is the most violent form of violence — just as I condemn violence as a method of winning political liberty.'[15]

The *Swarajist* activity in the legislatures was spectacular by any standards. It inspired the politicized persons and kept their political interest alive. People were thrilled every time the all-powerful foreign bureaucracy was humbled in the councils.

Simultaneously, during 1923-24, Congressmen captured a large number of municipalities and other local bodies. Das became the Mayor of Calcutta (with Subhas Bose as his Chief Executive Officer), and Vithalbhai Patel, the President of Bombay Corporation, Vallabhbhai Patel of Ahmedabad Municipality, Rajendra Prasad of Patna Municipality, and Jawaharlal Nehru of Allahabad Municipality. The no-changers actively joined in these ventures since they believed that local bodies could be used to promote the constructive programme.

Despite their circumscribed powers, many of the municipalities and district boards, headed by a galaxy of leaders, set out to raise, however little, the quality of life of the people. They did excellent work in the fields of education, sanitation, health, anti-untouchability, and *khadi* promotion, won the admiration of friend and foe, and quite often aroused popular enthusiasm.

The *Swarajists* suffered a major loss when C.R. Das died on 16 June 1925. Even more serious were a few other political developments. In the absence of a mass movement, communalism raised its ugly head and the political frustrations of the people began to find expression in communal riots. Actively encouraged by the colonial authorities, the communalists of all hues found a fertile field for their activities.

Its preoccupation with parliamentary politics also started telling on the internal cohesion of the *Swaraj* Party. For one, the limits of politics of obstruction were soon reached. Having repeatedly outvoted the

Government and forced it to certify its legislation, there was no way of going further inside the legislatures and escalating the politics of confrontation. This could be done only by a mass movement outside. But the *Swarajists* lacked any policy of coordinating their militant work in the legislatures with mass political work outside. In fact, they relied almost wholly on newspaper reporting.

The *Swarajists* also could not carry their coalition partners for ever and in every respect, for the latter did not believe in the *Swarajists* tactic of 'uniform, continuous and consistent obstruction.' The logic of coalition politics soon began to pull back the *Swarajists* from militant obstructionism. Some of the *Swarajist* legislators could also not resist the pulls of parliamentary perquisites and positions of status and patronage.

The Government's policy of creating dissension among the nationalists by trying to separate the *Swarajists* from the Liberals, militant *Swarajists* from the more moderate *Swarajists*, and Hindus from Muslims began to bear fruit. In Bengal, the majority in the *Swaraj* Party failed to support the tenants' cause against the *zamindars* and, thereby, lost the support of its pro-tenant, mostly Muslim, members. Nor could the *Swaraj* Party avoid the intrusion of communal discord in its own ranks.

Very soon, a group of Responsivists arose in the party who wanted to work the reforms and to hold office wherever possible. The Responsivists joined the Government in the Central Provinces. Their ranks were soon swelled by N.C. Kelkar, M.R. Jayakar and other leaders. Lajpat Rai and Madan Mohan Malaviya too separated themselves from the *Swaraj* Party on Responsivist as well as communal grounds.

To prevent further dissolution and disintegration of the party, the spread of parliamentary 'corruption,' and further weakening of the moral fibre of its members, the main leadership of the party reiterated its faith in mass civil disobedience and decided to withdraw from the legislatures in March 1926. Gandhiji, too, had resumed his critique of council-entry. He wrote to Srinivasa Iyengar in April 1926: 'The more I study the Councils' work, the effect of the entry into the Councils upon public life, its repercussions upon the Hindu-Muslim question, the more convinced I become not only of the futility but the inadvisability of Council-entry.'[16]

*

The *Swaraj* Party went into the elections held in November 1926 as a party in disarray — a much weaker and demoralized force. It had to face the Government and loyalist elements and its own dissenters on the one side and the resurgent Hindu and Muslim communalists on the other. A virulent communal and unscrupulous campaign was waged against the *Swarajists*. Motilal Nehru was, for example, accused of sacrificing Hindu interests, of favouring cow-slaughter, and of eating beef. The Muslim communalists were no less active in branding the *Swarajists* as anti-Muslim. The result was a severe weakening of the *Swaraj* Party. It succeeded in winning forty seats at the centre and half the seats in Madras but was severely mauled in all other provinces, especially in U.P., C.P., and Punjab. Moreover, both Hindu and Muslim communalists increased their representation in the councils. The *Swarajists* also could not form a nationalist coalition in the legislatures as they had done in 1923.

Once again the *Swarajists* passed a series of adjournment motions and defeated the Government on a number of bills. Noteworthy was the defeat of the Government on the Public Safety Bill in 1928. Frightened by the spread of socialist and communist ideas and influence and believing that the crucial role in this respect was being played by British and other foreign agitators sent to India by the Communist International, the Government proposed to acquire the power to deport 'undesirable' and 'subversive' foreigners. Nationalists of all colours, from the moderates to the militants, united in opposing the Bill. Lala Lajpat Rai said: 'Capitalism is only another name for Imperialism . . . We are in no danger from Bolshevism or Communism. The greatest danger we are in, is from the capitalists and exploiters.'[17] Motilal Nehru narrated his experiences in the Soviet Union and condemned anti-Soviet propaganda. He described the Public Safety Bill as 'a direct attack on Indian nationalism, on the Indian National Congress' and as 'the Slavery of India, Bill No. 1.'[18] T. Prakasam said that the Bill's main aim was to prevent the spread of nationalism among workers and peasants.[19] Diwan Chaman Lall, then a firebrand protege of Motilal, declared: 'If you are trying to preach against socialism, if you are demanding powers to suppress socialism, you will have to walk over our dead bodies before you can get that power.'[20] Even the two spokesmen of the capitalist class, Purshottamdas Thakurdas and G.D. Birla, firmly opposed the Bill.

In March 1929, having failed to get the Bill passed, the Government arrested thirty-one leading communists, trade unionists and other left-wing leaders and put them on trial at Meerut. This led to strong criticism of the Government by the nationalists. Describing the arrests as presaging 'a period of terrorism,' Gandhiji said that 'the motive behind these prosecutions is not to kill Communism, it is to strike terror.' He added: 'Evidently it (the Government) believes in a periodical exhibition of its capacity to supersede all law and to discover to a trembling India the red claws which usually remain under cover.'21 The *Swarajists* finally walked out of the legislatures in 1930 as a result of the Lahore Congress resolution and the beginning of civil disobedience.

Their great achievement lay in their filling the political void at a time when the national movement was recouping its strength. And this they did without getting coopted by the colonial regime. As Motilal Nehru wrote to his son: 'We have stood firm.' While some in their ranks fell by the wayside as was inevitable in the parliamentary framework, the overwhelming majority proved their mettle and stood their ground. They worked in the legislatures in an orderly disciplined manner and withdrew from them whenever the call came. Above all, they showed that it was possible to use the legislatures in a creative manner even as they promoted the politics of self-reliant anti-imperialism. They also successfully exposed the hollowness of the Reform Act of 1919 and showed the people that India was being ruled by 'lawless laws.'

*

In the meanwhile, the no-changers carried on laborious, quiet, undemonstrative, grass-roots constructive work around the promotion of *khadi* and spinning, national education and Hindu-Muslim unity, the struggle against untouchability and the boycott of foreign cloth. This work was symbolized by hundreds of ashrams that came up all over the country where political cadres got practical training in *khadi* work and work among the lower castes and tribal people. For example, there was the Vedchi Ashram in Bardoli *taluqa*, Gujarat, where Chimanlal Mehta, Jugatram Dave and Chimanlal Bhatt devoted their entire life to the spread of education among the adivasis or *kaliparaj*; or the work done by Ravishankar Maharaj among the lower caste *Baraiyas* of Kheda district.

In fact, Gandhian constructive work was multi-faceted in its content. It brought some much-needed relief to the poor; it promoted the process of the nation-in-the-making; and it made the urban-based and upper caste cadres familiar with the conditions of villages and lower castes. It provided Congress political workers or cadres continuous and effective work in the passive phases of the national movement, helped build their bonds with those sections of the masses who were hitherto untouched by politics, and developed their organizing capacity and self-reliance. It filled the rural masses with a new hope and increased Congress influence among them.

Without the uplift of the lower castes and *Adivasis* there could be no united struggle against colonialism. The boycott of foreign cloth was a stroke of genius which demonstrated to rulers and the world the Indian people's determination to be free. National schools and colleges trained young men in an alternative, non-colonial ideological framework. A large number of young men and women who dropped out in 1920-21 went back to the officially recognized educational institutions but many often became wholetime cadres of the movement.

As a whole, constructive work was a major channel for the recruitment of the soldiers of freedom and their political training — as also for the choosing and testing of their 'officers' and leaders. Constructive workers were to act as the steelframe of the nationalist movement in its active *satyagraha* phase. It was, therefore, not accidental that *khadi bhandar* workers, students and teachers of national schools and colleges, and Gandhian ashrams' inmates served as the backbone of the civil disobedience movements both as organizers and as active *Satyagrahis*.

The years 1922-27 were a period of contradictory developments. While the *Swarajists* and Gandhian constructive workers were quite active in their own separate ways, there simultaneously prevailed virulent factionalism and indiscipline in both the camps. By 1927, on the whole, an atmosphere of apathy and frustration had begun to prevail. Gandhiji wrote in May 1927: 'My only hope therefore lies in prayer and answer to prayer.'22

But underneath, after years of rest and recoupment, the forces of nationalism were again getting ready to enter a period of active struggle. This became evident in the rise of youth power and the national response to the Simon Commission.

20 *Bhagat Singh, Surya Sen and the Revolutionary Terrorists*

The revolutionary terrorists were severely suppressed during World War I, with most of their leaders in jail or absconding. Consequently, in order to create a more harmonious atmosphere for the Montagu-Chelmsford reforms, the Government released most of them under a general amnesty in early 1920. Soon after, the National Congress launched the Non-Cooperation Movement and on the urging of Gandhiji, C.R.Das and other leaders most of the revolutionary terrorists either joined the movement or suspended their own activities in order to give the Gandhian mass movement a chance.

But the sudden suspension of the Non-Cooperation Movement shattered the high hopes raised earlier. Many young people began to question the very basic strategy of the national leadership and its emphasis on non-violence and began to look for alternatives. They were not attracted by the parliamentary politics of the *Swarajists* or the patient and undramatic constructive work of the No-Changers. Many were drawn to the idea that violent methods alone would free India. Revolutionary terrorism again became attractive. It is not accidental that nearly all the major new leaders of the revolutionary terrorist politics, for example, Jogesh Chandra Chatterjea, Surya Sen, Jatin Das, Chandrashekhar Azad, Bhagat Singh, Sukhdev, Shiv Varma, Bhagwati Charan Vohra and Jaidev Kapur, had been enthusiastic participants in the non-violent Non-Cooperation Movement.

Gradually two separate strands of revolutionary terrorism developed — one in Punjab, U.P. and Bihar and the other in Bengal. Both the strands came under the influence of several new social forces. One was the upsurge of working class trade unionism after the War. They could see the revolutionary potential of the new class and desired to harness it to the nationalist revolution. The second major influence was that of the Russian Revolution and the success of the young Socialist State in consolidating itself. The youthful revolutionaries were keen to learn from and take the help of the young Soviet State and its ruling Bolshevik Party. The third influence was that of the newly sprouting Communist groups with their emphasis on Marxism, Socialism and the proletariat.

*

The revolutionaries in northern India were the first to emerge out of the mood of frustration and reorganize under the leadership of the old veterans, Ramprasad Bismil, Jogesh Chatterjea and Sachindranath Sanyal whose *Bandi Jiwan* served as a textbook to the revolutionary movement. They met in Kanpur in October 1924 and founded the Hindustan Republican Association (or Army) to organize armed revolution to overthrow colonial rule and establish in its place a Federal Republic of the United States of India whose basic principle would be adult franchise.

Before armed struggle could be waged, propaganda had to be organized on a large scale, men had to be recruited and trained and arms had to be procured. All these required money. The most important 'action' of the HRA was the Kakori Robbery. On 9 August 1925, ten men held up the 8-Down train at Kakori, an obscure village near Lucknow, and looted its official railway cash. The Government reaction was quick and hard. It arrested a large number of young men and tried them in the Kakori Conspiracy Case. Ashfaqulla Khan, Ramprasad Bismil, Roshan Singh and Rajendra Lahiri were hanged, four others were sent to the Andamans for life and seventeen others were sentenced to long terms of imprisonment. Chandrashekhar Azad remained at large.

The Kakori case was a major setback to the revolutionaries of northern India; but it was not a fatal blow. Younger men such as Bejoy Kumar Sinha, Shiv Varma and Jaidev Kapur in U.P., Bhagat Singh, Bhagwati Charan Vohra and Sukhdev in Punjab set out to reorganize the HRA under the overall leadership of Chandrashekhar Azad. Simultaneously, they were being influenced by socialist ideas. Finally, nearly all the major young revolutionaries of northern India met at Ferozeshah Kotla Ground at Delhi on 9 and 10 September 1928, created a new collective leadership, adopted socialism as their official goal and changed the name of the party to the Hindustan Socialist Republican Association (Army).

*

Even though, as we shall see, the HSRA and its leadership was rapidly moving away from individual heroic action and assassination and towards mass politics, Lala Lajpat Rai's death, as the result of a brutal lathi-charge when he was leading an anti-Simon Commission demonstration at Lahore on 30 October 1928, led them once again to take to individual assassination. The death of this great Punjabi leader, popularly known as Sher-e-Punjab, was seen by the romantic youthful leadership of the HSRA as a direct challenge. And so, on 17 December 1928, Bhagat Singh, Azad and Rajguru assassinated, at Lahore, Saunders, a police official involved in the lathi-charge on Lala Lajpat Rai. In a poster, put up by the HSRA after the assassination, the assassination was justified as follows: 'The murder of a leader respected by millions of people at the unworthy hands of an ordinary police official . . . was an insult to the nation. It was the bounden duty of young men of India to efface it . . . We regret to have had to kill a person but he was part and parcel of that inhuman and unjust order which has to be destroyed.'[1]

The HSRA leadership now decided to let the people know about its changed objectives and the need for a revolution by the masses. Bhagat Singh and B.K.Dutt were asked to throw a bomb in the Central Legislative Assembly on 8 April 1929 against the passage of the Public Safety Bill and the Trade Disputes Bill which would reduce the civil liberties of citizens in general and workers in particular. The aim was not to kill, for the bombs were relatively harmless, but, as the leaflet they threw into the Assembly hall proclaimed, 'to make the deaf hear'. The objective was to get arrested and to use the trial court as a forum for propaganda so that people would become familiar with their movement and ideology.

Bhagat Singh and B.K. Dutt were tried in the Assembly Bomb Case. Later, Bhagat Singh, Sukhdev, Rajguru and tens of other revolutionaries were tried in a series of famous conspiracy cases. Their fearless and defiant attitude in the courts — every day they entered the court-room shouting slogans '*Inquilab Zindabad,*' '*Down, Down with Imperialism,*'

'*Long Live the Proletariat*' and singing songs such as '*Sarfaroshi ki tamanna ab hamare dil mei hai*' (our heart is filled with the desire for martyrdom) and '*Mera rang de basanti chola*' (dye my clothes in saffron colour (the colour of courage and sacrifice)) — was reported in newspapers; unsurprisingly this won them the support and sympathy of people all over the country including those who had complete faith in non-violence. Bhagat Singh became a household name in the land. And many persons, all over the country, wept and refused to eat food, attend schools, or carry on their daily work when they heard of his hanging in March 1931.

The country was also stirred by the prolonged hunger strike the revolutionary under-trials undertook as a protest against the horrible conditions in jails. They demanded that they be treated not as criminals but as political prisoners. The entire nation rallied behind the hunger-strikers. On 13 September, the 64th day of the epic fast, Jatin Das, a frail young man with an iron-will, died. Thousands came to pay him homage at every station passed by the train carrying his body from Lahore to Calcutta. At Calcutta, a two-mile-long procession of more than six lakh people carried his coffin to the cremation ground.

A large number of revolutionaries were convicted in the Lahore Conspiracy Case and other similar cases and sentenced to long terms of imprisonment; many of them were sent to the Andamans. Bhagat Singh, Sukhdev and Rajguru were sentenced to be hanged. The sentence was carried out on 23 March 1931.

*

In Bengal, too, the revolutionary terrorists started reorganizing and developing their underground activities. At the same time, many of them continued to work in the Congress organization. This enabled them to gain access to the vast Congress masses; on the other hand, they provided the Congress with an organizational base in small towns and the countryside. They cooperated with C.R. Das in his Swarajist work. After his death, as the Congress leadership in Bengal got divided into two wings, one led by Subhas Chandra Bose and the other by J.M. Sengupta, the Yugantar group joined forces with the first and Anushilan with the second.

Among the several 'actions' of the reorganized groups was the attempt to assassinate Charles Tegart, the hated Police Commissioner of Calcutta, by Gopinath Saha in January 1924. By an error, another Englishman named Day was killed. The Government came down on the people with a heavy hand. A large number of people, suspected of being terrorists, or their supporters, were arrested under a newly promulgated ordinance. These included Subhas Chandra Bose and many other Congressmen. Saha was hanged despite massive popular protest. The revolutionary activity suffered a severe setback.

Another reason for stagnation in revolutionary terrorist activity lay in the incessant factional and personal quarrels within the terrorist groups, especially where Yugantar and Anushilan rivalry was concerned. But very soon younger revolutionaries began to organize themselves in new groups, developing fraternal relations with the active elements of both the Anushilan and Yugantar parties. Among the new 'Revolt Groups,' the most active and famous was the Chittagong group led by Surya Sen.

Surya Sen had actively participated in the Non-Cooperation Movement and had become a teacher in a national school in Chittagong, which led to his being popularly known as Masterda. Arrested and imprisoned for two years, from 1926 to 1928, for revolutionary activity, he continued to work in the Congress. He and his group were closely associated with the Congress work in Chittagong. In 1929, Surya Sen was the Secretary and five of his associates were members of the Chittagong District Congress Committee.

Surya Sen, a brilliant and inspiring organizer, was an unpretentious, soft-spoken and transparently sincere person. Possessed of immense personal courage, he was deeply humane in his approach. He was fond of saying: 'Humanism is a special virtue of a revolutionary.' He was also very fond of poetry, being a great admirer of Rabindranath Tagore and Kazi Nazrul Islam.

Surya Sen soon gathered around himself a large band of revolutionary youth including Anant Singh, Ganesh Ghosh and Lokenath Baul. They decided to organize a rebellion, on however small a scale, to demonstrate that it was possible to challenge the armed might of the British empire in India. Their action plan was to include occupation of the two main armouries in Chittagong and the seizing of their arms with which a large band of revolutionaries could be formed into an armed detachment; the destruction of the telephone and telegraph systems of the city; and the dislocation of the railway communication system between Chittagong and the rest of Bengal. The action was carefully planned and was put into execution at 10 o'clock on the night of 18 April 1930. A group of six revolutionaries, led by Ganesh Ghosh, captured the Police Armoury, shouting slogans such as *Inquilab Zindabad, Down with Imperialism* and *Gandhiji's Raj has been established*. Another group of ten, led by Lokenath Paul, took over the Auxiliary Force Armoury along with its Lewis guns and 303 army rifles. Unfortunately they could not locate the ammunition. This was to prove a disastrous setback to the revolutionaries' plans. The revolutionaries also succeeded in dislocating telephone and telegraph communications and disrupting movement by train. In all, sixty-five were involved in the raid, which was undertaken in the name of the Indian Republican Army, Chittagong Branch.

All the revolutionary groups gathered outside the Police Armoury where Surya Sen, dressed in immaculate white *khadi* dhoti and a long coat and stiffly ironed Gandhi cap, took a military salute, hoisted the National Flag among shouts of *Bande Mataram* and *Inquilab Zindabad*, and proclaimed a Provisional Revolutionary Government.

It was not possible for the band of revolutionaries to put up a fight in the town against the army which was expected. They, therefore, left Chittagong town before dawn and marched towards the Chittagong hill ranges, looking for a safe place. It was on the Jalalabad hill that several thousand troops surrounded them on the afternoon of 22 April. After a fierce fight, in which over eighty British troops and twelve revolutionaries died, Surya Sen decided to disperse into the neighbouring villages; there they formed into small groups and conducted raids on Government personnel and property. Despite severe repressive measures and combing operations by the authorities, the villagers, most of them Muslim, gave food and shelter to the revolutionary outlaws and enabled them to survive for three years. Surya Sen was finally arrested on 16 February 1933, tried and hanged on 12 January 1934. Many of his co-fighters were caught and sentenced to long terms of imprisonment.

The Chittagong Armoury Raid had an immense impact on the people of Bengal. As an official publication remarked, it 'fired the imagination of revolutionary-minded youth' and 'recruits poured into the various terrorist groups in a steady stream.' The year 1930 witnessed a major revival of revolutionary activity, and its momentum carried over to 1931 and 1932. There were numerous instances of death-defying heroism. In Midnapore district alone, three British magistrates were assassinated. Attempts were made on the lives of two Governors;

two Inspectors- General of Police were killed. During this three-year period, twenty-two officials and twenty non-officials were killed.

The official reaction to the Armoury Raid and the revival of revolutionary terrorist activity was initially one of panic and, then, of brutal reprisals. The Government armed itself with twenty repressive Acts and let loose the police on all nationalists. In Chittagong, it burnt several villages, imposed punitive fine on many others, and in general established a reign of terror. In 1933, it arrested and sentenced Jawaharlal Nehru to a two-year term in jail for sedition. He had in a speech in Calcutta condemned imperialism, praised the heroism of revolutionary youth (even while criticizing the policy of terrorism as futile and out-of-date) and condemned police repression.

A remarkable aspect of this new phase of the terrorist movement in Bengal was the large-scale participation of young women. Under Surya Sen's leadership, they provided shelter, acted as messengers and custodians of arms, and fought, guns in hand. Pritilata Waddedar died while conducting a raid, while Kalpana Dutt (now Joshi) was arrested and tried along with Surya Sen and given a life sentence. In December 1931, two school girls of Comilla, Santi Ghosh and Suniti Chowdhury, shot dead the District Magistrate. In February 1932, Bina Das fired point blank at the Governor while receiving her degree at the Convocation.

Compared to the old revolutionary terrorists, as also Bhagat Singh and his comrades, the Chittagong rebels made an important advance. Instead of an individual's act of heroism or the assassination of an individual, theirs was a group action aimed at the organs of the colonial state. But the objective still was to set an example before the youth, and to demoralize the bureaucracy. As Kalpana Joshi (Dutt) has put it, the plan was that when, after the Chittagong rebellion, 'the Government would bring in troops to take back Chittagong they (the terrorists) would die fighting — thus creating a legend and setting an example before their countrymen to emulate.'[2] Or as Surya Sen told Ananda Gupta: 'A dedicated band of youth must show the path of organized armed struggle in place of individual terrorism. Most of us will have to die in the process but our sacrifice for such a noble cause will not go in vain.'[3]

The Bengal revolutionaries of the 1920s and 1930s had shed some of their earlier Hindu religiosity — they no longer took religious oaths and vows. Some of the groups also no longer excluded Muslims — the

Chittagong IRA cadre included many Muslims like Sattar, Mir Ahmad, Fakir Ahmad Mian, Tunu Mian and got massive support from Muslim villagers around Chittagong. But they still retained elements of social conservatism, nor did they evolve broader socio-economic goals. In particular, those revolutionary terrorists, who worked in the *Swaraj* party, failed to support the cause of Muslim peasantry against the *zamindars*.

*

A real breakthrough in terms of revolutionary ideology and the goals of revolution and the forms of revolutionary struggle was made by Bhagat Singh and his comrades. Rethinking had, of course, started on both counts in the HRA itself. Its manifesto had declared in 1925 that it stood for 'the abolition of all systems which make the exploitation of man by man possible.'[4] Its founding council, in its meeting in October 1924, had decided 'to preach social revolutionary and communistic principles.'[5] Its main organ, *The Revolutionary*, had proposed the nationalization of the railways and other means of transport and large-scale industries such as steel and ship building. The HRA had also decided 'to start labour and peasant organizations' and to work for 'an organized and armed revolution.'[6]

In a message from the death-cell, Ramprasad Bismil had appealed to the youth to give up 'the desire to keep revolvers and pistols,' 'not to work in revolutionary conspiracies,' and to work in 'the open movement.' He had asked the people to establish Hindu-Muslim unity and unite all political groups under the leadership of the Congress He had also affirmed his faith in communism and the principle that 'every human being has equal rights over products of nature.'[7]

Bhagat Singh, born in 1907 and a nephew of the famous revolutionary Ajit Singh, was a giant of an intellectual. A voracious reader, he was one of the most well-read of political leaders of the time. He had devoured books in the Dwarkadas Library at Lahore on socialism, the Soviet Union and revolutionary movements, especially those of Russia, Ireland and Italy. At Lahore, he organized several study circles with the help of Sukhdev and others and carried on intensive political discussions. When the HSRA office was shifted to Agra, he immediately set up a library and urged members to read and discuss socialism and other revolutionary ideas. His shirt pockets always bulged with books which he constantly offered to lend his comrades. After his arrest he transformed the jail into a veritable university. Emphasizing the role of ideas in the making of revolution, he declared before the Lahore High Court: 'The sword of revolution is sharpened on the whetting- stone of ideas.'[8] This atmosphere of wide reading and deep thinking pervaded the ranks of the HSRA leadership. Sukhdev, Bhagwati Charan Vohra, Shiv Varma, Bejoy Sinha, Yashpal, all were intellectuals of a high order. Nor would even Chandrashekar Azad, who knew little English, accept any idea till it was fully explained to him. He followed every major turn in the field of ideas through discussion. The draft of the famous statement of revolutionary position, *The Philosophy of the Bomb*, was written by Bhagwati Charan Vohra at the instance of Azad and after a full discussion with him.

Bhagat Singh had already, before his arrest in 1929, abandoned his belief in terrorism and individual heroic action. He had turned to Marxism and had come to believe that popular broad-based mass movements alone could lead to a successful revolution; in other words revolution could only be achieved 'by the masses for the masses.' That is why Bhagat Singh helped establish the Punjab Naujawan Bharat Sabha in 1926 (becoming its founding Secretary), as the open wing of the revolutionaries. The Sabha was to carry out open political work among the youth, peasants and workers. It was to open branches in the villages. Under its auspices, Bhagat Singh used to deliver political lectures with the help of magic lantern slides. Bhagat Singh and Sukhdev also organized the Lahore Students Union for open, legal work among the students.

Bhagat Singh and his comrades also gave expression to their understanding that revolution meant the development and organization of a mass movement of the exploited and suppressed sections of society by the revolutionary intelligentsia in the course of their statements from 1929 to 1931 in the courts as well as outside. Just before his execution, Bhagat Singh declared that 'the real revolutionary armies are in the villages and in factories.'[9] Moreover, in his behest to young political workers, written on 2 February 1931, he declared: 'Apparently,I have acted like a terrorist. But I am not a terrorist. . . . Let me announce with all the strength at my command, that I am not a terrorist and I never was, except perhaps in the beginning of my revolutionary career. And I am convinced that we cannot gain anything through those methods.'[10]

Then why did Bhagat Singh and his comrades still take recourse to individual heroic action? One reason was the very rapidity of the changes in their thinking. The past formed a part of their present, for these young men had to traverse decades within a few years. Moreover, effective acquisition of a new ideology is not an event; it is not like a religious conversion; it is always a prolonged historical process. Second, they were faced with a classic dilemma: From where would come the cadres, the hundreds of full-time young political workers, who would fan out among the masses? How were they to be recruited? Patient intellectual and political work appeared to be too slow and too akin to the Congress style of politics which the revolutionaries wanted to transcend. The answer appeared to be to appeal to the youth through 'propaganda by deed,' to recruit the initial cadres of a mass revolutionary party through heroic dramatic action and the consequent militant propaganda before the courts. In the last stage, during 1930 and 1931, they were mainly fighting to keep the glory of the sacrifice of their comrades under sentence shining as before. As Bhagat Singh put it, he had to ask the youth to abandon revolutionary terrorism without tarnishing the sense of heroic sacrifice by appearing to have reconsidered his politics under the penalty of death[11]. Life was bound to teach, sooner or later, correct politics; the sense of sacrifice once lost would not be easy to regain.

Bhagat Singh and his comrades also made a major advance in broadening the scope and definition of revolution. Revolution was no longer equated with mere militancy or violence. Its first objective was national liberation — the overthrow of imperialism. But it must go beyond and work for a new socialist social order, it must 'end exploitation of man by man.'[12] *The Philosophy of the Bomb*, written by Bhagwati Charan Vohra, Chandrashekhar Azad and Yashpal, defined revolution as 'Independence, social, political and economic' aimed at establishing 'a new order of society in which political and economic exploitation will be an impossibility'[13]. In the Assembly Bomb Case, Bhagat Singh told the court: '"Revolution," does not necessarily involve sanguinary strife, nor is there any place in it for individual vendetta. It is not the cult of the bomb and the pistol. By "Revolution" we mean that the present order of things, which is based on manifest injustice, must change.'[14] In a letter from jail, he wrote: 'The peasants have to liberate themselves not only from foreign yoke but also from the yoke of landlords and capitalists.'[15] In his last message of 3 March 1931, he declared that the struggle in India would continue so long as 'a handful of exploiters go on exploiting the labour of common people for their own ends. It matters little whether these exploiters are purely British capitalists, or British and Indians in alliance, or even purely Indians.'[16] Bhagat Singh defined socialism in a scientific manner — it must mean abolition of capitalism and class domination. He fully accepted Marxism and the class approach to society. In fact, he saw himself above all as a precursor and not maker of the revolution, as a propagator of the ideas of socialism and communism, as a humble initiator of the socialist movement in India.[17]

Bhagat Singh was a great innovator in two areas of politics. Being fully and consciously secular, he understood, more clearly than many of his contemporaries, the danger that communalism posed to the nation and the national movement. He often told his audience that communalism was as big an enemy as colonialism.

In April 1928, at the conference of youth where Naujawan Bharat Sabha was reorganized, Bhagat Singh and his comrades openly opposed the suggestion that youth belonging to religious- communal organizations should be permitted to become members of the Sabha. Religion was one's private concern and communalism was an enemy to be fought, argued Bhagat Singh.[18] Earlier in 1927, condemning communal killings as barbaric, he had pointed out that communal killers did not kill a person because he was guilty of any particular act but simply because that person happened to be a Hindu, Muslim or Sikh. But, wrote Bhagat Singh, a new group of youth was coming forward who did not recognize any differences based on religion and saw a person first as a human being and then as an Indian.[19]

Bhagat Singh revered Lajpat Rai as a leader. But he would not spare even Lajpat Rai, when, during the last years of his life, Lajpat Rai turned to communal politics. He then launched a political-ideological campaign against him.[20] Because Lajpat Rai was a respected leader, he would not publicly use harsh words of criticism against him. And so he printed as a pamphlet Robert Browning's famous poem, 'The Lost Leader,' in which Browning criticizes Wordsworth for turning against liberty. The poem begins with the line 'Just for a handful of silver he left us.' A few more of the poem's lines were: 'We shall march prospering, — not thro' his presence; Songs may inspirit us, — not from his lyre,' and 'Blot out his name, then, record one lost soul more.' There was not one word of criticism of Lajpat Rai. Only, on the front cover, he printed Lajpat Rai's photograph!

Significantly, two of the six rules of the Naujawan Bharat Sabha, drafted by Bhagat Singh, were: 'To have nothing to do with communal bodies or other parties which disseminate communal ideas' and 'to create the spirit of general toleration among the public considering religion as a matter of personal belief of man and to act upon the same fully.'[21]

Bhagat Singh also saw the importance of freeing the people from the mental bondage of religion and superstition. A few weeks before his death, he wrote the article 'Why I am an Atheist' in which he subjected religion and religious philosophy to a scathing critique. He traced his own path to atheism, how he first gave up belief 'in the mythology and doctrines of Sikhism or any other religion,' and in the end lost faith in the existence of God. To be a revolutionary, he said, one required immense moral strength, but one also required 'criticism and independent thinking.' In the struggle for self-emancipation, humanity had to struggle against 'the narrow conception of religion' as also against the belief in God. 'Any man who stands for progress,' he wrote, 'has to criticise, disbelieve and challenge every item of the old faith. Item by item he has to reason out every nook and corner of the prevailing faith.' Proclaiming his own belief in atheism and materialism, he asserted that he was 'trying to stand like a man with an erect head to the last; even on the gallows.'[22]

*

Government action gradually decimated the revolutionary terrorist ranks. With the death of Chandrashekhar Azad in a shooting encounter in a public park at Allahabad in February 1931, the revolutionary terrorist movement virtually came to an end in Punjab, U.P. and Bihar. Surya Sen's martyrdom marked an end to the prolonged saga of revolutionary terrorism in Bengal. A process of rethinking in jails and in the Andamans began. A large number of the revolutionaries turned to Marxism and the idea of a socialist revolution by the masses. They joined the Communist Party, the Revolutionary Socialist Party, and other Left parties. Many others joined the Gandhian wing of the Congress.

The politics of the revolutionary terrorists had severe limitations — above all theirs was not the politics of a mass movement; they failed to politically activate the masses or move them into political actions; they could not even establish contact with the masses. All the same, they made an abiding contribution to the national freedom movement. Their deep patriotism, courage and determination, and sense of sacrifice stirred the Indian people. They helped spread nationalist consciousness in the land; and in northern India the spread of socialist consciousness owed a lot to them.

21 *The Gathering Storm 1927-1929*

In the years following the end of the Non-Cooperation Movement in
1922, the torch of nationalism had been kept alive by the Gandhian
constructive workers who dug their roots deep into village soil, by the
Swarajists who kept the Government on its toes in the legislatures, by
the Koya tribals in Andhra who heroically fought the armed might of
the colonial state under the leadership of Ramachandra Raju from 1922-
24, by the Akalis in Punjab, by the *Satyagrahis* who flocked to defend
the honour of the national flag in Nagpur in 1923, and countless others
who engaged themselves in organizational, ideological and agitational
activities at a variety of levels.

*

It was, however, from the latter part of 1927 that the curve of the mass
anti-imperialist upsurge began to take a marked upward turn. As with
the Rowlatt Bills in 1919, it was the British Government that provided
a catalyst and a rallying ground by an announcement on 8 November
1927 of an all-White commission to recommend whether India was
ready for further constitutional progress and on which lines. Indian
nationalists had for many years declared the constitutional reforms of
1919 as inadequate and had been clamouring for an early reconsideration
of the constitutional question, but the Government had been adamant
that the declared period of ten ears must lapse before fresh proposals
were considered. In 1927, however, the Conservative Government of
Britain, faced with the prospect of electoral defeat at the hands of the

Labour Party, suddenly decided that it could not leave an issue which concerned the future of the British Empire in the irresponsible hands of an inexperienced Labour Government; and it was thus that the Indian Statutory Commission, popularly known as the Simon Commission after its Chairman, was appointed.

The response in India was immediate and unanimous. That no Indian should be thought fit to serve on a body that claimed the right to decide the political future of India was an insult that no Indian of even the most moderate political opinion was willing to swallow. The call for a boycott of the Commission was endorsed by the Liberal Federation led by Tej Bahadur Sapru, by the Indian Industrial and Commercial Congress, and by the Hindu Mahasabha; the Muslim League even split on the issue, Mohammad Ali Jinnah carrying the majority with him in favour of boycott.

It was the Indian National Congress, however, that turned the boycott into a popular movement. The Congress had resolved on the boycott at its annual session in December 1927 at Madras, and in the prevailing excitable atmosphere, Jawaharlal Nehru had even succeeded in getting passed a snap resolution declaring complete independence as the goal of the Congress. But protest could not be confined to the passing of resolutions, as Gandhiji made clear in the issue of *Young India* of 12 January 1928: 'It is said that the Independence Resolution is a fitting answer. . . The act of appointment (of the Simon Commission) needs for an answer, not speeches, however heroic they may be, not declarations, however brave they may be, but corresponding action. . .'[1]

The action began as soon as Simon and his friends landed at Bombay on 3 February 1928. That day, all the major cities and towns observed a complete *hartal*, and people were out on the streets participating in mass rallies, processions and black-flag demonstrations. In Madras, a major clash with the police resulted in firing and the death of one person. T. Prakasam symbolized the defiant spirit of the occasion by baring his chest before the armed policemen who tried in vain to stop him from going to the scene of the killing. Everywhere that Simon went — Calcutta, Lahore, Lucknow, Vijayawada, Poona — he was greeted by a sea of black-flags carried by thousands of people. And ever new ways of defiance were being constantly invented. The youth of Poona, for example, took advantage of the fact that for a long stretch between Lonavala and Poona the road and the rail-track ran within sight of each other. They climbed into a lorry and drove alongside the train that was carrying Simon and Company, waving black flags at them all the way from Lonavala to Poona. In Lucknow, Khaliquzzaman executed the brilliant idea of floating kites and balloons imprinted with the popular slogan 'Go Back Simon' over the reception organized in Kaiserbagh by the *taluqdars* for members of the Commission.[2]

If humour and creativity was much in evidence, so too was popular anger at the manner in which the police dealt with the protesters. Lathi charges were becoming all too frequent, and even respected and senior leaders were not spared the blows. In Lucknow, Jawaharlal and Govind Ballabh Pant were beaten up by the police. But the worst incident happened in Lahore where Lala Lajpat Rai, the hero of the Extremist days and the most revered leader of Punjab, was hit on the chest by lathis on 30 October and succumbed to the injuries on 17 November 1928. It was his death that Bhagat Singh and his comrades were seeking to avenge when they killed the white police official, Saunders, in December 1928.

*

The Simon boycott movement provided the first taste of political action to a new generation of youth. They were the ones who played the most active role in this protest, and it was they who gave the movement its militant flavour. And although a youth movement had already begun to take shape by 1927, it was participation in the Simon agitation that gave a real fillip to the formation of youth leagues and associations all over the country. Jawaharlal Nehru and Subhas Bose emerged as the leaders of this new wave of youth and students, and they travelled from one province to another addressing and presiding over innumerable youth conferences.

The upsurge among the youth also proved a fruitful ground for the germination and spread of the new radical ideas of socialism that had begun to reach Indian shores. Jawaharlal Nehru had returned from Europe in 1927 after representing the Indian National Congress at the Brussels Congress of the League Against Imperialism. He also visited the Soviet Union and was deeply impressed by socialist ideas. It was with the youth that he first shared his evolving perspective. Although Jawaharlal Nehru's was undoubtedly the most important role, other groups and individuals too played a crucial part in the popularization of the socialist vision. Subhas Bose was one such individual, though his notion of socialism was nowhere as scientific and clear as Jawaharlal's. Among groups, the more important ones were the Naujawan Bharat

Sabha in Lahore, and the small group of Communists who had formed the Workers' and Peasants' Parties with the specific aim of organizing workers and peasants and radicalizing the Congress from within. As a result, the young people who were being drawn into the anti-imperialist movement were also simultaneously becoming sympathetic to the ideas of socialism, and youth groups in some areas even developed links with workers' and peasants' struggles.

*

Lord Birkenhead, the Conservative Secretary of State responsible for the appointment of the Simon Commission, had constantly harped on the inability of Indians to formulate a concrete scheme of constitutional reforms which had the support of wide sections of Indian political opinion. This challenge, too, was taken up and meetings of the All-Parties Conference were held in February, May and August 1928 to finalize a scheme which popularly came to be known as the Nehru Report after Motilal Nehru, its principal author. This report defined Dominion Status as the form of government desired by India. It also rejected the principle of separate communal electorates on which previous constitutional reforms had been based. Seats would be reserved for Muslims at the Centre and in provinces in which they were in a minority, but not in those where they had a numerical majority. The Report also recommended universal adult suffrage, equal rights for women, freedom to form unions, and dissociation of the state from religion in any form. A section of the Muslim League had in any case dissociated itself from these deliberations, but by the end of the year it became clear that even the section led by Jinnah would not give up the demand for reservation of seats for Muslims especially in Muslim majority provinces. The dilemma in which Motilal Nehru and other secular leaders found themselves was not one that was easy to resolve: if they conceded more to Muslim communal opinion, then Hindu communalists would withdraw support and if they satisfied the latter, then Muslim leaders would be estranged. In the event, no further concessions were forthcoming and Jinnah withdrew his support to the report and went ahead to propose his famous 'Fourteen Points' which were basically a reiteration of his objections to the Nehru Report.

*

Young and radical nationalists led by Jawaharlal Nehru had their own, very different, objections to the Nehru Report. They were dissatisfied with its declaration of Dominion Status on the lines of the self-governing dominions as the basis of the future constitution of India. Their slogan was 'Complete Independence.' And it was in December 1928, at the annual session of the Congress at Calcutta, that the battle was joined. Jawaharlal Nehru, Subhas Bose and Satyamurti, backed by a large number of delegates, pressed for the acceptance of *'Purna Swaraj'* or complete independence as the goal of the Congress. Gandhiji, Motilal Nehru and many other older leaders felt that the national consensus achieved with such great difficulty on Dominion Status should not be abandoned in such haste and a period of two years be given to the Government for accepting this. Under pressure, the grace period for the Government was reduced to a year and, more important, the Congress decided that if the Government did not accept a constitution based on Dominion Status by the end of the year, the Congress would not only adopt complete independence as its goal, but it would also launch a civil disobedience movement to attain that goal. A resolution embodying this proposal won over the majority of the delegates, and further amendments seeking immediate adoption of complete independence were defeated.

*

If civil disobedience was to be launched after the end of 'the present year of probation and grace,' as Gandhiji called it, then preparations had to begin in right earnest. Gandhiji cancelled his plans for a European tour, and explained in the issue of *Young India* dated 31 January, 1929: 'I feel that I would be guilty of desertion if I now went away to Europe . . . The voice within me tells me that I must not only hold myself in readiness to do what comes my way, but I must even think out and suggest means of working out what to me is a great programme. Above all I must prepare myself for next year's struggle, whatever shape it may take.'[3]

Gandhiji had of course been preparing the people for the future struggle in multifarious ways. For one, since his release from jail in 1924 on medical grounds, he had been travelling incessantly through the country. By the beginning of 1929, he had already toured Kathiawad, Central Provinces, Bengal, Malabar, Travancore, Bihar, United

Provinces, Kutch, Assam, Maharashtra, Karnataka, Tamil Nadu, and Orissa, many of them not once but twice. In 1929, in his sixtieth year, he began a tour of Sind, then proceeded via Delhi to Calcutta, then on to Burma, and back to Calcutta. In April, he began a six-week tour of Andhra Pradesh in which he visited 319 villages. In June, he was in Almora in the hills of U.P., and in September he covered the U.P. plains. The end of the year saw him in Lahore for the annual Congress session. He had also planned a visit to Kohat in the North-West Frontier Province, but was refused permission by the Government.

The significance of these mass contact tours was expressed by Gandhiji in these words: 'I travel because I fancy that the masses want to meet me. I certainly want to meet them. I deliver my simple message to them in few words and they and I are satisfied. It penetrates the mass mind slowly but surely.'[4]

While in his pre-1929 tours Gandhiji's emphasis had been on the constructive programme — *khadi*, Hindu-Muslim unity, and the removal of untouchability — he now began to prepare the people for direct political action. In Sind, for example, he told the youth to prepare for 'the fiery ordeal,' and it was at his instance that the Congress Working Committee constituted a Foreign Cloth Boycott Committee to promote an aggressive programme of boycott and public burning of foreign cloth. In Calcutta, on 4 March, 1929, Gandhiji took the lead in initiating the campaign of public burning of foreign cloth by lighting a bonfire in a public park before a crowd of thousands. The Government issued warrants for his arrest, but allowed him to go to Burma on his scheduled tour and face trial on his return. His arrest sparked off bonfires of foreign cloth all over the country. And when he returned to face trial, another wave of bonfires was lit to defy the government. Gandhiji warned the people that while they must carry on all manner of preparations for civil disobedience, they must remember that civil disobedience had not yet begun, and that they must as yet remain within the law as far as possible.

Apart from the preparations which the Congress carried on at various levels, there were a number of other developments that kept political excitement in 1929 at fever-pitch. On 20 March, 1929, in a major swoop, the Government arrested thirty-one labour leaders, most of them Communists, and marched them off to Meerut, in U.P., for trial. Their arrest was condemned by all sections of the national movement including Gandhiji and the Congress. Youth organizations organized protest demonstrations. On 8 April, 1929,, Bhagat Singh and Batukeswar Dutt of the Hindustan Socialist Republican Army (HSRA) threw harmless bombs in the Central Legislative Assembly and were arrested. In jail, the members of the HSRA went on a prolonged hunger strike demanding better treatment for political prisoners, and in September the death of one of them, Jatin Das, on the 64th day of the hunger strike led to some of the biggest demonstrations the country had ever witnessed.

Meanwhile, in May 1929, a Labour Government headed by Ramsay MacDonald took power in Britain and Lord Irwin, the Viceroy, was called to London for consultations. The sequel was an announcement on 31 October: 'I am authorized on behalf of His Majesty's Government to state clearly that in their judgement it is implicit in the Declaration of 1917 that the natural issue of India's progress as there contemplated, is the attainment of dominion status.'[5] He also promised a Round Table Conference as soon as the Simon Commission submitted its report. Two days later, a conference of major national leaders met and issued what came to be known as the Delhi manifesto, in which they demanded that it should be made clear that the purpose of the Round Table Conference was not to discuss when Dominion Status should be granted, but to formulate a scheme for its implementation. A debate in the House of Lords on 5 November, 1929 on this question had already raised serious doubts about British intentions; and, finally, on 23 December Irwin himself told Gandhiji and the others that he was in no position to give the assurance they demanded. The stage of negotiations was over and the stage of confrontation was about to begin.

*

The honour of hosting what was, perhaps, the most memorable of the Congress annual sessions went to Lahore, the capital city of Punjab, and the honour of declaring '*Purna Swaraj*' as the only honourable goal Indians could strive for went to the man who had done more than any other to popularize the idea — Jawaharlal Nehru. It was Gandhiji again who was the decisive voice in investing Jawaharlal Nehru with the office of President in what was to be a critical year of mass struggle. Only three out of eighteen Provincial Congress Committees had wanted Jawaharlal, but recognizing the appositeness of the occasion, and the upsurge of the youth who had made such a glorious success of the Simon Boycott, Gandhiji insisted and as usual got his way. The critics he countered by an assurance: 'Some fear in this transference of power from the old to the young, the doom of the Congress. I do not . . . "He is rash and impetuous," say some. This quality is an additional qualification, at the present moment. And if he has the dash and the rashness of a warrior, he has also the prudence of a statesman . . . He is undoubtedly an extremist thinking far ahead of his surroundings. But he is humble and practical enough not to force the pace to the breaking point.'[6] He added: 'Older men have had their innings. The battle of the future has to be fought by younger men and women. And it is but meet that they are led by one of themselves . . . Responsibility will mellow and sober the youth, and prepare them for the burden they must discharge. Pandit Jawaharlal has everything to recommend him. He has for years discharged with singular ability and devotion the office of secretary of the Congress. By his bravery, determination, application, integrity and grit, he has captivated the imagination of the youth of the land. He has come in touch with labour and the peasantry. His close acquaintance with European politics is a great asset in enabling him to assess ours.'[7]

To those who argued that he should himself assume the office because of the delicate nature of the negotiations that would have to be carried out with other parties and the Government, especially on the Hindu-Muslim question, he said: 'So long as I retain the affection and the confidence of our people, there is not the slightest danger of my not being able without holding office to make the fullest use of such powers as I may possess. God has enabled me to affect the life of the country since 1920 without the necessity of holding office.'[8] And to the youth he said: 'They may take the election of Jawaharlal Nehru as a tribute to their service . . . (and as) proof of the trust the nation reposes in its youth . . . Let them prove worthy of the trust.'[9]

Jawaharlal Nehru's Presidential Address was a stirring call to action: 'We have now an open conspiracy to free this country from foreign rule and you, comrades, and all our countrymen and countrywomen are invited to join it.'[10] Nehru also made it known that in his view liberation did not mean only throwing off the foreign yoke: 'I must frankly confess that I am a socialist and a republican, and am no believer in kings and princes, or in the order which produces the modern kings of industry, who have greater power over the lives and fortunes of men than even the kings of old, and whose methods are as predatory as those of the old feudal aristocracy.'[11] He also spelt out the methods of struggle: 'Any great movement for liberation today must necessarily be a mass movement, and mass movements must essentially be peaceful, except in times of organized revolt . . . And if the principal movement is a peaceful one, contemporaneous attempts at sporadic violence can only distract attention and weaken it.'[12]

On the banks of the river Ravi, at midnight on 31 December 1929, the tricolour flag of Indian independence was unfurled amidst cheers and jubiliation. Amidst the excitement, there was also a grim resolve, for the year to follow was to be one of hard struggle.

*

The first task that the Congress set itself and the Indian people in the new year was that of organizing all over the country, on 26 January, public meetings at which the Independence Pledge would be read out and collectively affirmed. This programme was a huge success, and in villages and towns, at small meetings and large ones, the pledge was read out in the local language and the national flag was hoisted. The text of the pledge bears quoting in full[13]: 'We believe that it is the inalienable right of the Indian people, as of any other people, to have freedom and to enjoy the fruits of their toil and have the necessities of life, so that they may have full opportunities of growth. We believe also that if any government deprives a people of these rights and oppresses them, the people have a further right to alter it or to abolish it. The British Government in India has not only deprived the Indian people of their freedom but has based itself on the exploitation of the masses, and has ruined India economically, politically, culturally and spiritually. We believe, therefore, that India must sever the British connection and attain *Purna Swaraj* or Complete Independence.

'India has been ruined economically. The revenue derived from our people is out of all proportion to our income. Our average income is seven pice, less than two pence, per day, and of the heavy taxes we pay, twenty per cent are raised from the land revenue derived from the peasantry and three per cent from the salt tax, which falls most heavily on the poor.

'Village industries, such as hand-spinning, have been destroyed, leaving the peasantry idle for at least four months in the year, and dulling their intellect for want of handicrafts, and nothing has been substituted, as in other countries, for the crafts thus destroyed.

'Customs and currency have been so manipulated as to heap further burdens on the peasantry. The British manufactured goods constitute the bulk of our imports. Customs duties betray clear partiality for British manufactures, and revenue from them is used not to lessen the burden on the masses, but for sustaining a highly extravagant administration. Still more arbitrary has been the manipulation of the exchange ratio which has resulted in millions being drained away from the country.

'Politically, India's status has never been so reduced, as under the British regime. No reforms have given real political power to the people. The tallest of us have to bend before foreign authority. The rights of free expression of opinion and free association have been denied to us, and many of our countrymen are compelled to live in exile abroad and they cannot return to their homes. All administrative talent is killed, and the masses have to be satisfied with petty village offices and clerkships.

'Culturally, the system of education has torn us from our moorings, our training has made us hug the very chains that bind us.

'Spiritually, compulsory disarmament has made us unmanly, and the presence of an alien army of occupation, employed with deadly effect to crush in us the spirit of resistance, has made us think that we cannot look after ourselves or put up a defence against foreign aggression, or defend our homes and families from the attacks of thieves, robbers, and miscreants.

'We hold it to be a crime against man and God to submit any longer to a rule that has caused this four-fold disaster to our country. We recognize, however, that the most effective way of gaining our freedom is not through violence. We will prepare ourselves, by withdrawing, so far as we can, all voluntary association from the British Government, and will prepare for civil disobedience including non-payment of taxes. We are convinced that if we can but withdraw our voluntary help, stop payment of taxes without doing violence, even under provocation, the end of this inhuman rule is assured. We, therefore, hereby solemnly resolve to carry out the Congress instructions issued from time to time for the purpose of establishing *Purna Swaraj*.'

22 *Civil Disobedience 1930-1931*

The Lahore Congress of 1929 had authorized the Working Committee to launch a programme of civil disobedience including non-payment of taxes. It had also called upon all members of legislatures to resign their seats. In mid-February, 1930, the Working Committee, meeting at Sabarmati Ashram, invested Gandhiji with full powers to launch the civil disobedience movement at a time and place of his choice. The acknowledged expert on mass struggle was already 'desperately in search of an effective formula.'[1] His ultimatum of 31 January to Lord Irwin, stating the minimum demands in the form of 11 points, had been ignored, and there was now only one way out: civil disobedience.

*

By the end of February, the formula began to emerge as Gandhiji began to talk about salt: 'There is no article like salt outside water by taxing which the State can reach even the starving millions, the sick, the maimed and the utterly helpless. The tax constitutes therefore the most inhuman poll tax the ingenuity of man can devise.'[2] On 2 March, he addressed his historic letter to the Viceroy in which he first explained at great length why he regarded British rule as a curse: 'It has impoverished the dumb millions by a system of progressive exploitation . . . It has reduced us politically to serfdom. It has sapped the foundations of our culture . . . it has degraded us spiritually.'[3] He then informed the Viceroy of his plan of action, as he believed every true *Satyagrahi* must: '. . . on the 11th day of this month, I shall proceed with such co-workers of the Ashram as I can take, to disregard the provisions of the salt laws . . . It is, I know, open to you to frustrate my design by arresting me. I hope that there will be tens of thousands ready, in a disciplined manner, to take up the work after me, and, in the act of disobeying the Salt Act to lay themselves open to the penalties of a law that should never have disfigured the Statute-book.'4

The plan was brilliantly conceived though few realized its significance when it was first announced. Gandhiji, along with a band of seventy-eight members of the Sabarmati Ashram, among whom were men belonging to almost every region and religion of India, was to march from his headquarters in Ahmedabad through the villages of Gujarat for 240 miles. On reaching the coast at Dandi, he would break the salt law by collecting salt from the beach. This deceptively innocuous move was to prove devastatingly effective. Even before the march began, thousands began to throng the Sabarmati Ashram in anticipation of the dramatic events that lay ahead. And Gandhiji painstakingly explained his plans, gave directions for future action, impressed on the people the necessity for non-violence, and prepared them for the Government's response: 'Wherever possible, civil disobedience of salt laws should be started . . . Liquor and foreign-cloth shops can be picketed. We can refuse to pay taxes if we have the requisite strength. The lawyers can give up practice. The public can boycott the courts by refraining from litigation. Government servants can resign their posts . . . I prescribe only one condition, viz., let our pledge of truth and non-violence as the only means for the attainment of *swaraj* be faithfully kept.'5

Explaining the power of civil disobedience, he said: 'Supposing ten persons in each of the 700,000 villages in India come forward to manufacture salt and to disobey the Salt Act, what do you think this Government can do? Even the worst autocrat you can imagine would not dare to blow regiments of peaceful civil resisters out of a cannon's mouth. If only you will bestir yourselves just a little, I assure you we should be able to tire this Government out in a very short time.'6

He also explained how non-violence enabled the widest participation of the people, and put the Government in an unenviable quandary. To a crowd who came to the ashram on 10 March , he said: 'Though the battle is to begin in a couple of days, how is it that you can come here quite fearlessly? I do not think any one of you would be here if you had to face rifle-shots or bombs. But you have no fear of rifle-shots or bombs? Why? Supposing I had announced that I was going to launch a violent campaign (not necessarily with men armed with rifles, but even with sticks or stones), do you think the Government would have left me free until now? Can you show me an example in history (be it in England, America or Russia) where the State has tolerated violent defiance of authority for a single day? But here you know that the Government is puzzled and perplexed.'[7]

And as Gandhiji began his march, staff in hand, at the head of his dedicated band, there was something in the image that deeply stirred the imagination of the people. News of his progress, of his speeches, of the teeming crowds that greeted and followed the marchers, of the long road lovingly strewn with leaves and festooned with banners and flags, of men and women quietly paying their homage by spinning yarn on their *charkas* as Gandhiji passed, of the 300 village officials in Gujarat who resigned their posts in answer to his appeal, was carried day after day by newspapers to readers across the country and broadcast live by thousands of Congress workers to eager listeners. By the time Gandhiji reached Dandi, he had a whole nation, aroused and expectant, waiting restlessly for the final signal. On 6 April 1930, by picking up a handful of salt, Gandhiji inaugurated the civil disobedience movement, a movement that was to remain unsurpassed in the history of the Indian national movement for the country-wide mass participation it unleashed.

*

While Gandhiji was marching to Dandi, Congress leaders and workers had been busy at various levels with the hard organizational task of enrolling volunteers and members, forming grass-roots Congress Committees, collecting funds, and touring villages and towns to spread the nationalist message. Preparations for launching the salt *Satyagraha* were made, sites chosen, volunteers prepared, and the logistics of battle worked out.[8]

Once the way was cleared by Gandhiji's ritual beginning at Dandi, the defiance of salt laws started all over the country. In Tamil Nadu, C. Rajagopalachari, led a salt march from Trichinopoly to Vedaranniyam on the Tanjore coast. By the time he was arrested on 30 April he had collected enough volunteers to keep the campaign going for quite some time. In Malabar, K. Kelappan, the hero of the Vaikom *Satyagraha*, walked from Calicut to Payannur to break the salt law. A band of

Satyagrahis walked all the way from Sylhet in Assam to Noakhali on the Bengal Coast to make salt. In Andhra, a number of *sibirams* (military-style camps) were set up in different districts to serve as the headquarters of the salt *Satyagraha*, and bands of *Satyagrahis* marched through villages on their way to the coastal centres to defy the law. On their return journeys, they again toured through another set of villages. The Government's failure to arrest Gandhiji for breaking the salt law was used by the local level leaders to impress upon the people that 'the Government are afraid of persons like ourselves,' and that since the starting of the salt *Satyagraha* the Government 'has disappeared and hidden itself somewhere, and that Gandhi Government has already been established.'[9] Jawaharlal Nehru's arrest on 14 April, for defiance of the salt law, was answered with huge demonstrations and clashes with the police in the cities of Madras, Calcutta and Karachi.

On 23 April, the arrest of Congress leaders in the North West Frontier Province led to a mass demonstration of unprecedented magnitude in Peshawar. Khan Abdul Gaffar Khan had been active for several years in the area, and it was his mass work which lay behind the formation of the band of non-violent revolutionaries, the Khudai Khidmatgars, popularly known as the Red Shirts — who were to play an extremely active role in the Civil Disobedience movement. The atmosphere created by their political work contributed to the mass upsurge in Peshawar during which the city was virtually in the hands of the crowd for more than a week. The Peshawar demonstrations are significant because it was here that the soldiers of the Garhwali regiments refused to fire on the unarmed crowd.

*

It was becoming increasingly clear that the Government's gamble — that non-interference with the movement would result in its spending itself out, that Gandhiji's salt strategy would fail to take off — had not paid off. In fact, the Government had never been clear on what course it should follow, and was, as Gandhiji had predicted, 'puzzled and perplexed.'[10] The dilemma in which it found itself was a dilemma that the Gandhian strategy of non-violent civil disobedience was designed to create. The Government was placed in a classic 'damned if you do, damned if you don't' fix, i.e., if it did not suppress a movement that brazenly defied its laws, its administrative authority would be seen to be undermined and its control would be shown to be weak, and if it did suppress it, it would be seen as a brutal, anti-people administration that used violence on non-violent agitators. 'If we do too much, Congress will cry "repression". . . if we do too little, Congress will cry "victory," ' — this is how a Madras civilian expressed the dilemma in early 1930.[11] Either way, it led to the erosion of the hegemony of the British government.

The rapid spread of the movement left the Government with little choice but to demonstrate the force that lay behind its benevolent facade. Pressures from officials, Governors and the military establishment started building up, and, on 4 May , the Viceroy finally ordered Gandhiji's arrest. Gandhiji's announcement that he would now proceed to continue his defiance of the salt laws by leading a raid on the Dharasana Salt Works certainly forced the Government's hand, but its timing of Gandhiji's arrest was nevertheless ill-conceived. It had neither the advantages of an early strike, which would have at least prevented Gandhiji from carefully building up the momentum of the movement, nor did it allow the Government to reap the benefits of their policy of sitting it out. Coming as it did at a high point in the movement, it only acted as a further spur to activity, and caused endless trouble for the Government.[12]

There was a massive wave of protest at Gandhiji's arrest. In Bombay, the crowd that spilled out into the streets was so large that the police just withdrew. Its ranks were swelled by thousands of textile and railway workers. Cloth-merchants went on a six-day *hartal*. There were clashes and firing in Calcutta and Delhi. But it was in Sholapur, in Maharashtra, that the response was the fiercest. The textile workers, who dominated the town went on strike from 7 May, and along with other residents, burnt liquor shops and proceeded to attack all symbols of Government authority — the railway station, law courts, police stations and municipal buildings. They took over the city and established a virtual parallel government which could only be dislodged with the imposition of martial law after 16 May.

*

But it was non-violent heroism that stole the show as the salt *Satyagraha* assumed yet another, even more potent form. On May 21, with Sarojini Naidu, the first Indian woman to become President of the

Congress, and Imam Saheb, Gandhiji's comrade of the South African struggle, at the helm, and Gandhiji's son, Manilal, in the front ranks, a band of 2000 marched towards the police cordon that had sealed off the Dharasana salt works. As they came close, the police rushed forward with their steel-tipped lathis and set upon the non-resisting *Satyagrahis* till they fell down. The injured would be carried away by their comrades on make-shift stretchers and another column would take their place, be beaten to pulp, and carried away. Column after column advanced in this way; after a while, instead of walking up to the cordon the men would sit down and wait for the police blows. Not an arm was raised in defence, and by 11 a.m., when the temperature in the shade was 116 degrees farenheit, the toll was already 320 injured and two dead. Webb Miller, the American journalist, whose account of the Dharasana *Satyagraha* was to carry the flavour of Indian nationalism to many distant lands, and whose description of the resolute heroism of the *Satyagrahis* demonstrated effectively that non-violent resistance was no meek affair, summed up his impressions in these words: 'In eighteen years of my reporting in twenty countries, during which I have witnessed innumerable civil disturbances, riots, street fights and rebellions, I have never witnessed such harrowing scenes as at Dharasana.'[13]

This new form of salt *Satyagraha* was eagerly adopted by the people, who soon made it a mass affair. At Wadala, a suburb of Bombay, the raids on the salt works culminated on 1 June in mass action by a crowd of 15,000 who repeatedly broke the police cordon and triumphantly carried away salt in the face of charges by the mounted police. In Karnataka, 10,000 invaded the Sanikatta salt works and faced lathis and bullets. In Madras, the defiance of salt laws led to repeated clashes with the police and to a protest meeting on 23 April on the beach which was dispersed by lathi charges and firing, leaving three dead. This incident completely divided the city on racial lines, even the most moderate of Indians condemning the incident, and rallying behind the nationalists. In Andhra bands of village women walked miles to carry away a handful of salt, and in Bengal, the old Gandhian ashrams, regenerated by the flood of volunteers from the towns, continued to sustain a powerful salt *Satyagraha* in Midnapore and other coastal pockets. The districts of Balasore, Puri and Cuttack in Orissa remained active centres of illegal salt manufacture.

*

But salt *Satyagraha* was only the catalyst, and the beginning, for a rich variety of forms of defiance that it brought in its wake. Before his arrest, Gandhiji had already called for a vigorous boycott of foreign cloth and liquor shops, and had especially asked the women to play a leading role in this movement. 'To call woman the weaker sex is a libel; it is man's injustice to woman,'[14] he had said; and the women of India certainly demonstrated in 1930 that they were second to none in strength and tenacity of purpose. Women who had never stepped unescorted out of their homes, women who had stayed in purdah, young mothers and widows and unmarried girls, became a familiar sight as they stood from morning to night outside liquor shops and opium dens and stores selling foreign cloth, quietly but firmly persuading the customers and shopkeepers to change their ways.

Along with the women, students and youth played the most prominent part in the boycott of foreign cloth and liquor. In Bombay, for example, regular Congress sentries were posted in business districts to ensure that merchants and dealers did not flout the foreign cloth boycott. Traders' associations and commercial bodies were themselves quite active in implementing the boycott, as were the many millowners who refused to use foreign yarn and pledged not to manufacture coarse cloth that competed with *khadi*. The recalcitrant among them were brought in line by fines levied by their own associations, by social boycott, by Congress black-listing, and by picketing.

The liquor boycott brought Government revenues from excise duties crashing down; it also soon assumed a new popular form, that of cutting off the heads of toddy trees. The success of the liquor and drugs boycott was obviously connected with the popular tradition of regarding abstinence as a virtue and as a symbol of respectability. The depth of this tradition is shown by the fact that lower castes trying to move up in the caste hierarchy invariably tried to establish their upper caste status by giving up liquor and eating of meat.

*

Eastern India became the scene of a new kind of no-tax campaign — refusal to pay the *chowkidara* tax. *Chowkidars*, paid out of the tax levied specially on the villages, were guards who supplemented the small police force in the rural areas in this region. They were particularly hated because they acted as spies for the Government and often also as retainers for the local landlords. The movement against this tax and calling for the resignation of *chowkidars*, and of the influential members of *chowkidari* panchayats who appointed the *Chowkidars*, first started in Bihar in May itself, as salt agitation had not much scope due to the land-locked nature of the province. In the Monghyr, Saran and Bhagalpur districts, for example, the tax was refused, *chowkidars* induced to resign, and social boycott used against those who resisted. The Government retaliated by confiscation of property worth hundreds and thousands in lieu of a few rupees of tax, and by beatings and torture. Matters came to a head in Bihpur in Bhagalpur on May 31 when the police, desperate to assert its fast-eroding authority, occupied the Congress ashram which was the headquarters of nationalist activity in the area. The occupation triggered off daily demonstrations outside the ashram, and a visit by Rajendra Prasad and Abdul Bari from Patna became the occasion for a huge mass rally, which was broken up by a lathi charge in which Rajendra Prasad was injured. As elsewhere, repression further increased the nationalists' strength, and the police just could not enter the rural areas.

In Bengal, the onset of the monsoon, which made it difficult to make salt, brought about a shift to anti-*chowkidara* and anti-Union Board agitation. Here too, villagers withstood severe repression, losing thousands of rupees worth of property through confiscation and destruction, and having to hide for days in forests to escape the wrath of the police.

In Gujarat, in Kheda district, in Bardoli *taluqa* in Surat district, and in Jambusar in Broach, a determined no-tax movement was in progress — the tax refused here was the land revenue. Villagers in their thousands, with family, cattle and household goods, crossed the border from British India into the neighbouring princely states such as Baroda and camped for months together in the open fields. Their houses were broken into, their belongings destroyed, their lands confiscated. The police did not even spare Vallabhbhai Patel's eighty-year-old mother, who sat cooking in her village house in Karamsad; her cooking utensils were kicked about and filled with kerosene and stone. Vallabhbhai, on his brief sojourns out of jail throughout 1930, continued to provide encouragement and solace to the hard-pressed peasants of his native land. Though their meagre resources were soon exhausted, and weariness set in, they stuck it out in the wilderness till the truce in March 1931 made it possible for them to return to their homes.

Defiance of forest laws assumed a mass character in Maharashtra, Karnataka and the Central Provinces, especially in areas with large tribal populations who had been the most seriously affected by the colonial Government's restrictions on the use of the forest. At some places the size of the crowd that broke the forest laws swelled to 70,000 and above.

In Assam, a powerful agitation led by students was launched against the infamous 'Cunningham circular' which forced students and their guardians to furnish assurances of good behaviour.

The people seemed to have taken to heart Jawaharlal Nehru's message when he unfurled the national flag at Lahore in December 1929: 'Remember once again, now that this flag is unfurled, it must not be lowered as long as a single Indian, man, woman, or child lives in India.'(15) Attempts to defend the honour of the national flag in the face of severe brutalities often turned into heroism of the most spectacular variety. At Bundur, on the Andhra Coast, Tota Narasaiah Naidu preferred to be beaten unconscious by a fifteen-member police force rather than give up the national flag. In Calicut, P. Krishna Pillai, who later became a major Communist leader, suffered lathi blows with the same determination. In Surat, a group of children used their ingenuity to defy the police. Frustrated by the repeated snatching of the national flag from their hands, they came up with the idea of stitching *khadi* dresses in the three colours of the national flag, and thereafter these little, 'living flags' triumphantly paraded the streets and defied the police to take away the national flag!16 The national flag, the symbol of the new spirit, now became a common sight even in remote villages.

U.P. was the setting of another kind of movement — a no-revenue, no-rent campaign. The no-revenue part was a call to the *zamindars* to refuse to pay revenue to the Government, the no-rent a call to the tenants not to pay rent to the *zamindars*. In effect, since the *zamindars* were largely loyal to the Government, this became a no-rent struggle. The Civil Disobedience Movement had taken a firm hold in the province in the initial months, but repression had led to a relative quiet, and though no-rent was in the air, it was only in October that activity picked up again when Jawaharlal Nehru, out of jail for a brief period, got the U.P. Congress Committee to sanction the no-rent campaign. Two months of preparation and intensive propaganda led to the launching of the campaign in December; by January, severe repression had forced many peasants to flee the villages. Among the important centres of this campaign were the districts of Agra and Rae Bareli.

The movement also popularized a variety of forms of mobilization. *Prabhat pheris*, in which bands of men, women and children went around at dawn singing nationalist songs, became the rule in villages and towns. *Patrikas*, or illegal news-sheets, sometimes written by hand and sometimes cyclostyled, were part of the strategy to defy the hated Press Act, and they flooded the country. Magic lanterns were used to take the nationalist message to the villages. And, as before, incessant tours by individual leaders and workers, and by groups of men and women, and the holding of public meetings, big and small, remained the staple of the movement. Children were organized into *vanar senas* or monkey armies and at least at one place the girls decided they wanted their own separate *manjari sena* or cat army![17]

*

The Government's attitude throughout 1930 was marked by ambivalence. Gandhiji's arrest itself had come after much vacillation. After that, ordinances curbing the civil liberties of the people were freely issued and provincial governments were given the freedom to ban civil disobedience organizations. But the Congress Working Committee was not declared unlawful till the end of June and Motilal Nehru, who was functioning as the Congress President, also remained free till that date. Many local Congress Committees were not banned till August. Meanwhile, the publication of the report of the Simon Commission, which contained no mention of Dominion Status and was in other ways also a regressive document, combined with the repressive policy, further upset even moderate political opinion. Madan Mohan Malaviya and M.S. Aney courted arrest. In a conciliatory gesture, the Viceroy on 9 July suggested a Round Table Conference and reiterated the goal of Dominion Status. He also accepted the suggestion, made by forty members of the Central Legislature, that Tej Bahadur Sapru and M.R. Jayakar be allowed to explore the possibilities of peace between the Congress and the Government. In pursuance of this, the Nehrus, father and son, were taken in August to Yeravada jail to meet Gandhiji and discuss the possibilities of a settlement. Nothing came of the talks, but the gesture did ensure that some sections of political opinion would attend the Round Table Conference in London in November. The proceedings in London, the first ever conducted between the British and Indians as equals, at which virtually every delegate reiterated that a constitutional discussion to which the Congress was not a party was a meaningless exercise, made it clear that it the Government's strategy of survival was to be based on constitutional advance, then an olive branch to the Congress was imperative. The British Prime Minister hinted at this possiblity in his statement at the conclusion of the Round Table Conference. He also expressed the hope that the Congress would participate in the next round of deliberations to be held later in the year. On 25 January, the Viceroy announced the unconditional release of Gandhiji and all the other members of the Congress Working Committee, so that might be to respond to the Prime Minister's statement 'freely and fearlessly.'

After deliberating amongst itself for close to three weeks, and after long discussions with delegates who had returned from London, and with other leaders representing a cross-section of political opinion, the Congress Working Committee authorized Gandhiji to initiate discussions with the Viceroy. The fortnight-long discussions culminated on 5 March 1931 in the Gandhi-Irwin Pact, which was variously described as a 'truce' and a 'provisional settlement.'

The Pact was signed by Gandhiji on behalf of the Congress and by Lord Irwin on behalf of the Government, a procedure that was hardly popular with officialdom as it placed the Congress on an equal footing with the Government. The terms of the agreement included the immediate release of all political prisoners not convicted for violence, the remission of all fines not yet collected, the return of confiscated lands not yet sold to third parties, and lenient treatment for those government employees who had resigned. The Government also conceded the right to make salt for consumption to villages along the coast, as also the right to peaceful and non-aggressive picketing. The Congress demand for a public inquiry into police excesses was not accepted, but Gandhiji's insistent request for an inquiry was recorded in the agreement. The Congress, on its part, agreed to discontinue the Civil Disobedience Movement. It was also understood that the Congress would participate in the next Round Table Conference.

*

The terms on which the Pact was signed, its timing, the motives of

Gandhiji in signing the Pact, his refusal to make the Pact conditional on the commutation of the death-sentences of Bhagat Singh and his comrades, (even though he had tried his best to persuade the Viceroy to do so), have generated considerable controversy and debate among contemporaries and historians alike. The Pact has been variously seen as a betrayal, as proof of the vacillating nature of the Indian bourgeoisie and of Gandhiji succumbing to bourgeois pressure. It has been cited as evidence of Gandhiji's and the Indian bourgeoisie's fear of the mass movement taking a radical turn; a betrayal of peasants' interests because it did not immediately restore confiscated land, already sold to a third party, and so on.

However, as with arguments relating to the withdrawal of the Non-Cooperation Movement in 1922 after Chauri Chaura, these perceptions are based on an understanding which fails to grasp the basic strategy and character of the Indian national movement. For one, this understanding ignores the fact which has been stressed earlier — that mass movements are necessarily short-lived, they cannot go on for ever, the people's capacity to sacrifice, unlike that of the activists', is not endless. And signs of exhaustion there certainly were, in large and important sectors of the movement. In the towns, while the students and other young people still had energy to spare, shopkeepers and merchants were finding it difficult to bear any more losses and the support from these sections, so crucial in making the boycott a success, had begun to decline by September of 1930. In rural India as well, those areas that had begun their resistance early in the year were fairly quiet in the second half. Though sporadic incidents of resistance and attacks on and clashes with police continued, this was as true of Bengal and Bihar as it was of Andhra and Gujarat. Those areas like U.P., which began their no-rent campaigns only at the end of 1930, still had more fight left in them, but the few instances of militant resistance that carried on and the ability of one or two regions to sustain activity can hardly be cited as proof of the existence of vast reserves of energy all over the country. And what was the guarantee that when those reserves were exhausted, as they were bound to be sooner rather than later, the Government would still be willing to talk? 1931 was not 1946; and as 1932 was to show, the Government could change tack and suppress with a ferocity that could effectively crush the movement. No doubt the youth were disappointed, for they would have preferred their world to end 'with a bang' rather than 'with a whimper';[18] and surely the peasants of Gujarat were not happy that some of their lands did not come back to them immediately (they were returned after the Congress Ministry assumed office in Bombay in 1937). But the vast mass of the people were undoubtedly impressed that the mighty British Government had had to treat their movement and their leader as an equal and sign a pact with him. They saw this as a recognition of their own strength, and as their victory over the Government. The thousands who flocked out of the jails as a result of the pact were treated as soldiers returning from a victorious battle and not as prisoners of war returning from a humiliating defeat. They knew that a truce was not a surrender, and that the battle could be joined again, if the enemy so wanted. Meanwhile, their soldiers could rest and they could all prepare for the next round: they retained their faith in their General, and in themselves.

*

The civil disobedience movement of 1930-31, then, marked a critically important stage in the progress of the anti-imperialist struggle. The number of people who went to jail was estimated at over 90,000 — more than three times the figure for the Non-Cooperation movement of 1920-22. Imports of cloth from Britain had fallen by half; other imports like cigarettes had suffered a similar fate. Government income from liquor excise and land revenue had been affected. Elections to the Legislative Assembly had been effectively boycotted. A vast variety of social groups had been politicized on the side of Indian nationalism — if urban elements like merchants and shopkeepers and students were more active in TamilNadu and Punjab, and in cities in general, peasants had come to the forefront in Gujarat, U.P., Bengal, Andhra, and Bihar, and tribals in the Central Provinces, Maharashtra, Karnataka and Bengal. Workers had not been missing from the battle either — they joined numerous mass demonstrations in Bombay, Calcutta, and Madras and were in the forefront in Sholapur.

The participation of Muslims in the Civil Disobedience Movement was certainly nowhere near that in 1920-22. The appeals of communal leaders to stay away, combined with active Government encouragement of communal dissension to counter the forces of nationalism, had their effect. Still, the participation of Muslims was not insignificant, either. Their participation in the North-West Frontier Province was, as is well known, overwhelming. In Bengal, middle class Muslim participation was quite important in Senhatta, Tripura, Gaibandha, Bagura and Noakhali, and, in Dacca, Muslim students and shopkeepers as well as people belonging to the lower classes extended support to the movement. Middle and upper class Muslim women were also active.[19] The Muslim weaving community in Bihar, and in Delhi and Lucknow the lower classes of Muslims were effectively mobilized as were many others in different parts of the country.

The support that the movement had garnered from the poor and the illiterate, both in the town and in the country, was remarkable indeed. Their participation was reflected even in the government statistics of jail-goers — and jail-going was only one of the many forms of participation. The Inspector-General of Police in Bengal, E.J. Lowman, expressed the general official bewilderment when he noted: 'I had no idea that the Congress organization could enlist the sympathy and support of such ignorant and uncultivated people . . .'[20]

For Indian women, the movement was the most liberating experience to date and can truly be said to have marked their entry into the public space.

23 From Karachi to Wardha: The Years From 1932 -1934

The Congress met at Karachi on 29 March 1931 to endorse the Gandhi-Irwin or Delhi Pact. Bhagat Singh, Sukhdev and Rajguru had been exe-cuted six days earlier. Even though Gandhiji had made every attempt to save their lives, there was anger among the people, especially the youth, as to why he had not refused to sign the Pact on this question. All along Gandhiji's route to Karachi he was greeted with black flag demonstrations. The Congress passed a resolution drafted by Gandhiji by which it, 'while dissociating itself from and disapproving of politi-cal violence in any shape or form,' admired 'the bravery and sacrifice' of the three martyrs. [1] The Congress endorsed the Delhi Pact and reiterated the goal of *Purna Swaraj*.

The Karachi session became memorable for its resolution on Fundamental Rights and the National Economic Programme. Even though the Congress had from its inception fought for the economic interests, civil liberties and political rights of the people, this was the first time that the Congress defined what *Swaraj* would mean for the masses. It also declared that, 'in order to end the exploitation of the masses, political freedom must include real economic freedom of the starving millions.' The resolution guaranteed the basic civil rights of free speech, free press, free assembly, and freedom of association; equal-ity before the law irrespective of caste, creed or sex; neutrality of the state in regard to all religions; elections on the basis of universal adult franchise; and free and compulsory primary education. It promised sub-stantial reduction in rent and revenue, exemption from rent in case of uneconomic holdings, and relief of agricultural indebtedness and control of usury; better conditions for workers including a living wage, limited hours of work and protection of women workers; the right to organize and form unions to workers and peasants; and state ownership or control of key industries, mines and means of transport. It also maintained that 'the culture, language and script of the minorities and of the different linguistic areas shall be protected.'[2] The Karachi resolution was to remain in essence the basic political and economic programme of the Congress in later years.

*

Gandhiji sailed for London on 29 August 1931 to attend the Second Round Table Conference. Nothing much was expected from the Conference for the imperialist political and financial forces, which ultimately controlled the British Government in London, were opposed to any political or economic concessions being given to India which could lead to its independence from their control. Winston Churchill, leader of the virulent right-wing, had strongly objected to the British Government negotiating on terms of equality with the 'seditious fakir' and demanded strong government in India.[3] The Conservative *Daily Mail* declared that 'Without India, the British Commonwealth would fall to pieces. Commercially, economically, politically and geographically it is our greatest imperial asset. To imperil our hold on it would be the worst treason any Briton could commit.'[4] In India, Irwin was replaced by Willingdon as the Viceroy. In Britain, after December 1931, the Laborite Ramsay MacDonald headed a Conservative-dominated Cabinet with the weak and reactionary Samuel Hoare as the Secretary of State for India. Apart from a few able individuals, the overwhelming majority of Indian delegates to the Round Table Conference(RTC), hand-picked by the Government, were loyalists, communalists, careerists, and place-hunters, big landlords and representatives of the princes. They were used by the Government to claim that the Congress did not represent the interests of all Indians vis-a-vis imperialism, and to neutralize Gandhiji and all his efforts to confront the imperialist rulers with the basic question of freedom.

The great Gujarati poet, Meghani, in a famous poem gave expression to the nationalist misgivings regarding the RTC. Addressing Gandhiji on the eve of his departure for London, he sang in the first line: *'Chchello Katoro Jerno Aa: Pi Jayo, Bapu!'* (Even this last cup of poison, you must drink, Bapu!) Gandhiji himself said: 'When I think of the prospects in London, when I know that all is not well in India . ... there is nothing wanting to fill me with utter despair . . . There is every chance of my returning empty-handed.'5 That is exactly what happened in London. The British Government refused to concede the basic Indian demand for freedom. Gandhiji came back at the end of December 1931 to a changed political situation.

*

The higher British officials in India had drawn their own lessons from the political impact of the Delhi Pact which had raised the political prestige of the Congress and the political morale of the people and undermined and lowered British prestige. They, as well as the new Viceroy, believed that the Government had made a major error in negotiating and signing a truce with the Congress, as if between two equal powers. They were now determined to reverse it all. No pact, no truce, no Gandhi-Viceroy meetings, no 'quarter for the enemy' became the watchwords of Government policy.

The British policy was now dominated by three major considerations: (a)Gandhiji must not be permitted to build up the tempo for a massive and protracted mass movement, as he had done in 1919, 1920-1 and 1930. (b)The Government functionaries — village officials, police and higher bureaucrats — and the loyalists — 'our friends' — must not feel disheartened that Gandhiji was being 'resurrected as a rival authority to the Government of India,' and that the Government was losing the will to rule. As the Home Member, H.G.Haig, put it: 'We can, in my view, do without the goodwill of the Congress, and in fact I do not believe for a moment that we shall ever have it, but we cannot afford to do without the confidence of those who have supported us in the long struggle against the Congress.'6 (c)In particular, the nationalist movement must not be permitted to gather force and consolidate itself in rural areas, as it was doing all over India, especially in U.P., Gujarat, Andhra, Bihar, Bengal and NWFP.

While Gandhiji was in London, the Government of India prepared, in secret, plans for the coming showdown with the nationalist forces. It decided to launch 'a hard and immediate blow' against any revival of the movement and to arrest Gandhiji at the very outset. It drafted a series of ordinances which would usher in virtual martial law, though under civilian control.

The shape of things to come had been overshadowed by what happened in UP, NWFP and Bengal during the truce period. In U.P. the Congress was leading a campaign for reduction of rent, remission of arrears of rent and prevention of eviction of tenants for non-payment of rents. By the first week of December, the Congress had launched a no-rent, no-revenue campaign in five districts. The Government's response was to arrest Jawaharlal on 26 December when he was going to Bombay to meet Gandhiji. In the North-Western Frontier Province, the Government continued its severe repression against the non-violent Khudai Khidmatgars (servants of God), also known as Red Shirts because of the colour of their shirts, and the peasants they led against the Government's policy of extracting revenue through cruel methods and torture. On 24 December, their leader, Abdul Ghaffar Khan, was arrested and Peshawar district was occupied by the army. In Bengal, the Government was ruling through draconian ordinances and detaining thousands of political workers in the name of fighting terrorism. In September, the police fired upon political prisoners in Hijli jail, killing two.

*

Gandhiji landed in Bombay on 28 December. The Congress Working Committee met the next day and decided to resume civil disobedience. On the 31st, Gandhiji asked the Viceroy for a meeting, offering to suspend the decision on civil disobedience till such a meeting. The Viceroy refused to see Gandhiji — the first of many such refusals during the next five years. On 4 January 1932, the Government launched its pre-emptive strike against the national movement by arresting Gandhiji, promulgating ordinances which gave the authorities unlimited power — thus initiating what a historian has described as 'Civil Martial Law.' Civil liberties no longer existed and the authorities could seize people and property at will. Within a week, leading Congressmen all over the country were behind bars.

The Indian people responded with anger. Even though the Congress entered the battle rather unprepared, the popular response was massive. In the first four months, over 80,000 *Satyagrahis*, most of them urban and rural poor, were jailed, while lakhs took to the picketing of shops selling liquor and foreign cloth. Illegal gatherings, non-violent demonstrations, celebrations of various national days, and other forms of defiance of the ordinances were the rule of the day.

The non-violent movement was met by relentless repression. The Congress and its allied organizations were declared illegal and their offices and funds seized. Nearly all the Gandhi Ashrams were occupied by the police. Peaceful picketers, *Satyagrahis* and processionists were lathi-charged, beaten and often awarded rigorous imprisonment and heavy fines, which were realized by selling their lands and property at throw away prices. Prisoners in jail were barbarously treated. Whipping as punishment became frequent. The no-tax campaigns in different parts of rural India were treated with great severity. Lands, houses, cattle, agricultural implements, and other property were freely confiscated. The police indulged in naked terror and committed innumerable atrocities. At Ras, a village in Gujarat, the non-tax paying peasants were stripped naked, publicly whipped and given electric shocks. The wrath of the Government fell with particular harshness on women. Conditions in jails were made extraordinarily severe with the idea of scaring away women from the *Satyagraha*. The freedom of the Press to report or comment on the movement, or even to print pictures of national leaders or *Satyagrahis*, was curtailed. Within the first six months of 1932 action was taken against 109 journalists and ninety-eight printing presses. Nationalist literature — poems, stories and novels — was banned on a large scale.

The people fought back. But Gandhiji and other leaders had no time to build up the tempo of the movement and it could not be sustained for long. The movement was effectively crushed within a few months. In August 1932, the number of those convicted came down to 3,047 and by August 1933 only 4,500 *Satyagrahis* were in jail. However, the movement continued to linger till early April 1934 when the inevitable decision to withdraw it was taken by Gandhiji.

*

Political activists despaired at the turn the movement had taken. What have we achieved, many asked? Even a buoyant and active person like Jawaharlal gave voice to this sense of despair — accentuated by his separation from his sick wife — by copying a verse in his jail diary in June 1935: 'Sad winds where your voice was; Tears, tears where my heart was; and ever with me, Child, ever with me, Silence where hope was.'[7] Earlier, when Gandhiji had withdrawn the movement, Jawaharlal had felt 'with a stab of pain' that his long association with Gandhiji was about to come to an end.[8] Subhas Chandra Bose and Vithalbhai Patel had been much more critical of Gandhiji's leadership. In a strong statement from Europe they had said in 1933 that 'Mr. Gandhi as a political leader has failed' and called for 'a radical reorganization of the Congress on a new principle with a new method, for which a new leader is essential.'[9]

The enemies of Indian nationalism gloated over this frustration among the nationalists — and grossly misread it. Willingdon declared in early 1933: 'The Congress is in a definitely less favourable position than in 1930, and has lost its hold on the public.'[10] But Willingdon and company had completely failed to understand the nature and strategy of the Indian national movement — it was basically a struggle for the minds of men and women. Seen in this light, if the colonial policy of negotiations by Irwin had failed earlier, so had the policy of ruthless suppression by Willingdon. People had been cowed down by superior force; they had not lost faith in the Congress. Though the movement from 1930 to 1934 had not achieved independence and had been temporarily crushed, the Indian people had been further transformed. The will to fight had been further strengthened; faith in British rule had been completely shattered. H.N. Brailsford, Laborite journalist, wrote, assessing th results of the nationalists' most recent struggle, that the Indians 'had freed their own minds, they had won independence in their hearts.'[11]

And, as we have seen earlier, this hiatus in the movement too was primarily to rest and regroup. Withdrawl of the movement did not mean defeat or loss of mass support; it only meant, as Dr. Ansari put it, 'having fought long enough we prepare to rest,' to fight another day a bigger battle with greater and better organized force.[12] Symbolic of the real outcome, the real impact of the civil disobedience, was the heroes' welcome given to prisoners on their release in 1934. And this became evident to all when the Congress captured a majority in six out of eleven provinces in the elections in 1937 despite the restricted nature of the franchise.

Alone among his contemporaries, Gandhiji understood the true nature and outcome of the Civil Disobedience Movement. To Nehru, he wrote in September 1933: 'I have no sense of defeat in me and the hope in me that this country of ours is fast marching towards its goal is burning as bright as it did in 1920.'[13] He reiterated this view to a group of Congress leaders in April 1934: 'I feel no despondency in me . . . I am not feeling helpless . . . The nation has got energy of which you have no conception but I have.'[14] He had, of course, an advantage over most other leaders. While they needed a movement to sustain their sense of political activism, he had always available the alternative of constructive work.

*

The British policy of 'Divide and Rule' found another expression in the announcement of the Communal Award in August 1932. The Award allotted to each minority a number of seats in the legislatures to be elected on the basis of a separate electorate, that is Muslims would be elected only by Muslims and Sikhs only by Sikhs, and so on. Muslims, Sikhs and Christians had already been treated as minorities. The Award declared the Depressed Classes (Scheduled Castes of today) also to be a minority community entitled to separate electorate and thus separated them from the rest of the Hindus.

The Congress was opposed to a separate electorate for Muslims, Sikhs and Christians as it encouraged the communal notion that they formed separate groups or communities having interests different from the general body of Indians. The inevitable result was to divide the Indian people and prevent the growth of a common national consciousness. But the idea of a separate electorate for Muslims had been accepted by the Congress as far back as 1916 as a part of the compromise with the Muslim League. Hence, the Congress took the position that though it was opposed to separate electorates, it was not in favour of changing the Award without the consent of the minorities. Consequently, though strongly disagreeing with the Communal Award, it decided neither to accept it nor to reject it.

But the effort to separate the Depressed Classes from the rest of Hindus by treating them as separate political entities was vehemently opposed by all the nationalists. Gandhiji, in Yeravada jail at the time, in particular, reacted very strongly.[15] He saw the Award as an attack on Indian unity and nationalism, harmful to both Hinduism and the Depressed Classes, for it provided no answers to the socially degraded position of the latter. Once the Depressed Classes were treated as a separate community, the question of abolishing untouchability would not arise, and the work of Hindu social reform in this respect would come to a halt.

Gandhiji argued that whatever harm separate electorates might do to Muslims or Sikhs, it did not affect the fact that they would remain Muslims or Sikhs. But while reformers like himself were working for the total eradication of untouchability, separate electorates would ensure that 'untouchables remain untouchables in perpetuity.' What was needed was not the protection of the so-called interests of the Depressed Classes in terms of seats in the legislatures or jobs but the 'root and branch' eradication of untouchability.

Gandhiji demanded that the representatives of the Depressed Classes should be elected by the general electorate under a wide, if possible universal, common franchise. At the same time he did not object to the demand for a larger number of the reserved seats for the Depressed Classes. He went on a fast unto death on 20 September 1932 to enforce his demand. In a statement to the Press, he said: 'My life, I count of no consequence. One hundred lives given for this noble cause would, in my opinion, be poor penance done by Hindus for the atrocious wrongs they have heaped upon helpless men and women of their own faith.'

While many political Indians saw the fast as a diversion from the ongoing political movement, all were deeply concerned and emotionally shaken. Mass meetings took place almost everywhere. The 20th of September was observed as a day of fasting and prayer. Temples, wells, etc., were thrown open to the Depressed Classes all over the country. Rabindranath Tagore sent a telegraphic message to Gandhiji: 'It is worth sacrificing precious life for the sake of India's unity and her social integrity . . . Our sorrowing hearts will follow your sublime penance with reverence and love.' Political leaders of different political persuasions, including Madan Mohan Malaviya, M.C. Rajah and B.R. Ambedkar, now became active. In the end they succeeded in hammering out an agreement, known as the Poona Pact, according to which the idea of separate electorates for the Depressed Classes was abandoned but the seats reserved for them in the provincial legislatures were increased from seventy-one in the Award to 147 and in the Central Legislature to eighteen per cent of the total.

*

Regarding the Poona agreement, Gandhiji declared after breaking his fast: 'I would like to assure my Harijan friends . . . that they may hold my life as a hostage for its due fulfilment.' He now set out to redeem his pledge. First from jail and then from outside, for nearly two years he gave up all other pre- occupations and carried on a whirlwind campaign against untouchability. After his release from prison, he had shifted to *Satyagraha* Ashram at Wardha after abandoning Sabarmati Ashram at Ahmedabad for he had vowed in 1930 not to return to Sabarmati till *Swaraj* was won. Starting from Wardha on 7 November 1933 and until 29 July 1934, for nearly nine months, he conducted an intensive 'Harijan tour' of the country travelling over 20,000 kilometres by train, car, bullock cart, and on foot, collecting money for the recently founded Harijan Sewak Sangh, propagating the removal of untouchability in all its forms and practices, and urging social workers to leave all and go to the villages for the social, economic, cultural and political uplift of the Harijans — his name for the Depressed Classes.

In the course of his Harijan campaign, Gandhiji undertook two major fasts on 8 May and 16 August 1933 to convince his followers of the importance of the issue and the seriousness of his effort. 'They must either remove untouchabilty or remove me from their midst.' He justified these fasts as answers to his 'inner voice,' which, he said, could also be described as 'dictates of reason.' These fasts created consternation in the ranks of the nationalists, throwing many of them into an emotional crisis. The fast of 8 May 1933 was opposed even by Kasturba, his wife. As the hour of the fast approached, Miraben sent a telegram: '*Ba* wishes me to say she is greatly shocked, Feels the decision very wrong but you have not listened to any others and so will not hear her. She sends her heartfelt prayers.' Gandhiji's reply was characteristic: 'Tell *Ba* her father imposed on her a companion whose weight would have killed any other woman. I treasure her love. She must remain courageous to the end.'

Throughout Gandhiji's Harijan campaign, he was attacked by orthodox and social reactionaries. They met him with black flag demonstrations and disrupted his meetings. They brought out scurrilous and inflammatory leaflets against him, putting fantastic utterances in his mouth. They accused him of attacking Hinduism. They publicly burnt his portraits. On 25 June 1934, at Poona, a bomb was thrown on a car believed to be carrying Gandhiji, injuring its seven occupants. The protesters offered the Government full support against the Congress and the Civil Disobedience Movement if it would not support the anti-untouchability campaign. The Government obliged by defeating the

Temple Entry Bill in the Legislative Assembly in August 1934.

Throughout his fast, Harijan work and Harijan tour, Gandhiji stressed on certain themes. One was the degree of oppression practised on the Harijans; in fact, day after day he put forward a damning indictment of Hindu society: 'Socially they are lepers. Economically they are worse. Religiously they are denied entrance to places we miscall houses of God. They are denied the use, on the same terms as Hindus, of public roads, public schools, public hospitals, public wells, public taps, public parks and the like . . . They are relegated for their residence to the worst quarters of cities and villages where they get no social services.' A second theme was that of the 'root and branch removal of untouchability.' Symbolic or rather the entering wedge in this respect was to be the throwing open of all temples to Harijans.

Gandhiji's entire campaign was based on the grounds of humanism and reason. But he also argued that untouchability, as practised at present, had no sanction in the Hindu *Shastras*. But even if this was not so, the Harijan worker should not feel daunted. Truth could not be confined within the covers of a book. The *Shastras* should be ignored if they went against human dignity.

A major running theme in Gandhiji's writings and speeches was the need for caste Hindus to do 'penance' and 'make reparations . . . for the untold hardships to which we have subjected them (the Harijans)for centuries.' For this reason, he was not hostile to Dr. Ambedkar and other Harijans who criticized and distrusted him. 'They have every right to distrust me,' he wrote. 'Do I not belong to the Hindu section miscalled superior class or caste Hindus, who have ground down to powder the so-called untouchables?' At the same time, he repeatedly warned caste Hindus that if this atonement was not made, Hinduism would perish: 'Hinduism dies if untouchability lives, and untouchability has to die if Hinduism is to live.' (This strong theme of 'penance' largely explains why caste Hindus born and brought up in pre-1947 India so readily accepted large scale reservations in jobs, enrolment in professional colleges and so on for the Scheduled Castes and Scheduled Tribes after independence).

Gandhiji was not in favour of mixing up the issue of the removal of untouchability with the issues of inter-dining and inter-marriage. Restriction on the latter should certainly go, for 'dining and marriage restrictions stunt Hindu society.' But they were also practised by caste Hindus among themselves as also the Harijans among themselves. The present all-India campaign, he said, had to be directed against the disabilities which were specific to the Harijans. Similarly, he distinguished between the abolition of caste system and the abolition of untouchability. He disagreed with Dr. Ambedkar when the latter asserted that 'the outcaste is a by-product of the caste system. There will be outcastes as long as there are castes. And nothing can emancipate the outcaste except the destruction of the caste system.' On the contrary, Gandhiji said that whatever the 'limitations and defects' of the Varnashram, 'there is nothing sinful about it, as there is about untouchability.' He believed that purged of untouchability, itself a product of 'the distinction of high and low' and not of the caste system, this system could function in a manner that would make each caste 'complementary of the other and none inferior or superior to any other.' In any case, he said, both the believers in and the critics of the Varna system should join hands in fighting untouchability, for opposition to the latter was common to both.

Gandhiji also stressed the positive impact that the struggle against untouchability would have on the communal and other questions. Non-Hindus were treated by Hindus as untouchables 'in some way or the other,' especially in matters of food and drink, and non-Hindus certainly took note of this fact. Hence, 'if untouchability is removed, it must result in bringing all Indians together.' Increasingly, he also began to point out that untouchability was only one form of the distinctions that society made between man and man; it was a product of the grading of society into high and low. To attack untouchability was to oppose 'this high-and-lowness.' That is why 'the phase we are now dealing with does not exhaust all the possibilities of struggle.'

In keeping with his basic philosophy of non-violence, and being basically a 19th century liberal and believer in rational discussion, Gandhiji was opposed to exercising compulsion even on the orthodox supporters of untouchability, whom he described as the Sanatanists. Even they had to be tolerated and converted and won over by persuasion, 'by appealing to their reason and their hearts.' His fasts, he said, were not directed against his opponents or meant to coerce them into opening temples and wells etc.; they were directed towards friends and followers to goad them and inspire them to redouble their anti-untouchability work.

Gandhiji's Harijan campaign included a programme of internal reform by Harijans: promotion of education, cleanliness and hygiene, giving up the eating of carrion and beef, giving up liquor and the abolition of untouchability among themselves. But it did not include a militant struggle by the Harijans themselves through *Satyagraha*, breaking of caste taboos, mass demonstrations, picketing, and other forms of protest. At the same time, he was aware that his Harijan movement 'must cause daily increasing awakening among the Harijans' and that in time 'whether the *savarna* Hindus like it or not, the Harijans would make good their position.'

Gandhiji repeatedly stressed that the Harijan movement was not a political movement but a movement to purify Hinduism and Hindu society. But he was also aware that the movement 'will produce great political consequences;' just as untouchability poisoned 'our entire social and political fabric.' In fact, not only did Harijan work, along with other items of constructive work, enable the Congress cadre to keep busy in its non-mass movement phases, it also gradually carried the message of nationalism to the Harijans, who also happened to be agricultural labourers in most parts of the country, leading to their increasing participation in the national as well as peasant movements.

24 The Rise of the Left-Wing

A powerful left-wing group developed in India in the late 1920s and 1930s contributing to the radicalization of the national movement. The goal of political independence acquired a clearer and sharper social and economic content. The stream of national struggle for independence and the stream of the struggle for social and economic emancipation of the suppressed and the exploited began to come together. Socialist ideas acquired roots in the Indian soil; and socialism became the accepted creed of Indian youth whose urges came to be symbolized by Jawaharlal Nehru and Subhas Chandra Bose. Gradually there emerged two powerful parties of the Left, the Communist Party of India (CPI) and the Congress Socialist Party (CSP).

*

Seminal in this respect was the impact of the Russian Revolution. On 7 November 1917, the Bolshevik (Communist) party, led by V.I. Lenin, overthrew the despotic Czarist regime and declared the formation of the first socialist state. The new Soviet regime electrified the colonial world by unilaterally renouncing its imperialist rights in China and other parts of Asia. Another lesson was driven home: If the common people — the workers and peasants and the intelligentsia — could unite and overthrow the mighty Czarist empire and establish a social order where there was no exploitation of one human being by another, then the Indian people battling against British imperialism could also do so. Socialist doctrines, especially Marxism, the guiding theory of the

Bolshevik Party, acquired a sudden attraction, especially for the people of Asia. Bipin Chandra Pal, the famous Extremist leader, wrote in 1919: 'Today after the downfall of German militarism, after the destruction of the autocracy of the Czar, there has grown up all over the world a new power, the power of the people determined to rescue their legitimate rights — the right to live freely and happily without being exploited and victimized by the wealthier and the so-called higher classes.'[1] Socialist ideas now began to spread rapidly especially because many young persons who had participated actively in the Non-Cooperation Movement were unhappy with its outcome and were dissatisfied with Gandhian policies and ideas as well as the alternative *Swarajist* programme. Several socialist and communist groups came into existence all over the country. In Bombay, S.A. Dange published a pamphlet *Gandhi and Lenin* and started the first socialist weekly, *The Socialist*; in Bengal, Muzaffar Ahmed brought out *Navayug* and later founded the *Langal* in cooperation with the poet Nazrul Islam; in Punjab, Ghulam Hussain and others published *Inquilab*; and in Madras, M. Singaravelu founded the *Labour-Kisan Gazette*.

Student and youth associations were organized all over the country from 1927 onwards. Hundreds of youth conferences were organized all over the country during 1928 and 1929 with speakers advocating radical solutions for the political, economic and social ills from which the country was suffering. Jawaharlal Nehru and Subhas Bose toured the country attacking imperialism, capitalism, and landlordism and preaching the ideology of socialism. The Revolutionary Terrorists led by Chandra Shekhar Azad and Bhagat Singh also turned to socialism. Trade union and peasant movements grew rapidly throughout the 1920s. Socialist ideas became even more popular during the 1930s as the world was engulfed by the great economic depression. Unemployment soared all over the capitalist world. The world depression brought the capitalist system into disrepute and drew attention towards Marxism and socialism. Within the Congress the left-wing tendency found reflection in the election of Jawaharlal Nehru as president for 1936 and 1937 and of Subhas Bose for 1938 and 1939 and in the formation of the Congress Socialist Party.

*

It was above all Jawaharlal Nehru who imparted a socialist vision to the national movement and who became the symbol of socialism and socialist ideas in India after 1929. The notion that freedom could not be defined only in political terms but must have a socio-economic content began increasingly to be associated with his name.

Nehru became the president of the historic Lahore Congress of 1929 at a youthful forty. He was elected to the post again in 1936 and 1937. As president of the Congress and as the most popular leader of the national movement after Gandhiji, Nehru repeatedly toured the country, travelling thousands of miles and addressing millions of people. In his books (*Autobiography* and *Glimpses of World History*), articles and speeches, Nehru propagated the ideas of socialism and declared that political freedom would become meaningful only if it led to the economic emancipation of the masses; it had to, therefore, be followed by the establishment of a socialist society. Nehru thus moulded a whole generation of young nationalists and helped them accept a socialist orientation.

Nehru developed an interest in economic questions when he came in touch with the peasant movement in eastern U.P. in 1920-21. He then used his enforced leisure in jail, during 1922-23, to read widely on the history of the Russian and other revolutions. In 1927, he attended the International Congress against Colonial Oppression and Imperialism, held at Brussels, and came into contact with communists and anti-colonial fighters from all over the world. By now he had begun to accept Marxism in its broad contours. The same year he visited the Soviet Union and was deeply impressed by the new socialist society. On his return he published a book on the Soviet Union on whose title page he wrote Wordsworth's famous lines on French Revolution: 'Bliss was it in that dawn to be alive, but to be young was very heaven.' Jawaharlal returned to India, in the words of his biographer S. Gopal, 'a self-conscious revolutionary radical.'[2]

In 1928, Jawaharlal joined hands with Subhas to organize the Independence for India League to fight for complete independence and 'a socialist revision of the economic structure of society.' At the Lahore session of the Congress in 1929, Nehru proclaimed: 'I am a socialist and a republican, and am no believer in kings and princes, or in the order which produces the modern kings of industry, who have greater power over the lives and fortunes of men than even the kings of old, and whose methods are as predatory as those of the old feudal aristocracy.' India, he said, would have to adopt a full 'socialistic programme' if she was 'to end her poverty and inequality.' It was also not possible for the Congress to hold the balance between capital and labour and landlord and tenant, for the existing balance was 'terribly weighted' in favour of the capitalists and landlords.3

Nehru's commitment to socialism found a clearer and sharper expression during 1933-36. Answering the question 'Whither India' in October 1933, he wrote: 'Surely to the great human goal of social and economic equality, to the ending of all exploitation of nation by nation and class by class.'4 And in December 1933 he wrote: 'The true civic ideal is the socialist ideal, the communist ideal.'5 He put his commitment to socialism in clear, unequivocal and passionate words in his presidential address to the Lucknow Congress in April 1936: 'I am convinced that the only key to the solution of the world's problems and of India's problems lies in socialism, and when I use this word I do so not in a vague humanitarian way but in the scientific, economic sense . . . I see no way of ending the poverty, the vast unemployment, the degradation, and the subjection of the Indian people except through socialism. That involves vast and revolutionary changes in our political and social structure . . . That means the ending of private property, except in a restricted sense, and the replacement of the present profit system by a higher ideal of cooperative service.'6 During these years, Nehru also emphasized the role of class analysis and class struggle.

Nehru developed a complex relationship with Gandhiji during this period. He criticized Gandhiji for refusing to recognize the conflict of classes, for preaching harmony among the exploiters and the exploited, and for putting forward the theories of trusteeship by, and conversion of, the capitalists and landlords. In fact, Nehru devoted a whole chapter in his *Autobiography* to gently combating some of the basic aspects of Gandhian ideology. At the same time, he fully appreciated the radical role that Gandhiji had played and was playing in Indian society. Defending Gandhiji against his left-wing critics, Jawaharlal contended in an article written in January 1936 that 'Gandhi has played a revolutionary role in India of the greatest importance because he knew how to make the most of the objective conditions and could reach the heart of the masses; while groups with a more advanced ideology functioned largely in the air.' Moreover, Gandhiji's actions and teachings had 'inevitably raised mass consciousness tremendously and made social issues vital. And his insistence on the raising of the masses at the cost, wherever necessary, of vested interests has given a strong orientation to the national movement in favour of the masses.'[7] Nehru's advice to other Leftists in 1939 regarding the approach to be adopted towards Gandhiji and the Congress has been well summed up by Mohit Sen: Nehru believed that 'the overwhelming bulk of the Congress was composed of amorphous centrists, that Gandhiji not only represented them but was also essential for any genuinely widespread mass movement, that on no account should the Left be at loggerheads with him or the centrists, but their strategy should rather be to pull the centre to the left — possibilities for which existed, especially as far as Gandhiji was concerned.'[8]

But Nehru's commitment to socialism was given within a framework that recognized the primacy of the political, anti-imperialist struggle so long as India was ruled by the foreigner. In fact the task was to bring the two commitments together without undermining the latter. Thus, he told the Socialists in 1936 that the two basic urges that moved him were 'nationalism and political freedom as represented by the Congress and social freedom as represented by socialism'; and that 'to continue these two outlooks and make them an organic whole is the problem of the Indian socialist.'[9]

Nehru, therefore, did not favour the creation of an organization independent of or separate from the Congress or making a break with Gandhiji and the right-wing of the Congress. The task was to influence and transform the Congress as a whole in a socialist direction. And this could be best achieved by working under its banner and bringing in workers and peasants to play a greater role in its organization. And in no case, he felt, should the Left become a mere sect apart from the mainstream of the national movement.

*

Attracted by the Soviet Union and its revolutionary commitment, a large number of Indian revolutionaries and exiles abroad made their way there. The most well-known and the tallest of them was M.N. Roy, who along with Lenin, helped evolve the Communist International's policy towards the colonies. Seven such Indians, headed by Roy, met at Tashkent in October 1920 and set up a Communist Party of India. Independently of this effort, as we have seen, a number of left-wing and communist groups and organizations had begun to come into existence in India after 1920. Most of these groups came together at Kanpur in

December 1925 and founded an all-India organization under the name the Communist Party of India (CPI). After some time, S.V. Ghate emerged as the general secretary of the party. The CPI called upon all its members to enroll themselves as members of the Congress, form a strong left-wing in all its organs, cooperate with all other radical nationalists, and make an effort to transform the Congress into a more radical mass-based organization.

The main form of political work by the early Communists was to organize peasants' and workers' parties and work through them. The first such organization was the Labour-Swaraj Party of the Indian National Congress organized by Muzaffar Ahmed, Qazi Nazrul Islam, Hemanta Kumar Sarkar, and others in Bengal in November 1925. In late 1926, a Congress Labour Party was formed in Bombay and a Kirti-Kisan Party in Punjab. A Labour Kisan Party of Hindustan had been functioning in Madras since 1923. By 1928 all of these provincial organizations had been renamed the Workers' and Peasants' Party (WPP) and knit into an all-India party, whose units were also set up in Rajasthan, UP and Delhi. All communists were members of this party. The basic objective of the WPPs was to work within the Congress to give it a more radical orientation and make it 'the party of the people' and independently organize workers and peasants in class organizations, to enable first the achievement of complete independence and ultimately of socialism.The WPPs grew rapidly and within a short period the communist influence in the Congress began to grow rapidly, especially in Bombay. Moreover, Jawaharlal Nehru and other radical Congressmen welcomed the WPPs' efforts to radicalize the Congress. Along with Jawaharlal and Subhas Bose, the youth leagues and other Left forces, the WPPs played an important role in creating a strong left-wing within the Congress and in giving the Indian national movement a leftward direction. The WPPs also made rapid progress on the trade union front and played a decisive role in the resurgence of working class struggles during 1927-29 as also in enabling the Communists to gain a strong position in the working class.

The rapid growth of communist and WPP influence over the national movement was, however, checked and virtually wiped out during 1929 and after by two developments. One was the severe repression to which Communists were subjected by the Government. Already in 1922-24, Communists trying to enter India from the Soviet Union had been tried in a series of conspiracy cases at Peshawar and sentenced to long periods of imprisonment. In 1924, the Government had tried to cripple the nascent communist movement by trying S.A. Dange, Muzaffar Ahmed, Nalini Gupta and Shaukat Usmani in the Kanpur Bolshevik Conspiracy Case. All four were sentenced to four years of imprisonment.

By 1929, the Government was deeply worried about the rapidly growing communist influence in the national and trade union movements. It decided to strike hard. In a sudden swoop, in March 1929, it arrested thirty-two radical political and trade union activists, including three British Communists — Philip Spratt, Ben Bradley and Lester Hutchinson — who had come to India to help organize the trade union movement. The basic aim of the Government was to behead the trade union movement and to isolate the Communists from the national movement. The thirty-two accused were put up for trial at Meerut. The Meerut Conspiracy Case was soon to become a *cause celebre*. The defence of the prisoners was to be taken up by many nationalists including Jawaharlal Nehru, M.A. Ansari and M.C. Chagla. Gandhiji visited the Meerut prisoners in jail to show his solidarity with them and to seek their cooperation in the coming struggle. Speeches of defence made in the court by the prisoners were carried by all the nationalist newspapers thus familiarizing lakhs of people for the first time with communist ideas. The Government design to isolate the Communists from the mainstream of the national movement not only miscarried but had the very opposite consequence. It did, however, succeed in one respect. The growing working class movement was deprived of its leadership. At this early stage, it was not easy to replace it with a new leadership.

As if the Government blow was not enough, the Communists inflicted a more deadly blow on themselves by taking a sudden lurch towards what is described in leftist terminology as sectarian politics or 'leftist deviation'.

Guided by the resolutions of the Sixth Congress of the Communist International, the Communists broke their connection with the National Congress and declared it to be a class party of the bourgeoisie. Moreover, the Congress and the bourgeoisie it supposedly represented were declared to have become supporters of imperialism. Congress plans to organize a mass movement around the slogan of *Purna Swaraj* were seen as sham efforts to gain influence over the masses by bourgeois leaders who were working for a compromise with British imperialism. Congress left leaders, such as Nehru and Bose, were described as 'agents of the bourgeoisie within the national movement' who were out to 'bamboozle the mass of workers' and keep the masses under bourgeois influence. The Communists were now out to 'expose' all talk of non-violent struggle and advance the slogan of armed struggle against imperialism. In 1931, the Gandhi-Irwin Pact was described as a proof of the Congress betrayal of nationalism.

Finally, the Workers' and Peasants' Party was also dissolved on the ground that it was unadvisable to form a two-class (workers' and peasant') party for it was likely to fall prey to petty bourgeois influences. The Communists were to concentrate, instead, on the formation of an 'illegal, independent and centralized' communist party. The result of this sudden shift in the Communists' political position was their isolation from the national movement at the very moment when it was gearing up for its greatest mass struggle and conditions were ripe for massive growth in the influence of the Left over it. Further, the Communists split into several splinter groups. The Government took further advantage of this situation and, in 1934, declared the CPI illegal.

The Communist movement was, however, saved from disaster because, on the one hand, many of the Communists refused to stand apart from the Civil Disobedience Movement (CDM) and participated actively in it, and, on the other hand, socialist and communist ideas continued to spread in the country. Consequently, many young persons who participated in the CDM or in Revolutionary Terrorist organizations were attracted by socialism, Marxism and the Soviet Union, and joined the CPI after 1934.

The situation underwent a radical change in 1935 when the Communist Party was reorganized under the leadership of P.C. Joshi. Faced with the threat of fascism the Seventh Congress of the Communist International, meeting at Moscow in August 1935, radically changed its earlier position and advocated the formation of a united front with socialists and other anti-fascists in the capitalist countries and with bourgeois-led nationalist movements in colonial countries. The Indian Communists were to once again participate in the activities of the mainstream of the national movement led by the National Congress. The theoretical and political basis for the change in communist politics in India was laid in early 1936 by a document popularly known as the Dutt-Bradley Thesis. According to this thesis, the National Congress could play 'a great part and a foremost part in the work of realizing the anti-imperialist people's front.'[10]

The Communist Party now began to call upon its members to join the Congress and enroll the masses under their influence to the Congress. In 1938, it went further and accepted that the Congress was 'the central mass political organization of the Indian people ranged against imperialism.'[11] And, in 1939, P.C. Joshi wrote in the party weekly, *National Front*, that 'the greatest class struggle today is our national struggle' of which Congress was the 'main organ.'[12] At the same time, the party remained committed to the objective of bringing the national movement under the hegemony of the working class, that is, the Communist Party. Communists now worked hard inside the Congress. Many occupied official positions inside the Congress district and provincial committees; nearly twenty were members of the All-India Congress Committee. During 1936-42, they built up powerful peasant movements in Kerala, Andhra, Bengal and Punjab. What is more important, they once again recovered their popular image of being the most militant of anti-imperialists.

*

The move towards the formation of a socialist party was made in the jails during 1930-31 and 1932-34 by a group of young Congressmen who were disenchanted with Gandhian strategy and leadership and attracted by socialist ideology. Many of them were active in the youth movement of the late 1920s. In the jails they studied and discussed Marxian and other socialist ideas. Attracted by Marxism, communism and Soviet Union, they did not find themselves in agreement with the prevalent political line of the CPI. Many of them were groping towards an alternative. Ultimately they came together and formed the Congress Socialist Party (CSP) at Bombay in October 1934 under the leadership of Jayaprakash Narayan, Acharya Narendra Dev and Minoo Masani.From the beginning, all the Congress socialists were agreed upon four basic propositions: that the primary struggle in India was the national struggle for freedom and that nationalism was a necessary stage on the way to socialism; that socialists must work inside the National Congress because it was the primary body leading the national struggle and, as Acharya Narendra Dev put it in 1934, 'it would be a suicidal policy for us to cut ourselves off from the national movement that the Congress undoubtedly represents; that they must give the Congress and the national movement a socialist direction; and that to achieve this objective they must organize the workers and peasants in their class organizations, wage struggles for their economic demands and make them the social base of the national struggle.'13

The CSP from the beginning assigned itself the task of both transforming the Congress and of strengthening it. The task of transforming the Congress was understood in two senses. One was the ideological sense. Congressmen were to be gradually persuaded to adopt a socialist vision of independent India and a more radical pro-labour and pro-peasant stand on current economic issues. This ideological and programmatic transformation was, however, to be seen not as an event but as a process. As Jayaprakash Narayan repeatedly told his followers in 1934: 'We are placing before the Congress a programme and we want the Congress to accept it. If the Congress does not accept it, we do not say we are going out of the Congress. If today we fail, tomorrow we will try and if tomorrow we fail, we will try again.'14

The transformation of the Congress was also seen in an organizational sense, that is, in terms of changes in its leadership at the top. Initially, the task was interpreted as the displacement of the existing leadership, which was declared to be incapable of developing the struggle of the masses to a higher level. The CSP was to develop as the nucleus of the alternative socialist leadership of the Congress. As the Meerut Thesis of the CSP put it in 1935, the task was to 'wean the anti-imperialist elements in the Congress away from its present bourgeois leadership and to bring them under the leadership of revolutionary socialism.'15

This perspective was, however, soon found to be unrealistic and was abandoned in favour of a 'composite' leadership in which socialists would be taken into the leadership at all levels. The notion of alternate Left leadership of the Congress and the national movement came up for realization twice at Tripuri in 1939 and at Ramgarh in 1940. But when it came to splitting the Congress on a Left-Right basis and giving the Congress an exclusive left-wing leadership, the CSP (as also the CPI) shied away. Its leadership (as also CPI's) realized that such an effort would not only weaken the national movement but isolate the Left from the mainstream, that the Indian people could be mobilized into a movement only under Gandhiji's leadership and that, in fact, there was at the time no alternative to Gandhiji's leadership. However, unlike Jawaharlal Nehru, the leadership of the CSP, as also of other Left groups and parties, was not able to fully theorize or internalize this understanding and so it went back again and again to the notion of alternative leadership.

The CSP was, however, fairly well grounded in the reality of the Indian situation. Therefore, it never carried its opposition to the existing leadership of the Congress to breaking point. Whenever it came to the crunch, it gave up its theoretical position and adopted a realistic approach close to that of Jawaharlal Nehru's. This earned it the condemnation of the other left-wing groups and parties — for example, in 1939, they were chastized for their refusal to support Subhas Bose in his confrontation with Gandhiji and the Right wing of the Congress. At such moments, the socialists defended themselves and revealed flashes of an empiricist understanding of Indian reality. Jayaprakash Narayan, for example, said in 1939 after Tripuri: 'We Socialists do not want to create factions in the Congress nor do we desire to displace the old leadership of the Congress and to establish rival leadership. We are only concerned with the policy and programme of the Congress. We only want to influence the Congress decisions. Whatever our differences with the old leaders, we do not want to quarrel with them. We all want to march shoulder to shoulder in our common fight against imperialism.'[16]

From the beginning the CSP leaders were divided into three broad ideological currents: the Marxian, the Fabian and the current influenced by Gandhiji. This would not have been a major weakness — in fact it might have been a source of strength — for a broad socialist party which was a movement. But the CSP was already a party, and a cadre-based party at that, within a movement that was the National Congress. Moreover, the Marxism of the 1930s was incapable of accepting as legitimate such diversity of political currents on the Left. The result was a confusion which plagued the CSP till the very end. The party's basic ideological differences were papered over for a long time because of the personal bonds of friendship and a sense of comradeship among most of the founding leaders of the party, the acceptance of Acharya Narendra Dev and Jayaprakash Narayan as its senior leaders, and its commitment to nationalism and socialism.

*

Despite the ideological diversity among the leaders, the CSP as a whole accepted a basic identification of socialism with Marxism. Jayaprakash

Narayan, for example, observed in his book *Why Socialism?* that 'today more than ever before it is possible to say that there is only one type, one theory of Socialism — Marxism.'[17] Gradually, however, as Gandhiji's politics began to be more positively evaluated, large doses of Gandhian and liberal democratic thought were to become basic elements of the CSP leadership's thinking.

Several other groups and currents developed on the Left in the 1930s. M.N. Roy came back to India in 1930 and organized a strong group of Royists who underwent several political and ideological transformations over the years. Subhas Bose and his left-wing followers founded the Forward Bloc in 1939 after Bose was compelled to resign from the Presidentship of the Congress. The Hindustan Socialist Republican Association, the Revolutionary Socialist Party, and various Trotskyist groups also functioned during the 1930s. There were also certain prestigious left-wing individuals, such as Swami Sahajanand Saraswati, Professor N.G. Ranga, and Indulal Yagnik, who worked outside the framework of any organized left-wing party.

The CPI, the CSP and Jawaharlal Nehru, Subhas Bose and other Left groups and leaders all shared a common political programme which enabled them, despite ideological and organizational differences, to work together after 1935 and make socialism a strong current in Indian politics. The basic features of this programme were: consistent and militant anti-imperialism, anti-landlordism, the organization of workers and peasants in trade unions and *kisan sabhas*, the acceptance of a socialist vision of independent India and of the socialist programme of the economic and social transformation of society, and an anti-fascist, anti-colonial and anti-war foreign policy.

Despite the fact that the Left cadres were among the most courageous, militant and sacrificing of freedom fighters, the Left failed in the basic task it had taken upon itself — to establish the hegemony of socialist ideas and parties over the national movement. It also failed to make good the promise it held out in the 1930s. This is, in fact, a major enigma for the historian.

Several explanations for this complex phenomenon suggest themselves. The Left invariably fought the dominant Congress leadership on wrong issues and, when it came to the crunch, was either forced to trail behind that leadership or was isolated from the national movement. Unlike the Congress right-wing, the Left failed to show ideological and tactical flexibility. It sought to oppose the right-wing with simplistic formulae and radical rhetoric. It fought the right-wing on slippery and wrong grounds. It chose to fight not on questions of ideology but on methods of struggle and on tactics. For example, its most serious charge against the Congress right-wing was that it wanted to compromise with imperialism, that it was frightened of mass struggle, that its anti-imperialism was not wholehearted because of bourgeois influence over it. The right-wing had little difficulty in disposing of such charges. The people rightly believed it and not the Left. Three important occasions may be cited as examples. In 1936-37, the Left fought the Right within the Congress on the issue of elections and office acceptance which was seen as a compromise with imperialism. In 1939-42, the fight was waged on the issue of the initiation of a mass movement, when Gandhiji s reluctance was seen as an aspect of his soft attitude towards imperialism and as the missing of a golden opportunity. And, in 1945-47, the Left confronted the dominant Congress leadership, including Jawaharlal Nehru and Maulana Azad, on the question of negotiations for the transfer of power, which were seen as British imperialism's last ditch effort to prolong their domination and the tired Congress leadership's hunger for power or even betrayal.

The Left also failed to make a deep study of Indian reality. With the exception of Jawaharlal Nehru, the Left saw the dominant Congress leadership as bourgeois, its policy of negotiations as working towards a 'compromise' with imperialism, any resort to constitutional work as a step towards the 'abandonment of the struggle for independence.' It took recourse to a simplistic model of analyzing Indian social classes and their political behaviour. It saw all efforts to guide the national movement in a disciplined manner as imposing restrictions on the movement. It constantly counterposed armed struggle to non-violence as a superior form and method of struggle, rather than concentrating on the nature of mass involvement and mobilization and ideology. It was convinced that the masses were ever ready for struggles in any form if only the leaders were willing to initiate them. It constantly overestimated its support among the people. Above all, the Left failed to grasp the Gandhian strategy of struggle.

A major weakness of the Left was the failure of the different Left parties, groups and individuals to work unitedly except for short periods. All efforts at forging a united front of left-wing elements ended in frustration. Their doctrinal disputes and differences were too many and too passionately held, and the temperamental differences among the leaders overpowering. Nehru and Bose could not work together for long and bickered publicly in 1939. Nehru and the Socialists could not coordinate their politics. Bose and the Socialists drifted apart after 1939. The CSP and the Communists made herculean efforts to work together from 1935 to 1940. The CSP opened its doors to Communists and Royists in 1935 so that the illegal Communist Party could have legal avenues for political work. But the Socialists and Communists soon drifted apart and became sworn enemies. The inevitable result was a long-term schism between the Socialists who suffered from an anti-Communist phobia and Communists who saw every Socialist leader as a potential bourgeois or (after 1947) American agent.

*

The Left did succeed in making a basic impact on Indian society and politics. The organization of workers and peasants, discussed elsewhere, was one of its great achievements. Equally important was its impact on the Congress. Organizationally, the Left was able to command influence over nearly one-third of the votes in the All-India Congress Committee on important issues. Nehru and Bose were elected Congress presidents from 1936 to 1939. Nehru was able to nominate three prominent Socialists, Acharya Narendra Dev, Jayaprakash Narayan and Achyut Patwardhan, to his Working Committee. In 1939, Subhas Bose, as a candidate of the Left, was able to defeat Pattabhi Sitaramayya in the presidential election by a majority of 1580 to 1377.

Politically and ideologically, the Congress as a whole was given a strong Left orientation. As Nehru put it, Indian nationalism had been powerfully pushed 'towards vital social changes, and today it hovers, somewhat undecided, on the brink of a new social ideology.'[18] The Congress, including its right-wing, accepted that the poverty and misery of the Indian people was the result not only of colonial domination but also of the internal socio-economic structure of Indian society which had, therefore, to be drastically transformed. The impact of the Left on the national movement was reflected in the resolution on Fundamental Rights and Economic Policy passed by the Karachi session of the Congress in 1931, the resolutions on economic policy passed at the Faizpur session in 1936, the Election Manifesto of the Congress in 1936, the setting up of a National Planning Committee in 1938, and the increasing shift of Gandhiji towards radical positions on economic and class issues. * The foundation of the All-India Students' Federation and the Progressive Writers' Association and the convening of the first All-India States' People's Conference in 1936 were some of the other major achievements of the Left. The Left was also very active in the All-India Women's Conference. Above all, two major parties of the Left, the Communist Party and the Congress Socialist Party, had been formed, and were being built up.

---

* Discussed in Chapters 23, 25 and 39.

25 The Strategic Debate 1934-1937

A major debate on strategy occurred among the nationalists in the period following the withdrawal of the Civil Disobedience Movement. In the first stage of the debate, during 1934-35, the issue was what course the national movement should take in the immediate future, that is, during its phase of non-mass struggle. How was the political paralysis that it had sunk into to be overcome? There were two traditional responses. Gandhiji emphasized constructive work in the villages, especially the revival of village crafts. Constructive work, said Gandhiji, would lead to the consolidation of people's power, and open the way to the mobilization of millions in the next phase of mass struggle.[1]

Another section of Congressmen advocated the revival of the constitutional method of struggle and participation in the elections to the Central Legislative Assembly to be held in 1934. Led this time by Dr. M.A. Ansari, Asaf Ali, Satyamurthy, Bhulabhai Desai and B.C. Roy, the new Swarajists argued that in a period of political apathy and depression, when the Congress was no longer in a position to sustain a mass movement, it was necessary to utilize elections and work in the legislative councils to keep up the political interest and morale of the people. This did not amount, they said, to having faith in the capacity of constitutional politics to achieve freedom. It only meant opening up another political front which would help build up the Congress, organizationally extend its influence, and prepare the people for the next mass struggle. C.Rajagopalachari, an erstwhile No-Changer, recommended the *Swarajist* approach to Gandhiji with the additional proviso that the Congress should itself, directly, undertake parliamentary work. A properly organized parliamentary party, he said, would enable the Congress to 'develop a certain amount of prestige and confidence among the masses even as (happened) . . . during the short period when the Gandhi-Irwin Pact was in force.' Since the Government was opposed to a similar pact, a strong Congress presence in the legislatures would serve the movement as 'its equivalent.'

*

But, unlike in the 1920s, a third tactical perspective, based on an alternative strategy, made its appearance at this time. The strong Left trend that had developed in the early 1930s was critical of both the Council-entry programme and the suspension of civil disobedience and its replacement by the constructive programme. Both of them, the leftists said, would sidetrack direct mass action and political work among the masses and divert attention from the basic issue of struggle against colonial rule. The leftists instead favoured the continuation or resumption of the non-constitutional mass movement since they felt that the situation continued to be revolutionary because of the continuing economic crisis and the readiness of the masses to fight.

It was Jawaharlal Nehru who represented at this time at its most cogent and coherent this new leftist alternative to the Gandhian anti-imperialist programme and strategy. Accepting the basic analytical framework of Marxism, Nehru put forward the Left paradigm in a series of speeches, letters, articles and books and his Presidential addresses to the Lucknow and Faizpur sessions of the Congress in 1936. The basic goal before the Indian people, as also before the people of the world, he said, had to be the abolition of capitalism and the establishment of socialism. While we've already looked at the pragmatic aspect of Nehru's challenge two of its other aspects have to be understood.

To Nehru, the withdrawal of the Civil Disobedience Movement and Council-entry and the recourse to constructive programmes represented a 'spiritual defeat' and a surrender of ideals, a retreat from the revolutionary to the reformist mentality, and a going back to the pre-1919 moderate phase. What was worse, it seemed that the Congress was giving up all social radicalism and 'expressing a tender solicitude for every vested interest.' Many Congress leaders, he said, 'preferred to break some people's hearts rather than touch others' pockets. Pockets are, indeed, more valuable and more cherished than hearts and brains and bodies and human justice and dignity!'[2] His alienation from Gandhiji also seemed to be complete. He wrote in his jail diary in April 1934:

'Our objectives are different, our ideals are different, our spiritual outlook is different and our methods are likely to be different.'[3]

The way out, said Nehru, lay in grasping the class basis of society
and the role of class struggle and in 'revising vested interests in favour
of the masses.' This meant taking up or encouraging the day-to-day
class, economic demands of the peasants and workers against the landlords and capitalists, organizing the former in their class organizations
— *kisan sabhas* and trade unions — and permitting them to affiliate
with the Congress and, thus, influence and direct its policies and activities. There could be, said Nehru, no genuine anti-imperialist struggle
which did not incorporate the class struggle of the masses.

Throughout these years, Nehru pointed to the inadequacy of the
existing nationalist ideology and stressed the need to inculcate a new,
socialist or Marxist ideology, which would enable the people to study
their social condition scientifically. Several chapters of his
Autobiography, published in 1935, were an ideological polemic against
Gandhiji even though conducted in a friendly tone.

Jawaharlal also challenged the basic Gandhian strategy of struggle.[4]

Under the Gandhian strategy, which may be described as Struggle —
Truce — Struggle (S-T-S'), phases of a vigorous extra-legal mass
movement and confrontation with colonial authority alternate with
phases, during which direct confrontation is withdrawn, political concessions or reforms, if any, wrested from the colonial regime, are willy-
nilly worked and silent political work carried on among the masses
within the existing legal framework, which, in turn, provides scope for
such work. Both phases of the movement are to be utilized, each in its
own way, to undermine the twin ideological notions on which the colonial regime rested — that British rule benefits Indians and that it is too
powerful to be challenged and overthrown — and to recruit and train
cadres and to build up the people's capacity to struggle. The entire
political process of S-T-S' was an upward spiralling one, which also
assumed that the freedom struggle would pass through several stages,
ending with the transfer of power by the colonial regime itself.[5]

Nehru did not subscribe to this strategy and believed that, whatever
might have been the case in the past, the Indian national movement had
now reached a stage where there should be a permanent confrontation
and conflict with imperialism till it was overthrown. He accepted that
the struggle had to go through setbacks and phases of upswing and
downswing; but these should not lead to a passive phase or a stage of

compromise or 'cooperation' with the colonial framework towards which permanent hostility and non-cooperation had to be maintained. The Congress, said Nehru, must maintain 'an aggressive direct action policy.' This meant that even if the mass movement was at a low ebb or remained at a symbolic plane, it should be continued. There could be no interposition of a constitutional phase when the existing constitutional framework was worked; nor could there be a diversion from political and economic class issues to the constructive programme. Furthermore, said Nehru, every movement sooner or later reached a stage when it endangered the existing order. The struggle then became perpetual and could go forward only through unconstitutional and illegal means. This also happened when the masses entered politics. No compromise or half- way house was then left. This stage had been reached in India with the Lahore Resolution for *Purna Swaraj*. There was now no alternative to permanent continuation of the struggle. For this reason, Nehru attacked all moves towards the withdrawal of the Civil Disobedience Movement. This would lead, he warned, to 'some form of compromise with imperialism' which 'would be a betrayal of the cause.' Hence, 'the only way out is to struggle for freedom without compromise or going back or faltering.' Nehru also attacked the notion of winning freedom through stages. Real power could not be won gradually 'bit by bit' or by 'two annas and four annas.' 'The citadel' — State power — had to be seized, though through a non-violent mass struggle. Thus, to S-T- S' he counterposed the strategy of S-V ('V' standing for victory) or the permanent waging of mass struggle till victory was won.

*

So sharp were the differences between Nehru and the leftists on the one side and proponents of council-entry on the other that many — the nationalists with apprehension and the British officials with hope — expected a split sooner or later. But Gandhiji once again moved into the breach and diffused the situation. Though believing that *Satyagraha* alone was capable of winning freedom, he conciliated the proponents of council- entry by acceding to their basic demand that they should be permitted to enter the legislatures. He also defended them from accusations of being lesser patriots. Parliamentary politics, he said, could not lead to freedom but those large number of Congressmen who could not for some reason or the other offer *Satyagraha* or devote themselves to constructive work should not remain unoccupied. They could give expression to their patriotic energies through council work in a period when there was no mass movement, provided they were not sucked into constitutionalism or self-serving. As he put it in a letter to Sardar Patel on 23 April 1934: 'Realities cannot be wished away. At the most we can improve them a little. We may exercise control. We can do neither more nor less.'6

Consequently, under Gandhiji's guidance, the AICC meeting at Patna decided in May 1934 to set up a parliamentary board to fight elections under the aegis of the Congress itself. To the Left-wing critics of the resolution, Gandhiji replied: 'I hope that the majority will always remain untouched by the glamour of council work . . . *Swaraj* will never come that way. *Swaraj* can only come through an all-round consciousness of the masses.'7

At the same time, he assured Nehru and the leftists that the withdrawal of the civil disobedience was dictated by the reality of the political situation. But this did not mean following a policy of drift or bowing down before political opportunists or compromising with imperialism. Only civil disobedience had been discontinued, the war continued. The new policy, he said, 'is founded upon one central idea — that of consolidating the power of the people with a view to peaceful action.'8 Moreover, he told Nehru in August 1934: 'I fancy that I have the knack for knowing the need of the time.'9 He also appeased the Left by strongly backing Nehru for the Presidentship of the Lucknow Congress despite contrary pressure from C. Rajagopalachari and other right-wing leaders.

Gandhiji was at the same time convinced that he was out of tune with powerful trends in the Congress. He felt that a large section of the intelligentsia favoured parliamentary politics with which he was in fundamental disagreement. Another section of the intelligentsia felt estranged from the Congress because of his emphasis on the spinning wheel as 'the second lung of the nation,' on Harijan work based on a moral and religious approach, and on other items of the constructive programme. Similarly, the socialist group, whose leader was Jawaharlal, was growing in influence and importance but he had fundamental differences with it. Yet the Socialists felt constrained by the weight of his personality. As he put it: 'But I would not, by reason of the moral pressure I may be able to exert, suppress the spread of the ideas propounded in their literature.' Thus, vis-a- vis both groups, 'for me to dominate the Congress in spite of these fundamental differences is almost a species of violence which I must refrain from.' Hence, in October 1934, he announced his resignation from the Congress 'only to serve it better in thought, word and deed.'[10]

Nehru and the Socialists responded with no less a patriotic spirit. While enemies of the Congress hoped that their radicalism would lead to their breaking away from the Congress, they had their priorities clearly worked out. The British must first be expelled before the struggle for socialism could be waged. And in the anti-imperialist struggle, national unity around the Congress, still the only anti-imperialist mass organization, was indispensable. Even from the socialist point of view, argued Nehru and other leftists, it was far better to gradually radicalize the Congress, where millions upon millions of the people were, than to get isolated from these millions in the name of political or ideological purity. Nehru, for example, wrote: 'I do not see why I should walk out of the Congress leaving the field clear to social reactionaries. Therefore, I think it is up to us to remain there and try to force the pace, thereby either converting others or making them depart.'[11] The Right was no less accommodating. C. Rajagopalachari wrote: 'The British, perhaps, hope for a quarrel among Congressmen over this (socialism). But we hope to disappoint them.'[12]

Elections to the Central Legislative Assembly were held in November 1934. Of the seventy-five elected seats for Indians, the Congress captured forty-five. 'Singularly unfortunate; a great triumph for little Gandhi,'wailed the Viceroy, Willingdon.[13]

*

Even though the Government had successfully suppressed the mass movement during 1932-33, it was aware that suppression could only be a short-term tactic, it could not prevent the resurgence of another powerful movement in the years to come. For that it was necessary to permanently weaken the movement. This could be achieved if the Congress was internally divided and large segments of it coopted or integrated into the colonial constitutional and administrative structure. The phase of naked suppression should, therefore, be followed, decided the colonial policy makers, by another phase of constitutional reforms.

. In August 1935, the British Parliament passed the Government of

India Act of 1935. The Act provided for the establishment of an All-India Federation to be based on the union of the British Indian provinces and Princely States. The representatives of the States to the federal legislature were to be appointed directly by the Princes who were to be used to check and counter the nationalists. The franchise was limited to about one-sixth of the adults. Defence and foreign affairs would remain outside the control of the federal legislature, while the Viceroy would retain special control over other subjects.

The provinces were to be governed under a new system based on provincial autonomy under which elected ministers controlled all provincial departments. Once again, the Governors, appointed by the British Government, retained special powers. They could veto legislative and administrative measures, especially those concerning minorities, the rights of civil servants, law and order and British business interests. The Governor also had the power to take over and indefinitely run the administration of a province. Thus both political and economic power remained concentrated in British hands; colonialism remained intact. As Linlithgow, Chairman of the Joint Parliamentary Committee on the Act of 1935 and the Viceroy of India from 1936, stated later, the Act had been framed 'because we thought that was the best way . . . of maintaining British influence in India. It is no part of our policy, I take it, to expedite in India constitutional changes for their own sake, or gratuitously to hurry the handing over of the controls to Indian hands at any pace faster than that which we regard as best calculated, on a long view, to hold India to the Empire.'14

The long-term strategy, followed by the British Government from 1935 to 1939, had several major components. Reforms, it was hoped, would revive the political standing of the Liberals and other moderates who believed in the constitutional path, and who had lost public favour during the Civil Disobedience Movement. Simultaneously, in view of the severe repression of the movement, large sections of Congressmen would be convinced of the ineffectiveness of extra-legal means and the efficacy of constitutionalism. They would be weaned away from mass politics and guided towards constitutional politics. It was also hoped that once the Congressmen in office had tasted power and dispensed patronage they would be most reluctant to go back to the politics of sacrifice.

Another aspect of the colonial strategy was equally complex and masterly. Reforms could be used to promote dissensions and a split within the demoralized Congress ranks on the basis of constitutionalist vs non-constitutionalist and Right vs Left. The constitutionalists and the Right wing were to be placated through constitutional and other concessions, lured into the parliamentary game, encouraged to gradually give up agitational politics and coalesce with the moderate Liberals and landlords and other loyalists in working the constitution, and enabled to increase their weight in the nationalist ranks. The Left and radical elements, it was hoped, would see all this as a compromise with imperialism and abandonment of mass politics and would, therefore, become even more strident. Then, either the leftists (radicals) would break away from the Congress or their aggressive anti-Right politics and accent on socialism would lead the Right wing to kick them out. Either way, the Congress would be split and weakened. Moreover, isolated from the Right wing and devoid of the protection that a united national movement gave them, the leftist (radical) elements could be crushed through police measures.

It was as a part of this strategy that the Government reversed its policy, followed during 1933-34, of suppressing the anti-constitutionalists in order to weaken the opposition to constitutionalism. Once division between the Left and the Right began to grow within the Congress, the Government refrained from taking strong action against revolutionary agitation by Left-wing Congressmen. This happened from 1935 onwards. Above all the Government banked on Nehru's strong attacks on the constitutionalists and the Right wing and his powerful advocacy of socialism and revolutionary overthrow of colonial rule to produce a fissure in the nationalist ranks. Officials believed that Nehru and his followers had gone so far in their radicalism that they would not retreat when defeated by the Right wing in the AICC and at the Lucknow Congress. It was for this reason that nearly all the senior officials advised the Viceroy during 1935-36 not to arrest him. Erskine, the Governor of Madras, for example, advised: 'The more speeches of this type that Nehru makes the better, as his attitude will undoubtedly cause the Congress to split. Indeed, we should keep him in cotton wool and pamper him, for he is unwittingly smashing the Congress organization from inside.'[15]

Provincial autonomy, it was further hoped, would create powerful provincial leaders in the Congress who would wield administrative power in their own right, gradually learn to safeguard their administrative prerogatives, and would, therefore, gradually become autonomous centres of political power. The Congress would, thus, be provincialized; the authority of the central all-India leadership would be weakened if not destroyed. As Linlithgow wrote in 1936, 'our best hope of avoiding a direct clash is in the potency of Provincial Autonomy to destroy the effectiveness of Congress as an All-India instrument of revolution.'[16]

The Act of 1935 was condemned by nearly all sections of Indian opinion and was unanimously rejected by the Congress. The Congress demanded instead, the convening of a Constituent Assembly elected on the basis of adult franchise to frame a constitution for an independent India.

*

The second stage of the debate over strategy occurred among Congressmen over the question of office acceptance. The British, after imposing the Act of 1935, decided to immediately put into practice provincial autonomy, and announced the holding of elections to provincial legislatures in early 1937. Their strategy of cooption or absorption into the colonial constitutional framework was underway. The nationalists were faced with a new political reality. All of them agreed that the 1935 Act must be opposed root and branch; but the question was how to do so in a period when a mass movement was not yet possible.

Very sharp differences once again emerged in the ranks of the Congress leaders. There was, of course, full agreement that the Congress should fight the coming elections on the basis of a detailed political and economic programme, thus deepening the anti-imperialist consciousness of the people. But what was to be done after the elections? If the Congress got a majority in a province, should it agree to form the Government or not? Basic questions of the strategy of the national movement and divergent perceptions of the prevailing political situation were involved. Moreover, the two sides to the debate soon got identified with the emerging ideological divide along Left and Right lines.

Jawaharlal Nehru, Subhas Bose, the Congress Socialists and the Communists were totally opposed to office acceptance and thereby working the 1935 Act. The Left case was presented effectively and passionately by Nehru, especially in his Presidential Address at Lucknow in early 1936. Firstly, to accept office, was 'to negative our rejection of it (the 1935 Act) and to stand self-condemned.' It would mean assuming responsibility without power, since the basic state structure would remain the same. While the Congress would be able to do little for the people, it would be cooperating 'in some measure with the repressive apparatus of imperialism, and we would become partners in this repression and in the exploitation of our people.'

Secondly, office acceptance would take away from the revolutionary character of the movement imbibed since 1919. Behind this issue, said Nehru, lay the question 'whether we seek revolutionary changes in India or (whether we) are working for petty reforms under the aegis of British imperialism.' Office acceptance would mean, in practice, 'a surrender' before imperialism. The Congress would get sucked into parliamentary activity within the colonial framework and would forget the main issues of freedom, economic and social justice, and removal of poverty. It would be coopted and deradicalized. It would fall into 'a pit from which it would be difficult for us to come out.'[17]

The counter-strategy that Nehru and the leftists recommended was the older, *Swarajists* one: enter the assemblies with a view to creating deadlocks and making the working of the Act impossible. As a long term strategy, they put forward the policy of increasing reliance on workers and peasants and their class organizations, integration of these class organizations with the Congress, imparting a socialist direction to the Congress, and preparing for the resumption of a mass movement.

Those who favoured office acceptance said that they were equally committed to combating the 1935 Act. They denied that they were constitutionalists; they also believed that 'real work lies outside the legislature' and that work in the legislatures had to be a short-term tactic, for it could not lead to freedom — for that a mass struggle outside the legal framework was needed. But, they said, the objective political situation made it necessary to go through a constitutional phase, for the option of a mass movement was not available at the time. The Congress should, therefore, combine mass politics with work in the legislatures and ministries in order to alter an unfavourable political situation. In other words, what was involved was not a choice between principles but a choice between the two alternative strategies of S-T-S' and S-V. The case of the Right wing was put with disarming simplicity by Rajendra Prasad in a letter to Nehru in December 1935: 'So far as I can judge, no one wants to accept offices for their own sake. No one wants to work the constitution as the Government would like it to be worked. The questions for us are altogether different. What are we to do with this Constitution? Are we to ignore it altogether and go our way? Is it possible to do so? Are we to capture it and use it as we would like to use it and to the extent it lends itself to be used in that way. . . . It is not a question to be answered *a priori* on the basis of pre-conceived notions of a so-called pro- changer or no-changer, cooperator or obstructionist.' And he assured Nehru that 'I do not believe that anyone has gone back to pre-non-cooperation mentality. I do not think that we have gone back to 1923-28. We are in 1928-29 mentality and I have no doubt that better days will soon come.' [18] Similarly, speaking at the Lucknow Session of the Congress, J.B. Kriplani said: 'Even in a revolutionary movement there may be time of comparative depression and inactivity. At such times, whatever programmes are devised have necessarily an appearance of reformatory activity but they are a necessary part of all revolutionary strategy.'[19] Nor was the issue of socialism involved in the debate. As T. Vishwanatham of Andhra put it: 'To my socialist comrades, I would say, capture or rejection of office is not a matter of socialism. I would ask them to realize that it is a matter of strategy.'[20]

The pro-office acceptance leaders agreed that there were pitfalls involved and that Congressmen in office could give way to wrong tendencies. But the answer, they said, was to fight these wrong tendencies and not abandon offices. Moreover, the administrative field should not be left clear to pro-Government forces. Even if the Congress rejected office, there were other groups and parties who would readily form ministries and use them to weaken nationalism and encourage reactionary and communal policies and politics. Lastly, despite their limited powers, the provincial ministries could be used to promote constructive work especially in respect of village and Harijan uplift, *khadi*, prohibition, education and reduction of burden of debt, taxes and rent on the peasants.

The basic question that the ministerialists posed was whether office acceptance invariably led to cooption by the colonial state or whether ministries could be used to defeat the colonial strategy. The answer, in the words of Vishwanatham was: 'There is no office and there is no acceptance . . . Do not look upon ministries as offices, but as centres and fortresses from which British imperialism is radiated . . . The Councils cannot lead us to constitutionalism, for we are not babies; we will lead the Councils and use them for Revolution.'[21]

Though Gandhiji wrote little on the subject, it appears that in the Working Committee discussions he opposed office acceptance and posed the alternative of quiet preparation in the villages for the resumption of civil disobedience. But by the beginning of 1936 he felt that the latter was still not feasible; he was, therefore, willing to give a trial to the formation of Congress ministries, especially as the overwhelming mood of the party favoured this course.

*

The Congress decided at Lucknow in early 1936 and at Faizpur in late 1936 to fight the elections and postpone the decision on office acceptance to the post-election period. Once again, as in 1922-24 and 1934 , both wings of the Congress, having mutual respect and trust in their commitment to the anti-imperialist struggle and aware of the damage to the movement that a split would cause, desisted from dividing the party. Though often out- voted, the Left fought every inch of the way for acceptance of their approach but would not go to breaking point.

The Congress went all out to win the elections to the provincial assemblies held in February 1937. Its election manifesto reaffirmed its total rejection of the 1935 Act. It promised the restoration of civil liberties, the release of political prisoners, the removal of disabilities on grounds of sex and untouchability, the radical transformation of the agrarian system, substantial reduction in rent and revenue, scaling down of the rural debts, provision of cheap credit, the right to form trade unions and the right to strike.

The Congress election campaign received massive response and once again aroused the political consciousness and energy of the people. Nehru's country-wide election tour was to acquire legendary proportions. He travelled nearly 80,000 kilometres in less than five months and addressed more than ten million people, familiarizing them with the basic political issues of the time. Gandhiji did not address a single election meeting though he was very much present in the minds of the voters.

The Congress won a massive mandate at the polls despite the narrow franchise. It won 716 out of 1,161 seats it contested. It had a majority in most of the provinces. The exceptions were Bengal, Assam, the NWPF, Punjab and Sind; and in the first three, it was the largest single party. The prestige of the Congress as the alternative to the colonial state rose even higher. The election tour and election results heartened Nehru, lifted him from the slough of despondency, and made him reconcile to the dominant strategy of S-T-S'.

26 Twenty-eight Months of Congress Rule

After a few months' tussle with the Government, the Congress Working Committee decided to accept office under the Act of 1935. During July, it formed Ministries in six provinces: Madras, Bombay, Central Provinces, Orissa, Bihar and U.P. Later, Congress Ministries were also formed in the North-West Frontier Province and Assam. To guide and coordinate their activities and to ensure that the British hopes of the provincialization of the Congress did not materialize, a central control board known as the Parliamentary Sub-Committee was formed, with Sardar Patel, Maulana Abul Kalam Azad and Rajendra Prasad as members. Thus began a novel experiment — a party which was committed to liquidate British rule took charge of administration under a constitution which was framed by the British and which yielded only partial state power to the Indians; this power could moreover be taken away from the Indians whenever the imperial power so desired. The Congress was now to function both as a government in the provinces and as the opposition vis-a-vis the Central Government where effective state power lay. It was to bring about social reforms through the legislature and administration in the provinces and at the same time carry on the struggle for independence and prepare the people for the next phase of mass struggle. Thus the Congress had to implement its strategy of Strugle-Truce-Struggle (S-T-S') in a historically unique situation.[1]

As Gandhiji wrote on the meaning of office acceptance in *Harijan* on 7 August 1937: 'These offices have to be held lightly, not tightly. They are or should be crowns of thorns, never of renown. Offices have been taken in order to see if they enable us to quicken the pace at which we are moving towards our goal.'[2] Earlier he had advised Congressmen to use the Act of 1935 'in a manner not expected by them (the British) and by refraining from using it in the way intended by them'[3]

*

The formation of the Ministries by the Congress changed the entire psychological atmosphere in the country. People felt as if they were breathing the very air of victory and people's power, for was it not a great achievement that *khadi* clad men and women who had been in prison until just the other day were now ruling in the secretariat and the officials who were used to putting Congressmen in jail would now be taking orders from them? The exhilarating atmosphere of the times is, perhaps, best brought out by the following passage from Jawaharlal Nehru's *Discovery of India*: 'There was a sense of immense relief as of the lifting of a weight which had been oppressing the people; there was a release of long-suppressed mass energy which was evident everywhere . . . At the headquarters of the Provincial Governments, in the very citadels of the old bureaucracy, many a symbolic scene was witnessed . . . Now , suddenly, hordes of people, from the city and the village, entered these sacred precincts and roamed about almost at will.They were interested in anything; they went into the Assembly Chamber, where the sessions used to be held ; they even peeped into the Ministers' rooms. It was difficult to stop them for they no longer felt as outsiders; they had a sense of ownership in all this . . . The policemen and the orderlies with shining daggers were paralyzed; the old standards had fallen; European dress, symbol of position and authority, no longer counted. It was diffiult to distinguish between members of the Legislatures and the peasants and townsmen who came in such large numbers.'[4]

There was an immense increase in the prestige of the Congress as an alternative power that would look after the interests of the masses, especially of the peasants. At the same time, the Congress had got an opportunity to demonstrate that it could not only lead the people in mass struggles but also use state power for their benefit.

The responsibility was, of course, tremendous. However, there were limitations on the Congress Ministries' power and financial resources. They could obviously not change the basically imperialist character of the administration; they could not introduce a radical era. But, within the narrow limits of their powers, and the time available to them (their tenure lasted only two years and four months), they did try to introduce some reforms, take some ameliorative measures, and make some improvement in the condition of the people — to give the people a glimpse of the future *Swaraj*.

The Congress Ministers set an example in plain living. They reduced their own salaries drastically from Rs.2000 to Rs. 500 per month. They were easily accessible to the common people. And in a very short time, they did pass a very large amount of ameliorative legislation, trying to fulfil many of the promises made in the Congress election manifesto.

*

The commitment of the Congress to the defence and extension of civil liberties was as old as the Congress itself, and it is hardly surprising, therefore, that the Congress Ministries registered major achievements in this sphere. All emergency powers acquired by the provincial governments during 1932, through Public Safety Acts and the like, were repealed; bans on illegal political organizations such as the Hindustan Seva Dal and Youth Leagues and on political books and journals were lifted. Though the ban on the Communist Party remained, since it was imposed by the Central Government and could only be lifted on its orders, the Communists could in effect now function freely and openly in the Congress provinces. All restrictions on the press were removed. Securities taken from newspapers and presses were refunded and pending prosecutions were withdrawn. The blacklisting of newspapers for purposes of government advertising was given up. Confiscated arms were returned and forfeited arms licenses were restored.

Of all the British functionaries, the ones the people were most afraid of, as also hated, were the police. On 21 August 1937, after the formation of the Ministries, Gandhiji wrote, 'Indeed, the triumph of the Congress will be measured by the success it achieves in rendering the police and military practically idle . . . The best and the only effective way to wreck the existing Constitution is for the Congress to prove conclusively that it can rule without the aid of the military and with the least possible assistance of the police . . .'[5] In the Congress provinces, police powers were curbed ,and the reporting of public speeches and the shadowing of political workers by CID (Central Investigation Department) agents stopped.

One of the first acts of the Congress Government was to release thousands of political prisoners and detenus and to cancel internment and deportation orders on political workers. Many of the revolutionaries involved in the Kakori and other conspiracy cases were released. But problems remained in U.P. and Bihar where several revolutionaries convicted of crimes involving violence remained in jails. Most of these prisoners had earlier been sent to *kala pani* (Cellular Jail in Andamans) from where they had been transferred to their respective provinces after they had gone on a prolonged hunger strike during July 1937. In February 1938, there were fifteen such prisoners in U.P. and twenty-three in Bihar. Their release required consent by the Governors which was refused. But the Congress Ministries were determined to release them. The Ministries of U.P. and Bihar resigned on this issue on 15 February. The problem was finally resolved through negotiations. All the prisoners in both provinces were released by the end of March.

The difference between the Congress provinces and the non-Congress provinces of Bengal and Punjab was most apparent in this realm. In the latter, especially in Bengal, civil liberties continued to be curbed and revolutionary prisoners and detenus, kept for years in prison without trial, were not released despite repeated hunger strikes by the prisoners and popular movements demanding their release.

In Bombay, the Government also took steps to restore to the original owners lands which had been confiscated by the Government as a result of the no-tax campaign during the Civil Disobedience Movement in 1930. It, too, had to threaten resignation before it could persuade the Governor to agree. The pensions of officials dismissed during 1930 and 1932 for sympathizing with the movement were also restored. There were, however, certain blemishes on the Congress ministerial record in this respect. In July 1937, Yusuf Meherally, a Socialist leader, was prosecuted by the Madras Government for making an inflammatory speech in Malabar, though he was soon let off. In October 1937, the Madras Government prosecuted S.S.Batliwala, another Congress Socialist leader, for making a seditious speech and sentenced him to six months'imprisonment. There was a furore in the Congress ranks led by Jawaharlal Nehru, for this action went against the well-known Congress position that nobody should be prosecuted for making a speech and least of all for a speech against colonial rule. During the discussion on the subject in the Congress Working Committee, Nehru, reportedly, asked C.Rajagopalachari, the Premier of Madras (the head of the Provincial ministry was then known as Premier and not Chief Minister as now is the case): 'Do you mean to say that if I come to Madras and make a similar speech you would arrest me?' 'I would,' the latter is said to have replied.[6] In the end Batliwala was released and went around Madras Presidency making similar speeches. The affair proved to be an exception; but it bred a certain suspicion regarding the future attitude of the Congress Right wing.

Much worse was the mentality of a few of the right-wing Congress ministers. For instance, K.M. Munshi, the Home Minister of Bombay, and a light-weight within the Congress leadership, used the CID to watch the Communists and other left-wing Congressmen, earning a rebuke from Jawaharlal Nehru: 'You have already become a police officer.'[7]The Madras Government, too, used the police to shadow radical Congressmen. These blemishes have, however, to be seen in the larger context of the vast expansion of civil liberties even in Bombay and Madras. Moreover, the mass of Congressmen were vigilant on this question. Led by the Left wing, they exerted intense pressure on the right-wing Congress ministers to avoid tampering with civil liberties.

*

The Congress Ministries tried to give economic relief to the peasants and the workers as quickly as possible. The Congress had succeeded, in the past, in acquiring massive support among them by exposing the roots of their poverty in colonial structure and policy, appealing to their nationalism, leading them in anti- imperialist struggles, and organizing and supporting their struggles around their economic demands. Now that the Congress had acquired some elements of state and administrative power, it was necessary to use these powers to improve their economic condition, and, thus, consolidate Congress support.

The strategy of Congress agrarian legislation was worked out within certain broad parameters. First, the Congress was committed by its election manifesto and the election campaign to a policy of agrarian reform through reform of the system of land tenures and the reduction of rent, land revenue and the burden of debt. The Congress had asked rural voters to vote for its candidates by making large promises in this respect, The voters had taken them seriously; for example, according to government reports from Pratapgarh in U.P., on election day 'a very large number of voters had brought with them pieces of dried cow dung to the various polling stations where these were lighted and, according to the tenants, *"bedakhlis"* ,i.e., ejectment orders, were burnt once for all'[8].

The Congress could not attempt a complete overhaul of the agrarian structure by completely eliminating the *zamindari* system. This, for two reasons. According to the constitutional structure of the 1935 Act, the provincial Ministries did not have enough powers to do so. They also suffered from an extreme lack of financial resources, for the lion's share of India's revenues was appropriated by the Government of India. The Congress Ministries could also not touch the existing administrative structure, whose sanctity was guarded by the Viceroy's and Governor's powers. What is more important, the strategy of class adjustment also forebade it. A multi-class movement could develop only by balancing or adjusting various, mutually clashing class interests. To unite all the Indian people in their struggle against colonialism, the main enemy of the time, it was necessary to make such an adjustment. The policy had to be that of winning over or at least neutralizing as large a part of the landlord classes as possible so as to isolate the enemy and deprive him of all social support within India. This was even more necessary because, in large parts of the country, the smaller landlords were active participants in the national movement. This was recongnized by most of the leaders of the time. Swami Sahajanand, the militant peasant leader of Bihar, for example, wrote in his memoirs: 'As a national organization, the Congress is the forum of all classes. All the classes are a part of the Congress. It represents all sections and classes. This is the claim of the Congress and this is desirable also . . . The major function of the Congress is to maintain harmony between different classes and to further its struggle while doing so.'[9]

There was also the constraint of time. The Congress leadership knew that their Ministries would not last long and would have to quit soon as the logic of their politics was to confront imperialism and not cooperate with it. As Nehru put it later in his *Discovery of India* , a 'sense of impending crisis was always present; it was inherent in the situation.'[10] Even when the Congress had accepted office, the usual figure given for longevity of the policy was two years. The time constraint became even more apparent as war clouds gathered in Europe from 1938 onwards. The Congress Ministries had, therefore, to act rapidly and achieve as much as possible in the short time available to them.

Further, nearly all the Congress-run states (that is, U.P., Bihar, Bombay, Madras and Assam) had reactionary second chambers in the form of legislative councils, which were elected on a very narrow franchise — while the number of voters for the assemblies in these states was over 17.5 million, it was less than 70 thousand for the second chambers. These were, therefore, dominated by landlords, capitalists and moneylenders, with the Congress forming a small minority. As a majority in the lower house was not enough, in order to get any legislation passed through the second chamber, the Congress had to simultaneously pressurise their upper class elements and conciliate them. Thus the Bihar Government negotiated a compromise with the *zamindars* on its tenancy bills while the U.P. Government conciliated the moneylender and merchant members of its upper house by going slow on debt legislation so that their support could be secured for tenancy legislation.

Finally, the agrarian structure of various parts of India had developed over the centuries and was extremely complex and complicated. There was not even enough information about its various components — land rights, for instance. The problem of debt and moneylending was also integrated with peasant production and livelihood in too complex a manner to be tackled by an easy one-shot solution. Consequently, any effort at structural reform was bound to be an extremely formidable and time-consuming operation, as was to be revealed later after independence when the Congress and the Communists attempted to transform the agrarian structure in different states of the Indian union.

Within these constraints, the agrarian policy of the Congress Ministries went a long way towards promoting the interests of the peasantry. Agrarian legislation by these Ministries differed from province to province depending on differing agrarian relations, the mass base of the Congress, the class composition and the outlook of the provincial Congress organization and leadership and the nature and extent of peasant mobilization. In general, it dealt with questions of tenancy rights, security of tenure and rents of the tenants and the problem of rural indebtedness.

To enumerate the achievements of the Ministries, in this regard, briefly: In U.P. a tenancy act was passed in October 1939 which gave all statutory tenants both in Agra and Oudh full hereditary rights in their holdings while taking away the landlord's right to prevent the growth of occupancy. The rents of hereditary tenants could be changed only after ten years, while restrictions were placed on the right of landlords to enhance rents even after this period. A tenant could no longer be arrested or imprisoned for non-payment of rent. All illegal exactions such as *nazrana* (forced gifts) and *begar* (forced unpaid labour) were abolished. In Bihar, the new tenancy legislation was passed mainly in 1937 and 1938, that is, more quickly than in U.P. More radical than that of U.P in most respects, its main provisions were: All increases in rent made since 1911 were abolished; this was estimated to mean a reduction of about twenty-five per cent in rent. The rent was also reduced if the prices had fallen, during the currency of the existing rent, the deterioration of soil and the neglect of irrigation by the landlord. Occupancy *ryots* were given the absolute right to transfer their holding on the payment of a nominal amount of two per cent of rent to the landlord. A point of radical departure was the grant to under- *Ryots* of occupancy rights if they had cultivated the land for twelve years. Existing arrears of rent were substantially reduced and the rate of interest on arrears was reduced from 12.5 to 6.25 per cent . The landlord's share in case of share-cropping was not to exceed 9/20 of the produce. Lands which had been sold in the execution of decrees for the payment of arrears between 1929 and 1937 (*bakasht* land) were to be restored to previous tenants on payment of half the amount of arrears. The landlord's power to realize rent was greatly reduced — the tenant could no longer be arrested or imprisoned on this account, nor could his immovable property be sold without his consent. Landlords were forbidden from charging illegal dues; any violation would lead to six months' imprisment. Occupancy tenants could no longer be ejected from their holdings for non-payment of rent. In fact, the only right that the landlord retained was the right to get his rent which was reduced significantly.

In Orissa, a tenancy bill was passed in May 1938 granting the right of free transfer of occupancy holdings, reducing the interest on arrears of rent from 12.5 to 6 per cent and abolishing all illegal levies on tenants. Another bill passed in February 1938 reduced all rents in the *zamindari* areas, transferred in the recent past from Madras presidency to Orissa, to the rate of land revenue payable for similar lands in the nearest *ryotwari* areas plus 12.5 per cent as compensation to the *zamindars*. The Governor refused to give assent to the bill as it would have reduced the *zamindars*' incomes by fifty to sixty per cent.

In Madras, a committee under the chairmanship of T.Prakasam (1872-1957), the Revenue Minister, recommended that in the areas under Permanent *Zamindari* Settlement the *ryot* and not the *zamindar* was the owner of the soil and that therefore the level of rents prevailing when the Settlement was made in 1802 should be restored.This would have reduced the rents by about two -thirds and would have meant virtual liquidation of the *zamindari* system. The Premier, C.Rajagopalachari, gave full support to the report. He also rejected the idea of compensating the *zamindars*. The Legislative Assembly passed, in January 1939, a resolution accepting the recommendations, but before a bill could be drafted, the Ministry resigned.

Measures of tenancy reform, usually extending security of tenure to tenants in landlord areas, were also carried in the legislatures of Bombay, the Central Provinces and the North-West Frontier Province. The agrarian legislation of the Congress Ministries thus improved and secured the status of millions of tenants in *zamindari* areas. The basic system of landlordism was, of course, not affected. Furthermore, it was, in the main,statutory and occupancy tenants who benefited. The interests of the sub-tenants of the occupancy tenants were overlooked. Agricultural labourers were also not affected. This was partially because these two sections had not yet been mobilized by the k*isan sabhas*, nor had they become voters because of the restricted franchise under the Act of 1935. Consequently, they could not exert pressure on the Ministries through either elections or the peasant movement.

Except for U.P and Assam, the Congress Governments passed a series of stringent debtors' relief acts which provided for the regulation of the moneylenders' business — provisions of the acts included measures such as the cancellation or drastic reduction of accumulated interest ranging from 6.25 per cent in Madras to 9 per cent in Bombay and Bihar . These Governments also undertook various rather modest rural reconstruction programmes. In Bombay 40,000 *dublas* or tied serfs were liberated . Grazing fees in the forests were abolished in Bombay and reduced in Madras. While the tenancy bills were strongly opposed by the landlords, the debtors' relief bills were opposed not only by the moneylenders but also by lawyers, otherwise supporters of the Congress, because they derived a large part of their income from debt litigation.

*

The Congress Ministries adopted ,in general, a pro-labour stance. Their basic approach was to advance workers' interests while promoting industrial peace, reducing the resort to strikes as far as possible, establishing conciliation machinery, advocating compulsory arbitration before resorting to strikes, and creating goodwill between labour and capital with the Congress and its ministers assuming the role of intermediaries, while, at the same time, striving to improve the conditions of the workers and secure wage increases. This attitude alarmed the Indian capitalist class which now felt the need to organize itself to press the 'provincial governments to hasten slowly' on such matters.[11]

Immediately after assuming office,the Bombay Ministry appointed a Textile Enquiry Committee which recommended, among other improvements, the increase of wages amounting to a crore of rupees. Despite millowners protesting against the recommendations, they were implemented. In November 1938, the Governments passed the Industrial Disputes Act which was based on the philosophy of 'class collaboration and not class conflict,' as the Premier B.G Kher put it. The emphasis in the Act was on conciliation, arbitration and negotiations in place of direct action. The Act was also designed to prevent lightning strikes and lock-outs. The Act empowered the Government to refer an industrial dispute to the Court of Industrial Arbitration. No strike or lock-out could occur for an interim period of four months during which the Court would give its award . The Act was strongly opposed by Left Congressmen, including Communists and Congress Socialists, for restricting the freedom to strike and for laying down a new complicated procedure for registration of trade unions, which, they said, would encourage unions promoted by employers. In Madras, too, the Government promoted the policy of 'internal settlement' of labour disputes through government sponsored conciliation and arbitration proceedings. In U.P., Kanpur was the seat of serious labour unrest as the workers expected active support from the popularly elected Government. A major strike occurred in May 1938 . The Government set up a Labour Enquiry Committee , headed by Rajendra Prasad. The Committee's recommendations included an increase in workers' wages with a minimum wage of Rs.15 per month, formation of an arbitration board, recruitment of labour for all mills by an independent board, maternity benefits to women workers, and recognition of the Left-dominated Mazdur Sabha by the employers. But the employers, who had refused to cooperate with the Committee, rejected the report. They did, however, in the end, because of a great deal of pressure from the Government, adopt its principal recommendations. A similar Bihar Labour Enquiry Committee headed by Rajendra Prasad was set up in

1938. It too recommended the strengthening of trade union rights, an improvement in labour conditions, and compulsory conciliation and arbitration to be tried before a strike was declared.

*

The Congress Governments undertook certain other measures of social reform and welfare. Prohibition was introduced in selected areas in different states. Measures for the advancement of untouchables or Harijans (children of God), as Gandhiji called them, including the passing of laws enabling Harijans to enter temples, and to get free access to public offices, public sources of water such as wells and ponds, roads, means of transport, hospitals, educational and other similar institutions maintained out of public funds, and restaurants and hotels. Morover, no court or public authority was to recognize any custom or usage which imposed any civil disability on Harijans. The number of scholarships and freeships for Harijan students was increased. Efforts were made to increase the number of Harijans in police and other government services.

The Congress Ministries paid a lot of attention to primary, technical and higher education and public health and sanitation. Education for girls and Harijans was expanded. In particular, the Ministries introduced basic education with an emphasis on manual and productive work. Mass literacy campaigns among adults were organized. Support and subsidies were given to *khadi*, spinning and village industries. Schemes of prison reforms were taken up. The Congress Governments removed impediments in the path of indigenous industrial expansion and, in fact, actively attempted to promote several modern industrial ventures such as automobile manufacture.

The Congress Governments also joined the effort to develop planning through the National Planning Committee appointed in 1938 by the Congress President Subhas Bose.

*

It was a basic aspect of the Congress strategy that in the non-mass struggle phases of the national movement, mass political activity and popular mobilization were to continue, though within the four-walls of legality. In fact, it was a part of the office- acceptance strategy that offices would be used to promote mass political activity. Jawaharlal Nehru, as the president of the Congress, for example, sent a circular to all Congressmen on 10 July, 1937 emphasizing that organizational and other work outside the legislature was to remain the major occupation of the Congress for 'without it legislative activity would have little value' and that 'the two forms of activity must be coordinated together and the masses should be kept in touch with whatever we do and consulted about it. The initiative must come from the masses.'[12]

The question was the forms this mass political activity should take, and how work in administration and legislature was to be coordinated with political work outside and, equally important, what attitude the populary elected government should adopt towards popular agitations, especially those which stepped outside the bounds of existing legality? There were no historical precedents to learn from or to follow. Different answers were found in different provinces. Unfortunately, the subject has not been studied in any depth by historians, except in a case study of U.P. by Visalakshi Menon.[13] According to Menon, the coordination of legislative and administrative activities and extra-parliamentary struggles was quite successful in U.P. There was widespread mass mobilization which took diverse forms, from the organization of Congress committees in villages to the setting up of popular organs of authority in the form of Congress police stations and panchayats dispensing justice under the leadership of local Congress committees, from organizing of mass petitions to officials and Ministers to setting up of Congress grievance committees in the districts to hear local grievances and reporting them to MLAs and Ministers, from mass literacy campaigns to explain to the people the working of the Ministries, and from organization of local, district and provincial camps and conferences to celebration of various days and weeks. Local Congress committees, members of Legislative Assembly ,provincial and all-India level leaders and even ministers were involved in many of these extra-parliamentary mass mobilization programmes. More detailed research is likely to show that not all Congress Governments were able to coordinate administration with popular mobilization, especially where the Right wing dominated the provincial Congress and the Government. Moreover, even in U.P., mass mobilization was losing steam by 1939.

However, the dilemma also arose in another manner. Political work outside the legislatures would involve organizing popular protest. How far could a movement go in organizing protests and agitations against itself? Could a party which ran a government be simultaneously the organizer of popular movements and enforcer of law and order? And what if some of the protests took a violent or extra-legal form? Could civil liberties have their excess? How should the governmental wing of the movement then respond, since it is one of the functions of any government — colonial or nationalist, leftist or rightist or centrist — to see that the existing laws are observed. In fact, the issue looks at the very question of the of role of the state in modern society, whether capitalist or socialist. Moreover, part of the strategy of increasing Congress influence or rather hegemony among the people was dependent on the demonstration, by the party leading the national movement, of its ability to govern and the capacity to rule. At the same time, existing laws were colonial laws. How far could a regime committed to their overthrow go in enforcing them? Furthermore, it was inevitable that, on the one hand, the long suppressed masses would try to bring pressure on the Ministries to get their demands fulfilled as early as possible, especially as they looked upon the Congress Ministries with 'a sense of ownership' while, on the other, the satisfaction of these demands by the Ministries would be slow because of the constraints inherent in working through constitutional processes. The issue was, perhaps, posed as an easily solvable problem so far as Congressmen committed to non-violence were concerned, but there were many other Congressmen — for example, Communists, Socialists, Royists and Revolutionary Terrorists — and non- Congressmen who were not so committed, who felt that expanded civil liberties should be used to turn the masses towards more militant or even violent forms of agitation, and who tried to prove through such agitations the inadequacy of non-violence, the Congress strategy of S-T-S' and the policy of the working of reforms. Could governance and tolerance, if not promotion, of violent forms of protest coexist?

There was one other problem. While many Congressmen agitated within the perspective of accepting the Congress Ministries as their own and their role as one of strengthening them and the Congress through popular agitations and refrained from creating situations in which punitive action by the Government would become necessary, many others were out to expose the 'breaches of faith and promises' by these Ministries and show up the 'true' character of the Congress as the political organ of the upper classes and one which was, perhaps, no different from the imperialist authorities so far as the masses and their agitations were concerned. In their turn, many of the Congressmen looked upon all hostile critics and militants as forces of disorder and all situations in which people expressed their feelings in an angry manner as 'getting out of hand.' Moreover, Congressmen like C. Rajagopalachari and K.M. Munshi did not hesitate to use their respective state apparatuses in a politically repressive manner. Unfortunately, the full dimensions of this dilemma have not been adequately explored by historians so far. Today they can, perhaps, be usefully analyzed in a comparative framework vis-a-vis the functioning of the Communists and other radical parties as ruling parties in several states of the Indian Union after 1947, or as parts of ruling groups as seen in France or Portugal, or as rulers in socialist countries.

The formation of Congress Ministries and the vast extension of civil liberties unleashed popular energies everywhere. *Kisan sabhas* sprang up in every part of the country and there was an immense growth in trade union activity and membership. Student and youth movements revived and burgeoned. A powerful fillip was given to the state peoples' movement. Left parties were able to expand manifold. Even though it was under a Central Government ban, the Communist Party was able to bring out its weekly organ, *The National Front*, from Bombay. The CSP brought out *The Congress Socialist* and several other journals in Indian languages. Of particular interest is the example of *Kirti Lehar* which the Kirti Communists of Punjab brought out from Meerut, U.P, because they could not do so in Unionist-ruled Punjab.

Inevitably, many of the popular movements clashed with the Congress Governments. Even though peasant agitations usually took the form of massive demonstrations and spectacular peasant marches, in Bihar, the *kisan* movement often came into frontal confrontation with the Ministry, especially when the *Kisan Sabha* asked the peasants not to pay rent or to forcibly occupy landlords' lands. There were also cases of physical attacks upon landlords, big and small, and the looting of crops. *Kisan Sabha* workers popularized Sahajanand's militant slogans: *Lagan Lenge Kaise, Danda Hamara Zindabad* (How will you collect rent, long live our lathis or sticks) and *Lathi Meri Sathi* (Lathi is my companion). Consequently, there was a breach in relations between the Bihar *Kisan Sabha* and the provincial Congress leadership.

In Bombay, the AITUC, the Communists, and the followers of Dr. B.R. Ambedkar organized a strike on 7 November 1938, in seventeen out of seventy-seven textile mills against the passage of the Industrial

Disputes Act. There was some 'disorder' and large-scale stone throwing at two mills and some policemen were injured. The police opened fire, killing two and injuring over seventy. The Madras Government (as also the Provincial Congress Committee) too adopted a strong policy towards strikes, which sometimes took a violent turn. Kanpur workers struck repeatedly, sometimes acting violently and attacking the police. But they tended to get Congress support.

Congress Ministries did not know how to deal with situations where their own mass base was disaffected, They tried to play a mediatory role which was successful in U.P. and Bihar and to a certain extent in Madras, but not in Bombay. But, in general, they were not able to satisfy the Left-wing critics. Quite often they treated all militant protests, especially trade union struggles, as a law and order problem. They took recourse to Section 144 of the Criminal Code against agitating workers and arrested peasant and trade union leaders, even in Kanpur.

Jawaharlal Nehru was privately unhappy with the Ministries' response to popular protest but his public stance was different. Then his answer was: 'We cannot agitate against ourselves.' He tended 'to stand up loyally for the ministers in public and protect them from petty and petulant criticism.'[14] To put a check on the growing agitations against Congress Ministries, the All India Congress Committee passed a resolution in September 1938, condemning those, 'including a few Congressmen,' who 'have been found in the name of civil liberty to advocate murder, arson, looting and class war by violent means.'

'The Congress,' the resolution went on, 'will, consistently with its tradition, support measures that may be undertaken by Congress governments for the defence of life and property.'[15]

The Left was highly critical of the Congress Governments' handling of popular protest; it accused them of trying to suppress peasants' and workers' organizations. The Communist critique of the Congress Ministries was later summed up by R.Palme Dutt: 'The experience of the two years of Congress Ministries demonstrated with growing acuteness the dangers implicit in entanglement in imperialist administration under a leadership already inclined to compromise. The dominant moderate leadership in effective control of the Congress machinery and of the Ministries was in practice developing an increasing cooperation with imperialism, was acting more and more openly in the interests of the upper-class landlords and industrialists, and was showing an increasingly marked hostility to all militant expression and forms of mass struggle . . . Hence a new crisis of the national movement began to develop.'[16]

Gandhiji too thought that the policy of ministry formation was leading to a crisis. But his angle of vision was very different from that of the Communists. To start with, he opposed militant agitations because he felt that their overt or covert violent character threatened his basic strategy based on non-violence. At the beginning of office acceptance, as pointed out earlier, he had advised the Congress Ministries to rule without the police and the army. Later he began to argue that 'violent speech or writing does not come under the protection of civil liberty.'[17] But even while bemoaning the militancy and violence of the popular protest agitations and justifying the use of existing legal machinery against them, Gandhiji objected to the frequent recourse to colonial laws and law and order machinery to deal with popular agitations. He wanted reliance to be placed on the political education of the masses against the use of violence. He questioned, for example, the Madras Government's resort to the Criminal Law Amendment Act, especially to its 'obnoxious clauses.' While criticizing Left-wing incitement to class violence, he constantly sought to curb Right-wing confrontation with the Left. He also defended the right of the Socialists and the Communists to preach and practise their politics in so far as they abided by Congress methods. Gandhiji was able to see the immense harm that the Congress would suffer in terms of erosion of popular support, especially of the workers and peasants, because of the repeated use of law and order machinery to deal with their agitations. This would make it difficult to organize the next wave of extra-legal mass movement against colonial rule. He thus perceived the inherent dilemma in the situation and dealt with it in a large number of articles in *Harijan* during 1938-39. This was one major reason why he began to question the efficacy of continuing with the policy of office acceptance.[18] He wrote in December 1938 that if the Congress Ministries 'find that they cannot run the State without the use of the police and the military, it is the clearest possible sign, in terms of non-violence, that the Congress should give up office and again wander in the wilderness in search of the Holy Grail.'[19]

*

The period of the Congress Ministries witnessed the emergence of serious weaknesses in the Congress. There was a great deal of factional strife and bickering both on ideological and personal bases, a good example of which was the factional squabbles within the Congress Ministry and the Assembly party in the Central provinces which led to the resignation of Dr.N.B.Khare as premier. The practice of bogus membership made its appearance and began to grow. There was a scramble for jobs and positions of personal advantage. Indiscipline among Congressmen was on the increase everywhere. Opportunists, self-seekers and careerists, drawn by the lure of associating with a party in power, began to enter the ranks of the Congress at various levels. This was easy because the Congress was an open party which anybody could join. Many Congressmen began to give way to casteism in their search for power.

Gandhiji began to feel that 'We seem to be weakening from within.' Full of despondency, Gandhiji repeatedly lashed out in the columns of *Harijan* against the growing misuse of office and creeping corruption in Congress ranks. 'I would go to the length of giving the whole Congress organization a decent burial, rather than put up with the corruption that is rampant,' he told the Gandhi Seva Sangh workers in May 1939.[20] Earlier, in November 1938, he had written in *Harijan*: 'If the Congress is not purged of illegalities and irregularities, it will cease to be the power it is today and will fail to fulfil expectations when the real struggle faces the country.'[21] Gandhiji, of course, saw that this slackening of the movement and weakening of the moral fibre of Congressmen was in part inevitable in a phase of non-mass struggle. He, therefore, advised giving up of offices and starting preparations for another phase of *Satyagraha*.

Jawaharlal too had been feeling for some time that the positive role of the Ministries was getting exhausted. He wrote to Gandhiji on 28 April 1938:'I feel strongly that the Congress ministries are working inefficiently and not doing much that they could do. They are adapting themselves far too much to the old order and trying to justify it. But all this, bad as it is, might be tolerated. What is far worse is that we are losing the high position that we have built up, with so much labour, in the hearts of the people. We are sinking to the level of ordinary politicians who have no principles to stand by and whose work is governed by a day to day opportunism . . . I think there are enough men of goodwill in the Congress . . . But their minds are full of party conflicts and the desire to crush this individual or that group.'[22]

The Congress Ministries resigned in October 1939 because of the political crisis brought about by World War II. But Gandhiji welcomed the resignations for another reason — they would help cleanse the Congress of the 'rampant corruption.' He wrote to C. Rajagopalachari on 23 October 1939: 'I am quite clear in my mind that what has happened is best for the cause. It is a bitter pill I know. But it was needed. It will drive away all the parasites from the body. We have been obliged to do wrong things which we shall be able to avoid.'[23] The resignations produced another positive effect. They brought the Left and the Right in the Congress closer because of a common policy on the question of participation in the war.

*

In the balance, the legislative and administrative record of the Congress Ministries was certainly positive. As R. Coupland was to remark in 1944: 'The old contention that Indian self-government was a necessity for any really radical attack on the social backwardness of India was thus confirmed.'[24] And Nehru, a stern critic of the Congress Ministries in 1938-39, wrote in 1944: 'Looking back, I am surprised at their achievements during a brief period of two years and a quarter, despite the innumerable difficulties that surrounded them.'[25] Even though the Left was critical, in the long view even its expectations were fulfilled in a large measure. In 1935, Wang Ming, in his report on the revolutionary movements in colonial countries at the 6th Congress of the Communist International, said in the section on India: 'Our Indian comrades in attempting to establish a united anti-imperialist front with the National Congress in December last year put before the latter such demands as "the establishment of an Indian workers' and peasants' soviet republic," "confiscation of all lands belonging to the *zamindars* without compensation," "a general strike as the only effective progrmme of action," etc. Such demands on the part of our Indian comrades can serve as an example of how not to carry on the tactics of the anti-imperialist united front . . . The Indian communists must formulate a programme of popular demands which could serve as a platform for a broad anti-imperialist united front . . . this programme for struggle in the immediate future should include approximately the following demands: 1) against the slavish constitution, 2) for the immediate liberation of all political prisoners, 3) for the abolition of all extraordinary laws etc., 4) against the lowering of wages, the lenghtening of working day and discharge of workers, 5}against burdensome taxes, high land rents and against confiscation of peasants' lands for non-payment of debts and obligations, and 6} for the establishment of democratic rights.'26

Certainly, the Congress Ministries fulfilled this agenda more or less in entirety.

One of the great achievements of the Congress Governments was their firm handling of the communal riots.They asked the district magistrates and police officers to take strong action to deal with a communal outbreak.

The Congress leadership foiled the imperialist design oᵢ using constitutional reforms to weaken the national movement and, instead, demonstrated how the constitutional structure could be used by a movement aiming at capture of state power to further its own aims without getting coopted. Despite certain weaknesses, the Congress emerged stronger from the period of office acceptance. Nor was the national movement diverted from its main task of fighting for self government because of being engaged in day-to-day administration. Offices were used successfully for enhancing the national consciousness and increasing the area of nationalist influence and thus strengthening ʳhe movement's capacity to wage a mass struggle in the future. The movement's influence was now extended to the bureaucracy, especiaⅰly at the lower levels. And the morale of the ICS (Indian Civil Service), one of the pillars of the British empire, suffered a snattering blow. Many ICS officers came to believe that the British departure from India was only a matter of time. In later years, especiaⅰly during the Quit India Movement, the fear that the Congress might again assume power in the future, a prospect made real by the fact that Congress Ministries had already been in power once, helped to neutralize many otherwise hostile elements, such as landlords and even bureaucrats, and ensured that many of them at least sat on the fence.

One may quote in thiϲ respect Visalakshi Menon's judgement: 'From the instance of the United Provinces,it is obvious that there was no popular disillusionment with the Congress during the period of the Ministry. Rather, the people were able to perceive, in more concrete terms, the shape of things to come, if independence were won.'27

There was also no growth of provincialism or lessening of the sense of Indian unity, as the framers of the Act of 1935 and of its provision for Provincial Autonomy had hoped. The Ministries succeeded in evolving a common front before the Government of India. Despite factionalism, the Congress organization as a whole remained disciplined. Factionalism, particularly at the top, was kept within bounds with a strong hand by the central leadership. When it came to the crunch, there was also no sticking to office. Acceptance of office thus did prove to be just one phase in the freedom struggle. When an all- India political crisis occurred and the central Congress leadership wanted it, the Ministries promptly resigned. And the opportunists started leaving. As the Congress General Secretary said at the time: 'The resignations of the ministries demonstrated o all those who had any doubts that Congress was not out for power and office but for the emancipation of the people of India from the foreign yoke.'28

The Congress also avoided a split between its Left and Right wings — a split which the British were trying to actively promote since 1934. Despite strong critiques of each other by the two wings, they not only remained united but tended to come closer to each other, as the crisis at Tripuri showed.

Above all, the Congress gained by influencing all sections of the people. The process of the growth of Congress and nationalist hegemony in Indian society was advanced. If mass struggles destroyed one crucial element of the hegemonic ideology of British colonialism by demonstrating that British power was not invincible, then the sight of Indians exercising power shattered another myth by which the British had held Indians in subjection: that Indians were not fit to rule.

27 Peasant Movements in the 1930s and '40s

The 1930s bore witness to a new and nation-wide awakening of Indian peasants to their own strength and capacity to organize for the betterment of their living conditions. This awakening was largely a result of the combination of particular economic and political developments: the great Depression that began to hit India from 1929-30 and the new phase of mass struggle launched by the Indian National Congress in 1930.

The Depression which brought agricultural prices crashing down to half or less of their normal levels dealt a severe blow to the already impoverished peasants burdened with high taxes and rents. The Government was obdurate in refusing to scale down its own rates of taxation or in asking *zamindars* to bring down their rents. The prices of manufactured goods, too, didn't register comparable decreases. All told, the peasants were placed in a situation where they had to continue to pay taxes, rents, and debts at pre-Depression rates while their incomes continued to spiral steadily downward.

The Civil Disobedience movement was launched in this atmosphere of discontent in 1930, and in many parts of the country it soon took on the form of a no-tax and no-rent campaign. Peasants, emboldened by the recent success of the Bardoli *Satyagraha* (1928), joined the protest in large numbers. In Andhra, for example, the political movement was soon enmeshed with the campaign against re-settlement that threatened an increase in land revenue. In U.P., no-revenue soon turned into no-rent and the movement continued even during the period of truce following the Gandhi-Irwin Pact. Gandhiji himself issued a manifesto to the U.P *kisans* asking them to pay only fifty per cent of the legal rent and get receipts for payment of the full amount.[1] Peasants in Gujarat, especially in Surat and Kheda, refused to pay their taxes and went on *hijrat* to neighbouring Baroda territory to escape government repression. Their lands and movable property were confiscated. In Bihar and Bengal, powerful movements were launched against the hated *chowkidara* tax by which villagers were made to pay for the upkeep of their own oppressors. In Punjab, a no-revenue campaign was accompanied by the emergence of *kisan sabhas* that demanded a reduction in land revenue and water-rates and the scaling down of debts. Forest *satyagrahas* by which peasants, including tribals, defied the forest laws that prohibited them from use of the forests, were popular in Maharashtra, Bihar and the Central Provinces. Anti- *zamindari* struggles emerged in Andhra, and the first target was the Venkatagiri *zamindari* in Nellore district.

*

The Civil disobedience movement contributed to the emerging peasant movement in another very important way: a whole new generation of young militant, political cadres was born from its womb. This new generation of political workers, which first received its baptism of fire in the Civil Disobedience Movement, was increasingly brought under the influence of the Left ideology that was being propagated by Jawaharlal Nehru, Subhas Bose, the Communists and other Marxist and Left individuals and groups. With the decline of the Civil Disobedience Movement, these men and women began to search for an outlet for their political energies and many of them found the answer in organizing the peasants.

Also in 1934, with the formation of the Congress Socialist Party (CSP), the process of the consolidation of the Left forces received a significant push forward. The Communists, too, got the opportunity, by becoming members of the CSP, to work in an open and legal fashion. This consolidation of the Left acted as a spur to the formation of an all-India body to coordinate the *kisan* movement, a process that was already under way through the efforts of N.G Ranga and other *kisan* leaders. The culmination was the establishment of the All-India Kisan Congress in Lucknow in April 1936 which later changed its name to the All-India *Kisan Sabha*. Swami Sahajanand, the militant founder of the Bihar Provincial *Kisan Sabha* (1929), was elected the President, and N.G.Ranga, the pioneer of the *kisan* movement in Andhra and a renowned scholar of the agrarian problem, the General Secretary. The first session was greeted in person by Jawaharlal Nehru. Other participants included Ram Manohar Lohia, Sohan Singh Josh, Indulal Yagnik, Jayaprakash Narayan, Mohanlal Gautam, Kamal Sarkar, Sudhin Pramanik and Ahmed Din. The Conference resolved to bring out a *Kisan* Manifesto and a periodic bulletin edited by Indulal Yagnik.

A *Kisan* Manifesto was finalized at the All-India *Kisan* Committee session in Bombay and formally presented to the Congress Working Committee to be incorporated into its forthcoming manifesto for the 1937 elections. The *Kisan* Manifesto considerably influenced the agrarian programme adopted by the Congress at its Faizpur session, which included demands for fifty per cent reduction in land revenue and rent, a moratorium on debts, the abolition of feudal levies, security of tenure for tenants, a living wage for agricultural labourers, and the recognition of peasant unions.[2]

At Faizpur, in Maharashtra, along with the Congress session, was held the second session of the All India *Kisan* Congress presided over by N.G.Ranga. Five hundred *kisans* marched for over 200 miles from Manmad to Faizpur educating the people along the way about the objects of the *Kisan* Congress. They were welcomed at Faizpur by Jawaharlal Nehru, Shankar Rao Deo, M.N.Roy, Narendra Dev, S.A. Dange, M.R.Masani, Yusuf Meherally, Bankim Mukherji and many other *Kisan* and Congress leaders. Ranga, in his Presidential Address, declared: 'We are organizing ourselves in order to prepare ourselves for the final inauguration of a Socialist state and society.'[3]

*

The formation of Congress Ministries in a majority of the provinces in early 1937 marked the beginning of a new phase in the growth of the peasant movement. The political atmosphere in the country underwent a marked change: increased civil liberties, a new sense of freedom born of the feeling that 'our own people are in power, 'a heightened sense of expectation that the ministries would bring in pro-people measures — all combined to make the years 1937-39 the high-water-mark of the peasant movement. The different Ministries also introduced varying kinds of agrarian legislation — for debt relief, restoration of lands lost during the Depression, for security of tenure to tenants — and this provided an impetus for the mobilization of the peasantry either in support of proposed legislation or for asking for changes in its content.[4]

The chief form of mobilization was through the holding of *kisan* conferences or meetings at the *thana*, *taluqa*, district and provincial levels at which peasant demands would be aired and resolutions passed. These conferences would be addressed by local, provincial and all-India leaders. They would also usually be preceded by a campaign of mobilization at the village level when *kisan* workers would tour the villages, hold meetings, enroll Congress and *kisan sabha* members, collect subscriptions in money and kind and exhort the peasants to attend the conferences in large numbers. Cultural shows would be organized at these conferences to carry the message of the movement to the peasants in an appealing manner. The effect on the surrounding areas was powerful indeed, and peasants returned from these gatherings with a new sense of their own strength and a greater understanding of their own conditions.

In Malabar, in Kerala, for example, a powerful peasant movement developed as the result of the efforts mainly of CSP activists, who had been working among the peasants since 1934, touring villages and setting up *Karshaka Sanghams* (peasant associations). The main demands, around which the movement cohered, were for the abolition of feudal levies or *akramapirivukal*, renewal fees or the practice of *policceluthu*, advance rent, and the stopping of eviction of tenants by landlords on the ground of personal cultivation. Peasants also demanded a reduction in the tax, rent, and debt burden, and the use of proper measures by landlords when measuring the grain rent, and an end to the corrupt practices of the landlords' managers.

The main forms of mobilization and agitation were the formation of village units of the *Karshaka Sanghams*, conferences and meetings. But a form that became very popular and effective was the marching of *jathas* or large groups of peasants to the houses of big *jenmies* or landlords, placing the demands before them and securing immediate redressal. The main demand of these *jathas* was for the abolition of feudal levies such as *vasi*, *nuri*, etc.

The *Karshaka Sanghams* also organized a powerful campaign around the demand for amending the Malabar Tenancy Act of 1929. The 6th of November, 1938 was observed as the Malabar Tenancy Act Amendment Day, and meetings all over the district passed a uniform resolution pressing the demand. A committee headed by R. Ramachandra Nedumgadi was appointed by the All Malabar *Karshaka Sangham* to enquire into the tenurial problem, and its recommendations were endorsed by the Kerala Pradesh Congress Committee on 20 November 1938. In December, two *jathas* of five hundred each started from Karivallur in north Malabar and Kanjikode in the south and, after being received and hosted by local Congress Committees en route, converged at Chevayur near Calicut where the All Malabar *Karshaka Sangham* was holding its conference. A public meeting was held the same evening at Calicut beach presided over by P. Krishna Pillai,the CSP and later Communist leader, and resolutions demanding amendments in the Tenancy Act were passed. In response to popular pressure, T.Prakasam, the Andhra Congress leader who was the Revenue Minister in the Congress Ministry in Madras Presidency, toured Malabar in December 1938 to acquaint himself with the tenant problem. A Tenancy Committee was set up which included three left-wing members. The *Karshaka Sangham* units and Congress committees held a series of meetings to mobilize peasants to present evidence and to submit memoranda to the Committee. But, by the time the Committee submitted its report in 1940, the Congress Ministries had already resigned and no immediate progress was possible. But the campaign had successfully mobilized the peasantry on the tenancy question and created an awareness that ensured that in later years these demands would inevitably have to be accepted. Meanwhile, the Madras Congress Ministry had passed legislation for debt relief, and this was welcomed by the *Karshaka Sangham.*[5]

In coastal Andhra, too, the mobilization of peasants proceeded on an unprecedented scale. The Andhra Provincial Ryots Association and the Andhra Zamin Ryots Association already had a long history of successful struggle against the Government and *zamindars*. In addition, N.G.Ranga had, since 1933, been running the Indian Peasants' Institute in his home village of Nidobrolu in Guntur district which trained peasants to become active workers of the peasant movement. After 1936, left-wing Congressmen, members of the CSP, many of whom were to later join the CPI also joined in the effort to organize the peasants, and the name of P. Sundarayya was the foremost among them.

The defeat of many *zamindar* and pro-*zamindar* candidates in the 1937 elections by Congress candidates dealt a blow to the *zamindars'* prestige and gave confidence to the *zamindari ryots*. Struggles were launched against the Bobbili and Mungala *zamindaris*, and a major struggle erupted against the Kalipatnam *zamindari* over cultivation and fishing rights.

In coastal Andhra, the weapon of peasant marches had already been used effectively since 1933. Peasant marchers would converge on the district or *taluqa* headquarters and present a list of demands to the authorities. But in 1938, the Provincial Kisan Conference organized, for the first time, a march on a massive scale — a true long march in which over 2,000 *kisans* marched a distance of over 1,500 miles, starting from Itchapur in the north, covering nine districts and walking for a total of 130 days. En route, they held hundreds of meetings attended by lakhs of peasants, and collected over 1,100 petitions; these were then presented to the provincial legislature in Madras on 27 March 1938. One of their main demands was for debt relief, and this was incorporated in the legislation passed by the Congress Ministry and was widely appreciated in Andhra. In response to the peasants' demands the Ministry had appointed a *Zamindari* Enquiry Committee, but the legislation based on its recommendations could not be passed before the Congress Ministries resigned.

Another notable feature of the movement in Andhra was the organization of Summer Schools of Economics and Politics for peasant activists. These training camps, held at Kothapatnam, Mantenavaripalam and other places were addressed by many of the major Left Communist leaders of the time including P.C.Joshi, Ajoy Ghosh and R.D. Bhardwaj. Lectures were delivered on Indian history, the history of the national struggle, on Marxism, on the Indian economy and numerous associated subjects. Money and provisions for running these training camps were collected from the peasants of Andhra. The celebration of various *kisan* and other 'days,' as well as the popularization of peasant songs, was another form of mobilization.[6]

Bihar was another major area of peasant mobilization in this period . Swami Sahajanand, the founder of the Bihar Provincial *Kisan Sabha* and a major leader of the All India *Kisan Sabha*, was joined by many other left-wing leaders like Karyanand Sharma, Rahul Sankritayan, Panchanan Sharma, and Yadunandan Sharma in spreading the *kisan sabha* organization to the villages of Bihar.

The Bihar Provincial *Kisan Sabha* effectively used meetings, conferences, rallies, and mass demonstrations, including a demonstration of one lakh peasants at Patna in 1938, to popularize the *kisan sabha* programme. The slogan of *zamindari* abolition, adopted by the Sabha in 1935, was popularized among the peasants through resolutions passed at these gatherings. Other demands included the stopping of illegal levies, the prevention of eviction of tenants and the return of *bakasht* lands.

The Congress Ministry had initiated legislation for the reduction of rent and the restoration of *bakasht* lands. *Bakasht* lands were those which the occupancy tenants had lost to *zamindars*, mostly during the Depression years, by virtue of non-payment of rent, and which they often continued to cultivate as share-croppers. But the formula that was finally incorporated in the legislation on the basis of an agreement with the *zamindars* did not satisfy the radical leaders of the *kisan sabha*. The legislation gave a certain proportion of the lands back to the tenants on condition that they pay half the auction price of the land. Besides, certain categories of land had been exempted from the operation of the law.

The *bakasht* lands issue became a major ground of contention between the *kisan sabha* and the Congress Ministry. Struggles, such as the one already in progress in Barahiya tal in Monghyr district under the leadership of Karyanand Sharma, were continued and new ones emerged. At Reora, in Gaya district, with Yadunandan Sharma at their head, the peasants won a major victory when the District Magistrate gave an award restoring 850 out of the disputed 1,000 *bighas* to the tenants. This gave a major fillip to the movement elsewhere. In Darbhanga, movements emerged in Padri, Raghopore, Dekuli and Pandoul. Jamuna Karjee led the movement in Saran district, and Rahul Sankritayana in Annawari. The movements adopted the methods of *Satyagraha*, and forcible sowing and harvesting of crops. The *zamindars* retaliated by using *lathials* to break up meetings and terrorize the peasants. Clashes with the *zamindars'* men became the order of the day and the police often intervened to arrest the leaders and activists. In some places, the government and other Congress leaders intervened to bring a compromise. The movement on the *bakasht* issue reached its peak in late 1938 and 1939, but by August 1939 a combination of concessions, legislation and the arrest of about 600 activists succeeded in quietening the peasants. The movement was resumed in certain pockets in 1945 and and continued in one form or another till *zamindari* was abolished.[7]

Punjab was another centre of *kisan* activity. Here, too, the *kisan sabhas* that had emerged in the early 1930s, through the efforts of Naujawan Bharat Sabha, *Kirti Kisan*, Congress and Akali activists, were given a new sense of direction and cohesion by the Punjab *Kisan* Committee formed in 1937. The pattern of mobilization was the familiar one — *kisan* workers toured villages enrolling *kisan sabha* and

Congress members, organizing meetings, mobilizing people for the *tehsil*, district and provincial level conferences (which were held with increasing frequency and attended by an array of national stars). The main demands related to the reduction of taxes and a moratorium on debts. The target of attack was the Unionist Ministry, dominated by the big landlords of Western Punjab.

The two issues that came up for an immediate struggle were the re-settlement of land revenue of Amritsar and Lahore districts and the increase in the canal tax or water-rates. *Jathas* marched to the district headquarters and huge demonstrations were held. The culmination was the Lahore Kisan Morcha in 1939 in which hundreds of *kisans* from many districts of the province courted arrest. A different kind of struggle broke out in the Multan and Montgomery canal colony areas. Here large private companies that had leased this recently-colonized land from the government and some big landlords insisted on recovering a whole range of feudal levies from the share-croppers who tilled the land. The *kisan* leaders organized the tenants to resist these exactions which had recently been declared illegal by a government notification and there were strikes by cultivators in some areas in which they refused to pick cotton and harvest the crops. Many concessions were won as a result. The tenants' struggle, suspended as a result of the War, was resumed in 1946-47.

The peasant movement in Punjab was mainly located in the Central districts, the most active being the districts of Jullundur, Amritsar, Hoshiarpur, Lyallpur and Sheikhupura. These districts were the home of the largely self-cultivating Sikh peasantry that had already been mobilized into the national struggle via the Gurdwara Reform Movement of the early 1920s and the Civil Disobedience Movement in 1930-32. The Muslim tenants- at-will of Western Punjab, the most backward part of the province, as well as the Hindu peasants of South-eastern Punjab (the present-day Haryana) largely remained outside the ambit of the *Kisan* Movement. The tenants of Montgomery and Multan districts mobilized by the *kisan* leaders were also mostly emigrants from Central Punjab. Baba Sohan Singh, Teja Singh Swatantar, Baba Rur Singh, Master Hari Singh, Bhagat Singh Bilga, and Wadhawa Ram were some of the important peasant leaders.[8]

The princely states in Punjab also witnessed a major outbreak of peasant discontent. The most powerful movement emerged in Patiala and was based on the demand for restoration of lands illegally seized by a landlord-official combine through various forms of deceit and intimidation. The *muzaras* (tenants) refused to pay the *batai* (share rent) to their *biswedars* (landlords) and in this they were led by Left leaders like Bhagwan Singh Longowalia and Jagir Singh Joga and in later years by Teja Singh Swatantar. This struggle continued intermittently till 1953 when legislation enabling the tenants to become owners of their land was passed.[9]

In other parts of the country as well, the mobilization of peasants around the demands for security of tenure, abolition of feudal levies, reduction of taxes and debt relief, made major headway. In Bengal, under the leadership of Bankim Mukherji, the peasants of Burdwan agitated against the enhancement of the canal tax on the Damodar canal and secured major concessions. *Kisans* of the 24-Parganas pressed their demands by a march to Calcutta in April 1938. In Surma Valley, in Assam, a no-rent struggle continued for six months against *zamindari* oppression and Karuna Sindhu Roy conducted a major campaign for amendment of the tenancy law. In Orissa, the Utkal Provincial *kisan sabha*, organized by Malati Chowdhury and others in 1935, succeeded in getting the *kisan* manifesto accepted by the PCC as part of its election manifesto, and the Ministry that followed introduced significant agrarian legislation. In the Orissa States, a powerful movement in which tribals also participated was led on the question of forced labour, rights in forests, and the reduction of rent. Major clashes occurred in Dhenkanal and thousands fled the state to escape repression. The *kisans* of Ghalla Dhir state in the North-west Frontier Province protested against evictions and feudal exactions by their Nawab . In Gujarat the main demand was for the abolition of the system of *hali* (bonded labour) and a significant success was registered. The Central Provinces *Kisan Sabha* led a march to Nagpur demanding the abolition of the *malguzari* system, reduction of taxes and moratorium on debts.

*

The rising tide of peasant awakening was checked by the outbreak of World War II which brought about the resignation of the Congress Ministries and the launching of severe repression against left-wing and *kisan sabha* leaders and workers because of their strong anti-War stance. The adoption by the CPI of the Peoples' War line in December 1941 following Hitler's attack on the Soviet Union created dissensions between the Communist and non-Communist members of the *kisan sabha*. These dissensions came to a head with the Quit India Movement, in which Congress Socialist members played a leading role. The CPI because of its pro-War People's War line asked its cadres to stay away, and though many local level workers did join the Quit India movement, the party line sealed the rift in the *kisan sabha* ranks, resulting in a split in 1943. In these years three major leaders of the All India *Kisan Sabha*. N.G.Ranga, Swami Sahajanand Saraswati and Indulal Yagnik, left the organization.

Nevertheless, during the War years the *kisan sabha* continued to play an important role in various kinds of relief work, as for example in the Bengal Famine of 1943, and helped to lessen the rigour of shortages of essential goods, rationing and the like. It also continued its organizational work, despite being severely handicapped by its taking the unpopular pro-War stance which alienated it from various sections of the peasantry.

*

The end of the War, followed by the negotiations for the transfer of power and the anticipation of freedom, marked a qualitatively new stage in the development of the peasant movement. A new spirit was evident and the certainty of approaching freedom with the promise of a new social order encouraged peasants, among other social groups, to assert their rights and claims with a new vigour.

Many struggles that had been left off in 1939 were renewed. The demand for *zamindari* abolition was pressed with a greater sense of urgency. The organization of agricultural workers in Andhra which had begun a few years earlier took on the form of a struggle for higher wages and use of standard measures for payment of wages in kind.

The peasants of Punnapra-Vayalar in Travancore fought bloody battles with the administration. In Telengana, the peasants organized themselves to resist the landlords' oppression and played an important role in the anti-Nizam struggle. Similar events took place in other parts of the country.

But in British India, it was the *tebhaga* struggle in Bengal that held the limelight. In late 1946, the share-croppers of Bengal began to assert that they would no longer pay a half share of their crop to the *jotedars* but only one-third and that before division the crop would be stored in their *khamars* (godowns) and not that of the *jotedars*. They were no doubt encouraged by the fact that the Bengal Land Revenue Commission, popularly known as the Floud Commission, had already made this recommendation in its report to the government. The Hajong tribals were simultaneously demanding commutation of their kind rents into cash rents. The *tebhaga* movement, led by the Bengal Provincial *Kisan Sabha* , soon developed into a clash between *jotedars* and *bargadars* with the *bargadars* insisting on storing the crop in their own *khamars*.

The movement received a great boost in late January 1947 when the Muslim League Ministry led by Suhrawardy published the Bengal Bargadars Temporary Regulation Bill in the *Calcutta Gazette* on 22 January 1947. Encouraged by the fact that the demand for *tebhaga* could no longer be called illegal, peasants in hitherto untouched villages and areas joined the struggle. In many places, peasants tried to remove the paddy already stored in the *jotedars' khamars* to their own, and this resulted in innumerable clashes.

The *jotedars* appealed to the Government, and the police came in to suppress the peasants. Major clashes ensued at a few places, the most important being the one at Khanpur in which twenty peasants were killed. Repression continued and by the end of February the movement was virtually dead. A few incidents occurred in March as well, but these were only the death pangs of a dying struggle.

The Muslim League Ministry failed to pursue the bill in the Assembly and it was only in 1950 that the Congress Ministry passed a Bargadars Bill which incorporated, in substance, the demands of the movement.

The main centres of the movement were Dinajpur, Rangpur, Jalpaiguri, Mymensingh, Midnapore, and to a lesser extent 24-Parganas and Khulna. Initially, the base was among the Rajbansi Kshatriya peasants, but it soon spread to Muslims, Hajongs, Santhals and Oraons. Among the important leaders of this movement were Krishnobinode Ray, Abani Lahiri, Sunil Sen, Bhowani Sen, Moni Singh, Ananta Singh, Bhibuti Guha, Ajit Ray, Sushil Sen, Samar Ganguli, and Gurudas Talukdar. [10]

*

To draw up a balance sheet of such a diverse and varied struggle is no easy task, but it can be asserted that perhaps the most important contribution of the peasant movements that covered large areas of the sub-continent in the 30s and 40s was that even when they did not register immediate successes, they created the climate which necessitated the post-Independence agrarian reforms. *Zamindari* abolition, for example, did not come about as a direct culmination of any particular struggle, but the popularization of the demand by the *kisan sabha* certainly contributed to its achievement.

The immediate demands on which struggles were fought in the pre-Independence days were the reduction of taxes, the abolition of illegal cesses or feudal levies and *begar* or *vethi*, the ending of oppression by landlords and their agents, the reduction of debts, the restoration of illegally or illegitimately seized lands, and security of tenure for tenants. Except in a few pockets like Andhra and Gujarat, the demands of agricultural labourers did not really become part of th movement. These demands were based on the existing consciousness of the peasantry of their just or legitimate rights, which was itself a product of tradition, custom, usage, and legal rights. When landlords or the Government demanded what was seen by peasants as illegitimate — high taxes, exorbitant rents, illegal cesses, forced labour or rights over land which the peasants felt was theirs — they were willing to resist if they could muster the necessary organizational and other resources. But they were also willing to continue to respect what they considered legitimate demands[11].

The struggles based on these demands were clearly not aimed at the overthrow of the existing agrarian structure but towards alleviating its most oppressive aspects. Nevertheless, they corroded the power of the landed classes in many ways and thus prepared the ground for the transformation of the structure itself. The *kisan* movement was faced with the task of transforming the peasants' consciousness and building movements based on a transformed consciousness.

It is also important to note that, by and large, the forms of struggle and mobilization adopted by the peasant movements in diverse areas were similar in nature as were their demands. The main focus was on mobilization through meetings, conferences, rallies, demonstrations, enrolment of members, formation of *kisan sabhas* or *ryotu* and *karshaka sanghams*. Direct action usually involved *Satyagraha* or civil disobedience, and non-payment of rent and taxes. All these forms had become the stock-in-trade of the national movement for the past several years.

As in the national movement, violent clashes were the exception and not the norm. They were rarely sanctioned by the leadership and were usually popular responses to extreme repression.

The relationship of the peasant movement with the national movement continued to be one of a vital and integral nature. For one, areas where the peasant movement was active were usually the ones that had been drawn into the earlier national struggles. This was true at least of Punjab, Kerala, Andhra, U.P and Bihar. This was hardly surprising since it was the spread of the national movement that had created the initial conditions required for the emergence of peasant struggles — a politicized and conscious peasantry and a band of active political workers capable of and willing to perform the task of organization and leadership .

In its ideology as well, the *kisan* movement accepted and based itself on the ideology of nationalism. Its cadres and leaders carried the message not only of organization of the peasantry on class lines but also of national freedom. As we have shown earlier, in most areas *kisan* activists simultaneously enrolled *kisan sabha* and Congress members.

True, in some regions, like Bihar, serious differences emerged between sections of Congressmen and the *kisan sabha* and at times the *kisan* movement seemed set on a path of confrontation with the Congress, but this tended to happen only when both left- wing activists and right-wing or conservative Congressmen took extreme positions and showed an unwillingness to accommodate each other. Before 1942 these differences were usually contained and the *kisan* movement and the national movement occupied largely common ground. With the experience of the split of 1942, the *kisan* movement found that if it diverged too far and too clearly from the path of the national movement, it tended to lose its mass base, as well as create a split within the ranks of its leadership. The growth and development of the peasant movement was thus indissolubly linked with the national struggle for freedom.

28 The Freedom Struggle in Princely India

The variegated pattern of the British conquest of India, and the different stratagems through which the various parts of the country were brought under colonial rule, had resulted in two-fifths of the sub-continent being ruled by Indian princes. The areas ruled by the princes included Indian States like Hyderabad, Mysore and Kashmir, that were equal in size to many European countries, and numerous small States who counted their population in the thousands. The common feature was that all of them, big and small, recognized the paramountcy of the British Government.

In return, the British guaranteed the Princes against any threat to their autocratic power, internal or external. Most of the princely States were run as unmitigated autocracies, with absolute power concentrated in the hands of the ruler, or his favourites. The burden of the land tax was usually heavier than in British India, and there was usually much less of the rule of law and civil liberties. The rulers had unrestrained power over the state revenues for personal use, and this often led to ostentatious living and waste. Some of the more enlightened rulers and their ministers did make attempts, from time to time, to introduce reforms in the administration, the system of taxation and even granted powers to the people to participate in government. But the vast majority of the States were bastions of economic, social, political and educational backwardness, for reasons not totally of their own making.

Ultimately, it was the British Government that was responsible for the situation in which the Indian States found themselves in the twentieth century. As the national movement grew in strength, the Princes were increasingly called upon to play the role of 'bulwarks of reaction.'

Any sympathy with nationalism, such as that expressed by the Maharaja of Baroda, was looked upon with extreme disfavour. Many a potential reformer among the rulers was gradually drained of initiative by the constant surveillance and interference exercised by the British residents. There were honourable exceptions, however, and some States, like Baroda and Mysore, succeeded in promoting industrial and agricultural development, administrative and political reforms, and education to a considerable degree.

*

The advance of the national movement in British India, and the accompanying increase in political consciousness about democracy, responsible government and civil liberties had an inevitable impact on the people of the States. In the first and second decade of the twentieth century, runaway terrorists from British India seeking shelter in the States became agents of politicization. A much more powerful influence was exercised by the Non-Cooperation and Khilafat movement launched in 1920; around this time and under its impact, numerous local organizations of the States' people came into existence. Some of the States in which *praja mandals* or States' People's Conferences were organized were Mysore, Hyderabad, Baroda, the Kathiawad States, the Deccan States, Jamnagar, Indore, and Nawanagar. This process came to a head in December 1927 with the convening of the All India States' People's Conference (AISPC) which was attended by 700 political workers from the States. The men chiefly responsible for this initiative were Balwantrai Mehta, Maniklal Kothari and G.R. Abhayankar.

The policy of the Indian National Congress towards the Indian States had been first enunciated in 1920 at Nagpur when a resolution·calling upon the Princes to grant full responsible government in their States had been passed. Simultaneously, however, the Congress, while allowing residents of the States to become members of the Congress, made it clear that they could not initiate political activity in the States in the name of Congress but only in their individual capacity or as members of the local political organizations. Given the great differences in the political conditions between British India and the States, and between the different States themselves, the general lack of civil liberties including freedom of association, the comparative political backwardness of the people, and the fact that the Indian States were legally independent entities, these were understandable restraints imposed in the interest of the movements in the States as well as the movement in British India. The main emphasis was that the people of the States should build up their own strength and demonstrate their capacity to struggle for their demands. Informal links between the Congress and the various organizations of the people of the States, including the AISPC, always continued to be close. In 1927, the Congress reiterated its resolution of 1920, and in 1929, Jawaharlal Nehru, in his presidential address to the famous Lahore Congress, declared that 'the Indian states cannot live apart from the rest of India . . . the only people who have a right to determine the future of the states must be the people of those states'.[1] In later years, the Congress demanded that the Princes guarantee fundamental rights to their people.

In the mid thirties, two associated developments brought about a distinct change in the situation in the Indian States. First, the Government of India Act of 1935 projected a scheme of federation in which the Indian States were to be brought into a direct constitutional relationship with British India and the States were to send representatives to the Federal Legislature. The catch was that these representatives would be nominees of the Princes and not democratically elected representatives of the people. They would number one-third of the total members of the Federal legislature and act as a solid conservative block that could be trusted to thwart nationalist pressures. The Indian National Congress and the AISPC and other organizations of the States' people clearly saw through this imperialist manoeuvre and demanded that the States be represented not by the Princes' nominees but by elected representatives of the people. This lent a great sense of urgency to the demand for responsible democratic government in the States.

The second development was the assumption of office by Congress Ministries in the majority of the provinces in British India in 1937. The fact that the Congress was in power created a new sense of confidence and expectation in the people of the Indian States and acted as a spur to greater political activity. The Princes too had to reckon with a new political reality — the Congress was no longer just a party in opposition but a party in power with a capacity to influence developments in contiguous Indian States.

The years 1938-39, in fact, stand out as years of a new awakening in the Indian States and were witness to a large number of movements demanding responsible government and other reforms. *Praja mandals* mushroomed in many States that had earlier no such organizations. Major struggles broke out in Jaipur, Kashmir, Rajkot, Patiala, Hyderabad, Mysore, Travancore, and the Orissa States.

These new developments brought about a significant change in Congress policy as well. Whereas, even in the Haripura session in 1938, the Congress had reiterated its policy that movements in the States should not be launched in the name of the Congress but should rely on their own independent strength and fight through local organizations, a few months later, on seeing the new spirit that was abroad among the people and their capacity to struggle, Gandhiji and the Congress changed their attitude on this question. The radicals and socialists in the Congress, as well as political workers in the States, had in any case been pressing for this change for quite some time.

Explaining the shift in policy in an interview to the *Times of India* on 24 January, 1939, Gandhiji said: 'The policy of non-intervention by the Congress was, in my opinion, a perfect piece of statesmanship when the people of the States were not awakened. That policy would be cowardice when there is all-round awakening among the people of the States and a determination to go through a long course of suffering for the vindication of their just rights . . . The moment they became ready, the legal, constitutional and artificial boundary was destroyed.'[2]

Following upon this, the Congress at Tripuri in March 1939 passed a resolution enunciating its new policy: 'The great awakening that is taking place among the people of the States may lead to a relaxation, or to a complete removal of the restraint which the Congress imposed upon itself, thus resulting in an ever increasing identification of the Congress with the States' peoples'.[3] Also in 1939, the AISPC elected Jawaharlal Nehru as its President for the Ludhiana session, thus setting the seal on the fusion of the movements in Princely India and British India.

The outbreak of the Second World War brought about a distinct change in the political atmosphere. Congress Ministries resigned, the Government armed itself with the Defence of India Rules, and in the States as well there was less tolerance of political activity. Things came to a head again in 1942 with the launching of the Quit India movement. This time the Congress made no distinction between British India and the Indian States and the call for struggle was extended to the people of the States. The people of the States thus formally joined the struggle for Indian independence, and in addition to their demand for responsible government they asked the British to quit India and demanded that the States become integral parts of the Indian nation.

The negotiations for transfer of power that ensued after the end of the War brought the problem of the States to the centre of the stage. It was, indeed, to the credit of the national leadership, especially Sardar Patel, that the extremely complex situation created by the lapse of British paramountcy — which rendered the States legally independent — was handled in a manner that defused the situation to a great degree. Most of the States succumbed to a combination of diplomatic pressure, arm-twisting, popular movements and their own realization that independence was not a realistic alternative, and signed the Instruments of Accession. But some of the States like Travancore, Junagadh, Kashmir and Hyderabad held out till the last minute. Finally, only Hyderabad held out and made a really serious bid for independence.

To illustrate the pattern of political activity in the Indian States, it is instructive to look more closely at the course of the movements in two representative States, Rajkot and Hyderabad — one among the smallest and the other the largest, one made famous by Gandhiji's personal intervention and the other by its refusal to accede to the Indian Union in 1947, necessitating the use of armed forces to bring about its integration.

*

Rajkot, a small state with a population of roughly 75,000, situated in the Kathiawad peninsula, had an importance out of all proportion to its size and rank among the States of Western India because Rajkot city was the seat of the Western India State Agency from where the British Political Agent maintained his supervision of the numerous States of the area.

Rajkot had enjoyed the good fortune of being ruled for twenty years — till 1930 — by Lakhajiraj, who had taken great care to promote the industrial, educational and political development of his state. Lakhajiraj encouraged popular participation in government by inaugurating in 1923 the Rajkot Praja Pratinidhi Sabha. This representative assembly consisted of ninety representatives elected on the basis of universal adult franchise, something quite unusual in those times. Though the Thakore Sahib, as the ruler was called, had full power to veto any suggestion, yet under Lakhajiraj this was the exception rather than the rule and popular participation was greatly legitimized under his aegis.

Lakhajiraj had also encouraged nationalist political activity by giving permission to Mansukhlal Mehta and Amritlal Sheth to hold the first Kathiawad Political Conference in Rajkot in 1921 which was presided over by Vithalbhai Patel. He himself attended the Rajkot and Bhavnagar (1925) sessions of the Conference, donated land in Rajkot for the starting of a national school that became the centre of political activity and, in defiance of the British Political Agent or Resident, wore *khadi* as a symbol of the national movement. He was extremely proud of Gandhiji and his achievements and often invited 'the son of Rajkot' to the Durbar and would then make Gandhiji sit on the throne while he himself sat in the Durbar. He gave a public reception to Jawaharlal Nehru during his visit to the State.

Lakhajiraj died in 1930 and his son Dharmendra Singhji, a complete contrast to the father, soon took charge of the State. The new Thakore was interested only in pleasure, and effective power fell into the hands of Dewan Virawala, who did nothing to stop the Thakore from frittering away the State's wealth, and finances reached such a pass that the State began to sell monopolies for the sale of matches, sugar, rice, and cinema licences to individual merchants. This immediately resulted in a rise in prices and enhanced the discontent that had already emerged over the Thakore's easy-going life-style and his disregard for popular participation in government as reflected in the lapse of the Pratinidhi Sabha as well as the increase in taxes.

The ground for struggle had been prepared over several years of political work by political groups in Rajkot and Kathiawad. The first group had been led by Mansukhlal Mehta and Amritlal Sheth and later by Balwantrai Mehta, another by Phulchand Shah, a third by Vrajlal Shukla, and a fourth group consisted of Gandhian constructive workers who, after 1936, under the leadership of U.N. Dhebar, emerged as the leading group in the Rajkot struggle.

The first struggle emerged under the leadership of Jethalal Joshi, a Gandhian worker, who organized the 800 labourers of the state-owned cotton mill into a labour union and led a twenty-one day strike in 1936 to secure better working conditions. The Durbar had been forced to concede the union's demands. This victory encouraged Joshi and Dhebar to convene, in March 1937, the first meeting of the Kathiawad Rajakiya Parishad to be held in eight years. The conference, attended by 15,000 people, demanded responsible government, reduction in taxes and state expenditure.

There was no response from the Durbar and, on 15 August 1938, the Parishad workers organized a protest against gambling (the monopoly for which had been sold to a disreputable outfit called Carnival) at the Gokulashtmi Fair. According to a pre- arranged plan, the protesters were severely beaten with lathis first by the Agency police and then by the State police. This resulted in a complete *hartal* in Rajkot city, and a session of the Parishad was held on 5 September and presided over by Sardar Patel. In a meeting with Dewan Virawala, Patel, on behalf of the Parishad, demanded a committee to frame proposals for responsible government, a new election to the Pratinidhi Sabha, reduction of land revenue by fifteen percent, cancellation of all monopolies or *ijaras*, and a limit on the ruler's claim on the State treasury. The Durbar, instead of conceding the demands, asked the Resident to appoint a British officer as Dewan to deal effectively with the situation, and Cadell took over on 12 September. Meanwhile, Virawala himself became Private Adviser to the Thakore, so that he could continue to operate from behind the scenes.

The *Satyagraha* now assumed major proportions and included withholding of land revenue, defiance of monopoly rights, boycott of all goods produced by the State, including electricity and cloth. There was a run on the State Bank and strikes in the state cotton mill and by students. All sources of income of the state, including excise and custom duties, were sought to be blocked.

Sardar Patel, though most of the time not physically present in Rajkot, kept in regular touch with the Rajkot leaders by telephone every evening. Volunteers began to arrive from other parts of Kathiawad, from British Gujarat and Bombay. The movement demonstrated a remarkable degree of organization: a secret chain of command ensured that on the arrest of one leader another took charge and code numbers published in newspapers informed each *Satyagrahi* of his arrival date and arrangements in Rajkot.

By the end of November, the British were clearly worried about the implications of a possible Congress victory in Rajkot. The Viceroy, Linlithgow, wired to the Secretary of State: 'I have little doubt that if Congress were to win in the Rajkot case the movement would go right through Kathiawad, and that they would then extend their activities in other directions . . .'[4]

But the Durbar decided to ignore the Political Department's advice and go ahead with a settlement with Sardar Patel. The agreement that was reached on 26 December, 1938, provided for a limit on the Thakore's privy purse and the appointment of a committee of ten State subjects or officials to draw up a scheme of reforms designed to give the widest possible powers to the people. A separate letter to the Sardar by the Thakore contained the informal understanding that 'seven members of the Committee . . . are to be recommended by Sardar Vallabhbhai Patel and they are to be nominated by us' [5] All prisoners were released and the *Satyagraha* was withdrawn.

But such open defiance by the Thakore could hardly be welcomed by the British government. Consultations involving the Resident, the Political Department, the Viceroy and the Secretary of State were immediately held and the Thakore was instructed not to accept the Sardar's list of members of the Committee, but to select another set with the help of the Resident. Accordingly, the list of names sent by Patel was rejected, the excuse being that it contained the names of only Brahmins and Banias, and did not gave any representation to Rajputs, Muslims and the depressed classes.

The breach of agreement by the State led to a resumption of the *Satyagraha* on 26 January 1939. Virawala answered with severe repression. As before, this soon led to a growing concern and sense of outrage among nationalists outside Rajkot, Kasturba, Gandhiji's wife, who had been brought up in Rajkot, was so moved by the state of affairs that she decided, in spite of her poor health and against everybody's advice, to go to Rajkot. On arrival, she and her companion Maniben Patel, the Sardar's daughter, were arrested and detained in a village sixteen miles from Rajkot.

But Rajkot was destined for even more dramatic events. The Mahatma decided that he, too, must go to Rajkot. He had already made it clear that he considered the breach of a solemn agreement by the Thakore Sahib a serious affair and one that it was the duty of every *Satyagrahi* to resist. He also felt that he had strong claims on Rajkot because of his family's close association with the State and the Thakore's family, and that this justified and prompted his personal intervention.

In accordance with his wishes, mass *Satyagraha* was suspended to prepare the way for negotiations. But a number of discussions with the Resident, the Thakore and Dewan Virawala yielded no results and resulted in an ultimatum by Gandhiji that if, by 3 March, the Durbar did not agree to honour its agreement with the Sardar, he would go on a fast unto death. The Thakore, or rather Virawala, who was the real power behind the throne, stuck to his original position and left Gandhiji with no choice but to begin his fast.

The fast was the signal for a nation-wide protest. Gandhiji's health was already poor and any prolonged fast was likely to be dangerous. There were *hartals*, an adjournment of the legislature and finally a threat that the Congress Ministries might resign. The Viceroy was bombarded with telegrams asking for his intervention. Gandhiji himself urged the Paramount Power to fulfil its responsibility to the people of the State by persuading the Thakore to honour his promise. On 7 March, the Viceroy suggested arbitration by the Chief Justice of India, Sir Maurice Gwyer, to decide whether in fact the Thakore had violated the agreement. This seemed a reasonable enough proposition, and Gandhiji broke his fast.

The Chief Justice's award, announced on 3 April, 1939, vindicated the Sardar's position that the Durbar had agreed to accept seven of his nominees. The ball was now back in the Thakore's court. But there had been no change of heart in Rajkot. Virawala continued with his policy of propping up Rajput, Muslim and depressed classes' claims to representation and refused to accept any of the proposals made by Gandhiji to accommodate their representatives while maintaining a majority of the Sardar's and the Parishad's nominees.

The situation soon began to take an ugly turn, with hostile demonstrations by Rajputs and Muslims during Gandhiji's prayer meetings, and Mohammed Ali Jinnah's and Ambedkar's demand that the Muslims and depressed classes be given separate representation. The Durbar used all this to continue to refuse to honour the agreement in either its letter or spirit. The Paramount Power, too, would not intervene because it had nothing to gain and everything to lose from securing an outright Congress victory. Nor did it see its role as one of promoting responsible government in the States.

At this point, Gandhiji, analyzing the reasons for his failure to achieve a 'change of heart' in his opponents, came to the conclusion that the cause lay in his attempt to use the authority of the Paramount Power to coerce the Thakore into an agreement. This, for him, smacked of violence; non-violence should have meant that he should have directed his fast only at the Thakore and Virawala, and relied only on the strength of his suffering to effect a 'change of heart'. Therefore, he released the Thakore from the agreement, apologized to the Viceroy and the Chief Justice for wasting their time, and to his opponents, the Muslims and the Rajputs, and left Rajkot to return to British India.[6]

The Rajkot *Satyagraha* brought into clear focus the paradoxical situation that existed in the States and which made the task of resistance a very complex one. The rulers of the States were protected by the might of the British Government against any movements that aimed at reform and popular pressure on the British Government to induce reform could always be resisted by pleading the legal position of the autonomy of the States. This legal independence, however, was usually forgotten by the British when the States desired to follow a course that was unpalatable to the Paramount Power. It was, after all, the British Government that urged the Thakore to refuse to honour his agreement with the Sardar. But the legal separation of power and responsibility between the States and the British Government did provide a convenient excuse for resisting pressure, an excuse that did not exist in British India. This meant that movements of resistance in the States operated in conditions that were very different from those that provided the context for movements in British India. Perhaps, then, the Congress had not been far wrong when for years it had urged that the movements in Princely India and British India could not be merged. Its hesitation to take on the Indian States was based on a comprehension of the genuine difficulties in the situation, difficulties which were clearly shown up by the example of Rajkot.

Despite the apparent failure of the Rajkot *Satyagraha*, it exercised a powerful politicizing influence on the people of the States, especially in Western India. It also demonstrated to the Princes that they survived only because the British were there to prop them up, and thus, the struggle of Rajkot, along with others of its time, facilitated the process of the integration of the States at the time of independence. Many a Prince who had seen for himself that the people were capable of resisting would hesitate in 1947 to resist the pressure for integration when it came. In the absence of these struggles, the whole process of integration would inevitably have been arduous and protracted. It is hardly a matter for surprise that the man who was responsible more than any other for effecting the integration in 1947-48 was the same Sardar who was a veteran of many struggles against the Princes.

*

But there was one State that refused to see the writing on the wall — Hyderabad. Hyderabad was the largest princely State in India both by virtue of its size and its population. The Nizam's dominions included three distinct linguistic areas: Marathi-speaking (twenty-eight percent), Kannada-speaking (twenty two) and Telugu-speaking (fifty per cent). Osman Ali Khan, who became Nizam in 1911 and continued till 1948, ruled the State as a personalized autocrary. The *sarf khas*, the Nizam's own estate, which accounted for ten per cent of the total area of the State, went directly to meet the royal expenses. Another thirty per cent of the States' area was held as *jagirs* by various categories of the rural population and was heavily burdened by a whole gamut of illegal levies and exactions and forced labour or *vethi*.

Particularly galling to the overwhelmingly Hindu population of the State was the cultural and religious suppression practised by the Nizam. Urdu was made the court language and all efforts were made to promote it, including the setting up of the Osmania University. Other languages of the State — Telugu, Marathi and Kannada — were neglected and even private efforts to promote education in these languages were obstructed. Muslims were given a disproportionately large share of the jobs in the administration, especially in its upper echelons. The Arya Samaj movement that grew rapidly in the 1920s was actively suppressed and official permission had to be sought to set up a *havan kund* for Arya Samaj religious observances. The Nizam's administration increasingly tried to project Hyderabad as a Muslim state, and this process was accelerated after 1927 with the emergence of the *Ittehad ul Muslimin*, an organization that based itself on the notion of the Nizam as the 'Royal Embodiment of Muslim Sovereignty in the Deccan.'

It is in this context of political, economic, cultural and religious oppression that the growth of political consciousness and the course of the States' People's Movement in Hyderabad has to be understood.

As in other parts of India, it was the Non-Cooperation and Khilafat Movement of 1920-22 that created the first stirrings of political activity. From various parts of the State, there were reports of *charkhas* being popularized, national schools being set up, of propaganda against drink and untouchability, of badges containing pictures of Gandhiji and the Ali brothers being sold. Public meetings were not much in evidence, except in connection with the Khilafat movement, which could take on a more open form because the Nizam hesitated to come out openly against it. Public demonstration of Hindu-Muslim unity was very popular in these years.

This new awakening found expression in the subsequent years in the holding of a series of Hyderabad political conferences at different venues outside the State. The main discussion at these conferences centered around the need for a system of responsible government and for elementary civil liberties that were lacking in the State. Oppressive practices like *vethi* or *veth begar* and exorbitant taxation, as well as the religious and cultural suppression of the people, were also condemned.

Simultaneously, there began a process of regional cultural awakening, the lead being taken by the Telengana area. A cohesion to this effort was provided by the founding of the Andhra Jana Sangham which later grew into the Andhra Mahasabha. The emphasis initially was on the promotion of Telugu language and literature by setting up library associations, schools, journals and newspapers and promoting a research society. Even these activities came under attack from the State authorities, and schools, libraries and newspapers would be regularly shut down. The Mahasabha refrained from any direct political activity or stance till the 1940s.

The Civil Disobedience Movement of 1930-32, in which many people from the State participated by going to the British areas, carried the process of politicization further. Hyderabad nationalists, especially many of the younger ones, spent time in jail with nationalists from British India and became part of the political trends that were sweeping the rest of the nation. A new impatience was imparted to their politics, and the pressure for a more vigorous politics became stronger.

In 1937, the other two regions of the State also set up their own organizations — the Maharashtra Parishad and the Kannada Parishad. And, in 1938, activists from all three regions came together and decided to found the Hyderabad State Congress as a state-wide body of the people of Hyderabad. This was not a branch of the Indian National Congress, despite its name, and despite the fact that its members had close contacts with the Congress. But even before the organization could be formally founded, the Nizam's government issued orders banning it, the ostensible ground being that it was a communal body of Hindus and that Muslims were not sufficiently represented in it. Negotiations with the Government bore no fruit, and the decision was taken to launch a *Satyagraha*.

The leader of this *Satyagraha* was Swami Ramanand Tirtha, a

Marathi-speaking nationalist who had given up his studies during the Non-Cooperation Movement, attended a national school and college, worked as a trade unionist in Bombay and Sholapur and finally moved to Mominabad in Hyderabad State where he ran a school on nationalist lines. A Gandhian in his life- style and a Nehruite in his ideology, Swamiji emerged in 1938 as the leader of the movement since the older and more established leaders were unwilling or unable to venture into this new type of politics of confrontation with the State.

The *Satyagraha* started in October 1938 and the pattern adopted was that a group of five *Satyagrahis* headed by a popular leader and consisting of representatives of all the regions would defy the ban by proclaiming themselves as members of the State Congress. This was repeated thrice a week for two months and all the *Satyagrahis* were sent to jail. Huge crowds would collect to witness the *Satyagraha* and express solidarity with the movement. The two centres of the *Satyagraha* were Hyderabad city and Aurangabad city in the Marathwada area.

Gandhiji himself took a keen personal interest in the developments, and regularly wrote to Sir Akbar Hydari, the Prime Minister, pressing him for better treatment of the *Satyagrahis* and for a change in the State's attitude. And it was at his instance that, after two months, in December 1938, the *Satyagraha* was withdrawn.

The reasons for this decision were to be primarily found in an accompanying development — the *Satyagraha* launched by the Arya Samaj and the Hindu Civil Liberties Union at the same time as the State Congress *Satyagraha*. The Arya Samaj *Satyagraha*, which was attracting *Satyagrahis* from all over the country, was launched as a protest against the religious persecution of the Arya Samaj, and it had clearly religious objectives. It also tended to take on communal overtones. The State Congress and Gandhiji increasingly felt that in the popular mind their clearly secular *Satyagraha* with distinct political objectives was being confused with the religious-communal *satyagraha* of the Arya Samaj and that it was, therefore, best to demarcate themselves from it by withdrawing their own *Satyagraha*. The authorities were in any case lumping the two together and seeking to project the State Congress as a Hindu communal organization.

Simultaneously, there was the emergence of what came to be known as the Vande Mataram movement. Students of colleges in Hyderabad city organized a protest strike against the authorities' refusal to let them sing *Vande Mataram* in their hostel prayer rooms. This strike rapidly spread to other parts of the State and many of the students who were expelled from the Hyderabad colleges left the State and continued their studies in Nagpur University in the Congress-ruled Central Provinces where they were given shelter by a hospitable Vice-Chancellor. This movement was extremely significant because it created a young and militant cadre that provided the activists as well as the leadership of the movement in later years.

The State Congress, however, continued to be banned, and the regional cultural organizations remained the main forums of activity. The Andhra Mahasabha was particularly active in this phase, and the majority of the younger newly-politicized cadre flocked to it. A significant development that occurred around the year 1940 was that Ravi Narayan Reddy, who had emerged as a major leader of the radicals in the Andhra Mahasabha and had participated in the State Congress *Satyagraha* along with B. Yella Reddy, was drawn towards the Communist Party. As a result, several of the younger cadres also came under Left and Communist influence, and these radical elements gradually increased in strength and pushed the Andhra Mahasabha towards more radical politics. The Mahasabha began to take an active interest in the problems of the peasants.

The outbreak of the War provided an excuse to the government for avoiding any moves towards political and constitutional reforms. A symbolic protest against the continuing ban was again registered by Swami Ramanand Tirtha and six others personally selected by Gandhiji. They were arrested in September 1940 and kept in detention till December 1941. A resumption of the struggle was ruled out by Gandhiji since an all-India struggle was in the offing and now all struggles would be part of that.

The Quit India movement was launched in August 1942 and it was made clear that now there was no distinction to be made between the people of British India and the States: every Indian was to participate. The meeting of the AISPC was convened along with the AICC session at Bombay that announced the commencement of struggle. Gandhiji and Jawaharlal Nehru both addressed the AISPC Standing Committee, and Gandhiji himself explained the implications of the Quit India movement and told the Committee that henceforth there would be one movement. The movement in the States was now to be not only for responsible government but for the independence of India and the integration of the States with British India.

The Quit India movement got a considerable response from Hyderabad, especially the youth. Though arrests of the main leaders, including Swamiji, prevented an organized movement from emerging, many people all over the State offered *Satyagraha* and many others were arrested. On 2 October 1942, a batch of women offered *Satyagraha* in Hyderabad city, and Sarojini Naidu was arrested earlier in the day. Slogans such as *'Gandhi Ka Charkha Chalana Padega, Goron ko London Jana Padega'* (Gandhiji's wheel will have to be spun, while the Whites will have to return to London) became popular. In a state where, till a few years agom even well-established leaders had to send their speeches to the Collector in advance and accept deletions made by him, the new atmosphere was hardly short of revolutionary.

But the Quit India movement also sealed the rift that had developed between the Communist and non-Communist radical nationalists after the Communist Party had adopted the slogan of People's War in December 1941. Communists were opposed to the Quit India movement as it militated against their understanding that Britain must be supported in its anti-Fascist War. The young nationalists in Telengana coalesced around Jamalpuram Keshavrao but a large section went with Ravi Narayan Reddy to the Communists. The Communists were also facilitated by the removal of the ban on the CPI by the Nizam, in keeping with the policy of the Government of India that had removed the ban because of the CPI's pro-War stance. Therefore, while most of the nationalists were clamped in jail because of their support to the Quit India movement, the Communists remained free to extend and consolidate their base among the people. This process reached a head in 1944 when a split occurred in the Andhra Mahasabha session at Bhongir, and the pro-nationalist as well as the liberal elements walked out and set up a separate organization. The Andhra Mahasabha now was completely led by the Communists and they soon launched a programme of mobilization and organization of the peasantry. The end of the War in 1945 brought about a change in the Peoples' War line, and the restraint on organizing struggles was removed.

The years 1945-46, and especially the latter half of 1946, saw the growth of a powerful peasant struggle in various pockets in Nalgonda district, and to some extent in Warangal and Khammam. The main targets of attack were the forced grain levy, the practice of *veth begar*, illegal exactions and illegal seizures of land. Clashes took place initially between the landlords' *goondas* and the peasants led by the *Sangham* (as the Andhra Mahasabha was popularly known), and later between the armed forces of the State police and peasants armed with sticks and stones. The resistance was strong, but so was the repression, and by the end of 1946 the severity of the repression succeeded in pushing the movement into quietude. Thousands were arrested and beaten, many died, and the leaders languished in jails. Yet, the movement had succeeded in instilling into the oppressed and downtrodden peasants of Telengana a new confidence in their ability to resist.

On 4 June 1947, the Viceroy, Mountbatten, announced at a press conference that the British would soon leave India for good on 15 August. On 12 June, the Nizam announced that on the lapse of British paramountcy he would become a sovereign monarch. The intention was clear: he would not accede to the Indian Union. The first open session of the Hyderabad State Congress which demanded accession to the Indian Union and grant of responsible government was held from 16 to 18 June. The State Congress, with the full support of the Indian National Congress, had also thwarted an attempt by the Nizam, a few months earlier, to foist an undemocratic constitution on the people. The boycott of the elections launched by them had received tremendous support. With this new confidence, they began to take a bold stand against the Nizam's moves.

The decision to launch the final struggle was taken by the leaders of the State Congress in consultation with the national leaders in Delhi. As recorded by Swami Ramanand Tirtha in his *Memoirs of Hyderabad Freedom Struggle*: 'That (the) final phase of the freedom struggle in Hyderabad would have to be a clash of arms with the Indian Union, was what we were more than ever convinced of. It would have to be preceded by a *Satyagraha* movement on a mass scale'.[7]

After the preliminary tasks of setting up the Committee of Action under the Chairmanship of D.G. Bindu (which would operate from outside the State to avoid arrest), the establishment of offices in Sholapur, Vijayawada, Gadag and a central office at Bombay, mobilization of funds in which Jayaprakash Narayan played a crucial role, the struggle was formally launched on 7 August which was to be celebrated as 'Join Indian Union Day'. The response was terrific, and meetings to defy the bans were held in towns and villages all over the State. Workers and students went on strike, including 12,000 Hyderabadi workers in Bombay. Beatings and arrests were common. On 13 August, the Nizam banned the ceremonial hoisting of the national flag. Swamiji gave the call: 'This order is a challenge to the people of Hyderabad and I hope they will accept it'. Swamiji and his colleagues were arrested in the early hours of 15 August, 1947, soon after the dawn of Indian Independence. But, despite tight security arrangements, 100 students rushed out of the Hyderabad Students' Union office and hoisted the flag in Sultan Bazaar as scheduled. In subsequent days, the hoisting of the Indian national flag became the major form of defiance and ingenious methods were evolved. Trains decorated with national flags would steam into Hyderabad territory from neighbouring Indian territory. Students continued to play a leading role in the movement, and were soon joined by women in large numbers, prominent among them being Brij Rani and Yashoda Ben.

As the movement gathered force and gained momentum, the Nizam and his administration cracked down on it. But the most ominous development was the encouragement give to the storm troopers of the *Ittihad ul Muslimin*, the Razakars, by the State to act as a para-military force to attack the peoples' struggle. Razakars were issued arms and let loose on protesting crowds; they set up camps near rebellious villages and carried out armed raids.

On 29 November 1947, the Nizam signed a Standstill Agreement with the Indian Government, but simultaneously the repression was intensified, and the Razakar menace became even more acute. Many thousands of people who could afford to do so fled the State and were housed in camps in neighbouring Indian territory. The people increasingly took to self-defence and protected themselves with whatever was available. In organizing the defence against the Razakars and attacks on Razakar camps, the Communists played a very important role, especially in the areas of Nalgonda, Warangal and Khammam that were their strongholds. Peasants were organized into *dalams*, given training in arms, and mobilized for the anti-Nizam struggle. In these areas, the movement also took an anti-landlord stance and many cruel landlords were attacked, some even killed, and illegally occupied land was returned to the original owners. Virtually all the big landlords had run away, and their land was distributed to and cultivated by those with small holdings or no land.

The State Congress, too, organized armed resistance from camps on the State's borders. Raids were made on customs' outposts, police stations and Razakar camps. Outside the Communist strongholds in the

Telengana areas, it was the State Congress that was the main vehicle for organizing popular resistance. Over 20,000 *Satyagrahis* were in jail and many more were participating in the movement outside.

By September 1948, it became clear that all negotiations to make the Nizam accede to the Union had failed. On 13 September, 1948, the Indian Army moved in and on 18 September the Nizam surrendered. The process of the integration of the Indian Union was finally complete. The people welcomed the Indian Army as an army of liberation, an army that ended the oppression of the Nizam and the Razakars. Scenes of jubilation were evident all over, and the national flag was hoisted. The celebration was, however, marred by the decision of the Communists to refuse to lay down arms and continue the struggle against the Indian Union, but that is another long story that falls outside the scope of our present concerns.[8]

*

The case of Hyderabad, and that of Rajkot, are good examples of how methods of struggle evolved to suit the conditions in British India, such as non-violent mass civil disobedience or *Satyagraha*, did not have the same viability or effectiveness in the Indian States. The lack of civil liberties, and of representative institutions, meant that the political space for hegemonic politics was very small, even when compared to the conditions prevailing under the semi-hegemonic and semi-repressive colonial state in British India. The ultimate protection provided by the British enabled the rulers of the States to withstand popular pressure to a considerable degree, as happened in Rajkot. As a result, there was a much greater tendency in these States for the movements to resort to violent methods of agitation — this happened not only in Hyderabad, but also in Travancore, Patiala, and the Orissa States among others. In Hyderabad, for example, even the State Congress ultimately resorted to violent methods of attack, and, in the final count, the Nizam could only be brought into line by the Indian Army.

This also meant that those such as the Communists and other Left groups, who had less hesitation than the Congress in resorting to violent forms of struggle, were placed in a more favourable situation in these States and were able to grow as a political force in these areas. Here, too, the examples of Hyderabad, Travancore, Patiala and the Orissa States are quite striking.

The differences between the political conditions in the States and British India also go a long way in explaining the hesitation of the Congress to merge the movements in the States with those in British India. The movement in British India adopted forms of struggle and a strategy that was specifically suited to the political context. Also, political sagacity dictated that the Princes should not be unnecessarily pushed into taking hard positions against Indian nationalism, at least till such time as this could be counter-balanced by the political weight of the people of the States.

29 Indian Capitalists And The National Movement

Among the various groups that participated in the national movement were several individual capitalists who joined the Congress. They fully identified with the movement, went to jails and accepted the hardships that were the lot of Congressmen in the colonial period. The names of Jamnalal Bajaj, Vadilal Lallubhai Mehta, Samuel Aaron, Lala Shankar Lal, and others are well known in this regard. There were other individual capitalists who did not join the Congress but readily gave financial and other help to the movement. People like G.D. Birla, Ambalal Sarabhai and Walchand Hirachand, fall into this category. There were also a large number of smaller traders and merchants who at various points came out in active support of the national movement. On the other hand, there were several individual capitalists or sections of the class who either remained neutral towards the Congress and the national movement or even actively opposed it.

In this chapter, we shall examine the overall strategy of the Indian capitalist class, as a class, towards the national movement, rather than highlight the role of various individuals or sections within the class who did not necessarily represent the class as a whole, or even its dominant section.

*

At the outset it must be said that the economic development of the Indian capitalist class in the colonial period was substantial and in many ways the nature of its growth was quite different from the usual experience in other colonial countries. This had important implications regarding the class's position vis-a-vis imperialism. First, the Indian capitalists class grew from about the mid 19th century with largely an independent capital base and not as junior partners of foreign capital or as compradors. Second, the capitalist class on the whole was not tied up in a subservient position with pro-imperialist feudal interests either economically or politically. In fact, a wide cross section of the leaders of the capitalist class actually argued, in 1944-45, in their famous Bombay plan (the signatories to which were Purshottamdas Thakurdas, J.R.D. Tata, G.D. Birla, Ardeshir Dalal, Sri Ram, Kasturbhai Lalbhai, A.D. Shroff and John Mathai) for comprehensive land reform, including cooperativization of production, finance and marketing.[1]

Third, in the period 1914-1947, the capitalist class grew rapidly, increasing its strength and self-confidence. This was achieved primarily through import substitution; by edging out or encroaching upon areas of European domination, and by establishing almost exclusive control over new areas thus accounting for the bulk of the new investments made since the 1920s. Close to independence, indigenous enterprise had already cornered seventy two to seventy three per cent of the domestic market and over eighty per cent of the deposits in the organized banking sector.[2]

However, this growth, unusual for a colonial capitalist class, did not occur, as is often argued, as a result or by-product of colonialism or because of a policy of decolonization. On the contrary it was achieved in spite of and in opposition to colonialism — by waging a constant struggle against colonialism and colonial interests, i.e., by wrenching space from colonialism itself.[3]

There was, thus, nothing in the class position or the economic interest of the Indian capitalists which, contrary to what is so often argued,[4] inhibited its opposition to imperialism. In fact, by the mid 1920s, Indian capitalists began to correctly perceive their long-term class interest and felt strong enough to take a consistent and openly anti-imperialist position. The hesitation that the class demonstrated was not in its opposition to imperialism but in the choice of the specific path to fight imperialism. It was apprehensive that the path chosen should not be one which, while opposing imperialism, would threaten its own existence, i.e., undermine capitalism itself.

*

Before we go on to discuss the capitalist class's position vis-a-vis imperialism and vis-a-vis the course of the anti-imperialist movement, we should look at the emergence of the class as a political entity — a 'class for itself.'

Since the early 1920s, efforts were being made by various capitalists like G.D. Birla and Purshottamdas Thakurdas to establish a national level organization of Indian commercial, industrial and financial interests (as opposed to the already relatively more organized European interests in India) to be able to effectively lobby with the colonial government. This effort culminated in the formation of the Federation of Indian Chambers of Commerce and Industry (FICCI) in 1927, with a large and rapidly increasing representation from all parts of India. The FICCI was soon recognized by the British government as well as the Indian public in general, as representing the dominant opinion as well as the overall consensus within the Indian capitalist class.

The leaders of the capitalist class also clearly saw the role of the FICCI as being that of 'national guardians of trade, commerce and industry,' performing in the economic sphere in colonial India the functions of a national government.[5] In the process, Indian capitalists, with some of the most astute minds of the period in their ranks, developed a fairly comprehensive economic critique of imperialism in all its manifestations, whether it be direct appropriation through home charges or exploitation through trade, finance, currency manipulation or foreign investments, including in their sweep the now fashionable concept of unequal exchange occurring in trade between countries with widely divergent productivity levels. (G.D. Birla and S.P. Jain were talking of unequal exchange as early as the 1930s).[6] The Congress leaders quite often saw their assistance as invaluable and treated their opinions and expertise on many national economic issues with respect.

The FICCI was, however, not to remain merely a sort of trade union organization of the capitalist class fighting for its own economic demands and those of the nation. The leaders of the capitalist class now clearly saw the necessity of, and felt strong enough for, the class to effectively intervene in politics. As Sir Purshottamdas, President of FICCI, declared at its second annual session in 1928: 'We can no more separate our politics from our economics.' Further, involvement of the class in politics meant doing so on the side of Indian nationalism. 'Indian commerce and industry are intimately associated with and are, indeed, an integral part of the national movement — growing with its growth and strengthening with its strength.'[7] Similarly G.D. Birla was to declare a little later in 1930: 'It is impossible in the present . . . political condition of our country to convert the government to our views . . . the only solution . . . lies in every Indian businessman strengthening the hands of those who are fighting for the freedom of our country.'[8]

*

However, as mentioned earlier, the Indian capitalist class had its own notions of how the anti-imperialist struggle ought to be waged. It was always in favour of not completely abandoning the constitutional path and the negotiating table and generally preferred to put its weight behind constitutional forms of struggle as opposed to mass civil disobedience. This was due to several reasons.

First, there was the fear that mass civil disobedience, especially if it was prolonged, would unleash forces which could turn the movement revolutionary in a social sense (i.e., threaten capitalism itself). As Lalji Naranji wrote to Purshottamdas in March 1930, 'private property,' itself could be threatened and the 'disregard for authority' created could have 'disastrous after effects' even for the 'future government of Swaraj.'[9] Whenever the movement was seen to be getting too dangerous in this sense, the capitalists tried their best to bring the movement back to a phase of constitutional opposition.

Second, the capitalists were unwilling to support a prolonged all-out hostility to the government of the day as it prevented the continuing of day-to-day business and threatened the very existence of the class.

Further, the Indian capitalists' support to constitutional participation, whether it be in assemblies, conferences or even joining the Viceroy's Executive Council, is not to be understood simply as their getting coopted into the imperial system or surrendering to it. They saw all this as a forum for maintaining an effective opposition fearing that boycotting these forums completely would help 'black legs' and elements who did not represent the nation to, without any opposition, easily pass measures which could severely affect the Indian economy and the capitalist class. However, there was no question of unconditionally accepting reforms or participating in conferences or assemblies. The capitalists were to 'participate on (their) own terms,' with 'no compromise on fundamentals,' firmly rejecting offers of cooperation which fell below their own and the minimum national demands.[10] It was on this ground that the FICCI in 1934 rejected the 'Report of the Joint Parliamentary Committee on Constitutional Reforms for India' as 'even more reactionary than the proposals contained in the White Paper.'[11]

Further, however keen the capitalists may have been to keep constitutional avenues open, they clearly recognized the futility of entering councils, etc., 'unless,' as N.R. Sarkar, the President of FICCI, noted in 1934, 'the nation also decides to enter them.'[12] They also generally refused to negotiate with the British Government, and certainly to make any final commitments, on constitutional as well as economic issues, behind the back of the Congress, i.e., without its participation or at least approval. In 1930, the FICCI (in sharp contrast to the Liberals) advised its members to boycott the Round Table Conference (RTC) stating that '. . . no conference . . . convened for the purpose of discussing the problem of Indian constitutional advance can come to a solution . . . unless such a conference is attended by Mahatma Gandhi, as a free man, or has at least his approval.'[13] This was partially because the capitalists did not want India to present a divided front at the RTC and because they knew only the Congress could actually deliver the goods. As Ambalal Sarabhai put it in November 1929, 'Minus the support of the Congress, the government will not listen to you.'[14]

Finally, it must be noted that for the capitalist class constitutionalism was not an end in itself, neither did it subscribe to what has often been called 'gradualism,' in which case it would have joined hands with the Liberals and not supported the Congress which repeatedly went in for non- constitutional struggle including mass civil disobedience. The capitalist class itself did not rule out other forms of struggle, seeing constitutional participation as only a step towards the goal, to achieve which other steps could be necessary. For example, G.D. Birla, who had worked hard for a compromise leading to the Congress accepting office in 1937, warned Lord Halifax and Lord Lothian that the 'Congress was not coming in just to work the constitution, but to advance towards their goal,' and if the 'Governors and the Services' did not play 'the game' or 'in case there was no (constitutional) advance after two or three years, then India would be compelled to take direct action,' by which he meant 'non-violent mass civil disobedience.'[15]

*

This brings us to the Indian capitalists' attitude towards mass civil disobedience, which was very complex. While, on the one hand, they were afraid of protracted mass civil disobedience, on the other hand, they clearly saw the utility, even necessity of civil disobedience in getting crucial concessions for their class and the nation. In January 1931, commenting on the existing civil disobedience movement, G.D. Birla wrote to Purshottamdas, 'There could be no doubt that what we are being offered at present is entirely due to Gandhiji . . . if we are to achieve what we desire, the present movement should not be allowed to slacken.'[16]

When, after the mass movement had gone on for considerable time, the capitalists, for reasons discussed above, sought the withdrawal of the movement and a compromise (often mediating between the Government and Congress to secure peace), they were quite clear that this was to be only after extracting definite concessions, using the movement, or a threat to re-launch it, to bargain. In their 'anxiety for peace,' they were not to surrender or 'reduce (their) demands.'[17] The dual objective of achieving conciliation without weakening the national movement, which after all secured the concessions, was aptly described by G.D. Birla in January 1931: 'We should . . . have two objects in view: one is that we should jump in at the most opportune time to try for a conciliation and the other is that we should not do anything which might weaken the hands of those through whose efforts we have arrived at this stage.'[18]

Further, however opposed the capitalist class may have been at a point of time to mass civil disobedience, it never supported the colonial government in repressing it. In fact, the capitalists throughout pressurized the government to stop repression, remove the ban on the Congress and the press, release political prisoners and stop arbitrary rule with ordinances as a first step to any settlement, even when the Congress was at the pitch of its non-constitutional mass phase. The fear of Congress militancy or radicalization did not push the capitalists (especially after the late 1920s) to either supporting imperialism in repressing it or even openly condemning or dissociating themselves from the Congress.

The Indian capitalists' attitude had undergone significant changes on this issue over time. During the Swadeshi movement (1905-08), the capitalists remained opposed to the boycott agitation. Even during the Non-Cooperation Movement of the early '20s, a small section of the

capitalists, including Purshottamdas, openly declared themselves enemies of the Non- Cooperation Movement. However, during the 1930s'
Civil Disobedience Movement, the capitalists largely supported the
movement and refused to respond to the Viceroy's exhortations (in
September 1930) to publicly repudiate the Congress stand and his offer
of full guarantee of government protection against any harrassment for
doing so.[19] In September 1940, Purshottamdas felt that, given the
political stance of the British, the Congress was 'left with no other
alternative than to launch non- cooperation.'[20] On 5 August 1942, four
days before the launching of the Quit India movement, Purshottamdas,
J.R.D. Tata and G.D. Birla wrote to the Viceroy that the only solution
to the present crisis, the successful execution of the war and the prevention of another civil disobedience movement was 'granting political
freedom to the country . . . even during the midst of war.'[21]

*

It must be emphasized at this stage that though, by the late 1920s, the
dominant section of the Indian capitalist class began to support the
Congress, the Indian national movement was not created, led or in any
decisive way influenced by this class, nor was it in any sense crucially
dependent on its support. In fact, it was the capitalist class which
reacted to the existing autonomous national movement by constantly
trying to evolve a strategy towards it. Further, while the capitalist class
on the whole stayed within the nationalist camp (as opposed to lining
up with the loyalists), it did so on the most conservative end of the
nationalist spectrum, which certainly did not call the shots of the
national movement at any stage.

However, the relative autonomy of the Indian national movement
has been repeatedly not recognized, and it has been argued that the capitalists, mainly by using the funds at their command, were able to
pressurize the Congress into making demands such as a lower Rupee-
Sterling ratio, tariff protection, reduction in military expenditure, etc.,
which allegedly suited only their class.[22] Further, it is argued that the
capitalists were able to exercise a decisive influence over the political
course followed by the Congress, even to the extent of deciding whether
a movement was to be launched, continued or withdrawn. The examples
quoted are of the withdrawal of civil disobedience in 1931 with the
Gandhi- Irwin Pact and the non-launching of another movement

between 1945-47.[23]

These formulations do not reflect the reality, and this for several reasons. First, a programme of economic nationalism vis- a-vis imperialism, with demands for protection, fiscal and monetary autonomy, and the like, did not represent the interest of the capitalist class alone, it represented the demands of the entire nation which was subject to imperialist exploitation. Even the leftists — Nehru, Socialists, and Communists — in their struggle against imperialism had to and did fight for these demands.

Second, the detailed working out of the doctrine of economic nationalism was done by the early nationalists nearly half a century before the Indian capitalists got constituted as a class and entered the political arena and began fighting for these demands. So there was no question of the Congress being bought, manipulated or pressurized into these positions by the capitalist class.

Third, while it is true that the Congress needed and accepted funds from the business community, especially during constitutional (election) phases, there is no evidence to suggest that through these funds the businessmen were able to, in any basic way, influence the party's policy and ideology along lines which were not acceptable to it independently. Even the Congress dependence on funds (in the days when it was a popular movement) has been grossly exaggerated. The Director of the Intelligence Bureau, in reply to a query from the Viceroy, noted in March 1939, 'Congress has also very important substitutes for regular finance. The "appeal to patriotism" saves a lot of cash expenditures . . . Both for normal Congress activities and for election purposes, the moneybags (capitalists) are less important than the Gandhian superstition . . . local Congress organizations can command so much support from the public . . . that they are in a position to fight elections without needing much money.'[24] In non-election phases, an overwhelming majority of Congress cadres maintained themselves on their own and carried on day-to-day agitations with funds raised through membership fees and small donations.

Gandhiji's position on capitalist support is very revealing in this context. As early as 1922, while welcoming and even appealing for support from merchants and millowners, he simultaneously maintained that, 'whether they do so or not, the country's march to freedom cannot be made to depend on any corporation or groups of men. This is a mass manifestation. The masses are moving rapidly towards deliverance and they must move whether with the aid of the organized capital or without. This must therefore be a movement independent of capital and yet not antagonistic to it. Only if capital came to the aid of the masses, it would redound to the credit of the capitalists and hasten the advent of the happy day.'[25] (Gandhiji's attitude towards the capitalists was to harden further over time, especially during World War II when a large number of them were busy profiteering while the national movement was facing untold repression and the people shortages and famines).

Lastly, as for the capitalists' determining the course of the Congress-led movements (many of them in specific areas led or supported by socialists and Communists), again there is little evidence to support this view. The Congress launched or withdrew movements based on its own strategic perceptions arising out of its understanding of the nature of the colonial state and its current postures, the organizational, political and ideological preparedness of the people, the staying power of the masses, especially when faced with repression, and so on. It did not do so at the behest, and not even on behalf of the capitalist class. In fact, almost each time the Congress launched mass movements, e.g., in 1905-08, 1920-22, 1930, 1932 and 1942, it did so without the approval of either the capitalist class as a whole or a significant section of it. However, once the movements were launched, the capitalist class reacted to it in a complex and progressively changing fashion, as discussed above.

Quite significantly, the Indian capitalists never saw the Congress as their class party or even as a party susceptible only to their influence. On the contrary, they saw the Congress as an open-ended organization, heading a popular movement, and in the words of J.K. Mehta, Secretary, Indian Merchants' Chamber, with 'room in it for men of all shades of political opinion and economic views,'[26] and therefore, open to be transformed in either the Left or the Right direction.

*

In fact, it was precisely the increasing radicalization of the Congress in the Left direction in the 1930s, with the growing influence of Nehru, and the Socialists and Communists within the Congress, which spurred the capitalists into becoming more active in the political field. The fear of radicalization of the national movement, however, did not push the capitalists into the 'lap of imperialism,' as predicted by contemporary radicals and as actually happened in some other colonial and semi-colonial countries. Instead, the Indian capitalists evolved a subtle, many-sided strategy to contain the Left, no part of which involved a sell-out to imperialism or imperial interests.

For example, when in 1929 certain capitalists, to meet the high pitch of Communist activity among the trade unions, attempted to form a class party, where European and Indian capitalists would combine, the leaders of the capitalist class firmly quashed such a move. As G.D. Birla put it, 'The salvation of the capitalists does not lie in joining hands with reactionary elements' (i.e., pro-imperialist European interests in India) but in 'cooperating with those who through constitutional means want to change the government for a national one' (i.e. conservative nationalists).[27] Similarly, in 1928, the capitalists' refused to support the Government in introducing the Public Safety Bill, which was intended to contain the Communists, on the ground that such a provision would be used to attack the national movement.

Further, the capitalists were not to attempt to 'kill Bolshevism and Communism with such frail weapons' as frontally attacking the Left with their class organizations which would carry no weight with 'the masses' or even the 'middle classes.' As Birla explained, 'I have not the least doubt in my mind that a purely capitalist organization is the last body to put up an effective fight against communism.'[28] A much superior method, he argued later (in 1936), when Nehru's leftist attitude was seen as posing a danger, was to 'let those who have given up property say what you want to say.' The strategy was to 'strengthen the hands' of those nationalist who, in their ideology, did not transcend the parameters of capitalism or, preferably, even opposed socialism.[29]

The capitalists also realized, as G.L. Mehta, the president of FICCI, argued in 1943, that 'A consistent . . . programme of reforms' was the 'most effective remedy against social upheavals.'[30] It was with this reform perspective that the 'Post War Economic Development Committee,' set up by the capitalists in 1942, which eventually drafted the Bombay Plan, was to function. Its attempt was to incorporate 'whatever is sound and feasible in the socialist movement' and see 'how far socialist demands could be accommodated without capitalism surrendering any of its essential features.'[31] The Bombay Plan, therefore, seriously took up the question of rapid economic growth and equitable distribution, even arguing for the necessity of partial nationalization, the public sector, land reform and a series of workers' welfare schemes.

One may add that the basic assumption made by the Bombay planners was that the plan could be implemented only by an independent national government.

Clearly the Indian capitalist class was anti-socialist and bourgeois but it was not pro-imperialist.

The maturity of the Indian capitalist class in identifying its long term interests, correctly understanding the nature of the Congress and its relationship with the different classes in Indian society, its refusal to abandon the side of Indian nationalism even when threatened by the Left or tempted by imperialism, its ability to project its own class interests as societal interests, are some of the reasons (apart from the failure of the Left in several of the above directions) which explain why, on the whole, the Indian national movement remained, till independence, under bourgeois ideological hegemony, despite strong contending trends within it.

30 The Development of a Nationalist Foreign Policy

In the course of their own anti-imperialist struggle, the Indian people evolved a policy of opposition to imperialism as also the expression and establishment of solidarity with anti-imperialist movements in other parts of the world. From the beginning, the Indian nationalists opposed the British policy of interfering in the internal affairs of other countries and the use of the Indian army and India's resources to promote, extend and defend British imperialism in Africa and Asia.

*

The broad basis for the nationalist foreign policy was laid in the initial years of the national movement, which coincided with a particularly active phase of British imperial expansionism. From 1878 onwards, the Government of India undertook a number of large-scale military expeditions outside India's frontiers and its armed forces were used in some of the wars waged by the British Government in Asia and Africa. These wars and expeditions were a major source of the rapid and massive increase in India's military expenditure. The early Indian national leaders condemned India's involvement in each of these wars and expeditions because of the financial burden on the Indian people, and on grounds of political morality, and also on the basis that these involved not Indian interests and purposes but British imperialist schemes of territorial and commercial expansion. They invariably demanded that the British Government should bear their entire cost. They also argued that India's interests would be best secured by a policy of peace.

The Second Afghan War was waged in 1878-80. Voicing the Indian opinion, Surendranath Banerjea publicly branded the war as an act of sheer aggression and 'as one of the most unrighteous wars that have blackened the pages of history.'[1] The Indians demanded that since the unjust war was waged in pursuance of Imperial aims and policies, Britain should meet the entire cost of the war. The *Amrita Bazar Patrika* of 19 March 1880 wrote in its usual vein of irony: 'Nothing throws an Englishman into a passion as when his pocket is touched and nothing pleases him more than when he can serve his own interests at the expense of others.'

In 1882, the Government of India participated in the expedition sent by England to Egypt to put down the nationalist revolt led by Colonel Arabi. Condemning the 'aggressive' and 'immoral' British policy in Egypt, the Indian nationalists said that the war in Egypt was being waged to protect the interests of British capitalists, merchants and bond-holders.

At the end of 1885, the Government of India attacked and annexed Burma. With one voice the Indian nationalists condemned the war upon the Burmese people as being immoral, unwarranted, unjust, arbitrary and an act of uncalled for aggression. The motive force behind the policy was once again seen to be the promotion of British commercial interests in Burma and its northern neighbour, China. The nationalists opposed the annexation of Burma and praised the guerrilla fight put up by the Burmese people in the succeeding years.

In 1903, Lord Curzon launched at attack upon Tibet. The nationalist attitude was best summarized by R.C. Dutt's denunciation of the 'needless, cruel, and useless war in Tibet,' once again motivated by commercial greed and territorial aggrandizement.[2]

Above all, it was the expansionist, 'forward' policy followed by the Government during the 1890s on India's north-western frontier that aroused the Indians' ire. Claiming to safeguard India against Russian designs, the Government of India got involved, year after year, in costly expeditions leading to the deployment of over 60,000 troops against rebellious tribesmen which led to the annexation of more and more new territory and, at the same time, to the continuous draining of the Indian treasury. The Indians claimed, on the one hand, that Anglo-Russian rivalry was the result of the clash of interests of the two imperialisms in Europe and Asia, and, on the other hand, that Russian aggression was a bogey, 'a monstrous bugbear,' raised to justify imperialist expansion. The nationalist justified the resistance put up by the frontier tribes in defending their independence. Refusing to accept the official propaganda that the Government's armed actions were provoked by the lawlessness and blood-thirstiness of the frontier tribesmen, they condemned the Government for its savage measures in putting down the tribal uprisings. They were quite caustic about the claim of the British Prime Minister, Lord Salisbury, that the frontier wars were 'but the surf that marks the edge and the advance of the wave of civilization.' 'Philanthropy, it is said,' quipped Tilak's *Mahratta* on 17 October 1897, 'is the last resort of the scoundrel and the statesman. It is the straw at which they will catch when reason is exhausted and sophistry is exposed.'

The Indian leaders argued that the expansionist policy of the Government on India's frontiers, a product of Britain's world-wide imperialist policy, was the most important cause of the maintenance of a large standing army, the increase in Indian military expenditure, the deplorable financial position of the Government, and the consequent increase of taxation in India after 1815. The Indians advocated, instead, a policy of peace, the demand for which was made by C. Sankaran Nair, the Congress President, in 1897 in words that have a remarkably modern and familiar ring: 'Our true policy is a peaceful policy . . . With such capacity for internal development as our country possesses, with such crying need to carry out the reforms absolutely necessary for our well-being, we want a period of prolonged peace.'3

Three other major themes in the area of nationalist foreign policy emerged during the period 1880-1914. One was that of sympathy and support for people fighting for their independence and liberation. Thus, sentiments of solidarity with the people of Ireland, Russia, Turkey, Burma, Afghanistan, Egypt and Sudan, Ethiopia and other people of Africa were vigorously expressed and popularized through the Press. Foreign intervention in China during the I Ho-Tuan (Boxer) Uprising was vigorously opposed and the despatch of Indian troops to China condemned.

The second theme was that of Asia-consciousness. It was during their opposition to the Burma war in 1885 that consciousness of an Asian identity emerged, perhaps for the first time. Some of the nationalist newspapers bemoaned the disappearance of an independent, fellow Asian country. The rise of modern Japan as an industrial power after 1868 was hailed by Indians as proof of the fact that a backward Asian country could develop itself without Western control. But despite their admiration for Japan, the nationalist newspapers criticized it for attacking China in 1895 and for participating in the international suppression of the I Ho-Tuan Uprising. The imperialist effort to partition China was condemned because its success would lead to the disappearance of a major independent Asian power. The defeat of Czarist Russia by Japan further exploded the myth of European solidarity and led to the resurgence of a pan-Asian feeling.

Indians also began to understand and expound the economic rationale, including the role of foreign capital exports, behind the resurgence of imperialism in the last quarter of the 19th century. Thus, commenting on the reasons behind the attack upon Burma, the *Mahratta* of 15 November 1885, edited at the time by Tilak and Agarkar, wrote: The truth was 'that England with its superfluous human energy and overflowing capital cannot but adhere to the principle of political conduct — might is right — for centuries to come in order to find food for her superfluous population and markets for her manufactures.' Similarly, the *Hindu* of 23 September 1889 remarked: 'Where foreign capital has been sunk in a country, the administration of that country becomes at once the concern of the bond-holders.'

*

World War I broke out in June 1914. The Indian nationalist leaders, including Lokamanya Tilak, decided to support the war effort of the Government. Sentiments of loyalty to the empire and of the desire to defend it were loudly and widely expressed. But, as Jawaharlal Nehru has pointed out in his *Autobiography*: 'There was little sympathy with the British in spite of loud professions of loyalty. Moderate and Extremist alike learnt with satisfaction of German victories. There was no love for Germany, of course, only the desire to see our own rulers humbled.'[4] The hope was that a grateful Britain would repay India's loyalty with economic and political concessions enabling India to take a long step towards self-government, that Britain would apply to India the principles of democracy for which she and the Allies were claiming to be fighting the War.

After the War, the nationalists further developed their foreign policy in the direction of opposition to political and economic imperialism and cooperation of all nations in the cause of world peace. As part of this policy, at its Delhi session in 1919, the Congress demanded India's representation at the Peace Conference through its elected representatives.

Indians also continued to voice their sympathy for the freedom-fighters of other countries. The Irish and Egyptian people and the Government of Turkey were extended active support. At its Calcutta session in 1920, the Congress asked the people not to join the army to fight in West Asia. In May 1921, Gandhiji declared that the Indian people would oppose any attack on Afghanistan. The Congress branded the Mandate system of the League of Nations as a cover for imperialist greed. In 1921, the Congress congratulated the Burmese people on their struggle for freedom. Burma was at that time a part of India, but the Congress announced that free India favoured Burma's independence from India. Gandhiji wrote in this context in 1922: 'I have never been able to take pride in the fact that Burma has been made part of British India. It never was and never should be. The Burmese have a civilization of their own.'5 In 1924, the Congress asked the Indian settlers in Burma to demand no separate rights at the cost of the Burmese people.

In 1925, the Northern March of the Chinese Nationalist army began under Sun Yat-Sen's leadership and the foreign powers got ready to intervene. The Congress immediately expressed a strong bond of sympathy with the Chinese people in their struggle for national unity and against the common enemy and protested against the dispatch of Indian troops to China. In 1925, Gandhiji described the use of Indian soldiers to shoot the innocent Chinese students as a 'humiliating and degrading spectacle.' 'It demonstrates also most forcibly that India is being kept under subjection, not merely for the exploitation of India herself, but that it enables Great Britain to exploit the great and ancient Chinese nation.'6

In January 1927, S. Srinivasa Iyengar moved an adjournment motion in the Central Legislative Assembly to protest against Indian troops being used to suppress the Chinese people. The strong Indian feelings on the question were repeatedly expressed by the Congress during 1927 (including at its Madras session). The Madras Congress advised Indians not to go to China to fight or work against the Chinese people who were fellow fighters in the struggle against imperialism. It also asked for the withdrawal of Indian troops from Mesopotamia and Iran and all other foreign countries. In 1928, the Congress assured the people of Egypt, Syria, Palestine, Iraq, and Afghanistan of its full support in their national liberation struggles.

Sentiments of the solidarity of the Indian people with the colonial people and the awareness of India's role as the gendarme of British imperialism the world over were summed up by Dr. M.A. Ansari in his presidential address at the Congress session of 1927: 'The history of this philanthropic burglary on the part of Europe is written in blood and suffering from Congo to Canton . . . Once India is free the whole edifice (of imperialism) will collapse as she is the key-stone of the arch of Imperialism.'[7]

*

In 1926-27, Jawaharlal Nehru travelled to Europe and came into contact with left-wing European political workers and thinkers. This had an abiding impact on his political development, including in the field of foreign affairs. This was, of course, not the first time that major Indian political leaders had made an effort to establish links with, and get the support of, the anti-imperialist sections of British and European public opinion. Dadabhai Naoroji was a close friend of the socialist H.M. Hyndman. He attended the Hague session of the International Socialist Congress in August 1904 and after describing imperialism as a species of barbarism declared that the Indian people had lost all faith in British political parties and parliament and looked for cooperation only to the British working class. Lajpat Rai also established close relations with American socialists during his stay in the US from 1914-18. In 1917, he opposed US participation in the World War because of the War's imperialistic character. Gandhiji also developed close relations with outstanding European figures such as Tolstoy and Romain Rolland.

The highlight of Jawaharlal's European visit was his participation as a representative of the Congress in the International Congress against Colonial Oppression and Imperialism held in Brussels in February 1927. The basic objective of the Conference was to bring together the colonial people of Africa, Asia and Latin America struggling against imperialism and the working people of the capitalist countries fighting against capitalism. Nehru was elected one of the honorary presidents of the Conference along with Albert Einstein, Romain Rolland, Madame Sun Yat-sen and George Lansbury. In his speeches and statements at the Conference, Nehru emphasized the close connection between colonialism and capitalism and the deep commitment of Indian nationalism to internationalism and to anti-colonial struggles the world over. A major point of departure from previous Indian approaches was his understanding of the significance of US imperialism as a result of his discussions with Latin American delegates. In his confidential report on the Conference to the Congress Working Committee, he wrote: 'Most of us, specially from Asia, were wholly ignorant of the problems of South America, and of how the rising imperialism of the United States, with its tremendous resources and its immunity from outside attack, is gradually taking a stranglehold of Central and South America. But we are not likely to remain ignorant much longer for the great problem of the near future will be American imperialism, even more than British imperialism.'[8]

The Brussels Conference decided to found the League Against Imperialism and for National Independence. Nehru was elected to the Executive Council of the League. The Congress also affiliated to the League as an associated member. At its Calcutta session, the Congress declared that the Indian struggle was a part of the worldwide struggle against imperialism. It also decided to open a Foreign Department to develop contacts with other peoples and movements fighting against imperialism. Nor was this understanding confined to Nehru and other leftists. Gandhiji, for example, wrote to Nehru in September 1933: 'We must recognize that our nationalism must not be inconsistent with progressive internationalism . . . I can, therefore, go the whole length with you and say that "we should range ourselves with the progressive forces of the world."'[9]

*

A very active phase of nationalist foreign policy began in 1936. From then onwards, there was hardly an important event in the world to which the Congress and its leaders did not react. Fascism had already triumphed in Italy, Germany and Japan and was raising its ugly head in other parts of the capitalist world. The Congress condemned it as the most extreme form of imperialism and racialism. It fully recognized that the future of India was closely interlinked with the coming struggle between Fascism and the forces of freedom, socialism and democracy. It extended full support to the people of Ethiopia, Spain, China and Czechoslovakia in their struggle against fascist aggression.

The nationalist approach to world problems was clearly enunciated by Jawaharlal Nehru, the chief Congress spokesperson on world affairs, in his presidential address to the Lucknow Congress in 1936. Nehru analysed the world situation in detail and focused on the Indian struggle in the context of the coming world struggle against Fascism. 'Our struggle was but part of a far wider struggle for freedom, and the forces that moved us were moving people all over the world into action ... Capitalism, in its difficulties, took to fascism ... what its imperialist counterpart had long been in the subject colonial countries. Fascism and imperialism thus stood out as the two faces of the now decaying capitalism.' And again: 'Thus we see the world divided up into two vast groups today — the imperialist and fascist on one side, the socialist and nationalist on the other. Inevitably we take our stand with the progressive forces of the world which are ranged against fascism and imperialism.'[10]. Nehru went back to these themes again and again in the later years. 'The frontiers of our struggle lie not only in our own country but in Spain and China also,' he wrote in January 1939.[11]

Gandhiji, too, gave expression to strong anti-fascist feelings. He condemned Hitler for the genocide of the Jews and for 'propounding a new religion of exclusive and militant nationalism in the name of which any inhumanity becomes an act of humanity.' 'If there ever could be a justifiable war in the name of and for humanity,' he wrote, 'a war against Germany, to prevent the wanton persecution of a whole race, would be completely justified.'[12]

When Ethiopia was attacked by fascist Italy in early 1936, the Congress declared the Ethiopian people's struggle to be part of all exploited people's struggle for freedom. The Congress declared 9 May to be Ethiopia Day on which demonstrations and meetings were held all over India expressing sympathy and solidarity with the Ethiopians. On his way back from Europe, Jawaharlal refused to meet Mussolini, despite his repeated invitations, lest the meeting was used for fascist propaganda.

The Congress expressed strong support for Spanish Republicans engaged in a life and death struggle with fascist Franco in the Spanish Civil War. In his presidential address to the Faizpur Congress in December 1936, Nehru emphasized that the struggle going on in Spain was not merely between Republicans and Franco or even Fascism and democracy but between forces of progress and reaction throughout the world. 'In Spain today,' he declared, 'our battles are being fought and we watch this struggle not merely with the sympathy of friendly outsiders, but with the painful anxiety of those who are themselves involved in it.'[13] In June 1938, he visited Spain accompanied by Krishna

Menon, visited the battlefront and spent five days in Barcelona which was under constant bombardment. On 13 October 1938, Gandhiji sent a message to Juan Negrin, Prime Minister of Spain: 'My whole heart goes out to you in sympathy. May true freedom be the outcome of your agony.'[14]

In late 1938, Hitler began his diplomatic and political aggression against Czechoslovakia leading to its betrayal by Britain and France at Munich. The Congress Working Committee, meeting in Nehru's absence, passed a resolution viewing 'with grave concern the unabashed attempt that is being made by Germany to deprive Czechoslovakia of its independence or to reduce it to impotence,' and sending its 'profound sympathy to the brave people of Czechoslovakia.'[15] Gandhiji wrote in the *Harijan*: 'Let the Czechs know that the Working Committee wrung itself with pain while their doom was being decided.' Speaking for himself, Gandhiji wrote that the plight of the Czechs 'moved me to the point of physical and mental distress.'[16] Nehru, then in Europe, refused to visit Germany as a state guest and went to Prague instead. He was angry with the British Government for encouraging Germany. In a letter to the *Manchester Guardian* he wrote: 'Recent developments in Czechoslovakia and the way the British Government, directly and through its mediators, had baulked and threatened the Czech Government at every turn has produced a feeling of nausea in me.'[17] He was disgusted with the Munich Agreement and in an article in the *National Herald* of 5 October 1938, he described it as 'the rape of Czechoslovakia by Germany with England and France holding her forcibly down!'[18] His interpretation of this betrayal of Czechoslovakia was that Britain and France wanted to isolate the Soviet Union and maintain Fascism in Europe as a counterpoise to it. At Tripuri, in early 1939, the Congress passed a resolution dissociating itself 'entirely from the British foreign policy, which has consistently aided the fascist Powers and helped the destruction of the democratic countries.'

In 1937, Japan launched an attack on China. The Congress passed a resolution condemning Japan and calling upon the Indian people to boycott Japanese goods as a mark of their sympathy with the Chinese people. At its Haripura session in early 1938, the Congress reiterated this call while condemning 'the aggression of a brutal imperialism in China and horrors and frightfulness that have accompanied it.' It warned that the invasion of China was 'fraught with the gravest consequences for the future of the world peace and of freedom in Asia.' As an expression of its solidarity with the Chinese people, 12 June was celebrated throughout India as China Day. The Congress also sent a medical mission, headed by Dr. M. Atal, to work with the Chinese armed forces. One of its members, Dr. Kotnis, was to lay down his life working with the Eighth Route Army under Mao Ze-Dong's command.

The complexity, the humanist approach, and anti-imperialist content of the Indian nationalist foreign policy were brought out in the approach to the problem of Palestine. While Arabs were fighting against British imperialism in Palestine, many of the Jews, hunted and killed in Nazi Germany and discriminated against and oppressed all over Europe, were trying to carve out under Zionist leadership a homeland in Palestine with British support. Indians sympathized with the persecuted Jews, victims of Nazi genocide, but they criticized their efforts to deprive the Arabs of their due. They supported the Arabs and urged the Jews to reach an agreement with the Arabs directly. The Congress observed 27 September 1936 as Palestine Day. In October 1937, the Congress protested against the reign of terror in Palestine and the proposal to partition it and assured the Arabs of the solidarity of the Indian people. In September 1938, it again condemned the partition decision, urged the British to 'leave the Jews and Arabs to amicably settle the issues between them,' and appealed to the Jews 'not to take shelter behind British imperialism.' Gandhiji reiterated all these views in December 1938 in an important editorial in the *Harijan* on the plight of the Jews in Europe. 'My sympathies are all with the Jews,' he wrote. But it would also be 'wrong and inhuman to impose the Jews on the Arabs . . . It would be a crime against humanity to reduce the proud Arabs.' Appealing to the Jews to reason with the Arabs and 'discard the help of the British bayonet,' he pointed out that 'as it is, they are co-sharers with the British in despoiling a people who have done no wrong to them.'[19] Nehru gave expression to similar views on the Palestinian question from 1936 to 1939.

A major aspect of the nationalists' world outlook, especially of the youth, was the admiration and immense goodwill for the Soviet Union. Nearly all the major Indian political leaders of the time — for example, Lokamanya Tilak, Lajpat Rai, Bipin Chandra Pal — had reacted favourably to the Russian Revolution during 1917-18, seeing in it the success of an oppressed people. During the 1920s, the rising socialist and communist groups and young intellectuals were attracted by the Soviet Union, its egalitarianism, socialist idealism, anti-imperialism, and the

Five Year Plan and were full of admiration for the socialist homeland. In November 1927, Jawaharlal and Motilal visited the Soviet Union. On his return, Jawaharlal wrote a series of articles for the *Hindu* which were also published in book form. His reaction was very positive and idealistic and was reflected in the lines he put on the title page of the book: 'Bliss was it in that dawn to be alive, but to be young was very heaven.' In 1928 and after Nehru repeatedly praised the Soviet Union 'as the greatest opponent of imperialism.' This admiration for the Soviet Union was to deepen as he came more and more under the influence of Marxism. At Lucknow, in 1936, he said that though he was pained by and disagreed with much that was happening in the Soviet Union, he looked upon 'that great and fascinating unfolding of a new order and a new civilization as the most promising feature of our dismal age.' In fact, 'if the future is full of hope it is largely because of Soviet Russia.'[20] The mass trials and purges of Stalin's opponents in the late 1930s repelled him, but he still retained his faith in the Soviet regime, especially as, in his view, it 'stood as the one real effective bulwark against fascism in Europe and Asia.'[21]

Other Congress leaders, for example, C.R. Das and Gandhiji were also friendly to the Soviet Union but were put off by what they believed to be the Communist emphasis on the role of violence. This was particularly true of Gandhiji. But he, too, gradually began to change his appraisal. In a discussion with students of Gujarat Vidyapith in late 1928, Gandhiji, on the one hand, praised the Bolshevik ideal of the abolition of the institution of private property and, on the other, condemned the Bolsheviks for accomplishing it through violence. While predicting the downfall of the Bolshevik regime, he said: 'if it continued to base itself on violence, there is no questioning the fact that the Bolshevik ideal has behind it the purest sacrifice of countless men and women who have given up their all for its sake, and an ideal that is sanctified by the sacrifices of such master spirits as Lenin cannot go in vain; the noble example of their renunciation will be emblazoned for ever and quicken and purify the ideal as time passes.'[22]

Goodwill, admiration and support for the Soviet Union were to acquire major proportions during the 1930s as the Communist Party, the Congress Socialist Party, the *kisan sabhas*, and trade unions developed and in their propaganda and agitation cited the Soviet Union as an example of what workers' and peasants' power could achieve.

*

War clouds had begun to gather again around the world since the late 1920s. The Congress had declared at its Madras session in 1927 that India could not be a party to an imperialist war and in no case should India be made to join a war without the consent of its people. This declaration was to become one of the foundations of nationalist foreign policy in the later years and was repeated time and again. The rise of Fascism and the threat it posed to peace, democracy and socialism and to the independence of nations transformed the situation to a certain extent. As pointed out earlier, the Indian national leadership was firmly opposed to Fascism and the fascist drive towards war and conquest. At the same time, it was afraid that Britain would go to war, when it did, not in defence of peace and democracy but to protect its imperialist interests. Indians could not support an imperialist war. Moreover, imperialism itself was a major cause of war. Imperialism must disappear if the fascist threat was to be successfully met; and lasting peace could be established only if the domination and exploitation of one nation by another was ended. The character of the war in which Britain participated would be determined by its attitude towards India's freedom. For enslaved India could not fight for the freedom of others. India could, and would, actively support an anti-fascist war provided its independence was immediately recognized. On the other hand, the Congress repeatedly declared, during 1936-39, it would resist every effort to use Indian men, money and resources in a war to serve British imperialism. Summing up the nationalist position, Nehru wrote on 18 April 1939: 'For us in India our path is clear. It is one of complete opposition to the fascists; it is also one of opposition to imperialism. We are not going to line up under Chamberlainism; we are not going to throw our resources in defence of empire. But we would gladly offer those very resources for the defence of democracy, the democracy of a free India lined up with other free countries.'[23] This position was reiterated by the Congress Working Committee meeting in the second week of August 1939, virtually on the eve of war. Because of his commitment to non-violence, Gandhiji had a basic difference with this approach. But he agreed to go along. The Congress position was to be sorely tested in the coming three years.

31 The Rise and Growth of Communalism

Before we discuss the growth of communalism in modern India, it is perhaps useful to define the term and point to certain basic fallacies regarding it. Communalism is basically an ideology with which we have lived so long that it appears to be a simple, easily understood notion. But this is, perhaps, not so.

Communalism or communal ideology consists of three basic elements or stages, one following the other. First, it is the belief that people who follow the same religion have common secular interests, that is, common political, economic, social and cultural interests. This is the first bedrock of communal ideology. From this arises the notion of socio-political communities based on religion. It is these religion-based communities, and not classes, nationalities, linguistic-cultural groups, nations or such politico-territorial units as provinces or states, that are seen as the fundamental units of Indian society. The Indian people, it is believed, can act socially and politically and protect their collective or corporate or non-individual interests only as members of these religion-based communities. These different communities are alleged to have their own leaders. Those who talk of being national, regional, or class leaders are merely masquerading; beneath the mask they are only leaders of their own communities. The best they can do is to unite as communal leaders and then serve the wider category of the nation or country.

The second element of communal ideology rests on the notion that in a multi-religious society like India, the secular interests, that is the social, cultural, economic and political interests, of the followers of one religion are dissimilar and divergent from the interests of the followers of another religion.

The third stage of communalism is reached when the interests of the followers of different religions or of different 'communities' are seen to be mutually incompatible, antagonistic and hostile. Thus, the communalist asserts at this stage that Hindus and Muslims *cannot* have common secular interests, that their secular interests are bound to be opposed to each other.

Communalism is, therefore, basically and above all an ideology on which communal politics is based. Communal violence is a conjunctural consequence of communal ideology. Similarly, Hindu, Muslim, Sikh or Christian communalisms are not very different from each other; they belong to a single species; they are varieties of the same communal ideology.

Communal ideology in a person, party or movement starts with the first stage. Many nationalists fell prey to it or thought within its digits even while rejecting the two other elements of communalism, that is, the notion of the mutual divergence or hostility of the interests of different religion-based communities. These were the persons who saw themselves as Nationalist Hindus, Nationalist Muslims, Nationalist Sikhs, etc., and not as simple nationalists.

The second stage of communalism may be described as liberal communalism or, in the words of some, moderate communalism. The liberal communalist was basically a believer in and practitioner of communal politics; but he still upheld certain liberal, democratic, humanist and nationalist values. Even while holding that India consisted of distinct religion-based communities, with their own separate and special interests which sometimes came into conflict with each other, he continued to believe and profess publicly that these different communal interests could be gradually accommodated and brought into harmony within the overall, developing national interests, and India built as a nation. Most of the communalists before 1937 — the Hindu Mahasabha, the Muslim League, the Ali Brothers after 1925, M.A. Jinnah, Madan Mohan Malaviya, Lajpat Rai, and N.C. Kelkar after 1922 — functioned within a liberal communal framework.

Extreme communalism, or communalism functioning broadly within a fascist syndrome, formed the third or last stage of communalism. Extreme communalism was based on fear and hatred, and had a tendency to use violence of language, deed or behaviour, the language of war and enmity against political opponents. It was at this stage that the communalists declared that Muslims, 'Muslim culture' and Islam and Hindus, 'Hindu culture,' and Hinduismwere in danger of being suppressed and exterminated. It was also at this stage that both the Muslim and Hindu communalists put forward the theory that Muslims and Hindus constituted separate nations whose mutual antagonism was permanent and irresolvable. The Muslim League and the Hindu Mahasabha after 1937 and the Rashtriya Swayamsevak Sangh (RSS) increasingly veered towards extreme or fascistic communalism.

Though the three stages of communalism were different from one another, they also interacted and provided a certain continuum. Its first element or stage fed liberal and extreme communalism and made it difficult to carry on a struggle against them. Similarly, the liberal communalist found it difficult to prevent the ideological transition to extreme communalism.

We may take note of several other connected aspects. While a communalist talked of, or believed in, defending his 'community's' interests, in real life no such interests existed outside the field of religion. The economic and political interests of Hindus, Muslims, and others were the same. In that sense they did not even constitute separate communities. As Hindus or Muslims they did not have a separate political-economic life or interests on an all-India or even regional basis. They were divided from fellow Hindus or Muslims by region, language, culture, class, caste, social status, social practices, food and dress habits, etc., and united on these aspects with followers of other religions. An upper class Muslim had far more in common, even culturally, with an upper class Hindu than with a lower class Muslim. Similarly, a Punjabi Hindu stood closer culturally to a Punjabi Muslim than to a Bengali Hindu; and, of course, the same was true of a Bengali Muslim in relation to a Bengali Hindu and a Punjabi Muslim. The unreal communal division, thus, obscured the real division of the Indian people into linguistic-cultural regions and social classes as well as their real, emerging and growing unity into a nation.

If communal interests did not exist, then communalism was not a partial or one-sided or sectional view of the social reality; it was its wrong or unscientific view. It has been suggested, on occasions, that a communalist, being narrow-minded, looks after his own community's interests. But if no such interests existed, then he could not be serving his 'community's' or co-religionists' interests either. He could not be the 'representative' of his 'community.' In the name of serving his community's interests, he served knowingly or unknowingly some other interests. He, therefore, either deceived others or unconsciously deceived himself. Thus, communal assumptions, communal logic and communal answers were wrong. What the communalist projected as problems were not the real problems, and what the communalist said was the answer was not the real answer.

Sometimes, communalism is seen as something that has survived from the past, as something that the medieval period has bequeathed to the present or at least as having roots in the medieval period. But while communalism uses, and is based on, many elements of ancient and medieval ideologies, basically it is a modern ideology and political trend that expresses the social urges and serves the political needs of modern social groups, classes and forces. Its social roots as also its social, political and economic objectives lie very much in the modern period of Indian history. It was brought into existence and sustained by contemporary socio-economic structure.

*

Communalism emerged as a consequence of the emergence of modern politics which marked a sharp break with the politics of the ancient or medieval or pre-1857 periods. Communalism, as also other modern views such as nationalism and socialism, could emerge as politics and as ideology only after politics based on the people, politics of popular participation and mobilization, politics based on the creation and mobilization of public opinion had come into existence. In pre-modern politics, people were either ignored in upper-class based politics or were compelled to rebel outside the political system and, in case of success, their leaders incorporated into the old ruling classes. This was recognized by many perceptive Indians. Jawaharlal Nehru, for example, noted in 1936: 'One must never forget that communalism in India is a latter-day phenomenon which has grown up before our eyes.'[1] Nor was there anything unique about communalism in the Indian context. It was not an inevitable or inherent product of India's peculiar historical and social development. It was the result of conditions which have in other societies produced similar phenomena and ideologies such as Fascism, anti-Semitism, racism, Catholic-Protestant conflict in Northern Ireland, or Christian-Muslim conflict in Lebanon.

The communal consciousness arose as a result of the transformation of Indian society under the impact of colonialism and the need to struggle against it. The growing economic, political and administrative unification of regions and the country, the process of making India into a nation, the developing contradiction between colonialism and the Indian people and the formation of modern social classes and strata called for new ways of seeing one's common interests. They made it necessary to have wider links and loyalties among the people and to form new identities. This also followed from the birth of new politics during the last half of the 19th century. The new politics was based on the politicization and mobilization of an ever increasing number of the Indian people.

The process of grasping the new, emerging political reality and social relations and the adoption of new uniting principles, new social and political identities with the aid of new ideas and concepts was bound to be a difficult and gradual process. The process required the spread of modern ideas of nationalism, cultural-linguistic development and class struggle. But wherever their growth was slow and partial, people inevitably used the old, familiar pre-modern categories of self-identity such as caste, locality, region, race, religion, sect and occupation to grasp the new reality, to make wider connections and to evolve new identities and ideologies. Similar developments have occurred all over the world in similar circumstances. But often such old, inadequate and false ideas and identities gradually give way to the new, historically necessary ideas and identities of nation, nationality and class. This also occurred on a large scale in India, but not uniformly among all the Indian people. In particular, religious consciousness was transformed into communal consciousness in some parts of the country and among some sections of the people. This was because there were some factors in the Indian situation which favoured its growth; it served the needs of certain sections of society and certain social and political forces. The question is why did communalism succeed in growing during the 20th century? What aspects of the Indian situation favoured this process? Which social classes and political forces did it serve? Why did it become such a pervasive part of Indian reality? Though it was not inherent or inevitable in the situation, it was not a mere conspiracy of power-hungry politicians and crafty administrators either. It had socio-economic and political roots. There was a social situation which was funneling it and without which it could not have survived for long.

*

Above all, communalism was one of the by-products of the colonial character of Indian economy, of colonial underdevelopment, of the incapacity of colonialism to develop the Indian economy. The resulting economic stagnation and its impact on the lives of the Indian people, especially the middle classes, produced conditions which were conducive to division and antagonism within Indian society as also to its radical transformation.

Throughout the 20th century, in the absence of modern industrial development and the development of education, health and other social and cultural services, unemployment was an acute problem in India, especially for the educated middle and lower middle classes who could not fall back on land and whose socio-economic conditions suffered constant deterioration. These economic opportunities declined further during the Great Depression after 1928 when large scale unemployment prevailed.

In this social situation, the nationalist and other popular movements worked for the long-term solution to the people's problems by fighting for the overthrow of colonialism and radical social transformation. In fact, the middle classes formed the backbone both of the militant national movement from 1905 to 1947 and the left-wing parties and groups since the 1920s. Unfortunately there were some who lacked a wider social vision and political understanding and looked to their narrow immediate interests and short-term solutions to their personal or sectional problems such as communal, caste, or provincial reservation in jobs or in municipal committees, legislatures, and so on.

Because of economic stagnation, there was intense competition among individuals for government jobs, in professions like law and medicine, and in business for customers and markets. In an attempt to get a larger share of existing economic opportunities, middle class individuals freely used all the means at their disposal — educational qualifications, personal merit as also nepotism, bribery, and so on. At the same time, to give their struggle a wider base, they also used other group identities such as caste, province and religion to enhance their capacity to compete. Thus, some individuals from the middle classes could, and did, benefit, in the short run, from communalism, especially in the field of government employment. This gave a certain aura of validity to communal politics. The communalist could impose his interpretation of reality on middle class individuals because it did have a basis, however partial, perverted and short-term, in the social existence and social experience of the middle classes.

Gradually, the spread of education to well-off peasants and small landlords extended the boundaries of the job-seeking middle class to the rural areas. The newly educated rural youth could not be sustained by land whether as landlords or peasants, especially as agriculture was totally stagnant because of the colonial impact. They flocked to the towns and cities for openings in government jobs and professions and tried to save themselves by fighting for jobs through the system of communal reservations and nominations. This development gradually widened the social base of communalism to cover the rural upper strata of peasants and landlords.

Thus, the crisis of the colonial economy constantly generated two opposing sets of ideologies and political tendencies among the middle classes. When anti-imperialist revolution and social change appeared on the agenda, the middle classes enthusiastically joined the national and other popular movements. They then readily advocated the cause and demands of the entire society from the capitalists to the peasants and workers. Individual ambitions were then sunk in the wider social vision. But when prospects of revolutionary change receded, when the anti-imperialist struggle entered a more passive phase, many belonging to the middle classes shifted to short-term solutions of their personal problems, to politics based on communalism and other similar ideologies. Thus with the same social causation, large sections of the middle classes in several parts of the country constantly oscillated between anti-imperialism and communalism or communal-type politics. But there was a crucial difference in the two cases. In the first case, their own social interests merged with the interests of general social development and their politics formed a part of the broader anti-imperialist struggle. In the second case, they functioned as a narrow and selfish interest group, accepted the socio-political status quo and objectively served colonialism.

To sum up this aspect: communalism was deeply rooted in and was an expression of the interests and aspirations of the middle classes in a social situation in which opportunities for them were grossly inadequate. The communal question was, therefore a middle class question par excellence. The main appeal of communalism and its main social base also lay among the middle classes. It is, however, important to remember that a large number of middle class individuals remained, on the whole, free of communalism even in the 1930s and 1940s. This was, in particular, true of most of the intellectuals, whether Hindu, Muslim or Sikh. In fact, the typical Indian intellectual of the 1930s tended to be both secular and broadly left-wing.

*

There was another aspect of the colonial economy that favoured communal politics. In the absence of openings in industry, commerce, education and other social services, and the cultural and entertainment fields, the Government service was the main avenue of employment for the middle classes. Much of the employment for teachers, doctors and engineers was also under government control. As late as 1951, while 1.2 million persons were covered by the Factory Acts, 3.3 millions got employment in government service. And communal politics could be used to put pressure on the Government to reserve and allocate its jobs as also seats in professional colleges on communal and caste lines. Consequently, communal politics till 1937 was organized around government jobs, educational concessions, and the like as also political positions — seats in legislative councils, municipal bodies, etc.— which enabled control over these and other economic opportunities. It may also be noted that though the communalists spoke in the name of their 'communities,' the reservations, guarantees and other 'rights' they demanded were virtually confined to these two aspects. They did not take up any issues which were of interest to the masses.

*

At another plane, communalism often distorted or misinterpreted social tension and class conflict between the exploiters and the exploited belonging to different religions as communal conflict. While the discontent and clash of interests was real and was due to non-religious or non-communal factors, because of backward political consciousness it found a distorted expression in communal conflict. As C.G.Shah has put it: 'Under the pressure of communal propaganda, the masses are unable to locate the real causes of their exploitation, oppression, and suffering and imagine a fictitious communal source of their origin.'[2]

What made such communal (and later casteist) distortion possible was a specific feature of Indian social development — in several parts of the country the religious distinction coincided with social, and class distinctions. Here most often the exploiting sections — landlords, merchants and moneylenders, — were upper caste Hindus while the poor and exploited were Muslims or lower caste Hindus. Consequently, propaganda by the Muslim communalists that Hindus were exploiting Muslims or by the Hindu communalists that Muslims were threatening Hindu property or economic interests could succeed even while wholly incorrect. Thus, for example, the struggle between tenant and landlord in East Bengal and Malabar and the peasant-debtor and the merchant-moneylender in Punjab could be portrayed by the communalists as a struggle between Muslims and Hindus. Similarly, the landlord-moneylender oppression was represented as the oppression of Muslims by Hindus, and the attack by the rural poor on the rural rich as an attack by Muslims on Hindus. For example, one aspect of the growth of communalism in Punjab was the effort of the big Muslim landlords to protect their economic and social position by using communalism to turn the anger of their Muslim tenants against Hindus traders and moneylenders, and the use of communalism by the latter to protect their threatened class interests by raising the cry of Hindu interests in danger. In reality, the struggle of the peasants for their emancipation was inevitable. The question was what type of ideological-political content it would acquire. Both the communalists and the colonial administrators stressed the communal as against the class aspects of agrarian exploitation and oppression. Thus, they held that the Muslim peasants and debtors were being exploited not as peasants and debtors but because they were Muslims.

In many cases, a communal form is given to the social conflict not by the participants but by the observer, the official, the journalist, the politician, and, finally, the historian, all of whom provide a post-facto communal explanation for the conflict because of their own conscious or unconscious outlook. It is also important to note that agrarian conflicts did not assume a communal colour until the 20th century and the rise of communalism and that too not in most cases. In the Pabna agrarian riots of 1873, both Hindu and Muslim tenants fought *zamindars* together. Similarly, as brought out in earlier chapters, most of the agrarian struggles after 1919 stayed clear of communal channels. The peasants and workers and the radical intelligentsia succeeded in creating powerful secular peasants' and workers' movements and organizations which became important constituents of the anti-imperialist struggle.

It is important to note in this context that Hindu *zamindars* in Bengal had acquired control over land not because they were Hindus but as a result of the historical process of the spread of Islamic religion in Bengal among the lower castes and classes. Hindu *zamindars* and businessmen acquired economic dominance over landed capital in Bengal at the beginning of the 18th century during the rule of Murshid Quli Khan, religiously the most devout of Aurangzeb's officials and followers. Under his rule, more than seventy-five per cent of the *zamindars* and most of the *taluqdars* were Hindus. The Permanent Settlement of 1793 further strengthened the trend by eliminating on a large scale both the old Hindu and Muslim *zamindar* families and replacing them with new men of commerce who were Hindus. Similarly, the predominance of Hindus among bankers, traders and moneylenders in northern India dated to the medieval period. The dominance these strata acquired over rural society under British rule was the result not of their being Hindus but of the important economic role they acquired in the colonial system of exploitation. In other words, colonial history guaranteed the growth and economic domination of merchant-moneylenders; medieval history had guaranteed that they would be mostly Hindus.

Communalism represented, at another level, a struggle between two upper classes or strata for power, privileges and economic gains. Belonging to different religions (or castes) these classes or strata used communalism to mobilize the popular support of their co-religionists in their mutual struggles. This was, for example, the case in Western Punjab where the Muslim landlords opposed the Hindu moneylenders and in East Bengal where the Muslim *jotedars* (small landlords) opposed the Hindu *zamindars*.

*

Above all, communalism developed as a weapon of ecomomically and politically reactionary social classes and political forces — the semi-feudal landlords and ex-bureaucrats (whom Dr. K.M. Ashraf has called the *jagirdari* classes)[3] merchants and moneylenders and the colonial state. Communal leaders and parties were, in general, allied with these classes and forces. The social, economic and political vested interests deliberately encouraged or unconsciously adopted communalism because of its capacity to distort and divert popular struggles, to prevent the masses from understanding the socio-economic and political forces responsible for their social condition, to prevent unity on national and class lines, and to turn them away from their real national and socio-economic interests and issues and mass movements around them. Communalism also enabled the upper classes and the colonial rulers to unite with sections of the middle classes and to utilize the latter's politics to serve their own ends.

*

British rule and its policy of Divide and Rule bore special responsibility for the growth of communalism in modern India, though it is also true that it could succeed only because of internal social and political conditions. The fact was that the state, with its immense power, could promote either national integration or all kinds of divisive forces. The colonial state chose the latter course. It used communalism to counter and weaken the growing national movement and the welding of the Indian people into a nation. Communalism was presented by the colonial rulers as the problem of the defence of minorities. Hindu-Muslim disunity — and the need to protect the minorities from domination and suppression by the majority — was increasingly offered as the main justification for the maintenance of British rule, especially as theories of civilizing mission, white man's burden, welfare of the ruled, etc., got increasingly discredited.

Communalism was, of course, not the only constituent of the policy of Divide and Rule. Every existing division of Indian society was encouraged to prevent the emerging unity of the Indian people. An effort was made to set region against region, province against province, caste against caste, language against language, reformers against the orthodox, the moderate against the militant, leftist against rightist, and even class against class. It was, of course, the communal division which survived to the end and proved the most serviceable. In fact, near the end, it was to become the main prop of colonialism, and colonial authorities were to stake their all on it. On the other hand, communalism could not have developed to such an extent as to divide the country, if it did not have the powerful support of the colonial state. In this sense, communalism may be described as the channel through which the politics of the middle classes were placed at the service of colonialism and the *jagirdari* classes. In fact, communalism was the route through which colonialism was able to extend its narrow social base to sections of workers, peasants, the middle classes and the bourgeoisie whose interests were otherwise in contradiction with colonialism.

What were the different ways and policies, or acts of omission and commission, through which the British encouraged and nurtured communalism? First, by consistently treating Hindus, Muslims and Sikhs as separate communities and socio-political entities which had little in common. India, it was said, was neither a nation or a nation-in-the-making, nor did it consist of nationalities or local societies, but consisted of structured, mutually exclusive and antagonistic religion-based communities. Second, official favour and patronage were extended to the communalists. Third, the communal Press and persons and agitations were shown extraordinary tolerance. Fourth, communal demands were readily accepted, thus politically strengthening communal organizations and their hold over the people. For example, while the Congress could get none of its demands accepted from 1885- 1905, the Muslim communal demands were accepted in 1906 as soon as they were presented to the Viceroy. Similarly, in 1932, the Communal Award accepted all the major communal demands of the time. During World War II, the Muslim communalists were given a complete veto on any political advance. Fifth, the British readily accepted communal organizations and leaders as the real spokespersons for their 'communities,' while the nationalist leaders were treated as representing a microscopic minority — the elite. Sixth, separate electorates served as an important instrument for the development of communal politics. Lastly, the colonial government encouraged communalism through a policy of non-action against it. Certain positive measures which the state alone could undertake were needed to check the growth of communalism. The failure to undertake them served as an indirect encouragement to communalism. The Government refused to take action against the propagation of virulent communal ideas and communal hatred through the Press, pamphlets, leaflets, literature, public platform and rumours. This was in sharp contrast with the frequent suppression of the nationalist Press, literature, civil servants, propaganda, and so on. On the contrary, the Government freely rewarded communal leaders, intellectuals and government servants with titles, positions of profit, high salaries, and so on. The British administrators also followed a policy of relative inactivity and irresponsibility in dealing with communal riots. When they occurred, they were not crushed energetically. The administration also seldom made proper preparations or took preventive measures to meet situations of communal tension, as they did in case of nationalist and other popular protest movements.

To sum up: So long as the colonial state supported communalism, a solution to the communal problem was not easily possible while the colonial state remained; though, of course, the overthrow of the colonial state was only the *necessary* but not a *sufficient* condition for a successful struggle against communalism.

*

A strong contributory factor in the growth of communalism was the pronounced Hindu tinge in much of nationalist thought and propaganda in the beginning of the 20th century.

Many of the Extremists introduced a strong Hindu religious element in nationalist thought and propaganda. They tended to emphasize ancient Indian culture to the exclusion of medieval Indian culture. They tried to provide a Hindu ideological underpinning to Indian nationalism or at least a Hindu idiom to its day-to-day political agitation. Thus, Tilak used the Ganesh Puja and the Shivaji Festival to propagate nationalism; and the anti-partition of Bengal agitation was initiated with dips in the Ganges. What was much worse, Bankim Chandra Chatterjea and many other writers in Bengali, Hindi, Urdu and other languages often referred to Muslims as foreigners in their novels, plays, poems, and stories, and tended to identify nationalism with Hindus. This type of literature, in which Muslim rulers and officials were often portrayed as tyrants, tended to produce resentment among literate Muslims and alienate them from the emerging national movement. Moreover, a vague Hindu aura pervaded much of the nationalist agitation because of the use of Hindu symbols, idioms, and myths.

Of course, the nationalist movement remained, on the whole, basically secular in its approach and ideology, and young nationalist Muslims like M.A.Jinnah and Maulana Abul Kalam Azad had little difficulty in accepting it as such and in joining it. This secularism became sturdier when leaders like Gandhiji, C.R.Das, Motilal Nehru, Jawaharlal Nehru, Maulana Azad, Dr. M.A. Ansari, Subhas Bose, Sardar Patel and Rajendra Prasad came to the helm. The Hindu tinge was not so much a cause of communalism as a cause of the nationalist failure to check its growth. It made it slightly more difficult to win over Muslims to the

national movement. It enabled the Government and Muslim communalists to use it to keep large sections of Muslims away from the
nationalist movement and to instil among them the feeling that the success of the movement would mean 'Hindu supremacy' in the country.

This Hindu tinge also created ideological openings for Hindu communalism and made it difficult for the nationalist movement to
eliminate Hindu communal political and ideological elements within its
own ranks. It also helped the spread of a Muslim tinge among Muslim
nationalists.

*

A communal and distorted unscientific view of Indian history, especially of its ancient and medieval periods, was a major instrument for
the spread of communal consciousness as also a basic constituent of
communal ideology. The teaching of Indian history in schools and colleges from a basically communal point of view made a major
contribution to the rise and growth of communalism. For generations,
almost from the beginning of the modern school system, communal
interpretations of history of varying degrees of virulence were propagated, first by imperialist writers and then by others. So deep and
widespread was the penetration of the communal view of history that
even sturdy nationalists accepted, however unconsciously, some of its
basic digits. All this was seen by many contemporary observers.
Gandhiji, for example, wrote: 'Communal harmony could not be permanently established in our country so long as highly distorted versions
of history were being taught in her schools and colleges, through the
history textbooks'[4]. Over and above the textbooks, the communal view
of history was spread widely through poetry, drama, historical novels
and short stories, newspapers and popular magazines, pamphlets, and
above all, orally through the public platform, classroom teaching,
socialization through the family, and private discussion and
conversation.

A beginning was made in the early 19th century by the British historian, James Mill, who described the ancient period of Indian history as
the Hindu period and the medieval period as the Muslim period.[5]
(Though he failed to characterize the modern period as the Christian period!). Other British and Indian historians followed him in this respect.
Furthermore, though the Muslim masses were as poor, exploited and

oppressed as the Hindu masses, and there were Hindu *zamindars*, nobles and rulers along with Muslim ones, these writers declared that all Muslims were rulers in medieval India and all Hindus were the ruled. Thus, the basic character of a polity in India was identified with the religion of the ruler. Later the culture and society of various periods were also declared to be either Hindu or Muslim in character.

The Hindu communalist readily adopted the imperialist view that medieval rulers in India were anti-Hindu, tyrannized Hindus and converted them forcibly. All communalist, as also imperialist, historians saw medieval history as one long story of Hindu-Muslim conflict and believed that throughout the medieval period there existed distinct and separate Hindu and Muslim cultures. The Hindu communalists described the rule of medieval Muslim rulers as foreign rule because of their religion. The talk of 'a thousand years of slavery' and 'foreign rule' was common rhetoric, sometimes even used by nationalists. Above all, the Hindu communal view of history relied on the myth that Indian society and culture had reached great, ideal heights in the ancient period from which they fell into permanent and continuous decay during the medieval period because of 'Muslim' rule and domination. The basic contribution of the medieval period to the development of the Indian economy and technology, religion and philosophy, arts and literature, and culture and society was denied.

In turn the Muslim communalists harked back to the 'Golden Age of Islamic achievement' in West Asia and appealed to its heroes, myths and cultural traditions. They propagated the notion that all Muslims were the rulers in medieval India or at least the beneficiaries of the so-called Muslim rule. They tended to defend and glorify all Muslim rulers, including religious bigots like Aurangzeb. They also evolved their own version of the 'fall' theory. While Hindus were allegedly in the ascendant during the 19th century, Muslims, it was said, 'fell' or declined as a 'community' throughout the 19th century after 'they' lost political power.

*

A major factor in the growth of communalism according to some authors was the religious pluralism or the existence of several religions in India. This is not so. It is not true that communalism must arise inevitably in a multi-religious society. Religion was not an underlying or basic cause of communalism, whose removal was basic to tackling or solving the communal problem. Here we must distinguish between religion as a belief system, which people follow as a part of their personal belief, and the ideology of a religion-based socio-political identity, that is, communalism. In other words, religion is not the 'cause' of communalism, even though communal cleavage is based by the communalist on differences in religion — this difference is then used to mask or disguise the social needs, aspirations, conflicts, arising in non-religious fields. Religion comes into communalism to the extent that it serves politics arising in spheres other than religion. K.M.Ashraf put this aspect in an appropriate phrase when he described communalism as '*Mazhab ki siyasi dukandari*' (political trade in religion).[6] Communalism was not inspired by religion, nor was religion the object of communal politics — it was only its vehicle.

Religion was, however, used as a mobilizing factor by the communalists. Communalism could become a popular movement after 1939, and in particular during 1945-47, only when it adopted the inflammable cry of religion in danger. Moreover, differing religious practices were the immediate cause of situations of communal tension and riots. We may also note that while religion was not responsible for communalism, religiosity was a major contributory factor. (Religiosity may be defined as intense emotional commitment to matters of religion and the tendency to let religion and religious emotions intrude into non-religious or non-spiritual areas of life and beyond the individual's private and moral world). Religiosity was not communalism but it opened a person to the appeal of communalism in the name of religion. Secularization did not, therefore, mean removing religion but it did mean reducing religiosity or increasingly narrowing down the sphere of religion to the private life of the individual.

32 *Communalism*
   — The Liberal Phase

There was hardly any communalism in India before the last quarter of the 19th century. As is well-known, Hindus and Muslims had fought shoulder to shoulder in the Revolt of 1857. The notion of Hindu-Muslim distinction at the non-religious plane, not to speak of the clash of interests of Hindus and Muslims was by and large non-existent in the Press during the 1860s. The identity that the North Indian newspapers emphasised was that of the Hindustanees, especially vis-a-vis Europeans or British rulers.

Even when some Muslim intellectuals began to notice that Muslims in some parts of the country were lagging behind Hindus in modern education and in government jobs, they blamed not Hindus but the Government's anti-Muslim policy and the neglect of modern education by upper class Muslims. Syed Ahmed Khan, undoubtedly one of the outstanding Indians of the 19th century, began his educational activities without any communal bias. The numerous scientific societies he founded in 1860s involved both Hindus and Muslims. The Aligarh College he specially founded to fight the bias against modern education among Muslims, received financial support from moneyed Hindus; and its faculty and students had a large Hindu component. Syed Ahmed loudly preached the commonness of Hindus and Muslims till the founding of the Congress in 1885. Thus, for example, he said in 1884: 'Do you not inhabit this land? Are you not buried in it or cremated on it? Surely you live and die on the same land. Remember that Hindus and Muslims are religious terms. Otherwise Hindus, Muslims and Christians who live in this country are by virtue of this fact one *qaum*' (nation or community).'[1]

*

Ironically, communalism in India got its initial start in the 1880s when Syed Ahmed Khan counterposed it to the national movement initiated by the National Congress. In 1887, Dufferin, the Viceroy, and A. Colvin the Lieutenant-Governor of U.P., launched a frontal public attack on the National Congress, once its anti-imperialist edge became clear. Syed Ahmed, believing that the Muslims' share in administrative posts and in professions could be increased only by professing and proving loyalty to the colonial rulers, decided to join in the attack. Furthermore, he felt that he needed the active support of big *zamindars* and the British officials for the Aligarh College. Initially he made an attempt with the help of Shiva Prasad, Raja of Bhinga, and others to organize along caste, birth, class and status lines the feudal (*jagirdari*) and bureaucratic elements in opposition to the rising democratic national movement. However, this attempt failed to get off the ground.

Syed Ahmed now set out to organize the *jagirdari* elements among Muslims as Muslims or the Muslim *qaum* (community). He and his followers gradually laid down the foundation of all the basic themes of the communal ideology as it was to be propagated in the first half of the 20th century. A basic theme was that Hindus, because they were a majority, would dominate Muslims and 'totally override the interests of the smaller community' if representative, democratic goverment was introduced or if British rule ended and power was transferred to Indians.[2] The British were needed to safeguard Muslims as a minority. In the Indian context, said Syed Ahmed, they were the best guardians of Muslim interests.[3] Muslims must, therefore, remain loyal and oppose the National Congress. The theme of a permanent clash of 'Hindu' and 'Muslim' interests was also brought forth. Giving up his earlier views, he now said that India could not be considered a nation.[4] He declared that the Congress was a Hindu body whose major objectives were 'against Muslim interest.' Simultaneously, he criticized the Congress for basing itself on the principle of social equality among the 'lowly' and the 'highly' born.[5] Objecting to the Congress demand for democratic elections, Syed Ahmed said that this would mean that Muslims would not be able to guard their interests, for 'it would be like a game of dice in which one man had four dice and the other only one.'[6] Any system of elections, he said, would put power into the hands of 'Bengalis or of Hindus of the Bengali type' which would lead to Muslims falling into 'a condition of utmost degradation' and 'the ring of slavery' being put on them by Hindus.[7] Syed Ahmed and his co-workers also demanded safeguards for Muslims in Government jobs, legislative councils, and district boards and recognition of the historical role and political importance of Muslims so that their role in legislative councils should not be less than that of Hindus. At the same time, Syed Ahmed and his followers did not create a counter communal political organization, because the British authorities at the time frowned upon any politicization of the Indian people. Syed Ahmed held that any agitational politics would tend to become anti-government and seditious and to create suspicion of disloyalty among the rulers. He, therefore, asked Muslims to shun all politics and remain politically passive, i.e., non-agitational, in their approach.[8] The colonial rulers were quick to see the inherent logic of communalism and the theory of the official protection of the minorities and from the beginning actively promoted and supported communalism.

The Muslim communalists continued to follow the politics of loyalty after Syed Ahmed's death. They openly sided with the Government during the Swadeshi Movement in Bengal during 1905-6 and condemned the Muslim supporters of the movement as 'vile traitors' to Islam and as 'Congress touts.'

But the attempt to keep the growing Muslim intelligentsia politically passive or loyalist was not wholly successful. Badruddin Tyabji presided over the Congress session in 1887, and the number of Muslim delegates to the Congress increased in the succeeding years. R.M. Sayani, A. Bhimji, Mir Musharaff Hussain, Hamid Ali Khan and numerous other Muslim intellectuals from Bombay, Bengal and Northern India joined the Congress. They pointed out that not even one of the Congress demands was communal or for Hindus only. The nationalist trend continued to spread among Muslims all over the country till the end of the 19th century. Abdul Rasul and a large number of other Bengali Muslim intellectuals gave active support to the Swadeshi agitation against the partition of Bengal. In fact, the nationalist trend remained dominant among Muslims in Bengal till the late 1920s.

Once the Swadeshi Movement brought mass politics to India, a large section of the Muslim intelligentsia could not be kept away from the Congress; the British Government felt compelled to offer some constitutional concessions, and it became impossible to continue to follow the policy of political passivity. The communalists, as also their official supporters, felt that they had to enter the political arena. At the end of 1907, the All India Muslim League was founded by a group of big *zamindars*, ex-bureaucrats and other upper class Muslims like the Aga Khan, the Nawab of Dacca and Nawab Mohsin-ul-Mulk. Founded as a loyalist, communal and conservative political organization, the League supported the partition of Bengal, raised the slogan of separate Muslim interests, demanded separate electorates and safeguards for Muslims in government services, and reiterated all the major themes of communal politics and ideology enunciated earlier by Syed Ahmed and his followers. Viqar-ul-Mulk, for example, said: 'God forbid, if the British rule disappears from India, Hindus will lord it over it; and we will be in constant danger of our life, property and honour. The only way for the Muslims to escape this danger is to help in the continuance of the British rule.'9 He also expressed the fear 'of the minority losing its identity.' One of the major objectives of the Muslim League was to keep the emerging intelligentsia among Muslims from joining the Congress. Its activities were directed against the National Congress and Hindus and not against the colonial regime.

*

Simultaneously, Hindu communalism was also being born. From the1870s, a section of Hindu *zamindars*, moneylenders and middle class professionals began to arouse anti-Muslim sentiments. Fully accepting the colonial view of Indian history, they talked of the 'tyrannical' Muslim rule in the medieval period and the 'liberating' role of the British in 'saving' Hindus from 'Muslim oppression.' In U.P. and Bihar, they took up the question of Hindi and gave it a communal twist, declaring that Urdu was the language of Muslims and Hindi of Hindus. All over India, anti-cow slaughter propaganda was undertaken in the early 1890s, the campaign being primarily directed not against the British but against Muslims; the British cantonments, for example, were left free to carry on cow slaughter on a large scale. Consequently, this agitation invariably took a communal turn, often resulting in communal riots. The anti-cow slaughter agitation died down by 1896, to be revived again in a more virulent form in the second decade of the 20th century. The Hindu communalists also carried on a regular agitation for a 'Hindu' share of seats in legislatures and in government services.

The Punjab Hindu Sabha was founded in 1909. Its leaders, U.N.

Mukerji and Lal Chand, were to lay down the foundations of Hindu communal ideology and politics. They directed their anger primarily against the National Congress for trying to unite Indians into a single nation and for 'sacrificing Hindu interests' to appease Muslims. In his booklet, *Self-Abnegation in Politics*, Lal Chand described the Congress as the 'self-inflicted misfortune' of Hindus. Hindus, he wrote, were moving towards extinction because of 'the poison imbibed for the last 25 years.' They could be saved only if they were willing to 'purge' the poison and get rid of the 'evil.' He accused the Congress of making 'impossible' demands on the Government, leading to its justifiable anger against the Congress and Hindus. Instead Hindus should try to neutralize the third party, the Government, in their fight against Muslims. It was also essential that Hindus abandon and 'end' the Congress. 'A Hindu,' Lal Chand declared, 'should not only believe but make it a part and parcel of his organism, of his life and of his conduct, that he is a Hindu first and an Indian after.'[10]

The first session of the All-India Hindu Mahasabha was held in April 1915 under the presidentship of the Maharaja of Kasim Bazar. But it remained for many years a rather sickly child compared to the Muslim League. This was for several reasons. The broader social reason was the greater and even dominant role of the *zamindars*, aristocrats and ex-bureaucrats among Muslims in general and even among the Muslim middle classes. While among Parsis and Hindus, increasingly, it was the modern intelligentsia, with its emphasis on science, democracy and nationalism, and the bourgeois elements in general, which rapidly acqired intellectual, social, economic and political influence and hege-mony, among Muslims the reactionary landlords and *mullahs* continued to exercise dominant influence or hegemony. Landlords and traditional religious priests, whether Hindu or Muslim, were conservative and sup-porters of established, colonial authority. But while among Hindus, they were gradually losing positions of leadership, they continued to dominate among Muslims. In this sense the weak position of the mid-dle class among Muslims and its social and ideological backwardness contributed to the growth of Muslim communalism.

There were other reason for the relative weakness of Hindu commu-nalism. The colonial Government gave Hindu communalsim few concessions and little support, for it banked heavily on Muslim com-munalism and could not easily simultaneously placate both communalisms.

*

The colonial authorities and the communalists together evolved another powerful instrument for the spread and consolidation of communalism in seperate electorates which were introduced in the Morley-Minto Reforms of 1907. Under this system, Muslim voters (and later Sikhs and others) were put in separate constituencies from which only Muslims could stand as candidates and for which only Muslims could vote. Separate electorates turned elections and legislative councils into arenas for communal conflict. Since the voters were exclusively the followers of one religion, the candidates did not have to appeal to voters belonging to other religions. They could, therefore, make blatantly communal appeals and voters and others who listened to these appeals were gradually trained to think and vote communally and in general to think in terms of 'communal' power and progress and to express their socio-economic grievances in communal terms. The system of reservation of seats and weightage in legislatures, government services, educational institutions etc., also had the same consequences.

*

A slight detour at this stage is perhaps necessary. When discussing the history of the origins and growth of communalism and communal organizations, one particular error is to be avoided. Often a communalist ascribed — or even now ascribes in historical writings — the origins of one communalism to the existence of and as a reaction to the other communalism. Thus, by assigning the 'original' blame to the other communalism a sort of backdoor justification for one's own communalism is (or was) provided. Thus the Hindu, Muslim or Sikh communalists justified their own communalism by arguing that they were reacting to the communalism initiated by others. In fact, to decide which communalism came first is like answering the question: which came first, the chicken or the egg? Once communalism arose and developed, its different variants fed and fattened on each other.

The younger Muslim intellectuals were soon dissatisfied with the loyalist, anti-Hindu and slavish mentality of the upper class leadership of the Muslim League. They were increasingly drawn to modern and radical nationalist ideas. The militantly nationalist Ahrar movement was founded at this time under the leadership of Maulana Mohammed Ali, Hakim Ajmal Khan, Hasan Imam, Maulana Zafar Ali Khan, and Mazhar-ul-Haq. In their efforts, they got support from a section of orthodox *ulama* (scholars), especially those belonging to the Deoband school. Another orthodox scholar to be attracted to the national movement was the young Maulana Abul Kalam Azad, who was educated at the famous Al Azhar University at Cairo and who propagated his rationalist and nationalist ideas in his newspaper *Al Hilal* which he brought out in 1912 at the age of twenty-four. After an intense struggle, the nationalist young Muslims came to the fore in the Muslim League. They also became active in the Congress. In 1912, the brilliant Congress leader, M.A.Jinnah, was invited to join the League which adopted self-government as one of its objectives. In the same year, the Aga Khan resigned as the President of the League.

From 1912 to 1924, the young nationalists began to overshadow the loyalists in the League which began to move nearer to the policies of the Congress. Unfortunately, their nationalism was flawed in so far as it was not fully secular (except with rare exceptions like Jinnah). It had a strong religious and pan-Islamic tinge. Instead of understanding and opposing the economic and political consequences of modern imperialism, they fought it on the ground that it threatened the Caliph (khalifa) and the holy places. Quite often their appeal was to religious sentiments. This religious tinge or approach did not immediately clash with nationalism. Rather, it made its adherents anti-imperialist; and it encouraged the nationalist trend among urban Muslims. But in the long run it proved harmful as it inculcated and encouraged the habit of looking at political questions from a religious point of view.

*

The positive development within the Congress — discussed in an earlier chapter — and within the Muslim League soon led to broad political unity among the two, an important role in this being played by Lokamanya Tilak and M.A. Jinnah. The two organizations held their sessions at the end of 1916 at Lucknow, signed a pact known as the Lucknow Pact, and put forward common political demands before the

Government including the demand for self-government for India after the war. The Pact accepted separate electorates and the system of weightage and reservation of seats for the minorities in the legislatures. While a step forward in many respects — and it enthused the political Indians — the Pact was also a step back. The Congress had accepted separate elec- torates and formally recognized communal politics. Above all, the Pact was tacitly based on the assumption that India consisted of different communities with separate interests of their own. It, therefore, left the way open to the future resurgence of communalism in Indian politics.

The nationalist movement and Hindu-Muslim unity took giant steps forward after World War I during the agitation against the Rowlatt Acts, and the Khilafat and the Non-Cooperation Movements. As if to declare before the world the principle of Hindu-Muslim unity in political action , Swami Shradhanand, a staunch Arya Samajist, was asked by Muslims to preach from the pulpit of the Jama Musjid at Delhi, while Dr. Saifuddin Kitchlu, a Muslim, was given the keys to the Golden Temple, the Sikh shrine at Amritsar. The entire country resounded to the cry of '*Hindu-Muslim ki Jai*'. The landlord-communalists and ex- bureaucrats increasingly diassociated themselves from the Muslim League, while the League itself was overshadowed by the Khilafat Committee as many of the League leaders — as also many of the old Congress leaders — found it difficult to keep pace with the politics of a mass movement. Even though the Khilafat was a religious issue, it resulted in raising the national, anti-imperialist consciousness of the Muslim masses and middle classes. Moreover, there was nothing wrong in the nationalist movement taking up a demand that affected Muslims only, just as the Akali movement affected the Sikhs only and the anti - untouchability campaign Hindus only.

But there were also certain weaknesses involved. The nationalist leadership failed to some extent in raising the religious political con- sciousness of Muslims to the higher plane of secular political consciousness. The Khilafat leaders, for example, made appeals to relig- ion and made full use of *fatwas* (opinion or decision on a point of Islamic law given by a religious person of standing) and other religious sanctions. Consequently, they strengthened the hold of orthodoxy and priesthood over the minds of men and women and encouraged the habit of looking at political questions from the religious point of view. By doing so and by emphasizing the notion of Muslim solidarity, they kept an opening for communal ideology and politics to grow at a later stage.

*

The Non-Cooperation Movement was withdrawn in February 1922. As
the people felt disillusioned and frustrated and the Dyarchy became oper-
ational, communalism reared its ugly head and in the post-1922 years
the country was repeatedly plunged into communal riots. Old communal organizations were revived and fresh ones founded. The Muslim
League once again became active and was cleansed of radical and nationalist elements. The upper class leaders with their open loyalism and
frankly communal ideology once again came to the fore. The Hindu
Mahasabha was revived in 1923 and openly began to cater to anti-
Muslim sentiments. Its proclaimed objective became 'the maintenance,
protection and promotion of Hindu race, Hindu culture and Hindu civilization for the advancement of Hindu Rashtra.'

The Hindu as well as Muslim communalists tried to inculcate the
psychology of fear among Hindus and Muslims — the fear of being
deprived, surpassed, threatened, dominated, suppressed, beaten down, and
even exterminated. It was during these years that *Sangathan* and *Shuddhi*
movements among Hindus and *Tanzeem* and *Tabligh* movements
among Muslims, working for communal consolidation and religious
conversion, came up. The nationalists were openly reviled as apostates
and as enemies of their own religion and co-religionists.

A large number of nationalists were not able to withstand communal
pressure and began to adopt communal or semi-communal positions.
The Swarajists were split by communalism. A group known as
'responsivists' offered cooperation to the Government so that the so-
called Hindu interests might be safeguarded. Lajpat Rai, Madan Mohan
Malaviya and N.C. Kelkar joined the Hindu Mahasabha and argued for
Hindu communal solidarity. The less responsible 'responsivists' and
Hindu Mahasabhaites carried on a virulent campaign against secular
Congressmen. They accused Motilal Nehru of letting down Hindus, of
being anti-Hindu and an Islam-lover, of favouring cow-slaughter, and of
eating beef. Many old Khilafatists also now turned communal. The
most dramatic shift was that of Maulanas Mohammed Ali and Shaukat
Ali who now accused the Congress of trying to establish a Hindu
Government and Hindus of wanting to dominate and suppress Muslims.
The most vicious expression of communalism were communal riots
which broke out in major North Indian cities during 1923-24.

According to the Simon Commission Report, nearly 112 major communal riots occurred between 1922 and 1927.

*

The nationalist leadership made strenuous efforts to oppose communal political forces, but was not able to evolve an effective line of action. What was the line of action that it adopted and why did it fail? Its basic strategy was to try to bring about unity at the top with communal leaders through negotiations. This meant that either the Congress leaders acted as mediators or intermediaries between different communal groups or they themselves tried to arrive at a compromise with Muslim communal leaders on questions of 'protection' to and 'safeguards' of the interests of the minorities in terms of reservation of seats in the legislatures and of jobs in the government.

The most well-known of such efforts was made during 1928. As an answer to the challenge of the Simon Commission, Indian political leaders organized several all-India conferences to settle communal issues and draw up an agreed constitution for India. A large number of Muslim communal leaders met at Delhi in December 1927 and evolved four basic demands known as the Delhi Proposals. These proposals were: (1) Sind should be made a separate province; (2) the North-West Frontier Province should be treated constitutionally on the same footing as other provinces; (3) Muslims should have 33 1/3 per cent representation in the central legislature; (4) in Punjab and Bengal, the proportion of representation should be in accordance with the population, thus guaranteeing a Muslim majority, and in other provinces, where Muslims were a minority, the existing reservation of seats for Muslims should continue.

The Congress proposals came in the form of the Nehru Report drafted by an all-parties committee. The Report was put up for approval before an All-Party Convention at Calcutta at the end of December 1928. Apart from other aspects, the Nehru Report recommended that India should be a federation on the basis of linguistic provinces and provincial autonomy, that elections be held on the basis of joint electorates and that seats in central and provincial legislatures be reserved for religious minorities in proportion to their population. The Report recommended the separation of Sind from Bombay and constitutional reform in the North-West Frontier Province.

The Report could not be approved unanimously at the Calcutta Convention. While there were wide differences among Muslim communalists, a section of the League and the Khilafatists were willing to accept joint electorates and other proposals in the Report provided three amendments, moved by M.A. Jinnah, were accepted. Two of these were the same as the third and fourth demands in the Delhi Proposals, the first and second of these demands having been conceded by the Nehru Report. The third was a fresh demand that residuary powers should vest in the provinces. A large section of the League led by Mohammed Shafi and the Aga Khan and many other Muslim communal groups refused to agree to these amendments; they were not willing to give up separate electorates. The Hindu Mahasabha and the Sikh League raised vehement objections to the parts of the Report dealing with Sind, North-West Frontier Province, Bengal and Punjab. They also refused to accept the Jinnah amendments. The Congress leaders were not willing to accept the weak centre that the Jinnah proposals envisioned.

Most of the Muslim communalists now joined hands and Jinnah too decided to fall in line. Declaring that the Nehru Report represented Hindu interests, he consolidated all the communal demands made by different communal organizations at different times into a single document which came to be known as Jinnah's Fourteen Points. The Fourteen Points basically consisted of the four Delhi Proposals, the three Calcutta amendments and demands for the continuation of separate electorates and reservation of seats for Muslims in government services and self-governing bodies. The Fourteen Points were to form the basis of all future communal propaganda in the subsequent years.

This strategy of trying to solve the communal problem through an agreement or pact with the Hindu, Muslim and Sikh communal leaders proved a complete failure and suffered from certain inherent weaknesses. Above all it meant that the Congress tacitly or by implication accepted, to a certain extent, the claim of the communal leaders that they were representatives of the communal interests of their respective 'communities,' and, of course, that such communal interests and religious communites existed in real life. By negotiating with communal leaders, the Congress legitimized their politics and made them respectable. It also weakened its right, as well as the will, to carry on a hard political-ideological campaign against communal parties and individuals. Constant negotiations with Muslim communal leaders weakened the position of secular, anti-imperialist Muslims and Muslim leaders like

Azad, Ansari and Asaf Ali. They also made it difficult to oppose and expose the communalism and semi-communalism of leaders like Madan Mohan Malaviya, Lajpat Rai and Maulana Mohammed Ali who often worked within the Congress ranks.

The strategy of negotiations at the top required generous concessions by the majority to the minority communalism on the question of jobs and seats in the legislatures. But communalism was quite strong among the Hindu middle classes which too suffered from the consequences of colonial underdevelopment. The Congress leadership found it politically difficult to force concessions to Muslim communalism down the throat of Hindu and Sikh communalists. Thus, the failure to conciliate the Muslim communalists helped them gain strength, while any important concessions to them tended to produce a Hindu communal backlash. In any case, even if by a supreme effort in generosity and sagacity a compromise with communal leaders had been arrived at, it was likely to prove temporary as was the case with the Lucknow Pact and to some extent the Nehru Report. Not one communal leader or group or party had enough authority over other communal groups and individuals to sign a lasting agreement. Concessions only whetted the appetite of the communalists. As soon as one group was appeased, a more 'extreme' or recalcitrant leader or group emerged and pushed up the communal demands. Consequently, often the more 'reasonable' leader or group felt his communal hold over the followers weakening and found it necessary to go back even on the earlier partial or fuller agreement. This is what repeatedly happened during 1928-29 — and Jinnah's was a typical example. The fact was that so long as communal ideology flourished or the socio-political conditions favouring communal politics persisted, it was difficult to appease or conciliate communal leaders permanently or for any length of time.

The real answer lay in an all-out opposition to communalism in all arenas — ideological, cultural, social and political. Based on a scientific understanding of its ideology, its social and ideological sources and roots, its social base, and the reasons for its growth in the face of the nationalist work in favour of Hindu-Muslim unity, an intense political-ideological struggle had to be waged against communalism and communal political forces. Moreover, it was necessary to take up the peasants' cause where their class struggle was being distorted into communal channels. All this was not done, despite the deep commitment to secularism of the bulk of the nationalist leadership from Dadabhai Naoroji to Gandhiji and Nehru. The need was to direct the debate with the communalists into hard, rational, analytical channels so that the latter were forced to fight on the terrain of reason and science and not of emotion and bias. Gandhiji and the Congress did make Hindu-Muslim unity one of the three basic items of the nationalist political platform. They also, at crucial moments, refused to appease the Hindu communalists. Gandhiji several times staked his life for the secular cause. But Gandhiji and the Congress provided no deeper analysis of the communal phenomenon.

*

Despite the intensified activities of communal parties and groups during the 1920s, communalism was not yet very pervasive in Indian society. Communal riots were largely confined to cities and their number, keeping in view the size of the country, was not really large. The Hindu communalists commanded little support among the masses. The social base of the Muslim communalists was also quite narrow. The nationalist Muslims, who were part of the Congress, still represented a major political force. The rising trade union, peasant and youth movements were fully secular. The reaction to the Simon Commission further revealed the weakness of communal forces when both the Muslim League and the Hindu Mahasabha got divided, some in favour of a boycott of the Commission and others for cooperating with it.

The anti-Simon Commission protest movement and then the Second Civil Disobedience Movement from 1930 to 1934 swept the entire country and once again pushed the communalists as a whole into the background. Led by the Congress, Jamiat-ul-Ulama-i-Hind, Khudai Khidmatgars and other organizations, thousands of Muslims went to jail. The national movement engulfed for the first time two new major areas with a Muslim majority — the North-West Frontier Province and Kashmir.

The communal leaders got a chance to come into the limelight during the Round Table Conferences of the early 1930s. At these conferences, the communalists joined hands with the most reactionary sections of the British ruling classes. Both the Muslim and Hindu communalists made efforts to win the support of British authorities to defend their so-called communal interests. In 1932, at a meeting in the House of Commons, the Aga Khan, the poet Mohammed Iqbal and the historian Shafaat Ahmad Khan stressed 'the inherent impossiblity of securing any merger of Hindu and Muslim, political, or indeed social interests' and 'the impracticability of ever governing India through anything but a British agency.'[11] Similarly, in 1933, presiding over the Hindu Mahasabha session, Bhai Parmanand made a plea for cooperation between Hindus and the British Government and said: 'I feel an impulse in me that Hindus would willingly cooperate with Great Britain if their status and responsible position as the premier community in India is recognized in the political institutions of new India.'[12]

The communal parties and groups remained quite weak and narrow based till 1937. Most of the Muslim as also Hindu young intellectuals, workers and peasants joined the mainstreams of nationalism and socialism in the early 1930s. In Bengal, many joined the secular and radical Krishak Praja Party. Moreover, in 1932, in an effort to bolster the sagging Muslim communalism, the British Government announced the Communal Award which accepted virtually all the Muslim communal demands embodied in the Delhi Proposals of 1927 and Jinnah's Fourteen Points of 1929. The communal forces were faced with an entirely new situation; they could not carry on as before. The question was where would they go from here.

Communalism remained at the second, liberal stage till 1937 when it increasingly started assuming a virulent, extremist or fascist form. The liberal communalist argued that India consisted of distinct religion-based communities which had their own separate and special interests which often came into mutual conflict. But he also accepted that the ultimate destiny of Indian politics was the merger of the different communities into a single nation. Thus, the liberal communalist demanded separate communal rights, safeguards, reservations, etc., within the broad concept of one Indian nation-in-the-making. He accepted national unity as the ultimate goal as also the concept of the ultimate common interests of Hindus, Muslims, Sikhs and Christians. Liberal communalism had also a rather narrow social base. Politically, it was based mainly on the upper and middle classes.

*

Extreme communalism was based on the politics of hatred, fear psychosis and irrationality. The motifs of domination and suppression, always present in communal propaganda as we have shown earlier, increasingly became the dominant theme of communal propaganda. A campaign of hatred against the followers of other religions was unleashed. The interests of Hindus and Muslims were now declared to be permanently in conflict. The communalists attacked the other 'communities' with, in W.C. Smith's words, 'fervour, fear, contempt and bitter hatred,' in the extremist or fascist phase of communalism after 1937. Phrases like oppression, suppression, domination, being crushed, even physical extermination and extinction were used. The communalists increasingly operated on the principle: the bigger the lie the better. They poured venom on the National Congress and Gandhiji, and, in particular, they viciously attacked their co-religionists among the nationalists.

Communalism also now, after 1937, increasingly acquired a popular base, and began to mobilize popular mass opinion. It was now sought to be organized as a mass movement around aggressive, extremist communal politics among the urban lower middle classes. This also required an issue or a slogan which could arouse mass emotion. Because of the reactionary, upper class base of communalism, an appeal to radical social issues could not be made. In other words, communalism could not base itself on a radical socio-economic, or political or ideological programme. Hence, inevitably, an appeal was made to religion and to irrational sentiments of fear and hatred.

Liberal communalism was transformed into extremist communalism for several reasons. As a consequence of the growth of nationalism and, in particular, of the Civil Disobedience Movement of 1930-34, the Congress emerged as the dominant political force in the elections of 1937. Various political parties of landlords and other vested interests suffered a drastic decline. Moreover, as we have seen, the youth as also the workers and peasants were increasingly turning to the Left, and the national movement as a whole was getting increasingly radicalized in its economic and political programme and policies. The *zamindars* and landlords — the *jagirdari* elements — , finding that open defence of landlords' interests was no longer feasible, now, by and large, switched over to communalism for their class defence. This was not only true in U.P. and Bihar but also in Punjab and Bengal. In Punjab, for example, the big landlords of West Punjab and the Muslim bureaucratic elite had supported the semi-communal, semi-casteist and loyalist Unionist Party. But they increasingly felt that the Unionist Party, being a provincial party, could no longer protect them from Congress radicalism, and so, during the years 1937-45, they gradually shifted their support to the Muslim League which eagerly promised to protect their interests. Very similar was the case of Muslim *zamindars* and *jotedars* in Bengal. Hindu *zamindars* and landlords and merchants and moneylenders in northern and western India too began to shift towards Hindu communal parties and groups. To attract them, V.D. Savarkar, the Hindu Mahasabha President, began to condemn the 'selfish' class tussle between landlords and tenants. Similarly, in Punjab, the Hindu communalists became even more active than before in defending moneylending and trading interests.

Communalism also became, after 1937, the only political recourse of colonial authorities and their policy of divide and rule. This was because, by this time, nearly all the other divisions, antagonisms and divisive devices promoted and fostered earlier by the colonial authorities had been overcome by the national movement, and had become politically non-viable from the colonial point of view. The Non-Brahmin challenge in Maharashtra and South India had fizzled out. The Scheduled Castes and other backward castes could no longer be mobilized against the Congress except in stray pockets. The Right and Left wings of the Congress also refused to split. Inter-provincial and inter-lingual rivalries had exhausted themselves much earlier, after the Congress accepted the validity of linguistic states and the cultural diversity of the Indian people. The effort to pit the *zamindars* and landlords against the national movement had also completely failed. The elections of 1937 showed that nearly all the major social and political props of colonialism lay shattered. The communal card alone was available for playing against the national movement and the rulers decided to use it to the limit, to stake all on it. They threw all the weight of the colonial state behind Muslim communalism, even though it was headed by a man — M.A. Jinnah — whom they disliked and feared for his sturdy independence and outspoken anti-colonialism.

The outbreak of World War II, on 1 September, 1939 further strengthened the reliance on the communal card. The Congress withdrew its ministries and demanded that the British make a declaration that India would get complete freedom after the War and transfer of effective government power immediately. For countering the nationalist demand and dividing Indian opinion, reliance was placed on the Muslim League whose politics and demands were counterposed to the nationalist politics and demands. The League was recognized as the sole spokesperson for Muslims and given the power to veto any political settlement. India could not be given freedom, it was said, so long as Hindus and Muslims did not unite. But such unity was made impossible by the wholesale official backing of Muslim communalism. The Muslim League, in turn, agreed to collaborate with the colonial authorities and serve as their political instrument for its own reasons. The Hindu Mahasabha and other Hindu and Sikh communal organizations also offered to support the colonial Government during the War. But the colonial authorities, while accepting their support, could no longer divide their loyalties; their commitment to Muslim communalism was to remain total during the course of the War, and even after.

Both the Muslim League and the Hindu Mahasabha had run the election campaign of 1937 on liberal communal lines — they had incorporated much of the nationalist programme and many of the Congress policies, except those relating to agrarian issues, in their election manifestoes. But they had fared poorly in the elections. The Muslim League, for example, won only 109 out of the 482 seats alloted to Muslims under separate electorates, securing only 4.8 per cent of the total Muslim votes. The Hindu Mahasabha fared even worse.

The communalists now realized that they would gradually wither away if they did not take to militant, mass-based politics. Hitherto, organized mass movements and cadre-based politics had been built by radical, anti-status quo nationalists. The conservatives had shied away from mass movements. In the 1930s, a successful right-wing model of mass politics, which would not frighten away the vested interests, became available in the form of the fascist movement. Both Hindu and Muslim communalists decided to follow this model. Moreover, the Congress had not yet acquired firm roots among all the masses, especially among the Muslim masses; now was the time to take advantage of their political immaturity, before it was too late. Urgency was added to the need to shift to extreme Muslim communalism because the Congress decided to initiate, under Jawaharlal Nehru's guidance, a massive campaign to work among the Muslim masses, known as the Muslim Mass Contact Programme.

The logic of communalism also inexorably led to extreme communalism. The Congress had gone quite far in the late 1920s in accepting Muslim communal demands. In 1932, the Communal Award and then the Government of India Act of 1935 accepted nearly all the liberal communal demands. Nor did the National Congress oppose these concessions to the communalists. But such concessions would have no cast iron guarantee behind them once the foreign rulers disappeared from the scene and the country came to be ruled democratically. Moreover, what would the communalists do next? Since their demands had been accepted, they had either to dissolve their political organizations, give up communalism and commit political *harakiri* or discover new demands, new threats to their communities, and inexorably and without necessarily, a conscious design turn towards extreme communalism. Similarly, the Hindu communalists had failed to grow. Further, till

1937, the Congress had permitted both Hindu and Muslim liberal communalists to work within the Congress organization. Under Jawaharlal Nehru's and the Left's pressure the Congress was frontally attacking the communalists. Not only did it not accommodate them in the elections of 1934 and 1937, it moved towards expelling them from the Congress, and finally did so in 1938. The Hindu communalists were facing political extinction. They also had to find a new basis and a new programme for their survival and growth.

*

The propositions that communalism has a logic of its own and, if not checked in its early stages, inevitably develops into its 'higher' stages is illustrated by the life history of Mohammed Ali Jinnah. His case shows how communalism is an inclined plane on which a constant slide down becomes inevitable unless counter steps are taken. Once the basic digits of communal ideology are accepted, the ideology takes over a person bit by bit, independent of the subjective desires of the person. This is how a person who started as the 'Ambassador of Hindu-Muslim Unity' ended up by demanding Pakistan.

M.A. Jinnah came back to India after becoming a Barrister in 1906 as a secular, liberal nationalist, a follower of Dadabhai Naoroji. On his return, he immediately joined the Congress and acted as Dadabhai's secretary at the Calcutta session of the Congress in 1906. He was an opponent of the Muslim League then being founded. The Aga Khan, the first president of the League, was to write later that Jinnah was 'our toughest opponent in 1906' and that he 'came out in bitter hostility toward all that I and my friends had done and were trying to do . . . He said that our principle of separate electorates was dividing the nation against itself.'[1] From 1906 onwards, Jinnah propagated the theme of national unity in the meetings that he addressed, earning from Sarojini Naidu the title 'Ambassador of Hindu-Muslim Unity.'

The first step towards communalism was taken without any desire of his own and perhaps against his own wishes when he entered the Central Legislative Council from Bombay as a Muslim member under the system of separate electorates. The real slide down began when from a nationalist pure and simple he became a communal nationalist in 1913 when he joined the Muslim League. This, of course, meant that he was still basically a nationalist. He remained in the Congress and still opposed separate electorates arguing that it would divide India into 'two watertight compartments.' But he also started assuming the role of a spokesperson of the Muslim 'community' as a whole. These dual roles reached the height of their effectiveness in the Lucknow Congress-League Pact of which he and Tilak were the joint authors. Acting as the spokesperson of Muslim communalism, he got the Congress to accept separate electorates and the system of communal reservations. But he still remained fully committed to nationalism and secular politics. He resigned from the Legislative Council as a protest against the passing of the Rowlatt Bill. He refuted the communal assumption that self-government in India would lead to Hindu rule; and argued that the real political issue in India was Home Rule or 'transfer of power from bureaucracy to democracy.'[2]

In 1919-20, the Congress took a turn towards mass politics based on the peaceful breaking of existing laws. Jinnah disagreed and did not find it possible to go along with Gandhi. Along with many other liberals, who thought like him — persons such as Surendranath Banerjea, Bipin Chandra Pal, Tej Bahadur Sapru, C. Sankaran Nair, and many more — Jinnah left the Congress. But he could also see that mere liberal politics had no future. And he was not willing to go into political oblivion. Unlike most of the other liberals, he turned to communal politics. He became a liberal communalist. The logic of communalism had asserted itself and transformed him first from a nationalist into a communal nationalist and then into a liberal communalist.

During the 1920s, Jinnah's nationalism was not fully swallowed by communalism. He revived the down-and-out Muslim League in 1924 and started building it upon and around the demand for safeguarding 'the interests and rights of the Muslims.' His politics were now based on the basic communal idea that 'Muslims should organize themselves, stand united and should press every reasonable point for the protection of their community.'[3] At the same time, he still pleaded for Hindu-Muslim unity on the basis of a fresh Lucknow Pact so as to fight the British together, and he cooperated with the *Swarajists* in opposing Government policies and measures in the Central Legislative Assembly. As late as 1925, he told a young Muslim, who said that he was a Muslim first: 'My boy, no, you are an Indian first and then a Muslim.'[4] In 1927-28, he supported the boycott of the Simon Commission, though he would not join in the mass demonstrations against it.

But by now his entire social base comprised communal-minded persons. He could not give up communalism without losing all political influence. This became apparent in 1928-29 during the discussions on the Nehru Report. Step by step he surrendered to the more reactionary communalists, led by the Aga Khan and M. Shafi, and in the end became the leader of Muslim communalism as a whole, losing in the bargain the support of nationalist leaders like M.A. Ansari, T.A.K. Sherwani, Syed Mahmud and his own erstwhile lieutenants like M.C. Chagla. His slide down was symbolized by his becoming the author of the famous 14 demands incorporating the demands of the most reactionary and virulent sections of Muslim communalism.

Jinnah was further alienated from the main currents of nationalism as the Congress organized the massive mass movement of 1930 and started moving towards a more radical socio-economic programme. Moreover, the Muslim masses especially the younger generation were increasingly shifting to nationalist and left-wing politics and ideologies. Jinnah was faced with a dilemma. He saw little light; and decided to stay mostly in Britain.

But Jinnah was too much of a man of action and of politics to stay there. He returned to India in 1936 to once again revive the Muslim League. He initially wanted to do so on the basis of liberal communalism. Throughout 1936, he stressed his nationalism and desire for freedom and spoke for Hindu-Muslim cooperation. For example, he said at Lahore in March 1936: 'Whatever I have done, let me assure you there has been no change in me, not the slightest, since the day when I joined the Indian National Congress. It may be I have been wrong on some occasions. But it has never been done in a partisan spirit. My sole and only object has been the welfare of my country. I assure you that India's interest is and will be sacred to me and nothing will make me budge an inch from that position.'5 On the one hand, he asked Muslims to organize separately, on the other hand, he asked them to 'prove that their patriotism is unsullied and that their love of India and her progress is no less than that of any other community in the country.'6

Jinnah's plan perhaps was to use the Muslim League to win enough seats to force another Lucknow Pact on the Congress. He also assumed that by participating in the 1937 elections the Congress was reverting to pre-Gandhian constitutional politics. Partially because of these assumptions and partially because the bag of communal demands was empty — nearly all the communal demands having been accepted by the

Communal Award — Jinnah and the League fought elections on a semi-nationalist Congress-type of programme, the only 'Muslim' demands being protection and promotion of the Urdu language and script, and adoption of measures for the amelioration of the general conditions of Muslims.

But the poor election results showed that none of Jinnah's assumptions were correct. Jinnah had now to decide what to do: To stick to his semi-nationalist, liberal communal politics which seemed to have exhausted its potentialities or to abandon communal politics. Both would mean going into political wilderness. The third alternative was to take to mass politics which in view of the semi-feudal and semi-loyalist social base of the League and his own socially, economically, and politically conservative views could only be based on the cries of Islam in danger and the danger of a Hindu raj. Jinnah decided in 1937-38 to opt for this last option. And once he took this decision he went all the way towards extreme communalism putting all the force and brilliance of his personality behind the new politics based on themes of hate and fear. From now on, the entire political campaign among Muslims of this tallest of communal leaders would be geared to appeal to his co-religionists' fear and insecurity and to drive home the theme that the Congress wanted not independence from British imperialism but a Hindu raj in cooperation with the British and domination over Muslims and even their extermination as also the destruction of Islam in India.

Let us take a few examples. In his presidential address to the League in 1938, Jinnah said: 'The High Command of the Congress is determined, absolutely determined, to crush all other communities and cultures in this country and establish Hindu raj in this country.'[7]. In March 1940, he told the students at Aligarh: 'Mr. Gandhi's hope is to subjugate and vassalize the Muslims under a Hindu raj.'[8] Again at Aligarh in March 1941: 'Pakistan is not only a practicable goal but the only goal if you want to save Islam from complete annihilation in this country.'[9] In his presidential address on April 1941, Jinnah declared that in a united India 'the Muslims will be absolutely wiped out of existence.'[10] Regarding the interim government in 1946, on 18 August, Jinnah referred to 'the caste Hindu Fascist Congress,' which wanted to 'dominate and rule over Mussalmans and other minor communities of India with the aid of British bayonets.' [11] In 1946, asking Muslims to vote for the League he said: 'If we fail to realize our duty today you will be reduced to the status of *Sudras* and Islam will be vanquished from

India.'[12]

If a leader of the stature of Jinnah could take up politics and agitation at this low level, it was inevitable that the average communal propagandist would be often even worse. Men like Z.A. Suleri and F.M. Durrani surpassed themselves in Goebbelsian demagogy.[13] Even Fazl-ul-Huq, holding a responsible position as the Premier of Bengal, told the 1938 session of the League: 'In Congress provinces, riots had laid the countryside waste. Muslim life, limb and property have been lost and blood has freely flowed . . . There the Muslims are leading their lives in constant terror, overawed and oppressed by Hindus . . . There mosques are being defiled and the culprit never found nor is the Muslim worshipper unmolested.'[14] M.H.Gazdar, a prominent League leader of Sind, told a League meeting in Karachi in March 1941: 'The Hindus will have to be eradicated like the Jews in Germany if they did not behave properly.'[15] Jinnah was however in no position to pull up such people, for his own speeches often skirted the same territory.

The Muslim communalists now launched a vicious campaign against nationalist Muslims. Maulana Abul Kalam Azad and other nationalist Muslims were branded as 'show boys' of the Congress, traitors to Islam and mercenary agents of the Hindus. They were submitted, during 1945-47, to social terror through appeals to religious fanaticsm and even to physical attacks. Jinnah himself in his presidential address to the League in April 1943 described Khan Abdul Ghaffar Khan as being 'in-charge of the Hinduizing influences and emasculation of the martial Pathans.'[16]

Religion was also now brought into the forefront of propaganda. In 1946, Muslims were asked to vote for the League because 'a vote for the League and Pakistan was a vote for Islam.' League meetings were often held in the mosques after Friday prayers. Pakistan, it was promised, would be ruled under the *Sharia*. Muslims were asked to choose between a mosque and a temple. The Quran was widely used as the League's symbol; and the League's fight with the Congress was portrayed as a fight between Islam and *Kufr* (infidelity).

*

Hindu communalism did not lag behind. Its political trajectory was of course different. The two main liberal communal leaders during the 1920s were Lajpat Rai and Madan Mohan Malaviya. Lajpat Rai died in

1928 and Malaviya, finding himself in 1937 in the sort of situation in which Jinnah found himself in the same year, decided to retire from active politics, partly on grounds of health. But Hindu communalism would also not commit suicide; it too advanced to the extremist or the fascist phase. The logic of communalism brought other communal leaders to the fore. The Hindu Mahasabha made a sharp turn in the fascist direction under V.D. Savarkar's leadership. The RSS (Rashtriya Swayamsevak Sangh) had been from the very beginning organized on fascist lines; it now began to branch out beyond Maharashtra.

Year after year, V.D. Savarkar warned Hindus of the dangers of being dominated by Muslims. He said in 1937 that Muslims 'want to brand the forehead of Hindudom and other non-Muslim sections in Hindustan with a stamp of self-humiliation and Muslim domination' and 'to reduce the Hindus to the position of helots in their own land.'[17] In 1938, he said that 'we Hindus are (already) reduced to be veritable helots throughout our land.'[18]

It was, however, the RSS which became the chief ideologue and propagator of extreme communalism. The head of the RSS, M.S. Golwalkar, codified the RSS doctrines in his booklet, *We*. In 1939, he declared that if the minority demands were accepted, 'Hindu National life runs the risk of being shattered.'[19]. Above all, the RSS attacked Muslims and the Congress leaders. Golwalkar attacked the nationalists for 'hugging to our bosom our most inveterate enemies (Muslims) and thus endangering our very existence.'[20] Condemning the nationalists for spreading the view by which Hindus 'began to class ourselves with our old invaders and foes under the outlandish name — Indian,' he wrote: 'We have allowed ourselves to be duped into believing our foes to be our friends . . . That is the real danger of the day, our self-forgetfulness, our believing our old and bitter enemies to be our friends.'[21] To Muslims and other religious minorities, Golwalkar gave the following advice: 'The non-Hindu peoples in Hindusthan must either adopt the Hindu culture and language, must learn to respect and hold in reverence Hindu religion, must entertain no ideas but those of glorification of the Hindu race and culture, i.e., they must not only give up their attitude of intolerance and ungratefulness towards this land and its age long traditions but must also cultivate the positive attitude of love and devotion instead — in one word, they must cease to be foreigners, or may stay in the country, wholly subordinated to the Hindu nation, claiming nothing, deserving no privileges, far less any preferential treatment — not even citizen's rights.'[22] Going further, he wrote; 'We Hindus are at war at once with the Muslims on the one hand and British on the other.'[23] He said that Italy and Germany were two countries where 'the ancient Race spirit' had 're-risen.' 'Even so with us: our Race spirit has once again roused itself,' thus giving Hindus the right of excommunicating Muslims.[24] The RSS launched an even more vicious attack on the Congress leaders during 1946-47. Provocatively accusing the Congress leaders in the true fascist style of asking Hindus to 'submit meekly to the vandalism and atrocities of the Muslims' and of telling the Hindu 'that he was imbecile, that he had no spirit, no stamina to stand on his own legs and fight for the independence of his motherland and that *all this had to be injected into him in the form of Muslim blood,*', he said in 1947, pointing his finger at Gandhiji: 'Those who declared "No *Swaraj* without Hindu-Muslim unity" have thus perpetrated *the greatest treason on our society.* They have committed the most heinous sin of killing the life-spirit of a great and ancient people.' He accused Gandhiji of having declared:' "There is no *Swaraj* without Hindu-Muslim unity and the simplest way in which this unity can be achieved is for all the Hindus to become Muslims." '[25]

The Hindu communalists also tried to raise the cries of 'Hinduism in danger,' 'Hindu faith in danger,' and 'Hindu culture or *sanskriti* in danger.'

*

The bitter harvest of this campaign of fear and hatred carried on by the Hindu and Muslim communalists since the end of the 19th century, and in particular after 1937, was reaped by the people in the Calcutta killings of August 1946 in which over 5,000 lost their lives within five days, in the butchery of Hindus at Noakhali in Bengal and of Muslims in Bihar, the carnage of the partition riots and the assassination of Gandhiji by a communal fanatic.

But, perhaps, the heaviest cost was paid by Muslims who remained in or migrated to Pakistan. Once Pakistan was formed, Jinnah hoped to go back to liberal communalism or even secularism. Addressing the people of Pakistan, Jinnah said in his Presidential address to the Constituent Assembly of Pakistan on 11 August 1947: 'You may belong to any religion or caste or creed — that has nothing to do with the business of the State . . . We are starting with this fundamental principle that we are all citizens and equal citizens of one State . . . Now, I think we should keep that in front of us as our ideal, and you will find that in course of time Hindus would cease to be Hindus and Muslims would cease to be Muslims, not in the religious sense, because that is the personal faith of each individual, but in the political sense as citizens of the State.'[26] But it was all too late. Jinnah had cynically spawned a monster which not only divided India, but would, in time, eat up his own concept of Pakistan and do more harm to Muslims of Pakistan than the most secular of persons could have predicted or even imagined. On the other hand, despite the formation of Pakistan and the bloody communal riots of 1947, nationalist India did succeed in framing a secular constitution and building a basically secular polity, whatever its weaknesses in this respect may be. In other words, ideologies have consequences.

*

Two major controversies have arisen in the last thirty years or so around the communal problem. One is the view that the communal problem would have disappeared or been solved if Jinnah had been conciliated during 1937-39 and, in particular, if a coaliation government with the Muslim League had been formed in U.P. in 1937. The rebuff to Jinnah's political ambitions, it is said, embittered him and made him turn to separatism.

Let us first look at the general argument. It entirely ignores the fact that before he was 'rebuffed' Jinnah was already a full-fledged liberal communalist. Second, every effort was made by the Congress leaders from 1937 to 1939 to negotiate with Jinnah and to conciliate him. But Jinnah was caught in the logic of communalism. He was left without any negotiable demands which could be rationally put forward and argued. Consequently, and it is very important to remember this historical fact, he refused to tell the Congress leaders what the demands were whose acceptance would satisfy him and lead him to join the Congress in facing imperialism. The impossible condition he laid down to even start negotiations was that the Congress leadership should first renounce its secular character and declare itself a Hindu communal body and accept the Muslim League as the sole representative of the Muslims. The Congress could not have accepted this demand. As Rajendra Prasad put it, for the Congress to accept that it was a Hindu body 'would be denying its own past, falsifying its history, and betraying its future'[27] — in fact, it would be betraying the Indian people and their future. If the Congress had accepted Jinnah's demand and 'conciliated' him, we might well have been living under a Hindu replica of Pakistan or a Hindu fascist state. So no serious negotiations could even begin.

Jinnah, too, all the while, was following the logic of his ideology and politics. But this posture could also not be maintained for long. The move towards Pakistan was then inevitable, for separatism was the only part of the communal ideological programme left unfulfilled. The alternative was to abandon communal politics. And so Jinnah and the Muslim League took the ultimate step in early 1940 and, basing themselves on the theory that Hindus and Muslims were two separate nations which must have separate homelands, put forward the demand for Pakistan. Hindu communalism too had moved in the same direction. Its separatism could not take the form of demanding a part of India as Hindusthan — that would be playing into the hands of Muslim communalism. It, therefore, increasingly asserted that Hindus were the only nation living in India and Muslims should either be expelled from India or live in it as second-class citizens.

Something similar was involved in the U.P. decision of 1937. Jinnah and the League were firmly opposed to mass politics. To have joined hands with them would have meant retreating to constitutional politics in which people had little role to play. Much before the ministerial negotiations occurred or broke down, Jinnah had declared Muslims to be a distinct third party in India, as distinguished from the British and Indian nationalism represented by the Congress. As S. Gopal has put it:'Any coalition with the League implied the Congress accepting a Hindu orientation and renouncing the right to speak for all Indians.'[28] It would have also meant the betrayal of nationalist Muslims, who had firmly taken their stand on the terrain of secular nationalism. Furthermore, it would have meant abandonment of the radical agrarian programme adopted at Faizpur in 1936 to which the Congress Ministry was fully committed, for the League was equally committed to the landlords' interests. With their representatives in the Government, no pro-peasant legislation could possibly have been passed. In fact, it was the Congress Socialists and the Communists, quite important in the U.P. Congress at the time, who put pressure on Nehru to reject any coalition with the League and threatened to launch a public campaign on the issue if their demand was rejected. Interestingly, even before negotiations for the formation of a Congress Ministry in U.P. had begun, the Muslim League had raised the cry of 'Islam in Danger' in its campaign against Congress candidates in the by-elections to U.P. assembly during May 1937. Jinnah himself had issued appeals to voters in the name of Allah and the Quran.

In any case, if a leader could turn into a vicious communalist and separatist because his party was not given two seats in a provincial ministry, then how long could he have remained conciliated? To argue in this fashion is, perhaps, to treat history and politics as a joke or as the play of individual whims. The fact is that communalism is basically an ideology which could not have been, and cannot be, appeased; it had to be confronted and opposed, as we have brought out earlier. The failure to do so was the real weakness of the Congress and the national movement. Interestingly, the Communists did try to appease the Muslim League from 1942 to 1946, hoping to wean away its better elements. They not only failed but in the bargain lost some of their best cadres to Muslim communalism. The effort to have a coalition with it turned out to be a one way street from which the Communists had the wisdom to withdraw in 1946. In fact, the negotiations by the Congress leaders as also the Left were based on the false assumption that liberal communalists could be conciliated and then persuaded to fight extreme communalism which was anti-national. After 1937 it was only the nationalist Hindus and Muslims who firmly opposed communalism. Liberal communalists like Malaviya, Shyama Prasad Mukherjee and N.C. Chatterji failed to oppose Savarkar or the RSS. Similarly, the liberal Iqbal or other liberal communal Muslims did not have the courage to oppose the campaign of hatred that Jinnah, Suleri, Fazl-ul-Huq and others unleashed after 1937. At the most, they kept quiet where they did not join it.

*

It is also not true that the Congress failure regarding communalism occurred in 1947 when it accepted the partition of the country. Perhaps, there was no other option at the time. Communalism had already advanced too far. There was, it can be argued, no other solution to the communal problem left, unless the national leadership was willing to see the nation plunged in a civil war when the armed forces and the police were under the control of the foreign rulers and were themselves ready to join the civil war.

The fact is that not all historical situations have an instant solution. Certainly, no such solution existed in 1947. There is never an instant solution to a socio-political problem like communalism. Conditions and forces for a solution have to be prepared over a number of years and even decades. This the Congress and the national movement failed to do. Despite their commitment to secularism, despite Gandhiji's constant emphasis on Hindu-Muslim unity and his willingness to stake his life for its promotion, and despite Nehru's brilliant analysis of the socio-economic roots of communalism, the Indian nationalists failed to wage a mass ideological-political struggle against all forms of communalism on the basis of patient and scientific exposure of its ideological content, socio-economic roots, and political consequences. In fact, the Congress relied too heavily on negotiations with the communal leaders and failed to evolve a viable and effective long-term strategy to combat communalism at the political, ideological and cultural levels. The Congress and its leadership have to be faulted on this count.

34 The Crisis at Tripuri to the Cripps Mission

The Congress victory in the 1937 election and the consequent formation of popular ministries changed the balance of power within the country vis-a-vis the colonial authorities. The growth of left-wing parties and ideas led to a growing militancy within the nationalist ranks. The stage seemed to be set for another resurgence of the nationalist movement. Just at this time, the Congress had to undergo a crisis at the top — an occurrence which plagued the Congress every few years.

*

Subhas Bose had been a unanimous choice as the President of the Congress in 1938. In 1939, he decided to stand again — this time as the spokesperson of militant politics and radical groups. Putting forward his candidature on 21 January 1939, Bose said that he represented the 'new ideas, ideologies, problems and programmes' that had emerged with 'the progressive sharpening of the anti-imperialist struggle in India.' The presidential elections, he said, should be fought among different candidates 'on the basis of definite problems and programmes.'[1] On 24 January, Sardar Patel, Rajendra Prasad, J.B.Kripalani and four other members of the Congress Working Committee issued a counter statement, declaring that the talk of ideologies, programmes and policies was irrelevant in the elections of a Congress president since these were evolved by the various Congress bodies such as the AICC and the Working Committee, and that the position of the Congress President was like that of a constitutional head who represented and symbolized the unity and solidarity of the nation.[2] With the blessings of Gandhiji, these and other leaders put up Pattabhi Sitaramayya as a candidate for the post. Subhas Bose was elected on 29 January by 1580 votes against 1377. Gandhiji declared that Sitaramayya's defeat was 'more mine than his.'

But the election of Bose resolved nothing, it only brought the brewing crisis to a head at the Tripuri session of the Congress. There were two major reasons for the crisis. One was the line of propaganda adopted by Bose against Sardar Patel and the majority of the top Congress leadership whom he branded as Rightists. He openly accused them of working for a compromise with the Government on the question of federation, of having even drawn up a list of prospective central ministers and therefore of not wanting a leftist as the president of the Congress 'who may be a thorn in the way of a compromise and may put obstacles in the path of negotiations.' He had, therefore, appealed to Congressmen to vote for a leftist and 'a genuine anti-federationist.'[3] In the second part of his autobiography, Subhas put forward his thinking of the period even more crudely: 'As Congress President, the writer did his best to stiffen the opposition of the Congress Party to any compromise with Britain and this caused annoyance in Gandhian circles who were then looking forward to an understanding with the British Government.' The Gandhiists, he wrote, 'did not want to be disturbed in their ministerial and parliamentary work' and 'were at that time opposed to any national struggle.'[4]

The Congress leaders, labelled as compromisers, resented such charges and branded them as a slander. They pointed out in a statement: 'Subhas Babu has mentioned his opposition to the federation. This is shared by all the members of the Working Committee. It is the Congress policy.'[5] After Subhas's election, they felt that they could not work with a president who had publicly cast aspersions on their nationalist bonafides. Twelve of them refused to join the Working Committee. Earlier, Gandhiji had issued a statement on 31 January saying: 'I rejoice in this defeat' because 'Subhas Babu, instead of being President on the sufferance of those whom he calls rightists, is now President elected in a contested election. This enables him to choose a homogeneous cabinet and enforce his programme without let or hindrance.'[6]

Jawaharlal Nehru did not resign along with the twelve other Working Committee members. He did not like the idea of confronting Bose publicly. But he did not agree with Bose either. Before the elections, he had said that in the election no principles or programmes were at stake. He had been unhappy with Bose's aspersions on his colleagues. Nor did he agree that the fight was between the Left and the Right . His letter to Subhas on 4 February 1939 would bear a long quotation:'I do not know who you consider a leftist and who a rightist. The way these words were used by you in your statements during the presidential contest seemed to imply that Gandhiji and those who are considered as his group in the Working Committee are the rightist leaders. Their opponents, whoever they might be, are the leftists. That seems to me an entirely wrong description. It seems to me that many of the so-called leftists are more right than the so-called rightists. Strong language and a capacity to criticize and attack the old Congress leadership is not a test of leftism in politics . . .I think the use of the words left and right has been generally wholly wrong and confusing. If, instead of these words, we talked about policies it would be far better. What policies do you stand for? Anti-federation, well and good. I think that the great majority of the members of the Working Committee stand for that and it is not fair to hint at their weakness in this respect.'7

However, more importantly, basic differences of policy and tactics were involved in the underlying Bose-Gandhi debate. They were partially based on differing perceptions of the political reality, and differing assessments of the strength and weakness of the Congress and the preparedness of the masses for struggle. Differing styles regarding how to build up a mass movement were also involved.

Subhas Bose believed that the Congress was strong enough to launch an immediate struggle and that the masses were ready for such struggle. He was convinced, as he wrote later, 'that the country was internally more ripe for a revolution than ever before and that the coming international crisis would give India an opportunity for achieving her emancipation, which is rare in human history.'8 He, therefore, argued in his presidential address at Tripuri for a programme of immediately giving the British Government a six-months ultimatum to grant the national demand for independence and of launching a mass civil disobedience movement if it failed to do so.9

Gandhiji's perceptions were very different. He, too, believed that another round of mass struggle was necessary to win freedom, for Indians were facing 'an impossible situation.' Already, in the middle of July 1938, he had written: 'The darkness that seems to have enveloped me will disappear, and that, whether with another battle more brilliant than the Dandi March. or without, India will come to her own.'10 But, he believed, the time was not yet ripe for an ultimatum because neither the Congress nor the masses were yet ready for struggle. Indians should first 'put our own house in order.' Making his position clear in an interview on 5 May 1939, Gandhiji declared: 'He (Subhas Bose) holds that we possess enough resources for a fight. I am totally opposed to his views. Today we possess no resources for a fight . . .There is no limit to communal strife . . . We do not have the same hold among the peasants of Bihar as we used to . . .If today I am asked to start the "Dandi March," I have not the courage to do so. How can we do anything without the workers and peasants? The country belongs only to them. I am not equipped to issue an ultimatum to the Government. The country would only be exposed to ridicule.'[11]

Gandhiji's views were above all based on his assessment of the Congress organization. He was convinced that corruption and indiscipline had vitiated its capacity to fight. As we have seen earlier, during 1938 and early 1939, he repeatedly and publicly raised the issues of mutual rivalries and bickerings among Congressmen, bogus membership and impersonation at party elections, efforts to capture Congress Committees, and the general decline of authority in the Congress.

*

The internal strife reached its climax at the Tripuri session of the Congress, held from 8 to 12 March 1939. Bose had completely misjudged his support and the meaning of his majority in the presidential election. Congressmen had voted for him for diverse reasons, and above all because he stood for militant politics, and not because they wanted to have him as the supreme leader of the national movement. They were not willing to reject Gandhiji's leadership or that of other older leaders who decided to bring this home to Subhas. Govind Ballabh Pant moved a resolution at Tripuri expressing full confidence in the old Working Committee, reiterating full faith in Gandhiji's leadership of the movement and the Congress policies of the previous twenty years, and asking Subhas to nominate his Working Committee 'in accordance with the wishes of Gandhiji.' The rsolution was passed by a big majority, but Gandhiji did not approve of the resolution and refused to impose a Working Committee on Subhas. He asked him to nominate a Committee of his own choice.

Subhas Bose refused to take up the challenge. He had placed himself in an impossible situation. He knew that he could not lead the organization on his own, but he was also not willing to accept the leadership of the majority. To place the best construction on his policy, he wanted Gandhiji to be the leader of the coming struggle but he wanted Gandhiji to follow the strategy and tactics laid down by him and the left-wing parties and groups. Gandhiji, on the other hand, would either lead the Congress on the basis of his own strategy and style of politics or surrender the position of the leader. As he wrote to Bose: 'If your prognosis is right, I am a back number and played out as the generalissimo of *satyagraha*.'[12] In other words, as Rajendra Prasad later wrote in his *Autobiography*, Gandhiji and the older leaders would not accept a situation where the strategy and tactics were not theirs but the responsibility for implementing them would be theirs.[13]

Bose could see no other way out but to resign from the presidentship. Nehru tried to mediate between the two sides and persuade Bose not to resign, while asking Gandhiji and the older leaders to be more accommodative. But Bose would not resile from his position. On the one hand, he insisted that the Working Committee should be representative of the new radical trends and groups which had elected him, on the other, he would not nominate his own Working Committee. He preferred to press his resignation. This led to the election of Rajendra Prasad in his place. The Congress had weathered another storm.

Bose could also not get the support of the Congress Socialists and the Communists at Tripuri or after for they were not willing to divide the national movement and felt that its unity must be preserved at all costs. Explaining its position, the CPI declared after Tripuri that the interests of the anti-imperialist struggle 'demanded not the exclusive leadership of one wing but a united leadership under the guidance of Gandhiji.'[14] P.C. Joshi, General Secratary of the CPI, wrote in April 1939 that 'the greatest class struggle today is our national struggle,' that the Congress was the main organ of this struggle, and that the preservation of its unity was a primary task.[15]

Subsequently, in May, Subhas Bose and his followers formed the Forward Bloc as a new party within the Congress. And when he gave a call for an all-India protest on 9 July against an AICC resolution, the Working Committee took disciplinary action against him, removing him from the presidentship of the Bengal Provincial Congress Commitee and debarring him from holding any Congress office for three years.

*

World War II broke out on 1 September 1939 when Nazi Germany invaded Poland. Earlier Germany had occupied Austria in March 1938 and Czechoslovakia in 1939. Britain and France, which had been following a policy of appeasement towards Hitler, were now forced to go to Poland's aid and declare war on Germany. This they did on 3 September 1939. The Government of India immediately declared India to be at war with Germany without consulting the Congress or the elected members of the central legislature.

The Congress, as we have seen earlier, was in full sympathy with the victims of fascist aggression, and its immediate reaction was to go to the aid of the anti-fascist forces. Gandhiji's reaction was highly emotinal. He told the Viceroy that the very thought of the possible destruction of the House of Parliament and Westminster Abbey produced a strong emotional reaction in him and that, fully sympathizing with the Allied cause, he was for full and unquestioning cooperation with Britain. But a question most of the Congress leaders asked was — how was it possible for an enslaved nation to aid others in their fight for freedom? The official Congress stand was adopted at a meeting of the Congress Working Committee held at Wardha from 10 to 14 September to which, in keeping with the nationalist tradition of accommodating diversity of opinion, Subhas Bose, Acharya Narendra Dev, and Jayaprakash Narayan were also invited. Sharp differences emerged in this meeting. Gandhiji was for taking a sympathetic view of the Allies. He believed that there was a clear difference between the democratic states of Western Europe and the totalitarian Nazi state headed by Hitler. The Socialists and Subhas Bose argued that the War was an imperialist one since both sides were fighting for gaining or defending colonial territories. Therefore, the question of supporting either of the two sides did not arise. Instead the Congress should take advantage of the situation to wrest freedom by immediately starting a civil disobedience movement.

Jawaharlal Nehru had a stand of his own. He had been for several years warning the world against the dangers of Nazi aggression, and he made a sharp distinction between democracy and Fascism. He believed that justice was on the side of Britain, France and Poland. But he was also convinced that Britain and France were imperialist countries and that the War was the result of the inner contradictions of capitalism maturing since the end of World War I. He, therefore, argued that India should neither join the War till she herself gained freedom nor take advantage of Britain's difficulties by starting an immediate struggle. Gandhiji found that his position was not supported by even his close followers such as Sardar Patel and Rajendra Prasad. Consequently, he decided to support Nehru's position which was then adopted by the Working Committee. Its resolution, while unequivocally condemning the Nazi attack on Poland as well as Nazism and Fascism, declared that India could not be party to a war which was ostensibly being fought for democratic freedom while that freedom was being denied to her. If Britain was fighting for democracy and freedom, she should prove this by ending imperialism in the colonies and establishing full democracy in India. In particular, she should declare how her war aims would be implemented in India at the end of the War. Indians would then gladly join other democratic nations in the war effort of starting a mass struggle, but it warned that the decision could not be delayed for long. As Nehru put it, the Congress leadership wanted 'to give every chance to the Viceroy and the British Government.'

The British Government's response was entirely negative. Linlithgow, the Viceroy, in his well considered statement of 17 October 1939 harped on the differences among Indians, tried to use the Muslim League and the Princes against the Congress, and refused to define Britain's war aims beyond stating that Britain was resisting aggression. As an immediate measure, he offered to set up a consultative committee whose advice might be sought by the Government whenever it felt it necessary to do so. For the future, the promise was that at the end of the War the British Government would enter into consultations with 'representatives of several communities, parties, and interests in India, and with the Indian princes' as to how the Act of 1935 might be modified. In a private communication to Zetland, the Secretary of State, Linlithgow was to remark a few months later: 'I am not too keen to start talking about a period after which British rule will have ceased in India. I suspect that that day is very remote and I feel the least we say about it in all probability the better.'[16] On 18 October, Zetland spoke in the House of Lords and stressed differences among Indians, especially among Hindus and Muslims. He branded the Congress as a purely Hindu organization.[17] It, thus, became clear that the British Government had no intention of loosening their hold on India during or after the War and that it was willing, if necessary, to treat the Congress as an enemy.

The reaction of the Indian people and the national leadership was sharp. The angriest reaction came from Gandhiji who had been advocating more or less unconditional support to Britain. Pointing out that the British Government was continuing to pursue 'the old policy of divide and rule,' he said: 'The Indian declaration (of the Viceroy) shows clearly that there is to be no democracy for India if Britain can prevent it . . . The Congress asked for bread and it has got a stone.' Referring to the question of minorities and special interests such as those of the princes, foreign capitalists, *zamindars*, etc., Gandhiji remarked: 'The Congress will safeguard the rights of every minority so long as they do not advance claims inconsistent with India's independence.' But, he added, 'independent India will not tolerate any interests in conflict with the true interests of the masses.'[18]

The Working Committee, meeting on 23 October, rejected the Viceregal statement as a reiteration of the old imperialist policy, decided not to support the War, and called upon the Congress ministries to resign as a protest. This they did as disciplined soldiers of the national movement. But the Congress leadership still stayed its hand and was reluctant to give a call for an immediate and a massive anti-imperialist struggle. In fact, the Working Committee resolution of 23 October warned Congressmen against any hasty action.

*

While there was agreement among Congressmen on the question of attitude to the War and the resignation of the ministries, sharp differences developed over the question of the immediate starting of a mass *satyagraha*. Gandhiji and the dominant leadership advanced three broad reasons for not initiating an immediate movement. First, they felt that since the cause of the Allies — Britain and France — was just, they should not be embarrassed in the prosecution of the War. Second, the lack of Hindu-Muslim unity was a big barrier to a struggle. In the existing atmosphere any civil disobedience movement could easily degenerate into communal rioting or even civil war. Above all, they felt that there did not exist in the country an atmosphere for an immediate struggle. Neither the masses were ready nor was the Congress organizationally in a position to launch a struggle. The Congress organization was weak and had been corrupted during 1938-39. There was indiscipline and lack of cohesion within the Congress ranks. Under these circumstances, a mass movement would not be able to withstand severe repressive measures by the Government. It was, therefore, necessary to carry on intense political work among the people, to prepare them for struggle, to tone up the Congress organization and purge it of weaknesses, to negotiate with authorities till all the possibilities of a negotiated settlement were exhausted and the Government was clearly seen by all to be in the wrong. The time for launching a struggle would come when the people were strong and ready for struggle, the Congress organization had been put on a sound footing, and the Government took such aggressive action that the people felt the absolute necessity of going into mass action. This view was summed up in the resolution placed by the Working Committee before the Ramgarh Session of the Congress in March 1940. The resolution, after reiterating the Congress position on the War and asserting that 'nothing short of complete independence can be accepted by the people,' declared that the Congress would resort to civil disobedience 'as soon as the Congress organization is considered fit enough for the purpose, or in case circumstances so shape themselves as to precipitate a crisis.'[19]

An alternative to the position of the dominant leadership came from a coalition of various left-wing groups: Subhas Bose and his Forward Bloc, the Congress Socialist Party, the Communist Party, the Royists, etc. The Left characterized the War as an imperialist war and asserted that the war-crisis provided an opportunity to achieve freedom through an all-out struggle against British imperialism. It was convinced that the masses were fully ready for action and were only waiting for a call from the leadership. They accepted that hurdles like the communal problem and weaknesses in the Congress organization existed; but they were convinced that these would be easily and automatically swept away once a mass struggle was begun. Organizational strength, they said, was not to be built up prior to a struggle but in the course of the struggle. Making a sharp critique of the Congress leadership's policy of 'wait and see,' the Left accused the leadership of being afraid of the masses, of having lost the zest for struggle, and consequently of trying to bargain and compromise with imperialism for securing petty concessions. They urged the Congress leadership to adopt immediate measures to launch a mass struggle.

While agreeing on the need for an immediate struggle, the Left was internally divided both in its understanding of political forces and on the course of political action in case the dominant leadership of the Congress did not accept the line of immediate struggle. Subhas Bose wanted the Left to split the Congress if it did not launch a struggle, to organize a parallel Congress and to start a struggle on its own. He was convinced that the masses and the overwhelming majority of Congress would support the Left-led parallel Congress and join the movement it would launch. The CSP and the CPI differed from this view. They were convinced that Bose was grossly overestimating the influence of the Left and no struggle could be launched without the leadership of Gandhiji and the Congress. Therefore an attempt should be made not to split the Congress and thus disrupt the 'national united front' but persuade and pressurize its leadership to launch a struggle.

Jawaharlal Nehru's was an ambivalent position. On the one hand, he could clearly see the imperialistic character of the Allied countries, on the other, he would do nothing that might lead to the triumph of Hitler and the Nazis in Europe. His entire personality and political thinking led to the line of an early commencement of civil disobedience, but he would do nothing that would imperil the anti-Nazi struggle in Europe and the Chinese people's struggle against Japanese aggression. In the end, however, the dilemma was resolved by Nehru going along with Gandhiji and the majority of the Congress leadership.

*

But politics could not go on on this placid note for too long. The patience of both the Congress leadership and the masses was getting exhausted. The Government refused to budge and took up the position that no constitutional advance could be made till the Congress came to an agreement with the Muslim communalists. It kept issuing ordinance after ordinance taking away the freedom of speech and the Press and the right to organize associations. Nationalist workers, especially those belonging to the left-wing, were harassed, arrested and imprisoned all over the country. The Government was getting ready to crush the Congress if it took any steps towards a mass struggle.

In this situation, the Indians felt that the time had come to show the British that their patience was not the result of weakness. As Nehru put it in an article entitled 'The Parting of the Ways,' the British rulers believed that 'in this world of force, of bombing aeroplanes, tanks, and armed men how weak we are! Why trouble about us? But perhaps, even in this world of armed conflict, there is such a thing as the spirit of man, and the spirit of a nation, which is neither ignoble nor weak, and which may not be ignored, save at peril.'[20] Near the end of 1940, the Congress once again asked Gandhiji to take command. Gandhiji now began to take steps which would lead to a mass struggle within his broad strategic perspective. He decided to initiate a limited *satyagraha* on an individual basis by a few selected individuals in every locality. The demand of a *satyagrahi* would be for the freedom of speech to preach against participation in the War. The *satyagrahi* would publicly declare: 'It is wrong to help the British war-effort with men or money. The only worthy effort is to resist all war with non-violent resistance.' The *satyagrahi* would beforehand inform the district magistrate of the time and place where he or she was going to make the anti-war speech. The carefully chosen *satyagrahis* — Vinoba Bhave was to be the first *satyagrahi* on 17 October 1940 and Jawaharlal Nehru the second — were surrounded by huge crowds when they appeared on the platform, and the authorities could often arrest them only after they had made their speeches. And if the Government did not arrest a *satyagrahi*, he or she would not only repeat the performance but move into the villages and start a trek towards Delhi, thus participating in a movement that came to be known as the *'Delhi Chalo'* (onwards to Delhi) movement.

The aims of the Individual *Satyagraha* conducted, as S.Gopal has put it, 'at a low temperature and in very small doses'[21] were explained as follows by Gandhiji in a letter to the Viceroy: 'The Congress is as much opposed to victory for Nazism as any Britisher can be. But their objective cannot be carried to the extent of their participation in the war. And since you and the Secretary of State for India have declared that the whole of India is voluntarily helping the war effort, it becomes necessary to make clear that the vast majority of the people of India are not interested in it. They make no distinction between Nazism and the double autocracy that rules India.'[22]

Thus, the Individual *Satyagraha* had a dual purpose — while giving expression to the Indian people's strong political feeling, it gave the British Government further opportunity to peacefully accept the Indian demands. Gandhiji and the Congress were, because of their anti-Nazi feelings, still reluctant to take advantage of the British predicament and embarrass her war effort by a mass upheaval in India. More importantly, Gandhiji was beginning to prepare the people for the coming struggle. The Congress organization was being put back in shape; opportunist elements were being discovered and pushed out of the organization; and above all the people were being politically aroused, educated and mobilized.

By 15 May 1941, more than 25,000 *satyagrahis* had been convicted for offering individual civil disobedience. Many more — lower level political workers — had been left free by the Government.

*

Two major changes in British politics occurred during 1941. Nazi Germany had already occupied Poland, Belgium, Holland, Norway and France as well as most of Eastern Europe. It attacked the Soviet Union on 22 June 1941. In the East, Japan launched a surprise attack on the American fleet at Pearl Harbour on 7 December. It quickly overran the Phillipines, Indo-China, Indonesia, Malaysia and Burma. It occupied Rangoon in March 1942. War was brought to India's doorstep. Winston Churchill, now the British Prime Minister, told the King that Burma, Ceylon, Calcutta and Madras might fall into enemy hands.

The Indian leaders, released from prisons in early December, were worried about the safety and defence of India. They also had immense concern for the Soviet Union and China. Many felt that Hitler's attack on the Soviet Union had changed the character of the War. Gandhiji had earlier denounced the Japanese slogan of 'Asia for Asiatics' and asked the people of India to boycott Japanese products. Anxious to defend Indian territory and to go to the aid of the Allies, the Congress Working Committee overrode the objections of Gandhiji and Nehru and passed a resolution at the end of December offering to fully cooperate in the defence of India and the Allies if Britain agreed to give full independence after the War and the substance of power immediately. It was at this time that Gandhiji designated Jawaharlal as his chosen successor. Speaking before the AICC on 15 January 1941, he said : 'Somebody suggested that Pandit Jawaharlal and I were estranged. It will require much more than differences of opinion to estrange us. We have had differences from the moment we became co-workers, and yet I have said for some years and say now that not Rajaji (C.Rajagopalachari) but Jawaharlal will be my successor. He says that he does not understand my language, and that he speaks a language foreign to me. This may or may not be true. But language is no bar to a union of hearts. And I know this that when I am gone he will speak my language.'23

*

As the war situation worsened, President Roosevelt of the USA and President Chiang Kai-Shek of China as also the Labour Party leaders of Britain put pressure on Churchill to seek the active cooperation of Indians in the War. To secure this cooperation the British Government sent to India in March 1942 a mission headed by a Cabinet minister Stafford Cripps, a left-wing Labourite who had earlier actively supported the Indian national movement. Even though Cripps announced that the aim of British policy in India was 'the earliest possible realization of self-government in India,' the Draft Declaration he brought with him was disappointing. The Declaration promised India Dominion Status and a constitution-making body after the War whose members would be elected by the provincial assemblies and nominated by the rulers in case of the princely states. The Pakistan demand was accommodated by the provision that any province which was not prepared to accept the new constitution would have the right to sign a separate agreement with Britain regarding its future status. For the present the British would continue to exercise sole control over the defence of the country. Amery, the Secretary of State, described the Declaration as in essence a conservative, reactionary and limited offer.24 Nehru, a friend of Cripps, was to write later: 'When I read those proposals for the first time I was profoundly depressed.'25

Negotiations between Cripps and the Congress leaders broke down. The Congress objected to the provision for Dominion Status rather than full independence, the representation of the princely states in the constituent assembly not by the people of the states but by the nominees of the rulers, and above all by the provision for the partition of India. The British Government also refused to accept the demand for the immediate transfer of effective power to the Indians and for a real share in the responsibility for the defence of India. An important reason for the failure of the negotiations was the incapacity of Cripps to bargain and negotiate. He had been told not to go beyond the Draft Declaration. Moreover, Churchill, the Secretary of State, Amery, the Viceroy, Linlithgow, and the Commander-in-Chief, Wavell, did not want Cripps to succeed and constantly opposed and sabotaged his efforts to accommodate Indian opinion. Stafford Cripps returned home in the middle of April leaving behind a frustrated and embittered Indian people. Though they still sympathized with the anti-fascist forces, especially the people of China and the Soviet people, they felt that the existing situation in the country had become intolerable. The time had come, they felt, for a final assault on imperialism. xisting situation in the country had become intolerable. The time had come, they felt, for a final assault on imperialism.

'Quit India,' 'Bharat Choro'. This simple but powerful slogan launched the legendary struggle which also became famous by the name of the 'August Revolution.' In this struggle, the common people of the country demonstrated an unparalleled heroism and militancy. Moreover, the repression that they faced was the most brutal that had ever been used against the national movement. The circumstances in which the resistance was offered were also the most adverse faced by the national movement until then — using the justification of the war effort, the Government had armed itself with draconian measures, and suppressed even basic civil liberties. Virtually any political activity, however peaceful and 'legal,' was at this time an illegal and revolutionary activity.

Why had it become necessary to launch a movement in these difficult conditions, when the possibility of brutal repression was a certainty?

*

For one, the failure of the Cripps Mission in April 1942 made it clear that Britain was unwilling to offer an honourable settlement and a real constitutional advance during the War, and that she was determined to continue India's unwilling partnership in the War effort. The empty gesture of the 'Cripps offer' convinced even those Congressmen like Nehru and Gandhiji, who did not want to do anything to hamper the anti-fascist War effort (and who had played a major role in keeping in check those who had been spoiling for a fight since 1939), that any further silence would be tantamount to accepting the right of the British

Government to decide India's fate without any reference to the wishes of her people. Gandhiji had been as clear as Nehru that he did not want to hamper the anti-fascist struggle, especially that of the Russian and Chinese people. But by the spring of 1942 he was becoming increasingly convinced of the inevitability of a struggle. A fortnight after Cripps' departure, Gandhiji drafted a resolution for the Congress Working Committee calling for Britain's withdrawal and the adoption of non-violent non-cooperation against any Japanese invasion. Congress edged towards Quit India while Britain moved towards arming herself with special powers to meet the threat. Nehru remained opposed to the idea of a struggle right till August 1942 and gave way only at the very end.[1]

Apart from British obduracy, there were other factors that made a struggle both inevitable and necessary. Popular discontent, a product of rising prices and war-time shortages, was gradually mounting. High-handed government actions such as the commandeering of boats in Bengal and Orissa to prevent their being used by the Japanese had led to considerable anger among the people.

The popular willingness to give expression to this discontent was enhanced by the growing feeling of an imminent British collapse. The news of Allied reverses and British withdrawals from South-East Asia and Burma and the trains bringing wounded soldiers from the Assam-Burma border confirmed this feeling.

Combined with this was the impact of the manner of the British evacuation from Malaya and Burma. It was common knowledge that the British had evacuated the white residents and generally left the subject people to their fate. Letters from Indians in South-East Asia to their relatives in India were full of graphic accounts of British betrayal and their being left at the mercy of the dreaded Japanese. Was it not only to be expected that they would repeat the performance in India, in the event of a Japanese occupation? In fact, one major reason for the leadership of the national movement thinking it necessary to launch a struggle was their feeling that the people were becoming demoralized and, that in the event of a Japanese occupation, might not resist at all. In order to build up their capacity to resist Japanese aggression, it was necessary to draw them out of this demoralized state of mind and convince them of their own power. Gandhiji, as always, was particularly clear on this aspect.

The popular faith in the stability of British rule had reached such a low that there was a run on the banks and people withdrew deposits from post-office savings accounts and started hoarding gold, silver and coins. This was particularly marked in East U.P and Bihar, but it also took place in Madras Presidency.

So convinced was Gandhiji that the time was now ripe for struggle that he said to Louis Fischer in an interview in the beginning of June: 'I have become impatient . . . I may not be able to convince the Congress . . . I will go ahead nevertheless and address myself directly to the people.'[2] He did not have to carry out his threat and, as before, the Congress accepted the Mahatma's expert advice on the timing of a mass struggle.

*

Though Gandhiji himself had begun to talk of the coming struggle for some time now, it was at the Working Committee meeting at Wardha on 14 July, 1942 that the Congress first accepted the idea of a struggle. The All-India Congress Committee was then to meet in Bombay in August to ratify this decision.

The historic August meeting at Gowalia Tank in Bombay was unprecedented in the popular enthusiasm it generated. Huge crowds waited outside as the leaders deliberated on the issue. And the feeling of anticipation and expectation ran so high that in the open session, when the leaders made their speeches before the many thousands who had collected to hear them, there was pin-drop silence.

Gandhiji's speech,[3] delivered in his usual quiet and unrhetorical style, recount many who were in the audience, had the most electrifying impact. He first made it clear that 'the actual struggle does not commence this moment. You have only placed all your powers in my hands. I will now wait upon the Viceroy and plead with him for the acceptance of the Congress demand. That process is likely to take two or three weeks.' But, he added: 'you may take it from me that I am not going to strike a bargain with the Viceroy for ministries and the like. I am not going to be satisfied with anything short of complete freedom. Maybe, he will propose the abolition of salt tax, the drink evil, etc. But I will say: "Nothing less than freedom."' He followed this up with the now famous exhortation: 'Do or Die.' To quote: 'Here is a *mantra*, a short one, that I give you. You may imprint it on your hearts and let every breath of yours give expression to it. The *mantra* is: "Do or Die."

We shall either free India or die in the attempt; we shall not live to see the perpetuation of our slavery.'

Gandhiji's speech also contained specific instructions for different sections of the people. Government servants would not yet be asked to resign, but they should openly declare their allegiance to the Congress, soldiers were also not to leave their posts, but they were to 'refuse to fire on our own people.' The Princes were asked to 'accept the sovereignty of your own people,' 'instead of paying homage to a foreign power.' And the people of the Princely States were asked to declare that they '(were) part of the Indian nation and that they (would) accept the leadership of the Princes, if the latter cast their lot with the People, but not otherwise.' Students were to give up studies if they were sure they could continue to remain firm till independence was achieved. On 7 August, Gandhiji had placed the instructions he had drafted before the Working Committee, and in these he had proposed that peasants 'who have the courage, and are prepared to risk their all' should refuse to pay the land revenue. Tenants were told that 'the Congress holds that the land belongs to those who work on it and to no one else.' 'Where the *zamindari* system prevails ... if the *zamindar* makes common cause with the ryot, his portion of the revenue, which may be settled by mutual agreement, should be given to him. But if a *zamindar* wants to side with the Government, no tax should be paid to him.'4 These instructions were not actually issued because of the preventive arrests, but they do make Gandhiji's intentions clear.

*

The Government, however, was in no mood to either negotiate with the Congress or wait for the movement to be formally launched. In the early hours of 9 August, in a single sweep, all the top leaders of the Congress were arrested and taken to unknown destinations. The Government had been preparing for the strike since the outbreak of the War itself, and since 1940 had been ready with an elaborate Revolutionary Movements Ordinance. On 8 August, 1940, the Viceroy, Linlithgow, in a personal letter to the Governors made his intentions clear: 'I feel very strongly that the only possible answer to a 'declaration of war' by any section of Congress in the present circumstances must be a declared determination to crush the organization as a whole.'5 For two years, Gandhiji had avoided walking into the trap set for him by refusing to make a rash and premature strike and had carefully built up the tempo through the Individual Civil Disobedience Movement, organizational revamping and a consistent propaganda campaign. But now, the Government was unwilling to allow him any more time to pursue his strategy. In anticipation of the A.I.C.C's passing the Quit India resolution, instructions for arrests and suppression had gone out to the provinces.

The sudden attack by the Government produced an instantaneous reaction among the people. In Bombay, as soon as the news of arrests spread, lakhs of people flocked to Gowalia Tank where a mass meeting had been scheduled and there were clashes with the authorities. There were similar disturbances on 9 August in Ahmedabad and Poona. On the 10th, Delhi and many towns in U.P. and Bihar, including Kanpur, Allahabad, Varanasi and Patna followed suit with *hartals*, public demonstrations and processions in defiance of the law. The Government responded by gagging the press. The *National Herald* and *Harijan* ceased publication for the entire duration of the struggle, others for shorter periods.

Meanwhile, many provincial and local level leaders who had evaded arrest returned to their homes through devious routes and set about organizing resistance. As the news spread further in the rural areas, the villagers joined the townsmen in recording their protest. For the first six or seven weeks after 9 August, there was a tremendous mass upsurge all over the country. People devised a variety of ways of expressing their anger. In some places, huge crowds attacked police stations, post offices, *kutcheries* (courts), railway stations and other symbols of government authority. National flags were forcibly hoisted on public buildings in defiance of the police. At other places, groups of *satyagrahis* offered arrest in *tehsil* or district headquarters. Crowds of villagers, often numbering a few hundred or even a couple of thousand, physically removed railway tracks. Elsewhere, small groups of individuals blew up bridges and removed tracks, and cut telephone and telegraph wires. Students went on strike in schools and colleges all over the country and busied themselves taking out processions, writing and distributing illegal news-sheets: hundreds of these '*patrikas*' came out all over the country. They also became couriers for the emerging underground networks. Workers too struck work: in Ahmedabad, the mills were closed for three and a half months, workers in Bombay stayed away from work for over a week following the 9 August arrests, in Jamshedpur there was a strike for thirteen days and workers in

Ahmednagar and Poona were active for several months.

The reaction to the arrests was most intense in Bihar and Eastern U.P., where the movement attained the proportions of a rebellion. From about the middle of August, the news reached the rural areas through students and other political activists who fanned out from the towns. Students of the Banaras Hindu University decided to go to the villages to spread the message of Quit India. They raised slogans of 'Thana jalao' (Burn the police station), 'Station phoonk do' (Burn the railway stations) 'Angrez bhag gaya' (Englishmen have fled). They hijacked trains and draped them in national flags. In rural areas, the pattern was of large crowds of peasants descending on the nearest tehsil or district town and attacking all symbols of government authority. There was government firing and repression, but the rebellion only gathered in momentum. For two weeks, Tirhut division in Bihar was totally cut off from the rest of the country and no Government authority existed. Control was lost over Patna for two days after firing at the Secretariat. Eighty percent of the police stations were captured or temporarily evacuated in ten districts of North and Central Bihar. There were also physical attacks on Europeans. At Fatwa, near Patna, two R.A.F. officers were killed by a crowd at the railway station and their bodies paraded through the town. In Monghyr, the crews of two R.A.F. planes that crashed at Pasraha on 18 August and Ruihar on 30 August were killed by villagers. Particularly important centres of resistance in this phase were Azamgarh, Ballia and Gorakhpur in East U.P. and Gaya, Bhagalpur, Saran, Purnea, Shahabad, Muzaffarpur and Champaran in Bihar.

According to official estimates, in the first week after the arrests of the leaders, 250 railway stations were damaged or destroyed, and over 500 post offices and 150 police stations were attacked. The movement of trains in Bihar and Eastern U.P. was disrupted for many weeks. In Karnataka alone, there were 1600 incidents of cutting of telegraph lines, and twenty-six railway stations and thirty-two post offices were attacked. Unarmed crowds faced police and military firing on 538 occasions and they were also machine-gunned by low-flying aircraft. Repression also took the form of taking hostages from the villages, imposing collective fines running to a total of Rs.90 lakhs (which were often realized on the spot by looting the people's belongings), whipping of suspects and burning of entire villages whose inhabitants had run away and could not be caught. By the end of 1942, over 60,000 persons had been arrested. Twenty-six thousand people were convicted and 18,000 detained under the Defence of India Rules. Martial law had not been proclaimed, but the army, though nominally working under the orders of the civilian authorities, often did what it wanted to without any reference to the district officers. The repression was as severe as it could have been under martial law.

*

The brutal and all-out repression succeeded within a period of six or seven weeks in bringing about a cessation of the mass phase of the struggle. But in the meantime, underground networks were being consolidated in various parts of the country. An all-India underground leadership with prominent members such as Achyut Patwardhan, Aruna Asaf Ali, Ram Manohar Lohia, Sucheta Kripalani, Chhotubhai Puranik, Biju Patnaik, R.P. Goenka and later, after his escape from jail, Jayaprakash Narayan had also begun to emerge. This leadership saw the role of the underground movement as being that of keeping up popular morale by continuing to provide a line of command and a source of guidance and leadership to activists all over the country. They also collected and distributed money as well as material like bombs, arms, and dynamite to underground groups all over the country. They, however, did not see their role as that of directing the exact pattern of activities at the local level. Here, the local groups retained the initiative. Among the places in which local underground organizations were active were Bombay, Poona, Satara, Baroda and other parts of Gujarat, Karnataka, Kerala, Andhra, U.P., Bihar and Delhi. Congress Socialists were generally in the lead, but also active were Gandhian ashramites, Forward Bloc members and revolutionary terrorists, as well as other Congressmen.

Those actually involved in the underground activity may have been few but they received all manner of support from a large variety of people. Businessmen donated generously. Sumati Morarjee, who later became India's leading woman industrialist, for example, helped Achyut Patwardhan to evade detection by providing him with a different car every day borrowed from her unsuspecting wealthy friends. Others provided hide-outs for the underground leaders and activists. Students acted as couriers. Simple villagers helped by refusing information to the police. Pilots and train drivers delivered bombs and other material across the country. Government officials, including those in police, passed on crucial information about impending arrests. Achyut Patwardhan testifies that one member of the three-man high level official committee formed to track down the Congress underground regularly informed him of the goings on in that committee.[6]

The pattern of activity of the underground movement was generally that of organizing the disruption of communications by blowing up bridges, cutting telegraph and telephone wires and derailing trains. There were also a few attacks on government and police officials and police informers. Their success in actually disrupting communications may not have been more than that of having nuisance value, but they did succeed in keeping up the spirit of the people in a situation when open mass activity was impossible because of the superior armed might of the state. Dissemination of news was a very important part of the activity, and considerable success was achieved on this score, the most dramatic being the Congress Radio operated clandestinely from different locations in Bombay city, whose broadcasts could be heard as far as Madras. Ram Manohar Lohia regularly broadcast on this radio, and the radio continued till November 1942 when it was discovered and confiscated by the police.[7]

*

In February 1943, a striking new development provided a new burst of political activity. Gandhiji commenced a fast on 10 February in jail. He declared the fast would last for twenty-one days. This was his answer to the Government which had been constantly exhorting him to condemn the violence of the people in the Quit India Movement. Gandhiji not only refused to condemn the people's resort to violence but unequivocally held the Government responsible for it. It was the 'leonine violence' of the state which had provoked the people, he said. And it was against this violence of the state, which included the unwarranted detention of thousands of Congressmen, that Gandhiji vowed to register his protest, in the only way open to him when in jail, by fasting.[8]

The popular response to the news of the fast was immediate and overwhelming.[9] All over the country, there were *hartals*, demonstrations and strikes. Calcutta and Ahmedabad were particularly active. Prisoners in jails and those outside went on sympathetic fasts. Groups of people secretly reached Poona to offer *satyagraha* outside the Aga Khan Palace where Gandhiji was being held in detention. Public meetings demanded his release and the Government was bombarded with thousands of letters and telegrams from people from all walks of life—students and youth, men of trade and commerce, lawyers, ordinary citizens, and labour organizations. From across the seas, the demand for his release was made by newspapers such as the *Manchester Guardian, New Statesmen, Nation, News Chronicle, Chicago Sun,* as well as by the British Communist Party, the citizens of London and Manchester, the Women's International League, the Australian Council of Trade Unions and the Ceylon State Council. The U.S. Government, too, brought pressure to bear.

A Leaders' Conference was held in Delhi on 19-20 February and was attended by prominent men, politicians and public figures. They all demanded Gandhiji's release. Many of those otherwise unsympathetic to the Congress felt that the Government was going too far in its obduracy. The severest blow to the prestige of the Government was the resignation of the three Indian members of the Viceroy's Executive Council, M.S. Aney, N.R. Sarkar and H.P. Mody, who had supported the Government in its suppression of the 1942 movement, but were in no mood to be a party to Gandhiji's death.

But the Viceroy and his officials remained unmoved. Guided by Winston Churchill's statement to his Cabinet that 'this our hour of triumph everywhere in the world was not the time to crawl before a miserable old man who had always been our enemy,'[10] they arrogantly refused to show any concern for Indian feeling. The Viceroy contemptuously dismissed the consequences of Gandhiji's possible death: 'Six months unpleasantness, steadily declining in volume, little or nothing at the end of it.' He even made it sound as if he welcomed the possibility: 'India would be far more reliable as a base for operations. Moreover, the prospect of a settlement will be greatly enhanced by the disappearance of Gandhi, who had for years torpedoed every attempt at a settlement.'[11]

While an anxious nation appealed for his life, the Government went ahead with finalizing arrangements for his funeral. Military troops were asked to stand by for any emergency. 'Generous' provision was made for a plane to carry his ashes and for a public funeral and a half-day holiday in offices.[12] But Gandhiji, as always, got the better of his opponents, and refused to oblige by dying.

The fast had done exactly what it had been intended to do. The public morale was raised, the anti-British feeling heightened, and an opportunity for political activity provided. A symbolic gesture of resistance had sparked off widespread resistance and exposed the Government's high-handedness to the whole world. The moral justification that the Government had been trying to provide for its brutal suppression of 1942 was denied to it and it was placed clearly in the wrong.

*

A significant feature of the Quit India movement was the emergence of what came to be known as parallel governments in some parts of the country. The first one was proclaimed in Ballia, in East U.P., in August 1942 under the leadership of Chittu Pande, who called himself a Gandhian. Though it succeeded in getting the Collector to hand over power and release all the arrested Congress leaders, it could not survive for long and when the soldiers marched in, a week after the parallel government was formed, they found that the leaders had fled.[13]

In Tamluk in the Midnapur district of Bengal, the *Jatiya Sarkar* came into existence on 17 December, 1942 and lasted till September 1944. Tamluk was an area where Gandhian constructive work had made considerable headway and it was also the scene of earlier mass struggles. The *Jatiya Sarkar* undertook cyclone relief work, gave grants to schools and organized an armed *Vidyut Vahini*. It also set up arbitration courts and distributed the surplus paddy of the well-to-do to the poor. Being located in a relatively remote area, it could continue its activities with comparative ease.[14]

Satara, in Maharashtra, emerged as the base of the longest-lasting and effective parallel government. From the very beginning of the Quit India movement, the region played an active role. In the first phase from August 1942, there were marches on local government headquarters, the ones on Karad, Tasgaon and Islampur involving thousands. This was followed by sabotage, attacks on post offices, the looting of banks and the cutting of telegraph wires. Y.B. Chavan, who had contacts with Achyut Patwardhan and other underground leaders, was the most important leader. But by the end of 1942, this phase came to an end with the arrest of about two thousand people. From the beginning of 1943, the underground activists began to regroup, and by the middle of the year, succeeded in consolidating the organization. A parallel government or *Prati Sarkar* was set up and Nana Patil was its most important leader. This phase was marked by attacks on Government collaborators, informers and *talatis* or lower-level officials and Robin Hood-style robberies. *Nyayadan Mandals* or people's courts were set up and justice dispensed. Prohibition was enforced, and 'Gandhi marriages' celebrated to which untouchables were invited and at which no ostentation was allowed. Village libraries were set up and education encouraged. The native state of Aundh, whose ruler was pro-nationalist and had got the constitution of his state drafted by Gandhiji, provided invaluable support by offering refuge and shelter to the *Prati Sarkar* activists. The *Prati Sarkar* continued to function till 1945.[15]

The Quit India Movement marked a new high in terms of popular participation in the national movement and sympathy with the national cause. As in earlier mass struggles, the youth were in the forefront of the struggle. Students from colleges and even schools were the most visible element, especially in the early days of August (probably the average age of participants in the 1942 struggle was even lower than that in earlier movements). Women, especially college and school girls, played a very important role. Aruna Asaf Ali and Sucheta Kripalani were two major women organizers of the underground, and Usha Mehta an important member of the small group that ran the Congress Radio. Workers were prominent as well, and made considerable sacrifice by enduring long strikes and braving police repression in the streets.

Peasants of all strata, well-to-do as well as poor, were the heart of the movement especially in East U.P. and Bihar, Midnapur in Bengal, Satara in Maharashtra, but also in other parts including Andhra, Gujarat and Kerala. Many smaller *zamindars* also participated, especially in U.P. and Bihar. Even the big *zamindars* maintained a stance of neutrality and refused to assist the British in crushing the rebellion. The most spectacular of these was the Raja of Darbhanga, one of the biggest *zamindars*, who refused to let his armed retainers be used by the Government and even instructed his managers to assist the tenants who had been arrested. A significant feature of the pattern of peasant activity was its total concentration on attacking symbols of British authority and a total lack of any incidents of anti-*zamindar* violence, even when, as in Bihar, East U.P., Satara, and Midnapur, the breakdown of Government authority for long periods of time provided the opportunity.[16] Government officials, especially those at the lower levels of the police and the administration, were generous in their assistance to the movement. They gave shelter, provided information and helped monetarily. In fact, the erosion of loyalty to the British Government of its own officers was one of the most striking aspects of the Quit India struggle. Jail officials tended to be much kinder to prisoners than in earlier years, and often openly expressed their sympathy.

While it is true that Muslim mass participation in the Quit India movement was not high, yet it is also true that even Muslim League supporters gave help by providing shelter to underground workers and did not act as informers. Also, there was a total absence of any communal clashes, a sure sign that though the movement may not have aroused much support from among the majority of the Muslim masses, it did not arouse their hostility either.

The powerful attraction of the Quit India movement and its elemental quality is also demonstrated by the fact that hundreds of Communists at the local and village levels participated in the movement despite the official position taken by the Communist Party. Though they sympathized with the strong anti-fascist sentiments of their leaders, yet they felt the irresistible pull of the movement and, for at least a few days or weeks, joined in it along with the rest of the Indian people.

*

The debate on the Quit India movement has centred particularly on two issues. First, was the movement a spontaneous outburst, or an organized rebellion? Second, how did the use of violence by the people in this struggle square with the overall Congress policy of non-violent struggle?

First, the element of spontaneity in the movement of 1942 was certainly larger than in the earlier movements, though even in 1919-22, as well as in 1930-31 and 1932, the Congress leadership allowed considerable room for popular initiative and spontaneity. In fact, the whole pattern of the Gandhian mass movements was that the leadership chalked out a broad programme of action and left its implementation at the local level to the initiative of the local and grass roots level political activists and the masses. Even in the Civil Disobedience Movement of 1930, perhaps the most organized of the Gandhian mass movements, Gandhiji signalled the launching of the struggle by the Dandi March and the breaking of the salt law; the leaders and the people at the local levels decided whether they were going to stop payment of land revenue and rent, or offer *satyagraha* against forest laws, or picket liquor shops, or follow any of the other items of the programme. Of course, in 1942, even the broad programme had not yet been spelt out clearly since the leadership was yet to formally launch the movement. But, in a way, the degree of spontaneity and popular initiative that was actually exercised had been sanctioned by the leadership itself. The resolution passed by the A.I.C.C. on 8 August 1942 clearly stated: 'A time may come when it may not be possible to issue instructions or for instructions to reach our people, and when no Congress committees can function. When this happens, every man and woman who is participating in this movement must function for himself or herself within the four corners of the general instructions issued. Every Indian who desires freedom and strives for it must be his own guide.'[17]

Apart from this, the Congress had been ideologically, politically and organizationally preparing for the struggle for a long time. From 1937 onwards, the organization had been revamped to undo the damage suffered during the repression of 1932-34. In political and ideological terms as well, the Ministries had added considerably to Congress support and prestige. In East U.P. and Bihar, the areas of the most intense activity in 1942 were precisely the ones in which considerable mobilization and organizational work had been carried out from 1937 onwards.[18] In Gujarat, Sardar Patel had been touring Bardoli and other areas since June 1942 warning the people of an impending struggle and suggesting that no-revenue campaigns could well be a part of it. Congress Socialists in Poona had been holding training camps for volunteers since June 1942.[19] Gandhiji himself, through the Individual Civil Disobedience campaign in 1940-41, and more directly since early 1942, had prepared the people for the coming battle, which he said would be 'short and swift.'[20]

In any case, in a primarily hegemonic struggle as the Indian national movement was, preparedness for struggle cannot be measured by the volume of immediate organizational activity but by the degree of hegemonic influence that the movement has acquired over the people.

How did the use of violence in 1942 square with the Congress policy of non-violence? For one, there were many who refused to use or sanction violent means and confined themselves to the traditional weaponry of the Congress. But many of those, including many staunch Gandhians, who used 'violent means' in 1942 felt that the peculiar circumstances warranted their use. Many maintained that the cutting of telegraph wires and the blowing up of bridges was all right as long as human life was not taken. Others frankly admitted that they could not square the violence they used, or connived at, with their belief in non-violence, but that they did it all the same. Gandhiji refused to condemn the violence of the people because he saw it as a reaction to the much bigger violence of the state. In Francis Hutchins' view, Gandhiji's major objection to violence was that its use prevented mass participation in a movement, but that, in 1942, Gandhiji had come round to the view that mass participation would not be restricted as a result of violence.[21]

The great significance of this historic movement was that it placed the demand for independence on the immediate agenda of the national movement. After 'Quit India,' there could be no retreat. Any future negotiations with the British Government could only be on the manner of the transfer of power. Independence was no longer a matter of bargain. And this became amply clear after the War.

*

With Gandhiji's release on 6 May 1944, on medical grounds, political activity regained momentum. Constructive work became the main form of Congress activity, with a special emphasis on the reorganization of the Congress machinery. Congress committees were revived under different names—Congress Workers Assemblies or Representative Assemblies of Congressmen—rendering the ban on Congress committees ineffective. The task of training workers, membership drives and fund collection was taken up. This re-organization of the Congress under the 'cover' of the constructive programme was viewed with serious misgivings by the Government which saw it as an attempt to rebuild Congress influence and organization in the villages in preparation for the next round of struggle.[22] A strict watch was kept on these developments, but no repressive action was contemplated and the Viceroy's energies were directed towards formulating an offer (known as the Wavell Offer or the Simla Conference) which would pre-empt a struggle by effecting an agreement with the Congress before the War with Japan ended. The Congress leaders were released to participate in the Simla Conference in June 1945. That marked the end of the phase of confrontation that had existed since August 1942.

*

Before we end this chapter, a brief look at the Indian National Army is essential. The idea of the INA was first conceived in Malaya by Mohan Singh, an Indian officer of the British Indian Army, when he decided not to join the retreating British army and instead went to the Japanese for help. The Japanese had till then only encouraged civilian Indians to form anti-British organizations, but had no conception of forming a military wing consisting of Indians.

Indian prisoners of war were handed over by the Japanese to Mohan Singh who then tried to recruit them into an Indian National Army. The fall of Singapore was crucial, for this brought 45,000 Indian POWs into Mohan Singh's sphere of influence. By the end of 1942, forty thousand men expressed their willingness to join the INA. It was repeatedly made clear at various meetings of leaders of the Indian community and of Indian Army officers that the INA would go into action only on the invitation of the Indian National Congress and the people of India. The INA was also seen by many as a means of checking the misconduct of the Japanese against Indians in South-East Asia and a bulwark against a future Japanese occupation of India.

The outbreak of the Quit India Movement gave a fillip to the INA as well. Anti-British demonstrations were organized in Malaya. On 1 September 1942, the first division of the INA was formed with 16,300 men. The Japanese were by now more amenable to the idea of an armed Indian wing because they were contemplating an Indian invasion. But, by December 1942, serious differences emerged between the Indian army officers led by Mohan Singh and the Japanese over the role that the INA was to play. Mohan Singh and Niranjan Singh Gill, the senior-most Indian officer to join the INA, were arrested. The Japanese, it turned out, wanted only a token force of 2,000 men, while Mohan Singh wanted to raise an Indian National Army of 200,000.

The second phase of the INA began when Subhas Chandra Bose was brought to Singapore on 2 July 1943, by means of German and Japanese submarines. He went to Tokyo and Prime Minister Tojo declared that Japan had no territorial designs on India. Bose returned to Singapore and set up the Provisional Government of Free India on 21 October 1943. The Provisional Government then declared war on Britain and the United States, and was recognised by the Axis powers and their satellites. Subhas Bose set up two INA headquarters, in Rangoon and in Singapore, and began to reorganize the INA. Recruits were sought from civilians, funds were gathered, and even a women's regiment called the Rani Jhansi regiment was formed. On 6 July 1944, Subhas Bose, in a broadcast on Azad Hind Radio addressed to Gandhiji, said: 'India's last war of independence has begun . . . Father of our Nation! In this holy war of India's liberation, we ask for your blessing and good wishes.'[23]

One INA battalion commanded by Shah Nawaz was allowed to accompany the Japanese Army to the Indo-Burma front and participate in the Imphal campaign. But the discriminatory treatment which included being denied rations, arms and being made to do menial work for the Japanese units, completely demoralized the INA men. The failure of the Imphal campaign, and the steady Japanese retreat thereafter, quashed any hopes of the INA liberating the nation. The retreat which began in mid-1944 continued till mid-1945 and ended only with the final surrender to the British in South-East Asia. But, when the INA men were brought back home and threatened with serious punishment, a powerful movement was to emerge in their defence.[24]

36 Post-War National Upsurge

The end of World War II marked a dramatic change. From then till the dawn of freedom in 1947 the political stage witnessed a wide spectrum of popular initiative. We are constrained to leave out of our purview the struggles of workers, peasants and people of the native states, which took the form of the country-wide strike wave, the Tebhaga movement, the Warlis revolt, the Punjab *kisan* morchas, the Travancore people's struggle (especially the Punnapra-Vayalar episode) and the Telengana movement. These movements had an anti-imperialist edge — as the direct oppressors they challenged were also the vested interests that constituted the social support of the Raj — but they did not come into direct conflict with the colonial regime. We shall confine ourselves to that stream of anti-imperialist activity which directly challenged the legitimacy of British rule and was perceived to be doing so by the colonial authorities.

*

The end of the War was greeted in India with a vast sigh of relief. Its few benefits such as windfall gains and super-profits for the capitalists and employment opportunities for the middle classes were far outweighed by the ravages and miseries wrought by it. The colony reeled under the heavy yoke of the war effort. Famine, inflation, scarcity, hoarding and blackmarketing plagued the land. The heroic action of a leaderless people notwithstanding, the Quit India Movement was snuffed out in eight weeks. Pockets of resistance, where the torch was kept ablaze, could not hold out for long.

When Congress leaders emerged from jail in mid-June 1945, they expected to find a demoralized people, benumbed by the repression of 1942, bewildered by the absence of leadership and battered by the privations that the War brought .To their surprise, they found tumultuous crowds waiting for them, impatient to do something, restless and determinedly anti-British. Repression had steeled the brave and stirred the conscience of the fence-sitter. Political energies were surfacing after more than three years of repression and the expectations of the people were now heightened by the release of their leaders. The popular belief was that the release would mark the beginning of a period of rapid political progress. Crowds thronged the gates of Almora jail on hearing that Jawaharlal Nehru was to be released. They waited a long while outside Bankura jail where Maulana Azad was lodged. When the Congress Working Committee met, more than half a million people lined the streets of Bombay, braving the rain to welcome their leaders. Similar scenes were witnessed when the leaders went to Simla to attend the conference called by the Viceroy. Villagers from places far away from Simla converged and sat atop trees, waiting for hours to catch a glimpse of their leaders.

The Labour Party, which had come to power in Britain after the War, was in a hurry to settle the Indian problem. As a result the ban on the Congress was lifted and elections declared. People were elated at the prospect of popular ministries and turned out in large numbers at election meetings — 50,000 on an average, and a lakh or so when all India leaders were expected. Nehru, a seasoned campaigner of the 1937 elections, confessed that he had not previously seen such crowds, such frenzied excitement. Except in constituencies where nationalist Muslims were put up, candidates did not really need to canvass for votes or spend money. The election results indicated that people had not only flocked to the meetings but had rallied behind the Congress at the ballot-box too. The Congress won over 90 percent of the general seats (including twenty-three of the thirty-six labour seats) in the provincial elections while the Muslim League made a similar sweep in the Muslim constituencies. But, perhaps, the most significant feature of the election campaign was that it sought to mobilize Indians against the British, not merely voters for the elections. This was evident from the two issues which were taken up and made the main plank of the election campaign — the repression in 1942 and the Indian National Army trials.

The question of official excesses during 1942 was taken up by Congress leaders soon after release from jail. Glorification of martyrs was one side of the coin, condemnation of official action the other. Congressmen lauded the brave resistance offered by the leaderless people, martyrs' memorials were erected in many places and relief funds organized for sufferers. Stories of repression were recounted in grim detail, the officials responsible condemned, often by name, promises of enquiries held out, and threats of punishment freely made. While such speeches, which the Government failed to check, had a devastating effect on the morale of the services, what was more alarming for the officials was the rising crescendo of demands for enquiries into official actions. The forthcoming elections were likely to bring the Congress ministries back to power, significantly in those provinces where repression had been most brutal. The U.P. Governor, Wylie, confessed on 19th February, 1946 that officials in U.P. in 1942 'used on occasion methods which I cannot condone and which, dragged out in the cold light of 1946, nobody could defend.'[1] The Viceroy concluded that only a 'gentleman's agreement' with the Congress could resolve the matter.

However, the issue which most caught the popular imagination was the fate of the members of Subhas Chandra Bose's Indian National Army (INA), who were captured by the British in the eastern theatre of War. An announcement by the Government, limiting trials of the INA personnel to those guilty of brutality or active complicity, was due to be made by the end of August, 1945. However, before this statement could be issued, Nehru raised the demand for leniency at a meeting in Srinagar on 16 August 1945 — making the proposed statement seem a response to his call rather than an act of generosity on the part of the Government. Hailing them as patriots, albeit misguided, Nehru called for their judicious treatment by the authorities in view of the British promise that 'big changes' are impending in India. Other Congress leaders soon took up the issue and the AICC, at its first post-War session held in Bombay from 21 to 23 September 1945, adopted a strong resolution declaring its support for the cause. The defence of the INA prisoners was taken up by the Congress and Bhulabhai Desai, Tej Bahadur Sapru, K.N. Katju, Nehru and Asaf Ali appeared in court at the historic Red Fort trials. The Congress organised an INA Relief and Enquiry Committee, which provided small sums of money and food to the men on their release, and attempted, though with marginal success, to secure employment for these men. The Congress authorized the

Central INA Fund Committee, the Mayor's Fund in Bombay, the AICC and the PCC offices and Sarat Bose to collect funds. The INA question was the main issue highlighted from the Congress platform in meetings held all over the country — in fact, very often it was difficult to distinguish between an INA and an election meeting. In view of Nehru's early championing of the INA cause and the varied involvement of the Congress later, the oft made charge that the Congress jumped on to the INA bandwagon and merely used the issue as an election stunt does not appear to have any validity.[2]

The INA agitation was a landmark on many counts. Firstly, the high pitch or intensity at which the campaign for the release of INA prisoners was conducted was unprecedented. This was evident from the press coverage and other publicity it got, from the threats of revenge that were publicly made and also from the large number of meetings held.

Initially, the appeals in the press were for clemency to 'misguided' men, but by November 1945, when the first Red Fort trials began, there were daily editorials hailing the INA men as the most heroic patriots and criticizing the Government stand. Priority coverage was given to the INA trials and to the INA campaign, eclipsing international news. Pamphlets, the most popular one being 'Patriots Not Traitors,' were widely circulated. '*Jai Hind*' and 'Quit India' were scrawled on walls of buildings in Ajmer. Posters threatening death to '20 English dogs' for every INA man sentenced, were pasted all over Delhi. In Banaras, it was declared at a public gathering that 'if INA men were not saved, revenge would be taken on European children.'[3] One hundred and sixty political meetings were held in the Central Provinces and Berar alone in the first fortnight of October 1945 where the demand for clemency for INA prisoners was raised. INA Day was observed on 12 November and INA Week from 5 to 11 November 1945. While 50,000 people would turn out for the larger meetings, the largest meeting was the one held in Deshapriya Park, Calcuuta. Organised by the INA Relief Committee, it was addressed by Sarat Bose, Nehru and Patel. Estimates of attendance ranged from to two to three lakhs to Nehru's five to seven lakhs.

The second significant feature of the INA campaign was its wide geographical reach and the participation of diverse social groups and political parties. This had two aspects. One was the generally extensive nature of the agitation, the other was the spread of pro-INA sentiment to social groups hitherto outside the nationalist pale. The Director of the

Intelligence Bureau conceded: 'There has seldom been a matter which has attracted so much Indian public interest, and, it is safe to say, sympathy.'[4] 'Anxious enquiries' and 'profuse sympathies' were forthcoming from the 'remotest villages' from all men, 'irrespective of caste, colour and creed.' Nehru confirmed the same: 'Never before in Indian history had such unified sentiments and feelings been manifested by various divergent sections of the Indian population as it has been done with regard to the question of the Azad Hind Fauj.'[5] While the cities of Delhi, Bombay, Calcutta and Madras and the towns of U.P. and Punjab were the nerve centres of the agitation, what was more noteworthy was the spreading of the agitation to places as distant as Coorg, Baluchistan and Assam.

Participation was of many kinds — some contributed funds, others attended or organized meetings, shopkeepers downed shutters and political parties and organizations raised the demand for the release of the prisoners. Municipal Committees, Indians abroad and Gurdwara committees subscribed liberally to INA funds. The Shiromani Gurdwara Prabandhak Committee, Amritsar donated Rs. 7000 and set aside another Rs. 10,000 for relief. The Poona City Municipality, the Kanpur City Fund and a local district board in Madras Presidency contributed Rs. 1,000 each. More newsworthy contributions were those by film stars in Bombay and Calcutta, by the Cambridge Majlis and the *tongawallas* of Amraoti. Students, whose role in the campaign was outstanding, held meetings and rallies and boycotted classes from Salem in the south to Rawalpindi in the north. Commercial institutions, shops and markets stopped business on the day the first trial began, 5 November 1945, on INA Day and during INA Week. Demands for release were raised at *kisan* Conferences in Dhamangaon and Sholapur on 16 November 1945 and at the tenth session of the All India Women's Conference in Hyderabad on 29 December 1945. 'Even English intellectuals, birds of a year or two's sojourn in India, were taking a keen interest in the rights and wrongs, and the degrees of wrong, of the INA men,' according to General Tuker of the Eastern Command.[6] Diwali was not celebrated in some areas in Punjab in sympathy with the INA men. Calcutta gurdwaras became a campaigning centre for the INA cause. The Muslim League, the Communist Party of India, the Unionist Party, the Akalis, the Justice Party, the Ahrars in Rawalpindi, the Rashtriya Swayamsevak Sangh, the Hindu Mahasabha and the Sikh League supported the INA cause in varying degrees. The Viceroy noted that 'all parties have taken the same line though Congress are more vociferous than the others.'[7]

The most notable feature of the INA agitation was the effect it had on the traditional bulwarks of the Raj. Significant sections of Government employees, loyalist sections and even men of the armed forces were submerged in the tide of pro-INA sentiment. Many officials saw in this a most disquieting trend. The Governor of North West Frontier Province warned that 'every day that passes now brings over more and more well-disposed Indians to the anti-British camp.'[8] The Director of the Intelligence Bureau observed that 'sympathy for the INA is not the monopoly of those who are ordinarily against Government,' and that it was 'usually the case that INA men belonged to families which had traditions of loyalty.'[9] In Punjab (to which province 48.07 per cent of the INA men released till February 1946 belonged) the return of the released men to their villages stimulated interest among groups which had hitherto remained politically unaffected. Local interest was further fuelled by virtue of many of the INA officers belonging to influential families in the region. P.K. Sehgal, one of the trio tried in the first Red Fort trial, was the son of Dewan Achhru Ram, an ex-Judge of the Punjab High Court. The gentlemen with titles who defended men accused of war time treason did not glorify the action of INA men — they appealed to the Government to abandon the trials in the interest of good relations between India and Britain. Government officials generally sympathized privately, but there were some instances, as in the Central Provinces and Berar, where railway officials collected funds.

The response of the armed forces was unexpectedly sympathetic, belying the official perception that loyal soldiers were very hostile to the INA 'traitors. Royal Indian Air Force (RIAF) men in Kohat attended Shah Nawaz's meetings and army men in U.P. and Punjab attended INA meetings, often in uniform. RIAF men in Calcutta, Kohat, Allahabad, Bamrauli and Kanpur contributed money for the INA defence, as did other service personnel in U.P. Apart from these instances of overt support, a 'growing feeling of sympathy for the INA' pervaded the Indian army, according to the Commander-in-Chief. He concluded that the 'general opinion in the Army is in favour of leniency' and recommended to Whitehall that leniency be shown by the Government.[10]

Interestingly, the question of the right or wrong of the INA men's action was never debated. What was in question was the right of Britain to decide a matter concerning Indians. As Nehru often stressed, if the

British were sincere in their declaration that Indo-British relations were to be transformed, they should demonstrate their good faith by leaving it to Indians to decide the INA issue. Even the appeals by liberal Indians were made in the interest of good future relations between India and Britain. The British realised this political significance of the INA issue. The Governor of North-West Frontier Province advocated that the trials be abandoned, on the ground that with each day the issue became 'more and more purely Indian versus British.'[11]

*

The growing nationalist sentiment, that reached a crescendo around the INA trials, developed into violent confrontations with authority in the winter of 1945-46. There were three upsurges — one on 21 November 1945 in Calcutta over the INA trials; the second on 11 February 1946 in Calcutta to protest against the seven year sentence given to an INA officer, Rashid Ali; and the third in Bombay on 18 February 1946 when the ratings of the Royal Indian Navy (RIN) went on strike. The upsurges followed a fairly similar pattern-an initial stage when a group (such as students or ratings) defied authority and was repressed, a second stage when people in the city joined in, and finally a third stage when people in other parts of the country expressed sympathy and solidarity.

The first stage began with the students' and ratings' challenge to authority and ended in repression. On 21 November 1945, a procession of students, consisting of Forward Bloc sympathizers and joined by Students Federation activists and Islamia College students, marched to Dalhousie Square, the seat of the Government in Calcutta, and refused to disperse. Upon a lathi-charge, the processionists retaliated with stones and brickbats which the police, in turn, met with firing and two persons died, while fifty-two were injured. On 11 February 1946, Muslim League students led the procession, Congress and Communist student organizations joined in and this time some arrests were made on Dharamatola Street. This provoked the large body of students to defy Section 144 imposed in the Dalhousie Square area and more arrests, in addition to a lathi-charge, ensued.

The RIN revolt started on 18 February when 1100 naval ratings of *HMIS Talwar* struck work at Bombay to protest against the treatment meted out to them — flagrant racial discrimination, unpalatable food and abuses to boot. The arrest of B.C. Dutt, a rating, for scrawling

'Quit India' on the *HMIS Talwar*, was sorely resented. The next day, ratings from Castle and Fort Barracks joined the strike and on hearing that the *HMIS Talwar* ratings had been fired upon (which was incorrect) left their posts and went around Bombay in lorries, holding aloft Congress flags, threatening Europeans and policemen and occasionally breaking a shop window or two.

The second stage of these upsurges, when people in the city joined in, was marked by a virulent anti-British mood and resulted in the virtual paralysis of the two great cities of Calcutta and Bombay. Meetings and processions to express sympathy, as also strikes and *hartals*, were quickly overshadowed by the barricades that came up, the pitched battles fought from housetops and by-lanes, the attacks on Europeans, and the burning of police stations, post offices, shops, tram depots, railway stations, banks, grain shops, and even a YMCA centre. This was the pattern that was visible in all the three cases. The RIN revolt and popular fury in Bombay alone accounted for, according to official estimates, the destruction of thirty shops, ten post offices, ten police *chowkis*, sixty-four foodgrain shops and 200 street lamps. Normal life in the city was completely disrupted. The Communist call for a general strike brought lakhs of workers out of their factories into the streets. *Hartals* by shopkeepers, merchants and hotel-owners and strikes by students and workers, both in industry and public transport services, almost brought the whole city to a grinding halt. Forcible stopping of trains by squatting on rail-tracks, stoning and burning of police and military lorries and barricading of streets did the rest.

The third phase was characterized by a display of solidarity by people in other parts of the country. Students boycotted classes, *hartals* and processions were organized to express sympathy with the students and ratings and to condemn official repression. In the RIN revolt, Karachi was a major centre, second only to Bombay. The news reached Karachi on 19 February, upon which the *HMIS Hindustan* alongwith one more ship and three shore establishments, went on a lightning strike. Sympathetic token strikes took place in military establishments in Madras, Vishakhapatnam, Calcutta, Delhi, Cochin, Jamnagar, the Andamans, Bahrain and Aden. Seventy eight ships and 20 shore establishments, involving 20,000 ratings, were affected. RIAF men went on sympathetic strikes in the Marine Drive, Andheri and Sion areas of Bombay and in Poona, Calcutta, Jessore and Ambala units. Sepoys at Jabalpur went on strike while the Colaba cantonment showed ominous 'restlessness.'

*

What was the significance of these events? There is no doubt that these three upsurges were significant in as much as they gave expression to the militancy in the popular mind. Action, however reckless, was fearless and the crowds which faced police firing by temporarily retreating, only to return to their posts, won the Bengal Governor's grudging admiration. The RIN revolt remains a legend to this day. When it took place, it had a dramatic impact on popular consciousness. A revolt in the armed forces, even if soon suppressed, had a great liberating effect on the minds of people. The RIN revolt was seen as an event which marked the end of British rule almost as finally as Independence Day, 1947.But reality and how men perceive that reality often proves to be different, and this was true of these dramatic moments in 1945-46. Contemporary perceptions and later radical scholarship have infused these historical events with more than a symbolic significance.[12] These events are imbued with an unrealized potential and a realized impact which is quite out of touch with reality. A larger than life picture is drawn of their militancy, reach and effectiveness. India is seen to be on the brink of a revolution. The argument goes that the communal unity witnessed during these events could, if built upon, have offered a way out of the communal deadlock.

When we examine these upsurges closely we find that the form they took, that of an extreme, direct and violent conflict with authority, had certain limitations. Only the more militant sections of society could participate. There was no place for the liberal and conservative groups which had rallied to the INA cause earlier or for the men and women of small towns and villages who had formed the backbone of the mass movements in earlier decades. Besides, these upsurges were short-lived, as the tide of popular fury surged forth, only to subside all too quickly. Interestingly, Calcutta, the scene of tremendous enthusiasm from 11 to 13 February 1946, was relatively quiet during the RIN revolt a week later. One lakh workers went on a one day strike, but the rest of the city, barring the organized working class, remained subdued, despite a seven-day ratings strike in Calcutta which had to be broken by a siege by troops. In addition, the upheavals were confined to a few urban centres, while the general INA agitation reached the remotest villages. This urban concentration made it easy for the authorities to deploy troops and effectively suppress the upsurge.

The communal unity witnessed was more organizational unity than unity of the people. Moreover, the organizations came together only for a specific agitation that lasted a few days, as was the case in Calcutta on the issue of Rashid Ali's trial. Calcutta, the scene of 'the almost revolution' in February 1946, according to Gautam Chattopadhaya[13], became the battle ground of communal frenzy only six months later, on 16 August 1946. The communal unity evident in the RIN revolt was limited, despite the Congress, League and Communist flags being jointly hoisted on the ships' masts. Muslim ratings went to the League to seek advice on future action, while the rest went to the Congress and the Socialists; Jinnah's advice to surrender was addressed to Muslim ratings alone, who duly heeded it. The view that communal unity forged in the struggles of 1945-46 could, if taken further, have averted partition, seems to be based on wishful thinking rather than concrete historical possibility. The 'unity at the barricades' did not show this promise.

Popular perceptions differ from reality when it comes to the response these upsurges, especially the RIN revolt, evoked from the colonial authorities. It is believed that 'the RIN revolt shook the mighty British Empire to its foundations.' In fact these upsurges demonstrated that despite considerable erosion of the morale of the bureaucracy and the steadfastness of the armed forces by this time, the British wherewithal to repress was intact. The soldier-Viceroy, Wavell, gave a clean chit to the army a few days after the naval strike: 'On the whole, the Indian army has been most commendably steady.'[15] Those who believed that the British would succumb to popular pressure if only it was exerted forcefully were proved wrong. It was one thing for the British Government to question its own stand of holding the INA trials when faced with opposition from the army and the people. It was quite another matter when they faced challenges to their authority. Challenges to the peace, the British were clear, had to be repressed.

Events in November 1945 in Calcutta had the troops standing by, but the Governor of Bengal preferred to and was able to control the situation with the police. Troops were called in on 12 February 1946 in Calcutta and thirty-six civilians were killed in the firing. Similarly, during the RIN revolt, ratings were forced to surrender in Karachi and six of them were killed in the process. Contrary to the popular belief that

Indian troops in Bombay had refused to fire on their countrymen, it was a Maratha battalion in Bombay that rounded up the ratings and restored them to their barracks. In Bombay, troops subdued not only the ratings but also the people, who had earlier supported the ratings with food and sympathy and later joined them in paralyzing Bombay. The British Prime Minister, Attlee, announced in the House of Commons that Royal Navy ships were on their way to Bombay. Admiral Godfrey of the R.I.N. gave the ratings a stern ultimatum after which troops circled the ships and bombers were flown over them. The *Amrit Bazar Patrika* referred to the virtual steel ring around Bombay. Two hundred and twenty eight civilians died in Bombay while 1046 were injured.

The corollary to the above argument is the attribution of the sending of Cabinet Mission to the impact of the RIN revolt. R.P. Dutt had yoked the two together many years ago — 'On February 18 the Bombay Naval strike began. On 19 February, Attlee in the House of Commons announced the decision to despatch the Cabinet Mission.'[16] This is obviously untenable. The decision to send out the Mission was taken by the British Cabinet on 22 January 1946 and even its announcement on 19 February 1946 had been slated a week earlier. Others have explained the willingness of the British to make substantial political concessions at this point of time to the combined impact of the popular, militant struggles. However, as we shall see in the next chapter, the British decision to transfer power was not merely a response to the immediate situation prevailing in the winter of 1945-46, but a result of their realization that their legitimacy to rule had been irrevocably eroded over the years. The relationship between these upsurges and the Congress is seen as one of opposition, or at best dissociation. These agitations are believed to have been led by the Communists, the Socialists or Forward Blocists, or all of them together. The Congress role is seen as one of defusing the revolutionary situation, prompted by its fear that the situation would go out of its control or by the concern that disciplined armed forces were vital in the free India that the party would rule soon. The Congress is seen to be immersed in negotiations and ministry-making and hankering for power. The belief is that if the Congress leaders had not surrendered to their desire for power, a different path to independence would have emerged.

In our view, the three upsurges were an extension of the earlier nationalist activity with which the Congress was integrally associated. It was the strong anti-imperialist sentiment fostered by the Congress through its election campaign, its advocacy of the INA cause and its highlighting of the excesses of 1942 that found expression in the three upsurges that took place between November 1945 and February 1946. The Home Department's provincial level enquiry into the causes of these 'disturbances' came to the conclusion that they were the outcome of the 'inflammatory atmosphere created by the intemperate speeches of Congress leaders in the last three months.'[17] The Viceroy had no doubt that the primary cause of the RIN 'mutiny' was the 'speeches of Congress leaders since September last.'[18] In fact, the Punjab CID authorities warned the Director of the Intelligence Bureau of the 'considerable danger,' while dealing with the Communists, 'of putting the cart before the horse and of failing to recognize Congress as the main enemy.'[19]

These three upsurges were distinguishable from the activity preceding them because the form of articulation of protest was different. They took the form of a violent, flagrant challenge to authority. The earlier activity was a peaceful demonstration of nationalist solidarity. One was an explosion, the other a groundswell.

The Congress did not give the call for these upsurges; in fact, no political organization did. People rallied in sympathy with the students and ratings as well as to voice their anger at the repression that was let loose. Individual Congressmen participated actively as did individual Communists and others. Student sympathizers of the Congress, the Congress Socialist Party, the Forward Bloc and the Communist Party of India jointly led the 21 November 1945 demonstration in Calcutta. The Congress lauded the spirit of the people and condemned the repression by the Government. It did not officially support these struggles as it felt their tactics and timing were wrong. It was evident to Congress leaders that the Government was able and determined to repress. Vallabhbhai Patel asked the ratings to surrender because he saw the British mobilization for repression in Bombay. He wrote to Nehru on 22 February 1946: 'The overpowering force of both naval and military personnel gathered here is so strong that they can be exterminated altogether and they have been also threatened with such a contingency.'[20] Congress leaders were not the only ones who felt the need to restore peace. Communists joined hands with Congressmen in advising the people of Calcutta in November 1945 and Feburary 1946 to return to their homes. Communist and Congress peace vans did the rounds of Karachi during the RIN revolt.

The contention that 'fear of popular excesses made Congress leaders cling to the path of negotiation and compromise, and eventually even accept Partition as a necessary price,'[21] has little validity. Negotiations were an integral part of Congress strategy, a possibility which had to be exhausted before a mass movement was launched. As late as 22 September 1945 this had been reiterated in a resolution on Congress policy passed by the AICC: 'The method of negotiation and conciliation which is the keynote of peaceful policy can never be abandoned by the Congress, no matter how grave may be the provocation, any more than can that of non-cooperation, complete or modified. Hence the guiding maxim of the Congress must remain: negotiations and settlement when possible and non-cooperation and direct action when necessary.'[22]

In 1946, exploring the option of negotiation before launching a movement was seen to be crucial since the British were likely to leave India within two to five years, according to Nehru. The Secretary of State's New Year statement and the British Prime Minister's announcement of the decision to send a Cabinet Mission on 19 February 1946 spoke of Indian independence coming soon. However, pressure had to be kept up on the British to reach a settlement and to this end preparedness for a movement (built steadily through 1945 by refurbishing the organization, electioneering and spearheading the INA agitation) was sought to be maintained. But the card of negotiation was to be played first, that of mass movement was to be held in reserve. Gandhiji, in three statements that he published in *Harijan* on 3 March 1946, indicated the perils of the path that had been recently taken by the people. 'It is a matter of great relief that the ratings have listened to Sardar Patel's advice to surrender. They have not surrendered their honour. So far as I can see, in resorting to mutiny they were badly advised. If it was for grievance, fancied or real, they should have waited for the guidance and intervantion of political leaders of their choice. If they mutinied for the freedom of India, they were doubly wrong. They could not do so without a call from a prepared revolutionary party. They were thoughtless and ignorant, if they believed that by their might they would deliver India from foreign domination ...

'Lokmanya Tilak has taught us that Home Rule or *swaraj* is our birthright. That *swaraj* is not to be obtained by what is going on now in Bombay, Calcutta and Karachi ...

'They who incited the mutineers did not know what they were doing. The latter were bound to submit ultimately ... .Aruna would "rather unite Hindus and Muslims at the barricade than on the constitution front." Even in terms of violence, this is a misleading proposition. If the union at the barricade is honest there must be union also at the constitutional front. Fighters do not always live at the barricade. They are too wise to commit suicide. The barricade life has always to be followed by the constitutional. That front is not taboo for ever. 'Gandhiji went on to outline the path that should be followed by the nation: 'Emphatically it betrays want of foresight to disbelieve British declarations and precipitate a quarrel in anticipation. Is the official deputation coming to deceive a great nation? It is neither manly nor womanly to think so. What would be lost by waiting? Let the official deputation prove for the last time that British declarations are unreliable. The nation will gain by trusting. The deceiver loses when there is correct response from the deceived . . . The rulers have declared their intention to 'quit' in favour of Indian rule . . .

'But the nation too has to play the game. If it does, the barricade must be left aside, at least for the time being.'[23]

37 *Freedom and Partition*

The contradictory nature of the reality of 15 August 1947 continues to intrigue historians and torment people on both sides of the border to this day. A hard-earned, prized freedom was won after long, glorious years of struggle but a bloody, tragic Partition rent asunder the fabric of the emerging free nation. Two questions arise. Why did the British finally quit? Why was Partition accepted by the Congress?

The imperialist answer is that independence was simply the fulfilment of Britain's self-appointed mission to assist the Indian people to self-government. Partition was the unfortunate consequence of the age-old Hindu-Muslim rift, of the two communities' failure to agree on how and to whom power was to be transferred. The radical view is that independence was finally wrested by the mass actions of 1946-47 in which many Communists participated, often as leaders. But the bourgeois leaders of the Congress, frightened by the revolutionary upsurge, struck a deal with the imperialist power by which power was transferred to them and the nation paid the price of Partition.

These visions of noble design or revolutionary intent, frustrated by traditional religious conflict or worldly profit, attractive as they may seem, blur, rather than illumine, the sombre reality. In fact, the Independence-Partition duality reflects the success-failure dichotomy of the anti-imperialist movement led by the Congress. The Congress had a two-fold task: structuring diverse classes, communities, groups and regions into a nation and securing independence from the British rulers for this emerging nation. While the Congress succeeded in building up a nationalist consciousness *sufficient* to exert pressure on the British to quit India, it could not complete the task of welding the nation and particularly failed to integrate the Muslims into this nation. It is this contradiction — the success and failure of the national movement — which is reflected in the other contradiction — Independence, but with it Partition.

*

The success of the nationalist forces in the struggle for hegemony over Indian society was fairly evident by the end of the War. The British rulers had won the war against Hitler, but lost the one in India. The space occupied by the national movement was far larger than that over which the Raj cast its shadow. Hitherto unpoliticized areas and apolitical groups had fallen in line with the rest of the country in the agitation over the INA trials. As seen in the previous chapter, men in the armed forces and bureaucracy openly attended meetings, contributed money, voted for the Congress and let it be known that they were doing so. The militancy of the politicized sections was evident in the heroic actions of 1942 and in the fearlessness with which students and others expressed their solidarity with INA and RIN men. The success of the national movement could be plotted on a graph of swelling crowds, wide reach and deep intensity of nationalist sentiment and the nationalist fervour of the people.

A corresponding graph could also be drawn of the demoralization of the British officials and the changing loyalties of Indian officials and loyalists, which would tell the same story of nationalist success, but differently. In this tale, nationalism would not come across as a force whose overwhelming presence left no place for the British. Rather, it would show the concrete way in which the national movement eroded imperialist hegemony, gnawed at the pillars of the colonial structure and reduced British political strategy to a mess of contradictions.[1]

An important point to be noted is that British rule was maintained in part on the basis of the consent or at least acquiescence of many sections of the Indian people. The social base of the colonial regime was among the *zamindars* and upper classes etc., the 'loyalists' who received the main share of British favours and offices. These were the Indians who manned the administration, supported government policy and worked the reforms the British reluctantly and belatedly introduced. The British also secured the consent of the people to their rule by successfully getting them to believe in British justice and fairplay, accept the British officer as the *mai-bap* of his people, and appreciate the prevalence of *Pax Brittanica*. Few genuinely believed in '*Angrezi Raj ki Barkaten*', but it sufficed for the British if people were impressed by the aura of stolidity the Raj exuded and concluded that its foundations were unshakable. The Raj to a large extent ran on prestige and the embodiment of this prestige was the district officer who belonged to the Indian Civil Service (ICS), the 'heaven-born service' much vaunted as 'the steel frame of the Raj.'

When the loyalists began to jump overboard, when prestige was rocked, when the district officer and secretariat official left the helm, it became clear that the ship was sinking, and sinking fast. It was the result of years of ravage wrought from two quarters — the rot within and the battering without.

Paucity of European recruits to the ICS, combined with a policy of Indianization (partly conceded in response to popular demand), ended British domination of the ICS as early as the First World War. By 1939 British and Indian members had achieved parity. Overall recruitment was first cut in order to maintain this balance, and later stopped in 1943. Between 1940 and 1946, the total number of ICS officials fell from 1201 to 939, that of British ICS officials from 587 to 429 and Indian ICS officials from 614 to 510. By 1946, only 19 British ICS officials were available in Bengal for 65 Posts.[2] Besides, the men coming in were no longer Oxbridge graduates from aristocratic families whose fathers and uncles were 'old India hands' and who believed in the destiny of the British nation to govern the 'child-people' of India. They were increasingly grammar school and polytechnic boys for whom serving the Raj was a career, not a mission. The War had compounded the problem. By 1945, war-weariness was acute and long absences from home were telling on morale. Economic worries had set in because of inflation. Many were due to retire, others were expected to seek premature retirement. It was a vastly-depleted, war-weary bureaucracy, battered by the 1942 movement, that remained.

However, much more than manpower shortage, it was the coming to the fore of contradictions in the British strategy of countering nationalism that debilitated the ICS and the Raj. The British had relied over the years on a twin policy of conciliation and repression to contain the growing national movement. But after the Cripps Offer of 1942, there was little left to be offered as a concession except transfer of power — full freedom itself. But the strategy of the national movement, of a multi-faceted struggle combining non-violent mass movement with working constitutional reforms proved to be more than a match for them. When non-violent movements were met with repression, the naked force behind the government stood exposed, whereas if government did not clamp down on 'sedition,' or effected a truce (as in 1931 when the Gandhi-Irwin Pact was signed) or conceded provincial autonomy under the Government of India Act 1935, it was seen to be too weak to wield control and its authority and prestige were undermined. On the other hand, the brutal repression of the 1942 movement offended the sensibilities of both liberals and loyalists. So did the government's refusal to release Gandhi, even when he seemed close to death during his 21 day fast in February-March 1943, and its decision to go ahead with the INA trials despite fervent appeals from liberals and loyalists to abandon them. The friends of the British were upset when the Government appeared to be placating its enemies — as in 1945-46, when it was believed that the Government was wooing the Congress into a settlement and into joining the government. The powerlessness of those in authority dismayed loyalists. Officials stood by, while the violence of Congress speeches rent the air. This shook the faith of the loyalists in the might of the 'Raj.'

If the loyalists' crisis was one of faith, the services' dilemma was that of action. Action could be decisive only if policy was clear-cut-repression or conciliation — not both. The policy mix could not but create problems when the same set of officials had to implement both poles of policy. This dilemma first arose in the mid-1930s when officials were worried by the prospect of popular ministries as the Congressmen they repressed during the civil disobedience movement were likely to become their political masters in the provincial Ministries. This prospect soon became a reality in eight provinces.

Constitutionalism wrecked services morale as effectively as the mass movement before it, though this is seldom realized. If fear of authority was exorcised by mass non-violent action, confidence was gained because of 'Congress Raj.' People could not fail to notice that the British Chief Secretary in Madras took to wearing *khadi* or that the Revenue Secretary in Bombay, on tour with the Revenue Minister, Morarji Desai, would scurry across the railway platform from his first-class compartment to the latter's third-class carriage so that the Honourable Minister may not be kept waiting. Among Indian officials, disloyalty was not evident, but where loyalty to the Raj was paraded earlier, 'it was the done thing to parade one's patriotism and, if possible, a third cousin twice removed who had been to jail in the civil disobedience movement.'3

But most importantly, the likelihood of Congress returning to power became a consideration with officials when dealing with subsequent Congress agitations. There was no refusal to carry out orders, but in some places this consideration resulted in half-hearted action against the individual disobedience movement in U.P. in 1940 and even against the 1942 rebels in East U.P. and Bihar. But action was generally harsh in 1942 and this was to create concrete entanglements between repression and conciliation at the end of the War when Congressmen were released and provincial Ministries were again on the cards. Morale of officials nosedived when Congressmen's demands for enquiries and calls for revenge were not proceeded against on the ground that some latitude had to be allowed during electioneering. The previous Viceroy, Linlithgow, had pledged that there would be no enquiries, but the services had little faith in the government's ability to withstand Congress pressure. The then Viceroy, Wavell, confessed that enquiries were the most difficult issue posed by the formation of provincial Ministries.

By the end of the War, the portents were clear to those officials and policy-makers who understood the dynamics of power and authority. The demand for leniency to INA men from within the army and the revolt in a section of the RIN further conveyed to the far-sighted officials, as much as a full-scale mutiny would to others more brashly confident, that the storm brewing this time may prove irrepressible. The structure was still intact, but it was feared that the services and armed forces may not be reliable if Congress started a mass movement of the 1942 type after the elections, which provincial Ministries would aid, not control. The Viceroy summed up the prospect: 'We could still probably suppress such a revolt' but 'we have nothing to put in its place and should be driven to an almost entirely official rule, for which the necessary numbers of efficient officials do not exist.'4

Once it was recognized that British rule could not survive on the old basis for long, a graceful withdrawal from India, to be effected after a settlement had been reached on the modalities of transfer of power and the nature of the post-imperial relationship between Britain and India, became the overarching aim of British policy-makers.5 The British Government was clear that a settlement was a must both for good future relations and to bury the ghost of a mass movement. Since failure could not be afforded, the concessions had to be such as would largely meet Congress demands. With the Congress demand being that the British quit India, the Cabinet Mission went out to India in March 1946 to negotiate the setting up of a national government and to set into motion a machinery for transfer of power. It was not an empty gesture like the Cripps Mission in 1942 — the Cabinet Mission was prepared for a long stay.

*

The situation seemed ripe for a settlement as the imperialist rulers were cognisant of the necessity of a settlement and the nationalist leaders were willing to negotiate with them. But rivers of blood were to flow before Indian independence, tacitly accepted in early 1946, became a reality in mid 1947. By early 1946 the imperialism nationalism conflict, being resolved in principle, receded from the spotlight. The stage was then taken over by the warring conceptions of the post-imperial order held by the British, the Congress and the Muslim League.

The Congress demand was for transfer of power to one centre, with minorities' demands being worked out in a framework ranging from autonomy to Muslim provinces to self-determination on secession from the Indian Union — but after the British left. The British bid was for a united India, friendly with Britain and an active partner in Commonwealth defence. It was believed that a divided India would lack depth in defence, frustrate joint defence plans and be a blot on Britain's diplomacy. Pakistan was not seen by Britain as her natural future ally, as the Government's policy of fostering the League ever since its inception in 1906 and the alignment today between Pakistan and the Western imperialist bloc may suggest.

British policy in 1946 clearly reflected this preference for a united India, in sharp contrast to earlier declarations. Attlee's 15 March 1946 statement that a 'minority will not be allowed to place a veto on the progress of the majority' was a far cry from Wavell's allowing Jinnah to wreck the Simla Conference in June-July 1945 by his insistence on nominating all Muslims. The Cabinet Mission was convinced that Pakistan was not viable and that the minorities' autonomy must somehow be safeguarded within the framework of a united India. The Mission Plan conceived three sections, A-comprising Madras, Bombay, Uttar Pradesh, Bihar, C.P. and Orissa; B-consisting of Punjab,

N.W.F.P. and Sind; and C—of Bengal and Assam—which would meet separately to decide on group constitutions. There would be a common centre controlling defence, foreign affairs and communications. After the first general elections a province could come out of a group. After ten years a province could call for a reconsideration of the group or union constitution. Congress wanted that a province need not wait till the first elections to leave a group, it should have the option not to join it in the first place. It had Congress-ruled provinces of Assam and N.W.F.P. (which were in Sections C and B respectively) in mind when it raised this question. The League wanted provinces to have the right to question the union constitution now, not wait for ten years. There was obviously a problem in that the Mission Plan was ambivalent on whether grouping was compulsory or optional. It declared that grouping was optional but sections were compulsory. This was a contradiction, which rather than removing, the Mission deliberately quibbled about in the hope of somehow reconciling the irreconcileable.

The Congress and League interpreted the Mission Plan in their own way, both seeing it as a confirmation of their stand. Thus, Patel maintained that the Mission's Plan was against Pakistan, that the League's veto was gone and that one Constituent Assembly was envisaged. The League announced its acceptance of the Plan on 6 June in so far as the basis of Pakistan was implied in the Mission's plan by virtue of the compulsory grouping. Nehru asserted the Congress Working Committee's particular interpretation of the plan in his speech to the A.I.C.C on 7 July 1946: 'We are not bound by a single thing except that we have decided to go into the Constituent Assembly.'[6] The implication was that the Assembly was sovereign and would decide rules of procedure. Jinnah seized the opportunity provided by Nehru's speech to withdraw the League's acceptance of the Mission Plan on 29th July, 1946.

The dilemma before the Government was whether to go ahead and form the Interim Government with the Congress or await League agreement to the plan. Wavell, who had opted for the second course at the Simla Conference an year earlier, preferred to do the same again. But His Majesty's Government, especially the Secretary of State, argued that it was vital to get Congress cooperation. Thus, the Interim Government was formed on 2nd September 1946 with Congress members alone with Nehru as *de facto* head. This was against the League's insistence that all settlements be acceptable to it. The British in 1946, in keeping with their strategic interests in the post-independence Indian subcontinent, took up a stance very different from their earlier posture of encouraging communal forces and denying the legitimacy of nationalism and the representative nature of the Congress. Continuance of rule had demanded one stance, withdrawal and post-imperial links dictated a contrary posture.

However, Jinnah had no intention of allowing the British to break with their past. His thinly veiled threat to Attlee that he should 'avoid compelling the Muslims to shed their blood . . . (by a) surrender to the Congress' had already been sent out and the weapon of Direct Action forged . Jinnah had become 'answerable to the wider electorate of the streets.'7 With the battle cry, *Lekar rahenge Pakistan, Larke lenge Pakistan,* Muslim communal groups provoked communal frenzy in Calcutta on 16 August 1946. Hindu communal groups retaliated in equal measure and the cost was 5000 lives lost. The British authorities were worried that they had lost control over the 'Frankenstein monster' they had helped to create but felt it was too late to tame it. They were frightened into appeasing the League by Jinnah's ability to unleash civil war. Wavell quietly brought the League into the Interim Government on 26 October 1946 though it had not accepted either the short or long term provisions of the Cabinet Mission Plan and had not given up its policy of Direct Action. The Secretary of State argued that without the League's presence in the Government civil war would have been inevitable. Jinnah had succeeded in keeping the British in his grip.

The Congress demand that the British get the League to modify its attitude in the Interim Government or quit was voiced almost from the time the League members were sworn in. Except Liaqat Ali Khan all the League nominees were second-raters, indicating that what was at stake was power, not responsibility to run the country. Jinnah had realized that it was fatal to leave the administration in Congress hands and had sought a foothold in the Government to fight for Pakistan. For him, the Interim Government was the continuation of civil war by other means. League Ministers questioned actions taken by Congress members, including appointments made, and refused to attend the informal meetings which Nehru had devised as a means of arriving at decisions without reference to Wavell. Their disruptionist tactics convinced Congress leaders of the futility of the Interim Goverment as an exercise in Congress-League cooperation. But they held on till 5th February 1947 when nine members of the Interim Government wrote to the Viceroy demanding that the League members resign. The League's demand for the dissolution of the Constituent Assembly that had met for the first time on 9th December 1946 had proved to be the last straw. Earlier it had refused to join the Constituent Assembly despite assurances from His Majesty's Government in their 6th December 1946 statement that the League's interpretation of grouping was the correct one. A direct bid for Pakistan, rather than through the Mission Plan, seemed to be the card Jinnah now sought to play.

This developing crisis was temporarily defused by the statement made by Attlee in Parliament on 20 February, 1947. The date for British withdrawal from India was fixed as 30 June 1948 and the appointment of a new Viceroy, Lord Mountbatten, was announced. The hope was that the date would shock the parties into agreement on the main question and avert the constitutional crisis that threatened. Besides, Indians would be finally convinced that the British were sincere about conceding independence, However, both these hopes were introduced into the terminal date notion after it had been accepted. The basic reason why the Attlee Government accepted the need for a final date was because they could not deny the truth of Wavell's assessment that an irreversible decline of government authority had taken place. They could dismiss the Viceroy, on the ground that he was pessimistic, which they did in the most discourteous manner possible. The news was common gossip in New Delhi before Wavell was even informed of it. But they could not dismiss the truth of what he said. So the 20 February statement was really an acceptance of the dismissed Viceroy, Wavell's reading of the Indian situation.

The anticipation of freedom from imperial rule lifted the gloom that had set in with continuous internal wrangling. The statement was enthusiastically received in Congress circles as a final proof of British sincerity to quit. Partition of the country was implied in the proviso that if the Constituent Assembly was not fully representative (i.e. if Muslim majority provinces did not join) power would be transferred to more than one central government. But even this was acceptable to the Congress as it meant that the existing Assembly could go ahead and frame a constitution for the areas represented in it. It offered a way out of the existing deadlock, in which the League not only refused to join the Constituent Assembly but demanded that it be dissolved. Nehru appealed to Liaqat Ali Khan: 'The British are fading out of the picture and the burden of this decision must rest on all of us here. It seems desirable that we should face this question squarely and not speak to each other from a distance.'[8] There seemed some chance of fulfilment of Attlee's hopes that the date would 'force the two political parties in India to come together.'[9]

This was an illusory hope, for Jinnah was more convinced than ever that he only had to bide his time in order to reach his goal. This is precisely what Conservative members of Parliament had warned would happen, in the contentious debate that followed the 20th February statement. Godfrey Nicolson had said of Cripps speech — 'if ever there was a speech which was a direct invitation to the Muslim League to stick their toes in and hold out for Pakistan, that was one.'[10] The Punjab Governor, Evan Jenkins, was equally emphatic — 'the statement will be regarded as the prelude to the final communal showdown,' with everyone out to 'seize as much power as they can — if necessary by force.'[11] Jenkins' prophecy took immediate shape with the League launching civil disobedience in Punjab and bringing down the Unionist-Akali- Congress coalition ministry led by Khizr Hayat Khan. Wavell wrote in his diary on 13th March 1947— 'Khizr's resignation was prompted largely by the statement of February 20.'[12]

This was the situation in which Mountbatten came to India as Viceroy. He was the last Viceroy and charged with the task of winding up the Raj by 30th June 1948. Mountbatten has claimed to have introduced the time limit into the 20 February settlement: 'I made the great point about it.. I had thought of the time limit, and I had great difficulty in bringing him (Attlee) upto it . . . I think the time limit was fundamental. I believe if I'd gone out without a time limit, I'd still be there.'[13] This is so obviously untrue that it should need no refutation, but Lapierre and Collins in *Freedom at Midnight* and others have passed off as history Mountbatten's self-proclamations of determining history single-handedly. The idea of a fixed date was originally Wavell's, 31 March 1948 being the date by which he expected a stage of responsibility without power to set in. Attlee thought mid—1948 should be the date aimed at. Mountbatten insisted it be a calendar date and got 30th June 1948.

Mountbatten's claim of having plenipotentiary powers, such that he need make no reference back to London, is equally misleading. It is true that he had more independence than the Viceroys preceding him and his views were given due consideration by the Labour Government. Yet he referred back to London at each stage of the evolution of his Plan, sent his aide Ismay to London and finally went himself to get Attlee and his Cabinet to agree to the 3rd June Plan.

Mountbatten had a clear cut directive from His Majesty's Government, he did not write his own ticket, as he has claimed. He was directed to explore the options of unity and division till October, 1947 after which he was to advise His Majesty's Government on the form transfer of power should take. Here again he soon discovered that he had little real choice. The broad contours of the scenario that was to emerge were discernible even before he came out. Mountbatten found out within two months of his arrival that more flogging would not push the Cabinet Mission Plan forward, it was a dead horse. Jinnah was obdurate that the Muslims would settle for nothing less than a sovereign state. Mountabatten found himself unable to move Jinnah from this stand: 'He gave the impression that he was not listening. He was impossible to argue with . . . He was, whatever was said, intent on his Pakistan.'[14]

The British could keep India united only if they gave up their role as mediators trying to effect a solution Indians had agreed upon. Unity needed positive intervention in its favour, including putting down communal elements with a firm hand. This they chose not to do. Attlee wrote later — 'We would have preferred a United India. We couldn't get it, though we tried hard'[15] They in fact took the easy way out. A serious attempt at retaining unity would involve identifying with the forces that wanted a unified India and countering those who opposed it. Rather than doing that, they preferred to woo both sides into friendly collaboration with Britain on strategic and defence issues. The British preference for a united Indian subcontinent that would be a strong ally in Commonwealth defence was modified to two dominions, both of which would be Britain's allies and together serve the purpose a united India was expected to do. The poser now was, how was friendship of *both* India and Pakistan to be secured?

Mountbatten's formula was to divide India but retain maximum unity. The country would be partitioned but so would Punjab and Bengal, so that the limited Pakistan that emerged would meet both the Congress and League's positions to some extent. The League's position on Pakistan was conceded to the extent that it would be created, but the Congress position on unity would be taken into account to make Pakistan as small as possible. Since Congress were asked to concede their main point i.e. a unified India, all their other points would be met.

Whether it was ruling out independence for the princes or unity for Bengal or Hyderabad's joining up with Pakistan instead of India, Mountbatten firmly supported Congress on these issues. He got His Majesty's Government to agree to his argument that Congress goodwill was vital if India was to remain in the Commonwealth.

The Mountbatten Plan, as the 3rd June, 1947 Plan came to be known, sought to effect an early transfer of power on the basis of Dominion Status to two successor states, India and Pakistan. Congress was willing to accept Dominion Status for a while because it felt it must assume full power immediately and meet boldly the explosive situation in the country. As Nehru put it, 'Murder stalks the streets and the most amazing cruelties are indulged in by both the individual and the mob.'16 Besides Dominion Status gave breathing time to the new administration as British officers and civil service officials could stay on for a while and let Indians settle in easier into their new positions of authority. For Britain, Dominion Status offered a chance of keeping India in the Commonwealth, even if temporarily, a prize not to be spurned. Though Jinnah offered to bring Pakistan into the Commonwealth, a greater store was laid by India's membership of the Commonwealth, as India's economic strength and defence potential were deemed sounder and Britain had a greater value of trade and investment there.

The rationale for the early date for transfer of power, 15th August 1947, was securing Congress agreement to Dominion Status. The additional benefit was that the British could escape responsibility for the rapidly deteriorating communal situation. As it is, some officials were more than happy to pack their bags and leave the Indians to stew in their own juice. As Patel said to the Viceroy, the situation was one where 'you won't govern yourself, and you won't let us govern.'17. Mountbatten was to defend his advancing the date to 15th August, 1947 on the ground that things would have blown up under their feet had they not got out when they did. Ismay, the Viceroy's Chief of Staff, felt that August, 1947 was too late, rather than too early. From the British point of view, a hasty retreat was perhaps the most suitable action. That does not make it the inevitable option, as Mountbatten and Ismay would have us believe. Despite the steady erosion of government authority, the situation of responsibility without power was still a prospect rather than a reality. In the short term the British could assert their authority, but did not care to, as Kripalani, then Congress

President, pertinently pointed out to Mountbatten.[18] Moreover, the situation, rather than warranting withdrawal of authority, cried out for someone to wield it.

If abdication of resposibility was callous, the speed with which it was done made it worse. The seventy-two day timetable, 3rd June to 15th August 1947, for both transfer of power and division of the country, was to prove disastrous. Senior officials in India like the Punjab Governor, Jenkins, and the Commander-in-Chief, Auchinleck, felt that peaceful division could take a few years at the very least. As it happened, the Partition Council had to divide assets, down to typewriters and printing presses, in a few weeks. There were no transitional institutional structures within which the knotty problems spilling over from division could be tackled. Mountbatten had hoped to be common Governor-General of India and Pakistan and provide the neccessary link but this was not to be as Jinnah wanted the position himself. Hence even the joint defence machinery set up failed to last beyond December 1947 by which time Kashmir had already been the scene of a military conflict rather than a political settlement.

The Punjab massacres that accompanied Partition were the final indictment of Mountbatten. His loyal aide, Ismay, wrote to his wife on 16 September 1947: 'Our mission was so very nearly a success: it is sad that it has ended up such a grim and total failure.'[19] The early date, 15th August 1947, and the delay in announcing the Boundary Commission Award, both Mountbatten's decisions, compounded the tragedy that took place. A senior army official, Brigadier Bristow, posted in Punjab in 1947, was of the view that the Punjab tragedy would not have occurred had partition been deferred for a year or so. Lockhart, Commander-in-Chief of the Indian Army from 15 August to 31 December 1947, endorsed this view: 'Had officials in every grade in the civil services, and all the personnel of the armed services, been in position in their respective new countries before Independence Day, it seems there would have been a better chance of preventing widespread disorder.'[20] The Boundary Commission Award was ready by 12th August, 1947 but Mountbatten decided to make it public after Independence Day, so that the responsibility would not fall on the British. Independence Day in Punjab and Bengal saw strange scenes. Flags of both India and Pakistan were flown in villages between Lahore and Amritsar as people of both communities believed that they were on the right side of the border. The morrow after freedom was to find them aliens in their own homes, exiled by executive fiat.

*

Why and how did the Congress come to accept Partition? That the League should assertively demand it and get its Shylockian pound of flesh, or that the British should concede it, being unable to get out of the web of their own making, seems explicable. But why the Congress, wedded to a belief in one Indian nation, accepted the division of the country, remains a question difficult to answer. Why did Nehru and Patel advocate acceptance of the 3rd June Plan and the Congress Working Committee and A.I.C.C. pass a resolution in favour of it? Most surprising of all, why did Gandhi acquiesce? Nehru and Patel's acceptance of Partition has been popularly interpreted as stemming from their lust for quick and easy power, which made them betray the people. Gandhiji's counsels are believed to have been ignored and it is argued that he felt betrayed by his disciples and even wished to end his life, but heroically fought communal frenzy single-handedly — 'a one man boundary force,' as Mountbatten called him.

It is forgotten that Nehru, Patel and Gandhiji in 1947 were only accepting what had become inevitable because of the long-term failure of the Congress to draw in the Muslim masses into the national movement and stem the surging waves of Muslim communalism, which, especially since 1937, had been beating with increasing fury. This failure was revealed with stark clarity by the 1946 elections in which the League won 90 percent Muslim seats. Though the war against Jinnah was lost by early 1946, defeat was conceded only after the final battle was mercilessly waged in the streets of Calcutta and Rawalpindi and the village lanes of Noakhali and Bihar. The Congress leaders felt by June 1947 that only an immediate transfer of power could forestall the spread of Direct Action and communal disturbances. The virtual collapse of the Interim Government also made Pakistan appear to be an unavoidable reality. Patel argued in the AICC meeting on 14th June, 1947 that we have to face up to the fact that Pakistan was functioning in Punjab, Bengal and in the Interim Government. Nehru was dismayed at the turning of the Interim Government into an arena of struggle. Ministers wrangled, met separately to reach decisions and Liaquat Ali Khan as Finance Member hamstrung the functioning of the other ministries. In the face of the Interim Government's powerlessness to check Governors from abetting the League and the Bengal provincial Ministry's inaction and even complicity in riots, Nehru wondered whether there was any point in continuing in the Interim Government while people were being butchered. Immediate transfer of power would at least mean the setting up of a government which could exercise the control it was now expected to wield, but was powerless to exercise.

There was an additional consideration in accepting immediate transfer of power to two dominions. The prospect of balkanisation was ruled out as the provinces and princes were not given the option to be independent — the latter were, in fact, much to their chagrin, cajoled and coerced into joining one or the other dominion. This was no mean achievement. Princely states standing out would have meant a graver blow to Indian unity than Pakistan was.

The acceptance of Partition in 1947 was, thus, only the final act of a process of step by step concession to the League's intransigent championing of a sovereign Muslim state. Autonomy of Muslim majority provinces was accepted in 1942 at the time of the Cripps Mission. Gandhiji went a step further and accepted the right of self-determination of Muslim majority provinces in his talks with Jinnah in 1944. In June 1946, Congress conceded the possibility of Muslim majority provinces (which formed Group B and C of the Cabinet Mission Plan) setting up a separate Constituent Assembly, but opposed compulsory grouping and upheld the right of NWFP and Asam not to join their groups if they so wished. But by the end of the year, Nehru said he would accept the ruling of the Federal Court on whether grouping was compulsory or optional. The Congress accepted without demur the clarification by the British Cabinet in December, 1946 that grouping was compulsory. Congress officially referred to Partition in early March 1947 when a resolution was passed in the Congress Working Committee that Punjab (and by implication Bengal) must be partitioned if the country was divided. The final act of surrender to the League's demands was in June 1947 when Congress ended up accepting Partition under the 3rd June Plan.

The brave words of the leaders contrasted starkly with the tragic retreat of the Congress. While loudly asserting the sovereignty of the Constituent Assembly, the Congress quietly accepted compulsory grouping and abandoned NWFP to Pakistan. Similarly the Congress leaders finally accepted Partition most of all because they could not stop communal riots, but their words were all about not surrendering to the blackmail of violence. Nehru wrote to Wavell on 22nd August 1946: 'We are not going to shake hands with murder or allow it to determine the country's policy.'[21]

What was involved here was a refusal to accept the reality that the logic of their past failure could not be reversed by their present words or action. This was hardly surprising at the time, for hardly anybody had either anticipated the quick pace of the unfolding tragedy or was prepared to accept it as irrevocable. It is a fact that millions of people on both sides of the new border refused to accept the finality of Partition long after it was announced, and that is one major reason why the transfer of population became such a frenzied, last-minute affair. Wishful thinking, clinging to fond hopes and a certain lack of appreciation of the dynamics of communal feeling characterized the Congress stand, especially Nehru's. The right of secession was conceded by the Congress as it was believed that 'the Muslims would not exercise it but rather use it to shed their fears.'[22] It was not realised that what was in evidence in the mid-1940s was not the communalism of the 1920s or even 1930s, when minority fears were being assiduously fanned, but an assertive 'Muslim nation,' led by an obdurate leader, determined to have a separate state by any means. The result was that each concession of the Congress, rather than cutting the ground from under the communalists' feet, consolidated their position further as success drew more Muslims towards them. Jinnah pitched his claim high, seeing that Congress was yielding. Hindu communalism got a chance to grow by vaunting itself as the true protector of Hindu interests, which, it alleged, the Congress was sacrificing at the altar of unity.

Another unreal hope was that once the British left, differences would be patched up and a free India built by both Hindus and Muslims. This belief underestimated the autonomy of communalism by this time — it was no longer merely propped up by the British, in fact it had thrown away that crutch and was assertively independent, defying even the British. Yet another fond hope was that Partition was temporary — it had became unavoidable because of the present psyche of Hindus and Muslims but was reversible once communal passions subsided and sanity returned. Gandhiji often told people that Pakistan could not exist for long if people refused to accept Partition in their hearts. Nehru wrote to Cariappa: 'But of one thing I am convinced that ultimately there will be a united and strong India. We have often to go through the valley of the shadow before we reach the sun-lit mountain tops.'[23]

The most unreal belief, given what actually happened, was the one that Partition would be peaceful. No riots were anticipated, no transfers of population planned, as it was assumed that once Pakistan was conceded, what was there to fight over? Nehru continued to believe as always in the goodness of his people, despite the spate of riots which plagued India from August 1946 onwards. The hope was that madness would be exorcised by a clean surgical cut. But the body was so diseased, the instruments used infected, that the operation proved to be terribly botchy. Worse horrors were to accompany Partition than those that preceded it.

What about Gandhiji? Gandhiji's unhappiness and helplessness have often being pointed out. His inaction has been explained in terms of his forced isolation from the Congress decision making councils and his inability to condemn his disciples, Nehru and Patel, for having succumbed to the lust for power, as they had followed him faithfully for many years, at great personal sacrifice.[24]

In our view, the root of Gandhiji's helplessness was neither Jinnah's intransigence nor his disciples' alleged lust for power, but the communalisation of his people. At his prayer meeting on 4th June 1947 he explained that Congress accepted Partition because the people wanted it: 'The demand has been granted because you asked for it. The Congress never asked for it . . . But the Congress can feel the pulse of the people. It realized that the Khalsa as also the Hindus desired it.'[25] It was the Hindus' and Sikhs' desire for Partition that rendered him ineffective, blind, impotent. The Muslims already considered him their enemy. What was a mass leader without masses who would follow his call? How could he base a movement to fight communalism on a communalised people? He could defy the leaders' counsels, as he had done in 1942, when he saw clearly that the moment was right for a struggle. But he could not 'create a situation,' as he honestly told N.K.Bose, who asked him to do so. His special ability, in his own words, only lay in being able to 'instinctively feel what is stirring in the hearts of the masses' and 'giving a shape to what was already there.' In 1947, there were no 'forces of good' which Gandhiji could 'seize upon' to 'build up a programme' — 'Today I see no sign of such a healthy feeling. And, therefore, I shall have to wait until the time comes.'[26] But political developments did not wait till a 'blind man . . . groping in the dark all alone' found a way to the light. The Mountbatten Plan confronted him and Gandhiji saw the inevitability of Partition in the ugly gashes left by riots on the country's face and in the *rigor mortis* the Interim Government had fallen into. He walked bravely into the AICC meeting on 14 June, 1947 and asked Congressmen to accept Partition as an unavoidable necessity in the given circumstances, but to fight it in the long run by not accepting it in their hearts. He did not accept it in his heart and kept alive, like Nehru, his faith in his people. He chose to plough a lonely furrow, walking barefoot through the villages of Noakhali, bringing confidence by his presence to the Muslims in Bihar and preventing riots by persuasion and threats of a fast in Calcutta. *Ekla Cholo* had long been his favourite song — 'if no one heeds your call, walk alone, walk alone.' He did just that.

15th August 1947, dawned revealing the dual reality of Independence and Partition. As always, between the two of them, Gandhiji and Nehru mirrored the feelings of the Indian people. Gandhiji prayed in Calcutta for an end to the carnage taking place. His close follower, Mridula Sarabhai, sat consoling a homeless, abducted 15-year-old girl in a room somewhere in Bombay. Gandhiji's prayers were reflective of the goings-on in the dark, the murders, abductions and rapes. Nehru's eyes were on the light on the horizon, the new dawn, the birth of a free India. 'At the stroke of the midnight hour when the world sleeps India shall awake to light and freedom.' His poetic words, 'Long years ago, we made a tryst with destiny,' reminded the people that their angry bewilderment today was not the only truth. There was a greater truth — that of a glorious struggle, hard-fought and hard-won, in which many fell martyrs and countless others made sacrifices, dreaming of the day India would be free. That day had come. The people of India saw that too, and on 15 August — despite the sorrow in their hearts for the division of their land — danced in the streets with abandon and joy.

38 The Long-Term Strategy of The National Movement[1]

A very basic aspect of the long-term dynamics of the Indian national movement was the strategy it adopted in its prolonged struggle against colonial rule. The capacity of a people to struggle depends not only on the fact of exploitation and domination and on its comprehension by the people but also on the strategy and tactics on which their struggle is based.

The existing writings on the subject have failed to deal with, or even discuss, the strategy adopted by the national movement. It appears as if the movement was a mere conglomeration of different struggles or, in the case of its Gandhian phase, certain principles such as non-violence and certain forms of struggle such as *satyagraha*, picketting, etc., but without an overall strategy. One reason for this failure in the existing writings on the subject is the largely untheorized character of the nationalist strategy. Unlike the leaders of the Russian and Chinese Revolutions, the leaders of the Indian national movement were not theoretically inclined and did not write books and articles putting forth their political strategy in an explicit form. But, in fact, the various phases of the struggle, phases of constitutional activity, constructive work, basic political decisions, forms of struggle, non-violence, *satyagraha*, etc., cannot be properly understood or historically evaluated unless they are seen as integral parts of a basic strategy.

Large elements of the nationalist strategy were evolved during the Moderate and the Extremist phases of the movement; it was structured and came to fruition during the Gandhian phase of the movement and in Gandhiji's political practice. Historians and other social scientists, as also contemporary commentators, have tended to concentrate on

Gandhiji's philosophy of life. But, in fact, his philosophy of life had only a limited impact on the people. It was as a political leader and through his political strategy and tactics of struggle that he moved millions into political action.

*

At the very outset, it is to be noted that the nationalist strategy was based on the specific nature and character of British rule and the colonial state. While fully grasping the exploitative and dominational character of colonial rule, Indian leaders also realized that the colonial state was semi-hegemonic, and semi-authoritarian in character. It was not like Hitler's Germany or Czarist Russia, or Chiang Kai-shek's China, or Batista's Cuba. Its character could, perhaps, be best described as legal authoritarianism.

The colonial state was established by force and force remained its ultimate sanction. Naked force was often used to suppress peaceful movements. But it was not based just on force. It was also based on the creation of certain civil institutions, such as elected assemblies, local government institutions, courts, and schools and colleges, and, above all, on the rule of law. It provided a certain amount of civil liberties in non-movement periods. Moreover, often, even while suppressing popular opposition, it observed certain rules of law and codes of administration. In other words it was semi-democratic, semi-authoritarian.

The semi-hegemonic character of the colonial state arose from the fact that it relied very heavily for the acquiescence of the Indian people in their rule on two notions carefully inculcated over a long period of time. One was the notion that the foreign rulers were benevolent and just, that they were the *Mai-Baap* of the people, that they were economically and socially and culturally developing or 'modernizing' India. The second notion was that the colonial rulers were invincible, that it was futile to oppose them, that the Indian people were too weak and disunited to oppose them successfully, that they would crush all opposition except to the extent they themselves permitted it, that all opposition had, therefore, to proceed along constitutional lines. The colonial rulers also offered constitutional, economic and other concessions to popular movements and did not rely on their repression alone; they followed a policy of the carrot and the stick.

It was in the context of and in opposition to this semi-hegemonic, semi-authoritarian colonial state that the national movement gradually evolved its strategy and tactics.

*

The basic strategic perspective of the national movement was to wage a long-drawn out hegemonic struggle, or, in Gramscian terms, a war of position. By hegemonic struggle, we mean a struggle for the minds and hearts of men and women so that the nationalist influence would continuously grow among the people through different channels and through the different phases and stages of the national movement. The movement alternated between phases of extra-legal or law-breaking mass movements and phases of functioning within the four walls of the law. But both phases were geared to expanding the influence of the national movement among the people. The basic strategy of the national movement was, moreover, not a strategy of gradual reform. It was a strategy of active struggle with the objective of wresting power from the colonial rulers.

The effectiveness and validity of the nationalist strategy lay in the active participation of the masses in the movement. The masses had, therefore, to be politicized and activized. The political passivity of the masses, especially in the villages, consciously inculcated and nurtured by the colonial authorities, was a basic factor in the stability of colonial rule. A major objective of the movements of the Gandhian era was to bring the masses into active politics and political action. As Gandhiji repeatedly declared, people 'can have *Swaraj* for the asking' when they 'have attained the power to take it.'[2]

The second objective of the nationalist strategy was to erode the hegemony or ideological influence of the colonial rulers inch by inch and in every area of life. Since the British did not rule primarily by force but by a carefully organized belief system or ideology, it was necessary to undermine and overthrow this belief system. The battle then had to be one of ideas. The objective was to have more and more people adopt nationalist ideas and ideology. A major objective of the hegemonic colonial ideology was to hide the face of the real enemy — colonialism — that is, to hide the primary contradiction between the interests of the Indian people and colonialism. The basic task of the counter hegemonic nationalist movement was to expose the face of the colonial enemy and the primary contradiction to the light of day. Hence the most important element of nationalist stragegy was its ideological-political work.

Above all, this meant the undermining of the twin notions of the benevolence and invincibility of British rule. The process of undermining the first, i.e., the notion of benevolence, and creating an intellectual framework for it was initiated and performed brilliantly by Dadabhai Naoroji, Justice Ranade, R.C. Dutt and other Moderates. This framework was carried to the lower middle classes by the Extremists and to the masses during the Gandhian era. The sturdily independent newspapers of the late 19th century, the work in the legislative councils by leaders like Pherozeshah Mehta and G.K. Gokhale, the bold propaganda of Lokamanya Tilak, Aurobindo Ghose and other Extremists, and the death-defying deeds of the Revolutionary Terrorists frontally challenged the notion of the invincibility of the colonial state. But it was the law-breaking mass movements of the post-1918 period which basically performed the task among the mass of the Indian people. The basic objective of these movements was to destroy the notion that British rule could not be challenged, to create among the people fearlessness and courage and the capacity to fight and make sacrifices, and to inculcate the notion that no people could be ruled without their consent.

A third objective of the Congress strategy was to undermine the hold of the colonial state on the members of its own state apparatuses — members of the civil services, the police and the armed forces — and to win them over to the nationalist cause or at least to weaken their loyalty and obedience to the colonial regime. The nationalist movement was, in fact, quite successful in this task. Gradually, the behaviour of the police and jail officials underwent a qualitative change. A large number of officials of all types actively helped the 1942 movement at great personal risk. As we have seen earlier, the virtual disappearance of loyalty among the police, army and bureaucracy after 1945 and the consequent disarray of the British administrative structure were major reasons for the British decision to finally quit India.

The national movement, from the beginning, made efforts to weaken the hegemony of colonial ideology among the British people and public opinion. There was a basic continuity in this respect from the work of the British Committee of the National Congress during the 1890s using the services of William Digby, William Wedderburn, and others to the work of the India League in which persons like V.K. Krishna Menon and Fenner Brockway were active.

This as well as efforts to win the support of non-Congress leaders and public opinion within India also aided the achievement of a fourth objective of the nationalist strategy: to constantly expand the semi-democratic political space, and to prevent the colonial authorities from limiting the existing space, within which legal activities and peaceful mass struggles could be organized.

*

The second major aspect of nationlist strategy was the long-drawn out character of the hegemonic struggle. Under this strategy, which may be described as Struggle-Truce-Struggle or S-T-S', a phase of vigorous extra-legal mass movement and open confrontation with colonial authority was followed by a phase during which direct confrontation was withdrawn, and political concessions, if any, wrested from the colonial regime were worked and shown to be inadequate. During this latter, more 'passive,' phase, intense political and ideological work was carried on among the masses within the existing legal and constitutional framework, and forces were gathered for another mass movement at a higher level. The culmination of this strategy of S-T-S' came with a call for 'Quit India' and the achievement of independence. Both phases of the movement were utilized, each in its own way, to undermine colonial hegemony, to recruit and train nationalist workers and to build up the people's capacity to struggle.

The entire political process of S-T-S' was an upward spiralling one. This strategy also assumed advance through stages. Each stage represented an advance over the previous one. At the same time, it was realized that the task of national liberation was incomplete till state power was transferred. Even an advanced stage of constitutional reforms did not mean that freedom had been partially transferred. Freedom was a whole; till it was fully won, it was not won at all. Any other view would tend to make Indians 'partners' of colonialism during the 'reform' phases of the movement, and the national movement would tend to be coopted by the colonial state. The Indian nationalists avioded this trap by treating the non-mass movement phases also as phases of political, anti-colonial struggle. The working of the reforms was not equated with the working of the colonial system. A basic feature of the nationalist strategy was to move from stage to stage without getting coopted by the colonial regime which was opposed and struggled against at each stage. Only the form of struggle changed. In the extra-legal mass-movement phases, laws were broken and civil disobedience was practised; in the non-mass movement or 'passive' phases, there was mass agitation, intense ideological work, including extensive tours by leaders, organization of public meetings on an extensive scale, and the organization of workers, peasants and students and youth and their struggles, mostly by the left-wing, during the late 1920s and the 1930s. Thus, both types of phases were seen as political phases of the anti-imperialist struggle, equally rich in anti-imperialist content, and parts of the same anti-imperialist strategy. So the political struggle was perpetual, only its forms underwent change. As Gandhiji put it, 'suspension of civil disobedience does not mean suspension of war. The latter can only end when India has a Constitution of her own making.'3

*

A basic question regarding the S-T-S' strategy is: why did there have to be two types of phases in the national movement? Why should a phase of non-mass movement or 'war of position' inevitably follow a phase of extra-legal mass struggle or 'war of movement' in Gramscian terms? Why could the national movement not take the form of one continuous mass struggle till freedom was won? Would this not have brought freedom much earlier? The nationalist strategy, under Gandhiji's leadership, was based on the assumptions that by its very nature a mass movement could not be carried on or sustained indefinitely or for a prolonged period, that a mass movement must ebb sooner or later, that mass movements had to be short lived, and that periods of rest and consolidation, of 'breathing time,' must intervene so that the movement could consolidate, recuperate and gather strength for the next round of struggle.

This was so because the masses on whom the movement was based invariably got exhausted after some time. Their capacity to confront the state or to face state repression — imprisonment, brutal lathi-charges, heavy fines, confiscation of houses, land and other property — or to make sacrifices was not unlimited. The national leadership made continuous efforts to increase the people's capacity to sacrifice and face colonial repression through ideological work. Simultaneously, it recognized the limits of their capactiy to suffer, and therefore did not overstrain this capacity over much. It also based its tactics on the fact that the colonial state was not yet, at least till 1945, in disarray, that its state apparatuses were still loyal to it, that it was till 1945 a strong state, and that it had, consequently, a considerable capacity to crush a movement, as it did in 1932-33 and 1942.

The strategic persepctive that there should be two types of phases of the national movement was also based on the perception that though a mass movement needed a 'standing army' or 'steel frame' of wholetime political workers, it could not be based only on them. Its real striking power could come only from the masses. The national movement produced thousands of these wholetime workers who devoted their entire lives to the freedom struggle. They spent their entire lives in jails, or Ashrams, or *khadi bhandars*, or trade union and *kisan sabha* offices. But while they played a crucial role in organizing and mobilizing the masses, the movement had to be based on the masses. Consequently, recourse to a mass movement that confronted the colonial state and then its shift to a phase of non-confrontation were an inherent part of a strategy of political struggle that was based on the masses. The Gandhian strategy was thus based on a specific understanding of the limits to which both the people and the Government could go.

Once it was realized that the S-T-S' strategy of the mass movement required the launching of a massive mass movement as well as shifting it to a non-mass movement phase, the decision to shift from one phase to the other became a purely tactical one and not a matter of principle. The question then was: When was the decision to make the shift to be made in keeping with the reality on the ground? In two of the rare instances when Gandhiji theorized his political practice, he gave an inkling of how he perceived the role of leadership in this context. He wrote in 1938: 'A wise general does not wait till he is actually routed; he withdraws in time in an orderly manner from a position which he knows he would not be able to hold.'[4] And again in 1939: 'An able general always gives battle in his own time on the ground of his choice. He always retains the initiative in these respects and never allows it to pass into the hands of the enemy. In a *satyagraha* campaign the mode of fight and the choice of tactics, e.g., whether to advance or retreat, offer civil resistance or organize non-violent strength through constructive work and purely selfless humanitarian service, are determined according to the exigencies of the situation.'[5]

In other words, the very important question of the timing of starting or withdrawing a movement was decided by Gandhiji and the national leadership on the basis of their perception of the strength or weakness of the movement, the staying power of the masses and the political and administrative reserves of the Government.

Similarly, the question was not whether negotiations with the Government should or should not be held. The question was — when one negotiated, how did one choose the right psychological moment to negotiate, how did one actually negotiate, what did one negotiate about, what would the outcome of the negotiations be, and what would the terms on which a truce was signed be, if there was a truce. As the AICC resolution on Congress Policy, adopted on 22 September 1945, stated: 'The method of negotiation and conciliation which is the key-note of peaceful policy can never be abandoned by the Congress, no matter how grave may be the provocation, any more than can that of non-cooperation, complete or modified. Hence, the guiding maxim of the Congress must remain: negotiation and settlement when possible and non-cooperation and direct action when necessary.'[6]

*

Constructive work played an important role in Gandhian (and even pre-Gandhian) strategy. It was primarily organized around the promotion of *khadi*, spinning and village industries, national education and Hindu-Muslim unity, the struggle against untouchability and the social upliftment of the Harijans, and the boycott of foreign cloth and liquor. Constructive work was symbolized by hundreds of Ashrams which came up all over the country, almost entirely in the villages.

Constructive work was basic to a war of position. It played a crucial role during the 'passive' or non-mass movement phase in filling the political space left vacant by the withdrawal of civil disobedience. It solved a basic problem that a mass movement faces — the sustenance of a sense of activism in the non-mass movement phases of the struggle. Constructive work had also the advantage of involving a large number of people. Parliamentary and intellectual work could be done by relatively few, constructive work could involve millions. Moreover, not all could go to jail. But constructive work was within the reach of all.

The hard core of constructive workers also provided a large cadre for the civil disobedience movement. They were Gandhiji's steel-frame or standing army.

*

Constitutional reforms and legislative councils formed a basic element of the complex colonial strategy to meet the challenge of Indian nationalism. The Indians had to evolve an equally complex approach towards legislatures. Complexity also arose from the fact that, on the one hand, the constitutional structure and constitutional reforms represented instruments of colonial domination and of colonial efforts to co-opt and derail the national movement; while, on the other hand, they represented the fruits of the anti-colonial struggle of the Indian people, a measure of the changing balance of forces and the widening of the democratic space in which the national movement could operate. The colonial authorities hoped that constitutional work would weaken the nationalist urge to take to mass politcs, promote dissensions and splits within the nationalist ranks on the basis of constitutionalist vs. non-constitutionalist and Right vs. Left.

In opposing the colonial strategy, the national leaders had to follow the logic of the constitutional reforms as well as the logic of their own strategy. Once colonialism was forced to yield a political space the space had to be occupied so that political-ideological struggle against colonialism could be waged from it. The reforms had to be worked; the question was in what manner. The answer, found after a great deal of experimentation and debate within the nationalist ranks, was to work the reforms but in a way that would upset imperialist calculations and advance the nationalist cause. In fact, the dominant sections of the national leadership from 1880 onwards looked upon the councils in the wider perspective of undermining colonial hegemony. Work in the legislative councils, municipal bodies, and, after 1937, through popular ministries was also used to promote reforms so as to give relief to the hard-pressed people, to built up confidence among the people in their capacity to govern themselves and to acquire prestige for the Congress and the national movement.

For a people who had been for long deprived of political power and subjected to the colonial ideology that they were incapable of exercising political power or challenging the colonial rulers, the strong speeches of a Pherozeshah Mehta, or a G.K. Gokhale, or a C.R. Das, or a Motilal Nehru in the legislative councils, the defeats of the Government in the legislatures during the 1920s, the wielding of elements of state power in the 1930s by the Congress ministries, and the nationalist exercise of municipal power in numerous cities, towns and districts, provided a boost to their sense of self-worth and self-confidence.

The nationalist strategy vis-a-vis legislative councils and constitutional reforms did register considerable success. Work in the councils did fill the political void at a time when the national movement was recouping its strength. And those working in the legislatures and municipal bodies did, on the whole, avoid getting co-opted or absorbed by the colonial state. They also successfully exposed the hollowness of colonial reforms and showed that India was, despite these reforms, being ruled from Britain in British interests and with the aid of 'lawless laws' whenever the rulers found it in their interests to do so.

The National Congress also successfully avoided a split once the lessons of the Surat split of 1907 had been learnt. All this was possible because Congressmen after 1919 were as a whole committed to mass politics and not to constitutional politics. Whenever the mass upsurge came, Congressmen abandoned the legislatures and plunged into the mass movement. They saw legislatures not as instruments of the gradual reform of the colonial structure but as arenas for the struggle against, or rather the struggle for the overthrow of, the colonial state.

*

For Gandhiji non-violence was a matter of principle. But for most of his contemporaries in the Congress — C.R. Das, Motilal Nehru, Jawaharlal Nehru, Maulana Azad, Sardar Patel, Acharya Narendra Dev, and so on — it was a matter of policy. As policy and as a form of political action and behaviour, it was an essential component of the overall strategy of the National Congress. In fact, non-violence was in some essential ways integral to the nature of the Indian national movement as a hegemonic movement based on wide mass mobilization. It was because of this hegemonic and mass character of the national movement that non-violence became one of its basic elements.

The adoption of non-violent forms of struggle enabled the participation of the mass of the people who could not have participated in a similar manner in a movement that adopted violent forms. This was particularly true of women's participation. Women would have found it difficult to join an armed struggle in large numbers. But when it came to undergoing suffering, facing lathi-charges, picketting for hours on end in the summer or the winter, women were probably stronger than men. Non-violence as a form of struggle and political behaviour was also linked to the semi-hegemonic, semi authoritarian character of the colonial state and the democratic character of the polity in Britain.

Non-violence meant above all fighting on the terrain of moral force. Non-violent mass movements placed the colonial authorities in the wrong and exposed the underpinning of colonial state power in brute force, when the authorities used armed force against peaceful *satyagrahis*. In fact, a non-violent mass movement put the rulers on the horns of a dilemma. If they hesitated to suppress it because it was peaceful, they lost an important part of their hegemony, because the civil resisters did break existing, colonial laws; not to take action against them amounted to the abdication of adminsitrative authority and a confession of the lack of strength to rule. If they suppressed the movement by use of force, they still lost, for it was morally difficult to justify the suppression of a peaceful movement and non-violent law-breakers through the use of force. They were in a no-win situation. The national movement had, on the other hand, a winning strategy: a semi-democratic rule had no answer to a mass movement that was non-violent and had massive popular support. In practice, the colonial authorities constantly vacillated between the two choices, usually plumping in the end for suppression. By taking recourse to suppression of a non-violent movement, they had to suffer constant erosion of hegemony by exposing the basic underpinnings of colonial rule in force and coercion. Consequently, the hegemony of colonial rule or its moral basis was destroyed bit by bit.

The adoption of non-violence was also linked to the fact that a disarmed people had hardly any other alternative. The colonial state had, through an elaborate system, completely disarmed the Indian people since 1858 and made it difficult, indeed nearly impossible, for them to obtain arms or training in their use. The leaders of the national movement understood from the beginning that Indians did not possess the material resources necessary to wage an armed struggle against the strong colonial state. In non-violent mass struggle, on the other hand, it was moral strength and the force of massive and mobilized public opinion that counted. And here the disarmed Indian people were not at a disadvantage. In other words, in a war of position, the non-violence of a mass movement was a way of becoming equal in political resources to the armed colonial state.

Basic here was also the understanding that the disarmed Indian people would not be able to withstand massive government repression, and that the use of violence would provide justification to the Government for launching a massive attack on the popular movement. Such heavy repression, it was believed, would demoralize the people and lead to political passivity.

Two further remarks may be made in this context. First, the question whether a mass movement could assume a violent form or as suggested by Jawaharlal Nehru and Bhagat Singh in short but pregnant statements, do mass movements in which millions participate — as distinguished from cadre-based movements — have to be, by their very nature, non-violent.[7] Second, in India's case, non-violent struggle was as revolutionary in character as an armed struggle in other contexts; a part of a revolutionary strategy of hegemonic struggle — of a Gramscian war of position — for changes in the structure of state and society.

*

Once the basic character and objectives of the nationalist strategy are grasped, once it is realised that both phases of the national movement were geared to the twin tasks of winning the hearts and minds of the Indian people and making them active participants in the movement and makers of their own history, the successes and failures of the different phases of the movement and of its basic strategy have to be evaluated in a new manner. The criterion of success or failure here is the extent to which the colonial hegemony over the Indian people was undermined and the people were politicized and prepared for struggle. Judged in this light, we would see that these objectives were progressively achieved through successive waves of mass movements alternating with phases of truce. Even when the mass movements were suppressed (1932, 1942), withdrawn (1922), ignored and suppressed (1940-41) or ended in compromise (1930-31) and were apparently defeated in terms of their stated objectives of winning freedom; in terms of hegemony, these movements were great successes, and marked leaps in mass political consciousness.

*

The strategic practice of the Indian national movement, especially during its leadership by Gandhiji, has a certain significance in world history comparable to that of the British, French, Russian, Chinese, Cuban and Vietnamese revolutions. India's is the only actual historical example of a semi-democratic or democratic type of state structure being replaced or transformed, of the broadly Gramscian theoretical perspective of a war of position being successfully practised. The study of its experience can yield many insights into the processes of historical change and state transformation, both in the past and the present, both to the historian and the political activist.

It is the one concrete example of a long-drawn out hegemonic struggle in which state power is not seized in a single historical moment of revolution but through a prolonged political process, in which the main terrain of popular struggle is the 'national-popular,' that is, the moral, political and ideological on a national or societal plane, in which the reserves of counter-hegemony are patiently built up over the years, in which mass movements are occasional but politics is perpetual, in which the struggle for state power goes through stages, each stage marking a step forward over the previous one, in which masses play an active part and do not depend upon a 'standing army' of cadres and yet the cadres play a critical role, in which the movement goes through the inevitable 'passive' phases but the popular political morale is not only kept up but enhanced. The problems of popular mobilization, of waging national-popular and hegemonic struggle or a war of position in societies functioning within the confines of the rule of law and a democratic and basically civil libertarian polity have something in common with the problems and circumstances of the Indian national movement. It is unquestionable that the study of the rich experience of the Indian national movement and in particular of Gandhian political strategy and style of leadership, as distinguished from Gandhian philosophy, has a certain significance for the revolutionary, that is, basic, transformation of democratic, hegemonic states and societies.

39 The Indian National Movement — The Ideological Dimension

The Indian national movement was basically the product of the central contradiction between colonialism and the interests of the Indian people. The leadership of the movement gradually arrived at, and based itself on, a clear, scientific and firm understanding of colonialism — that the British were using their political control to subordinate the Indian economy and society to the needs of the British economy and society. It began to perceive that overall the country was regressing and underdeveloping. On this basis, it evolved an understanding of the Indian reality and gradually generated and formed a clear-cut anti-colonial ideology.

Already, by the end of the 19th century, the founding fathers of the national movement had worked out a clear understanding of all the three modes of colonial exploitation: through plunder, taxation and the employment of Englishmen in India, through free and unequal trade, and through the investment of British capital. They had also grasped that India's colonial relationship was not an accident of history or a result of political policy but sprang rather from the very character of British society and India's subordination to it. Their entire critique of colonialism got its focus in the theory of the drain of wealth from India — the theory that a large part of India's capital and wealth were being transferred to Britain.

This understanding of the complex economic mechanism of modern imperialism was further advanced after 1918 under the impact of the anti-imperialist mass movements and the spread of Marxist ideas. The nationalist leadership also understood that the central contradiction could be resolved only through the transformation or overthrow of colonial economic relations. Moreover, at each stage of the movement's development, the leadership linked its analysis to the analysis of colonialism.

This anti-colonial world view was fully internalized by the lowermost cadres of the national movement. During the Gandhian era of mass politics, they disseminated this critique of colonialism among the common people in the urban as well as the rural areas. The twin themes of the drain of wealth and the use of India as a market for Britain's manufactured goods and the consequent destruction of the Indian handicraft industries formed the very pith and marrow of their agitation. This agitation undermined the foundations of colonial rule in the minds of the Indian people — it destroyed the carefully inculcated colonial myth that the British ruled India for the benefit of Indians, that they were the *Mai-Baap* of the common people.

Thus, if the primary contradiction provided the material or structural basis of the national movement, its grasping through the anti-colonial ideology provided its ideological basis. This opened the way to a firm and consistent anti-imperialist movement, which could follow highly flexible tactics precisely because of its rootedness in and adherence to the anti-colonial principle.

This strong anti-colonial basis of the movement was also very important because in any mass movement ideology plays a crucial role. In normal politics, passive support or opposition to, or voting for and against, a regime do not require very strong motivation. But active participation in a mass movement, involving immense sacrifice, cannot take place only on the basis of a sense of being poor or being exploited. It requires a strong, a very strong ideological commitment based on an understanding of the causes of the social condition. Therefore, it was the movement's scientific anti-colonial ideology which became the prime mover in its anti-imperialist struggle.

Along with the anti-colonial world view, certain other ideological elements constituted the broad socio-economic-political vision of the Indian national movement. Broadly speaking, this vision was that of bourgeois or capitalist independent economic development and a secular, republican, democratic, civil libertarian political order, both the economic and political order to be based on principles of social equality. Interestingly, this vision was to remain unquestioned throughout; the only controversy was confined to the capitalist character of the economic order, which was questioned in a serious manner after 1920.

*

The national movement was fully committed to parliamentary democracy and civil liberties. It provided the soil and climate in which these two could root themselves at a time when the colonial rulers were preaching that because of India's climate, the historical traditions of the Indian people and the nature of their religious and social institutions, democracy was not suited to India — that Indians must be ruled in an authoritarian and despotic manner. The British also increasingly tampered with and attacked the freedoms of speech and the Press.

Consequently, it was left to the national movement to fight for democracy and to internalize and indigenize it, that is to root it in the Indian soil. From the beginning it fought for the introduction of a representative form of government on the basis of popular elections. Tilak and other nationalists before 1920 and, then, Gandhiji and the Congress demanded the introduction of adult franchise so that all adult men and women could vote. From its inception, the Indian National Congress was organized along democratic lines. All its resolutions were publicly debated and then voted upon. The Congress permitted and encouraged minority opinion to freely express itself.

Some of the most important decisions in its history were taken after heated debates and on the basis of open voting. For example, the decision to start the Non-Cooperation Movement was taken in 1920 at Calcutta with 1886 voting for and 884 against Gandhiji's resolution. Similarly, at the Lahore Congress in 1929, a resolution sponsored by Gandhiji condemning the Revolutionary Terrorists' bomb attack on the Viceroy's train was passed by a narrow majority of 942 to 794. In 1942, thirteen Communist members of the AICC voted against the famous Quit India resolution. But instead of condemning these thirteen, Gandhiji, at the very beginning of his famous 'Do or Die' speech, said: 'I congratulate the thirteen friends who voted against the resolution, In doing so, they had nothing to be ashamed of. For the last twenty years we have tried to learn not to lose courage even when we are in a hopeless minority and are laughed at. We have learned to hold on to our beliefs in the confidence that we are in the right. It behoves us to cultivate this courage of conviction, for it ennobles man and raises his moral stature. I was, therefore, glad to see that these friends had imbibed the principle which I have tried to follow for the last fifty years and more.'[1]

*

The national movement was from the beginning zealous in defence of civil liberties. From the beginning, the nationalists fought against attack by the colonial authorities on the freedom of the Press, speech and association and other civil liberties. Lokamanya Tilak, for instance, often claimed that 'liberty of the Press and liberty of speech give birth to a nation and nourish it.'[2]

Gandhiji's commitment to civil liberties was also total. At the height of the Non-Cooperation Movement, he wrote in the *Young India* in January 1922: '*Swaraj*, the Khilafat, the Punjab occupy a subordinate place to the issue sprung upon the country by the Government. We must first make good the right of free speech and free association before we can make any further progress towards our goal . . . We must defend these elementary rights with our lives.' In another article soon after, he went on to explain these rights: 'Liberty of speech means that it is unassailed even when the speech hurts; liberty of the Press can be said to be truly respected only when the Press can comment in the severest terms upon and even misrepresent matters . . . Freedom of association is truly respected when assemblies of people can discuss even revolutionary projects.'[3] One other quotation from Gandhiji on the subject is of great relevance: 'Civil liberty consistent with the observance of non-violence is the first step towards *Swaraj*. It is the breath of political and social life. It is the foundation of freedom. There is no room there for dilution or compromise. It is the water of life.'[4]

Jawaharlal Nehru was, perhaps, the strongest champion of civil liberties. He assigned as much importance to them as he did to economic equality and socialism. The resolution on fundamental rights, passed by the Karachi Congress in 1931 and drafted by him, guaranteed the rights of free expression of opinion through speech and the Press and the freedom of association. In August 1936, as a result of his efforts, the Indian Civil Liberties Union was formed on non-party, non-sectarian lines to mobilize public opinion against all encroachments on civil liberties. He declared at this time: 'If civil liberties are suppressed, a nation loses all vitality and becomes impotent for anything substantial.'[5] And again in March 1940: 'The freedom of the Press does not consist in our permitting such things as we like to appear. Even a tyrant is agreeable to this type of freedom. Civil liberty and freedom of the Press consist in our permitting what we do not like, in our putting up with criticisms of ourselves, in our allowing public expression of views which seem to us even to be injurious to our cause itself.'6

Thus, over the years, the nationalist movement successfully created an ideology and culture of democracy and civil liberties based on respect for dissent, freedom of expression, the majority principle, and the right of minority opinions to exist and grow.

*

Secularism was from the beginning made a basic constituent of the nationalist ideology and a strong emphasis was laid on Hindu-Muslim unity. Although the national movement failed to eradicate communalism and prevent the partition of the country, this was due not to its deviance from a secular ideology but to weaknesses in its strategy for fighting communalism and its failure to fully grasp the socio-economic and ideological roots of communalism. The national movement also opposed caste oppression and after 1920 made abolition of untouchability a basic constituent of its programme and political work, though in this aspect too serious ideological flaws remained. In particular, a strong anti-caste ideology was not formed and propagated. The cause of women's liberation was also taken up seriously.

The national movement fully recognized the multifaceted diversity of the Indian people. That India was not yet a developed or structured nation, but a nation-in-the-making, was accepted and made the basis of political and ideological work and agitation. It was fully grasped that common subjection to colonial rule provided the material and emotional basis for nation-making and that one of the functions of the movement was to structure the nation through a common struggle against colonialism. It was also seen that the political and ideological practices of the movement would play a crucial role in the process of nation-in-the-making. Furthermore, it was clearly understood that the objective of unifying the Indian people into a nation would have to be realized by taking into account regional, religious, caste, ethnic and linguistic differences. The cultural aspirations of the different linguistic groups were given full recognition. From 1921, the Congress organized its provincial or area committees along linguistic lines and not according to the British-created multi-lingual provinces.

*

The Indian national movement accepted from the beginning, and with near unanimity, the objective of a complete economic transformation of the country on the basis of modern industrial and agricultural development. From Justice Ranade onwards, the nationalists were agreed that industrialization was the only means of overcoming the poverty of the people. Gandhiji was to some extent an exception to this near-unanimous opinion, but not wholly so. Nor did he counterpose his opinion to that of the rest of the national leadership. Moreover, his stand on the use of machines and large-scale industry has been grossly distorted. He was opposed to machines only when they displaced the labour of the many or enriched the few at the expense of the many. On the other hand, he repeatedly said that he would 'prize every invention of science made for the benefit of all.' He repeatedly said that he was not opposed to modern large-scale industry so long as it augmented, and lightened the burden of, human labour and not displaced it. Moreover, he laid down another condition: All large-scale industry should be owned and controlled by the state and not by private capitalists.[7]

The nationalists were fully committed to the larger goal of independent, self-reliant economic development to be based on independence from foreign capital, the creation of an indigenous capital goods or machine-making sector and the foundation and development of independent science and technology. Ever since the 1840s, British economists and administrators had argued for the investment of foreign capital as the major instrument for the development of India.[8] The Indian nationalists, from Dadabhai Naoroji and Tilak to Gandhiji and Nehru, disagreed vehemently. Foreign capital, they argued, did not develop a country but underdeveloped it. It suppressed indigenous capital and made its future growth difficult. It was also, the nationalists said, politically harmful because, sooner or later it began to wield an increasing and dominating influence over the administration.[9]

Starting with Dadabhai Naoroji and Ranade, the nationalists visualized a crucial role for the public sector in the building of an independent and modern economy. In the 1930s, Jawaharlal Nehru, Gandhiji, and the left-wing also argued for the public sector, especially in large-scale and key industries, as a means of preventing the concentration of wealth in a few hands. In the late 1930s, the objective of economic planning was also widely accepted. In 1938, the Congress, then under the presidentship of Subhas Chandra Bose, set up the National Planning Committee under the chairmanship of Nehru, to draw up a development plan for free India. During World War II, several other plans were devised, the most important being the Bombay Plan drawn up by the big three of the Indian capitalist world — J.R.D. Tata, G.D. Birla and Sri Ram. This plan too visualized far-reaching land reforms, a large public sector and massive public and private investment.

As brought out earlier, the world outlook of the national movement based on anti-colonialism, anti-Fascism, peace and national independence was a powerful element of its overall ideology.

*

From its early days, the national movement adopted a pro-poor orientation. The entire economic agitation of the Moderates and their critique of colonialism was linked to the growing poverty of the masses. This orientation was immensely strengthened by the impact of the Russian Revolution of 1917, the coming of Gandhiji on the political stage and the growth of powerful left-wing parties and groups during the 1920s and 1930s. The movement adopted policies and a programme of reforms during various stages of the struggle that were quite radical by contemporary standards.

Compulsory primary education, the lowering of taxation on the poor and middle classes, the reduction of the salt tax, land revenue and rent, relief from indebtedness and the provision of cheap credit to peasants, the protection of tenants' rights, workers' right to a living wage and a shorter working day, higher wages for low-paid government servants, including policemen, the defence of the right of workers' and peasants' to organize themselves, the protection and promotion of village industries, the promotion of modern science and technical education, the eradication of the drink evil, the improvement of the social position of women including their right to work and education and to equal political rights, the initiation of legal and social measures for the abolition of untouchability, and the reform of the machinery of law and order were some of the major reforms demanded by the Indian national movement.

The basic pro-people or pro-poor orientation of the national movement and the notion that politics must be based on the people, who must be politicized, activized and brought into politics, also made it easier to give it a socialist orientation.

But still, as pointed out earlier, the nationalist developmental perspective was confined within bourgeois parameters, that is, independent economic development was visualized within a capitalist framework. After 1919, when the national movement became a mass movement, Gandhiji evolved and propagated a different, non-capitalist, basically peasantist-artisanist outlook but his socio-economic programme and thought were not capable of challenging the basic hegemony of bourgeois ideology over the national movement.

It is true that the national movement, as an anti-colonial movement in a colony in which the primary contradiction pitted the entire society against colonialism, was a popular, people's movement; it was a multi-class movement which represented the interests of the different classes and strata of Indian society. However, the Indian people, though unified against colonialism and in the anti-imperialist struggle, were at the same time divided into social classes which had their own contradictions with colonialism as well as with each other. Different classes and strata had different levels and degrees of contradiction with colonialism as also different extent and manner of participation in the anti-imperialist struggle. The result was that the anti-colonial struggle could have several different class consequences. The final outcome of the struggle could see several different balances of class or political and ideological forces. This balance of forces would help decide in whose class interests would the primary contradiction get resolved as a result of the anti-imperialist struggle, that is, what sort of India would come into existence after freedom. In other words, freedom could result in a socialist or a capitalist societal order.

Beginning with the 1920s, a powerful socialist trend developed in the national movement. The bourgeois developmental perspective of the national movement was challenged in a serious manner by early Communist groups, Jawaharlal Nehru, Subhas Chandra Bose, and a large number of socialist-minded groups and individuals. The struggle for the spread of socialist ideas was intensified in the 1930s when these were joined by the Congress Socialist Party, a reorganized Communist Party and the Royists. The Great Depression of the 1930s in the capitalist world, the Russian Revolution and the success of the Soviet Five Year Plans, and the anti-fascist wave the world over during the 1930s made socialist ideas attractive. Most of the leaders of the youth movement of the late 1920s and a large number of Revolutionary Terrorists also made the turn to socialism. Throughout the 1920s, 1930s, and 1940s, the youthful nationalist cadres were increasingly turning to socialist ideas.

The left-wing tried to popularize the idea that constant class strug-gles were going on within India between peasants and landlords and workers and capitalists. It tried to organize these struggles through their class organizations — *kisan sabhas* and trade unions. But above all, it struggled to transform the national movement in a leftward, socialist ideological direction, to impart to the movement a vision of socialist India after independence.

Jawaharlal Nehru played a very important role in popularizing the vision of a socialist India both within the national movement and in the country at large. Nehru argued that political freedom must mean the economic emancipation of the masses. Throughout the 1930s, he pointed to the inadequacy of the existing nationalist ideology and the hegemony of bourgeois ideology over the national movement, and stressed the need to inculcate a new socialist or basically Marxist ideol-ogy, which would enable the people to study their social condition scientifically and to give the Congress a new socialist ideological orientation.

The 1930s were highly favourable to socialist ideas, and they spread widely and rapidly. But though the left-wing and socialist ideas grew in geometric proportions, they did not succeed in becoming the dominant ideological trend within the national movement. They did, however, succeed in becoming a basic constituent of the national movement and in constantly shifting it leftward. The national movement continuously defined itself further and further in a radical direction in terms of the popular element. Increasingly, freedom was defined in socio-economic terms which went far beyond the mere absence of foreign rule. By the late 1930s, the Indian national movement was one of the most radical of the national liberation movements.

This radicalism found reflection in the Congress resolutions at Karachi, Lucknow and Faizpur (in 1931 and 1936), in the election man-ifestoes of 1936 and 1945-46 and in the economic and social reforms of the Congress Ministries from 1937-39. In fact, the Congress progres-sively evolved in a radical socio-economic-political direction and increasingly adopted most of the demands put forward by the Left though with a time lag of a few years. The politics of the Left and workers' and peasants' struggles, of course, played a crucial role in this evolution. One result was that even the Congress Right was not only firmly anti-imperialist but also committed to basic changes in political and economic power even though it was opposed to socialism. It remained bourgeois in outlook but with a reformist outlook.

This becomes evident when we study the evolution of the agrarian policy of the Congress, for after all the key question in India was that of the social condition of the peasant. The Congress had always fought for the peasant demands vis-a-vis the colonial state. But goaded by the left-wing and the peasant movements, the Congress accepted at Faizpur in 1936 a programme of substantial reduction in rent and revenue, abolition of feudal dues and forced labour, fixity of tenure and a living wage for agricultural labourers. The Congress Ministries passed legislation, which varied in its radical content from province to province, to protect tenants' rights and prevent expropriation by the moneylenders. Finally, in 1945, the Congress Working Committee accepted the policy of the abolition of landlordism and of land belonging to the tiller when it declared: 'The reform of the land system involves the removal of intermediaries between the peasant and the state.'[10]

*

A major ideological dimension of the national movement was the overall social outlook of Gandhiji and the Gandhians. Gandhiji did not accept a class analysis of society and the role of class struggle. He was also opposed to the use of violence even in defence of the interests of the poor. But his basic outlook was that of social transformation. He was committed to basic changes in the existing system of economic and political power. Moreover, he was constantly moving in a radical direction during the 1930s and 1940s. In 1933, he agreed with Nehru that 'without a material revision of vested interests the condition of the masses can never be improved.'[11] He was beginning to oppose private property and thus radicalize his theory of trusteeship. He repeatedly argued for the nationalization of large-scale industry. He condemned the exploitation of the masses inherent in capitalism and landlordism. He was highly critical of the socio-economic role played by the middle classes.[12]

His emphasis on the removal of distinction and discrimination between physical and mental labour, his overall emphasis on social and economic equality and on the self-activity of the masses, his opposition to caste inequality and oppression, his active support to women's social liberation, and the general orientation of his thought and writing towards the exploited, the oppressed and the down-trodden tended in general to impart a radical ideological direction to the national movement.

The most remarkable development was Gandhiji's shift towards agrarian radicalism. In 1937, he said: 'That the land today does not belong to the people is too true . . . (But) Land and all property is his who will work it. Unfortunately the workers are or have been kept ignorant of this simple fact.'[13] In 1942, he again declared that 'the land belongs to those who will work on it and to no one else.'[14] Similarly, in June 1942 Gandhiji told Louis Fischer in answer to his question: 'What is your programme for the improvement of the lot of the peasantry?' that 'the peasants would take the land. We would not have to tell them to take it. They would take it.' And when Fischer asked, 'Would the landlords be compensated?' He replied: 'No, that would be fiscally impossible.' Fischer asked: 'Well, how do you actually see your impending civil disobedience movement?' Gandhiji replied: 'In the villages, the peasants will stop paying taxes. They will make salt despite official prohibition . . . Their next step will be to seize the land.' 'With violence?' asked Fischer. Gandhiji replied: 'There may be violence, but then again the landlords may cooperate . . . They might cooperate by fleeing.' Fischer said that the landlords 'might organize violent resistance.' Gandhiji's reply was: 'There may be fifteen days of chaos, but I think we could soon bring that under control.' Did this mean, asked Fischer, that there must be 'confiscation without compensation?' Gandhiji replied: 'Of course. It would be financially impossible for anybody to compensate the landlords.'[15]

*

Thus the national movement based itself on a clear-cut anti-colonial ideology and the vision of a civil libertarian, democratic, secular and socially radical society. The Indian economy was to be developed along independent, self-reliant lines. It was this vision, combined with anti-colonial ideology and a pro-poor radical socio-economic orientation that enabled the national movement to base itself on the politically awakened and politically active people and to acquire the character of a popular, people's movement.

Additional Reading

General: (A) Historical Background

1. Bipan Chandra, *Modern India*, New Delhi, 1971.
2. Tara Chand, *History of the Freedom Movement in India*, Vol.I, Delhi, 1961.
3. Percival Spear, *Oxford History of India*, New Delhi, 1974.
4. R.Palme Dutt, *India Today*, Bombay, 1949 edition.
5. A.R. Desai, *Social Background of Indian Nationalism*, Bombay, 1959 edition.

(B) National Movement

1. *A Centenary History of the Indian National Congress*, 3 Vols., B.N. Pande, general editor, New Delhi, 1985.
2. Sumit Sarkar, *Modern India 1885-1947*, Delhi, 1983.
3. A.R. Desai, *Social Background of Indian Nationalism*.
4. Bipan Chandra, Amales Tripathi and Barun De, *Freedom Struggle*, New Delhi, 1972.
5. S. Gopal, *Jawaharlal Nehru — A Biography*, Vol.One, London, 1975.
6. B.R. Nanda, *Mahatma Gandhi — A Biography*, London, 1958.
7. Bipan Chandra, *Indian National Movement: Long-term Dynamics*, New Delhi, 1988.

Introduction: (A) Gramsci and Hegemony

1. A.Gramsci, *Selections from the Prison Notebooks*, London, 1971.
2. Perry Anderson, 'The Antinomies of Antonio Gramsci,' New Left Review, 100, London, 1976-7.

3. C. Buci-Glucksmann, *Gramsci and the State*, London, 1979.

4. J. Femia, *Gramsci's Political Thought*, Oxford, 1981.

5. C.Mouffe, editor, *Gramsci and Marxist Theory*, London, 1979.

6. A.S. Sassoon, *Gramsci's Politics*, London, 1980.

7. Ernesto Laclau: *Politics and Ideology in Marxist Theory*, London, 1977.

(B) Historiographic Schools

1. V. Chirol, *Indian Unrest*, London, 1910.

2. Bruce T. McCully, *English Education and the Origins of Indian Nationalism*, New York, 1940.

3. Anil Seal, *The Emergence of Indian Nationalism: Competition and Collaboration in the Late 19th Century*, Cambridge, 1968.

4. J. Gallaghar, G.Johnson and A. Seal, editors, *Locality, Province and Nation*, Cambridge, 1973.

5. C.J. Baker, G.Johnson, A.Seal, editors, 'Power, Profit and Politics: Essays on Imperialism, Nationalism and Change in 20th Century India,' *Modern Asian Studies*, Cambridge, 1981.

6. Ranajit Guha, *Subaltern Studies*, I-IV, New Delhi, 1982-1986.

7. R.G. Pradhan, *India's Struggle for Swaraj*, Madras, 1929.

8. B. Pattabhi Sitaramayya, *The History of the Indian National Congress (1885-1935)*, Madras, 1935.

9. Bisheshwar Prasad, *Changing Modes of Indian National Movement*, New Delhi, 1966.

10. R.Falme Dutt, *India Today*.

11. A.R. Desai, *Social Background of Indian Nationalism*.

12. E.M.S. Namboodiripad, *History of Indian Freedom Struggle*, Trivandrum, 1986.

13. S. Gopal, 'Book Review,' *The Indian Economic and Social History Review*, New Delhi, Vol.XIV, No.3, July-September 1977.

14. Mridula Mukherjee, 'Book Review,' *Studies in History*, New Delhi, Vol.I, January-June, 1979.

15. Jayant Prasad, *'Neo-Liberal History or an Imperialist Apologia?'* *Social Scientist*, New Delhi, Vol.1, No.12, July 1973.

16. Tapan Raychaudhuri, 'Indian Nationalism as Animal Politics,' *The Historical Journal*, Cambridge, Vol.22, No.3, 1979.

17. Mridula Mukherjee, 'Peasont Resistance, and Consciousness: 'Subalterns' and Beyond,' *EPW*, 8 and 15 October, 1988.

1. The First Major Challenge: The Revolt of 1857

1. S.N. Sen, *Eighteen Fifty-Seven*, Delhi, 1957.

2. Harprasad Chattopadhyaya, *The Sepoy Mutiny — A Social Study*

and Analysis, Calcutta, 1957.

3. S.B. Chaudhuri, *Civil Rebellion in the Indian Mutinies 1857-59*, Calcutta, 1957.

4. Eric Stokes, *The Peasant and the Raj*, Cambridge, 1978.

5. P.C. Joshi, editor, *Rebellion, 1857: A Symposium*, Delhi, 1957.

6. Rudrangshu Mukherjee, *Awadh in Revolt 1857-1858*, Delhi, 1984.

2 & 3. Civil Rebellions and Tribal Uprisings and Peasant Movements and Uprisings After 1857

1. A.R. Desai, editor, *Peasant Struggles in India*, Delhi, 1979.

2. S.B. Chaudhuri, *Civil Disturbances during the British Rule in India*, Calcutta, 1955.

3. Ranajit Guha, *Elementary Aspects of Peasant Insurgency in Colonial India*, Delhi, 1983.

4. Blair B. Kling, *The Blue Mutiny — The Indigo Disturbances in Bengal 1859-1862*, Philadelphia, 1966.

5. Kalyan Kumar Sen Gupta, *Pabna Disturbances and the Politics of Rent 1873-1885*, New Delhi, 1974.

6. Ravinder Kumar, *Western India in the Nineteenth Century*, London, 1968.

7. Stephen Fuchs, *Rebellious Prophets: A Study of Messianic Movements in Indian Religions*, Bombay, 1965.

8. Suresh Singh, *The Dust-Storm and the Hanging Mist*, Calcutta, 1966.

9. Suresh Singh, 'Colonial Transformation of the Tribal Society in Middle India,' *Proceedings of the Indian History Congress*, 1977.

4 & 5. Foundation of the Congress: The Myth and Foundation of the Indian National Congress: The Reality

1. Briton Martin, *New India 1885*, Bombay, 1970.

2. B.L. Grover, *British Policy Towards Indian Nationalism 1885-1909*, Delhi, 1967.

3. S.R. Mehrotra, *Emergence of Indian National Congress*, Delhi, 1971.

4. William Wedderburn, *Allan Octavian Hume, C.B*, London, 1913.

5. Amitabh Mukherjee, 'Genesis of the Indian National Congress,' and Sita Ram Singh, 'Moderates and Extremists,' in a *A Centenary History of the Indian National Congress (1885-1985)*, General Editor, B.N. Pande, New Delhi, 1985, Vol.I: 1885-1919.

6. Socio-Religious Reforms and the National Awakening

1. Charles Hiemsath, *Indian Nationalism and Hindu Social Reform*, Princeton, 1964.
2. V.C. Joshi, editor, *Rammohan and the Process of Modernization in India*, Delhi, 1975.
3. Ashok Sen, *Elusive Milestones of Ishwarchandra Vidyasagar*, Calcutta, 1977.
4. K.N. Panikkar, Presidential Address, Modern Indian History, *Proceedings of the Indian History Congress*, 1975.
5. K.N. Panikkar, 'Intellectual and Cultural History of Colonial India: Some Conceptual and Historiographical Questions,' in S. Bhattacharya and Romila Thapar, editors, *Situating Indian History*, Delhi, 1986.
6. K.N. Panikkar, editor, *Studies in History*, Special Issue on 'Intellectual History of Colonial India,' Vol.3, No.1, January-June, 1987.

7. Economic Critique of Colonialism

1. R.C. Dutt, *The Economic History of India Under Early British Rule*, and *Economic History of India in the Victorian Age*, Delhi, 1960 reprint.
2. Bipan Chandra, *The Rise and Growth of Economic Nationalism in India*, New Delhi, 1984 reprint.
3. Bipan Chandra, 'British and Indian Ideas on Indian Economic Development, 1858-1905,' in his *Nationalism and Colonialism in Modern India*, New Delhi, 1987 reprint.
4. B.N. Ganguli, *Indian Economic Thought — Nineteenth Century Perspectives*, New Delhi, 1977.
5. J.R. McLane, *Indian Nationalsim and the Early Congress*, Princeton, 1977.

8. The Fight to Secure Press Freedom

1. G.P. Pradhan and A.K. Bhagwat, *Lokamanya Tilak — A Biography*, Bombay, 1958.
2. J. Natarajan, *History of Indian Journalism — Part II of the Report of the Press Commission*, New Delhi, 1955.
3. Surendranath Banerjea, *A Nation in the Making*, Calcutta, 1963 reprint.
4. Ram Gopal, *Lokamanya Tilak*, Bombay, 1965 reprint.

9. Propaganda in the Legislatures

1. B.R. Nanda *Gokhale, The Indian Moderates and the Raj*, Delhi, 1977.
2. Homi Mody, *Sir Pherozeshah Mehta, A Political Biography*, Bombay, 1963 reprint.
3. *Speeches and Writings of Gopal Krishna Gokhale* edited, by D.G. Karve and D.V. Ambekar, Bombay 1966, 3 Volumes.
4. Pherozeshah M. Mehta, *Speeches and Writings*, edited by C.Y. Chintamani, Allahabad, 1905.

10. The Swadeshi Movement — 1903-1908

1. Sumit Sarkar, *The Swadeshi Movement in Bengal, 1903-1908*, New Delhi, 1973.
2. S. Gopal, *British Policy in India, 1858-1905*, Cambridge, 1965.
3. Haridas and Uma Mukherjee, *India's Fight for Freedom or the Swadeshi Movement, 1905-1906*, Calcutta, 1958.
4. Amales Tripathi, *The Extremist Challenge*, Calcutta, 1967.
5. J.R. McLane, *Indian Nationalism and the Early Congress*, Princeton, 1977.

11. The Split in the Congress and the Rise of Revolutionary Terrorism

1. B.R. Nanda, *Gokhale*.
2. G.P. Pradhan and A.K. Bhagwat, *Lokamanya Tilak*.
3. Arun Chandra Guha, *First Spark of Revolution*, Bombay, 1971.
4. Biman Bihari Majumdar, *Militant Nationalism of India*, Calcutta, 1966.
5. Kalicharan Ghosh, *Roll of Honour*, Calcutta, 1965.
6. Budhadeva Bhattacharya, editor, *Freedom Struggle and Anushilan Samiti*, Vol. One, 1979.

12. World War I and Indian Nationalism: The Ghadar

1. Harish K. Puri, *Ghadar Movement*, Amritsar, 1983.
2. Emily C. Brown, *Har Dayal: Hindu Revolutionary and Rationalist*, Tucson, 1975.
3. Mark Juergensmeyer, 'The Ghadar Syndrome: Immigrant Sikhs and the Nationalist Pride,' in Mark Juergensmeyer and N.Gerald Barrier, editors, *Sikh Studies*, Berkeley, 1979.
4. A.C. Bose, *Indian Revolutionaries Abroad 1905-22*, Patna, 1971.

5. Sohan Singh Josh, *Hindustan Ghadar Party: A Short History*, New Delhi, 1977.

13. The Home Rule Movement and its Fallout

1. G.P. Pradhan and A.K. Bhagwat, *Lokamanya Tilak: A Biography*, Chs.13-17.
2. T.V. Parvate, *Bal Gangadhar Tilak*, Ahmedabad, 1958.
3. H.F. Owen, 'Towards Nation-wide Agitation and Organisation: The Home Rule Leagues, 1915-18,' in D.A. Low, editor, *Soundings in Modern South Asian History*, Berkeley and Los Angeles, 1968, pp. 159-95.
4. S. Vijayalakshmi, 'Healing the Breach and the Home Rule Movement,' in *A Centenary History of the Indian National Congress*, Vol.I.

14. Gandhi's Early Career and Activism

1. Chandran D.S Devanesan, *The Making of the Mahatma*, Madras, 1969.
2. R.A. Huttenback, *Gandhi in South Africa*, Ithaca, New York, 1971.
3. M.K. Gandhi, *An Autobiography:The Story of My Experiments with Truth*, London, 1966.
4. B.R. Nanda, *Mahatma Gandhi*, New Delhi, 1958, Chs. 4-21.
5. Ravinder Kumar, editor, *Essays on Gandhian Politics: The Rowlatt Satyagraha of 1919*, London, 1971.
6. David Hardiman, *Peasant Nationalists of Gujarat: Kheda District 1917-1934*, New Delhi, 1981, Chapter 5.

15. The Non-Cooperation Movement — 1920-22

1. Tendulkar, *Mahatma*, Vol.2.
2. Jawaharlal Nehru, *An Autobiography*, Bombay, 1962 reprint, Chs. 7-13.
3. P.C. Bamford, *Histories of Khilafat and Non-Cooperation Movements*, Delhi, 1925, reprinted 1985.
4. Sumit Sarkar, *Modern India*, New Delhi, 1983, pp.195-226.
5. *1921 Movement: Reminiscences*, New Delhi, 1971.
6. J.C. Jha, 'The Struggle for Swaraj (1919-1922),' in *A Centenary History of the Indian National Congress*, Vol.II.

16. Peasant Movements and Nationalism in the 1920s

1. Majid H. Siddiqi, *Agrarian Unrest in North India: The United Provinces (1918-22)*, New Delhi, 1978.

2. Kapil Kumar, *Peasants in Revolt: Tenants, Congress, Landlords and the Raj in Oudh, 1886-1922*, New Delhi, 1984.

3. S. Gopal, *Jawaharlal Nehru: A Biography*, Vol.One, Chapter 4.

4. K.N. Panikkar, 'Peasant Revolts in Malabar in the Nineteenth and Twentieth Centuries,' in A.R. Desai, editor, *Peasant Struggles in India.*

5. Shirin Mehta, *The Peasantry and Nationalism*, New Delhi, 1984.

6. Mahadev Desai, *The Story of Bardoli*, Ahmedabad, 1957.

17. The Indian Working Class and the National Movement

1. Bipan Chandra, *The Rise and Growth of Economic Nationalism in India*, Chapter VIII.

2. Sumit Sarkar, *The Swadeshi Movement in Bengal 1903-1908*, Chapter V.

3. Ravinder Kumar, 'From Swaraj to Purna Swaraj: Nationalist Politics in the City of Bombay, 1930-32,' in D.A. Low, ed., *Congress and the Raj: Facets of Indian Struggle 1917-47*, London, 1977.

4. Aditya Mukherjee, 'The Workers' and Peasants' Parties, 1926-30: An Aspect of Communism in India,' in Bipan Chandra, editor, *The Indian Left: Critical Appraisals*, New Delhi, 1983.

5. Lajpat Jagga, 'Colonial Railwaymen and British Rule — A Probe into Railway Labour Agitation in India, 1919-1922,' in Bipan Chandra, editor, *The Indian Left.*

6. V.V. Balabushevich and A.M. Dyakov, editors, *A Contemporary History of India*, New Delhi, 1964.

7. Sukomal Sen, *Working Class of India, History of Emergence and Movement, 1830-1970*, Calcutta, 1977.

18. The Struggles for Gurdwara Reforms and Temple Entry

1. Mohinder Singh, *The Akali Movement*, Delhi, 1978.

2. Tendulkar, *Mahatma*, Vol.2.

3. T.K. Ravindran, *Vaikkom Satyagraha and Gandhi*, Trivandrum, 1973.

4. Gail Omvedt, *Cultural Revolt in a Colonial Society: The Non-Brahmin Movement in Western India (1873-1930)*, Bombay, 1976.

5. D. Keer, *Dr. Ambedkar: Life and Mission*, Bombay, 1954.

6. E.M.S. Namboodiripad, *How I became a Communist*, Trivandrum, 1976.

7. E.Sa. Viswanathan, *The Political Career of E.V. Ramasami Naicker*, Madras, 1983.

19. The Years of Stagnation — Swarajists, No-Changers and Gandhiji

1. B.R. Nanda, *The Nehrus, Motilal and Jawaharlal*, London, 1962.
2. Hemendranath Gupta, *Deshbandhu Chittaranjan Das*, Delhi, 1960.
3. Manoranjan Jha, *Role of Central Legislature in the Freedom Struggle*, New Delhi, 1972.
4. Tendulkar, *Mahatma*, Vol.2.
5. B.R. Nanda, 'The Swarajist Interlude,' in *A Centenary History of the Indian National Congress*, Vol.II.

20. Bhagat Singh, Surya Sen and the Revolutionary Terrorists

1. *Challenge — A Saga for India's Struggle for Freedom*, edited by Nitish Ranjan Ray, *et.al.*, New Delhi, 1984.
2. Shiv Varma, editor, *Selected Writings of Shaheed Bhagat Singh*, New Delhi, 1986.
3. Budhadeva Bhattacharyya, editor, *Freedom Struggle and Anushilan Samiti*, Vol.One.
4. Bipan Chandra, 'The Ideological Development of the Revolutionary Terrorists in Northern India in the 1920s,' in his *Nationalism and Colonialism in Modern India*.

21. The Gathering Storm 1927-31

1. S. Gopal, *Jawaharlal Nehru: A Biography*, Vol.One, Chapter 9.
2. Tendulkar, *Mahatma*, Vol.2.
3. Subhas Bose, *The Indian Struggle*, Calcutta, 1964 edition.
4. Jawaharlal Nehru, *An Autobiography*, Chapters 24-27.
5. Sashi Joshi, 'Nehru and the Emergence of the Left Bloc, 1927-29,'in Bipan Chandra, editor, *The Indian Left*.

22. Civil Disobedience 1930-31

1. Tendulkar, *Mahatma*, Vol.3.
2. S. Gopal, *Jawaharlal Nehru: A Biography*, Volume One, Chapter 10.
3. Gyanendra Pandey, *The Ascendency of the Congress in Uttar Pradesh: 1926-34*, New Delhi, 1978.

4. D.A. Low, editor,*Congress and the Raj.*

5. David Hardiman, *Peasant Nationalists of Gujarat: Kheda District 1917-34*, Chapter 9.

6. A.K. Gopalan, *In the Cause of the People: Reminiscences*, Madras, 1973, Chapters 3-4.

7. Tanika Sarkar, 'The First Phase of Civil Disobedience in Bengal, 1930-1,' in *The Indian Historical Review*, New Delhi, July 1977, Vol.IV, No.1.

23 From Karachi to Wardha: The Years from 1932 to 1934

1. Tendulkar, *Mahatma*, Vol.3.

2. S. Gopal, *Jawaharlal Nehru — A Biography*, Vol.One, Chapters 11-13.

3. B.R. Nanda, *Mahatma Gandhi — A Biography*.

4. D. Keer, *Dr. Ambedkar: Life and Mission*, Bombay, 1954.

5. Jawaharlal Nehru, *An Autobiography*.

6. D.A. Low, editor, *Congress and the Raj*.

24. The Rise of the Left-Wing

1. Jawaharlal Nehru, *An Autobiography*.

2. Subhas Bose, *The Indian Struggle*.

3. S. Gopal, *Jawaharlal Nehru — A Biography*, Vol.One.

4. Bipan Chandra, editor, *The Indian Left*.

5. Girja Shankar, *Socialist Trends in Indian National Movement*, Meerut, 1987.

6. *Guidelines of the History of the Communist Party of India*, issued by Central Party Education Department, New Delhi, 1974.

7. Satyabrata Rai Chowdhury, *Leftist Movements in India: 1917-1947*, Calcutta, 1977.

25. The Strategic Debate (1934-37)

1. Tendulkar, *Mahatma*, Vol.4.

2. S. Gopal, *Jawaharlal Nehru — A Biography*, Vol.One, Chapters 14-15.

3. Jawaharlal Nehru, *An Autobiography*.

4. Bipan Chandra, 'Jawaharlal Nehru and the Capitalist Class, 1936,' in his *Nationalism and Colonialism in Modern India*.

5. Subhas Bose, *The Indian Struggle*.

26. Twenty-Eight Months of Congress Rule

1. Reginald Coupland, *Indian Politics, 1936-1942*, Bombay, 1944.
2. Visalakshi Menon, 'The Indian National Congress and Mass Mobilization — A Study of the U.P. 1937-39,' *Studies in History*, New Delhi, Vol.II, No.2, July-December 1980.
3. S. Gopal, *Jawaharlal Nehru — A Biography*, Vol. One, Chapters 14-15.
4. Kishori Mohan Patra, 'The First Congress Ministries: Problems and Prospects (1937-1939),' in *A Centenary History of the Indian National Congress*, Vol.III.
5. Tendulkar, *Mahatma*, Vols. 4 and 5.
6. Amalendu Guha, *Planter Raj to Swaraj: Freedom Struggle and Electoral Politics in Assam 1926-1947*, New Delhi, 1977.

27. Peasant Movements in the 1930s and '40s

1. K. Gopalan Kutty, 'The Integration of Anti-Landlord Movement with the Movement Against Imperialism,' in Bipan Chandra, editor, *The Indian Left*.
2. S. Henningham, *Peasant Movements in Colonial India: North Bihar, 1917-42*, Canberra, 1982, Chapter 6.
3. Sunil Sen, *Agrarian Struggle in Bengal*, New Delhi, 1972.
4. Mridula Mukherjee, 'Communists and Peasants in Punjab: A Focus on the Muzara Movement in Patiala, 1937-53,' in Bipan Chandra, editor, *The Indian Left*.
5. N.G. Ranga, *Fight for Freedom: Autobiography*, Delhi, 1968.
6. A.R. Desai, editor, *Peasant Struggles in India*.

28. The Freedom Struggle in Princely India

1. Urmila Phadnis, *Towards the Integration of Indian States, 1919-47*, Bombay, 1968.
2. John R. Wood, 'Rajkot: Indian Nationalism in the Princely Context: The Rajkot Satyagraha of 1938-9,' in Robin Jeffrey, editor, *People, Princes and Paramount Power*, New Delhi, 1978.
3. Tendulkar, *Mahatma*, Vol.5.
4. P. Sundarayya, *Telengana People's Struggle and Its Lessons*, Calcutta, 1972, Part I, Chapters 1-4.
5. Ramanand Tirtha, *Memoirs of Hyderabad Freedom Struggle*, Bombay, 1967.
6. Mridula Mukherjee, 'Communists and Peasants in Punjab: A Focus on

the Muzara Movement in Patiala, 1937-53,' in Bipan Chandra, editor, *The Indian Left.*

29. Indian Capitalists and the National Movement

1. Bipan Chandra, 'Indian Capitalist Class and Imperialism Before 1947,' and 'Jawaharlal Nehru and the Capitalist Class, 1936,' in his *Nationalism and Colonialism in Modern India.*

2. Aditya Mukherjee, 'The Indian Capitalist Class: Aspects of its Economic Political and Ideological Development in the Colonial Period, 1927-47,' in S. Bhattacharya and Romila Thapar, editors, *Situating Indian History.*

3. Aditya Mukherjee, 'Indian Capitalists and Congress on National Planning and Public Sector,' in K.N. Panikkar, editor, *National and Left Movements in India*, New Delhi, 1980.

4. Rajat Ray, *Industrialization in India, Growth and Conflict in the Private Corporate Sector, 1914-1947*, New Delhi, 1979.

5. B. Chatterjee, 'Business and Politics in the 1930s, Lancashire and the Making of the Indo-British Trade Agreement,' *Modern Asian Studies*, London, Vol.15, No.3, 1981.

6. Gokhale Institute, *Notes on the Rise of Business Communities in India*, New York, 1951.

7. H. Venkatasubbiah, *Enterprise and Economic Change, 50 Years of FICCI*, New Delhi, 1977.

8. A.K. Bagchi, *Private Investment in India, 1900-1939*, Cambridge, 1972.

30. The Development of a Nationalist Foreign Policy

1. Bimal Prasad, *The Origins of Indian Foreign Policy*, Calcutta, 1962 edition.

2. S. Gopal, *Jawaharlal Nehru — A Biography,* Volume One.

3. Bimal Prasad, 'Foreign Policy in the Making,' in *A Centenary History of the Indian National Congress*, Vol.III.

4. Bipan Chandra, 'Indian Nationalists and Foreign Wars and Expeditions, 1878-1903,' in *Homage to a Historian*, edited by N. Jagadeesan and S. Jeyapragasam, Madurai, 1976.

31 & 32 & 33. The Rise and Growth of Communalism and The Liberal Phase and Jinnah, Golwalkar and Extreme Communalism

1. Bipan Chandra, *Communalism in Modern India*, New Delhi, 1987 edition.

2. W.C. Smith, *Modern Islam in India*, Lahore, 1963 reprint.

3. K.B. Krishna, *The Problem of Minorities*, London, 1939.

4. Moin Shakir, *Khilafat to Partition — A Study of Major Political Trends among Indian Muslims during 1919-1941*, Delhi, 1983 edition.

5. Khalid B. Sayeed, *Pakistan — The Formative Phase 1857-1948*, London, 1968.

6. Peter Hardy, *The Muslims of British India*, Cambridge, 1972.

7. Francis Robinson, *Separatism Among Indian Muslims: The Politics of the United Provinces' Muslims, 1860-1923*, Delhi, 1975.

8. Mushirul Hasan, *Nationalism and Communal Politics in India, 1916-1928*, New Delhi, 1979.

9. Mushirul Hasan, editor, *Communal and Pan-Islamic Trends in Colonial India*, Delhi, 1981.

10. C.H. Philips and M.D. Wainwright, editors, *The Partition of India*, London, 1970.

11. Prabha Dixit, *Communalism — A Struggle for Power*, New Delhi, 1974.

12. Indra Prakash, *A Review of the History and Work of the Hindu Mahasabha and the Hindu Sangathan Movement*, New Delhi, 1938.

13. D.R. Goyal, *Rashtriya Swayamsewak Sangh*, New Delhi, 1979.

14. Beni Prasad, *The Hindu-Muslim Questions*, Allahabad, 1941.

15. *Report of the Kanpur Riots Enquiry Committee*, 1931, published as *Roots of Communal Politics*, edited by N.G. Barrier, New Delhi, 1976.

34. The Crisis at Tripuri to the Cripps Mission

1. S. Gopal, *Jawaharlal Nehru — A Biography*, Vol. One. Chapters 15-17.

2. Subhas Bose, *The Indian Struggle*.

3. Tendulkar, *Mahatma*, Vols. 5 and 6.

4. Bhupen Qanungo, 'Preparations for Civil Disobedience January-September 1940' and 'The Individual Civil Disobedience (October 1940-December 1941)' in *A Centenary History of the Indian National Congress*, Vol.III.

5. R.J. Moore, *Churchill, Cripps, and India 1939-1945*, Oxford, 1979.

35. The Quit India Movement and the INA

1. Tendulkar, *Mahatma*, Vol.6.

2. Francis Hutchins, *Spontaneous Revolution: The Quit India Movement*, New Delhi, 1971.

3. Bhupen Qanungo, 'The Quit India Movement, 1942,' in *A Centenary*

History of the Indian National Congress, Vol.III.

4. Max Harcourt, 'Kisan Populism and Revolution in Rural India: The 1942 Disturbances in Bihar and East United Provinces,' in D.A. Low, editor, *Congress and the Raj.*

5. Stephen Henningham, *Peasant Movements in Colonial India: North Bihar 1917-42*, Chapter 7.

6. K.K. Ghosh, *The Indian National Army*, Meerut, 1969.

7. Gail Omvedt, 'The Satara Parallel Government, 1942-47,' in D.N. Panigrahi, editor, *Economy, Society and Politics in Modern India*, New Delhi, 1985.

36. Post-War National Upsurge

1. Sumit Sarkar, 'Popular Movements and National Leadership, 1945-47,' in *Economic and Political Weekly*, Vol.XVII, Nos. 14-16, April 1982.

2. Sucheta Mahajan, 'British Policy, Nationalist Strategy and Popular National Upsurge, 1945-6,' in A.K. Gupta, editor, *Myth and Reality, Struggle for Freedom in India, 1945-47*, New Delhi, 1987.

3. Subrata Banerjee, *The R.I.N Strike*, New Delhi, 1981.

4. K.K. Ghosh, *The Indian National Army*, Meerut, 1969.

37. Freedom and Partition

1. S. Gopal, *Jawaharlal Nehru — A Biography*, Vol.One, Chapters 19-22.

2. R.J. Moore, *Escape from Empire*, Oxford, 1983.

3. Partha Sarathi Gupta, 'Imperial Strategy and Transfer of Power, 1939-51,' in A.K. Gupta, editor, *Myth and Reality, Struggle for Freedom in India, 1945-47*.

4. Simon Epstein, 'District Officers in Decline: The Erosion of British Authority in the Bombay Countryside, 1919-1947,' in *Modern Asian Studies*, Vol.16, No.3, 1982.

38. The Long-term Strategy of the National Movement

1. Bipan Chandra, *Indian National Movement: The Long-term Dynamics*, New Delhi, 1988.

2. Bipan Chandra, 'Elements of Continuity and Change in the Early Nationalist Activity' in his *Nationalism and Colonialism in Modern India*.

3. Tendulkar, *Mahatma*, 8 Vols.

4. S. Gopal, *Jawaharlal Nehru — A Biography*, Vol.One.

5. Joan V. Bondurant, *Conquest of Violence*, Berkeley, 1971.

6. B.R. Nanda, *Gandhi and His Critics*, Delhi, 1985.
7. Bimal Prasad, *Gandhi, Nehru and J.P*, Delhi, 1985.

39. The Indian National Movement — The Ideological Dimension

1. Bipan Chandra, *The Rise and Growth of Economic Nationalism in India*.
2. M.S. Buch, *Rise and Growth of Indian Liberalism*, Baroda, 1938.
3. G.P. Pradhan and A.K. Bhagat, *Lokamanya Tilak*.
4. B.R. Nanda, *Mahatma Gandhi — A Biography*.
5. S. Gopal, *Jawaharlal Nehru — A Biography*, Vol.One.
6. *Indian National Congress Resolutions on Economic Policy, Programme and Allied Matters*, New Delhi, 1969.
7. Gyorgy Kalmar, *Gandhism*, Budapest, 1977.
8. Francine R. Frankel, *India's Political Economy, 1947-1977: The Gradual Revolution*, Delhi, 1978.
9. S.G. Sardesai in M.B. Rao, editor, *The Mahatma, Marxist Evaluation*, New Delhi, 1969.
10. Mohit Sen, *The Indian Revolution, Review and Perspectives*, New Delhi, 1970.

Notes

Introduction

1. Anil Seal, *The Emergence of Indian Nationalism*, Cambridge, 1968, p.351.
2. *Ibid.*, p.342.
3. *Ibid*.
4. *Ibid*.
5. S. Gopal, *The Indian Economic and Social Review*, Vol.XIV, No. 3, July-September 1977, p.405.
6. Jawaharlal Nehru, *Discovery of India*, Calcutta, 1946, second edition, p.311.
7. *The Collected Works of Mahatma Gandhi* (hereafter referred to as Gandhi, *CW*), New Delhi, 1958-1984, Vol.57, p.454.

1. The First Major Challenge: The Revolt of 1857

1. R.C. Majumdar, editor, *British Paramountcy and Indian Renaissance*, Part I, Bombay, 1963, p.513.
2. S.N. Sen, *Eighteen Fifty-Seven*, Delhi, 1957, pp.5-10.
3. T.R. Holmes, *A History of the Indian Mutiny*, London, 1898, p.50.
4. Harprasad Chattopadhyaya, *Sepoy Mutiny, 1857 — A Social Study and Analysis*, Calcutta, 1957, p.1.
5. E.I.Brodkin, *Property Mutations and the Mutiny in Rohilkhand*, *Journal of Asian Studies*, August 1969, p.66.
6. Talmiz Khaldun, 'The Great Rebellion' in P.C.Joshi, editor, *Rebellion, 1857 — A Symposium*, Delhi, 1957, pp.36-44.

2. Civil Rebellions and Tribal Uprisings

1. L. Natrajan, 'The Santhal Insurrection: 1855-56,' in A.R. Desai, edi-

tor, *Peasant Struggles in India*, Delhi, 1979, p.137.

2. Ranajit Guha, *Elementary Aspects of Peasant Insurgency in Colonial India*, Delhi, 1983, pp.28,112.

3. L. Natrajan, *op.cit.*, p.143.

4. Suresh Singh, *The Dust Storm and the Hanging Mist*, Calcutta, 1966, pp.87 and 85.

3. Peasant Movements and Uprisings After 1857

1. Blair B. Kling, *The Blue Mutiny — the Indigo Disturbances in Bengal 1859-1862*, Philadelphia, 1966, p.145.

2. *Ibid.*, p.73.

3. *Ibid.*, p.120.

4. Foundation of the Congress: The Myth

1. Lajpat Rai, *Young India*, Delhi, 1965 edition, first published in 1916, pp.112-6.

2. R.Palme Dutt, *India Today*, Bombay, 1949 edition, pp.288 ff.

3. M.S. Golwalkar, *We or Our Nationhood Defined*, Nagpur, 1947 edition, first published in 1939.

4. William Wedderburn, *Allan Octavian Hume, C.B.*, London, 1913, pp.79 ff.

5. Lajpat Rai, *op.cit.*, p.114.

6. Gurmukh Nihal Singh, *Landmarks in Indian Constitutional and National Development*, Vol.I, 1600-1919, Delhi, 1952, third edition, p.105.

7. C.F. Andrews and Girija Mukerji, *The Rise and Growth of the Congress in India*, London, 1938, p.128.

8. R.Plame Dutt, *op.cit.*, p.291.

9. Briton Martin, *New India, 1885*, Bombay, 1970, pp.65 ff.

10. Dufferin to Kimberley, 20 Aug. 1986, *Dufferin Papers (DP)*, Vol. 37, Reel no. 525; Hume to Dufferin, 31 July 1886, *DP*; Vol.50, Reel no. 531; Dufferin to Hume, 8 Oct. 1887, *DP*, Vol. 52, Reel no. 532; Hume to A.P. MacDonnell, no date, Letter no. 521, *DP*, Vol. 54, Reel no. 534; Dufferin to Gratham Geary, 27 Oct. 1888, *DP*, Vol. 54, Reel no. 534.

11. *Hume to Dufferin*, 27 November 1886, *DP*, Vol.50, Reel no. 530.

12. *Ibid.*

13. W.C. Bonnerji, 'Introduction' to *Indian Politics*, Madras, 1898, p.VII.

14. Briton Martin, *op.cit.*, pp.74-5.

15. B.L. Grover, *British Policy Towards Indian Nationalism 1885-1909*,

Delhi, 1967, pp.181 ff.

16. Dufferin to Reay, 17 May 1885, *DP*, Vol.47, Reel no. 528.

17. Dufferin to Colvin, 9 October 1888, *DP*, Vol. 54, Reel no. 534.

18. Dufferin to Reay, 17 May 1885, *DP*, Vol. 47, Reel no.528.

19. Reay to Dufferin, 24 May 1885, and 4 June 1885, *DP*, Vol. 47, Reel no. 528.

20. Dufferin to Secretary of State, 3 February 1885, and 7 August 1885, *DP*, Volume 18, Reel no.517.

21. Dufferin to Northbrook, 23 June 1886; and Dufferin to Henry S. Maine, 9 May 1886, *DP*, Vol. 37, Reel no. 525.

5. Foundation of the Indian National Congress: The Reality

1. *Indian National Congress*, containing full texts of all Presidential Addresses, reprint of all the Congress Resolutions, etc., Madras, no date, Part I, p.386.

2. *Ibid.*, p.3.

3. I.P. Minayeff, *Trends in and Diaries of India and Burma*, Calcutta, no date, p.120.

4. S.R. Mehrotra, *Emergence of the Indian National Congress*, Delhi, 1971, p.418.

5. Indian National Congress, *op.cit.*, Part III, p.16.

6. *Ibid.*, Part III, pp.17-8.

7. *Ibid.*, Part I, pp.11-2.

8. G.K. Gokhale, *Speeches of Gopal Krishna Gokhale*, Madras, 1916, second edition, p.929.

9. R.G. Pradhan, *India's Struggle for Swaraj*, Madras, 1930, p.20.

10. *Indian National Congress*, Part I, *op.cit.*, p.3.

11. R.P. Masani, *Dadabhai Naoroji: The Grand Old Man of India*, London, 1939, p.441.

12. Gokhale, *Speeches*, p.1113.

13. W. Wedderburn, *Allan Octavian Hume*, pp.63-4.

6. Socio-Religious Reforms and the National Awakening

1. Sophia Dobson Collet, *Life and Letters of Rammohan Roy*, Calcutta, 1913, p.124.

2. *Life and Work of Brahmananda Keshav*, edited by P.S. Basu, Calcutta, 1940, p.63.

3. J.C. Ghose, editor, *English Works of Rammohan Roy*, Allahabad, 1906, p.312.

4. Mahadev Govind Ranade, *The Miscellaneous Writings*, Bombay, 1915, p.191.

5. P.S. Basu, *op.cit.*, p.147.

6. *Writings and Speeches of Sir Syed Ahmed Khan*, edited by Shan Mohammad, Meerut, 1972, p.117.

7. Dayanand Saraswati, *Satyartha Prakash*, English translation by Durga Prasad, New Delhi, 1972, p.83.

8. M.K. Sanoo, *Narayana Guru Swami*, in Malayalam, Irininjalakuda, 1976, p.441.

9. P.J. Thomas, *The Growth of Higher Education in Southern India*, Madras, no date, p.5.

7. An Economic Critique of Colonialism

1. For a short treatment of the subject, see Bipan Chandra, *The Rise and Growth of Economic Nationalism in India*, New Delhi, 1966, Chapter I. For details, see Dadabhai Naoroji, *Poverty and Un-British Rule in India*, London, 1901, and *Speeches and Writings*, Madras, no date.

2. R.C. Dutt, *Economic History of India in the Victorian Age*, London, sixth edition, first published in 1903, p.XVI.

3. G.V. Joshi, *Writings and Speeches*, Poona, 1912, p.616.

4. M.G.Ranade, *Essays on Indian Economics*, Bombay, 1898, p.96.

5. For a detailed treatment, see Bipan Chandra, *The Rise and Growth of Economic Nationalism in India*, Chapter III, Section I; and his 'British and Indian Ideas on Indian Economic Development, 1858-1905' in *Nationalism and Colonialism in Modern India*, New Delhi, 1987 reprint.

6. Curzon, *Speeches*, Vol.I, Calcutta, 1900, p.34.

7. Naoroji, *Poverty and Un-British Rule in India*, pp.34, 568-9, *Speeches*, p.169.

8. February 1903, p.193.

9. *New India*, 12 August 1901.

10. G.V. Joshi, *op.cit.*, pp.687-8.

11. Ram Gopal, *Lokamanya Tilak*, Bombay. 1965 reprint, p.148.

12. For details, see Bipan Chandra, *The Rise and Growth of Economic Nationalism in India*, Chapter XIII.

13. Naoroji, *Poverty and Un-British Rule in India*, p.216.

14. R.C. Dutt, *Economic History of India Under Early British Rule*, London, 1956, 8th impression, pp.xi and 420.

15. *Abstract of the Proceedings of the Council of the Governor-General of India*, 1896, Vol.XXXV, p.85.

16. Naoroji, *Speeches*, pp.328, 329.

17. Naoroji, *Poverty and Un-British Rule in India*, pp.224-5.

18. Naoroji, *Speeches*, p.389.
19. *India*, London, 2 September 1904.
20. Naoroji, *Speeches*, p.671.
21. *Ibid.*, p.73.

8. The Fight to Secure Press Freedom

1. J. Natrajan, *History of Indian Journalism — Part II of the Report of the Press Commission*, New Delhi, 1955, p.15.
2. Dufferin to Secretary of State, 21 March and 17 May 1886, *Dufferin Papers*.
3. Lord Curzon, *Speeches*, Vol. IV, Calcutta, 1906, p.75.
4. J. Natrajan, *op.cit.*, p.135.
5. D.V. Tahmankar, *Lokamanya Tilak*, London, 1956, p.73; and Ram Gopal, *Lokamanya Tilak*, p.133.
6. R.G. Pradhan and A.K. Bhagwat, *Lokamanya Tilak — A Biography*, Bombay, 1958, p.111.
7. D. Keer, *Lokamanya Tilak*, Bombay, 1969, p.141.
8. Pradhan and Bhagwat, *op.cit.*, pp.117-8.
9. *Ibid.*, pp.219-21.
10. *Ibid.*, p.222.
11. *Ibid.*, p.228.
12. V.I. Lenin, *Collected Works*, Moscow, 1963, Vol.15, p.184.
13. Gandhi, *CW*, Vol. 23, p.120.

9. Propaganda in the Legislatures

1. R.C. Majumdar, editor, *British Paramountcy and Indian Renaissance*, Part I, p.759.
2. Bipan Chandra, *The Rise and Growth of Economic Nationalism in India*, p.534 f.n.
3. *Ibid.*, p.553 f.n.
4. Madan Mohan Malaviya, *Speeches*, Madras, no date, pp.26-7, 30-1.
5. Pherozeshah M. Mehta, *Speeches and Writings*, edited by C.Y. Chintamani, Allahabad, 1905, pp.405-6.
6. Homi Mody, *Sir Pherozeshah Mehta, A Political Biography*, Bombay, 1963 edition, pp.185-6.
7. *Ibid.*, p.188.
8. Speeches and Writings *op.cit.*, pp.334, 348.
9. *Ibid.*, p.350.
10. *Ibid.*, p.663.
11. *Ibid.*, p.564.

12. Gokhale, *Speeches*, pp.1-29.

13. B.R. Nanda, *Gokhale, The Indian Moderates and the Raj*, Delhi, 1977, p.138.

14. *Ibid.*

15. Bipan Chandra, *The Rise and Growth of Economic Nationalism in India*, p.4 f.n.

16. *Abstract of the Proceedings of the Council of the Governor-General of India, assembled for the purpose of making Laws and Regulations*, 1904, Vol.XLIII, p.542.

17. Nanda, *Gokhale*, pp.358-9.

18. Pradhan and Bhagwat, *Lokamanya Tilak*, p.259.

10. The Swadeshi Movement — 1903-1908

1. B.L. Grover, *A Documentary Study of British Policy Towards Indian Nationalism, 1885-1909*, Delhi, pp.224-5.

2. S. Gopal, *British Policy in India, 1858-1905*, Cambridge, 1965, p.270.

3. *Ibid.*, pp.270-1.

4. *Ibid.*

5. Sumit Sarkar, *The Swadeshi Movement in Bengal, 1903-8*, New Delhi, 1973, p.20.

6. Haridas and Uma Mukherjee, *India's Fight in Freedom or the Swadeshi Movement, 1905-06*, Calcutta, 1958, p.162.

7. Sumit Sarkar, *op.cit.*, p.65.

8. *Indian National Congress*, containing full texts of all Presidential Addresses, etc., Part I, p.863.

9. Bipan Chandra, *Modern India*, New Delhi, 1969, p.244.

10. *Sandhya*, 21 November 1906, in Sumit Sarkar, op.cit., p.69.

11. Haridas and Uma Mukherjee, *op.cit.*, p.109.

11. The Split in the Congress and the Rise of Revolutionary Terrorism

1. Grover, *British Policy Towards Indian Nationalism*, p.183.

2. R.C. Majumdar, *History of Freedom Movement in India*, Vol.I, Calcutta, 1962, p.413.

3. Nanda, *Gokhale*, p.176.

4. Quoted in R.P. Masani, *Dadabhai Naoroji: The Grand Old Man of India*, p.459.

5. C.H. Philips, editor, *The Evolution of India and Pakistan 1858-1947 Select Documents*, London, 1965 edition, p.151.

6. Nanda, *Gokhale*, p.182.

7, *Speeches and Writings of Gopal Krishna Gokhale*, edited by D.G. Karve and D.V. Ambekar, Bombay, 1966, Vol. Two, p.243.

8. Nanda, *Gokhale*, p.283.

9. *Ibid.*, p.293.

10. *Ibid.*

11. *Lajpat Rai: Writings and Speeches*, edited by V.C. Joshi, 2 Vols., Delhi, 1966, Vol. I, p.180.

12. Nanda, *Gokhale*, p.288.

13. *Sri Aurobindo Karmayogin*, edited from Sri Aurobindo Ashram, Pondicherry, 1972, p.1.

14. C.H. Philips, *op.cit.*, p.85.

15. Haridas and Uma Mukherjee, *India's Fight for Freedom or the Swadeshi Movement 1905-1906*, Calcutta, 1958, p.166.

16. Hirendranath Mukherjee, *India Struggles for Freedom*, Bombay, 1948 edition, p.96.

12. World War I and Indian Nationalism: The Ghadar

1. Harish K. Puri, *Ghadar Movement*, Amritsar, 1983, pp.31-2.

2. 'Ghadar Conspiracy Report, 1913-16,' by Isemonger and Slattery, 1922, reproduced in Bhai Nahar Singh and Kirpal Singh, editors, *Struggle for Free Hindustan, (Ghadar Movement), Vol.I, 1905-1916*, New Delhi, 1986, pp.17-21.

3. *Ibid.*, pp.46-7.

4. Harish K. Puri, *op.cit.*, pp.69-70.

5. Sohan Singh Josh, *Baba Sohan Singh Bhakna: Life of the Founder of the Ghadar Party*, New Delhi, 1970, pp.30-1.

6. *Ghadar di Goonj*, No.1, poem 8, quoted in Harish K. Puri, *op.cit.*, pp.73-4.

7. Sohan Singh Josh, *op.cit.*, p.45.

8. Harish K. Puri, *op.cit.*, pp.121-2.

9. *Ibid.*, p.124.

10. *Ibid.*, p.113.

11. See, Emily C. Brown, *Har Dayal: Hindu Revolutionary and Rationalist*, Tuscon, 1975, for a full account of Har Dayal's life and ideas.

13. The Home Rule Movement and its Fallout

1. Letter to the Press, August 27, 1914, *Bal Gangadhar Tilak, His Writings and Speeches*, Madras, 1919, p.392.

2. Bombay Police 1915, par. 568 (b), cited in H.F. Owen, 'Towards Nation-Wide Agitation and Organisation: The Home Rule Leagues,

1915-18,' in D.A. Low, editor, *Soundings in Modern South Asian History*, Berkeley and Los Angeles, 1968, p.167, n.42.

3. G.P. Pradhan and A.K. Bhagwat, *Lokamanya Tilak: A Biography*, Bombay, 1959, pp.265-6.

4. *Ibid.*, p.266-7, Tilak's *Writings and Speeches*, pp.116-17, has a slightly different translation of the passage.

5. *Ibid.*, p.269. Tilak's *Writings and Speeches*, p.187, has a slightly different version.

6. Pradhan and Bhagwat, *op.cit.*, p.292.

7. *Ibid.*, p.306.

8. Home Rule Speech at Ahmednagar, May 31, 1916, Tilak's *Writings and Speeches*, p.142.

9. Pradhan and Bhagwat, *op.cit.*, p.271.

10. *Ibid.*, p.273.

11. A.M. Zaidi and S.G. Zaidi, *The Encyclopaedia of the Indian National Congress*, Vol.7, 1916-20, p.48.

12. Tilak's *Writings and Speeches*, pp.202-03.

13. Pradhan and Bhagwat, *op.cit.*, p.284.

14. Edwin S. Montagu, *Indian Diary*, London, 1930, p.157.

15. S.R. Mehrotra, *India and the Commonwealth, 1885-1929*, London, 1965, p.103.

14. Gandhi's Early Career and Activism

1. One of the best accounts of this journey is in Chandran D.S Devanesan, *The Making of the Mahatma*, Madras, 1969, pp.229-45.

2. Gandhi, *CW*, Vol.1, p.61.

3. B.R. Nanda, *Mahatma Gandhi*, New Delhi, 1958, p.117.

4. D.G. Karve and D.V. Ambekar, editors, *Speeches and Writings of Gopal Krishna Gokhale*, Volume 2: Political, p.444.

5. G.A. Natesan, 'Reminiscences,' in *Gandhi*, p.215, on Gandhi's 75th birthday in 1944, cited in B.R. Nanda, *op.cit.*, pp.154-5.

6. Gandhi, *CW*, Vol. XIV, p.340.

7. *Ibid*, p.339.

8. M.K. Gandhi, *An Autobiography OR The Story of My Experiments with Truth*, Ahmedabad, 14th Reprint, first published in 1927 and 1929, pp.365-6.

15. The Non-Cooperation Movement — 1920-22

1. Gandhi, *CW*, Vol.17, p.504.

2. Prabhudas Gandhi, 'Recalling Memories of 1921,' in Government of

India, *1921 Movement: Reminiscences*, New Delhi, 1971, p.85.

3. Prabhudas Gandhi, *op.cit.*, pp.86-7; and Gandhi, *CW*, Vol.21, pp.180-1.

4. D.G. Tendulkar, *Mahatma, Life of Mohandas Karamchand Gandhi*, 8 Volumes, New Delhi, 1969 reprint, Vol.2, p.52.

5. Hitesranjan Sanyal, 'Congress Movements in the Villages of Eastern Midnapore, 1921-31,' in *Asie du Sud, Traditions et Changements, Colloques Internationaux du Centre National de la Recherche Scientifique*, No.582, Paris.

6. Atlury Murali, *Social Change and Nature of Social Participation in National Movement in Andhra, 1905-1934*, Unpublished Ph.D. Thesis, Centre for Historical Studies, Jawaharlal Nehru University, New Delhi, 1985, pp.284-90.

7. See Chapter 16 below.

8. See Chapter 16 below.

9. See Chapter 18 below.

10. R.P. Dutt, *India Today*, pp.324-9.

11. Majid H. Siddiqi, *Agrarian Unrest in North India: The United Provinces, 1918-22*, New Delhi, 1978, p.201.

12. Atlury Murali, *op.cit.*, pp.288-90.

13. B.L. Grover, *British Policy Towards Indian Nationalism 1885-1909*, Delhi, 1967, pp.181 ff.

14. Gandhi, *CW*, Vol.22, p.457.

15. *Ibid.*, p.458.

16. Peasants Movements and Nationalism in the 1920s

1. For the Kisan Sabha and Eka movements in Avadh, see Majid H. Siddiqi, *Agrarian Unrest in North India: The United Provinces (1918-22)*, New Delhi, 1978; Kapil Kumar, *Peasants in Revolt: Tenants, Congress, Landlords and the Raj in Oudh, 1886-1922*, New Delhi, 1984; S.Gopal, *Jawaharlal Nehru: A Biography*, Vol.1, London, 1975, pp.42-57; Gyanendra Pandey, 'Peasant Revolt and Indian Nationalism,' in Ranajit Guha, editor, *Subaltern Studies I*, Delhi, 1982.

2. For the Mappila revolt in Malabar, see K.N. Pannikar, 'Peasant Revolts in Malabar in the Nineteenth and Twentieth Centuries,' in A.R. Deasi, editor, *Peasant Struggles in India*, New Delhi, 1979, pp.601-630; Conrad Wood, 'Peasant Revolt: An Interpretation of Moplah Violence in the 19th and 20th Centuries,' in Dewey and Hopkins, editors, *The Imperial Impact: Studies in the Economic History of India and Africa*, London, 1978; Stephen F. Dale, *Islamic Society on the South Asian Frontier: The Mappilas of Malabar,*

1498-1922, New York, 1980, Chapter 7.

3. For the no-tax movement in Bardoli, see Mahadev Desai, *The Story of Bardoli*, Ahmedabad, 1957; Shirin Mehta, *The Peasantry and Nationalism*, New Delhi, 1984; Ghanshyam Shah, 'Traditional Society and Political Mobilisation: The experience of Bardoli Satyagraha (1920-1928),' in *Contributions to Indian Sociology*, New Series, New Delhi, No.8, 1974, pp.89-107; and Interviews with Uttamchand Shah, Bardoli, 22 and 25 June 1985, Chimanlal Pranlal Bhatt, Vedchi, 26 June 1985, and Kasanbhai Ukabhai Choudhry, Vedchi, 26 June 1985, Khushalbhai Morarji Patel, Bardoli, 25 June 1985, Vallabhbhai Khushalbhai Patel, Sankri, 25 June 1985, Chhotubhai Gopalji Desai, Puni, 25 June 1985.

4. Interview with Kalyanji V. Mehta, cited in Shirin Mehta, *The Peasantry and Nationalism*, pp.88-9.

5. *Ibid.*, p.177.

6. *Ibid.*, pp.182-3.

7. Gandhi, *CW*, Vol. 36, p.73.

17. The Indian Working Class and the National Movement

1. *Indian National Congress*, containing full texts of all Presidential Addresses, etc., Part I, p.12.

2. Quoted in Bipan Chandra, *The Rise and Growth of Economic Nationalism in India*, pp.360-1.

3. G. Subramaniya Iyer, *Some Economic Aspects of British Rule in India*, Madras, 1903, pp.175-8, 218-32.

4. Sumit Sarkar, *The Swadeshi Movement in Bengal, 1903-1908*, pp.183-4.

5. *AITUC — Fifty Years, Documents*, New Delhi, 1973, pp.30, 35.

6. *Ibid.*, pp.78-9.

7. *Lala Lajpat Rai: Writings and Speeches*, Vol.II, p.57.

8. *Ibid.*, pp.60-1.

9. Quoted in Balabushevich and Dyakov, editors, *A Contemporary History of India*, New Delhi, 1964, p.150.

10. Lajpat Jagga, 'Colonial Railwaymen and British Rule: A Probe into Railway Labour Agitation in India, 1919-1922,' in Bipan Chandra, editor, *The Indian Left: Critical Appraisals*, New Delhi, 1983, pp.104-06.

11. Ravinder Kumar, 'From Swaraj to Purna Swaraj: Nationalist Politics in the city of Bombay, 1920-32,' in D.A. Low, editor, *Congress and the Raj, Facets of the Indian Struggle 1917-47*, London, 1977, p.88.

12. J.B. Kripalani, *Gandhi, His 'Life and Thought,'* p.78, quoted in Sukomal Sen, *(Working Class of India, History of Emergence and*

Movement 1830-1870), Calcutta, 1977, pp.152-3. In Chapter 39 below we see how in another context Gandhiji went beyond the trusteeship theory to argue that land belonged to the tiller and landlords could 'cooperate by running away.'

13. H. Williamson, *India and Communism*, National Archives of India (NAI), p.126. Williamson was the Director, Intelligence Bureau, Government of India. Also see, Home Political Department, Fl. 7/16/34 in Subodh Roy, editor, *Communism in India, Unpublished Documents, 1935-45*, Calcutta, 1976, p.103.

14. *Guidelines of the History of the Communist Party of India,* issued by Central Party Education Department, New Delhi, 1974, p.35.

15. Balabushevich and Dyakov, *op.cit.,* p.241.

16. Ibid., p.321; and Sukomal Sen, *op.cit.,* p.364.

18.The Struggles for Gurdwara Reform and Temple Entry

1. Mohinder Singh, *The Akali Movement*, Delhi, 1978, p.47.

2. *Ibid.,* Appendix IV.

3. *Ibid.,* pp.149-50.

4. A.K. Gopalan, *In the Cause of the People*, New Delhi, 1973, p.38.

5. E.M.S. Namboodiripad, *How I became a Communist*, Trivandrum, 1976, p.123.

19. The Years of Stagnation — Swarajists, No-changers and Gandhiji

1. Indian Annual Register, 1923, Vol.II, pp.143-4.

2. B.R. Nanda, *The Nehrus Motilal and Jawaharlal*, London, 1962, p.234.

3. *Ibid.,* pp.239-40.

4. Gandhi, *CW*, Vol.24, p.109.

5. *Ibid.,* Vol.25, p.310.

6. *Ibid.,* Vol. 23, p.341.

7. *Ibid.,* Vol.24, p.356.

8. *Ibid.,* Vol.25, p.275.

9. *Ibid.,* p.335.

10. *Ibid.,* p.310.

11. *Indian Annual Register,* 1923, Vol.II, p.217.

12. Manoranjan Jha, *Role of Central Legislature in the Freedom Struggle*, New Delhi, 1972, p.82.

13. *Ibid.,* p.87.

14. *Lajpat Rai: Writings and Speeches*, Vol.II, p.260.

15. Leonard A. Gordon, *Bengal: The Nationalist Movement 1876-1940*, Delhi, 1974, p.217.

16. Gandhi, *CW*, Vol.30, p.371.

17. *Lajpat Rai: Writings and Speeches*, Vol.II, pp.430, 437.

18. *The Voice of Freedom — Selected Speeches of Pandit Motilal Nehru*, edited by K.M. Pannikar and A. Pershad, Bombay, 1961, pp.371 ff., 401 ff.

19. Manoranjan Jha, *op.cit.*, p.142.

20. *Ibid.*, p.143.

21. Gandhi, *CW*, Vol.40, pp.201-2.

22. *Ibid.*, Vol. 33, p.347.

20. Bhagat Singh, Surya Sen and the Revolutionary Terrorists

Interviews with the following have been very useful: Shiv Varma, New Delhi, 12 and 14 September 1984; Jaidev Kapur, New Delhi, 10 and 14 September 1984; Kishorilal, Jullundhur (Punjab), 1 April 1985; Bejoy Kumar Sinha, Hyderabad, 17 June 1985; Durga Das Khanna, Chandigarh, 10 and 11 November 1983; Tridip Choudhry, New Delhi, 27 November 1983.

1. Jagmohan Singh and Chamanlal, *Bhagat Singh aur unke Sathiyon ke Dastavez* (The Documents of Bhagat Singh and His Comrades), New Delhi, 1986, in Hindi, p.266.

2. Kalpana Joshi (nee Dutt), 'Chittagong Uprising and the Role of Muslims,' in *Challenge — A Saga of India's Struggle for Freedom*, edited by Nitish Ranjan Ray, *et. al.*, New Delhi, 1984, p.51.

3. Anand Gupta, 'The Immortal Surya Sen,' in *Ibid.*, p.89.

4. Shiv Varma, editor, *Selected Writings of Shaheed Bhagat Singh*, New Delhi, 1986, Appendix I.

5. *Proceedings of the HRA Council Meeting*, 1924.

6. Shiv Varma, *op.cit.,*, Appendix II.

7. Ramprasad Bismil, *Autobiography*, edited by Banarsidas Chaturvedi, Delhi, 1966, in Hindi.

8. Shiv Varma, *op.cit.,*, p.95.

9. *Ibid.*, p.130.

10. *Ibid.*, pp.137-8.

11. *Ibid.*, p.137.

12. Jagmohan Singh and Chamanlal, *op.cit.,*, p.267.

13. Shiv Varma, *op.cit.,*, pp.190, 198-9.

14. *Ibid.*, p.74.

15. Quoted in Gopal Thakur, *Bhagat Singh: The Man and His Ideas*, New Delhi, 1952, p.39.
16. Vishwanath Vaishampayan, *Amar Shahid Chandrasekhar Azad*, Benaras, 1976, in Hindi, Parts 2-3, Appendix 5.
17. Shiv Varma, *op.cit.*, p.109.
18. Sohan Singh Josh, *My Meetings with Bhagat Singh and on Other Early Revolutionaries*, New Delhi, 1976, pp.13-5; and Jagmohan Singh and Chamanlal, *op.cit.*,, pp.186-9, 244-5.
19. Jagmohan Singh and Chamanlal, *op.cit.*, pp.190-3.
20. *Ibid.*, pp.248 ff.
21. Rules and Regulations of the Naujawan Bharat Sabha, Punjab, 1 May 1928, *Meerut Conspiracy Case*, 1929, Exhibit no.P 205 (T); Reports on the Naujawan Bharat Sabha, *Home (Political) Proceedings*, F.130 & KW (1930).
22. Bhagat Singh, *Why I am an Atheist*, with an introduction by Bipan Chandra, Delhi, 1979. Also in Shiv Varma, *op.cit.*, pp.139 ff. and pp.117 ff.

21. The Gathering Storm — 1927-29

1. Gandhi, *CW*, Vol. 35, pp.454-5.
2. Sumit Sarkar, *Modern India, 1885-1947*, New Delhi, 1983, p.266.
3. Gandhi, *CW*, Vol.38, p.416.
4. Tendulkar, *Mahatma*, Vol.2, p.176.
5. *Ibid*, p.381.
6. Gandhi, *CW*, Vol.41, p.499.
7. *Ibid.*, p.240.
8. *Ibid.*, pp.240-1.
9. *Ibid.*, pp.499-500.
10. *Selected Wroks of Jawaharlal Nehru*, general editor, S. Gopal, 15 volumes, New Delhi, 1972-1982, Vol.4, p.198. Hereafter referred to as Nehru, SW.
11. *Ibid.*, p.192.
12. *Ibid.*, p.195.
13. Tendulkar, *Mahatma*, Vol.3, pp.8-9.

22. Civil Disobedience — 1930-31

This account of the Civil Disobedience Movement owes a lot to our interviews with participants in the movement; in particular, Sita Poviah, Chitra Poviah and Lata Poviah, Bombay, 21 May 1985; Najuben Dastoor, Bomay, 16 June 1985; Pramodaben Gosalia, Bombay, 22 May

1985; Pashabhai Bhailalalbhai Amin, Anand (Gujarat), 4 July 1985; Tribhuvandas Patel, Anand, 1 and 5 July 1985; Umashankar Joshi, Ahmedabad, 9 July, 1985; Madhavlal Shankarlal Pandya, Piplov, Borsad (Gujrat), 3 July 1985; A.K. Raman Kutty, Palghat (Kerala), 20 May 1984; A.V. Kuttimalu Amma, Ernakulum, 23 May 1984; Bhaktavatsalam, Madras, 4 June 1984; K. Subramaniam 'Subri', Madras, 7 June 1984; Sadhu Ram Sharma, Amritsar, 28 March 1985; Tunmala Durgamba, Guntur, 23 June 1984; P.C. Sen, Calcutta, 19 January 1985; Atulya Ghosh, Calcutta, 27 July 1986; R.R. Diwakar, New Selhi, 4 May 1986; Madan Mohan Misra, Rae Bareili, 26 April 1986; Rampal Trivedi, Lucknow, 27 April 1986.

1. Gandhi, *CW*, Vol.42, p.389.
2. *Ibid.*, p.499.
3. Gandhi, CW, Vol.43, p.3.
4. *Ibid.*, p.7.
5. *Ibid.*, pp.46-7.
6. *Ibid.*, p.37.
7. *Ibid.*
8. For an example of the kind of effort that was made at the local level, see Atlury Murali, *Social Change and Nature of Social Participation in National Movement in Andhra, 1905-1934*, pp.653-60.
9. *Ibid.*, pp.659-60.
10. Gandhi, *CW*, Vol.43, p.37.
11. C.F.V. Williams, cited in David Arnold, 'The Politics of Coalescence: The Congress in Tamilnad, 1930-37,' in D.A. Low, editor, *Congress and the Raj*, p.264.
12. For a discussion of British Policy towards the Civil Disobedience Movement, see D.A. Low, 'Civil Martial Law, 1930-34,' in D.A. Low, editor, *Congress and the Raj*.
13. Tendulkar, *Mahatma*, Vol.3, p.41.
14. Gandhi, *CW*, Vol.43, p.219.
15. Nehru, *SW*, Volume 4, p.183.
16. Interview with Usha Mehta, Bombay, 18 May, 1985.
17. *Ibid.*
18. Jawaharlal Nehru had summed up his immediate reaction to the signing of the Gandhi-Irwin Pact in the famous lines of T.S. Eliot:
'This is the way the world ends
Not with a bang but with a whimper.'
Jawaharlal Nehru, *An Autobiography*, New Delhi, 1962 reprint, p.259.
19. Tanika Sarkar, 'The First Phase of Civil Disobedience in Bengal, 1930-1,' in *The Indian Historical Review*, New Delhi, July 1977, Vol.IV, No. 1, pp.90-92.

20. *Ibid.*, p.80.

23. From Karachi to Wardha: The Years from 1932 to 1934

1. Pattabhi Sitaramayya, *The History of Indian National Congress 1885-1935*, no place, 1935, p.768.
2. *Ibid.*, pp.779 ff; and *Indian National Congress
Resolutions on Economic Policy, Programme and Allied Matters*, New Delhi, 1969, pp.3 ff.
3. R.J. Moore, *The Crisis of Indian Unity 1917-1940*, Delhi, 1974, p.209.
4. B. R. Nanda, *Mahatma Gandhi — A Biography*, Delhi, 1981 reprint, p.314.
5. Gandhi, *CW*, Vol.47, p.369.
6. R.J. Moore, *op.cit.*, p.289.
7. Nehru, *SW*, Vol.6, p.372.
8. *Ibid.*, p.273.
9. Pattabhi Sitaramayya, *op.cit.*, p.942.
10. Nanda, *Mahatma Gandhi*, p.339.
11. Bisheshwar Prasad, *Bondage and Freedom*, Vol.II, New Delhi, 1979, p.423.
12. Nanda, *Mahatma Gandhi*, p.367.
13. Gandhi, *CW*, Vol.55, p.430.
14. *Ibid.*, Vol.57, pp.451,454.
15. Citations are too many for Sections V and VI. See *CW*, Vols. 51 to 56; or Tendulkar, Mahatma, Vol.3, pp.159-245; and Vol. 4, pp.14-63.

24. The Rise of the Left-wing

In writing this chapter, we have extensively used interviews with the following: S.A. Dange, 20 February 1984; S.M. Joshi, New Delhi, 29 February 1984; Achuta Menon, Trichur (Kerala), 21 May 1984; E.P. Gopalan, Pattambi (Kerala), 18 May 1984; Achyut Patwardhan, Bangalore, 7 December 1984; K. Lingaraju, Rajahmundry, 1 July 1984; Venkata Subiah, Pondicherry, 10 June 1984; Master Hari Singh, Chandigarh, 8 July 1982; N.C. Shekhar, Cannanore (Kerala), 15 and 16 May 1984; P. Balachandra Menon, Chittoor (Kerala), 20 May 1984; M. Govindan Nair, New Delhi, 24 May, 1984: K.C. George, Trivandrum, 27 May 1984; V.P. Chinthan, Madras, 15 June 1984; Karam Singh Mann, Jullundhur (Punjab), 2 April 1985; S.G. Sardesai, Pune, 6 June 1985; M.R. Masani, Bombay, 26 May and 10 June 1985; Rohit Dave, Bombay, 21 May 1985; S.Y. Kolhatkar, Bombay, 23 May 1985; Dinkar Mehta,

Bombay, 15 June 1985; Kamalashankar Pandya, Baroda, 29 and 30 June 1985; Ganga Saran Sinha, New Delhi, 16 December 1985;A.R. Desai, Bombay, 17 May and 13 June 1985; V.B. Karnik, Bombay, 20 May 1985; R.M. Jhambekar, Bombay, 22 May 1985; Batuk Desai, Bombay, 14 June 1985; P.B. Rangnekar, 28 May 1985; L.K. Oak, Bombay, 1985; Ramesh Sinha, Lucknow, 22 April 1986; Z.A. Ahmed, Lucknow, 29 April 1986; N.G. Gore, 29 December 1986; Prem Bhasin, New Delhi, 10 February 1987.

1. Jnananjan Pal, 'Bipin Chandra Pal,' in Atulchandra Gupta, editor, *Studies in the Bengal Renaissance*, Jadavpur, 1958, p.573.

2. S. Gopal, *Jawaharlal Nehru — a Biography*, Vol. One, p.109.

3. Nehru, *SW*, Vol.4, pp.192-3.

4. *Ibid.*, Vol.6, p.16.

5. *Ibid.*, p.124.

6. *Ibid.*, Vol.7, pp.180-1.

7. *Ibid.*, pp.76-7.

8. Mohit Sen, *The Indian Revolution, Review and Perspectives*, New Delhi, 1970, p.35.

9. Nehru, *SW*, Vol.7, pp.60-1.

10. *Guidelines of the History of the Communist Party of India*, issued by Central Party Education Department, New Delhi, 1974, p.46.

11. *Ibid.*, p.54.

12. Sumit Sarkar, *Modern India*, p.374.

13. Acharya Narendra Dev, *Socialism and the National Revolution*, Bombay, 1946, p.4.

14. Girja Shankar, *Socialist Trends in Indian National Movement*, Meerut, 1987, p.57.

15. *Ibid.*, Appendix V.

16. *Ibid.*, p.126.

17. Jayaprakash Narayan, *Why Socialism*, Benaras, 1936, p.1.

18. Nehru, *SW*, Vol.7, p.76.

25. The Strategic Debate — 1934-37

1. Gandhi, *CW*, Vol.55, p.429.

2. Nehru, *SW*, Vol.6, p.281.

3. *Ibid.*, p.271.

4. For detailed treatment, See Bipan Chandra, 'Jawaharlal Nehru and the Capitalist Class,' in his *Nationalism and Colonialism in Modern India*, pp.177 ff.

5. For detailed treatment, See Chapter 38 below and Bipan Chandra, *Indian National Movement: The Long-term Dynamics*, New Delhi, 1988.

6. Gandhi, *CW*, Vol.57, p.425.

7. *Ibid.*, Vol.58, p.11.

8. *Ibid*, Vol.61, p.439.

9. *Ibid.*, Vol.58, p.318.

10. *Ibid.*, Vol.59, pp.3-12; Vol.58, pp.405-06; and Tendulkar *Mahatma*, Vol.3, pp.318-9.

11. Nehru, *SW*, Vol.7, p.118.

12. Raj Mohan Gandhi, *A Warrior From the South — The Rajaji Story*, Bombay 1978, p.282.

13. D.A. Low, 'Civil Martial Law: The Government of India and the Civil Disobedience Movements, 1930-34,' in D.A. Low, editor, *Congress and the Raj*, p.190.

14. R.J. Moore, 'The Problem of Freedom with Unity: London's India Policy 1917-47,' in *Ibid.*, p.379.

15. Erskine to Craik, 20 April 1936, *Home Political Proceedings*, F.No.4/6/36 (National Archives of India).

16. John Glendevon, *The Viceroy at Bay — Lord Linlithgow in India, 1936-43*, London, 1971, p.52.

17. Nehru, *SW*, Vol.7, pp.185-7.

18. Jawaharlal Nehru — *A Bunch of Old Letters, Written mostly to Jawaharlal Nehru*, Bombay, 1958, pp.157 and 156.

19. A.M. Zaidi and S.G. Zaidi, *The Encyclopaedia of Indian National Congress*, Volume Eleven: 1936-1938, New Delhi, 1980, p.48.

20. *Ibid.*, p.42.

21. *Ibid.*, pp.41-2.

26. Twenty-Eight Months of Congress Rule

Our understanding of the period of Congress Ministries from 1937 to 1939 was enriched by interviews with large number of freedom fighters, in particular Keralyeean, Calicut, 25 February and 12 May 1984; E.P. Gopalan, Pattambi (Kerala), 18 May 1984; B. Gopal Reddy, Nellore (Andhra Pradesh), 16 June 1984; C. Subramaniam, Madras, 2 June 1984; Soli Batliwala, Bombay, 26 May 1985; M.R. Masani, Bombay, 26 May and 10 June 1985; Kamalashankar Pandya, Baroda, 29 and 30 June 1985; Shekhar Ganguly, Patna, 27 November 1985; Rameshwar Prasad Misra, Lucknow, 28 April 1986.

1. For detailed discussion of S-T-S', See Chapter 38 below.

2. Gandhi, *CW*, Vol.66, p.16.

3. *Ibid*, Vol.65, p.406.

4. Nehru, *Discovery of India*, pp.321-2.

5. Gandhi, *CW*, Vol.66, p.63.

6. Rajmohan Gandhi, *The Rajaji Story 1937-72*, Bombay, 1984, p.7.

7. S. Gopal, *Jawaharlal Nehru — A Biography*, Vol.One, p.230.

8. Quoted in Visalakshi Menon, 'The Indian National Congress and Mass Mobilization — A Study of U.P. 1937-39,' *Studies in History*, Vol.II, No.2, July-December 1980, New Delhi, p.115.

9. Quoted in Gyanesh Kudaisya, *Office Acceptance and the Congress 1937-1939: Premises and Perceptions*, M.Phil dissertation, Centre for Historical Studies, Jawaharlal Nehru University, New Delhi, pp.110 and 93.

10. Nehru, *Discovery of India*, p.321.

11. *Annual Report of the Federation of Indian Chambers of Commerce and Industry*, 1938, pp.27, 30, 83-7, 113, 117, 120-2.

12. AICC, G-13/1937. Nehru Memorial Museum and Library.

13. Visalakshi Menon, *op.cit.*

14. S. Gopal, *op.cit.*, p.231.

15. Tendulkar, *Mahatma*, Vol.4, p.276.

16. R. Palme Dutt, *India Today*, pp.491-2.

17. Gandhi, *CW*, Vol.68, pp.112-3. Also see *CW*, Vol.66, pp.268-9.

18. See, for example, *Ibid.*, Vol.66, pp.300-02.

19. *Ibid.*, Vol.68, p.195.

20. Tendulkar, *Mahatma*, Vol.5, p.94. A different translation is given in Gandhi, *CW*, Vol.69, p.210.

21. Gandhi, *CW*, Vol.68, p.125.

22. Nehru, *SW*, Vol.8, p.388.

23. Gandhi, *CW*, Vol.70, p.291.

24. R. Coupland, *Indian Politics 1936-1942*, Madras, 1944, p.156.

25. Nehru, *Discovery of India*, p.326.

26. *Guidelines of the History of the Communist Party of India*, p.45.

27. Visalakshi Menon, *op.cit.*, p.140.

28. A.M. Zaidi and S.G. Zaidi, editors, *The Encyclopaedia of Indian National Congress*, Vol. Twelve, p.255.

27. Peasant Movements in the 1930s and '40s

1. Gandhi, *CW*, Vol. 46, pp. 200-03.

2. For the text of the Congress Agrarian Programme see A.M. Zaidi and S.G. Zaidi, *The Encyclopaedia of the Indian National Congress*, Volume II, 1936-38, New Delhi, 1980, pp.212-3.

3. M.A. Rasul, *A History of the All India Kisan Sabha*, Calcutta, 1974, p.9.

4. See Chapter 26 above.

5. K. Gopalankutty, 'The Integration of Anti-Landlord Movement with the Movement Against Imperialism — The Case of Malabar, 1935-39,' in Bipan Chandra, editor, *The Indian Left: Critical Appraisals*, New Delhi, 1983; A.K. Gopalan, *In the Cause of the People: Reminiscences*, Madras, 1973, Chs.6-12, and Interviews with E.P. Gopalan, Pattambi, 18 May 1984, K. Madhavan, Kanhangad, 14 May 1984, K.P.R. Gopalan, Cannanore, 16 May 1984, K. Keralyeean, Calicut, 25 February and 17 May 1984, E.Nayanar, Trivandrum, 25 May 1984.

6. N.G. Ranga, *Fight for Freedom: Autobiography*, Delhi, 1968; P.Sundarayya, *Telangana Peoples' Struggle and its Lessons*, Calcutta, 1972, pp.139-147; M.A. Rasul, *op.cit.*, and Interviews with N.G. Ranga, Nidobrulu, 22 June 1984, Uddaraju Ramam, Vijayawada, 25 June, 1984, Kolah Venkaiah, Guntur, 5 July 1984.

7. Walter Hauser, *The Bihar Provincial Kisan Sabha, 1929-1942: A Study of an Indian Peasant Movement*, Unpublished Ph.D. dissertation, University of Chicago, 1962, Microfilm, Nehru Memorial Museum and Library, New Delhi; Gyan Prakash Sharma, *Congress, Peasant Movement and Tenancy Legislation in Bihar, 1937-1939*, Unpublished M.Phil dissertation, CHS, Jawaharlal Nehru University, New Delhi, 1979; Sahajanand Saraswati, *Mera Jeevan Sangharsh*, in Hindi, Delhi, 1985 edition.

8. Master Hari Singh, *Punjab Peasant in Freedom Struggle*, Volume 2, New Delhi, 1984; Bhagwan Josh, *Communist Movement in Punjab*, Delhi, 1979; Mridula Mukherjee, 'Communists and Peasants in Punjab: A Focus on the Muzara Movement in Patiala, 1937-53,' in Bipan Chandra, editor, *The Indian Left: Critical Appraisals*, pp.401-46; Interviews with Jagjit Singh Lyallpuri, Ludhiana, 29 May 1981, G.S. Randhawa, New Delhi, 14 September 1981, Master Hari Singh, Chandigarh, 8 July 1982, Bhagat Singh Bilga, Phillaur, 17 November 1983, Chain Singh Chain, Jullundur, 14 November 1983.

9. Mridula Mukherjee, *op.cit.*; Mridula Mukherjee, 'Peasant Movement in a Princely State: Patiala, 1937-48,' in *Studies in History*, New Delhi, Vol.1, No.2, 1979; Master Hari Singh, *op.cit.*, Ramesh Walia, *Praja Mandal Movement in East Punjab States*, Patiala, 1972; Interviews with Jagir Singh Joga, Joga, 16 May 1981, Brish Bhan, 18 May 1981, Bachittar Singh, Patiala, 14 April 1981, G.S. Randhawa, New Delhi, 14 September 1981, Vaid Chajju Mal, New Delhi, 27 February 1981, Giani Bachan Singh, Sunam, 2 May 1981.

10. Sunil Sen, *Agrarian Struggle in Bengal*, New Delhi, 1972; Abani Lahiri, 'Last Battle of Bengal Peasants Under British Rule,' in Nisith Ranjan Ray *et.al.*, editors, *Challenge: A Saga of India's Struggle for Freedom*, New Delhi, 1984, pp.374-86; Krishna Kant Sarkar, 'Kakdwip

Tebhaga Movement,' in A.R. Desai, editor, *Peasant Struggles in India*, pp.469-85; Ranjit Das Gupta, 'Peasants, Workers and Freedom Struggle, Jalpaiguri, 1945-47,' in Amit Kumar Gupta, editor, *Myth and Reality: The Struggle for Freedom in India, 1945-47*, New Delhi, 1987, pp.435-49.

28. The Freedom Struggle in Princely India

1. Jawaharlal Nehru, *SW*, Vol.4, pp.192-3.
2. Gandhi, *CW*, Vol. 68, pp.326-7.
3. A.M. Zaidi and S.G. Zaidi, *The Encyclopaedia of the Indian National Congress*, Volume 12, 1939-46, New Delhi, 1981, p.162.
4. John R. Wood, 'Rajkot: Indian Nationalism in the Princely Context: The Rajkot Satyagraha of 1938-9,' in Robin Jeffrey, editor, *People, Princes and Paramount Power*, New Delhi, 1978, p.260.
5. *Ibid.*
6. Gandhi,*CW*, Vol.69, pp.162-6 and 168-71.
7. Ramanand Tirtha, *Memoirs of Hyderabad Freedom Struggle*, Bombay, 1967, pp.176-7.
8. For the struggle in Hyderabad, see P. Sundarayya, *Telengana People's Struggle and Its Lessons*, Calcutta, 1972; Ravi Narayan Reddy, *Heroic Telengana: Reminiscences and Experiences*, New Delhi, 1973; Raj Bahadur Gour *et.al., Glorious Telengana Armed Struggle*, New Delhi, 1973; Ramanand Tirtha, *Memoirs of Hyderabad Freedom Struggle*, Bombay, 1967; N. Ramesan, editor, *The Freedom Struggle in Hyderabad*, Vol.IV (1921-1947), Hyderabad, 1966; and Interviews with Devapalli Venkateswara Rao, Hyderabad, 7 July, 1984, Ravi Narayan Reddy, Hyderabad, 8 July 1984, Arutla Ramachandra Reddy, Hyderabad, 6 and 9 July, 1984, Giri Prasad, Hyderabad, 9 July 1984, C. Thirumal Rao, Nalgonda, 16 July 1984, Mallu Swarajyam, Hyderabad, 10 July 1984, Bhimareddy Narsimhareddy, Hyderabad, 12 July 1984.

29. Indian Capitalists and the National Movement

1. Purshottamdas Thakurdas, *et.al., A Plan of Economic Development for India*, Pts. I & II, Penguin, London, 1945, popularly known as the *Bombay Plan*.
2. Aditya Mukherjee, 'The Indian Capitalist Class: Aspects of its Economic, Political and Ideological Development in the Colonial Period, 1927-47,' in S. Bhattacharya and Romila Thapar, editors, *Situating Indian History*, New Delhi, 1986, pp.246-7.
3. *Ibid.*, pp.250-1.
4. See for example, Sumit Sarkar, 'Logic of Gandhian Nationalism: Civil

Disobedience and the Gandhi-Irwin Pact (1930-31),' *The Indian Historical Review*, New Delhi, Vol.III, No.1, July 1976, pp.120-1, 146.

5. Sri Ram, *Annual Reports of the Federation of Indian Chambers of Commerce and Industry*, (hereafter referred to as FICCI, *A.R.*), 1943, p.150, and Muthiah Chettiar, President, FICCI, *A.R.*, 1944, p.205.

6. G.D. Birla, FICCI, *A.R.*, 1934, p.173; S.P. Jain and B.M. Birla in FICCI, *A.R.*, 1943, p.129 and 1946, pp.104-5 respectively.

7. Purshottamdas Thakurdas, President's Speech, FICCI, *A.R.*, 1928, p.4.

8. G.D. Birla, FICCI, *A.R.*, 1930, p.264.

9. Lalji Naranji to Purshottamdas, 28 March 1930, *Purshottamdas Thakurdas (PT) Papers*, fl. 91, part II, Nehru Memorial Museum and Library.

10. G.D. Birla to Purshottamdas, 16 Feb. 1932, *PT Papers*, fl. 104; Purshottamdas to N.R. Sarkar, 1 August 1942, *PT Papers*, fl.239, pt. II, and N.R. Sarkar, *Free Press Journal*, 24 July 1941.

11. FICCI, *Proccedings of the Executive Committee (Proc. of EC)*, 1934, pp.33-42.

12. FICCI, *A.R.*, 1935, pp.72-3.

13. FICCI, *Proc. of EC*, 1930-31, p.5.

14. Ambalal to Purshottamdas, 5 Nov. 1929, *PT Papers*, fl. 91, pt.1.

15. G.D. Birla to Mahadev Desai, 8 July 1937 and 22 July 1937 in, *In the Shadow of the Mahatma*, Calcutta, 1953, pp.219, 224-6.

16. G.D. Birla to Purshottamdas, 16 Jan. 1931, *PT Papers*, fl.42, pt. VII (emphasis mine).

17. *Ibid*.

18. *Ibid*.

19. Irwin to Purshottamdas, 29 Sept. 1930 and Purshottamdas to Irwin, 28 April 1930, *PT Papers*, fl. 99, pt.2.

20. Purshottamdas to G.D. Birla, 9 Sept. 1940 and G.D. Birla to Purshottamdas, 11 Sept. 1940, *PT Papers*, fl. 239, pt.I.

21. *PT Papers*, fl.239, pt.4.

22. A.D.D. Gordon, Business and Politics, *Rising Nationalism and Modernising Economy in Bombay, 1918-1933*, New Delhi, 1978, pp.179, 185-86, 192, 199. See also, Claude Markovits, *Indian Business and Nationalist Politics from 1931-1939*, unpublished D.phil dissertation, Cambridge, pp.96, 121, 172 ff.

23. For example, Sumit Sarkar, *op.cit.*, p.99; and 'Popular Movements and National Leadership 1945-47,' *Economic and Political Weekly*, Vol. XVII, Nos. 14-16, (annual no.), April 1982.

24. Home Political Department, F. no.4/14-A, 1940, National Archives of India.

25. Gandhi, *CW*, Vol.32, pp.459-60.

26. J.K. Mehta to Purshottamdas, 3 Feb. 1930, *PT Papers*, fl. 42, pt.8. For an understanding of the relationship of the capitalist class and the national movement, especially leaders like Gandhi, Sardar Patel and Nehru, the following interviews have proved very useful: J.R.D. Tata, Bombay, 23 May, 1985, R.K. Bajaj, Bombay, 17 June 1985, and Vadilal Lallubhai Mehta, 8 July 1985.

27. G.D. Birla to Purshottamdas, 30 July 1929, *PT Papers*, fl. 42, pt.5.

28. *Ibid*.

29.G.D. Birla to Walchand Hirachand, 26 May 1936, *PT Papers*, fl.177.

30. FICCI, *A.R.*, 1943, p.31.

31. John Mathai to Purshottamdas, 8 Dec. 1942 and enclosures, *PT Papers*, fl. 291, pt.1 and fl.42, pt.5.

30. The Development of a Nationalist Foreign Policy

1. S.N. Banerjea, *Speeches*, Vol. II, Calcutta, 1880, pp.215-6.

2. R.C. Dutt, *Economic History of India in the Victorian Age*, p.549.

3. *Indian National Congress*, containing full texts of all Presidential Addresses, reprint of all the Congress Resolutions, etc., Part I, p.386.

4. Jawaharlal Nehru, *An Autobiography*, p.31.

5. Gandhi, *CW*, Vol.22, p.246.

6. *Ibid*, Vol.27, p.450.

7. A.M. Zaidi and S.G. Zaidi, editors, *The Encyclopaedia of the Indian National Congress*, Volume Nine: 1925-1929, New Delhi, 1980, p.234.

8. Nehru, *SW*, Vol.2, p.281.

9. Gandhi, *CW*, Vol.55, p.427.

10. Nehru, *SW*, Vol.7, pp.172-3.

11. *Ibid*., Vol.9, p.235.

12. Gandhi, *CW*, Vol.68, p.138.

13. Nehru, *SW*, Vol.7, p.602.

14. Gandhi, *CW*, Vol.67, p.428.

15. Tendulkar, *Mahatma*, Vol.4, p.276.

16. Gandhi, *CW*, Vol.67, pp. 404, 414.

17. Nehru, *SW*, Vol.9, p.144.

18. *Ibid*., p.157.

19. Gandhi, *CW*, Vol. 68, pp. 137-40.

20. Nehru, *SW*, Vol. 7, p.181.

21. *Ibid*., Vol. 9, p.508.

22. Gandhi, *CW*, Vol. 37, p.380.
23. Nehru, *SW*, Vol. 9, p.292.

31. The Rise and Growth of Communalism

1. Nehru, *SW*, Vol.7, p.69.
2. C.G. Shah, *Marxism, Gandhism, Stalinism*, Bombay, 1963, p.185.
3. K.M. Ashraf, *Hindustani Muslim Siyasat Par Ek Nazar*, Bombay, 1959 reprint, in Urdu.
4. Quoted in A.N. Vidyalankar, *National Integration and Teaching of History*, New Delhi, no date, p.3.
5. James Mill, *The History of British India*, London, 1826. Since then the work has been reprinted several times.
6. K.M. Ashraf, *op.cit.*, p.73.

32. Communalism — The Liberal Phase

1. S. Abid Husain, *The Destiny of Indian Muslims*, Bombay, 1965, p.24.
2. *Ibid.*, pp.156-7.
3. Syed Ahmed Khan, *Writings and Speeches*, edited by Shan Mohammad, Bombay, 1972, pp.102 ff., 180 ff., 202 ff., 210 ff., 243.
4. *Ibid.*, pp.156-7, 184-5.
5. *Ibid*, pp.204, 207-10.
6. *Ibid.*, p.210.
7. *Ibid.*, p.242.
8. *Ibid.*, p.243.
9. Quoted in Ram Gopal, *Indian Muslims: A Political History (1858-1947)*, Bombay, 1959, p.101.
10. Lal Chand, *Self-abnegation in Politics*, Lahore, 1938 edition.
11. Report in the *Statesman*, 31 December 1932, quoted in Nehru, *SW*, Vol.6, p.163.
12. *Indian Annual Register*, 1933, Vol.II, p.206.

33. Jinnah, Golwalkar And Extreme Communalism

1. Stanley Wolpert, *Jinnah of Pakistan*, New York, 1984, p.26.
2. *Ibid.*, Chapters 4 and 5.
3. *Ibid.*, p.97.
4. Quoted in Raja of Mahmudabad, 'Some Memories,' in *The Partition of India*, edited by C.H. Philips and M.D. Wainright, London, 1970, p.385.
5. Quoted in S. Gopal, *Jawaharlal Nehru — A Biography*, Vol. One, 1889-1947, p.223, f.n.5.

6. Quoted in Z.H. Zaidi, 'Aspects of the Development of Muslim League Policy, 1937-47,' in *The Partition of India*, edited by C.H. Philips and M.D. Wainright, p.250.

7. M.A. Jinnah, *Speeches and Writings*, edited by Jamil-ud-Din, Vol.I, Lahore, 1960 edition, pp 69-70, 72-3.

8. *Ibid.*, p.127.

9. *Ibid.*, p.243.

10. *Ibid.*, p.248.

11. *Indian Annual Register*, 1946, Vol. II, p.226.

12. M.A. Jinnah, *Speeches and Writings*, edited by Jamil-ud-Din, Vol.II, Lahore, edition, 1964, pp.240-1.

13. Z.A. Suleri, *My Leader*, no place, 1946, third edition; F.K. Khan Durrani, *The Meaning of Pakistan*, Lahore, 1944.

14. Quoted in Ram Gopal, *Indian Muslims: A Political History (1858-1947)*, Bombay, 1959, p.258.

15. Quoted in W.C. Smith, *Modern Islam in India*, Lahore, 1963 reprint, p.299.

16. M.A. Jinnah, *op.cit.*, Vol.II, p.489.

17. V.D. Savarkar, *Hindu Rashtra Darshan, A Collection of the Presdential Speeches*, Bombay, 1949, pp.21-2.

18. *Ibid.*, p.77.

19. M.S. Golwalkar, *We or Our Nationhood Defined*, Nagpur, 1947 edition, first published in 1939, p.58.

20. *Ibid.*, p.73.

21. *Ibid.*, p.19.

22. *Ibid.*, pp.55-6.

23. *Ibid.*, p.19.

24. *Ibid.*, pp.40-1.

25. M.S. Golwalkar, *Bunch of Thoughts*, Bangalore, 1966 edition, pp.150-2.

26. Jinnah, *op.cit.*, Vol.II, pp.403-4.

27. Rajendra Prasad, *India Divided*, Bombay, 1947, third revised edition, p.153.

28. S. Gopal, *op.cit.*, p.227.

34. The Crisis at Tripuri to the Cripps Mission

1. Crossroads, *Being the Works of Subhas Chandra Bose 1938-40*, Bombay, 1962, p.87.

2. Tendulkar, *Mahatma*, Vol.5, pp.28-9.

3. *Crossroads*, pp.91-2.

4. Subhas Bose, *The Indian Struggle 1920-42*, Bombay, 1967 reprint,

p.332.
5. Tendulkar, *Mahatma*, Vol.5, p.28.
6. Gandhi, *CW*, Vol.68, p.359.
7. Nehru, *SW*, Vol.9, pp.481-2.
8. *The Indian Struggle*, p.335.
9. *Crossroads*, pp.108 ff.
10. *Gandhi*, CW, Vol.67, p.198.
11. *Ibid.*, Vol.69, pp.209-10.
12. *Ibid.*, p.98.
13. Rajendra Prasad, *Autobiography*, Bombay, 1957.
14. Gene D. Overstreet and Marshall Windmiller, *Communism in India*, Berkeley, 1959, p.168.
15. Sumit Sarkar, *Modern India*, p.374.
16. S. Gopal, *Jawaharlal Nehru — A Biography*, Vol.One, p.263.
17. *Indian Annual Register*, 1939, Vol.II, pp.389-93.
18. Gandhi, *CW*, Vol.70, pp.267-280.
19. *Ibid.*, Vol.71, Appendix VI.
20. Nehru, *SW*, Vol.II, p.106.
21. S. Gopal, *op.cit.*, p.268.
22. Gandhi, *CW*, Vol.73, p.72.
23. Tendulkar, *Mahatma*, Vol.6, p.43. Gandhi's *Collected Works*, Vol.75, p.224 has another version of the speech.
24. S. Gopal, *op.cit.*, p.278.
25. Nehru, *Discovery of India*, p.399.

35. The Quit India Movement and The INA

1. S. Gopal, *Jawaharlal Nehru: A Biography*, Vol. One, p.294.
2. Gandhi, *CW*, Vol.76, p.442. Gandhi is also reported to have told Jawaharlal Nehru, 'If you won't join, I'll do it without you.' S. Gopal, *op.cit.*, p.292.
3. For the full text of the speech, see Gandhi, *CW*, Vol.76, pp.384-96; the quotes in my text are to be found on pp.391, 392, 394 and 395.
4. *Ibid.*, p.367.
5. Francis Hutchins, *Spontaneous Revolution: The Quit India Movement*, New Delhi, 1971, p.191.
6. Interview with Achyut Patwardhan, Bangalore, 9 December 1984.
7. Interviews with Usha Mehta, Bombay, 18 May 1985; S.M. Joshi, New Delhi, 29 February 1984; Annadada Narde, Bombay, 25 May1985; Lalbhai Dayabhai Naik, Navsari (Gujarat), 27 June 1985; Jayanti Thakore, Ahmedabad, 7 and 8 July 1985; Hoshiar Singh, Baraut (U.P.), 14 April 1987.

8. Gandhiji first used the phrase 'leonine violence' in his letter of 29 January 1943 to the Viceroy. Gandhi, *CW*, Vol.77, p.56. For Gandhi's declaration of his intention to fast and the Viceroy's response, see Gandhi, *CW*, Vol.77, pp.49-51, and Mansergh and Lumby, editors, *Transfer of Power* (hereafter *TP*), 1942-7, Vols. 1-12, London, 1970-1983, Vol.3, pp.462-3 and 493.

9. The popular reaction to Gandhi's fast is detailed in *Government of India, Home Political Department*, file nos. 19/3/43, 19/4/43, 19/5/43 and 19/6/43, National Archives of India, New Delhi.

10. *TP*, Vol.3, p.632.

11. Linlithgow in a conversation with Louis Phillips, Special U.S. representative in New Delhi. *Ibid.*, p.690.

12. *Ibid.*, pp.684-6.

13. Radhika Singha, *Aspects of the Quit India Movement in Eastern U.P.*, Unpublished M.Phil dissertation, CHS, Jawaharlal Nehru University, New Delhi, 1986; Chandan Mitra, 'Countours of Popular Protest: The Quit India Movement of 1942,' paper presented at a Seminar on *A History of the Indian National Congress, 1885-1947*, at Nehru Memorial Museum and Library, 22-24 July 1985.

14. Sumit Sarkar, *Modern India*, pp.400-01.

15. Gail Omvedt, 'The Satara Parallel Government, 1942-47,' in D.N. Panigrahi, editor, *Economy, Society and Politics in Modern India*, New Delhi, 1985; and Interviews with Y.B. Chavan, New Delhi, 2 May 1984, V.S. Page, Bombay, 7 June 1985 and Vasantdada Patil, Bombay, 14 June 1985.

16. Stephen Hennigham, *Peasant Movements in Colonial India: North Bihar 1917-1942*, Canberra, 1982, pp.183-5; Interview with Paras Nath Misra, Lucknow, 20 and 21 April 1986.

17. Gandhi, *CW*, Vol.76, p.461.

18. Interviews with Paras Nath Misra, Lucknow, 20 and 21 April 1986, and Vishwanath Prasad Mardana, Lucknow, 24 April 1986.

19. Interview with Mrinalini Desai, Bombay, 22 May 1985, and Shirubhau Limaye, Pune, 5 June 1985, G.P. Pradhan, Pune, 6 June 1985.

20. Gandhi, *CW*, Vol. 76, p.295.

21. Francis Hutchins, *op.cit.*, pp.247-8.

22. *TP*, Vol.5, pp.166, 359, 615 and 754.

23. *Selected Speeches of Subhas Chandra Bose*, New Delhi, 1965, p.218.

24. For accounts of the I.N.A., see K.K. Ghosh, *The Indian National Army*, Meerut, 1969, and Interviews with P.K. Sehgal, Kanpur, 23 September, 1986, Laxmi Sehgal, 23 September, 1986, Colonel Mahboob Ahmed, Patna, November 1985, Niranjan Singh Gill, Amritsar, 2 and 3 April 1985.

36. Post-War National Upsurge

1. *TP*, Vol.6, p.109.
2. K.K. Ghosh, *The Indian National Army*, p.210.
3. *TP*, Vol.6, p.507.
4. *Ibid.*, p.512.
5. Nehru, *SW*, Vol.14, pp.279-80.
6. F. Tuker, *While Memory Serves*, London, 1950, p.54.
7. Wavell to Pethick Lawrence, 27 November 1945, *TP.*, Vol.6, p.552.
8. Cunningham to Wavell, 27 November 1945, *Ibid.*, p.546.
9. Note on INA Situation by Director, Intelligence Bureau, *TP*, Vol.6, p.512.
10. Commander-in-Chief to Viceroy, 24 and 26 November 1945, *TP*, Vol.6., pp.533 and 545.
11. *TP*, Vol.6, p.546.
12. R.P. Dutt, *India Today*, Bombay, 1949, pp.536-42; Sumit Sarkar, 'Popular Movements and National Leadership 1945-47,' *Economic and Political Weekly*, Vol.XVII, Nos. 14-16 (annual no.) April 1982; Gautam Chattopadhyay, 'The Almost Revolution: A Case Study of India in February 1946,' in *Essays in Honour of Professor S.C. Sarkar*, New Delhi, 1976.
13. Gautam Chattopadhyay, *op.cit.*
14. Subrata Banerjee, *The R.I.N Strike*, New Delhi, 1981, p.vii.
15. Viceroy to Secretary of State, 27 February 1946, *TP*, Vol.6, p.1076.
16. R.P. Dutt, *op.cit.*, p.542.
17. Government of India, *Home Political Department*, File No. 5/8/46, National Archives of India.
18. Viceroy to Prime Minister, 24 February 1946, *TP*, Vol.6, p.1055.
19. *Home Political Department*, File No. 7/1/46.
20. *Jawaharlal Nehru Correspondence*, Part I, Vol.81, Nehru Memorial Library.
21. Sumit Sarkar, *op.cit.*, p.2. Also see G. Chattopadhyay, *op.cit.*, p.428; and A.R. Desai, 'Introduction,' in A.R. Desai, editor *Peasant Struggles in India*, p.xx.
22. *Indian National Congress, March 1940 to September 1946: Being the Resolutions Passed by the Congress, the AICC and the Working Commitee*, published by the General Secretary, AICC.
23. Gandhi, *CW*, Vol.83, pp.171, 175, 183-4.

37. Freedom and Partition

1. For a fuller discussion of how this erosion took place and the conclusions drawn from it by the British, see Sucheta Mahajan, 'British Policy, Nationalist Strategy and Popular National Upsurge, 1945-6,' in A.K Gupta, editor, *Myth and Reality, Struggle for Freedom in India, 1945-7*, pp.57-63.
2. R.J. Moore, *Escape from Empire*, Oxford, 1983, p.22. Also see David Potter, 'Manpower Shortage and the End of Colonialism: The Case of the Indian Civil Service,' *Modern Asian Studies*, Vol.7, No.1, 1973.
3. R.P. Noronha, *Tale Told by an Idiot*, New Delhi, 1976, p.3.
4. *TP*, Vol.6, p.688.
5. The option of changing the nature of British rule to one of strong autocratic authority capable of maintaining British rule for another 15-20 years was ruled out by Attlee in late 1946. The considerations were that there were no British troops available, British and U.S. public opinion would not accept it and a disgraceful exit with a legacy of hostility would be the end result. TP, Vol.9, pp.68-9. Our understanding of the reasons for British withdrawl from India is also based on Interviews with contemporary officials as well as participants in the national movement, especially R.A. Gopalaswamy, Madras, 5 June 1984, S.R. Kaiwar, Madras, 2 June 1984, A.K. Das, Lucknow, 20 April 1986, K.K. Das, Lucknow, 26 April 1986, Achyut Patwardhan, Bangalore, 9 december 1984, N.G. Gore, 29 December 1984, Rohit Dave, Bombay, 21 May 1985.
6. *Bombay Chronicle*, 8 July 1946.
7. R.J. Moore, *op.cit.*, pp.156 and 163.
8. Nehru, *Selected Works*, edited by S. Gopal, Second Series, Vol.2, New Delhi, 1984, p.69.
9. Attle's statement in the Cabinet meeting of 18 February 1946, *TP*, Vol.9, London, 1980, p.750.
10. House of Commons Debate, 5 March 1947, *Parliamentary Debates* (Hansard).
11. Note by Jenkins, Punjab Governor, 16 February 1947, *TP*, Vol.9, p.729.
12. *Wavell: The Viceroy's Journal*, edited by Penderel Moon, New Delhi, 1977, p.428.
13. Collins and Lapierre, *Mountbatten and the Partition of India*, Sahibabad, 1983, pp.21 and 53.
14. Report of Viceroy's 13th Staff Meeting, 11 April *1947*, *TP*, Vol.10, p.190.

15. Francis Williams, *A Prime Minister Remembers*, London, 1961, p.212.
16. Nehru, *SW*, Second Series, Vol.1, p.207.
17. S. Gopal, *Jawaharlal Nehru — A Biography*, Vol.One, p.352.
18. Interview with Mountbatten, 17 April 1947, *TP*, Vol.10, p.309.
19. Ronald Wingate, *Lord Ismay, A Biography*, London, 1970, p.167.
20. Brigadier R.C.B. Bristow, *Memories of the British Raj — A Soldier in India*, London, 1974. Lockhart wrote the Foreword.
21. Nehru, *SW*, Vol.15, pp.306-07.
22. S. Gopal, *op.cit.*, p.307.
23. Nehru, *SW*, Second Series, Vol.2, p.377.
24. Bimal Prasad, *Gandhi, Nehru and J.P. Studies in Leadership*, Delhi, 1985; Sandhya Chaudhuri, *Gandhi and the Partition of India*, New Delhi, 1984, Sumit Sarkar, *Modern India*.
25. Gandhi, *CW*, Vol.88, p.75.
26. Bimal Prasad, *op.cit.*, p.31.

38. The Long-term Strategy of the National Movement

1. This Chapter is based on Bipan Chandra, *Indian National Movement: The Long-term Dynamics*, New Delhi, 1988.
2. Gandhi, *CW*, Vol.64, p.194. Also Vol.68, p.319.
3. Gandhi, *CW*, Vol.67, p.226.
4. *Ibid.*, p.420.
5. *Ibid*, Vol.69, p.60.
6. *Indian National Congress, March 1940 to September 1946: Being the Resolutions Passed by the Congress, AICC and the Working Committee*, New Delhi, 1946.
7. Nehru, *SW*, Vol.4, p.195; Bhagat Singh, *Why I am an Athiest*, p.12.

39. The Indian National Movement — The Ideological Dimension

1. Gandhi, *CW*, Vol.76, p.384.
2. *Kesari*, 16 June 1908, quoted in Ashis Kumar Dhuliya, *Aspects of Tilak's Political Strategy and His Struggle for Civil Liberties*, M.Phil Dissertation, Centre for Historical Studies, Jawaharlal Nehru University, New Delhi, 1984, p.269.
3. Gandhi, *CW*, Vol.22, pp.142 and 176-7.
4. *Ibid.*, Vol.69, p.356.
5. Nehru, *SW*, Vol.7, p.414.

6. *Ibid.*, Vol.11, p.367.

7. See, for example, Gandhi, *CW*, Vol.68, pp.258-9.

8. Bipan Chandra, 'British and Indian Ideas on Indian Economic Development, 1858-1905,' in Bipan Chandra *Nationalism and Colonialism in Modern India*, pp.92 ff.

9. *Ibid.*, pp.109 ff; and Bipan Chandra, *The Rise and Growth of Economic Nationalism in India*, pp.90 ff.

10. *Indian National Congress: Resolutions on Economic Policy, Programme and Allied Matters 1924-1969*, New Delhi, 1969, p.16.

11. Gandhi, *CW*, Vol.55, p.427.

12. References are too many. The reader may see Gyorgy Kalmar, *Gandhism*, Budapest, 1977; and Francine R. Frankel, *India's Political Economy 1947-1977: The Gradual Revolution*, Delhi, 1978, Chapters 1 and 2.

13. Gandhi, *CW*, Vol.64, p.192.

14. *Ibid.*, Vol.76, p.367.

15. *Ibid.*, pp.437, 445-6.

Index

Q